THE WHITE AFRICANS

THE WHITE AFRICANS

FROM COLONISATION TO LIBERATION

GERALD L'ANGE

JONATHAN BALL PUBLISHERS
JOHANNESBURG & CAPE TOWN

Published in 2005 in trade paperback by
JONATHAN BALL PUBLISHERS (PTY) LTD
PO Box 33977
Jeppestown
2043

ISBN 1 86842 219 4

Cover design and reproduction by
Flame Design, Cape Town

Maps by Ingrid Booysen

Typesetting and reproduction of text by
Triple M Design & Advertising, Johannesburg

Set in 11/13pt Bembo

Editing and index by
J Owen Hendry for Wordsmiths, Johannesburg

Printed and bound by
CTP Book Printers, Duminy Street, Parow, Cape

CONTENTS

LIST OF MAPS

AUTHOR'S NOTE

Much has been written about various aspects of the European experience in Africa, but this is believed to be the first attempt to pull it all together in a single book and to place it in the context of the creation of that modern phenomenon, the white Africans.

In telling their story, the book recounts the whole European experience in Africa from the 15th century to the formal ending of white supremacy, which is taken to be Nelson Mandela's inauguration as president of South Africa in 1994. The story is told, however, in brief – the size of the book reflects only the wide scope of the subject.

This is a journalistic rather than an academic work, a storyteller's rather than an historian's construction. Rather than being divided into the compartments appropriate to academic analysis, the story has been told more or less in the somewhat untidy form of chronological order in the belief that allowing it to unfold in its natural sequence more effectively traces the threads of cause and effect, more interestingly places events in the context of their period, showing the relationship between them – and, in the end, makes for a better read.

The book attempts to tell the white Africans' story as truthfully as possible, viewing it from a modern perspective and eschewing past historical falsities as well as more recent propagandising and political correctness.

The ethnic divisions cause problems of nomenclature in a work of this kind. Since the book is about the whites as Africans, it was impossible to use the term African in reference to the black people as well without causing confusion. Therefore those who are commonly called Africans are referred to as blacks, and the whites simply as whites (except, of course, when they are specifically called white Africans). As these two are commonly referred to without a capital letter, the same rule has been applied to those who are called coloureds. Indians or Asians as well as Chinese naturally get the capital.

In general, the nomenclature of the time has been used. The people in Ethiopia, for instance, are called Abyssinians when that is how they were commonly referred to at the time, and Ethiopians when they became known as such.

I am indebted to a number of people who helped me in the preparation of this book, not least to Barry Streek, Jonathan Ball Publishing's editor-in-chief, who unerringly detected initial faults in the manuscript, and to Francine Blum, the production manager, who steered it expertly and expeditiously to publication, helped me patiently over technical hurdles and generally guided my efforts with wisdom and warmth. I gratefully acknowledge the skill with which Owen Hendry edited the work. Much appreciation is owed to Kevin Shenton for the designing of this book. My greatest debt – and it is indeed a large one – is to Jonathan Ball himself for publishing this book.

Most of the historical research I did myself, drawing unreservedly on the works of professional historians and other writers, to whom I have made some acknowledgement, unavoidably inadequate, in the end notes. For some of the material on more recent times I have drawn on my own knowledge and experience as a journalist in Africa, at the United Nations and in Washington, and elsewhere. I owe a great debt of gratitude, however, to several persons, most of them journalists, who brought me up to date on later developments in Zimbabwe, Namibia and Kenya, where they respectively live. I do not know whether all of them would appreciate being identified with a book over whose writing they had no direct influence, for not even journalists can be certain of how a colleague will view or interpret information. I am especially hesitant to identify those who helped me in Zimbabwe, given the vindictive attitude of the government there to honest reporting. I therefore confine my open thanks to Fanie Kruger in Eldoret and to Des Erasmus and Dudley Viall in Namibia. The others will know if they read this that it records my gratitude to them.

I can with less inhibition thank those who helped provide the illustrations: Dr Rayda Becker of the Library of Parliament, Rowena Wilkinson and Gerda Viljoen of the Museum of Military History in Johannesburg, Melanie Guestyn of the National Library in Cape Town, Cathy Brookes of Museum Africa in Johannesburg, Lalou Meltzer of the Fehr Collection in Cape Town, Paul Smith of the Thomas Cook Archives in England, and the *Illustrated London News* office in London.

To my wife, Barbara, who endured my preoccupation with this book for the best part of seven years, I make a grateful salute.

CHRONOLOGY

1415 Portuguese seizure of Ceuta begins post-Roman intrusion by Europeans into sub-Saharan Africa.

1434 Gil Eanes sails beyond Cape Bojador, proving techniques for tacking against the wind and opening the way for maritime exploration of sub-Saharan African coastline – and the world.

1471 Portuguese reach 'Gold Coast'.

1482 Portuguese complete Elmina Fort on Gold Coast.

1488 Bartholomew Dias rounds Cape.

1493 Columbus completes first voyage to Americas.

1498 Vasco da Gama reaches India.

1553 English traders set up at Benin.

1637 Dutch capture Elmina.

1652 Van Riebeeck opens resupply station at Cape.
     Danes build Cape Coast Castle on Gold Coast.

1657 First white settlers placed on Liesbeeck River near Cape Town.

1660 English Company of Royal Adventurers given authority to license slavers on West African coast.

1688 First Huguenots arrive at Cape.

1702 First meeting of trekboers and Xhosas.

1720 Trans-Atlantic slave trade becomes established.

1737 George Schmidt establishes first mission station in Cape.

1770 James Bruce claims Blue Nile's source to be the Little Abbai River.

1776 American Declaration of Independence.

1778 Formation of Cape Patriots marks first organised opposition to Dutch rule at Cape.

1779 First Frontier War with Xhosas begins in South Africa.

1780 Free burgher population at Cape exceeds ten thousand.

1781 French begin four-year presence at Cape in alliance with Dutch.

1782 James Watt invents steam engine.

1787 Freed slaves established at Sierra Leone.

1788 British establish penal settlements in Australia.

1789 French Revolution.
     Second Frontier War with Xhosas.

1792 First white settlement in New Zealand.

1795 Burghers declare republic at Graaff-Reinet.
     Dutch East India Company collapses; Batavian Republic takes over Cape, which is then seized by British.
     London Missionary Society founded.
     Mungo Park reaches upper Niger River.

1798 Napoleon invades Egypt.

1799 Third Frontier War with Xhosas.

1800 Britain established as major trading power on Gold Coast.

1801 British oust French from Egypt.

1803 British leave Cape.
     Henry Shrapnel invents the artillery shell.

1805 Mungo Park begins second Niger expedition.

1806 British again occupy Cape.

1807 Slave trade outlawed by British.

1811 British drive Xhosas back across Fish River.

1820 English settlers land at Algoa Bay.

1821 Brazil declares independence from Portugal.

1822 Farewell and King establish Port Natal.

1822 Liberia founded.
1823 America's Monroe Doctrine forbids new colonial settlements in Western Hemisphere.
1824 McCartney killed in first British–Asante war.
1825 Stockton to Darlington railway opened in England.
1828 Shaka assassinated.
1829 Lander completes exploration of Niger River.
1830 French seize Algiers.
  Royal Geographic Society founded.
1831 Abd el-Kader leads Berber revolt in Algeria.
1834 Slaves emancipated at Cape.
1836 Great Trek begins in South Africa.
1837 Queen Victoria crowned.
1838 Voortrekkers defeat Zulus in Battle of Blood River, found Republic of Natalia.
1840 Exeter Hall meeting becomes milestone of British liberalism.
1841 British sovereignty proclaimed over Hong Kong.
  New Zealand proclaimed British colony.
1843 British annex Natal.
  French Foreign Legion establishes headquarters in Algeria.
1845 Maoris begin warfare against white settlement in New Zealand.
1847 German explorers Krupp and Rebman sight Mount Kilimanjaro.
  Abd el-Kader surrenders to the French in Algeria.
1849 Livingstone discovers Lake Ngami.
  First Byrne settlers arrive in Natal from Britain.
1850 Danes sell Accra fort to British.
1851 Great Exhibition at Crystal Palace in London.
  General Bugeaud destroys Algerian agriculture to force obedience to France.
1852 Transvaal Republic founded.
1854 Orange Free State Republic founded.
  Crimean War begins.
1855 Livingstone discovers Victoria Falls.
1856 Xhosas conduct Great Cattle Killing.
  Algeria's white population reaches

170 000.
1857 Burton and Speke discover Lakes Tanganyika and Victoria.
  Tukolors end resistance to French domination in West Africa.
  Indian Mutiny begins.
1858 Livingstone discovers Lake Nyasa.
1859 Dutch Reformed Church founded in South Africa.
  First railway opened in Cape Colony.
  Construction of Suez Canal begins.
1860 First indentured Indian labourers arrive in Natal Colony.
1862 Speke and Grant fix Nile source at Lake Victoria.
  RJ Gatling invents first machine-gun.
1864 Baker discovers Lake Albert.
1866 First diamond found near Orange River.
1868 Theodore defeated in Abyssinia.
  Basutoland annexed by Britain.
1869 Tunisia becomes French protectorate.
  Suez Canal opened.
1870 Baker sets out to annex upper Nile for Egypt.
1871 Stanley meets Livingstone at Ujiji.
  British annex diamond-rich Griqua territory.
  Cecil Rhodes arrives in Kimberley.
1872 Cape Colony gets self-government.
1873 Gold found in eastern Transvaal.
  Livingstone dies at Ilala.
1874 Wolseley leads campaign against the Asante.
  Stanley begins exploration of Great Lakes and Congo River.
  Gordon takes over from Baker as Ismail's upper-Nile agent.
1875 Verney Cameron completes cross-Africa march.
  De Brazza begins his exploration of Congo River.
  Ismail sells his Suez Canal interest to Britain.
1876 King Leopold calls conference to form International Africa Association.
1877 Stanley reaches Congo mouth, confirming the river's source and course.
  Gordon resigns, then returns as Sudan governor-general.

Britain annexes Transvaal.

1878 Britain annexes Walvis Bay.

1879 Stanley begins to establish Congo base for Leopold.

Western powers depose Ismail in Egypt.

British invade Zululand; battles of Isandlwana and Rorke's Drift.

1880 De Brazza establishes French foothold on Congo River.

Boers proclaim restoration of Transvaal sovereignty at Paardekraal, and repulse British at Bronkhorstspruit.

1881 British defeated by Boers at Majuba, recognise independence of South African Republic (Transvaal) with British 'suzerainty'.

French gain control of Tunis.

1882 Transvalers declare Goshen Republic.

Anti-European rioting in Alexandria; Wolseley invades Egypt and occupies Canal Zone and Cairo.

Maxim gun invented.

1883 Lüderitz establishes German presence at Angra Pequena.

Stellaland republic declared.

Paul Kruger becomes president of Transvaal.

Mahdi annihilates Hicks's force in Sudan.

1884 Gordon returns to Khartoum and is besieged by Mahdists; Wolseley begins rescue expedition.

British send Hewett to sign treaties in West Africa.

Carl Peters lands in East Africa on private treaty-signing mission.

Britain and Portugal sign Congo treaty.

Bismarck annexes Togo, Cameroon and Angra Pequena.

Berlin conference on African colonial acquisitions opens.

British force disbandment of Stellaland and Goshen republics.

Kruger signs London Convention regulating Transvaal boundaries.

1885 Wolseley's expedition fights battle of Abu Klea.

Mahdists storm Khartoum and kill Gordon.

Gladstone's government resigns.

Berlin conference adopts Act regulating colonial expansion in Africa.

Leopold gains personal control of Congo.

Bismarck declares German protectorate in East Africa.

1886 Gold discovered on Witwatersrand.

United Africa Company gets charter to trade on lower Niger River.

Britain and Germany agree on territorial division in East Africa.

1887 British East Africa Company gets charter.

Stanley begins expedition to save Emin Pasha.

Transvaal gets hunting and trading concession from Lobengula.

1888 Lobengula cedes mining rights in his territory to Rhodes, who gets royal charter for his BSA Company.

Gambia becomes British colony.

Rider Haggard publishes *King Solomon's Mines*.

1889 France declares Ivory Coast protectorate.

1890 Rhodes's Pioneer Column invades Mashonaland, founds Salisbury.

Germany concedes Uganda to Britain.

Leopold beats Rhodes in contest for concession to exploit Katanga copper.

1891 Hehe revolt in German East Africa.

1893 Jameson seizes Matabeleland for Rhodes; Lobengula commits suicide.

Natal granted self-government.

1894 Monteil expedition sets out to establish French presence on upper Nile.

1895 Opening of railway to Delagoa Bay gives Transvaal access to sea.

1896 Jameson's raid into Transvaal is defeated.

Matabeles and Shonas rebel in Rhodesia.

Italians defeated in Battle of Adowa (Adua).

Leopold sends expeditions to Lado enclave in bid to get Nile presence.

Kitchener advances up the Nile to recapture Sudan.

British forces impose protectorate on Asante.

1897 British celebrate Victoria's jubilee.

Britain offers land for white settlement in Kenya.

1898 French and British resolve armed confrontation over upper Niger.

Marchand occupies Fashoda on Nile for France.

Kitchener defeats Khalifa at Omdurman, recaptures Khartoum.

Britain and France hover on brink of war as Kitchener confronts Marchand at Fashoda.

Rhodesia gets legislative council.

1899 Anglo–Boer War begins.

1900 Asantes revolt and besiege British in Kumase fort.

Morel begins campaign against rubber-collecting brutality in Belgian Congo.

1901 British seize Benin to complete possession of lower Niger.

Australia bars non–white immigrants.

1902 Anglo–Boer War ends.

1903 Lugard conquers Kano to put northern Nigeria under British control.

1904 Hereros and Namas rebel in German South West Africa.

Agreement on disposition of Egypt and Morocco ends Anglo–French territorial rivalry in Africa.

1905 Maji-maji rebellion in German East Africa.

Bambata rebellion in Natal.

1906 Afrikaners begin taking advantage of British offer of land in Kenya.

Transvaal and Orange Free State get self-government.

Britain, France and Italy define 'areas of interest' in the Horn.

Algeciras conference clears way for eventual French control of Morocco.

1907 Belgian parliament backs removing Congo Free State from Leopold's control.

1910 Union of South Africa formed.

1912 Turkey cedes Tripolitania and Cyrenaica to Italy.

France declares protectorate over Morocco; Spain takes Spanish Sahara.

Southern Rhodesia's white population reaches 24 000.

South African Native National Congress formed.

1913 South Africa adopts Native Land Act reserving most of the land for whites.

1914 National Party formed in South Africa.

Parliament votes to fight for Britain in First World War, and South African

troops invade German South West Africa. Dissident Afrikaners rise in revolt in South Africa but are defeated in civil war.

1915 South Africa sends troops to fight Germans in East Africa, then in France.

Britain reserves Kenya's highlands for whites.

1918 President Wilson pledges American support for self-determination of nations.

1919 League of Nations mandates former German colonies to Britain, South Africa and Belgium.

White population of Kenya reaches 10 000.

Egyptians riot after Britain rejects Wafd's demand for independence.

First flight from Britain to South Africa.

Sol Plaatje leads black South African delegation to London to present grievances.

1920 Black miners go on strike in South Africa.

On Louis Botha's death, Smuts becomes prime minister of South Africa.

1922 Government uses aircraft, artillery and troops to quell revolt by white workers in South Africa.

South African forces bloodily put down Bondelswart rebellion in South West Africa.

In referendum Southern Rhodesian whites reject union with South Africa.

1923 Southern Rhodesia becomes self-governing colony.

SANNC becomes African National Congress of South Africa.

Devonshire Declaration affirms Kenya is primarily for Africans.

1924 Ethiopia (Abyssinia) joins League of Nations.

Rand strike.

National and Labour party coalition wins election in South Africa, forming Pact government.

1926 Imperial Conference recognises autonomy of Dominions.

1928 South Africa launches steel industry.

1930 White women get the vote in South Africa.

Land Apportionment Act reserves most

of Southern Rhodesia for whites.

British government's African paramountcy declaration for Kenya is extended to Northern Rhodesia.

1931 Britain goes off gold standard.

1933 League of Nations refuses South African request for incorporation of South West Africa.

1934 Hertzog and Smuts form United Party.

1935 Blacks in All-African Convention accept qualified vote in South Africa.

Italy invades Ethiopia.

1936 Natives' Representative Council formed to advise South African government on black affairs.

French parliament rejects Blum–Violette Bill that would have given qualified vote to Arabs in Algeria.

Britain grants independence to Egypt.

Native Trust and Land Act reserves only 13 per cent of South Africa for blacks.

1937 Census shows 55 per cent of blacks in South Africa live outside the reserves.

1938 Great Trek centenary is commemorated in South Africa with ox-waggon trek from Cape Town to Pretoria.

1939 Divided parliament commits South Africa to war against Germany.

1940 Italians drive British back in Egypt and Somaliland.

White South African troops and planes go into action against Italians in Somaliland and Abyssinia, backed by black non-combatant units.

Colonial Development and Welfare Act passed in Britain.

1941 Italians defeated in the Horn; South African troops join British forces in Western Desert.

Churchill and Roosevelt adopt Atlantic Charter.

1942 South African troops lead campaign against Vichy French in Madagascar.

1944 South African forces join Allied troops in Italy.

1945 South African Air Force in Berlin Airlift.

Anti-French rioting in Algeria.

1946 UN General Assembly rejects South Africa's bid to incorporate South West Africa.

1948 UN adopts Universal Declaration of Human Rights.

National and Afrikaner party alliance wins South African general election.

Alan Paton publishes *Cry, the Beloved Country*.

1950 South African Air Force serves with UN forces in Korea.

Communist Party banned in South Africa.

Group Areas Act passed in South Africa.

1951 White war veterans form Torch Commando, oppose apartheid.

British refusal to scrap Suez Canal treaty sparks rioting in Cairo.

Libya becomes independent.

1952 King Farouk deposed in Egypt, opening way for Nasser to take power.

Elizabeth II succeeds George VI on British throne.

Mau Mau rebellion begins in Kenya.

1953 Central African Federation joins the Rhodesias and Nyasaland.

1954 Ben Bella leads independence struggle in Algeria.

1955 Freedom Charter adopted at Kliptown, Johannesburg.

1956 Treason trial of Mandela and other Freedom Charter backers begins in South Africa.

Tunisia gets independence from France, and Morocco from Spain.

France offers responsible government to individual African colonies.

Nasser nationalises Suez Canal; invading British and French troops occupy canal, but are forced by international protests to withdraw.

Sudan gets independence outside the Commonwealth.

1957 Gold Coast gets independence as Ghana.

1958 Racial turmoil in Algeria, De Gaulle installed as head of French government, rebellion by conservative whites in Algeria.

In referendum, all other French African territories except Guinea choose independence within the French Community.

Verwoerd succeeds Malan as prime minister in South Africa.

1959 Bantustan legislation adopted in South Africa.

PAC and Progressive Party formed.

1960 Spate of independence in British colonies.

Belgian Congo gets independence, army mutinies, whites attacked, Katanga and Shaba attempt to secede, UN intervenes, Dag Hammarskjold killed in air crash, Lumumba murdered.

Macmillan makes 'winds of change' speech in South African parliament.

South Africa's South West Africa mandate challenged in World Court.

Pratt attempts to assassinate Verwoerd.

Sharpeville massacre; state of emergency declared in South Africa; ANC and PAC banned; parliamentary representation of blacks by whites ended.

1961 South Africa becomes a republic, leaves Commonwealth; treason trial ends; ANC forms *Umkhonto we Sizwe* (MK) and turns to insurgency; whites actively oppose apartheid through African Resistance Movement.

Angolans take up arms against Portuguese rule.

1962 Algerian settlement overwhelmingly accepted in referendum; whites begin to flee.

Mandela arrested in South Africa; Thabo Mbeki goes into exile.

Britain adopts legislation to restrict entry of former colonial subjects.

1963 Central African Federation dissolved.

Organisation of African Unity formed.

1964 Frelimo begins armed struggle in Mozambique.

Ian Smith becomes prime minister of Rhodesia.

Belgian paratroops dropped in Stanleyville as whites killed.

Mandela and other ANC leaders sentenced in Rivonia trial to life imprisonment.

1965 John Harris, convicted of exploding a bomb at Johannesburg railway station in 1964, becomes only white person hanged in South Africa for opposing apartheid.

Mobutu seizes power in Congo (Kinshasa).

Unilateral Declaration of Independence in Rhodesia.

1966 Swapo begins armed struggle in South West Africa.

Verwoerd assassinated, succeeded by Vorster.

1967 Wilson and Smith in HMS *Tiger* talks.

UN General Assembly revokes South Africa's South West Africa mandate.

Wilson and Smith in HMS *Fearless* talks.

1968 In Lusaka Manifesto, African leaders offer whites non-racist solutions.

1970 English cricket tour to South Africa cancelled because of apartheid.

1971 White House adopts 'Tar Baby' option on South Africa.

1972 Pearce Commission finds Rhodesian blacks reject incremental progress to democracy.

Armed struggle begins in Rhodesia.

1973 UN declares apartheid a crime against humanity.

General Assembly declares Swapo has sole authenticity in Namibia.

1974 Portuguese military oust Caetano regime.

South Africa barred from General Assembly.

Black Peoples Convention formed in South Africa.

Vorster introduces policy of détente with African states.

1975 Vorster, Kaunda and Rhodesian parties in Victoria Falls bridge talks.

Turnhalle talks begin in Windhoek.

Cuban troops intervene on MPLA's side in Angolan civil war; Soviet Union begins large-scale arms supplies.

South African troops invade Angola in Operation Savannah.

Clark Amendment in US Senate blocks arms supplies to FNLA and UNITA.

1976 Wilson government adopts NIBMAR policy on Rhodesia.

South African troops withdraw from Angola.

Students riot in Soweto over Afrikaans education.

Henry Kissinger begins southern African mediation efforts.

Rhodesian cabinet accepts majority rule within two years.

Carter wins US presidential election.

1977 Steve Biko killed by South African

Police interrogators.

European Union follows UK with moral code for investment in South Africa.

Western Powers form Contact Group on Namibia.

UN arms embargo against South Africa made mandatory.

South African cabinet decides to strike at Swapo deep inside Angola.

1978 Sullivan code for South African investment takes hold in US.

South African troops attack Swapo camp at Cassinga in Angola.

Security Council Resolution 435 offers new proposals for Namibian settlement.

Botha succeeds Vorster as South African prime minister.

Rhodesian troops in major raids into Zambia and Mozambique.

1979 South Africa makes nuclear weapons.

Botha proposes Constellation of Southern African States.

Black trade unionism legalised in South Africa.

In referendum white Rhodesians accept Smith government's 'internal settlement' proposals for majority rule with safeguards for whites. Bishop Abel Muzorewa's UANC wins election.

Thatcher government rejects 'internal settlement' and demands all-party negotiations.

Lancaster House talks reach agreement on new elections.

1980 Robert Mugabe's Zanu(PF) wins Zimbabwean election by landslide amid allegations of intimidation.

South Africa takes over Rhodesia's backing of Renamo insurgents in Mozambique.

Botha government adopts Total National Strategy policy.

Reagan defeats Carter in US presidential election.

1981 Chester Crocker activates constructive engagement policy, and links Namibian settlement with Cuban troop withdrawal from Angola.

Geneva conference fails to resolve Namibia dispute.

1982 In referendum South African whites accept power-sharing through tri-

cameral parliament separately representing whites, blacks and Asians.

Right-wingers split from National Party and form Conservative Party.

Mandela moved from Robben Island to Pollsmoor prison.

MK detonates two bombs at Koeberg nuclear power station.

South Africa blamed for sabotaging of Zimbabwean aircraft at Thornhill base, and for backing Super-ZAPU insurgents.

South African commandos in attacks on ANC targets in Maputo.

SADC formed.

1983 United Democratic Front formed to oppose new tricameral constitution in South Africa.

Mugabe's 5th Brigade launches pogrom in Matabeleland.

1984 South Africa and Mozambique sign Nkomati Accord on cooperation.

Warring parties sign Lusaka Agreement on troop withdrawal from southern Angola.

Anti-apartheid campaign in US escalates with sit-in at South African embassy in Washington.

Pretoria's hit-squads begin assassinating opponents of apartheid.

1985 South African commandos caught trying to sabotage Angolan oil installations.

Partial South African blockade of Lesotho triggers coup ousting prime minister Leabua Jonathan.

Shopping centres in South Africa bombed after ANC abandons policy of avoiding civilian targets.

Partial state of emergency declared in South Africa as resistance flares in townships.

Clark Amendment repealed in US Senate.

Botha's 'Rubicon' speech shatters high expectations of change.

US banks refuse to roll over South African loans.

Commonwealth appoints Eminent Persons Group to mediate on ending apartheid and South African administration of Namibia.

White businessmen meet ANC in

Lusaka.

South Africa intervenes militarily when Luanda forces begin big offensive against UNITA.

Documents captured by Frelimo reveal clandestine South African aid to Renamo.

Gorbachev's reforms in Soviet Union begin influencing affairs in southern Africa.

South African government members in secret talks with Mandela.

1986 Soviet general Shaganovitch sends Luanda forces on major offensive aimed at taking Mavinga and Jamba from UNITA.

SADF raids on supposed ANC targets in Gaborone, Lusaka and Harare neutralise EPG exercise.

President Machel of Mozambique killed in plane crash.

Botha extends state of emergency in South Africa.

Mbeki has secret talks in New York with Broederbond leader.

1987 Dissident Afrikaners in talks with ANC at Dakar.

Afrikaner leaders hold talks with ANC in England.

ANC prepares Operation Vula to seize power if negotiation fails.

Shaganovitch's second offensive fails as South African and UNITA forces prevent crossing of Lomba River.

Cubans put out feelers for negotiations.

South African security chief in secret talks with Mandela in prison.

1988 South African–UNITA attempts to drive Luanda forces east of Cuito River fail.

Cubans open new front in southern Angola and join peace talks.

Agreement on Cubans leaving Angola and South Africans quitting Namibia is signed in New York.

Emergency regulations tightened in South Africa.

ANC switches from supporting command economy to mixed economy.

White election makes Conservative Party the official opposition in South Africa.

1989 PW Botha has stroke, FW de Klerk becomes NP leader and president.

De Klerk frees Walter Sisulu and some other ANC leaders from jail, and has secret meeting with Mandela.

1990 De Klerk frees Mandela, unbans ANC and PAC, and ends state of emergency; ANC suspends armed struggle and begins formal talks with government; Groote Schuur Accord signed.

Namibia becomes independent under Swapo government.

1991 Government repeals apartheid laws and begins Codesa negotiations with ANC at Kempton Park. National Peace Accord signed in bid to halt escalating violence.

1992 In referendum, whites overwhelmingly back continued negotiation.

Codesa talks collapse; Boipatong and Bisho massacres; ANC begins 'rolling mass action' campaign; negotiators sign Record of Understanding; ANC proposes 'sunset clauses' to protect whites; PAC begins killing whites.

1993 Chris Hani assassinated; ANC pulls out of talks; agreement reached on election date and interim constitution; Transitional Executive Council takes office.

Mandela and De Klerk awarded Nobel Peace Prize.

Kempton Park negotiators agree on reabsorption of bantustans.

1994 IFP members killed in pro-Zulu marches in Johannesburg; some white right-wingers begin bombings and plan rebellion; others form Freedom Front to contest election; ANC wins South Africa's first democratic election; Mandela installed as president.

1995 Food riots in Zimbabwe.

Truth and Reconciliation Commission initiated in South Africa.

Maoris demonstrate in New Zealand and aboriginals in Australia over land claims.

1996 Government of National Unity (GNU) adopts new constitution for South Africa.

National Party withdraws from GNU.

1997 White farmers killed in South Africa.

War veterans in Zimbabwe demonstrate over government's looting of their compensation fund; in placatory move,

Mugabe awards large gratuities and offers white farms.

1999 Thabo Mbeki succeeds retiring Mandela as president of South Africa.

2000 Zimbabweans show dissatisfaction with Zanu(PF) by rejecting proposed new constitution in referendum; in reaction, government launches invasion of white farms by 'war veterans' and abolishes compensation for seized land.

Zanu(PF) narrowly wins election in Zimbabwe.

Zanu(PF) attacks courts after they declare land seizures illegal.

2000 White farmers jailed in Zimbabwe for opposing land seizures; white firms in towns attacked by Zanu(PF) gangs.

2002 African Union formed to replace OAU.

2003 Emigration has cut Zimbabwe's white population by two-thirds.

INTRODUCTION

In Africa, where human time began, the European occupation of the continent was but a drip in the ancient stream of the millennia. For the Africa of the period, however, it was a powerful phenomenon that changed the entire continent.

The rush for colonies at the end of the 19th century, popularly known as the Scramble for Africa, was especially transforming, sweeping across the continent like a tsunami, destroying existing states and creating new ones wholesale, splitting old communities and throwing diverse peoples into forced association, bringing social destruction but also, in its wake, a measure of development and infrastructure.

Never before or since has a continental map been so comprehensively redrawn, so many established societies so drastically reshaped, in so short a time.

Even before the Scramble, Europeans had settled in large numbers at the southern and northern extremities of the continent. Afterwards they came in even greater numbers and into east Africa as well, confident that they were taking Africa for their own by the right of innate superiority.

The colonial and settler intrusion of the Europeans ran for close on four centuries, peaking in the Scramble. Then the wave receded almost as precipitately as it had rushed in, leaving a genetic sediment, the white people who could not or would not leave Africa, the millions who either by choice or compulsion of circumstance have become Africans, white Africans.

The collapse first of colonialism and then of indigenous white supremacy has left the native-born whites facing a future of excruciating uncertainty. Hugely outnumbered by the black people whom they or their forebears dominated and often exploited, their very identity and culture are now in question. Seldom in history have so few people been able to dominate so many others for such a long time. And seldom has a dominant minority like that in South Africa so dramatically surrendered its power, putting its fate in the hands of those it formerly subjugated and often oppressed.

Once ostracised in the world, the white South Africans have been restored to international respectability, lauded even, for their courageous act and the example it has set for a world still fraught with racial intolerance and oppression.

As Africans themselves now, they must find ways to live with the black majority whose traditions and habits are in many ways starkly different from their own. By the same token, it is in the interests of the black majorities to make the most of what the whites can offer wherever the latter live, for their skills and material resources are rare and precious in their continent.

The future of the major community of white Africans, those in South Africa, must inevitably be sharply cleft from their past, for there is too much that is bad in the past for them to take much of it forward in their culture, too much that is resented by the black people with whom they must now live in brotherhood. There being no sound future, however, without knowledge of the past, they must know their own story, which often has been distorted or hidden for base purposes. The story is intertwined with the whole European experience in Africa, an experience as wide and dramatic as the continent itself, forming some of history's richest episodes.

PREFACE: THE HINGE OF DESTINY

There was a moment during the inauguration of Nelson Mandela as president of South Africa in May 1994 that came close to being sublime. In politics sublimity is rare indeed, but Mandela's installation went beyond politics. It was a carnival, a celebration of humanistic triumph shared by the world, and therefore especially open to notions of something beyond excellence.

The special moment came when the air force planes flew over, trailing smoke in the new colours of a nation ostensibly united, democratic and at peace after nearly three and a half centuries of racial division, conflict and oppression. For the delegates of the global community that had made the struggle against apartheid one of the main events of the century, it was the equivalent of the culinary cherry on top. For the South Africans it had deeper significance, giving credence to the evidence that apartheid was dead and to the expectation that it would be replaced by true democracy.

When the aircraft came Mandela had already taken over as head of state. The formalities were done, the pact sealed. What the serried warplanes did then was put the stamp on the seal: the assurance that the armed forces that had been deployed in defence of apartheid would now assert and defend black majority rule. Surely the power was now truly with the people if the armed forces that had once been the power of apartheid were now with the people. It could never again be held exclusively by the whites, even if some of them tried to reverse the process. It had gone too far now; there was no going back.

Freedom had, of course, been declared in the new constitution and demonstrated in the first election open to all. But it was never fully proven until Mandela was installed in office and the planes came over. Then it became tangible and credible for everyone, blacks and whites. The fly-past brought the biggest cheer of the day, but it was more than just delight at a stirring spectacle. It was blacks and whites cheering for different forms of release, but in the end for the same freedom. For the blacks, it was release from oppression. For the whites, it was release from a bad past, release from shame. And for both, it was freedom to enter a pristine future, freedom to jointly forge new relationships and create respectable social structures.

Some of those in the amphitheatre found it necessary to ram a knuckle up under the nose to keep from weeping. Some quietly wept; others openly screamed. It was about as close as a political event can get to being orgasmic.

Sublimity, ecstasy, euphoria – all are, like orgasm, short-lived, however. Their real significance often lies in their aftermath, and so it will be for the South Africans.

The climactic moment did not reach full sublimity because for many of the celebrants the rapture was shadowed by anxiety about what might follow for the nation, by uncertainty that the new democracy would survive in the harsh environment left by apartheid and the fight against it. For some, it was far from sublime, only painful, for the nature of the ceremony – a formal handover of power – required that the vanquished be there as well as the victors. It is doubtful that the joy was unequivocally shared, for instance, by all the chiefs of the armed forces who had directed the defence of white supremacy and who now stood in fealty behind the black man who was their new commander-in-chief. Or by FW de Klerk, probably the last white president of South Africa ever, standing beside Mandela to hand over the power, to officially end more than three centuries of segregation and white domination – and indeed looking rather unhappy.

Even the vanquished, however, could find a certain triumph in their surrender: the triumph of reason over their unworthy and hopeless cause. Even those whites who had not supported apartheid but had passively acquired its taint could now hope to wipe off the stain. All of them could know that they were no longer pariahs around the globe, that the world's doors were open to them again

Twice in the recent past, first in Rhodesia and then in Namibia, a minority of white citizens had surrendered power to a black majority after waging different versions of civil war to defend it. Now, in the last lair of white supremacy, the only remaining white oligarchy was peacefully handing the power to those it had oppressed – and doing so with no real guarantee, only with hope, that the power would be used wisely and without retribution. It was partly in salute of this act of sanity and courage that the representatives of the international community had come to the inauguration.

There was, however, a wider significance to the occasion than the formal ending of apartheid. The ceremony marked also an acute turn in a great sociocultural process that had begun five centuries earlier when Prince Henry the Navigator sent Portuguese sea captains out from Lisbon to find a sea route to India. From that initiative had come the first European settlements in sub-Saharan Africa, and half a millennium of transformation in the continent. The process was not ended by Mandela's inauguration; rather, the ceremony marked the start of a new phase of it, for the whites are still present in their millions. Their story is still unfolding.

A major part of it, however, the era of white domination – as distinct from white presence – in sub-Saharan Africa, was symbolically terminated on that day. It was an era that had begun with the almost simultaneous expansion into the hinterland of Portugal's coastal trading enclaves and of the Dutch settlement at the Cape of Good Hope. It had climaxed with what has been called the Scramble for Africa, the unseemly episode late in the 19th century in which the European powers descended on the continent in a colonial feeding frenzy. The era had waned with the advent of independence in the former colonies, and now had ended with the scrapping of apartheid.

Except for the tiny Spanish enclaves of Ceuta and Melilla in Morocco, Africa was now ruled by black people from Cairo to the Cape.

Mandela's inauguration marked the end not only of white domination but also of the struggle to throw it off, which had begun in earnest after the Second World War. The wave of liberation had stirred with anti-colonial riots in the Gold Coast, then swelled up in Kenya and Algeria, where the indigenous peoples showed that European domination might successfully be challenged by force of arms – by insurgency and terrorism. The wave had then swept peacefully but inexorably through the colonies and protectorates, impelled not only by black nationalism but in much of Africa by the colonial masters' readiness to surrender power. Bloodied again in Mozambique, Angola, Rhodesia, Namibia and South Africa, the wave had at last washed to Africa's southern tip and the continent was liberated from sea to sea.

So there was at Mandela's inauguration a powerful sense not only of present significance but also of history, of an epochal roll-over.

One could easily imagine the ghosts of white ascendancy gathered there to observe and ponder the magnitude of the occasion. Portuguese navigators like Vasco da Gama rubbing spectral shoulders with leaders of the Dutch settlement at the Cape, such as Jan van Riebeeck and Simon van der Stel. Perhaps Napoleon, whose fascination with the Egypt of the Nile led him to conquer it. And the missionaries, certainly Livingstone, driven by religious zeal and geographic curiosity to become one of the most renowned figures in history. The explorers would be there, Mungo Park, Baker, Burton and Speke, and others who experienced amazing hardships and adventures in the cause of 'discovering' for Europe what the natives had always known. There would perhaps be the ghosts of the point-men of the Scramble: the British/American Henry Morton Stanley, and the Francophone Italian, Pierre de Brazza. And imperialist visionaries such as Cecil Rhodes, who dreamed of an Africa British from Cairo to the Cape; Lord Lugard, who tightened Britain's grip on the continent from east coast to west; Gustave Borgnis-Desbordes, who did much the same for France in the west. Certainly there would be the stern ghost of Prince Otto von Bismarck, more opportunist than visionary, who triggered the Scramble in order to promote German interests against the other European powers.

There would have to be the soldiers, the stiff-backed martinets who in large numbers stamped colonialism on Africa. Perhaps Thomas-Robert Bugeaud, the private in Napoleon's army who became a Marshal of France and ruthlessly subdued Algeria. Sir Charles McCarthy, whose heart was eaten by the Asante he tried to conquer. Sir Garnet Wolseley, the dedicated militarist who led the British armies in 'Ashanti', on the Nile and in the Boer War. Charles Gordon, the mystic who lost his head to the Mahdi at Khartoum. Kitchener, who avenged Gordon and imposed Victorian pride and imperatives at both ends of the continent. Roberts, who in the same cause instituted atrocities against Afrikaner families. Assuredly there would be the Boer part-timers such as Botha, De Wet and Smuts who out-generalled the British professionals in the South African War. Somewhere in the ghostly assembly would be the Germans, Lothar von Trotha, who tried to exterminate the Herero nation, and Paul von Lettow-Vorbeck, who in turn out-generalled Smuts in East Africa.

There would, of course, be the spirits of Paul Kruger and the other Boer presidents who created white republics in lands claimed by the blacks, and fought to keep them from being seized by the British. There would surely be the merchant princes, perhaps George Goldie, who clamped British commerce firmly in West Africa, and Sir William Mackinnon who did the same in the east. Colonialism's developers might be represented by Ferdinand de Lesseps, builder of the Suez Canal.

The monarchs would be essential presences, Victoria herself, of course, and Kaiser Wilhelm. Also Leopold II of Belgium – if he dared show his disgraced face – who got rich from atrocity. There might even be that shabby latecomer to the colonial scramble, the fascist Mussolini, no monarch but kingly for a while in his empire-building. An inevitable though woebegone spectre would be that of Hendrik Verwoerd, watching the final dissolution of his apartheid dream.

Not only the famous would be there but also the infamous – the slavers, the land-grabbers and the Congo rubber barons who devised the production incentives of death and mutilation.

Also the loyal servants of European colonisation: the white bwanas – the governors and district commissioners. And the entrepreneurs – the traders, the prospectors, the white hunters – who helped fix Europe's grip on Africa and left their seed behind when the European powers released their hold and departed.

Somewhere in the ghostly assembly would surely be the souls of some of the thousands of Africa-born whites who left their native lands in answer to Britain's call in 1914 and again in 1939, and died on foreign fields and distant seas.

Spectrally or in memory, all these figures were present as Mandela's inauguration brought their saga to its close, and they will be recalled in these pages.

The inauguration stands now in history as an epochal pivot in the fortunes of the whites in Africa. The past axis of the pivot is the era of white intrusion, settlement and dominance. The future axis extends into uncertainty, an immediate period when the whites born and remaining in Africa can be sure only of minority status and political impotency. Living now in a state of existential anxiety, they know only that they must find fortitude and hope with which to replace the comfortable certainty once seemingly conferred by segregation and supremacy. They must come to terms with being Africans.

★ ★ ★ ★

The Africanisation of the whites was not, of course, an overnight transmutation catalysed by democracy. It took place gradually over the centuries. Still, the realisation probably came as a surprise to many when democracy snapped up the blinds.

Their ancestors came to Africa to colonise it and Europeanise it, but instead the colonisers have decamped and their descendants are being Africanised. In the lands of those ancestors they are now regarded as foreigners, entitled to no more consideration than any other foreigner.

The Afrikaners, of course, had long accepted their Africanisation, embracing it in their very name, but with a fundamental reservation: white Africans they might be, but whites above all else. The acceptance has come less easily to the whites of British extraction, for their ties with Europe were tighter than those of the Afrikaners, their bond with Africa looser.

All the whites were aware that the ethnic residuum they formed was unlike the others left by British colonialism in the United States, Canada, Australia and New Zealand, unlike even those deposits left by the Spanish in Latin America, in that they alone were a white minority among a majority whose skin colours and cultures were vastly different. The white settlers in all these other lands had been outnumbered at first by the natives, but all except those in Africa had ended up outnumbering the natives. It is arguable whether the reason is that the forebears of the others killed off more than did those of the South Africans.

In any event, once the European settlers in the Americas and Australia had conquered the natives and begun to outnumber them, they could afford largely to ignore them, which they did. The whites in Africa, on the other hand, were increasingly outnumbered and had always to live with the possibility of being overwhelmed – culturally, economically and politically if not physically – by the indigenous peoples. The fear of it was never strong enough to make the white settlers abandon the more temperate parts of Africa, but it did make them take extreme measures to protect themselves by way of dominating the black peoples. Parallel with the fear of being swamped by the blacks ran the desire to acquire ever more of their land and to exploit them as cheap labour. More than any others, these three factors shaped white behaviour from the first settlement to the inevitable advent of majority rule.

Now, of all the descendants of white settlers around the world, only those in Africa still face the possibility of cultural extinction, of an obliteration of custom and identity. There is some irony in this, given that the European presence in Africa preceded that in any of the other places of settlement. It was established (by the Portuguese) a decade before Columbus discovered the Americas and about half a century before the first such presence in Canada. The first permanent settlement at the Cape came more than a century before it happened in Australia and New Zealand.

The end of their domination left the whites with a choice between fleeing black rule or coming to terms with it. Most chose to stay, either opportunistically, or out of readiness to embrace African identity, or because they were too old or poor or their ancestors too long out of Europe to find a new home elsewhere.

Hybrids of a peculiar sort, the white Africans are deeply rooted in and adapted to their Third World environment and yet are endowed with much of the technology and practices of the First World. It was this technology, for instance, that in South Africa pioneered human heart transplanting, that built the southern hemisphere's first nuclear bombs and Africa's only nuclear power station. Their skills and capital gave South Africa assets possessed by no other African countries, certainly not on the same scale. In turn these assets gave black South Africans a unique chance to avoid following the many other African countries that had gone down the slippery slope from independence to economic ruin, corruption, civil war, dictatorship and despair – and perhaps a chance to help haul back those who had slipped.

Besides their material assets the whites also had relatively large numbers. These had declined somewhat from something over six million at the peak of white settlement in Africa, but they still numbered some five million, mostly in South Africa. Together they exceeded the populations of a number of sovereign countries elsewhere. There were at least as many of them as there were Danes and Finns, and they outnumbered the Norwegians, the native Irish and Lebanese, the New Zealanders, the Israelis, the Nicaraguans, the Jordanians, the Panamanians and others. When colonialism began to collapse there were nearly five million whites in South Africa, more than a million in Algeria, about three hundred thousand in Zimbabwe, some eighty-five thousand in Namibia, about eighty thousand in Kenya, and smaller pockets elsewhere in places as scattered as Zambia, Madagascar, Mauritius, Seychelles, Ivory Coast and Gabon. Not all were Africa-born or otherwise eligible for a white African identity, but the majority probably were.

The democratisation of South Africa, besides ending white supremacy, was widely seen to hold a brilliant promise: if blacks and whites could succeed in living and prospering together they would light a lamp for the world, one that would shine into the remaining dark corners of ethnic prejudice and conflict elsewhere on the planet.

Ten years later, the lamp remained lit, though burning with a flickering flame. The common white fear that black rule would send the country into disorder and decline had not come about. The fear had nonetheless driven thousands of whites to emigrate, depleting the pool of both skills and capital. For most of those who stayed, life went on much the same as before – but with greater anxiety than ever. Those who cannot or will not flee have become, in a sense, colonialism's castaways, stranded among people whose languages and culture few of them even now understand, but which they must now either adapt to or adopt.

The South Africans in particular form a unique community, one that has come out of a past filled with more violence and hatred, with perhaps more political conflict and warfare, with more social upheaval, than has been experienced in the ethnic residuums left by European migration elsewhere in the world. Previously vilified, ostracised and penalised in the world more than any other community in modern history, this one has now resumed a decent place in international society.

But in their own continent these people are now vulnerable as well as valuable. They can now only guess at what lies ahead for them, for their accustomed lifestyle, for their traditions, their languages, their cultural heritage, the whole of the separate, eurocentric world that their predecessors began to create more than four centuries ago, when Europe was emerging from the Middle Ages.

ETHNIC MOVEMENTS THAT SHAPED AFRICAN HISTORY

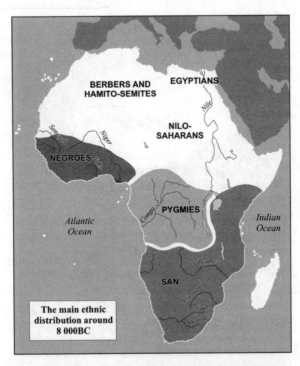

The main ethnic distribution around 8 000BC

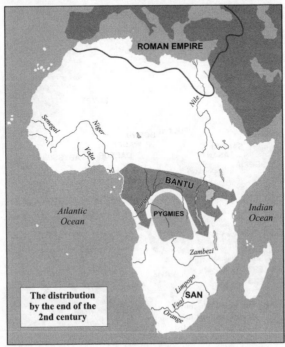

The distribution by the end of the 2nd century

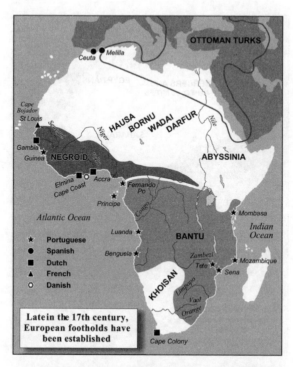

Late in the 17th century, European footholds have been established

Legend:
- ★ Portuguese
- ● Spanish
- ■ Dutch
- ▲ French
- ○ Danish

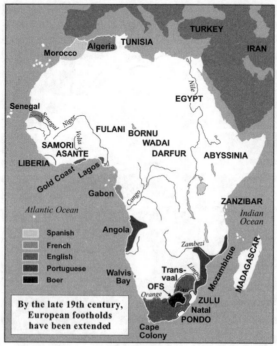

By the late 19th century, European footholds have been extended

Legend:
- Spanish
- French
- English
- Portuguese
- Boer

CHAPTER 1

SEA OF DARKNESS AND GHOSTS

Though the Europeans came early to Africa's shores, they went slowly round them and even more slowly into its interior. It took them nearly a century just to feel their way round the coastline from Portugal to the Arabian Sea. Another three centuries passed before they became seriously interested in what lay in the interior, let alone possessive about it.

As late as the middle of the 19th century much of the continent's middle was blank on the European maps, even though Europeans had lived in the Cape for two centuries and had been visiting or occupying north Africa for twenty-five.

When David Livingstone's party footslogged their dusty way in 1849 to Lake Ngami, his first major geographical 'discovery' in Africa, there were already more than three thousand kilometres of railways in England – more than twice the distance covered by Livingstone's trek. The Victorian era was into its second decade, and its technology was blooming. Ether was being used in anaesthesia, and safety matches were old hat. The world had got its first nightclub (in Paris).

By the time Livingstone stumbled across the Victoria Falls in 1855 the Europeans were already well into an industrial revolution lit by gas and driven by steam and soon to be powered and illuminated by electricity (the first light bulb having been invented the year before). They had begun planning the Suez Canal to cut the sailing time to the East – 'sailing' being a relative term since by then ships were being driven by steam. The first iron-hulled Cunard liner had in fact crossed the Atlantic, and in only nine and a half days. The British had laid the first undersea telegraphic cable across the English Channel and were busy laying another to America. Double-decker, horse-drawn trams were running in London, and work had begun on the city's underground railway system. The hypodermic syringe and cold storage were coming into use. The first elevator, which was to become known as the lift in England, had been installed in America.

Exploration of the hostile reaches of both the Arctic and Antarctic had begun almost two decades before Burton and Speke in 1858 'discovered' Lakes Victoria and Tanganyika in their warm tropical setting. At a time when the Europeans had pinpointed the position of the magnetic north pole they were uncertain about the source of the Nile, that ancient wellspring of some of their own civilisation.

The Europeans' ignorance of hinterland Africa was remarkable considering that they had been in contact with the continent even before Alexander the Great's conquest of Egypt. But not even Alexander's Greeks, or even the Romans after them, had ventured deep into Africa. Neither had taken their occupation much beyond the lower cataracts of the Nile, their further exploration presumably having been blocked by the Sudd, the great, shifting, mosquito-plagued swampland barring the river's upper reaches.

The Romans had some indirect knowledge of Africa's western coastline north of the 'bulge' but seem never to have explored it. Seeing no incentive to cross the hostile sands of the Sahara desert, they extended their empire along the entire Mediterranean littoral, defeating the Carthaginians, the descendants of Semitic Phoenicians who had brought their own sophisticated technology to the littoral. By the end of the 6th century the Romans had been expelled by the Arabs. Aside from fluctuating Spanish occupations of the area across the Gibraltar strait, Europeans would not again control any part of the region until Napoleon's invasion of Egypt in 1798.

Before then, however, they would establish a presence south of the Sahara that would bring revolutionary change to the continent. That presence would come not over the traditional routes across the Mediterranean and the Sahara but, startlingly for the Africans, from out of the unknown, from the stormy and unsailed Atlantic.

The Europeans came not with conquering armies but in small bands, tentatively, as trade-seeking explorers. Their interest was primarily commercial, overshadowing the lesser ones of religious zeal and of scientific and geographic curiosity. The religious motive was essentially to promote Christianity, if necessary at the expense of Islam, for the Crusades were still relatively recent and the rivalry still fierce. The Papal authorisation of war against Islam was still in effect and taken very seriously in Portugal and Spain.

The commercial interest was mainly in gold and ivory, later also in slaves. Gold, together with silver, was even in the late Middle Ages the principal medium of exchange in trade and the index of wealth. Ivory was the nearest thing to the plastics of the late 20th century, even if relatively more expensive. More versatile than bone, more durable than wood or ceramics, it was incomparable for making almost anything from sword hilts to buttons. Europe's enduring desire for ivory would profoundly influence the course of Africa's history.

The Europeans had known for centuries that gold and ivory came from somewhere south of the Sahara, transported by way of the caravan routes across the desert. It seemed possible that they could more efficiently and cheaply be obtained by sailing southward down the African coastline and fetching them back by the shipload. The possibility remained hypothetical well into the 15th century, however, since no-one was willing to try it for the reason that southern European sailors had not yet mastered the art of tacking against the wind.

This was not a serious problem on the relatively small and usually placid Mediterranean, where ships could be rowed by banks of oars in the absence of a favourable wind. But it was a serious handicap to marine exploration far out into the stormy Atlantic, where the prevailing winds blow from the north. Neither the Portuguese nor the Atlantic Spanish had ships of the right design, or the skills necessary, to sail far out to sea and come back against the wind, not even, it seems, by hugging the coastline. And none was willing to brave the unknown perils that might lie out in the Atlantic – giant sea monsters, perhaps, or ship-swallowing vortexes or perpetual storms. No-one had found the courage or the skills to sail much beyond the Canaries.

There was no lack of incentive to do so, though, not so much to find out what was beyond the Atlantic horizons but to find a sea route round Africa to the East Indies. Besides the desire for direct access to Africa's gold and ivory, the Europeans were eager to find a new way to reach the silks, precious stones and spices of the East. Spices, for one, meant a great deal more to the Europeans of the Middle Ages than they do to modern generations for the simple reason that they were the best means then available to preserve food and to make it still palatable when it was going off, a common occurrence before the invention of refrigeration. It would be an exaggeration to say that the Europeans' early exploration of Africa was motivated by their abhorrence of bad meat, but that certainly played a big part in it.

The spices and silks had to be carried expensively and perilously to Europe overland along the Silk Route from China, or from India by way of the eastern Mediterranean. All of this trade first went through points controlled by Muslims, the Ottoman Turks, and then through Venetian and Genoese middlemen, all of whom imposed prohibitive duties. The Portuguese, being at the wrong end of this line, developed a strong incentive to find a way to bypass Islam and the Venetians by sailing round Africa.

The Portuguese found themselves particularly well placed to respond to these incentives towards the middle of the 15th century. Not only had they thrown the invading Moors out of their own country, but they had taken the fight to Islam, crossing the Mediterranean to capture Ceuta in Morocco in 1415, an act some historians see as the beginning of Europe's exploitation of Africa. Having in addition firmly installed a new dynasty in the form of the house of Aziz, Portugal was then the only European nation-state besides Spain with the political stability and economic strength necessary to back foreign exploration and expansion, and possessing the technical skills to carry it out.

Technology made a fortuitous advance at this time with the development by the Portuguese of the caravel, a relatively small but highly seaworthy vessel with up to four masts. Rather than the rectangular, centrally-slung sails used by the Mediterranean sailors, the caravel had triangular sails copied from the lateen sails of the Arab dhows of the Red Sea. Easily pivoted to either side of the mast, the sails made seamen better able to counterpoise the force of the wind on the sail and the force of the water on the rudder, thereby squeezing the boat diagonally forward against the wind, tacking in a zigzag but always forward pattern.

Equipped now to take on the one-way winds of the Atlantic, the Portuguese began to venture further from shore, reaching Madeira in 1418 and the Azores 12 years later. But for decades no sea captain was willing to challenge what had always seemed to be the point of no return: Cape Bojador on the African mainland immediately south of the Canaries. Beyond Bojador was a sea 'of darkness and ghosts' into which none dared go.

The breakthrough came in 1434 when a daring seafarer, Gil Eanes, took his courage (not to mention that of his crew) in his hands and sailed some way past Cape Bojador, then turned about and zigzagged his way safely back home. Still, it took the Portuguese another half-century to make their coast-hugging way to the southern tip of Africa, which Bartholomeu Dias rounded in 1487. The exploration had been extraordinarily slow when measured by modern standards, but the perils and difficulties were still great. Though the Portuguese seamen had astrolabes and compasses and could navigate by the stars in the northern hemisphere, the night skies beyond the equator were strange to them and they were still feeling their way through the southern seas – or, more accurately, along the African coastline.

Not until 1498 did Vasco da Gama complete the voyage to India. Drawing on the experience of Dias, he followed a bold new plan that was in concept and execution a 15th-century equivalent of the 'slingshot' technique used in modern space exploration, in which a craft is rocketed off to orbit a distant body, gathering momentum to then shoot off from that for an even more distant objective. Instead of hugging the coast, Da Gama's flotilla headed south-west deep into the frighteningly unknown reaches of the Atlantic. Then, beyond Tristan da Cunha, it turned to run with the Westerlies to round the Cape.

Da Gama's first landfall three months into his voyage completed the longest open-sea voyage yet made by Europeans. More important, it established that the sailing time to the Cape could be halved by taking the slingshot route. Thereafter the route to India was relatively certain, and Da Gama anchored off Calicut 'with great rejoicing and with the sound of trumpets after dinner'. Ten months later he was back in Lisbon with the first cargoes of spices to be carried to Europe round the Cape. He had opened the way for the European colonisation of the East.

In the course of their search for the sea route to the east, the Portuguese had reached the coast of the main gold-producing hinterland, now modern Ghana, and gained direct access to the Akan and Black Volta goldfields. To defend their trade against the competition now coming from other European seafaring nations, the Portuguese built Elmina fort on what was to become known as the Gold Coast. Elmina, the first of the strongholds the Portuguese were to string along the west and east coasts, was completed in 1482, giving Europe its first toehold in sub-Saharan Africa.

The Portuguese had hoped that Christian kingdoms in north-eastern Africa would provide a base for Portuguese operations in the Indian Ocean. Christianity had not fared well in Africa, however. The Christian Nubians on the upper Nile had been overwhelmed by the Muslims, and the remaining Christians in Abyssinia were hard pressed. In an effort to save them, the Portuguese landed soldiers at Massawa on the Red Sea in 1541. The Muslims were driven back but 17 years later recaptured Massawa, isolating the Abyssinians in their mountain fastnesses.

To their great disappointment, the Portuguese had found no trace of Prester John, the Christian leader reputed to rule on or beyond Africa's east coast.

The rounding of the Cape meant that Africa's coastline was known, albeit only roughly. Portugal's acquaintance with Africa remained largely peripheral, however, for while its naval strength gave it control of the coastline, tropical diseases and strong African societies discouraged inland conquest.

Portugal's main concern in any case was to secure the sea route to the East against Arab or any other competitors, and then to exploit the African gold and ivory trade. To that end the Portuguese established a headquarters on Mozambique Island and bases on Zanzibar, Pemba and Lamu islands and, later, at Mombasa in addition to those at Elmina, Shama and Axim on the Gold Coast, Fernando Po and Sao Tome in the Gulf of Guinea, and at Luanda and Benguela on the Angolan coast. No serious effort was made to penetrate inland other than a tentative presence up the Congo River and a deeper and more permanent one up the Zambezi, in which bases were established at Sena and Tete, in order to gain control of the upriver gold trade.

★ ★ ★ ★

In their exploration of the African coastline the Portuguese became the first to pass through all of the great social divisions that geography and migration had created in Africa, the fundamental differentiation that dictates the continent's basic ethnic variety, making, for example, a Xhosa as different from a Hausa as a Finn is from a Spaniard.

First the Portuguese passed along the Atlantic end of the strip of Africa that had been known to the Europeans for centuries, the continent-wide stretch between the Mediterranean and the Sahara, inhabited by Egyptians, Arabs, Berbers, Moors and Bedouins. Rounding Africa's 'bulge', they encountered the Negroid societies who had to some extent been cut off by the Sahara from the powerful influences of the Mediterranean, though tenuously linked by the caravan routes across the desert. The further south they went the weaker became these influences, the societies there still making their own way through their Iron Age.

In Africa north of the equator, kingdoms and empires rose and fell for hundreds of years before the arrival of the Portuguese. The kingdoms had tended to agglomerate at the intersections of the great caravan trading routes, which for centuries had provided a link across the Sahara, bringing information and cultural influences from the Mediterranean, Egypt and the Middle East, notably the cultures of Islam. Though the Sahara discouraged any mass movement of people southwards from the Mediterranean, the caravan routes gave the African kingdoms a measure of overland contact with some of the sources of European civilisation long before the Portuguese came by sea.

When the Portuguese stepped ashore from their caravels there were in sub-Saharan Africa some highly organised states, with centralised systems of government and structures for collecting taxes and dispensing justice. Their armies had infantry, cavalry and archers.

On reaching the forested southern half of West Africa, their 'Guinea', the Portuguese came to the Negro states which, only tenuously linked to the caravan routes, had not become Islamised. Where present-day Ghana is situated the Portuguese found the gold-rich Akan states. In what is now Nigeria they came across the Yoruba states of Oyo, Ife and Benin and their now-famous bronze sculptures.

As elsewhere in tropical Africa, some Guinean communities engaged in human sacrifice and cannibalism. Further south, in what is now Gabon, the Fang people were especially noted for eating their fellows, and not only because of their custom of filing their teeth to points. Such habits, though rare, would later be seized on by Europeans as evidence of the lesser status they wished to impose on Africans. In this context, it is worth recalling the eminent Africanist Basil Davidson's comparison of Africa and Europe during the medieval period.

'If anything,' he wrote, 'the comparison between Africa and Europe is likely to be in Africa's favour. Throughout the medieval period most African forms of government were undoubtedly more representative than their European contemporaries. Most African wars were less costly in life and property. And most African ruling groups were less predatory. So far as the comparison has any value, daily life in medieval Europe was likely to be far more hazardous or disagreeable for the common man …'[1]

As they sailed further south the Portuguese encountered the people who had migrated far beyond the influence of the caravan routes during the great outpouring of negroid people from West Africa that has been described by some historians as the most important happening in African history. It was this slow but massive migration from the Negro heartland that filled most of the southern half of the continent with the Bantu people whose descendants occupy it today.

Supposedly triggered by growing population pressure in the Negroes' customary territory in the lower half of the bulge, the outflow began at the start of the first millennium, when the Roman empire embraced the Mediterranean littoral. Spreading east and south, the fecund flood met first with the pygmies, the little hunter-gatherers who at that time occupied most of the equatorial rain forests, and assimilated some.

Moving on into the savannah, the negroid migrants encountered other hunter-gatherers, the San (Bushmen) people who are believed to have occupied all of southern and eastern Africa up to the Horn, and whose tongue clicks are thought by some to have eventually entered the languages of the southern Bantu known as the Nguni. The migrants also met with the Caucasoid Hamites who had worked their way down from what is now commonly known as the Middle East, and whose intermarriage with the San is believed by some anthropologists to have created the Khoikhoi (Hottentots).

Pushing the San and the Khoikhoi before it, sometimes simply absorbing them, the negroid flood spread across from coast to coast. It also moved south until in the middle of the second millennium it had reached beyond the Tropic of Capricorn.

The migration crept rather than flooded into the lower two-thirds of the continent. Along the way, elements of the flood settled and jelled into ethnic groups that have developed different customs and beliefs but are mostly linked through common elements of language.

As they moved on round the continental tip, the Portuguese mariners came across the Khoikhoi and San peoples in their last refuge. Moving on eastwards and northwards, they encountered the southern vanguard of the great Bantu migration that had ousted the Khoikhoi and San: the Nguni peoples living in late-Iron Age societies in the south-east of present-day South Africa, which they had reached about four centuries earlier.

In most of southern Africa at this time the migration had generally formed not kingdoms but smaller chiefdoms. Since there was still enough room in the Khoikhoi and San lands into which the pastoral and agronomist Bantu could spread, the chiefdoms, rather than expanding by conquest into kingdoms, tended to split when they exceeded a convenient size. The offshoots then moved off to displace the hunter-gatherer San and the pastoral Khoikhoi. Only when the demand for land exceeded the supply did the stronger chiefdoms begin to incorporate smaller ones, most notably leading to the emergence of the militant Zulu kingdom under Shaka and its influence on the *mfecane* of the early 19th century.

In this reversal of the great southward migration, Nguni groups moved inland from the coastal Zulu kingdom, fleeing Shaka's indomitable regiments, to establish new societies in the interior. The great migration had run out of room and was rebounding off its own stalled front: the Xhosa tribes now firmly entrenched on the south-eastern coast. Further dispersal to the south was blocked by the northward expansion of the European settlers. To the west were the Tswana peoples, pressed up against the Kalahari and Namib deserts.

By the time of the *mfecane*, the Portuguese had been established in Mozambique for two centuries, though only shallowly. As their predecessors, the early Portuguese explorers, had made their way further up the coast beyond Mozambique they had found themselves dealing with Swahili and Arab people, and indirectly with the Nilotic and Bantu communities of the East African hinterland. The cultures of the coastal societies had been influenced by ancient trade across the Indian Ocean with the Arabs and Indians and, indirectly, the Chinese. The port of Kilwa, on the coast of what is now Tanzania, had for instance been founded by Muslims in the 10th century to handle the gold trade with the hinterland to the south. Yet, aside from the links with the Zambezi valley and Katanga, there was little intercourse with the wider hinterland.

When they reached Africa's Horn, the Portuguese came to the last of the great social divisions, the Somalis and Ethiopians whose societies had long been infused with Hamito-Semitic influences from beyond the Red Sea.

Beyond the few inland trade routes, the southern and central hinterland of Africa was largely unknown to the outside world when the Portuguese completed their coastal explorations. There is evidence in the writings of the Greek geographer Claudius Ptolemy that the traders of Alexandria in the 4th century had heard about the great lakes and even about snow-capped Mount Kilimanjaro. Still, the hinterland remained blank on European maps for centuries after the coast had become known to them.

CHAPTER 2

SHRINKING THE WORLD

When brave Gil Eanes sailed past Bojador and out into the unknown Atlantic he was making a great leap that was to have larger significance for humankind than the more celebrated one to the lifeless moon has yet had.

For Eanes's voyage did more than open the sea route to the Indies – it opened up the world. The lives of the great majority of succeeding generations everywhere on the planet were affected by it, indirectly if not directly. By proving the more effective sailing technique, Eanes's leap cleared the way for the Europeans to spread their technology and mercantilism around the globe. Besides a sizeable indigenous component, the Europeans' technology had largely been acquired through their special facility for emulating and improving on the discoveries of others, principally the Arabs and the Chinese. It was a facility that was to make them masters of the world, enabling them to subjugate other peoples who, for various reasons, were less imitative and innovative.

Trans-ocean sailing made possible a much wider acquisition of knowledge. With their guns, it also enabled the Europeans to extend economic and political dominance across the seas. Whether the rest of the world benefited more than it suffered from these initiatives is a matter of debate. The voyages of discovery that followed Eanes's great leap are, however, matters of fact. Before the century had turned, the sea route to the East had been opened, Columbus had made his first voyage (in 1492), John Cabot had explored the north American coast for the English (1497), and Amerigo Vespucci and others had sailed to South America. They were followed in the next century by Cordoba, Balboa, Cortes, Magellan, Cartier, Frobisher, Drake, and others in a host of seaborne pioneers.

In modern terms, the pace of discovery was slow. The 88 years that elapsed between Eanes's voyage and the first circumnavigation of the globe by Magellan's crews was more than seven times greater than the 12 years between the launching of the first Russian sputnik and the first moon landing. Nonetheless, the spurt of exploration that Eanes sparked was dramatic on the time scale of the age. The expansion of geographic knowledge in the 15 decades after his voyage was explosive in relation to what had gone on before. In terms of communication, the world suddenly shrank; meetings and exchanges were made possible between most of its peoples for the first time since their very distant ancestors had migrated in hunched and hirsute bands from mankind's presumed point of genesis in Africa.

Besides their technology, the Europeans took into the outer world their extraordinary commercial energy and competitiveness. In Africa as elsewhere it was the imperative of commerce more than any search for knowledge or power that was to drive them further and wider into new territories and ventures. The flag almost always followed trade, was at times even its servant, for it was trade that was powering the levitation of Europe out of the dead-end of the Middle Ages. The Renaissance was rising on the wings of commerce.

Spanish and Portuguese monopoly in the East Indies and the New World came to be challenged by Dutch, French and English entrepreneurs. It was brutal commerce, for the competition, unhampered by writ or regulation, was fierce, sometimes literally cut-throat. At times it became outright buccaneering, not only when pirates and privateers filled their own chests but even when blue-blooded Elizabethan sea-dogs like Drake, Hawkins and Raleigh promoted English trade in the Caribbean by cannon and cutlass. The takeover bids of the time were conducted not by stock acquisitions but by grapeshot, not quietly by boardroom vote but to gunpowder's roar.

While piracy could feed off trade it could not sustain it, and neither could the anarchous adventures of the privateers. It became imperative that the trade be made more orderly, and in both east and west this was done to a large extent by organising it under the banners of companies formed by the public sale of shares but operating in some cases under government or royal charter. Formation by the English of their East India Company in 1600 was followed two years later by the Dutch equivalent, the *Vereenigde Oost-Indische Compagnie (VOC)*, which was to play an important role in white settlement in Africa. It was followed by French and Danish companies. Separate Dutch and English companies were formed to operate in the New World.

In 1637 the Dutch, having largely expelled the Portuguese from the East Indies, turned their interest to Africa's Gold Coast and captured first Elmina and then the other forts, shutting the Portuguese out of the gold trade on the west coast. The Portuguese were left with a presence at the Luanda and Benguela forts in Angola, and a slightly deeper one in the Kongo kingdom. By the middle of the century the Danes had managed to get a toehold on the west coast, and the Swedes were also trying to horn in. Elsewhere in West Africa the French had established a presence at the mouth of the Senegal River, a beachhead that would in time expand into a colonial holding covering most of West Africa.

On Africa's east coast the Portuguese were successfully challenged by Arabs coming down from Oman until eventually their presence was confined more or less to the Mozambican coast and Zambezi valley.

Still there were no Europeans at the Cape. For all its temperate climate and physical beauty, the Cape held little interest for them. In the 15 decades since Da Gama had stopped at the Cape, European seamen had called intermittently to take on water and obtain slaughter cattle from the Khoikhoi. Other than that, however, the Cape seemed to have nothing of commercial value. It had no gold or other minerals, and it was populated by natives who were not always friendly, and were so primitive that they had no manufactured goods such as the fine cloths, jewels and perfumes of the Indies to offer in trade, and no spices. Whatever ivory, pelts and ostrich feathers they could offer were insufficient to excite the Europeans.

Neither the Portuguese, who had resupply stations in Angola and Mozambique, nor the French, who had them on Reunion and Madagascar, had any interest in establishing a station at the Cape. It did, however, become an important watering point for the Dutch and the English, both of whom followed 'slingshot' routes that took wide sweeps out into the ocean, coming close to land only at the Cape.

During the long voyages both lost seamen – as many as half the crew on a single voyage – to scurvy and, knowing that the disease could be prevented by the eating of fresh fruit and vegetables, both the Dutch and the English began to look more closely at the Cape as a station for resupplying their ships with greens. The Dutch had in addition begun to worry that one of the other European powers might establish a base there for the strategic purpose of controlling the growing shipping traffic round the Cape.

Amsterdam was aware that the English had almost beaten the Dutch to the Cape when in 1620 two officers of the English East India Company had landed there and taken formal possession in the name of King James I. The king, perhaps fearing it would be too expensive to maintain, had declined the gift, little knowing how his decision would shape the future of the sub-continent.

Amsterdam's corporate mind was made up by the experience of the crew of the Dutch ship *Haarlem*, which had been wrecked at the Cape in 1647. Forced to fend for themselves on land for a year before they were picked up by another Dutch ship, the crew began growing their own food. Thus the castaways inadvertently demonstrated the practicability of supplying the East Indiamen with fresh greens. Four years after the *Haarlem* survivors came home, Jan van Riebeeck was sent to the Cape to set up a resupply station.

His flotilla of five ships dropped anchor in Table Bay on 6 April 1652. For most of his party of about ninety men, women and children it was their first sight of the great slab-sided, flat-topped mountain in whose shadow would rise South Africa's first city.

Van Riebeeck's orders were not to found a permanent settlement but merely to provide food for the passing ships by growing vegetables and buying slaughter livestock from the Khoikhoi. He was to build a fort, mainly for defence against European competitors. The first earth-walled structure was ravaged by the winter rains. Work was started on a stone fort in 1665 when war broke out with England. Known as the Castle, it became the Company's headquarters at the Cape. Today, still in use, though not as a fort, surrounded by office blocks, hotels, shopping malls and reclaimed foreshore, the building stands as a memorial of the most consequential of all the European settlements in Africa.

Van Riebeeck was initially expected to take no more land than was necessary for his buildings and gardens. But *Jan Compagnie's* innocent little vegetable garden was to become something of a Jack's beanstalk, growing uncontrollably, taking on a life of its own, shucking off the Company and expanding into a colony whose own growth would spark wars. From it would hive off independent republics which in turn would ignite bigger wars until very little of the sub-continent would have been untouched by conflict with or among the Europeans.

Van Riebeeck's little band of gardeners would swell and subdivide into communities, sucking in more European settlers and setting off internal migrations and still more immigration that would carry white people on a tide of technological superiority deep into the heart of Africa, in a saga of conquest and domination that would remake the southern sub-continent. From it would emerge the most powerful nation in Africa – and also the most widely hated and contested racism in history.

The Cape station's switch from supply depot to colony was relatively quick. While easily providing the Company's ships with meat, fruit and vegetables and wine – dreadful stuff at first that gave no hint of the fine wines for which the Cape would in time become famous – the station had not succeeded in growing its own wheat or rice. These had to be imported at considerable cost, dashing the Company's hope that the base would be self-sufficient.

To overcome the problem the Company decided to set up former employees as private entrepreneurs on land on which they would produce wheat, cattle and wine for sale to the Company. Only five years after Van Riebeeck's landing, nine free burghers were established on small farms in the Liesbeeck Valley at Rondebosch, on the other side of Table Mountain. The revictualling station had become a colony. The first white settlers had come to sub-Saharan Africa. The white man was there to stay.

★ ★ ★ ★

The Liesbeeck settlers brought to Africa a new dynamic, expansive white settlement, that was to change the southern part of the continent forever.

The impetus came not from the Company that had placed them on the farms but from the settlers themselves. By their own choice, their settlement became an enrootment that meant cutting their ties with Europe and identifying themselves with Africa. And the further into Africa they went the closer became that identification, the looser their ties with Cape Town, the Company and Europe.

In this respect their ethos was fundamentally different from that of the Portuguese, who, despite having come to Africa more than a century earlier, had kept their cultural roots and loyalties in Portugal. In this sense the Portuguese were sojourners rather than true settlers, unlike even their cousins in Brazil who eventually declared independence from Portugal in 1822. On their way to the riches of the East the Portuguese had stopped at various places on Africa's tropical coasts to exploit gold, ivory, slaves and other commodities. These stoppages had became permanent footholds but, apart from the presences up the Zambezi and Congo rivers, had not been widely extended. Only when the European powers began to scramble for African territory late in the 19th century would Portugal fully extend the colonies of Mozambique and Angola and create the little new one of Portuguese Guinea (Guinea Bissau at independence).

So wherever the Portuguese stopped in Africa, they remained sons of Portugal. Lisbon in time declared the colonies to be parts of Portugal but hardly anybody accepted this fiction, least of all the original inhabitants, who contested it through the gun barrel. It was to be dramatically disproved when the toppling of the Caetano dictatorship in 1975 opened the way to independence for the colonies. Then 'Portugal in Africa' suddenly became empty of Portuguese, most fleeing to Portugal.

The Liesbeeck farmers were different. Their adoption of Africa as home in effect made them the first of the white Africans. They were the nucleus of a European expansion in Africa that would soon send white settlers driving vigorously into the interior, looking not so much for colonial advantage as for land – farmland, homeland, land for the putting down of roots. And for breaking free of control from Europe, or even from Cape Town – and especially from Cape Town after the British seized it in 1795.

The Cape settlement would lay the pattern of racial attitudes – white competition with, exploitation of and discrimination against blacks – that would shape South African life for centuries and perhaps even influence European attitudes towards Africa in general.

Jan Compagnie did not see the Liesbeeck settlement as enrootment; it was just a necessary adaptation in the matter of feeding the passing seamen. The farmers were instruments in a process, nothing more. It was almost as impersonal a deployment as the dumping of the English convicts in Australia in 1788; expediency rather than colonisation. That changed, though, as the settlers began to take Africa for their own, to implant themselves forever in the land.

Because the Company placed its interests above those of the settlers, and because it was beyond any kind of democratic accountability, its rule became as irksome to the Cape burghers as London's later did to the rebellious English colonists of America. Their resistance to the Company's dictates grew as they adapted to their often harsh environment and became increasingly self-sufficient. With or without the Company's consent, they expanded their settlement ever further into the hinterland. In a generation or two they developed an affinity with and a love of the country that left no desire to return to Europe, which had become as alien to them as the Cape had been to their pioneering fathers.

In taking their lifestyle into the hinterland the settler farmers were extending precedents set by the Company, beginning with the seizure of land from the Khoikhoi, whom the Dutch called Hottentots. Since the Khoikhoi's land ownership was communal and not recorded in any form of script (for they had none), their rights of ownership could be expressed only verbally or by occupation, which was not always constant as these pastoralists followed the grazing. Even less claim could be demonstrated by the hunter-gatherer San, for whom land ownership was an even more alien concept than it was for the Khoikhoi. For that reason, if not out of plain pioneering need, the Dutch never gave more than token recognition to the indigenous peoples' title to the land. The Khoikhoi resisted the taking of the land as best they could, but their Iron Age culture was no match for the Europeans' equestrian mobility and guns. They were defeated in two relatively major conflicts and many smaller scraps.

Having acquired enough land for his *raison d'être* of supplying the passing ships, Van Riebeeck had marked off a boundary by building three blockhouses along the Liesbeeck and planting a pole fence and a bitter-almond hedge between the sea (at Salt River mouth) and Table Mountain. That was the frontier, but it was soon left behind by the colony's expansion – an expansion led by the burghers, with the Company scrambling to catch up and impose its authority.

In its style and purpose the Europeans' seizure of the natives' land in the Cape was no different from that in the Americas and Australasia – except in one important respect: both Dutch and later English settlers in the Cape took not only land but, in effect, labour as well, coercing the indigenous people to work on their farms as serfs if not as slaves. While some native Americans and Australasians also ended up working for the whites who had taken their land, in the Cape it happened on a larger scale and was effected more systematically.

One reason may be that in the other countries of settlement there were fewer native people and they were less suited to work in European-style commercial farming, being mostly hunter-gatherers, often nomadic, or subsistence farmers. In contrast, the Khoikhoi – and the Bantu nations whom the Europeans were later to meet – were pastoralists. Peoples of the grasslands and the semi-desert, they were skilled cattlemen, managing large herds. As in the other grasslands of Africa, their herds were food, currency, wealth – the very nucleus of their lifestyle.

This culture must have made them more useful than the hunter-gatherer San to the intruding whites and less vulnerable to extermination, more open to exploitation as farmworkers when the settlers discovered the benefits of cheap labour and an easier life. The method of coercion into labour – depriving the Khoikhoi of their means of self-support by taking their land, their water sources and sometimes their cattle as well – was devised soon after white presence became white settlement.

A precedent of sorts was set with the introduction of slavery, a development that was perhaps an inevitable reflection of the prevailing mores of the age but one that would have social consequences far beyond it.

CHAPTER 3

BONDAGE BEGUN

The Dutch presence at the Cape began as an incidental scraping off the East India Company's great trade with the Far East as it swept past Africa's southern tip. Likewise the white settlement, and likewise the bringing of the slaves. All, however, took root and spread deep into the sub-continent, and with the expansion went the ethos of slavery and subjugation of the indigenous peoples.

Initially the slaves were brought to the Cape to provide labour for the Company's food-growing, the Khoikhoi having refused to work for the Dutch while they could still acquire the white man's manufactures by bartering the products of their own herding and hunting. Van Riebeeck proposed enslaving them but the Company refused, believing they had a greater value as suppliers of the meat for the ships. He was ordered to rely on the contracted workers the Company sent from Europe. These, however, proved unable to handle the growing volume of work, and after five years the Company agreed to send slaves to the Cape – but only to work on its own undertakings and not those of the free burghers. *Jan Compagnie* felt that giving slaves to the burghers would encourage them to become idle and unproductive.

But if the Company could use slaves, the burghers wanted them too. Their struggle to create viable farms out of the wild lands along the Liesbeeck was being hampered by the shortage of white labourers and their high cost. It was, however, only after some of the burghers gave up farming after a couple of years and returned to Holland that the Company, seeing the food production for the ships threatened, relented and allowed the remaining farmers to have slaves.

There was a continuous influx of slaves thereafter, from Madagascar, eastern Africa, the Guinea coast and Angola, and a steady flow from the East Indies – from Java, Malacca, Borneo, Burma, Ceylon, Bengal, Iran and almost all the lands of the Indian Ocean Rim. Some were Chinese – mostly convicts from the Company's Eastern territories serving long terms – and a few came from Japan.

From this unique and polyglot genesis came a community quite unlike any other on the continent. Neither European nor African, neither black nor white, the slaves brought from the Far East were to found a distinctive people synonymous with the Cape itself. Their blood would mix with that of Europeans, of slaves from elsewhere in Africa and of the Khoikhoi to create the people known as the Cape Coloureds, including, in a narrower genetic band, the Cape Malays.

There was steady but not large growth in the slave population from 1658, the first year of official slave importation, until slavery was formally abolished in 1835 under British occupation. At abolition there were 36 304 officially listed. Altogether, about sixty-five thousand slaves were imported into the Cape.[1] Slaves came to form a significant proportion of the total exotic population, at one point even the majority. By 1760 more than half of the slave population was locally born.[2]

Most slaves at the Cape came to be owned not by the Company but by the burghers and by Company officials, including Van Riebeeck. Some slaves enjoyed a comfortable life, but most had to endure the hardships and indignity basic to slavery. All were subject to harsh laws designed to keep them subservient. Severe penalties, including lashing, branding and amputations, were imposed for infractions and, for serious crimes, execution, sometimes by roasting or impalement, in which a long iron spike was thrust into the anus and up alongside the spine to come out at the neck. The other end was then fixed in the ground.

A story, possibly apocryphal, is told of an impaled slave who was offered a drink of brandy by a sympathetic onlooker to ease his agony. When another bystander protested that the slave might get drunk, the slave is said to have responded: 'Well, at least I can't fall down!'

The slaves ostensibly had basic rights of decent treatment and owners could be – and sometimes were – punished for maltreating them. Manumission (freeing) of slaves was infrequent, however, for they often constituted a large part of the owners' assets and could be hired out, mortgaged for loans, bequeathed in wills or given as wedding presents.

The morality of slavery was seldom challenged. It could hardly be questioned when the practice appeared to have the endorsement of the Dutch Reformed Church, some of whose ministers owned slaves.

For a great many of the Dutch at the Cape, especially those in rural and frontier areas, Christianity was synonymous with European identity and culture; it did not apply to black people. Thus the outlawing of slavery by the British was resented by many of the Cape Dutch not because it gave the blacks social equality but because it opened the way for them to be baptised. Proselytisation by the British missionaries was resented for the same reasons.

Often excluded from baptism and marriage in the Christian church, many slaves turned to Islam, which had been brought to the Cape by slaves from the East. Though most of the descendants of the slaves are Christians, Islam remains a major faith among the coloured people.

Slavery left a greater legacy, however, one not so benign, in its influence on the emergence of racial discrimination in the Cape society. There being no white slaves – the law specifically excluded it – slavery was associated with people of dark complexion. The social structure assumed a pyramidal form, rising progressively from the darkest skins to the lightest.

A significant proportion of the society comprised children born to female slaves of white fathers. A Company report of 1671 estimated that as many as three-quarters of the children born to the Company's slave women had European fathers

– Company employees, soldiers stationed at the Cape, and visiting seamen.[3] Quite often female slaves bore children fathered by their owners through the casual gratification of carnal desire. Only infrequently did an owner marry the slave who bore his children, even though mixed marriages were at first socially acceptable in the isolated and largely womanless expatriate society. Van Riebeeck in fact encouraged the practice, and a number of Europeans married Khoikhoi women. Cohabitation within or outside of marriage between whites and Khoikhoi created the light-skinned Baster people who in time established themselves near the Orange River.

Children of mixed marriages were at first accepted with little or no reservation into white society, but they came increasingly to be subjected to discrimination and rejection as a relatively wealthy elite formed among the descendants of the original settlers.

Ironically, some of apartheid's most ardent practitioners would later strive to deny the evidence of the African and Asian genes bequeathed to them – a darkness of skin or a kink in the hair – through their forebears' visits to the beds of slave women or through a liaison with a Khoikhoi girl. But recent research suggests that more than seven per cent of the white Afrikaner population has 'non-white' ancestry.

Racial discrimination grew partly from the dual stigmas of slavery and the primitivism ascribed by the Europeans to the Khoikhoi. It was accentuated by the need felt by the whites to find means to debase the enslaved in order to justify their enslavement. Male slaves, for instance, were forbidden to wear shoes or stockings, even in winter. Dress codes were imposed not only on slave women but also on free black women, who, in order that they should not outdo the whites, were denied fancy clothing, hairstyles or jewellery.

Land and labour – from the beginning of European settlement these were the prime elements in the shaping of social and political forms around racial discrimination in white-dominated Africa. It would always be about land and labour as much as about ethnic difference itself – and perhaps even more so.

★ ★ ★ ★

Appalling as it was in its content, in scale the Cape slavery was a sideshow to the main event to the north, the trans-Atlantic slave trade to the Americas.

That long-running atrocity, growing ever larger over more than two centuries, affected Africa more profoundly than any other activity of the Europeans except colonialism. The extent of the damage is argued to this day. Some hold that large parts of the western continent were stripped of their most vigorous people and left socially and economically debilitated for generations after slavery was abolished. At the opposite extreme of the polemic is an assertion that the profits of slavery brought a measure of prosperity to West Africa that it would not otherwise have had, and that social structures quickly recovered. What is not in dispute, though, is the suffering inflicted on those taken from Africa as slaves and on their descendants in the Americas.

Neither is there argument over the price paid by the descendants of the slave us-ers, certainly in the United States, in the form of intractable social problems and enduring agonies of conscience.

Both the Cape and the trans-Atlantic slaving contributed fundamentally to the prejudice against people of colour that shaped the attitudes of the Europeans as they built their colonial empires, and of the Americans as they grew into a world power.

Other factors did indeed contribute to the European view of Africans as inferior, factors that have to do with differences in appearance, culture, environment and technology rather than with innate ability. But slavery sealed the perception of blacks as lesser beings. Slavery required an excuse for its iniquity, one most easily found in ethnic difference. To justify slavery, the slave had to be made out to be of a lower order of life. The fact that some West Africans practised cannibalism was a useful clincher, the image eventually being stereotyped in cartoons of white missionaries and explorers being cooked in huge pots by blacks with bones through their noses.

Historians who hold that the European perception of African inferiority was neither justified nor inevitable point out that the first Europeans to arrive on the west coast, the maritime explorers from Portugal, respected the natives for their social organisation and commercial abilities.

At first the European presence was largely beneficent, bringing to the 'Guinea Coast' a measure of prosperity it had not known before. Living standards of many Africans were raised by the tools and other imports from Europe. Food production was improved by the introduction of rice, sugar cane and citrus from the East Indies, and of maize, cassava, sweet potatoes and tomatoes from the West Indies. Some historians credit these new foods with sparking something of a population explosion in a West Africa whose indigenous foods were not as nourishing or as prolific.

Soon another commodity was added to the list – the living, breathing commodity of slaves. It was then that the European impact on Africa switched from being largely benign to being malign as well.

The Europeans did not introduce slavery to Africa, they only extended it. Slavery was as ancient a practice in Africa as it was anywhere else in the world, but in the absence of labour-intensive industry and agriculture there was no big demand for large work forces. Slaving was therefore not an industry, as it was to become under the Europeans.

Before the white men came, slaves captured in the Sudan belt[*] were sold in North Africa to meet the demand there and in the Middle East. The Europeans, through the impact of their advanced technology and commercialism, radically transformed this pattern. It was their maritime technology that had enabled them to find the sea route round Africa to the East Indies and to discover the New World of the Americas. And then it was the cutting edge of their technology, the firearm, that had enabled them to subdue the native peoples of the new lands. Their technology enabled them to exploit the agricultural potential of these lands and to run

---

[*]Not the modern country of that name but the whole strip of territory immediately south of the Sahara, running from West Africa to the Nile.

transport efficiently to and from them, thereby expanding trade across the oceans in the produce of these lands.

Mining (mainly for diamonds) and the commercial production of sugar, cotton, tobacco, timber and the other products of the New World became vital to the development of the increasingly industrial economies of the European states. However, the labour-intensiveness of the plantation system created a shortage of workers. European men forced to labour as convicts in the tropics seldom lived long. The native Indians and Caribs of the New World generally objected to working for their conquerors. They were in any case too few for either purpose, many having been killed in the European conquest or by the diseases brought by the Europeans. They had, besides, been given a form of protection against slavery by a convention of theologians at Salamanca in 1550 which ruled that the Indians should not be used as slaves. The men of God decreed, however, that it was acceptable to enslave Africans (a decision, incidentally, that some might hold to belie the assertion that Africans were not regarded as inferior beings by the post-medieval Europeans).

The ruling was wonderfully convenient for the European planters and traders. Not only were the Africans native to the tropics and accustomed to its rigours, but they were numerous enough to meet the rising demand for slaves. Some were experienced in mining (for gold) or in tropical agriculture. Being situated directly across the Atlantic from the New World, it was relatively convenient to ship them over.

The African victims of the trade simply did not have the means to resist European technology: the gun as instrument of enforcement, and manufactured goods as means of payment. Africans themselves monopolised the traffic on land in Africa. European slaving agents had simply to set up coastal bases stocked with trade goods and barter these for slaves brought to them by local chiefs or slave-catchers.

The ethos that the white people applied to mass slavery might be seen as a human equivalent of mechanisation, with the slaves regarded not much differently than cogs and pistons were in the industrial revolution. Often they were in fact viewed less as humans than as machines, and were treated accordingly, to be pushed to the limit of their productive capacity and, if they broke down, to be mended if possible, otherwise scrapped and replaced by a new one. If they were looked after, it was in many cases to preserve their commercial value rather than for humanitarian reasons.

Estimates of the number of Africans torn from their homelands for slavery in the Americas go as high as fifteen million, an enormous proportion of the populations of the times. There seems little doubt that at least eleven million were shipped across between 1600 and the ending of slaving, a gradual process which commenced when the British outlawed slavery in 1807 but could not be said to have achieved final success for another thirty years or so.

Nearly twenty per cent of those packed and layered on board the slave ships died from illness or hardship and were dumped overboard, leaving trails of human bones across the seabed, unseen monuments to one of the greatest atrocities in history. It was criminality that went unpunished, for there were no power blocs or international organisations to stage Nuremberg-type trials.

In any case, in the rise to slavery's heyday relatively few non-Africans saw it as morally wrong. Either from conviction or defensively, as a shield against moral discomfort, white people in general accepted a lesser status and rights for black people.

Inevitably, however, the Africans' equal humanity came to be recognised, and the morality of trans-Atlantic slavery came increasingly into question. The issue became so controversial in America that the Americans fought a civil war over it, or partly over it, in which nearly one in thirty of them died. That, ironically, left a demographic gap in their country proportionately bigger than the one created in Africa by the American south's participation in the slavery.

African-American historians contend that there was a cardinal difference between the slavery conducted in the New World and the slavery traditional in Africa. The Africans, they argued, generally saw their slaves simply as less fortunate people, perhaps to be cruelly treated, perhaps to be well treated, but very often to be absorbed into the conquering society. In contrast, most Europeans and Americans rejected any notion of black slaves ever being taken into their society, not only believing them to be inferior in their present predicament but forever inferior, culturally and intellectually.

These historians hold that slavery and the colonialism that succeeded it left Africa crippled in almost every way – demographically, socially, economically, educationally, technically, scientifically. The Atlantic slave trade, by stripping western Africa of the cream of its able-bodied men, is held to have been largely responsible for a social and economic decline of the region as advances were made in these respects in Europe and America.

This claim might be extended in a lesser degree to eastern and central Africa, from where Arab slavers took large numbers of captives. It surely cannot be applied, though, to large regions in the south and elsewhere that were untouched by large-scale slavery but remained no less backward than West Africa.

Some British historians contend that the slaves taken to the Americas were almost always captives of war – wars that would have taken place even if there had been no demand for slaves across the Atlantic. Furthermore, since most of the trans-Atlantic slaves were men, a high proportion of the women seized in war remained behind in Africa, in whose generally polygynous societies they very likely had as many children as they would have had if they had not been captured. Hence there was no great denudation of population.

A British view is that it was the abolition of slavery that brought economic hardship to West Africa, prompting the British, for instance, to compensate by paying subsidies to promote the production of palm oil in the Niger delta. The closure of the slave markets of the Americas is said to have left a surplus of captives from African wars, resulting in an increase in execution, ritual sacrifice and cannibalism.

While Britons had been the prime movers in the Atlantic slave trade, it was they who took the lead in suppressing the traffic. In this is reflected the conflict between mercantile and moral imperatives that bothered the British for centuries, the one creating the Empire and the other contributing powerfully to its eventual dissolution. It was British commercial enterprise that had created the prime market for slaves in the New World and which largely fed it. King Charles II himself had shares in the Company of Royal Adventurers, to which his government in 1660 gave a monopoly for the sale of licences to British slavers operating in West Africa.

The moral sensibilities that drove the international campaign against slavery were not always nurtured by the Christian churches, certainly not by the 18th-century Church of England. One of its divines, Bishop Fleetwood, declared in 1711 that 'the laws of God did not forbid the keeping of slaves, nor do the laws of the land'. His belief was shared by the Anglican church's missionary arm, the Society for the Propagation of the Christian Gospel. When a planter bequeathed his estate in Barbados to the society, the new owners had the word 'Society' branded on the chest of each of its newly acquired slaves to affirm their possession.

British efforts to promote alternative forms of trade to compensate for the abolition of the slave trade made it necessary to establish consular offices on African soil, the first opening in 1849. Together with the incidental protection provided by the navy's anti-slavery patrols, these encouraged British merchants in their trade in commodities other than slaves. Thus did first slavery and then anti-slavery help blaze the trail for British colonisation.

The winding-down of the African slave trade, however, coincided with a decline in the supplies of both gold and ivory, and therefore with a general decline in European interest in the continent. Few Europeans saw much incentive to explore a hinterland that seemed singularly unattractive, a hostile world occupied by people who appeared to be primitive and savage, a place made miserable by humid heat and diseases. It was the Dark Continent, a world to be avoided, and avoided it was, except for the temperate extremity at the Cape of Good Hope, where the Dutch had unwittingly planted ineradicable seeds of European dominance.

★ ★ ★ ★

The other extremity, the Mediterranean littoral, was climatically as temperate as the Cape but for many years it was not considered a healthy place for Europeans because of the depredations of the piratical Arabs known as the Barbary corsairs. Not only did they rob the Europeans – and Americans – but they enslaved them as well.

Skilled seamen and able soldiers, and well armed, the Islamic corsairs plundered the shipping routes of the Mediterranean and North Atlantic, and even pillaged ashore in raids from Italy to Iceland. They are thought to have captured more than a million Europeans and Americans in a reign of terror lasting from the early 17th century to the second decade of the 19th. Operating from fortified strongholds at Sale in Morocco and at Algiers, Tunis and Tripoli, the Barbary pirates sent fleets marauding far and wide, in one sense waging a holy war against Christianity but primarily robbing the growing oceanic trade of the Europeans and raiding their countries for slaves – men, women and children. They brazenly sailed even into English seaports in Cornwall in 1625 to seize slaves. Capturing Lundy Island in the Bristol Channel, they used it as a base for more raids, defeating English warships sent to chase them away.

Many of the whites seized were sold to the slave markets of north Africa and the Middle East, forming a principal source of the corsairs' revenue. Of the others, a fortunate few were ransomed by their governments or families, but large numbers were made to labour for their captors, and subjected to extreme ill-treatment, horrific tortures and executions, such as, according to some accounts, being burned alive, crucified or progressively dismembered from the fingers and toes onwards.

Estimates of the number of whites taken into slavery vary, but the most authoritative account estimates that over two centuries some five thousand were seized each year.[4] In Algiers, where there was always the largest concentration, there were at any one time some twenty-five thousand, sometimes many more.

The Americans appear to have been specially angered by the attacks on their shipping in the Mediterranean, particularly by the ignominy of having their frigate, the *Philadelphia*, captured by the corsairs of Tripoli after becoming stuck on a reef. After years of attempting to deal with the pirates through appeasement and bribes, President Thomas Jefferson in 1804 sent an American fleet to bombard Tripoli, where the *Philadelphia* was being refitted by the corsairs. During the action a daring American party sneaked aboard the *Philadelphia* at night and burned the ship to the water. A year later a small American force reinforced with Greek and Arab mercenaries set out overland from Egypt to seize Tripoli, but was inexplicably recalled by Jefferson after capturing Derne.

The corsairs continued their depredations for another decade before the Americans and British were moved to put a stop at last to the piracy. In 1815 American ships under Commodore Stephen Decatur defeated an Algerian fleet off the coast of Spain and forced Algiers, Tunis and Tripoli to pay reparations and agree to stop attacking American shipping. It took a more destructive blow by the British to finally end the piracy and slavery.[5] As the Napoleonic Wars ended, a group calling themselves the Society of Knights Liberators of the White Slaves of Africa persuaded the British government to send a strong fleet to attack Algiers. It was hoped that by defeating the most powerful of the corsair leaders, the dey of Algiers, a stern warning would be sent to Morocco, Tunis and Tripoli to cease their piracy too. In a furious gun battle in 1816 the corsairs' shore batteries severely damaged the British ships, but much of Algiers was blasted to ruins by 50 000 British cannon balls, and the pirate fleet was destroyed. The dey surrendered and soon thereafter the other pirate capitals renounced slavery. Grateful governments of other European nations that had suffered from the marauding of the Barbary pirates showered honours on the commander of the British fleet, Admiral Sir Edward Pellew. And thousands of white slaves began returning to Europe.

Black slaves continued to be shipped from West Africa to the Americas for another three decades or more. The British, if not the Americans as well, presented their attacks on the Barbary pirates as a moral crusade against slavery, but a stronger reason probably was the need to end the plundering of their shipping. There was no such exigency in the case of the trans-Atlantic slavery, however, and so neither was a moral duty acknowledged.

CHAPTER 4

THE NEW AFRICANS

Compared with the heavy influx of Europeans into North America, white settlement in sub-Saharan Africa was small and slow. Africa, it seems, was too distant, strange and savage for the Europeans.

North America was not only closer but much more like Europe in its seasons, climate and vegetation. Africa was different. Only its coastal regions were known to the Europeans when they began their trans-Atlantic migrations. And the parts closer to Europe were either unbearably hot and dry for Europeans, or unbearably hot and humid and plagued by lethal diseases. Some were occupied by strong, well-ordered societies better able than the indigenous peoples of the Americas to resist European encroachment.

Even Africa's southern tip, for all its temperate climate and physical beauty, was less attractive than the Americas. The Dutch were in any case not much inclined to foreign colonisation; their population was simply too small to sustain it. The Company did try to encourage European immigration to the Cape by offering assisted passages to settlers from 1685, hoping settlers would alleviate the labour shortage, reduce the preponderance of slaves over Europeans, and help defend the Cape against the French and the English. But when the assisted passages were ended after 22 years slaves still outnumbered officials, burghers and their families.

The still small settler population received a stimulating injection of new blood from 1688 in the form of Huguenot refugees from France, who had fled to the Netherlands to escape Louis XIV's persecution of Protestants.

Only about two hundred Huguenots came, arriving in small groups, while larger numbers migrated elsewhere in the world. They were destined, however, to have a disproportionately large influence on the Cape's culture and economy, notably by transforming the viticulture. The French brought an element of sophistication to the Cape, an elegance that was to remain integral to its character long after the rebellious Dutch farmers had gone off to found republics in the far interior.

White numbers were increased somewhat by the immigrant European labourers known as *knechts*. Though generally unskilled they were paid wages. Some acquired enough experience and capital to set themselves up as farmers with their own slaves and become absorbed into the resident white community and assume its privileges.

Among those privileges was the assumed one that white people did not do manual labour. That was only for people of colour. The assumption, born out of slavery, was to persist through the centuries to the present day, broken only in exceptional circumstances, such as when the depression of the 1930s forced poor white men to accept pick-and-shovel work on government development projects. The assumption has been reflected up to the present time in the customary employment of black domestic servants in even the poorer white households.

Small though it was, the white immigration encroached inexorably inland. To help meet the growing demand for fresh produce for the ships, the Company enlarged the freehold allotments and by the early 18th century was allocating farms of up to six thousand acres. By 1750 the settler population exceeded the complement of Company officials. Thirty years later, the free burghers and their families numbered 10 500. Most of the burghers were now farmers.

Their demand for more land was exponentially increased by the effect of the Dutch custom of equal division of an estate among the heirs. Often, in order to keep a farm viable, one son would buy out his brothers, who would then seek farms of their own, usually in virgin lands deeper in the interior. Any Khoikhoi who happened to be in occupation were ousted, much as the Xhosas had displaced the Khoikhoi. From this grew a notion among the settlers' descendants of land endlessly available beyond the moving frontier and of a facility, almost a right, of acquiring it without purchase. The settlers brought to the frontier the European concept of individual land ownership and simply asserted it over the African custom of communal land use.*

Whites seldom bought land from the Khoikhoi, usually acquiring it either by simple occupation, by taking their cattle or by seizing their water sources. The Khoikhoi resisted by attacking the settlers' homesteads and herds. Unable to get adequate protection from the Company, the frontiersmen at times took the law into their own hands, banding together in groups of mounted riflemen to attack the Khoikhoi.

This may have been the beginning of the commando – the military arm of the farmers and their descendants for the next two centuries – although some historians place the commando's genesis in the local militia that had been organised in Van Riebeeck's time. Commando service became obligatory from 1739, and by the closing decades of the 18th century commandos were riding out almost every month at one point or another on the frontier.

Against the commandos' horses and guns, the spears and arrows of the Khoikhoi and San were ineffective. Their numbers drastically depleted by outbreaks of smallpox brought by the Europeans, the Khoikhoi were slowly driven off their customary lands and gradually lost their herds. Some of the Khoikhoi moved further inland, displacing the San. Thus one of the ancient social cycles of Africa – migration, conquest, displacement, migration – was repeated. These Khoikhoi in turn barred others displaced later by the whites, forcing them to return south to the control of the whites.

---

* Later, when there was no longer land for the taking, the younger members of large rural families often ended up working for their older brothers with little prospect of advancement, or drifting into the poor white population.

As the white farmlands spread further inland, the rising demand for labour made both slave and *knecht* more expensive to get and hold. So the farmers turned to enserfment of the Khoikhoi. Landless and herdless in the regions taken over by the white farmers, the Khoikhoi had little alternative but to give their skills as cattlemen in exchange for a piece of land for a crop patch, and grazing for a few cattle of their own.

From the expansion of white settlement emerged the trekboer, a personage whose ambitions and customs would powerfully influence the course of South African history for the next two centuries. The first trekboers moved inland to acquire land, and to this fundamental desire was later added the almost equally powerful urge to escape the authority first of the Company, which frequently was corrupt and inept, and later of the British colonial administrators, who could be equally inept.

Literally translated, trekboer means migrant farmer, but the term came more from his search for permanence – but independent permanence – than for any urge to move on for the sake of it. It is not possible to farm well and travel at the same time. Perpetual migration was not a way of life that the trekboers chose above settlement.

By the 1740s the trekboer vanguard had left the green Cape far behind and had crossed the mountains to enter the drier land beyond them, the Little Karoo. Two decades later they were deep into the wide scrub plains of the Great Karoo

Despite Cape Town's attempts to define the frontier, it remained open and mobile. And the further the trekboer moved from Cape Town, the more independent he was of the authority of the Castle and the more self-reliant he became, making his own housing, clothing, furniture, candles and many other essentials, and producing his own food. As a result, he became less susceptible to the Cape's social and cultural influences.

All these factors contributed to the development of a strongly patriarchal society among the trekboers. The large, widely dispersed rural families came close to being separate communities in themselves, with the head of the household ruling autocratically, even if often kindly, over his lineal dependants as well as his slaves and serfs. Frontier custom and the influence of the Bible made patriarchy the fundamental characteristic of trekboer society. Attempts by Cape Town to impose its authority were seen as interference in the rights and duties of the patriarch, as an intrusion into the sanctity of the household, and were resented accordingly.

Distant from the instruments and influence of state and church, the farming families tended to develop their own social and religious laws. The Calvinism brought by their forebears from Holland was the handfast to which their societies held as they adapted to an environment that was at the front edge of white settlement, sometimes beyond it. Their common faith was the binder that gave cohesion to those societies' loose and often quarrelsome elements. But in the absence of ministers of the church – there were fewer than ten Dutch Reformed ministers at the Cape by 1790 – it was the head of the family who interpreted the Bible and Calvinism's principles. By the time the organised church caught up with the trekboers deep in the hinterland, it sometimes found itself having to adapt to their beliefs and principles rather than the other way round. And in the absence of police and courts, it was the patriarch who dispensed justice, arbitrating disputes and deciding punishments.

Two centuries after Van Riebeeck's landing, by which time the trekkers had settled in the far interior and founded their independent republics, they had developed a culture that was as much indigenous as it was exotic. It had been moulded by generations of life in Africa, with Europe's influence growing progressively weaker and Africa's correspondingly stronger. But it was an isolated culture, cut off from its foreign roots, introverted and closed. It had been formed by adaptation to and identification with the physical environment but by dissociation from the human environment, the indigenous, black one.

As the trekboers widened their distance from Cape Town the Company's relatively moderating influence on racial attitudes weakened accordingly. The trekboers developed a strongly paternalistic attitude not only towards slaves but to all black people associated with their households. From this and other influences emerged a more rigid discrimination, a social code in which the black slave or serf was forever inferior and entirely dependent on the head of his household for whatever privileges and kindness came his way. That code came to be extended to people of colour outside the patriarchy. And it came to be fixed in the subconscious minds of many black as well as white people: blacks inferior, whites superior; that was ordained, that was the way of things.

Far from the Castle's ken, the trekboers not only enserfed the natives but they also enslaved them. San, Khoikhoi and later — when the frontier expanded far enough eastwards — even Xhosas were seized and forced into slavery on farms. So established was the practice that it was taken up by some of the English settlers who came to the eastern Cape in 1820. Enslavement of the indigenous people on the frontier continued through the 18th century, even increasing after the price of slaves went up as a result of the outlawing of the slave trade by the British in 1804.

Some of the enslaving was done by trekboers in the course of reprisal raids for cattle theft. Such reprisals could be especially vicious when launched against the San, whom most whites appeared to regard as more animal than human. Their contempt was mixed with fear, though — and therefore hatred — because of the San's use of poisoned arrows against the trekboers. The San were like gadflies to the trekboers in their resistance to the encroachment on their hunting lands. The San recognised no personal ownership of land or animals, including the trekboers' cattle and sheep, which had replaced much of the game the San had always depended on for a living. In turn the farmers hunted the San, winkling them out of their mountain hideouts, advancing behind outspread blankets held up to catch the venomous arrows.

Even as the farmers trekked inland, the Company lumbered after them, concerned not only to protect its lines of supply but also to retain control of the suppliers. Thirty years after the first settlement, the farmers had become established in the Stellenbosch area, 40 km from Cape Town, and the Company formally declared it a district and opened an administrative office. Sixty-five years later another district was proclaimed at Swellendam, 240 kilometres east along the coastal plain. After another 40 years the farmers were established at Graaff-Reinet on the Sundays River, some seven hundred kilometres from the Castle, in the heart of the Great Karoo, and another district was established there, in 1786.

As they probed beyond the Sundays River the frontiersmen began to encounter the Xhosas. Though lacking a national structure, and existing in clans that sometimes fought one another, the Xhosas were more numerous than the Khoikhoi, more aggressive, better organised and led, and more skilful at war. They were the southern tip of the great movement from the Negro heartland north of the equator. Their own migration down the coastal plain had taken their main body to the region of the Fish River by the time they encountered the trekboers. They had lived in the region for generations when the whites began edging in from the west, and their numbers were beginning to strain the comfortable capacity of their traditional lands. It was time for another onward move of the excess population, another step in the ancient pattern of migration.

This time, though, it was the whites, equipped with guns and horses, not the Khoikhoi or San, who were in the way. The Xhosas were in no mind to retreat, especially as behind them were the Zulus, soon to become rampantly expansive under the tyrannical genius, Shaka. And so began a sporadic testing, a pushing and shoving, between trekboers and Xhosas. Fluctuating between contest and coexistence, varying from bloody fighting to cattle raiding, it kept the frontier in a state of periodic agitation for decades.

The Company, its merchant soul disturbed by this disorder, tried to define the frontier and get the farmers and the Xhosas to respect it, but was largely ignored by both. The frontiersmen were becoming impatient with other aspects of Company rule too, as were the burghers in Cape Town. Both saw the Company as autocratic, tainted with corruption, and little concerned with the interests of the burghers. In 1778 members of the burgher elite in Cape Town, inspired in part by the Americans' fight for independence from Britain, formed a group known as the Cape Patriots with the purpose of presenting their grievances to the Company. Intentionally or not, it was a first step towards white independence in Africa.

Burgher dissatisfaction erupted into open rebellion in February 1795, inspired now by the French Revolution. The trekboers at Graaff-Reinet threw out Maynier the sheriff and declared an independent republic. The white African was for the first time hauling up his own flag, so to speak, in his adopted continent. Four months later the burghers of Swellendam back in the Little Karoo followed suit. These were the first of a number of mini-republics that the Boers were to form as they sought to take root in the hinterland – all destined to be short-lived.

The Company made no immediate effort to put down the Graaff-Reinet and Swellendam rebellions. It had steadily been losing interest in its expanding and rebellious colony as its own fortunes went into decline, eroded by the challenge of its European rivals. A few months after the rebellions the once-great Dutch East India Company acknowledged bankruptcy and was taken over by the Dutch state, which was itself having trouble with its political viability and, coming under the domination of the revolutionary French, became in 1795 the Batavian Republic.

CHAPTER 5

ENTER BRITANNIA

With imperatives swiftly changing and alliances suddenly shifting, European politics was like a mad game of musical chairs in the power struggles that convulsed Europe shortly before and during the time of Napoleon.

The Cape in effect become one of the chairs, for whoever occupied it sat in the halfway house to India and could put an interdictory foot into the shipping between the Far East and Europe. Not only was merchant shipping now carrying a large part of the world's trade, but naval traffic too was increasing as the trade went from merchanting to colonising as well.

The Dutch were still firmly seated when in 1748 the British came in force into Table Bay as allies in a joint expedition against the French in the Indian Ocean. The long-lasting Anglo-Dutch alliance collapsed in 1780 when, the French having intervened on George Washington's side in the War of American Independence, the Dutch refused a British call for assistance, and so the British declared war on them too.

With the British and the French at the same time locked in a struggle for dominance of India, the Cape's strategic importance heightened and it was only a matter of time before one of them attempted to secure control of it. Both made their move in the same year, 1781, that Washington's forces won their decisive victory at Yorktown in Virginia. Two fleets sailed simultaneously from Europe in a race for the Cape, the French expecting to be welcomed there and the British to seize it. Their courses converged off the Cape Verde islands, and after some heavy fighting the French sensibly sped on for the Cape. By the time the British fleet arrived the French were already ashore, toasting their success with the quite drinkable wine now being produced by their former countrymen, the Huguenots.

With a strong garrison stationed at the Cape and their ships needing supplies, the French brought a boom to the Cape for the next three years. The bubble burst when the French left in 1784, the Dutch having made peace with Britain. The economy of the Cape went into decline together with that of the Company.

The French Revolution in 1789 set off fresh bustle around Europe's political chairs. By 1793 France was at war with England and Holland. The matter of who occupied the Cape again became pressing when in 1795 the Netherlands came under the influence of the Jacobin French as the Batavian Republic, which took over the dying Dutch East India Company. The English were not prepared to see the

Cape again fall into French hands, not with India now become England's major foreign interest since the loss of America. They occupied the Cape, overcoming resistance by the Jacobin sympathisers among the Dutch there.

Britain now had the firmest foothold it had yet had in Africa, with control over a well-established community of more than sixty thousand people, including the only sizeable white community – numbering 20 000 – in Africa. Besides the whites, most of whom were Dutch, there were 25 000 slaves, 1 000 free blacks and 15 000 Khoikhoi living in an area stretching 700 km inland from Cape Town to Graaff-Reinet.

The British had got what they wanted: control of the strategic Cape and its naval base. With it they had acquired, wanted or not, a colony of doubtful commercial value occupied by refractory Dutch settlers and roiled by racially-based politics.

Up to now the English had established only shallow footholds in Africa. The Royal Company of Adventurers in Africa, to which King Charles II had given the monopoly for the issuing of the slaving licences, had expanded into other forms of trade as well. By 1672, when their organisation was renamed the Royal African Company, it was operating a string of fort-like trading stations, garrisoned by troops, on the coasts of what are now Gambia, Senegal, Ghana and Nigeria. When the royal warrant was abandoned in 1698 and the company abolished, the trading was continued by independent operators. These maintained the link that would in time allow the British government to return as a colonial power, but until then it was always a matter of trade, not occupation.

The British in 1758 had seized the French slaving stations at Fort Louis and Goree on the coast of Senegal, but these had been returned under the Peace of Versailles of 1783.

The Cape was thus Britain's first significant territorial acquisition in Africa. Besides the Cape and the slave trade, the British had no great interest in the continent. Their focus, like that of the other European powers, was on the West and East Indies. It was for the colonies there that they fought each other. By the end of the 18th century Britain's naval and industrial strength had gained her seemingly rich prizes from the French, Spanish and Dutch, including Quebec, Tobago, Martinique, Guadeloupe, St Lucia, Trinidad, Curacao and Ceylon. In all of sub-Saharan Africa, only the Cape of Good Hope had been considered worth seizing.

At the other extremity of the continent it was, of course, a different matter. Mediterranean Africa had long interested the Europeans, and now one of Europe's major figures, Napoleon Bonaparte, fixed a covetous eye on Egypt. By occupying Egypt, he reckoned, the French would open the way for seizing India, or at least making the British more vulnerable there. Napoleon's interests were more than strategic. Long fascinated by Egypt's past, he intended that the French should uncover more of the secrets of ancient Egypt for Europe and at the same time take European technology to Egypt. On board his invasion fleet in 1798 was a Commission of Arts and Sciences consisting of more than a hundred and fifty engineers, scientists, mathematicians and archaeologists.

Defeating the Turkish forces in the Battle of the Pyramids, Napoleon occupied

Egypt but then was left stranded when Horatio Nelson caught the French fleet napping at anchor off Alexandria and destroyed it in the Battle of the Nile. Napoleon went ahead with his colonisation nonetheless. He initiated civil engineering works and surveys. His archaeologists uncovered extensive writings that provided the foundation for modern Egyptology and led to the discovery of the Rosetta Stone, which provided the key to the deciphering of ancient Egyptian hieroglyphs.

Napoleon, however, was not one to meekly accept being bottled up by the British. After repulsing a Turkish attempt to regain Egypt, he slipped through the British blockade on a small ship and returned to France, leaving his occupying forces in place in Egypt. In France he went on to institute a military dictatorship and eventually to crown himself emperor.

Napoleon's invasion of Egypt had brought home to the British the vulnerability of the land route to India and the need to have control of Egypt. In 1801 they invaded the country and, with the help of Turkish allies, captured Cairo from the French. The next year France, Britain, Spain and Holland signed the Treaty of Amiens, under which, among other things, Egypt was to revert to Turkey and the Cape of Good Hope to the Batavian Republic.

During their eight years in possession of the Cape the British had run into the same problems that had bothered the Dutch East India Company. The first British governor, Major General James Craig, had brought the rebellious burghers to sullen obedience by the threat of cutting off their supplies of arms and ammunition. Any lingering thoughts of resistance were discouraged when a Batavian Republic fleet sent to recapture the Cape was defeated by the British in Saldanha Bay.

The frontier farmers, collectively known as the Boers, resumed their preoccupation with land. Soon they were demanding the right to occupy land beyond the Fish River. Craig responded in words that might have made modern South Africa a very different place had their sense been heeded then and by succeeding generations.

'With what face can you ask of me to allow you to occupy lands which belong to other people?' he asked. 'What right can I have to give to you the property of others? ... what would be your own sensations were you to hear that I was even debating on a proposal ... to turn you out of your farms and give them to others?'

The British had always to remember, however, that they relied on the settler farmers for the meat and other foodstuffs for their Cape base and for their passing ships. Craig, and the later British governor, Earl Macartney, tackled the frontier problem in the same way as the Company's governors had: by fixing the Fish River as the boundary and ordering both Boers and Xhosas (whom the British called the Kaffirs) to stay on their respective sides of it. Neither did, of course; the pressure on both sides for more land was too strong, and the British, like the Dutch before them, had no effective means of policing the divide.

Ensconced in the Castle at Cape Town, the British found themselves dealing with a local white population split between sympathisers (the *Anglomannen*) and opponents (the *Jacobynen*). Relations between the burghers and the occupying force varied from cordiality in Cape Town to surly acceptance in the hinterland, but were

29

cooperative overall.

The British found themselves dragged into the third of the nine Frontier Wars (until relatively recently known as the Kaffir Wars) that had begun in 1779 and were fought intermittently over the next hundred years. The Boer commandos reluctantly helped their British conquerors against the Xhosas. When the time came for the British to hand the Cape to the Batavian Republic in 1803 under the Treaty of Amiens, the frontier was still so unsettled that they had to call out the Boer commandos to cover the withdrawal of their troops.

The Batavians' administration was more liberal than that of the Company had been. Influenced by the egalitarianism of the French Revolution, they applied elements of the Enlightenment that was liberalising attitudes in Europe. In trying to bring order to the frontier, however, they were not much more resourceful or successful than their predecessors.

Only four years after reclaiming the Cape, the Batavians found themselves once again at war with Britain, dragged in through their alliance with France. Again it was only a matter of time before the Cape was occupied by the French or British, and this time the British got in first. In January 1806 an invasion force under Major General David Baird was hazardously put ashore through the surf at Blaauwberg, on the northern shore of Table Bay. After short resistance, Governor Jan Willem Janssens surrendered and was allowed to sail for Holland. With him went the last vestige of Dutch colonialism in Africa.

The twenty thousand or so people of Dutch, German and French descent who found themselves at the Cape through the enterprises of the Dutch East India Company were now irrevocably under British rule. They and their descendants would remain so for the next hundred years. Overnight, so to speak, they had become Dutch-speaking British subjects who, with few exceptions, did not understand the language of their overlords. Although the Cape would not be ceded to the British until 1814, their formal links with the homelands of their forefathers in Europe had been cut forever. In ethnic terms they were stranded in Africa. Most were not much bothered by this, though, certainly not those in the hinterland, for already they had become as much African as European, if not more so. They were less concerned about being abandoned by the Dutch than they were about being ruled by the British – a circumstance that neither they nor succeeding generations would ever accept with equanimity.

★ ★ ★ ★

The return of the British to the Cape set off a domino effect reaching far beyond their immediate preoccupations, a knock-on sequence running for longer than a century.

Like the Dutch, the British were drawn in beyond their primary concern, in their case, having a naval base to guard the sea route to India. In order to maintain that base they had to control the local sources of its food supplies. Over and above this was the fear that by limiting themselves to the Cape Town foothold the British would leave the coastline to the east intolerably open to military or commercial invasion by competing powers in Europe.

While the second British occupation was not necessarily intended to be permanent, the turn of events made it so, sending repercussions far beyond the Fish River. Three developments in particular brought profound change.

The first was the ripple effect of the Enlightenment in Europe, in time ending slavery but before that bringing to the Cape the British missionaries who would have a radical impact, both socially and politically.

The second was the arrival of the 5 000 British settlers of 1820, the largest influx of white immigrants that Africa had yet seen and proportionately the biggest it would ever know, increasing the white population by ten per cent in a matter of months.

The third was the concerted exodus of Boers from the Cape Colony in the Great Trek, which sent an even larger number of whites migrating deep into Africa, fleeing from British rule but more importantly seeking land and *lebensraum*.

These three European-inspired developments overlapped an indigenous one that also had enormous consequences: the *mfecane*, the violent tribal conflicts and migrations, emanating from the territory of the Zulus, that swirled devastatingly across the south-eastern part of the sub-continent.

The combined effect of these influences, added to later on by the discovery of great mineral wealth in the interior, would transform southern Africa, giving it a social and political volatility extraordinary to Africa and, indeed, the wider world.

Events in Africa were deeply coloured during this era by one other development: the ascent of Queen Victoria to the British throne in 1837. It is possible that the Victorian age would have been much the same with some other monarch in Buckingham Palace, for it was driven and shaped by social forces beyond the influence and perhaps even the ken of the palace. Still, as her reign extended, as teenage queen matured into autocratic empress, Victoria came to personify the nation, to understand its perception of destiny, to infuse her stiff yet sentimental personality into its psyche, and to serve as an enduring figurehead, a living symbol of unity, assurance and pride. It was the totem of Victoria that was carried – figuratively, of course – in the van of the British advance into Africa and implanted from its rearmost bases to its farthest outposts.

But Victoria was just a year-old babe and her uncle had just been crowned King George IV when John Bailie led the first party of British settlers ashore at Algoa Bay on 10 April 1820.

It would be a traumatic switch, they knew, from cobbled streets and tidy English fields to the wilds of Africa. Beyond that, though, neither Bailie nor the 255 members of his party had much idea of what might lie ahead as they made the difficult landing through the surf in longboats. Bailie, then aged 32, was pulling up roots that went deep in England, back to William the Conqueror's Normans in 1066, according to a legend preserved among his descendants. As a lieutenant in the Royal Navy, but fluent in French, he had been assigned by the Foreign Office to adjudicate claims against the French after the Battle of Waterloo. The legend holds that

Napoleon was so impressed with Bailie's fairness in carrying out this task that he presented him with a fine set of silverware, each piece marked with Napoleon's honeybee symbol. When he led his party to Africa the silverware went along with his other effects.

At Algoa Bay, Bailie's group, like the 59 other settler parties that followed his, was issued with rations, tents, implements and seeds – and then left with this advice from the local landdrost: 'When you go out to plough, never leave your guns at home.' It was with grave misgiving that the Boers commissioned to transport the settlers to their allotments left them standing lonely and bewildered among their boxes and bales in the bush, some still wearing the stovepipe hats and frock coats that had been everyday wear in London.

The British settlers learned to adapt, but at harsh cost. At least a hundred and twenty of the men were killed in encounters with Xhosas, mostly while serving as volunteers with British troops. One of John Bailie's sons was killed in the fighting, and most of his possessions lost in the Xhosa attacks, the Napoleonic silverware among them. The legend has it that during one of the raids the silver was hastily buried for safekeeping as the family fled to safety. Afterwards they could not find where it had been buried. If the story is true, the silver must still lie there somewhere in the African earth, a part of Africa now, like Bailie's later kin.

Whatever other motives might be ascribed to it, the 1820 settlement was essentially a cynical and callous dumping of women and children in the front line of the Frontier Wars in the hope that their menfolk would sufficiently reinforce the British troops and the burghers to keep the Xhosa from encroaching east of the Fish River. A lesser motive was the British government's hope of winning popularity at home by being seen to be doing something to tackle the unemployment, hunger and other hardships prevalent in Britain at the end of the Napoleonic Wars.

As far as Whitehall was concerned, the Cape station existed only to serve the greater British interest in India, and it was opposed to any form of territorial expansion in southern Africa. Had the government wanted to encourage emigration to the colonies it would have made more sense to channel it to Canada, where prospects were better, or even Australia or New Zealand. The scheme was motivated primarily by the government's reluctance to spend the money necessary to station enough troops at the frontier to keep the Xhosa from disrupting Boer farm production. The £50 000 voted by Parliament to settle white families there was the cheaper alternative.

The settlers for their part could hardly have been unaware of the hazards awaiting them, for all that some of the criticism of the scheme was exaggerated – such as a cartoon by George Cruikshank, the leading pictorial satirist of the day (and illustrator of some of Charles Dickens's novels), showing settlers being chomped alive by black cannibals.

Public interest in the scheme remained high and largely favourable, nonetheless. William Barrymore, progenitor of the family that was to achieve theatrical fame in America, ran a sketch entitled *Cape of Good Hope, or, Cafres and Settlers*, at a London theatre. Among its characters were 'Zomai, a Caffre chief' and 'Lily Piccaninny, a Hottentot slave'.

The idea of using civilians as a frontier buffer had been explored as early as 1807 when an assessment ordered by the Earl of Caledon had recommended that the Xhosa be forced back east of the Fish River and that European colonists be settled on the west side. The next governor, Sir John Cradock, had implemented the first part of the recommendation in 1811, driving an estimated twenty thousand Xhosas out of the region west of the Fish River, known as the Zuurveld. His successor, Somerset, had further secured the frontier with cavalry and infantry posts, but most of the 105 Boer families who had moved into the Zuurveld had soon fled in the face of Xhosa raiders slipping between the redcoats' guns.

In a determined effort to drive the Europeans out of the Zuurveld, 10 000 Xhosas had attacked Graham's Town, the main settler base, in 1819 but had been thrown back by the musket volleys and grapeshot of the 330 defenders. The action saved the Zuurveld for the whites, but in Cape Town it underlined the great cost of defending the frontier by military means. When London had withdrawn the artillery and cavalry for what was considered more urgent service in India, Somerset had revived the idea of creating a buffer of British civilian settlers.

Government offices in Britain were swamped with thousands of applications for settlement, but the funds voted by Parliament were enough for only 4 000. These set sail in 27 ships from London, Liverpool, Portsmouth and Bristol between December 1819 and March 1820. Although they were being settled as farmers, fewer than half the settlers had any farming skills. There were 12 medical doctors among them and a number of military officers on half pay, ranking from general down to lieutenant. About a third were artisans and mechanics, most of whom soon abandoned their allotments and went to practise their skills in the towns as these formed.

Africa was not kind to these innocents from Europe. Some had to run for their lives from elephants they tried to chase from their crops by peppering them with birdshot. A little girl out herding cattle was confronted by a maned lion which roared until the ground seemed to shake, then walked away, no doubt leaving her considerably more shaken than the ground had been. Some settlers had to walk fifty kilometres or more to fetch their government rations, at times dodging rhinos and other big game. Lions, wild dogs, leopards, hyenas and other predators ravaged the settlers' herds. One settler, trying to round up straying sheep, tied the feet of those he had caught and left his young daughter to watch over them while he went after the rest. He returned to find vultures devouring the tied sheep alive as the girl looked on in helpless horror.

Again and again the settlers' crops were wiped out by drought, flood, hail, pests and disease. Some were reduced to bartering their precious possessions for food from the Boers. Some wore crude clothing made from tent canvas or animal skins. When accounts of their plight reached Cape Town and England, relief funds were set up.

Three years after the landing, fewer than half of the settler men remained on their allotments to claim title. The rest had given up farming. Most remained in South Africa, though. They and their descendants spread throughout the country, exercising a strong cultural, commercial and political influence.

Though sometimes at heavy cost, the 1820 settlers did what the politicians in London had intended: they helped to stabilise the turbulent frontier and to check the advance of the Xhosa.

★ ★ ★ ★

Of all the forms in which European religion came to Africa, few were more contentious than that brought by the fundamentalist Protestant missionaries who came to the Cape with the first British occupation. Rather than as beneficent clerics, they seemingly saw themselves more as crusaders. Before long they were being viewed by burghers, trekboers and officials alike as something more like pyromaniacs let loose in a gunpowder magazine.

The missionaries brought a radical and aggressive morality to a British occupation that essentially had been a matter of political strategy. Sometimes eccentric, sometimes arrogant in their personalities as well as their faith, these single-minded men brought to the raw frontier the idealism of both the Enlightenment and the evangelical movement then flowering in Europe. Besides seeking converts to their faith they fought against the injustices and exploitation they perceived to be inflicted on the natives by the whites. Mixing religion with politics, they injected into Cape society an ethical element largely absent from the conventions of military governors, settlers and frontiersmen. And they did it with a vigour that at times shook the white social structure to its foundations.

At the Cape, white settlement preceded the church and often remained both physically and doctrinally beyond the Dutch mother church as the settlement spread inland, shaping Calvinism to its own circumstances. At the frontier, however, the settler ethos was overtaken by and clashed with the human rights principles imported by the missionaries from England.

Missionary work had not figured large in the designs of the Dutch settlement at the Cape, where the Dutch Reformed Church allowed its ministers – all employees of the Company – to own slaves. Serious missionary work was not begun by the DRC until the late 1850s, after slavery had been abolished. It was left to outsiders, the Moravians, to begin dedicated missionary work at the Cape. From the German arm of this Lutheran sect came George Schmidt in 1737 to set up South Africa's first mission station at Baviaanskloof, later known as Genadendal. Obstructed by the DRC because of his baptising of the Khoikhoi, he left the Cape in despair after seven years.

Into the vacuum left by Schmidt came the London Missionary Society, riding on the coat-tails of the British occupational forces. The LMS was representative of a number of missionary bodies formed in Britain around the turn of the 18th century. All had their genesis in the growth of industrialisation and the relative decline of the (slave) labour-intensive plantation economy, which led Britain to embrace free trade. The perceived need to create markets for British products among the colonial peoples required that they be emancipated and 'civilised', which in turn required that they be converted to Christianity. It was heaven-sent both for secular opponents of slavery and for missionaries.

Missionary societies mushroomed, the Baptist one arising in 1792, the LMS in 1795, the Glasgow one in 1796, the (Anglican) Church Missionary Society in 1799, the British and Foreign Bible Society in 1804, and the Wesleyan Methodist Missionary Society in 1813. In South Africa the Wesleyans established a series of mission stations stretching from the Cape Colony frontier to Port Natal. Other nationalities came in, too: the Rhenish, Berlin and Paris missionary societies and the American Board all operated within a region stretching from the eastern coast to Basutoland. By the time the whites spread inland in numbers with the Great Trek, the missionaries were deeply if not widely established there.

None, however, was quite like Johannes Theodosius van der Kemp. Once a high-living medical doctor in the Netherlands, Van der Kemp found religion after seeing his wife and child drown in a boating accident. Joining the LMS, he opened a mission station for the society at Bethelsdorp in 1797. He quickly antagonised both the burghers and the British brass. Conservative churchmen were pained by his literal application of Christian principles to relations with Khoikhoi, San and Xhosa. And they were appalled when he 'went native', living among the local peoples, dispensing with much of his European clothing and marrying a 14-year-old Madagascan slave girl.

Besides trying to convert the Khoikhoi, Van der Kemp and his fellow Bethelsdorp missionaries began to educate them, raising fears among the burghers that it would induce notions of equality. At the frontier the burghers were even more riled by the missionaries' unending complaints to the authorities about the way they recruited and treated their workers. In 1801 they assembled a commando and rode on Graaff-Reinet to drive the missionaries out, but were seen off by the British dragoons in the town, though not before firing a few shots at Van der Kemp.[1]

Though the LMS missionaries were allowed by the Batavian government to remain at the Cape, they were expelled from the frontier as burgher complaints against them mounted. Returning to Bethelsdorp when the British came back, the missionaries renewed their complaints, obliging the British to put some Boers on trial for mistreating their labourers.

Like their Batavian predecessors, the British governors saw the missionaries as troublemakers and tried to curb their activities. In this atmosphere the LMS mission in South Africa waned after Van der Kemp's death in 1811. The LMS looked for a strong restorative hand and found it in Dr John Philip.

The son of a Scottish schoolteacher, Philip had extraordinary determination and power of personality. Both burghers and colonial authorities at the Cape found him arrogant and professionally ambitious Arriving in 1819, he stirred and stung the colony's white inhabitants for the next 30 years.

Philip represented a Methodist school of thought that saw God best served not only through righteous living and good works but also through hard work and thrift, ideals that mirrored the simultaneous and interlinked rise of humanitarianism and industrialisation in Britain. Rejecting the then emerging concepts of scientific racism, the missionaries believed that Africans could be as competent, productive and inventive as Europeans if shown the way and given the chance.

Their beliefs were rejected by Dutch burghers convinced by Calvinist notions of predestination of the divinely ordained inferiority of the black people, and who in any event required them to be kept subservient as a source of labour. Whereas the missionaries' values had sprouted in the relative prosperity and liberalism associated with Britain's rising technocracy, those of the Boers had been shaped by adaptation to a crueller, more primal environment in which life remorselessly fed on other life, and human relations and ideals were dictated by fundamental imperatives of survival.

The missionaries' militancy also antagonised many of the British settlers at the frontier. Many had gone into business in the towns, and some speculated in land, covetously eyeing that of the Xhosa.

Philip's campaigning caused him to be called the most hated man in the Cape. He had an influential ally, however, in John Fairbairn, the Cape Town newspaper publisher who became his son-in-law. Fairbairn became the voice of the mercantile-humanitarian lobby in Cape Town, whose attitudes he reflected when he wrote: 'To stimulate Industry, to encourage civilisation, and convert the hostile natives into friendly customers, is … a more profitable speculation than to exterminate or reduce them to slavery.'

After the Xhosa attack on Grahamstown in 1819, Somerset declared the area between the Fish and Keiskamma rivers a no-man's-land. That measure proved unavailing in the pressure-cooker atmosphere created by rising demand for land on both sides of the frontier. In 1834 some twelve thousand Xhosas attacked on a broad front in the Sixth Frontier War.

After the Xhosa had been driven back across the frontier by the redcoats and colonial forces, the governor, Sir Benjamin D'Urban, widened the buffer by extending the no-go area all the way to the Kei River, calling the extension the Province of Queen Adelaide.

Angry protest shot forth from the missionaries and from humanitarians in England, prompting the secretary of state, Lord Glenelg, to take the view that the Xhosa had been justified in invading the colony. He castigated the frontier authorities for 'a long series of acts of injustice and spoliation' against the Xhosa.

Glenelg abolished the Province of Queen Adelaide, allowing the Xhosas to return, and instituted a system of dealing with them through treaties rather than military force.

In 1846 the border pressures again burst out in conflict, the Seventh Frontier War. By now the governor's seat was occupied by Sir Harry Smith, a fireball of a man with conservative views and a propensity for action before contemplation. He restored D'Urban's annexations under different names, making the territory between the Fish and the Keiskamma a district of the Cape Colony, calling it Victoria East in honour of the queen, then in the ninth year of her reign. The land between the Keiskamma and the Kei he annexed as the crown colony of British Kaffraria. Smith ceremonially terminated the treaty system, and soon land in Victoria East was being auctioned and eagerly bought by English settlers.

When Smith deposed Paramount Chief Sandile in 1850, the most bitter of the Frontier Wars erupted. Smith resorted to scorched earth tactics, destroying crops and seizing cattle to deprive the Xhosa of food, and burning their kraals to intimidate their families – tactics that were later to be used by the British against the Boers almost half a century later. About sixteen thousand Xhosa died in the war, and the Xhosa social infrastructure was ravaged.

Smith was replaced in 1852 by General Sir George Cathcart, who after a year in office castigated the settler merchants as 'a set of covetous, profligate, unscrupulous, land-jobbers of colonists' who sought to get rich by fomenting and supplying war with the Xhosas. Of the same group he later said: 'I am heartily disgusted and sick of these mean, dishonest people; the Kaffir is much the finer race of the two.'[2]

An even larger calamity than the eighth war befell the Xhosa when in 1857 many responded to a young girl's prophecy that if they planted no more crops and killed all their cattle, a whirlwind would sweep the British into the sea. Then dead heroes of the past would come to life, bringing cattle and grain. Many obeyed the injunction, and thousands starved to death as a result. The governor of the time, Sir George Grey, cleared the remaining Xhosa from east of the Kei River and opened it to white settlement. Although border troubles continued, Xhosa power was in effect broken and white hegemony firmly installed.

Under British rule the native peoples had acquired statutory freedom and overt equality, but in practice their subjugation had been completed. The whites had acquired effective control of land, labour and capital resources. The indigenous peoples had largely been deprived of the means to compete in a productive market.

The LMS missionaries, for their part, had only delayed and ameliorated the process of subjugation and dispossession. By the end of the eighth war their interests were in any case turning to new frontiers and opportunities to the north.

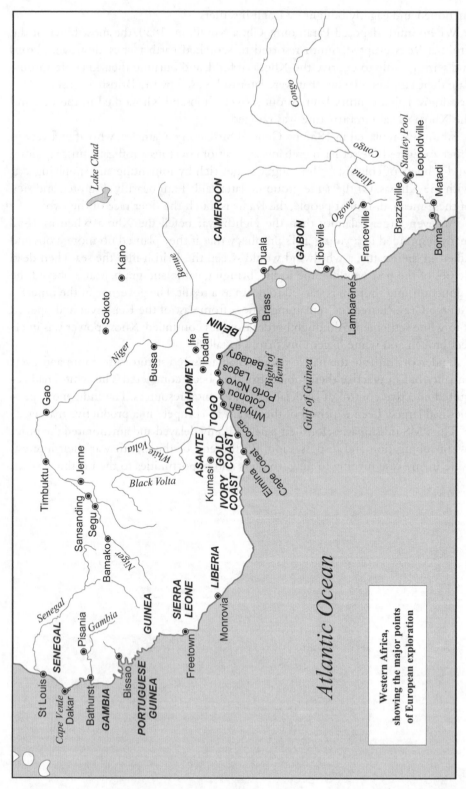

Western Africa,
showing the major points
of European exploration

CHAPTER 6

BIG WRONG-WAY RIVER

Beware, beware, the Bight of Benin
For few come out, though many go in.

They didn't come out because they died of heatstroke and tropical diseases, of parasites such as worms that burrowed through their bodies and came out through their eyes. Some perhaps died of drink and despair.

The old rhyme about the hazards Europeans faced when sojourning on the West African coast reflected their reluctance to penetrate inland for much of their time there. It was bad enough at the coast, with its relatively cool sea breezes; there was no good reason to go inland where it was even hotter, into the still and sodden jungles where the diseases were probably even deadlier, the parasites more prolific, and the natives sometimes hostile. Better to stay at the seaside and let the Africans bring in their slaves and other commodities of trade.

The few Europeans based at the coast lived an unhappy existence at the trading stations. Many of them went there in the first place out of desperation – poverty, escape from creditors or the law, that sort of thing – and stayed as briefly as possible. Many, if not most, never made it back, dying of malaria, blackwater fever, yellow fever, sleeping sickness or other afflictions. Not for nothing was West Africa called 'The White Man's Grave'.

Europeans did not begin to venture in numbers into Africa's tropical interior until some time after quinine (first isolated from the bark of the South American cinchona tree in 1820) was found in 1847 to offer protection against malaria. Long before then, however, hardy explorers began to venture into the interior in response to Europe's urgent and growing need for foreign raw materials and markets and to satisfy the basic curiosity that was fundamental to European development.

Explorers everywhere in the world generally followed the major rivers first, since they generally provided the easiest passage for both explorer and trader. Though few of Africa's rivers were navigable for far, and most were plagued by deadly diseases, efforts to explore them nevertheless began with the earliest coming of the Europeans. The Portuguese went some way up the Senegal, the Gambia and the Congo but, like most of those who came after them, were defeated by 'the fever' – the catchall term for all the feverish diseases but primarily for the biggest killer, malaria.

The Europeans were especially fascinated by the glamour and mysticism of the Nile – the river of the pharaohs and the pyramids, the river of the Bible, of Cleopatra and the Romans – and deeply curious about its source. Along its known length it was clear of malaria but the Europeans' early efforts to trace it further were foiled by the cataracts and the Sudd – and confused by the river having two sources. The major tributary, the White Nile, can be traced back certainly to Lake Victoria and arguably even further back to the Luvironza River, flowing into the lake from Burundi. The secondary tributary, the Blue Nile, flows from Lake Tana in the highlands of Ethiopia. But no-one knew that until it was confirmed in 1770 by James Bruce, one of the many Scots whose names pepper the annals of African exploration.

Large, loud and red-headed, Bruce became interested in the Nile while serving as British consul in Algiers. In 1768 he set out on a private expedition to find the river's origin, marching with a string of porters from Massawa on the Red Sea to Adowa, Axum and then Gondar. In a kingdom where violence and cruelty were endemic, the flamboyant Scottish giant survived through the force of his personality. It took him several years of adventure and hardship to establish that the Blue Nile flowed from Lake Tana and perhaps could be sourced from there back to the Little Abbai river. Bruce returned to Britain five years after he had set out on his quest. To his dismay, his story was disbelieved in England, and he retreated into bitter seclusion in Scotland, where he died falling down the stairs of his home.

Bruce had effectively mapped the Blue Nile but the more intriguing mystery, the source of the White Nile, had still to be solved.

Fascinated though they were by the Nile, the British were even more interested in finding the source and mapping the course of the Niger, evidently because the Niger's hinterland seemed to offer greater commercial opportunity than that of the Nile. No other river inspired more extraordinary efforts to map it than the Niger. And in no other exploration did so many die in the attempt.

The Europeans knew the river where it flowed into the sea, into the Bight of Benin, and split into a many-channelled delta 320 km wide, called the Oil Rivers delta because of the palm oil produced there. What lay upstream intrigued them for more than two centuries before they were able to find the answer.

Over this period, 19 expeditions were sent out by the British to establish the source and course of the river. At least seventy Europeans died in these attempts. When at last it was mapped, the Niger's odd course, curved back somewhat like a magnet, was aptly symbolic of its special attraction. It was that very shape, the great stream running first one way, away from the nearby sea, and then bending hugely to run in almost the opposite direction back to the sea, that baffled European explorers for decades and had fascinated and puzzled Arab geographers for centuries before them.

While the river's source, middle course and mouth were all known as separate entities, no-one had been able to link them up as a single river. The reason, besides its odd shape, was that the river traversed a vast area occupied by ruthlessly competing kingdoms that made travel between them hazardous and communication scanty.

European efforts to investigate the stories of a great river in the interior and to link it with one or other of the rivers emerging at the coast began in the early 17th century. The search was given impetus in 1788 when a group of prominent merchants led by Sir Joseph Banks founded the English African Association on a rising wave of interest in Africa. Rising with it was the recognition that commercial exploitation could not in the end be divorced from scientific and geographical exploration. The association was inclined to support the theory that the Oil Rivers delta was the mystery river's mouth. Three successive expeditions commissioned by the association failed, two of them with the death of the leaders.

Then in 1795 Mungo Park became the first to reach the upper Niger after setting out from a trading post on the Gambia and surviving fever, captivity and escape, starvation and exposure. At last, too weak to continue, he turned back and returned to England two years and seven months after he had set out. He became a celebrity, married, and opened a medical practice at Peebles. But Africa was not finished with him yet.

In the ten years following Park's return three more explorers sent out by the African Association failed, two dying of disease and the third being killed by robbers. Interest in Africa was growing, however, not only in business and academic circles but also in government, where some were beginning to perceive the probability of colonial competition with other European powers.

In 1803 the British government asked Park to go back and complete his survey of the river. He was given 36 British soldiers, two sailors and five ships' carpenters who, on reaching the river at Segu, were to build a boat in which the party would sail down to the sea. But by the time the party reached Segu nearly all the soldiers and four of the carpenters had died. Park carried on by canoe with the survivors, fighting off repeated attacks from the shore. At Bussa they were ambushed in rapids and all but one, a slave, drowned.

Park's journey had taken him nearly three thousand kilometres from the starting point on the Gambia, but he was still about fifteen hundred kilometres from the sea.

Park was posthumously enshrined as one of Britain's heroes. Few asked whether his achievements justified the cost in British lives; most had no doubt about the value of his journeys in increasing European knowledge of Africa, it being impossible to trade with parts that were unknown. Park had died promoting the interests of every British factory owner, every engineer and mechanic, every loom-minder, every grocer and innkeeper, every ship's chandler and miner. He was a hero not just because he was brave, determined and enterprising but because he was helping to create the means of British prosperity (and therefore security), which was what imperialism was all about.

That men should have risked their lives to find out where a river ran made more sense in Park's day than space exploration does today, for it promised more direct commercial benefits, greater in their time than those so far produced from probing beyond Earth.

In the next 25 years seven more expeditions, mostly led by military officers, were despatched by the British to solve the riddle of the Niger. All were defeated by disease and native hostility. In the end the mystery was solved by Richard Lander, the manservant of an earlier explorer, Lieutenant Hugh Clapperton, who had died of the fever at Sokoto.

Almost in desperation, the British government sent Lander back in a small and poorly financed expedition. With his brother John, Lander marched from Badagri in 1830, reached Bussa and travelled down the river by canoe. Close to the delta, they were seized by a local chief and John was held hostage while Richard was taken downriver to negotiate a ransom with a European ship. When Richard saw two sailing ships, one British, anchored in the delta he knew that the quest was over at last.

The brothers returned in the British ship to England and a heroes' welcome. Liverpool merchants formed a company to trade up the Niger with two woodburning steamboats. Besides trade, the company professed to be concerned with suppressing slavery and spreading 'true religion' and civilisation among the natives. To help achieve these objectives it equipped the steamers with cannons. The era of the gunboat had begun.

Sweeping aside the coastal middlemen with whom they had previously traded, the British opened direct trade links with the hinterland.

Only after the Lander brothers had completed the mapping of the Niger in 1830 did British trading begin to expand into the hinterland behind the Oil Rivers delta. Not until 1861, however, did the British feel obliged to annex Lagos, where they had much earlier set up an anti-slaving base. The Niger delta was not annexed until 24 years later. Even then the British did not move to expand these conquests into what became the colony of Nigeria until the Europeans commenced their 'scramble' for Africa in the late 19th century.

While palm oil gave the Niger delta an economic value to the British, it was the Gold Coast that they had coveted and fought for longer. Indeed, the campaigns against the native Asante people became one of the most enduring conflicts waged by the Europeans against a single nation in Africa.

★ ★ ★ ★

When British troops fought the Asante in 1824 the British commander, Sir Charles McCarthy, began the action by standing to attention in his scarlet jacket while his brass band played 'God Save the King'. The Asante responded loudly with drums and elephant-tusk horns. Then, apparently tiring of war by music, they opened fire with their flintlock muskets and the British responded with theirs.

McCarthy had taken a relatively small force against the Asante, evidently expecting an easy victory, but he was to be mortally disappointed. Before the day was out his British regulars and native militia had been routed, and McCarthy, badly wounded, had shot himself dead rather than be captured.

As they often did with enemies killed in battle, the Asante cut his heart out and ate it.[1] The top of his skull was preserved as a trophy to be kept in the Asante capital of Kumase with those of other eminent enemies.

Previous to McCarthy's battle, the Europeans on the west coast had tended to fight one another – over trade – rather than the natives. None of the Europeans trading there had previously made a serious attempt to extend their presence inland, for none fancied taking on the relatively strong African armies as well as the diseases, heat, rain and dense forests. The Europeans had named sectors of the West African coast according to their main trading activities: the Gold Coast (now Ghana), the Ivory Coast (now the Republic of the same name) the Grain Coast (where Liberia was implanted) and, on the western sector of the Bight of Benin, the Slave Coast, covering present-day Nigeria and Benin (formerly Dahomey). There was great interest in what might lie in the hinterland, as was evidenced by the determined efforts to trace the course of the Niger. But until the interior was opened up the Europeans saw little point in hinterland conquest away from the rivers, especially when the needs of trade were met at the coast by the African middlemen.

A different situation arose on the Gold Coast, however, when conflict between the Asante gold producers in the interior and the Fante middlemen at the coast threatened the free flow of trade. Intervention by the British traders or their government became inevitable.

Like many other early extensions of empire, the intervention, when it came, was not so much a matter of territorial ambition as of the government being hauled in to protect the foreign interests of its merchants – which in the end were those of government, too.

By 1824 the British dominated Gold Coast trading but had not acquired a monopoly. They had taken over the fort the Swedes had built in 1652, and were calling it Cape Coast Castle. The Dutch had long displaced the Portuguese and taken over their fort at Elmina. The Danes still occupied their own 17th-century fort at Accra, but both they and the Dutch were beginning to feel the pinch as the British suppression of slaving cut their income from this source. Both would sell out to the British before the turn of the century, but in its third decade they were still competitive and the British considered it important to protect their dominance on the Gold Coast. If that required subduing the Asante, who had unsuccessfully attacked Cape Coast Castle in 1807, then it would be done.

Britain was then beginning to establish herself as a major presence in Africa, having evicted the French from Egypt, occupied the Cape, and established dominance over the Gold Coast trade. The African Company of Merchants, which had replaced the old British Royal African Company in 1750, was taking a more expansive view of its operations. Though chartered and subsidised by the British government, the company ran its own show on the Gold Coast, with minimal interference from the Foreign Office.

Rather surprisingly, the company knew little about the Asante (whom the British persisted in calling the Ashanti) even though they were the dominant ethnic group in the region and produced most of the gold that was the principal commodity of trade. The British merchants were content to deal with the Fante who, living between the Asante and the coast, were able to act as middlemen. The Fante, also

Akans but nonetheless implacable rivals of the Asante, did their best to keep them apart from the British and to depict them as oppressors.

Only quite late in their acquaintance did the British come to know that the Asante had in many ways one of the most advanced civilisations in Africa, one that seemed at odds with their practices of human sacrifice and execution on a grand scale, and occasional cannibalism. Governance was carried out by a national assembly and cabinet, and an extensive civil service. The major towns were linked through the forest by gravelled paths. The British were impressed by the dominant aristocracy, whom they found striking physically and in their dress (silk robes and gold-studded sandals for formal occasions) and their habits. Their buildings were well constructed and ornamented, in some cases in stone with bas-relief designs, and, according to some accounts, many had indoor toilets that were flushed with boiling water.[2]

Britons granted an audience with the king, Osei Bonsu, in 1817 were literally dazzled by the sun reflecting off the masses of gold ornaments worn by him and his courtiers and guards. Gold, extracted both alluvially and from shallow mines, was liberally used in the Asante capital for ornamentation and artifact as well as for exchange.

Exasperated by the continuing friction between the merchants and the Asante, the British government terminated the African Company of Merchants' charter in 1822 and attached its assets. The government had in any event decided to establish British protection over the Gold Coast as the best way of ending the now illegal but persistent slaving. McCarthy, formerly governor of Sierra Leone, was appointed governor and decided that British interests required the subjugation of the Asante. In 1824 he led a force of 3 000 against an Asante army 10 000 strong, and paid for it with his life.

Malaria proved a more deadly enemy to the British troops than the Asante, however. After more than three hundred soldiers and many of their wives and children had perished in sickbeds, the British abandoned efforts to establish a redcoat garrison at Cape Coast. The defence of the coastal stations was entrusted to native militia led by British officers.

In 1829 the government, feeling that British interests could now be looked after by the merchants, handed control back to them. The merchants set up an administrative council and, in 1831, signed a treaty guaranteeing the protection of the Asante's coastal trade. Relative peace prevailed for the next three decades, during which the Danes saw their West African trading profits so reduced by the suppression of the slave trade that they sold out to the British, handing over the Accra fort in 1850.

A parliamentary select committee appointed in 1862 to look into British activities in West Africa as a whole recommended a severe reduction in British interests. The recommendation was largely ignored, however, by both politicians and merchants. There was not much sentiment in the City or Whitehall for abandoning one of the world's richest sources of gold, certainly not when Britain's arch rivals, the French, were expanding into the Senegal basin.

As it turned out, however, the British faced no competition on the Gold Coast from the French, though they had a fort at Ouidah not far along the coast in Dahomey. French trading was centred on their first fort, St Louis, at the mouth of the Senegal River, far to the west around Africa's bulge. In the long warring between the French and British, St Louis and the former slaving station on nearby Goree Island changed hands a number of times until they were finally returned to the French in 1814. The French in turn several times seized and lost Fort James, the British base in the Gambia, which the Royal Adventurers Trading in Africa had built towards the end of the 16th century. The French never made a grab for the Gold Coast, however, which was perhaps just as well for the British, considering the troubles they had not only with the Asante but with the Fante too.

In 1868 the Fante established an independent confederation, modelled on European lines. The British proscribed the confederacy and interned its leaders.

Not until 1900 were they finally able to put down Asante military resistance. Political resistance continued for another half-century, however, until the Gold Coast in 1957 became the first British colony in Africa to be granted independence, reverting to the ancient name of Ghana.

Elsewhere on the West African coast the British had developed another significant presence in Sierra Leone, where a philanthropic body, the Sierra Leone Company, had in 1787 resettled slaves who had sided with the British during the American War of Independence and had then been dumped in cold Canada. The Africans were being returned to the Africa from which their forefathers had been torn, but not to the same part of Africa. In effect they were foreign settlers, and behaved towards the natives almost as badly as the white settlers did elsewhere in Africa. Economic problems were to lead to the settlement being taken over by the British government and declared a Crown colony in 1808. The colony became a major centre of British administration and missionary activity in West Africa, with Gambia being administered from there until it, too, became a separate colony in 1888.

With the ending of the slave trade European interest in West Africa would have receded sharply but for the industrial revolution's growing need for raw materials and markets for manufactures. Commerce kept the Europeans looking to Africa and penetrating ever deeper into its unmapped centre. That penetration did not seriously begin, though, until some way into the 19th century, after the Europeans had been clinging to their commercial beachheads for some three hundred years.

CHAPTER 7

THE COMING OF THE SWALLOWS

A sudden shift in the coastal wind one day in 1823 brought far-reaching change to the eastern part of the sub-continent.

Frank Farewell and James Saunders King were sailing close inshore in the brig *Julia*, looking for an opening in the coastline of Natal where they might establish a post for trading for ivory. They knew nothing of the hinterland, for none of those who had been shipwrecked on this straight-edged coast had survived to tell what lay beyond the endless line of surf. Farewell and King knew only that it was the territory of the Zulus of fearsome repute.

Both lieutenants in the Royal Navy, they had seen their commissions become dormant after the Napoleonic Wars and had turned to making a living from ivory. More than three centuries after the demand for the elephant's tusk had led the first white men ashore in sub-Saharan Africa, ivory was still coveted for Europe's combs and fans and gewgaws, its knife handles and piano keys and billiard balls.

Farewell and King made their breakthrough when an unusual off-shore breeze one day persuaded them to anchor close inshore. But then the wind suddenly turned and began blowing hard from the sea and the little ship was driven inexorably towards the land, then over a sandbar and into a great, quiet lagoon.[1] They had found the bay on which was to rise Durban, South Africa's third-largest city and Africa's busiest port. Through this gateway would in time pour a stream of Europeans, almost all from Britain, to form in the hinterland one of Africa's largest communities of English-speaking whites. And in the early part of this process it would land the powerful British forces that would destroy Zulu power.

The Zulu king, Shaka, was then at the height of his power, ruthlessly presiding over an empire stretching thousands of square kilometres inland from the sea. An extraordinary man of high intelligence and powerful personality, Shaka had formed disparate Nguni clans into the Zulu nation through the exercise of his military genius and political skill; and through a belief that the clans, proud, pugnacious and quarrelsome, could be held together in a larger nation only by the ultimate discipline, the fear of death.

Frequently implementing that threat, he formed his warriors into regiments, rigorously trained in new fighting methods. Deployed with extraordinary tactical skill, his regiments were almost invincible. At the time of the white men's coming he commanded the largest and most effective army in all of southern and central Africa. It had taken him little more than five years to create his kingdom, rising from minor chief in 1816 to rule an empire reaching half-way across the sub-continent. His rampaging regiments had sent whole tribes fleeing into the interior, leading early historians to blame him for the *mfecane* (the crushing), as it was known among the Nguni-speaking peoples, or the *difaqane* (the great flight) among the Sotho-speakers.

The domino effect of the *mfecane* sent waves of upheaval from Zululand westwards to the Kalahari desert, southwards to the frontiers of white expansion in the Cape, and northwards into central and east Africa. For a decade it disrupted the hinterland as clans, tribes and breakaway Zulu warriors fled from stronger forces and in turn fell upon weaker ones in a fight for survival. When the convulsion subsided, vast regions in the interior were left bare of people, cattle and crops. Some of those fleeing the turmoil had established new homelands far from those of their birth, in some cases joining with different peoples to form new tribes.

Shaka is now held only partly accountable for the disastrous effects of the *mfecane*. While his wars of conquest were perhaps the main cause of the upheaval, they in turn arose from competition between four main groups that had formed among the Nguni clans in the area that later became known as Zululand. It appears that the clashing of these groups was in turn part of the process in which the great Bantu southward migration from West Africa turned in on itself when it collided with northward European expansion and ran out of space.

The *mfecane* is attributed by some historians also to the raids and flights associated with the slavery that Arabs were conducting from the north-east. Yet another cause is held to be competition for the ivory that fed the lucrative trade with the Portuguese at Delagoa Bay.

Whatever its causes, the *mfecane* gave the whites the impression of a largely uninhabited hinterland when they began to surge northwards in that other major phenomenon of the time, the Great Trek. On that basis the trekkers claimed possession of the land, a claim defended for generations thereafter with conviction but without incontrovertible foundation, for it is inconceivable that these temperate grasslands had always been unpopulated. It is much more probable that the previous occupants had only fled from the *mfecane* with the hope of returning if and when it was all over.

The fortunes of the whites were to become enmeshed with those of a number of the new tribes formed in the *mfecane's* cauldron. In one of the major episodes of the phenomenon, Mzilikazi, chief of the Kumalo clan, rebelled against Shaka and fled westwards with his army. Defeated by the Voortrekkers, he moved to the north, founding the Ndebeles, known by the whites as the Matabeles, a nation that became almost as formidable as the Zulus.

At the highest edge of South Africa's central plateau another remarkable leader, Moshoeshoe, gathered Sotho and other refugees of the *mfecane* round a mountain fortress and formed them into the Basotho nation.

The *mfecane* was still running strong when Farewell and his companions came face to face with Shaka. They were the first white persons the Zulu king had seen.

Their horses, which they had shipped up from Algoa Bay by the time they were granted their first audience, were likewise the first the Zulus had set eyes on. So, too, were the ships that were now crossing the bar into what the whites were calling Port Natal. Intrigued as he was by the pale newcomers and their steeds, Shaka was more fascinated by their technology. It seems that Shaka's great intelligence, which had not been fully challenged by his own limited environment, immediately appreciated the intellectual fecundity of a society that could produce such technology. Recognising the power that its ruler must exercise, he became obsessed with forming an alliance with King George – *Umjoji*, as Shaka called him.

Farewell and King, joined now in the Port Natal venture by Henry Francis Fynn, were recognised by Shaka as King George's representatives and given virtually open entre to the royal kraal. The Cape governor, Sir Charles Somerset, formed the impression, however, that Shaka, having subjugated the Pondos to the south of his territory, was planning to do the same to the Xhosas beyond them, which might see the frontier overwhelmed by refugees and the white settlers swamped by uncontrollable hordes. According to one account, Somerset asked Farewell to take a message to Shaka informing him of King George's desire for friendship but assuring him that the British would go to the aid of the Xhosas if he attacked them.[2]

Shaka valued what he saw as this pledge of friendship with the British, and for the rest of his reign he treated them as allies. He called them swallows because, like the birds, they built houses of clay rather than grass like the Zulus. None of the little group of traders at Port Natal or those at Shaka's kraal was ever harmed, while around them Zulus were executed in thousands for offending Shaka's codes or whims. In 1828 he sent an embassy of chiefs on an English trading ship to Algoa Bay to cement his alliance with King George.

Farewell was able to persuade Shaka to put his mark on a document giving him about one-sixth of present-day Natal. Authorities on Zulu custom have expressed doubt that Shaka attached the same meaning to it as Farewell. Nonetheless, Farewell hoisted the Union Jack at the bay and annexed the territory in the name of King George.

Shaka did indeed launch a southward assault that seemed aimed at the Xhosa, but when his impis got within a hundred kilometres of the Xhosa he ordered them to turn back. His reasons are unclear. Some weight must perhaps be given to accounts that his efficient intelligence service informed him of the mustering of the British troops to meet his assault, and he chose to keep to his resolve not to fight with King George.

Shaka's remarkable reign ended in September 1828 when he was assassinated by his brothers Dingane and Mhlangana. Dingane assumed the Zulu throne and immediately sent peace overtures to the British at the Cape. But the days of Zulu power were already numbered – as the dying Shaka had prophesied.

'You think you will rule this country,' he said to his assassins, 'but already I see the swallows coming. You will not rule it when I am dead. The white people have already arrived.'[3]

Indeed, within months the swallows were flocking in. English traders began to move in numbers to Port Natal. Farewell was murdered by a renegade Zulu chief, but the Union Jack he hoisted at Port Natal in 1824 continued to fly over the colony of Natal for most of the next 86 years, with only a relatively brief interruption when the Boers moved in and occupied the port and its hinterland in their search for a nation-state of their own.

★ ★ ★ ★

It had taken the trekboers nearly two centuries to edge their way from Cape Town across the Karoo to the east coast, a gradual advance that by 1835 had moved the frontier some nine hundred kilometres. Then, in five momentous years, thousands of Boers broke away from the frontier in a concerted migratory surge and staked out new lands as far as fifteen hundred kilometres to the north in land largely unknown to whites.

The migration had effects hugely disproportional to its relative brevity, arguably more transformative even than the *mfecane,* taking white domination into the heart of the sub-continent and radically changing its demography and social structures.

About fifteen thousand Boers left the Cape between 1835 and 1840, travelling in a number of separate expeditions. From the rootbole of the Cape the migration spread out like a tree, its branches eventually touching both coasts of the sub-continent and penetrating most of the hinterland between. Each main branch was a large party that divided into lesser branches and then into family twigs, each of which sought to make a homestead beyond sight of the neighbours' smoke. For the Voortrekkers, besides being individualistic by nature, had learned through their trekboer ancestors that the African south's fickle climate and relatively poor soil and vegetation mandated farming spread thin and wide.

This factor, together with the ready availability of big farms in the early days of the Cape, had contributed to the creation of the patriarchal Boer society composed of large families isolated from one another, rather than clustered in villages. It was a way of life that fostered independence and intolerance of external authority. There remained, of course, a need for social intercourse, a requirement that was met largely through the church – whenever it caught up with the migration. The lifestyle required also an element of cooperation for security – the need that produced the commando and the laager, the instant fortress formed by a ring of waggons when attack threatened.

In its broad character the Boer lifestyle was the antithesis of communality, contradistinct from that of Bantu communities living close-packed and close-knit in villages administered by a chief who decided who might do what with the communal land and herds. A lifestyle of the latter kind, what might be called the beehive social mode, is predicated primarily on security. For that reason it was retained by the Bantu peoples even when they migrated from the close tropical environment into the open plains of the savannah. Without guns, the Bantu relied on numbers of spears for defence against enemies, which made a communal way of life essential. They could not afford the luxury of space given the Boer by his guns and horses;

they had not only to see their neighbours' smoke but to breathe it too.

Communality had advantages besides security. It offered companionship and a labour force for agriculture and hut-building. It also provided a social safety net, an extended family system that had the capability of ensuring that no-one need starve or lie sick or die alone. At the same time it demanded conformity to the communal will and codes, creating a compliant society in which chiefs and also healers and soothsayers – the 'witchdoctors' of Western terminology – could acquire great power. This aspect of communality may have hampered individuality, inventiveness and enterprise and, ultimately, development – technological development, at any rate, thus putting the indigenous African at a disadvantage when the better-equipped European came seeking his land and its wealth.

Not that the white man always accepted that it was the black man's land. Disputes about who was there first have simmered in South Africa for generations, with conservative Afrikaners asserting that their forefathers did not seize the central part of the country from the natives but found it empty when they trekked in.

This need for justification was something peculiar to the whites of South Africa in their unique position as a dominant ethnic minority. The dominant white majorities in America, Australia, New Zealand, Argentina and other colonised parts seldom if ever found it necessary to justify their title to the land formerly occupied by indigenous peoples, who came to be outnumbered and politically powerless (and nowhere in the world was a white majority created kindly). In contrast, the white South African, the Afrikaner in particular, was always required to account for his possession and to have it challenged. The challenge came primarily from a black majority protesting against dispossession but whose superior numbers still made them an incipient threat to the dispossessors. It came also from the blacks' foreign sympathisers, whose own numbers grew as continuing white racism in South Africa stood in ever-starker contrast to its waning elsewhere.

The essence of the Afrikaner's thesis of possession was expressed in a guidebook for the monument that was built a century later at Pretoria to commemorate the Voortrekkers: 'It is nonsense to suppose that the interior of Southern Africa belonged to the Bantu and that the white man took it away from him. The Bantu penetrated from the north almost at the same time as the white man entered the south. They had equal title. The Voortrekkers wished to partition the country and live in peace because they had already experienced enough trouble in the Cape. But the Bantu was not amenable to reason. He respected only one thing and that was force.'

Such self-serving falsification of their own history was routinely fed to generations of white schoolchildren by historians and teachers bowing – even if subconsciously – to the imperatives of separateness. The claim of title to the land had continually to be asserted if segregation was to have any sustainable basis. It had to be based either on the grounds that the whites had arrived first in empty land or that whites and blacks had arrived simultaneously. Or, failing that, that the land was legally ceded to the whites by occupant blacks. There is some truth in all three versions, less in the first than the second, and less in the second than the third. Seldom was the most realistic claim, the right of conquest, advanced, even though it had always been the way in Africa, the only right the Bantu themselves could claim besides long tenure, having themselves displaced the Khoikhoi and San.

Nowhere can the whites truly claim first occupation, not even where they arrived at the Cape. European seamen had been dealing with the San and Khoikhoi for two centuries before Van Riebeeck's landing, and archaeological evidence of their habitation extends deep into the hinterland. Xhosas had been burying their fathers east of the Great Fish River for generations before the trekboers showed up on its western bank. There is likewise no doubting the long prior tenure further north of the other Ngunis such as the Zulus and Swazis and of the Vendas and Pedis and the Tswanas and other tribes.

White segregationists could most easily claim first possession in the central interior, for extensive tracts were indeed largely empty of people when the Voortrekkers arrived there. It is inconceivable, however, that neither the hunting San nor the pastoral Khoikhoi nor the mixed-farming Bantu peoples would not already have moved into the vast temperate grasslands of the interior plateau, rich in game and free of the tsetse fly that kills cattle and people in the tropical lowlands.

One theory holds that the indigenous inhabitants had been decimated by disease and the survivors had fled from it. Another, perhaps more tenable, is that much of the highlands had been scoured of settlement by the *mfecane*.

The Voortrekkers' migration to the wide-open spaces to the north was spurred partly by grievances against the British — their intervention in commando raids against Xhosa cattle raiders, and in slavery and other coercive labour practices; their autocratic governance; their efforts to suppress the Dutch language and to Anglicise the schools and churches. But, like the expansion of the trekboers, it was chiefly a matter of land. Even if neither the British nor their pesky missionaries had arrived at the Cape, the descendants of the Dutch settlers would inevitably have moved north in search of new lands as they found their expansion to the east and northeast blocked by the Xhosa.

Some Afrikaners have characterised the Great Trek as the birthing labour from which emerged the modern Afrikaner nation, but this ignores the fact that only about one in ten of the Dutch-descended in the Cape joined the exodus. For all the resentment over aspects of British rule, most preferred to remain under the British in the Cape Colony. Those who stayed behind also became Afrikaners, sharing the same language and culture. When the Boer War broke out 60 years later only a minority of the Cape Afrikaners left the colony to fight with the Boer forces. What the Great Trek did was spread Afrikanerdom wider, and the further north it went the more bitter and extreme its participants seemed to be.

The trekkers were in a sense dissidents not only against their governance but also against their church, for the DRC, the official church even under British rule, opposed the emigration, unwilling — or unable — to extend its ministrations beyond the colony. The Synod of the church in 1837 formally denounced the trek, and barred its ministers from accompanying it.[4] So in the wilderness the trekkers relied for spiritual guidance on their own leaders and their own interpretation of the Bible, increasingly identifying themselves with the Israelites wandering in the wilderness, the seekers after the promised land of Beulah, and with the concept of themselves as a race chosen for a divine purpose.

In 1859, having settled beyond the Orange River, some of the migrants split from the DRC to found their own church, the Nederduitsch Hervormde Kerk, which became known as the Voortrekker Church. From that body a third church, the Gereformeerde Kerk, splintered off in 1859 at Potchefstroom in the Transvaal to follow an even stricter Calvinist line. All three churches were to have a powerful influence on the shaping of Afrikaner political and racial attitudes.

The Voortrekkers have been likened to the pioneering settlers of the American West in that both left places of older coastal settlement and travelled in covered waggons to create new homes in the interior, using their guns to displace indigenous inhabitants. The American pioneers, however, seem to have been more predacious than the Voortrekkers, acquiring land through broken treaties and violent seizure. In this they had the advantage of having long thrown off British colonial authority, and being unhampered by the restraints of Victorian morality and colonialism that were imposed from London on the Boers.

The Afrikaners did have the convenience at a later stage of Zulu military power being broken by the British, but only at the cost of seeing the British take much of the Zulu land for themselves, and later the Afrikaners' land as well. Besides that, the British blocked Afrikaner expansion west and north of the Limpopo, and stopped them from acquiring direct access to the sea.

In the furthest extent of the Great Trek, a number of parties pushed across the Vaal River, some intending to go round the Zulus and establish a link with the Indian Ocean. Some parties were wiped out by malaria and hostile tribes. Others were halted by Mzilikazi's warriors, but eventually defeated him with their firepower and forced him to migrate again. It was then that he took his formidable spearmen on a destructive path across the Limpopo, and began subjugating the resident Shonas, establishing his new capital at what is now Bulawayo in Zimbabwe.

While the Great Trek was under way, Queen Victoria ascended the British throne in 1837. To those trekkers who learned of the event she was just another of the kingdom's long line of monarchs. But she would not long remain so.

Piet Retief, Gert Maritz and Piet Uys led their parties over the Drakensberg into what was to become Natal, where Dingane, Shaka's assassin and successor, is said to have promised to cede a large region to them. Dingane was in fact opposed to white intrusion. He had a delegation led by Retief killed, and then sent his warriors to wipe out the rest of their parties – more than five hundred in all. A commando that rode from the highveld to avenge these killings was ambushed and defeated.

Defensively laagered against further attack, the Voortrekkers began to set up a republic at a settlement, called Pietermaritzburg, at the foot of the misty inland hill country. Convinced now that they could not be safe without first smashing Dingane, they sent 500 men under Andries Pretorius to challenge him. The Zulus came on 16 December 1838 and went down in swathes before the hail of shot from within Pretorius's laager beside the Ncome River. Retreating, they left some three thousand of their number dead and the river running red, and thereafter known to the trekkers as Blood River.

The Blood River action was perhaps the most significant battle of the white migration into the northern interior, for it checked the strongest indigenous power (Zulu power was not broken until British troops defeated Cetewayo at Ulundi in 1879), opened the hinterland to white settlement, and sealed the subjugation of the native peoples.

Pretorius pursued the disorganised Zulus, forcing Dingane to abandon his kraal at Umgungundhlovu. There, beside Retief's remains, the Voortrekkers were said to have found a satchel containing the land treaty Dingane had signed. Some historians have suggested that the document subsequently produced was forged.

Forgery or not, the Voortrekkers used it as licence for their new state, the Republic of Natalia, the Afrikaners' first serious attempt to establish a republic outside the Cape Colony. But already the English were breathing down their necks.

★ ★ ★ ★

The search for a homeland in the continent of their genesis is the central theme of the Afrikaners' story as many of them see it. It is a tragic one in their perspective in that the search has never been fulfilled.

They see the theme running unbroken from the first ventures into the hinterland by the trekboers in the 17th century right up to the present time. An endless search, an elusive dream, briefly realised in the republics founded by the Voortrekkers and partly realised in apartheid South Africa, but each time crushed by the larger politics of the day: first by authority in Amsterdam, then by British imperialism, then by black majority rule imposed by domestic and international pressure.

Some Afrikaners still obsessively chase the dream, though it now appears hopeless, not only as a separate nation-state but even as a distinctive part of a multi-ethnic and democratic South Africa. In the land where they pioneered, the Afrikaners cannot even claim – as in many respects can the French Canadians of Quebec – a part, a province, dominated by their kind and their language. Only now may some perceive that the dream was lost because it was pursued at the expense of other people.

It was never a unanimous dream. More than independent statehood, many of the trekkers primarily wanted a lifestyle that had become traditional and land on which to live it. Like some of the trekboers who preceded them across the Orange, many had no strong objection to achieving this ambition under British rule.

Still, the dream was there and it appears to have become stronger the further the Afrikaners moved from the Cape, the more clearly they saw themselves as *het volk*, a people, the people, even as a chosen people when it seemed advantageous to claim divine warrant. Fulfilment of the dream first seemed really attainable to its followers when the victory at Blood River cleared the way for the founding of the Republic of Natalia.

But even as Pretorius went out to fight Dingane at Blood River, British troops landed at Port Natal with orders to stop both the battle and the formation of the republic. The colonial authorities had made some efforts to stop the trekkers from leaving the Cape, and still considered them British subjects. Their declaration of a republic was seen as rebellion. And their clashes with indigenous peoples were disturbing political stability in a sub-continent in which Britain perceived a special interest.

The redcoats arrived at the port too late to do anything about the battle at Blood River, and the governor at the Cape, Sir George Napier, withdrew them. But he did not abandon his hope of persuading the Voortrekkers to give up their migration and return to the Cape as loyal subjects of the Queen. The Colonial Office had added to its concerns a suspicion that the Netherlands was about to give formal backing to Natalia. The prospect of another power muscling in on a British sphere of interest, perhaps even establishing a presence on the sea route to India, was intolerable. Intervention was only a matter of time and excuse.

In setting up their republic the Voortrekkers had come squarely up against the South African whites' fundamental dilemma of not wanting to share a society with black people yet being unable to do without their labour. The Natalians approached the problem by instituting an early form of apartheid. The constitution of their new republic provided for a white society that would admit black people only as servants. All others would be moved to an area set aside for them along the southern border – one of South Africa's first 'native reserves'. Those blacks allowed to remain in white Natalia would have to carry passes.

Each white farmer was allowed five black families living on his farm to provide serf labour. Often this was not enough to meet the farmers' needs, and they extended their labour forces with children captured in actions against rebellious Zulus or simply abducted under the euphemism of apprenticeship.

Napier saw his chance to intervene when Natalia sent a commando down to the southern border to punish Pondo stock thieves and the Pondo called for British protection. Napier sent troops to attack the Boers at Port Natal, but the redcoats found themselves besieged instead and had to send Dick King on his famous 800-km ride to Grahamstown to fetch help. Reinforcements sailed, lifted the siege, and effectively ended Afrikaner republican ambitions in Natal.

Natal was made a district of the Cape Colony, with the stipulation that there was to be 'no distinction of colour, origin, race or creed'. Rather than accept British domination and an ethnic liberalism that they considered unrealistic for whites settling in Africa, most of the Boers dribbled back over the Drakensberg, abandoning their farms and their ambition of securing an outlet to the sea.

In the hinterland, serious attempts were now made by the Voortrekkers to set up republics. In Transorangia (the region north of the Orange River), Dr Philip popped up again to make life difficult for the Boers, asserting Griqua and Basotho rights to land. Trekkers challenging these claims clashed with British troops. When Sir Harry Smith became governor in 1847 he gave land claimed by the Griquas and the Basotho to Boer and British settlers. Most of the territory between the Orange and Vaal rivers he annexed as the British Orange River Sovereignty.

Trekkers opposed to British rule were outraged at the annexation, and chased Smith's representative, Major Henry Warden, back across the Orange. As the rebels prepared to march on Bloemfontein, Smith came bustling up from the Cape with a strong force and dispersed them in an action at Boomplaats.

British and Boer speculators were now snapping up land in both the Orange River Sovereignty and Natal. The farms vacated in Natal by the departing trekkers were got for as little as tuppence an acre, in many cases by companies based in the Cape. By now the original 400 Voortrekker families had dwindled to 60.

Some of the land was parcelled out to several thousand Britons who poured into Natal as settlers, mostly under a scheme sponsored by JC Byrne. At more than seven thousand five hundred, their influx, from 1849 to 1852, was even bigger than the 1820 settlement in the Cape. They, too, found the land allocations too small to be viable, and began drifting off to the towns.

Smith, discredited by his failure to bring order to the eastern Cape frontier and Transorangia, was replaced by Sir George Cathcart, with instructions to be more sympathetic to Boer aspirations for independent statehood. In January 1852 he signed the Sand River Convention, granting independence to the South African Republic (the Transvaal), and eschewed any British alliances with black leaders in the region. For the first time London was withdrawing support for indigenous people for whom it had tacitly accepted responsibility, and abandoning them to white domination.

The Orange River Sovereignty was dismantled and in February 1854 became a white republic, the Orange Free State, bounded on the north by the Vaal and in the south by the Orange. Many Britons remained in the republic and formed the majority in the capital, Bloemfontein.

Dispute continued over the Free State's border with Basutoland. Moshoeshoe held out against strong Boer attacks but eventually sought and won British protection. Basutoland was annexed to the Crown in 1868. The British returned some of the land conquered from the Basotho but still left them with less territory than they had originally held. The Free State retained the fertile west bank of the Caledon, while the Basotho were confined to the mainly unarable highlands. They ended up a few generations later having to sell their only resources, labour and water, to South Africa in order to survive.

While the Boers consolidated their hold on the plains that had been found almost empty by the Voortrekkers, they had recurring troubles with the African tribes that had largely been forced into the hills by the *mfecane* and which greatly outnumbered them. Even within their borders, the Boers were outnumbered by black majorities – twice as many as whites in the OFS, and three times as many in the Transvaal.

Both republics adopted constitutions and policies similar to those of Natalia, designed to segregate the races while ensuring that black people would be available as labourers. Blacks were denied citizenship and the vote, and were barred from owning land in white areas. This effectively barred them from private enterprise since where there was communal black land they could neither farm it extensively nor obtain credit against land holdings for development. In the Transvaal only 860 000 of the republic's 71-million morgen was set aside for blacks.

In both states blacks' movements were controlled by the issuing of passes, and they were induced to work for the whites by the levying of hut or poll taxes. The Transvaal added the refinement of higher taxes for the unemployed than for those with jobs. Indentured labour was used in both republics.

Limits were placed in both states on the number of black workers on any one farm. Urban workers were controlled by making them live in 'locations' outside the towns, allowing only those with jobs into the locations.

At a later stage, after Asians had joined the ethnic agglomeration, the Orange Free State imposed limitations on Asians as well as blacks. Responding in part to pressure from English-speaking traders, the Free State at first restricted Asians' trading rights in 1885, and then in 1890 barred Asians from the Republic altogether.

Racial discrimination was not exclusive to the Afrikaners. It was practised in effect also by the British authorities in Natal, and for the same reasons of self-preservation and exploitation. Even with the settler influx the whites were outnumbered there more than ten to one by blacks. The equal rights policy the British had imposed on the Boers at annexation was compromised when they came to govern the territory themselves and had to balance the rights of the indigenous peoples against the demands of the labour-hungry settlers.

In keeping with the strictures they had forced on the Natalia Boers, as well as with the prevailing sentiment in Britain, the British ostensibly extended the vote to all men in Natal, as in the Cape. But the qualification – ownership of immovable property worth 50 pounds or payment of an annual rent of ten pounds – meant that hardly any black people qualified. They were further disqualified by a law passed in 1865 (by which time Natal had limited self-government) confining the vote to blacks who had been exempted from customary (tribal) law. By 1905 only three blacks had won the right to vote.

The Britons in Natal became no less keen than the Boers on keeping the races apart while at the same time preserving a supply of cheap labour. To this end they created native reserves, otherwise known as locations. As in the Boer republics, a hut tax was levied, ostensibly to help meet the cost of administering the locations but effectively to force black people to work for the whites (blacks working for white farmers were exempted from the tax). From 1854, every black man entering Natal from outside was required to work on white farms for at least three years at fixed wages.

In placing the blacks under customary rather than the Roman–Dutch law applying to the whites, the British ostensibly were aiming to protect the blacks from exploitation, but this was turned against them in the measure denying the vote to those not exempted from customary law.

While the Voortrekkers put their stamp on the territory west of the Drakensberg, the British put theirs on Natal, setting up their administration in Pietermaritzburg. The streets, though retaining their Dutch names, came to be lined with British shopkeepers. In a park beside the Msunduze River, cricket was played by whiteflannelled men wearing caps striped with the colours of Eton and Cambridge. Military bands thumped out music from a bandstand while ladies carrying parasols strolled with red-coated officers beside sapling planes brought out from 'home'. It would be a long time before any of their descendants would think of Natal – or South Africa – as home.

CHAPTER 8

THE FOUNTAINS OF THE NILE

Almost as much as nature abhors a vacuum, 19th-century Europe could not abide blank spaces on the world map. They could be tolerated least of all by the Victorian Britons, expansive, ascendant, confident in their military and industrial might.

Unmapped regions stood almost as a reproach, certainly as a challenge, to a generation convinced of the near-omnipotence of British enterprise and technology – and spirit. Not only had these protected their island nation from its enemies, they had extended its power around the globe. The challenge could hardly be ignored when the triumphs of the British Empire and the marvels of British industry were being flaunted in the Great Exhibition of 1851, where beneath the immense glass curves of the Crystal Palace the latest inventions were displayed beside native artifacts from distant lands now flying the Union Jack.

No blank space was as taunting as those that by mid-century still spread across the interior of Africa. Most of the world's other geographic secrets had already been unveiled, yet middle Africa still lay hidden to Europe. The New World of the Americas was pretty well known from coast to coast, except for the Northwest Passage that hopefully would give to northern hemisphere shipping a westward access from the Atlantic to the Pacific. Australasia had been not only well mapped but colonised too. Captain Cook had long ago circumnavigated Antarctica. The Royal Geographical Society, dedicated to unravelling the secrets of the globe, was into its third decade. But inner Africa remained locked in mystery – the Nile's source was still unknown; the stories of snow-capped mountains on the equator were tantalisingly unproven; the tales of inland seas untested.

By mid-century, however, interest in Africa was growing fast, especially in Britain. Commercial bodies in Europe were keen to assess the possibilities of trade. Missionary interests were eager to spread the gospel. Scientific organisations thirsted for knowledge of the interior. And the public in general was deeply curious about what might lie in the mysterious depths of the 'Dark Continent'. Lacking electronic entertainment to feed them with simulated heroes and adventures, and having only books and theatre for diversion, they looked to accounts of the real thing for titillation and vicarious thrills. As one British historian has noted, 'Space exploration in the twentieth century has never succeeded in generating a quarter of the enthusiasm that the search for the Nile aroused in the nineteenth.'[1]

It was only a matter of time before the Europeans broke through the barriers

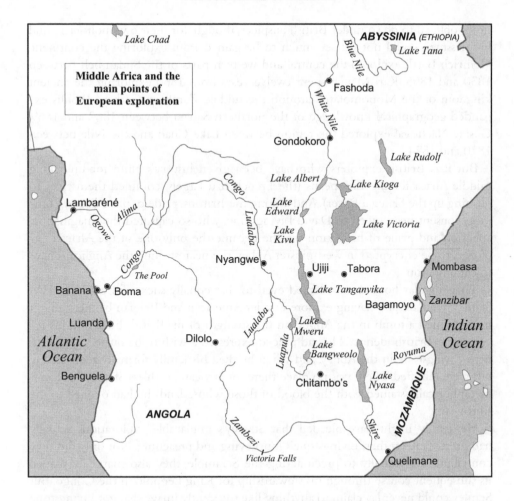

Middle Africa and the main points of European exploration

of climate, disease, topography and the strength of the indigenous peoples that had kept them tinkering around the coastal fringes of Africa for centuries. Not unexpectedly, the penetration came mainly from the east and south. In the north were still the barriers of the Sahara and the Sudd. The west, which the Europeans had come to first because it was closest and seemingly abundant in gold, ivory and slaves, had been shown to be desperately hard to explore with its debilitating climate and deadly diseases. It made more sense to approach from more temperate parts.

It was missionaries rather than traders who made the first inroads, religious fervour tending to be stronger even than commercial ambition, and often to be complemented by the geographical curiosity of the time. Two German members of the Church Missionary Society penetrated the eastern hinterland long before the British explorers who were to win later and greater fame. These two, Johann Krapf and Johann Rebmann, in 1847 became the first Europeans to set eyes on the fabled equatorial snow, the white peaks of Kilimanjaro and Mount Kenya.

Despite Germany's comparative lack of imperial ambition and resources at the time, Germans were remarkably energetic in exploring Africa. They were sometimes obliged to do so under British auspices, though, for their own politicians and businessmen could not yet see much to be gained from exploring the continent. Heinrich Barth explored the central and western parts of the Sudan belt between 1850 and 1855. Karl Mauch spent twelve years from 1860 exploring the ancient kingdom of the Monomotapas around the middle Zambezi. Gerhard Rohlfs expanded geographical knowledge of the northern Sahara between 1862 and 1869. Gustav Nachtigal explored the region between Lake Chad and the Nile between 1870 and 1874.

But it is British explorers who have been given history's plum for unlocking middle Africa for the Europeans (the French had largely confined themselves to pushing up the Senegal River). And among the Britons, pride of place has by common consent been given to David Livingstone, who so captured the imagination, affection and pride of his nation that he became the only one of the African explorers to be encrypted in Westminster Abbey, the nearest thing the Anglicans have to canonisation.

That singular honour was denied even to that equally successful explorer, HM Stanley, who, despite having explored under American and Belgian banners, might have claimed a tomb in the Abbey on the strength of his British birth and his reversion to British identity. He had indeed expressed a wish to be buried beside his hero Livingstone in the Abbey, and when he died his family formally requested it, but were rebuffed. There was no place there for arrogant, ruthless Stanley, his hands metaphorically stained with the blood of those whose lands he had opened to the Europeans.

His family might have pleaded that Stanley's implacable explorations actually had greater effects than Livingstone's journeying and preaching. Not only did they contribute substantially to precipitating the Scramble, they also markedly shaped its subsequent course through his stewardship for King Leopold in the Congo. But Stanley could never lay claim to anything like the saintly image that got Livingstone his place near the high altar of the British Establishment. Had Stanley, like Livingstone, died during his explorations there would have been no faithful black retainers to go to extraordinary lengths to get his body back to England, as they did for Livingstone. They would more likely have simply walked away from the corpse of the man who was accused by his contemporaries of shooting Africans 'as if they were monkeys'.

Livingstone saw the African as backward but capable of advancement and equally worthy of salvation through Christian faith. Stanley saw the African as a congenital inferior, to be Christianised, by all means if anyone wanted to do that, but to be exploited, too, if need be. These two represented the opposite extremes of the attitudes brought by the explorers to Africa as they revealed its long-hidden core to Europe. Besides clearing the way for the Scramble, the explorers contributed enormously to forming and fixing European opinions of the African at a time of intense controversy over whether he was more savage than civilised, or even worth civilising.

In the middle of the 19th century Europeans in general held very low opinions of those who weren't white, and lowest of all of those who were the least white –

the Africans. In part they were influenced by what they perceived to be the comparative backwardness of the Africans who had first been met on the coasts – a perception based more on the Africans' technological inferiority than on any other criterion. Perhaps the greatest moulder of their perception, though, was slavery, which had made disparagement of the Negro essential for its practitioners; slavery could be morally justified only by depicting the black person as inherently inferior, even sub-human.

Proponents of slavery favoured the theory of polygenesis, which held that the different races had separate origins and were therefore different species. Opponents supported the monogenesis theory that all humans were descended from the same source – Adam and Eve for those making a literal interpretation of the Bible. Polygenesists pounced on Darwin's *On the origin of Species* when it was published in 1859, arguing that it gave credence to theories of the fundamental difference and essential inferiority of the Negro.

Few of the explorers and even not all the missionaries regarded the Africans as equals in all respects; at best their attitude was patronising.

Livingstone himself was patronising in his belief that the African required upliftment and that the European was the one to do it. He was equally convinced, though, of the African's fundamental human equality, and his ability and right eventually to take his place alongside the European.

Livingstone scoffed at the 'heaps of nonsense' which had been written about the African intellect. 'In reference to the status of the Africans among the nations of the earth,' he wrote, 'we have seen nothing to justify the notion that they are of a different "breed" or "species" from the most civilised. The African is a man with every attribute of humankind.' He added, though, that 'centuries of barbarism' had had the same deteriorating effect on Africans as on some of the Irish.[2]

That Livingstone felt it necessary to make this defence illustrates the common European attitude to Africans at the time. Later historians have found it surprising 'how many of these (British) attitudes were set and hardened, rather than modified and corrected, during the decades which saw the great European exploration of the African continent.'[3]

Almost all the explorers brought to Africa the racial preconceptions of Europe, and in some cases reinforced its prejudices. The vision of salvation pursued by missionaries like Philip and Livingstone was not universally shared by their countrymen. While the missionaries mostly agreed with the common perception of the African as a primitive and wretched pagan, they believed he could be transformed into a civilised and even prosperous Christian through education and commerce.

That was the key: commerce. In Livingstone's view, 'give the people the opportunity (and) they will civilise themselves, and that more effectually than can be done by missionary societies'. As he saw it, the purpose of his explorations was to 'make an open path for Christianity and commerce' in Africa. He believed he was primarily a spiritual rather than a scientific geographer.

A revealing perspective of the racial attitudes prevailing in Britain is given by the opinions of Charles Dickens, who in many ways reflected the moral perceptions and prejudices of his age. Though he ardently condemned human exploitation in Victorian Britain and spoke out against the slave trade, he appears to have had as low an opinion of the African as he had of elements of the white society in America. He thought Livingstone was wasting his time in Africa, and discouraged efforts to help his cause. 'The history of all African effort hitherto,' Dickens wrote, 'is a history of wasted European life, squandered European money and blighted European hope'.[4] Dickens derided the concept of the 'noble savage' that was popular among British moralists, saying: 'His virtues are a fable, his happiness is a delusion, his nobility nonsense.'

Especially contemptuous of the African was Sir Samuel Baker, who was knighted for his African exploits and greatly influenced European attitudes with his prolific writings. His opinion was: 'Human nature when viewed in its crude state as pictured amongst African savages is quite on a level with that of the brute, and not to be compared with the noble character of the dog.'

In a lecture in 1874 Baker declared that the indigenous inhabitants of central Africa 'are unchanged from the prehistoric tribes who were the original inhabitants'. Sweepingly asserting that 'central Africa ... is without a history', he said there were no vestiges of the past, 'no ancient architecture, neither sculpture, nor even one chiselled stone', to show that 'the Negro savage of this day' had had a more civilised past. It is intriguing to speculate what his reaction would have been had he seen the impressive masonry of Great Zimbabwe.

That other knight of African exploration, Sir Richard Burton, also equated Africans with animals and believed they had very little capacity for self-improvement. His observations convinced him that they were irreformably childish, fundamentally savage and criminal, preoccupied with drunkenness, and without any religion, capable only of 'a vague and nameless awe'.

Sir Bartle Frere, who was prominent as a colonial administrator in India and South Africa, expressed a view widely held in Britain when he said: 'If you read the history of any part of the Negro population of Africa you will find nothing but a dreary recurrence of tribal wars and an absence of everything which forms a stable government, and year after year, generation after generation, century after century, those tribes go on obeying no law but that of force, and consequently never emerging from the state of barbarism in which we find them at present and in which they have lived, so far as we know, for a period long anterior to our own.'[5]

Frere, like most of his contemporaries, was overlooking the fact that the only histories of Africa that were available to European readers were the ones written by their own kind, largely based on their own preconceptions and interpretations. In the absence of script among Africans their histories were preserved orally, and since the Europeans mostly had not bothered to learn the African languages those histories were closed to them – apart from the glimpses given by the Arab travellers.

So widely was black inferiority assumed that racism was hardly a concept in mid-century Europe, certainly not in the pejorative sense in which the term is used today. The relevant morality consisted not so much in egalitarianism as in the upliftment of the inferiors to a higher – though not necessarily equal – status. Victorian Britain's espousal of high moral values was in any case often in conflict with its commercial imperialism. Efforts to reconcile the two inevitably produced extremes of hypocrisy.*

The dilemma was perhaps experienced with special intensity in Africa as the Europeans penetrated deeper and more exploitively into the continent. There were subtle shades to it, though, as was demonstrated by the Tory leader Sir Robert Peel (not yet prime minister) when in 1840 he addressed the meeting in Exeter Hall in London of the Society for the Extinction of the Slave Trade and for the Civilisation of Africa.** Britain, said Peel, never would be able 'to convince the black population of Africa of the superiority of their European fellow men' until slave trading had been eradicated from the continent.[6]

★ ★ ★ ★

The era of exploration propelled onto the African stage giant, eccentric figures, a disproportionate number of whom emerged from the misty wings of Scotland, notably James Bruce, Mungo Park and Livingstone.

It was both Livingstone's curse and his glory that his religious fervour was intertwined with a passion for exploration. He justified the latter with a conviction that slavery could never be stamped out as long as it was profitable, and the best way to end it was to replace it with more acceptable forms of commerce. To that end he dedicated himself to finding means of local production and opening trade routes to the sea.

In his search for commercial antidotes to slavery Livingstone covered thousands of kilometres, criss-crossing southern and middle Africa, mostly walking but occasionally using steam launches and canoes, and riding donkeys. His first major expedition, during which he 'discovered' the Victoria Falls in 1855, was undertaken under the auspices of the LMS. When the society demanded that he stop exploring and settle down to running mission stations, the Royal Geographical Society and the government became his sponsors.

As Livingstone exited the stage to great applause after his first expedition, Richard Burton and John Hanning Speke made their appearance. Theirs was a different act altogether. They had none of Livingstone's missionary ideals and fervour; they were geographers and adventurers pure and simple. Besides a background in the Indian Army and an ambition to find the source of the Nile, they had nothing in common. The odd couple of African exploration were they, Burton dark, sardonic and rakish, given to debauchery but a scholar and linguist; Speke blonde, blue-eyed, open-faced, abstemious, obsessed with fitness and keen on hunting.

Burton, the leader, had secured the sponsorship of the RGS for their expedition.

---

*Even as late as 1921, Dr Albert Schweitzer, who was to win the 1952 Nobel Peace Prize for his medical work among the Africans at Lambarene, wrote that: 'The Negro is a child, and with children nothing can be done without the use of authority ... With regard to Negroes, then, I have coined the formula: I am your brother, it is true, but your elder brother.'

**From this and other such meetings Exeter Hall became a code term, often disparaging, for the liberal and humanitarian attitudes to Africans that emerged alongside the growth of colonialism.

They led their 130-man caravan from Bagamoyo in 1857, discovered Lake Tanganyika, and established that it wasn't the source of the Nile. Leaving Burton, an ardent Arabist, revelling in the company of the slavers at Tabora, Speke went off on his own and discovered Lake Victoria. He was convinced the lake was the Nile's source but Burton disagreed, preferring Herodotus' suggestion that the river rose in fountains beneath snow-covered mountains.

Both contracted malaria, and on the journey back to England Burton stopped at Aden to recuperate while Speke hitched a ride on a passing British warship. Burton later said Speke had agreed not to disclose their discoveries until both were back home. As soon as Speke reached London, however, he told all to the RGS. When Burton came in 12 days later Speke was the hero of the hour, and the RGS was arranging for him to lead a new expedition to the source of the Nile. Burton was fast being forgotten.

In 1858, the same year Burton and Speke found their lakes, Livingstone set off on a marathon, six-year expedition during which he discovered Lake Nyasa and, weeping, buried his wife Mary beside the Zambezi, a victim of malaria.

Meanwhile, Speke had embarked on his new venture, accompanied now by James Grant, another Indian Army veteran, one who had been decorated for gallantry in the relief of Lucknow during the Indian Mutiny. Setting out from Bagamoyo in 1860, they tramped to the region where lay the kingdoms of Karagwe, Buganda and Bunyoro. In Buganda they were held up by the despotic King Mutesa. At last, in 1862, with Grant suffering from an ulcerated leg, Speke was allowed to go off on his own, and came to the cataract (now the Ripon Falls) where the Nile exits Lake Victoria.

Speke still could not be certain that Lake Victoria was the Nile's source until he had explored another big lake said to lie to the west, the Luta Nzige. But, with both their bodies and supplies near exhaustion, he and Grant decided to take a short cut to Gondokoro near present-day Juba on the Nile, where Austrian missionaries had set up a mission station after following the route pioneered through the Sudd by Arab slavers. Speke knew the RGS had sent supplies there for him.

When Speke and Grant staggered into Gondokoro they were surprised to be met by Samuel Baker, who had been commissioned by the RGS to search for them when nothing was heard from them. The wealthy Baker had happened to be in Khartoum at the time, pursuing his passion for hunting and a private ambition to find the source of the Nile.

Back in England, Speke and Grant were met with both adulation and scepticism. Burton and others, including Livingstone, held that Speke could not be sure he had found the Nile's source since he had not followed it from Lake Victoria to Gondokoro. After a year of raging public controversy, the British Association for the Advancement of Science arranged in 1864 for Burton and Speke to debate the issue at a meeting in Bath. As a distinguished assembly gathered for the great debate, word came that Speke had been killed by his own gun while hunting partridges. The inquest verdict was accidental death, but some privately preferred one of suicide rather than face Burton.

Baker had meanwhile pushed on from Gondokoro with his remarkable wife, Florence. The beautiful Florence is one of the unrecognised heroines of African exploration, all of whom have slipped through the cracks of male-dominated Victorian history. Florence, born to the upper-class Hungarian family of Szasz, was at a young age separated from her parents by war, and found herself growing up as a slave in a Turkish harem. When at the age of 14 she was put up for sale, Baker smuggled her to freedom and married her. Florence accompanied Baker on most of his explorations. She was as capable of wading through a mosquito-ridden African swamp in her husband's trousers as she was of charming diplomats at an elegant soiree beneath crystal chandeliers in Europe. She could manage a camel as well as she could a dinner party, and she did both with unfailing grace.

The Bakers experienced excruciating hardships in their search for the Luta Nzige. After being hauled from a quagmire into which she was sinking, Florence went into a coma for three days and then was delirious for two weeks. When they at last tottered to the shore of the lake, Baker named it after Albert, Victoria's consort, and the name has stuck.

In canoes, the Bakers crossed the lake and paddled up the Nile to what are now known as the Murchison Falls. Then, too sick and exhausted for further exploration, they made their painful way back home. At Khartoum they were welcomed as though returning from the dead, in which state they had been presumed to be since nothing had been heard from them for two years.

Reaching England late in 1865, Baker was awarded the gold medal of the RGS, and the following year was knighted. He acknowledged, however, that he could not claim to have solved the riddle of the Nile. He had found evidence that the river Speke had seen exiting Lake Victoria flowed into Lake Albert, and he had been told by the natives that it flowed out again to the north. But since he had not followed it to the known Nile he could not complete the connection.

In the same year Baker was knighted, the RGS sent Livingstone back to Africa to explore the sources of the Zambezi, Congo and Nile and report on the slave trade. He reached the Lualaba River and discovered Lakes Mweru and Bangweolo. An attempt to find whether the Lualaba was the Nile's source was frustrated by the pillaging of his supplies and by an encounter with Arab slavers, and he ended up destitute at Ujiji.

The Western world had heard nothing from Livingstone for three years, and a worshipful public was avid for news. To find Livingstone the *New York Herald* in 1869 sent Henry Morton Stanley, a tough man shaped by a hard life. Born a bastard of a Welsh father named Rowlands, tossed by his dissolute mother into a dismal English workhouse, he had worked a passage to America, where he had in effect been adopted by a wealthy cotton merchant named Stanley. He had served in the American Civil War, in the United States Navy, and with federal forces fighting the Indians, before joining the *Herald*.

Stanley began his quest for Livingstone in Zanzibar. In the eight months it took him to reach Ujiji he contracted malaria, fought with Arab traders, and saw his two white companions die.

Stanley's meeting with Livingstone on 10 November 1871 at Ujiji has become one of the favourite moments of Western history, and Stanley's stiff greeting – 'Dr Livingstone, I presume' – one of the favourite quotes. So captivated was he by Livingstone that he could not tear himself away to exploit his scoop. He accompanied Livingstone to the northern tip of Lake Tanganyika and then to Tabora, where supplies were to have been sent. Finding none, Stanley left Livingstone with some of his own supplies and marched for the coast to tell his story and arrange for fresh supplies for the explorer. An expedition sent out by the RGS to look for Livingstone turned back on meeting Stanley and learning his news.

Stanley's scoop – one of the greatest in journalistic history, despite his news being six months old – had a sensational impact when published in May 1872.

With the fresh supplies and porters sent by Stanley, Livingstone resumed his now obsessive search for the Nile's source. He determined to establish whether it rose in Herodotus' fountains (which he thought might be near Lake Bangweolo), whether the Lualaba was the link or whether it was the source of the Congo, and whether the Luapula had any connection with the Nile.

Passing down the eastern side of Lake Tanganyika, he began searching south of Lake Bangweolo for the fountains but became lost in the great swamplands at the height of the rainy season. Desperately sick, the great explorer headed erratically towards the Luapula. When he collapsed he was carried by his loyal retainers to the village of Ilala, where he died in an attitude of prayer.

In the mean time, nothing having been heard from Livingstone since Stanley's report, the RGS had in 1873 sent out Lieutenant Verney Lovett Cameron (yet another Scot) to find him. At Tabora, Cameron met Livingstone's retainers bearing his body to the coast. He decided to continue Livingstone's probing of the Lualaba but at the river his way was barred by Arabs fearful that European exploration would bring an end to their slaving.

Turning to the south-west, he carried on and in November 1875 reached Benguela on the Angolan coast, his supplies nearly all gone and his body wasted.

Cameron's reports to the RGS caused something of a flurry in commercial as well as geographic circles. He said that most of the country from Tanganyika to the west coast was 'one of almost unspeakable richness'. To give Britain first option to these riches, Cameron had signed treaties on behalf of the British government with chiefs in the Lualaba basin. The government, however, had no interest in becoming involved in uncertain colonial adventures in the heart of Africa; it had enough on its hands with the Cape, Natal and the Gold Coast, not to mention the French becoming ensconced in north Africa and especially in Egypt through building the Suez Canal.

Other, more perceptive, eyes, however, were keenly scanning Cameron's reports. These accounts had sparked a plot in the clever mind of King Leopold II of Belgium, but it would not finally take shape until Stanley had mapped the way with his own astonishing journey across Africa.

After the great scoop of finding Livingstone at Ujiji, Stanley had been sent to cover the latest campaign against the Asante, led by Sir Garnet Wolseley. But he, too, had been bewitched by the Nile. As soon as the Asante campaign was over he resolved to fill in the gaps left by the other explorers.

CHAPTER 9

LIBERTY, EQUALITY, FRATERNITY, COLONIALISM

Did the Bey of Algiers lash the French consul with his fly whisk or was it just a little tap? On such minutiae do international affairs sometimes swing. In this case it was enough to give the French militarists an excuse to seize the Bey's country, which in turn opened the way to one of the greatest of the colonial occupations and one of the major European migrations into Africa.

At the time, while European explorers were beginning to put Africa's long-hidden centre on the map, their home powers were encroaching deeper at the edges of the continent, though slowly and tentatively. The southern tip had been occupied by the British, and the whole of the Mediterranean littoral was becoming increasingly vulnerable to spillovers of the rivalry between the European powers. The French made their move in 1830, seizing Algiers.

Various justifications were presented by the French for their invasion. One was the need to put down Algiers-based piracy in the Mediterranean (it had in fact virtually ended). Another was that it was a necessary response to the 'insult' suffered by the French consul when the Turkish Bey 'struck' him with a fly whisk during a tiff over payment for French wheat purchases. Blow or tap, it was enough to give the French military excuse and opportunity to recover some of the prestige lost with Napoleon's decline. They sent a 35 000-strong invasion force and ousted the occupying Ottoman Turks. If that was a lot of tit for a little tat it didn't bother the French.

In the absence of any firm policy in Paris, the military commanders in Algeria began promoting French settlement. Within two years, the Berbers and Arabs, finding themselves being edged ever further into the barren hinterland, rose in a *jihad*, led by the man known to the Europeans as Abdelkader. Despite ruthless countermeasures by the military commander, General Bugeaud, the insurrection continued actively for the next 15 years, forcing the French to commit 100 000 troops to combat it. Abdelkader surrendered in 1847, but the resistance never fully ended until Algeria won independence from France in 1962.

France, her population increase limited by years of war, was unable to provide enough colonists to occupy the coastal plain. Others were therefore brought in from elsewhere, mainly from Spain, with smaller numbers coming from Italy, Sicily and Malta. Soon the non-French settlers outnumbered the French.

The Algerian influx was the third major wave of European immigration into the continent, coming after the Dutch colonisation of the Cape from 1652, and between the 1820 settlement of the eastern Cape Colony and the arrival of the Byrne settlers in Natal from 1849. By 1856 there were 170 000 Europeans in Algeria, about the same number as there were whites in South Africa.

Like the settlers in South Africa, those in Algeria soon began to identify themselves with their adopted country. Here, too, a white nation professing adherence to Christianity began to develop separately from the indigenous people of different faith. But whereas the independence-minded Boers in South African resented British domination, the Algerian colonists demanded political attachment to the colonial power, in their case France – but on their own terms, which amounted to guarantees of white segregation and supremacy. That posed a problem for the government of the nation dedicated to liberty, equality and fraternity – a problem that would recur elsewhere in Africa as the French expanded their colonial holdings.

Like the Boers, the Algerian settlers opposed efforts by the colonial power to protect the rights of the indigenous inhabitants. Their resistance was not always peaceful. In 1848 the settlers prevented General Changarnier, the new governor-general, from disembarking, and then held the old one, General Cavaignac, hostage in his palace for eight days.

Under Emperor Louis Napoleon, nephew of Napoleon Bonaparte, policy on Algeria vacillated as the emperor sought to respect the rights of the Arabs without displeasing the *colons*. In 1865 he declared the Muslims to be French and at the same time endorsed white settlement. He said Algeria was soil 'that is forever French', but he also said that France's first duty was to Algeria's three million Arabs. He ambiguously defined Algeria as 'an Arab kingdom, a European colony and a French camp'. Even when French citizenship was extended to the Arabs they were not immediately given equal rights with the colonists. (Full voting rights were not granted to them until 1958, after they had again risen in rebellion.)

Louis Napoleon's policy swung like a pendulum between direct rule from Paris and indirect rule through a military governor-general. Under the latter, the military came to be associated by the settlers with what they saw as the Arab-friendly policies of the emperor. When his Second Empire collapsed in 1870 with France's defeat by Prussia, the settlers formed defence committees to resist military rule. The military governor appointed by the new republic, General Walsin-Esterhazy, was chased from his palace by a mob and forced to flee to a ship in the harbour. Facing the possibility of a unilateral declaration of independence by the settlers, the government granted them concessions, including the formal annexation of Algeria to France.

The Muslims, seeing their position worsening, rose again in a brief but bloody revolt, attacking settler farms. By the time the rebellion had ruthlessly been put down, 2 700 French and many more Muslims had been killed. Harsh indemnity payments were extracted from the Arabs. They were specifically targeted with taxes and educational policies that seemed to them to be intended to keep them forever poor, unskilled and available as cheap labour for the white settlers – shades of South Africa.

European immigration and landholding were deliberately increased. As a result, many Arab farmers lost their lands and became *khammas*, tenant-labourers who got one-fifth of the produce. The Muslim system of justice was replaced by the French one, but a separate penal system, the *Code de l'Indigenat*, was applied to the Arabs. Like the pass system in South Africa, it required Arabs to get special permission to leave their districts. It also empowered the detention of Arabs without trial, the sequestration of their properties, and the imposition of collective penalties. To close any loopholes, the code created the catch-all offence of 'lack of respect' for authority.

In 1889 the settlers celebrated again when French nationality was extended to the children of all Europeans born in Algeria, whether their parents were French or not.

All of these measures, together with policies that weakened the influence of Muslim religious leaders, enabled the settlers to gain both political and economic dominance, and cemented the ethnic polarisation of the Algerian society.

Algeria's white population grew relatively quickly, not only through colonisation but also through local births – significantly adding to the numbers of the white Africans. By 1896 Algerian-born whites – the *pieds noirs* – for the first time outnumbered those who had come in as immigrants.

While France's main thrust across the Mediterranean was into Algeria, its interests were also growing elsewhere on the littoral, where the fading dominance of the Ottoman Turks was being replaced by British, French and Italian engagement. Trade was inevitably followed by the flag, first by a diplomatic and then by a colonial presence.

In Tunisia the way was opened for colonisation by the efforts of the beys, Ahmed and his successor, Mohammed, to modernise and develop their country, with the help of the European powers. The beys overreached themselves, however, and the government was heavily in debt by the time Mohammed Bey was succeeded by Sadiq Bey in 1859. Ten years later Tunisia was so thoroughly bankrupted that, in a parallel with what was to happen in Egypt, control of the country's finances was taken over by France, Britain and Italy, with France taking precedence as the largest creditor. Within another decade it was to become a French protectorate in one of the prefatory developments of the Scramble.

Simultaneously with their efforts to establish themselves in north Africa, the French were enlarging their presence in West Africa by pushing in from the old foothold of Senegal. As in the north, the motive for the expansion here was French desire to restore the empire lost in the Revolutionary and Napoleonic Wars. The driving force behind it was Louis Faideherbe, a hard-nosed professional soldier who before becoming governor of Senegal in 1854 had fought in the ferocious campaign against Abdelkader in Algeria.

Faideherbe had three objectives. Immediately, to put down 'Moors'* who had been bothering French traders in Senegal. In the medium term, to conquer the whole of the Senegal basin and turn it to agricultural production for the benefit of

---

*The term was generally applied to almost anyone in the Sahel who was not obviously Negroid or animist.

France. In the long term to establish a base at Bamako on the Niger from which the middle and lower Niger might be exploited by the French.

In this Faideherbe was following his own ideas rather than any precise instructions from Paris, but then that tended to be the style of French penetration in Africa – ambitious and energetic generals taking initiatives and then seeking official endorsement afterwards.

Between Faideherbe and his objectives stood the equally strong figure of Al Haj Umar, creator of the Islamic Tukolor empire and symbol of a recrudescence of Islam in Africa's Sudan. Faideherbe began his eastward expansion from the coast at about the same time as Umar began his westward expansion from the empire he had created in the region embracing the upper reaches of both the Niger and Senegal rivers. The decisive clash came in 1857 when Umar attacked the French fort at Medine, 500 kilometres up the Senegal River. Repulsed, Umar withdrew, leaving the French in control of the entire lower Senegal and its environs and southwards along the coast almost to the Gambia, where the British held sway. An unofficial truce came into effect between the French and the Tukolors. It continued after Umar was succeeded at his death by his son Ahmadu and after Faideherbe was recalled to Paris, putting in abeyance ambitions of French conquest of the Niger.

★ ★ ★ ★

On the world map it is an insignificant smudge of land, barely a hundred and fifty kilometres across. But for centuries it stood as a frustrating barrier between the Mediterranean Sea and the Indian Ocean, frustrating European and Levantine dreams of a canal to join the seas, to open a marine short cut to the Far East.

Not until the middle of the 19th century did the necessary coincidence of politics, finance and technology come about to grant possibility to the dream. And then the building of the Suez Canal put a new facet on world politics and trade.

Some might have expected that the canal would have been built by the British rather than the French, given the wide extent of Britain's interests in India, the Far East and Australasia, and the jealous watch the British kept over both the Cape sea route and the overland approaches to India from the north. It was to defend the latter from the expanding Russians that the British had fought them in the Crimean War, in alliance with France and the Ottoman Turks. But while the French were united with the British in their opposition to Russian expansion, they were at odds with them over both the Cape and Suez routes, in which they, too, had long had an interest as they sought to expand their own Far Eastern concerns.

Having been foiled at the Cape by the British occupation and ousted from India and Mauritius, the French turned to Suez, where Frenchmen had nursed ambitions for a canal as far back as the reign of Louis XIV. Napoleon Bonaparte had surveyed a route for a canal during his occupation of Egypt from 1798, but had had to shelve the idea when ousted from there.

The British, having the Cape under their control, were less urgently interested than the French in a canal across the Suez isthmus, especially as it might give rival powers easier access to the Far East. In the first half of the 19th century the British ran an overland horse-drawn service between the Mediterranean and the Red Sea, but it was intended to speed up the delivery of mail rather than freight. Even when a railway was built in the 1850s along the route – between Port Said and Alexandria – it could not compete in freight cost and volume with the ships passing round the Cape. In the days of sailing ships, a canal was a questionable proposition both because of the often unfavourable winds in the Red Sea and because of the difficulty of hauling windjammers along the hundred and sixty-odd kilometres of the canal's length. These problems disappeared, however, with the advent of self-propelled, ocean-going steamships in the late eighteen-hundreds.

In this light it was not surprising that it was a Frenchman who took the initiative for a canal. In 1854 the engineer Ferdinand de Lesseps obtained the necessary concession from Khedive Said on terms much more favourable to the French than to the Egyptians.

British merchants, envisaging faster passage for their goods, were pleased. Their government, however, was not happy with the prospect of the French gaining control of a short route to the East, one giving rival powers easy access to areas of special British interest, access less susceptible to British control than the Cape route. So the Foreign Office leaned on the Turkish sultan in Istanbul, persuading him to countermand the Egyptian backing for the construction of the canal. But by the time the sultan's order came into effect the project was already half-completed. The French government stepped in with its own funding and the canal was completed in 1869, only three years behind schedule. The Khedive had a 45 per cent shareholding, the rest being held mostly by the French government and French commercial interests.

The official opening was a lavish affair, giving the world not only a new sea route but also the opera *Aïda*, which Verdi was commissioned to write for the occasion.

In order to protect its interests, Britain was now compelled to strengthen its influence not only in the Red Sea and Persian Gulf but also in the Canal's African hinterland, notably the Nile and the Sudan. In this respect the Canal may have helped to precipitate the Scramble.

In other respects the Canal's significance in Africa was peripheral and incidental. It was not really an African thing, it was a means of taking the Europeans to the riches of Asia, avoiding the physical, religious and political obstacles that had sent the Portuguese navigators round the Cape. It was a means of getting across the bit of Africa that happened to be in the way. Even Ismael, who had become khedive on Said's death in 1863, proudly declared at the opening of the Canal: 'We are not now a country of Africa but a country of Europe.' He could not then appreciate the irony behind his words, that the Canal would more than ever make Egypt a sphere of European interest and European domination. Never a part of Europe, though. But perhaps never a part of Africa, either. Egypt, more Arab than African, had always been and would always be a part of the Middle East despite being a chunk of Africa, and despite its water lifeline rising in the continent's heart.

While much of the shipping that had formerly passed round the Cape was diverted through the Canal, the waterway did not destroy the Cape's strategic value, for the Canal was especially vulnerable to political and military interference. It could be blocked simply by sinking a couple of ships across it (as the Egyptians did nearly a century later in the 1967 war with Israel). So the Cape route remained a vital passage, even if a longer one, and the Royal Navy continued to maintain its main South Atlantic base at Simonstown.

★ ★ ★ ★

While the French were building the Suez Canal the British were engaged in a very different exercise at the other end of the Red Sea. It was in essence a rescue mission but an extraordinary one in its purpose and scope: a famous general leading a British army in an assault on a mountain-top fortress in Abyssinia to free diplomats held hostage by a mad emperor. It could have come straight from the pages of the *Boys' Own Paper*, the popular periodical of young Victorian males, but this was fact, not fiction.

Its singularity arose from the eccentricity of the man who caused it all, Tewodros, self-proclaimed emperor of Christian Abyssinia. Handsome, athletic, intelligent, brave, strong-willed and able, Tewodros, known to the Europeans as Theodore, might have become one of Africa's great leaders had he not also been emotionally unstable to a point close to, if not deep into, psychosis.

What became one of the most extensive military operations conducted by the Victorian British in Africa was initiated by the innocent suggestion of the British consul, Captain Charles Cameron, that the emperor conclude a treaty of friendship with Queen Victoria. Theodore enthusiastically endorsed the idea in a letter to the queen – which then became mislaid and forgotten in the files of the Foreign Office. Then Cameron went to the Sudan to investigate cotton growing to replace the supplies interrupted by the American Civil War. When Theodore, already miffed by Victoria's silence, learned that Cameron was visiting his arch foe, Islamic Sudan, his hurt turned to fury. He vengefully imprisoned the nearest Europeans, a group of missionaries. When Cameron returned he was thrown in with them, as was a British envoy sent with apologies when the Foreign Office realised what was happening.

After three years of dithering, London in August 1867 bit the bullet and gave Theodore an ultimatum to release the hostages. When he failed to respond, war was formally declared. General Napier, one of the heroes of the suppression of the Indian Mutiny and the leader of the British expedition to Peking in 1860, was put in command of the operation.

The campaign's singularity was compounded by the fact that in no way did the matter affect British interests. Abyssinia was peripheral to British concerns in the region. The French might control the Suez Canal but Britain, with the seizure of Aden in 1839, had acquired the means to control the southern approaches to it.

But now one man's eccentricity was calling up a war. A large army would be required to fight its way through kilometres of mountains to storm Theodore's lofty fortress and pluck out a handful of hostages, most of whom weren't even British citizens. There was no certainty that Theodore would not kill them even as his ey-rie was being overwhelmed. The material cost would be high. London could see no other way, however. British pride was at stake, as well as Britain's international image. If Theodore could get away with defying and insulting Britain, others might get similar ideas. Anyway, Cameron couldn't simply be abandoned to a death in Theodore's jail.

Napier turned the village of Zula, south of Massawa on the Red Sea, into a bustling port. From there he built a railway extending 30 kilometres inland. Then he sailed for Zula from India with a fleet of 280 ships carrying 13 000 troops (9 000 Indian and 4 000 European), 19 000 support staff, 55 000 horses, mules, camels and oxen and 44 elephants for carrying the heavy artillery.[1]

The march on Magdala began in January 1868, with the engineers building kilometres of roads and dozens of bridges to get Napier's column up through the mountains. Theodore meanwhile kept his army encamped on a high plateau below Magdala fortress. When the redcoats at last reached the plateau the Abyssinians charged but were mown down by volleys from the hastily formed British square.

Theodore offered reconciliation but Napier insisted on his surrender. After having scores of his Ethiopian prisoners tossed over a cliff, Theodore tried to shoot himself but the pistol misfired. With his troops deserting in droves, he freed the European hostages. The next day when the British stormed the fort they passed Theodore's corpse; this time the pistol had not misfired.

After loading loot from Theodore's treasury onto 15 elephants, Napier destroyed Magdala and withdrew, leaving nothing behind except two piers at Zula and a couple of rusting locomotives. The hostages had been rescued, and British pride and honour restored. But nothing had been changed in Africa or Britain, except that Theodore's hard-won kingdom had been returned to implacable contest among the clans and the British treasury was considerably depleted.

★ ★ ★ ★

Only half a decade after Napier's force had withdrawn from Ethiopia, an invading British army was again being landed in Africa, but this time on the other side of the continent and with a much more imperialist purpose. That purpose had been enthusiastically enunciated by the newspaper serving the British traders on the Gold Coast, the *African Times*. Whitehall's decision in 1873 to send a military expedition to subdue the Asante was reported by the newspaper under the headline: 'Ashanti War – Gold, Gold, Gold!'

For the traders, that was what it was mainly about: getting control of the gold at its hinterland source, the kingdom of the Asante. Whitehall shared that concern but in addition wanted to ensure that the Asante did not make an alliance with the French.

The man chosen to lead the expedition was certainly not one to put a euphemistic spin on the business of promoting British imperialism. Sir Garnet Wolseley had no scruples about subjugating the African, whom he viewed as 'an objectionable animal', fit only to serve the white man.[2]

Wolseley had already demonstrated his singular skill in exploiting the splendid opportunities for advancement that were offered to military men by the expansion of British foreign rule. Overcoming his lowly birth as the son of an Irish shopkeeper, Wolseley had had to bore his way up through the upper crust of British society and the British military. In the latter, upward mobility was often decided by lineage rather than ability, but Wolseley proved a striking exception. He would eventually become Britain's top soldier: field marshal, viscount and chief of the armed forces at the apogee of Victorian imperialism.

Wolseley served widely in the Empire but made his mark most notably in Africa. He blooded himself in the conquest of Burma in 1852, suffering a thigh wound that pained him for the rest of his life. Hardly was that campaign over than he was fighting in 1854 in the Crimea, where he lost an eye to a piece of Russian shrapnel. Within a year he was in the thick of the Indian Mutiny. Then it was on to China in 1860 for the wars to force opium addiction on the Chinese – compelling them to allow the British to bring opium into China and market it in order to get revenue to help finance the rule of the British Raj in India.

Wolseley did not see action again until 1870, when he quashed an attempt at independence by the Metis, a community of mixed Indian and European blood, in the Red River Colony (now Manitoba), Canada. His star was rising, but he needed a new war to give it impetus. He found it in 1873 in 'Ashanti'. By then, 20 years after joining the army, he had made it to colonel.

A year earlier, the British had bought Elmina station from the Dutch to gain exclusive control of trading on the Gold Coast. When the British refused to pay rent to the Asante for Elmina, as the Dutch had always done, the Asante invaded the protectorate the British had declared on the coast. They found themselves woefully outgunned, however, by the new breech-loading, rapid-fire, long-range rifles of the British. They nonetheless continued to make such a nuisance of themselves that Whitehall, nudged by the British traders at the coast, decided to send Wolseley to put them down once and for all.

Whitehall employed the favourite imperial device of pre-justifying conquest by making unacceptable demands on those to be conquered. The Asante were to withdraw from the coastal protectorate, eschew further hostilities, and make onerous reparations. To put a moral slant on what were essentially imperialistic and commercial demands, the Asante were directed to give up human sacrifice and slavery. Evidently to ensure that the Asante would reject the demands and give him the excuse to march on Kumase, Wolseley independently increased the reparations figure and demanded that King Kofi Kakari hand over his mother and other members of the royal family as hostages.

Forced by the rugged terrain to abandon his first plan to build a railway to carry his invasion force, Wolseley had to fall back on the basic means of transportation that everywhere opened up inner Africa to the Europeans – the indigenous porter carrying a load on his head.

Wolseley, who owed much of his success to careful preparation, sent advance parties to build elaborate camps along the route to Kumase, prompting one of the several newspaper correspondents with the force to observe: 'In no campaign has the British soldier ever had such comforts and luxuries on the march.' Among the correspondents was Henry Morton Stanley, famous for his 'discovery' of Livingstone, now covering the Asante campaign for his newspaper. In between these assignments, Stanley had covered Napier's campaign against Theodore.

Wolseley marched on Kumase in January 1874 with 2 500 British troops of the Black Watch, the Royal Welsh Fusiliers and the Rifle Brigade, and 1 000 black troops: Hausas from Nigeria and men of the West Indian Regiment. A flanking approach was made by a force of local militia under Captain John Glover.

The Asante resisted the advance as best they could with their muzzle-loading flintlocks, but in the end halted Wolseley by attacking the porters at the rear of his column, prompting them to down their loads. Wolseley took a gamble and raced to Kumase with a small force carrying its own supplies and ammunition. He seized the city but then, with supplies exhausted and rains threatening to flood the rivers and cut him off, he accepted defeat and retreated – but not before stripping Kumase of all the gold that could be found, blowing up the royal palace and putting the city to the torch.

Wolseley was well on the way back to the coast when envoys from the king arrived with his acceptance of the British terms. It turned out that Glover's black militias had fought their way into Kumase, battered and starving, shortly after Wolseley had marched out. The Asante assumed that Glover's force was the advance guard of an army of occupation, and decided further resistance was futile.

So Wolseley's reputation was saved by the African soldiers he held in contempt. Had they not reached Kumase he would have returned home in failure. Instead, he led his troops into Cape Coast through a beflowered victory arch while the warships offshore fired their guns in salute.

The reaction was of the same order in Britain, where Wolseley was musically immortalised as 'the very model of a modern major-general' in Gilbert and Sullivan's comic opera *The Pirates of Penzance*.

The Gold Coast was declared a British crown colony but the Asante, though riven by discord, remained recalcitrant.

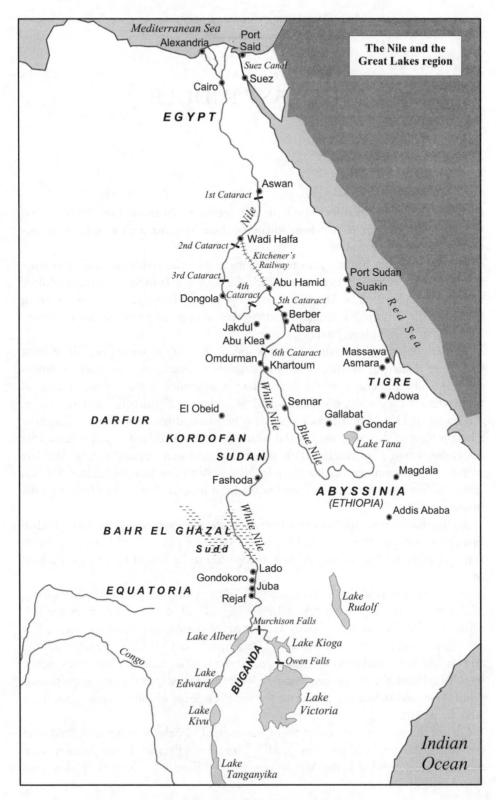

The Nile and the
Great Lakes region

Mediterranean Sea
Alexandria
Port Said
Suez Canal
Suez
Cairo
EGYPT
Aswan
1st Cataract
Nile
Wadi Halfa
2nd Cataract
Kitchener's Railway
3rd Cataract
Abu Hamid
Port Sudan
Suakin
4th Cataract
Dongola
5th Cataract
Berber
Jakdul
Atbara
Abu Klea
Omdurman
6th Cataract
Khartoum
Massawa
Asmara
TIGRE
Adowa
El Obeid
Sennar
Gallabat
Gondar
DARFUR
Lake Tana
KORDOFAN
Blue Nile
White Nile
SUDAN
Magdala
Fashoda
ABYSSINIA
(ETHIOPIA)
Addis Ababa
BAHR EL GHAZAL
White Nile
Sudd
Lado
Gondokoro
Juba
Lake Rudolf
EQUATORIA
Rejaf
Murchison Falls
Lake Albert
Lake Kioga
Congo
Owen Falls
BUGANDA
Lake Edward
Lake Victoria
Lake Kivu
Indian Ocean
Lake Tanganyika

Red Sea

CHAPTER 10

THE LAST RIDDLE

Early in 1875, HM Stanley stood on the southern shore of Lake Victoria and watched his men launch a 40-foot collapsible boat, the first such vessel ever to enter the lake's pristine waters.

The occasion was historic for other reasons besides the arrival of modern marine technology on Africa's largest water. With the boat was launched an extraordinary episode of exploration in Africa, the last great leap of European discovery, solving the last of the continent's geographic mysteries and opening the way for the white man into its long-hidden heart.

Stanley could not know then how significant his journey would be. Still, it must have been a stirring moment for him, strongly symbolic in a number of different ways, all represented by the boat. Here was Stanley, having climbed clear of his wretched childhood, now renowned as author and journalist and famous as the finder of Livingstone; now engaged to be married to a millionaire's daughter, a bright light of the New York social scene; now about to lead an expedition that hopefully would strip the last dark veils from the inner continent, win him the world's plaudits and cement his place in history. With this boat he figuratively was sailing to fame and fortune he could never have imagined as a child in the workhouse.

Stanley had named his boat the *Lady Alice* after his betrothed, the heiress Alice Pike. Made of Spanish cedar, the boat was in six sections that could be carried separately on overland marches, and bolted together to be rowed or sailed on inland waters.

Stanley's expedition was well timed, coinciding with the stirring and quickening of European interest in inner Africa. In the second half of the 19th century the Europeans had begun to get seriously acquisitive of the continent, which meant that they also became seriously competitive. Better protected against malaria by quinine and against native resistance by improved firearms, and guided by the maps drawn by the explorers, the Europeans began to look more closely at the opportunities for profit. They still lacked the platforms for the great leaps of the Scramble, but these were being laid.

One of the most significant of them was created by Stanley, more maligned than any of the African explorers yet possibly the most effective. It was Stanley who filled the great gaps left in the African map by the others, effectively establishing the source of the White Nile, defining the biggest of the great lakes, and proving that the Lualaba became the Congo. With these exploits, the passage of the Congo in particular, he cleared the way for European exploitation and colonisation of middle Africa.

Stanley was successful because he was both practical and determined to a point of ruthlessness. Also because he was particularly well supplied. His expeditions, meticulously planned, lavishly equipped and resolutely, even relentlessly, executed, stand in sharp contrast to Livingstone's saintly, often penurious and sometimes aimless wanderings. Livingstone, patient and principled, was the antithesis of Stanley of the polished boots, icy eyes and smoking gun. Livingstone followed his heart, Stanley followed his compass and his ego.

Beside Burton, Speke and Grant, officers and gentlemen all, Stanley is blunt and boorish. Yet within his scarred psyche there was a longing for goodness. It found purpose and expression in the profound effect Livingstone had on him when they travelled together in Africa. After serving as one of the pallbearers at Livingstone's funeral, Stanley professed to have resolved to devote himself to furthering Livingstone's cause of freeing Africans from their bonds of primitivism through commerce and development, in the cause of the Christian faith Stanley ostensibly embraced. He thought of himself as Livingstone's successor in 'opening up Africa to the shining light of Christianity', but through different methods. In his diary he wrote that 'the selfish and wooden-headed world requires mastering, as well as a loving charity'. There was much more of the former than the latter in the methods he chose.

As soon as Wolseley's Asante campaign was over, Stanley secured the joint and generous backing of the *New York Herald* and the *Daily Telegraph* of London for his venture to solve the remaining mysteries of middle Africa. He set out from Bagamoyo in November 1874 with three oddly chosen English companions, none of whom had any experience in African exploration or survived it long. Stanley's other 350 men were mainly porters but included a number of askaris equipped with the latest Snider rifles. Stanley had learned of the firepower of the large-calibre, breech-loading Sniders in the Asante campaign, where, abandoning any pretence of journalistic detachment, he had taken up a Snider and fired busily into the charging Asante in at least one battle.[1]

Stanley's caravan marched with three flags at its head. The red banner of the Sultan of Zanzibar signified the Sultan's consent to the expedition; the Union Jack and the Stars and Stripes represented Stanley's mixed citizenship and financial backing.

By the time the party reached the southern shore of Lake Victoria at Mwanza its numbers had been somewhat depleted by the afflictions standard to African exploration: disease, desertion and attacks by local Africans. In the reassembled *Lady Alice*, Stanley circumnavigated the lake, establishing that only one major river flowed in and only one out. Then he sailed northwards again to prepare for an exploration of Lake Albert to determine whether it had any link with Lake Tanganyika or the Nile.

Stanley paused at Bumbire to exact vengeance on a tribe that had half-heartedly attacked his party during their earlier voyage from Buganda. As the tribesmen gathered on the shore Stanley and his askaris poured volleys from the Sniders into the crowd. He later wrote about the incident with a relish that so offended many in England that protests were made to the Foreign Office and to the RGS. Stanley's trigger-happy image became ineradicable.

Stanley abandoned his proposed survey of Lake Albert when Mutesa reneged on his promise to provide warriors to escort the party through warring tribes that intervened. Instead, he took the *Lady Alice* to Lake Tanganyika and circumnavigated the lake, confirming that it had no outlet that could lead to the Nile. Speke seemingly had been proven right about the Nile's origin. Lake Victoria, with only one major outlet – at the Ripon Falls – must be presumed to be the source, but only if it could be shown that the source was not in fact the Lualaba.

Stanley thought it more likely that the Lualaba became the Congo, and he now set out to prove it. The ubiquitous *Lady Alice* was humped overland to Nyangwe on the Lualaba. Stanley's well-armed caravan was not as easily turned back by the Arabs there as Livingstone and Cameron had been. He hired the most prominent of the slavers, Mohammed bin Sayed, better known as Tippu Tib, to provide an escort for 60 days' march along the course of the river, which here was broken by rapids preventing the launching of the *Lady Alice*.

What followed was a nightmarish ordeal. The expedition had to hack its way through dense forest, several times fighting off Africans who mistook them for slavers. It was beset by disease and eventually hunger, and was deserted by Tippu Tib. The *Lady Alice* was relaunched but eventually abandoned at cataracts, and the expedition staggered forward on foot. Believing he was near the trading post at Boma near the Congo's mouth, Stanley sent four of the strongest men ahead with a letter asking for help. They tottered into Boma in August 1877, astonishing the traders. Nothing had been heard from Stanley for more than a year, and he had been written off as dead.

It had taken Stanley three years to complete his journey across Africa. Mixed with the plaudits now showered upon him was the bitter news that Alice Pike had married another man. But he would have little time for grieving, for Africa would soon make new demands on him.

★ ★ ★ ★

In the same year that Stanley launched the *Lady Alice* on Lake Victoria, a small expedition flying the Tricolor started out from the mouth of the Ogowe River, south of the French settlement at Libreville in Gabon. Leading the party was Pierre Savorgnan de Brazza, a young Italian of noble birth who had acquired French citizenship after being admitted to the French navy. Brazza believed the river might provide a better route into the hinterland than the Congo, which was barred to ships by the rapids near its mouth.

Having won French government backing, Brazza paddled up the Ogowe only to find that it rose in highlands about five hundred kilometres from the coast. Learning of a big river beyond, he crossed the watershed and soon came to a river the local people called the Alima. He followed it downstream but turned back when he ran out of ammunition during a fierce attack by local Africans.

Brazza suspected that the Alima was a tributary of the Congo, but five years would pass before he could test his theory. Then he would find himself in a race with Stanley to secure exclusive rights to the trade of the Congo basin. It would be a race that would set the pace for the Scramble.

★ ★ ★ ★

The Europeans got to dominate Africa not only by simple conquest but also by more ingenious practices. Trading and mining concessions, for instance, were useful tools for gaining a foothold which later could be expanded to possession. Even more effective was the clever manipulation of debt, and nowhere was this more effectively employed than on the Mediterranean littoral.

The efficacy of the debt tool had been proved in the European annexation of Tunisia's finances in 1869, and was to be even more dramatically demonstrated in Egypt, ruled by the Ottoman empire's ambitious satrap, Mohammed Ali.

After conquering Nubia as a colony of Egypt, Mohammed Ali began to overreach himself. His modernisation of Egypt began to exceed his ability to pay for it. The gold he had expected to find in Nubia was not there, and Egypt's agricultural economy was unable to finance his costly imports. By the time Mohammed Ali died in 1849 his government was uncomfortably in the red. This situation may have been crucial in influencing his second successor, Said, to grant De Lesseps the Suez Canal concession on terms outrageously unfavourable to Egypt.

When Said died in 1863 he was succeeded by his nephew Ismail, who turned out to be an even more enthusiastic developer – and borrower – than Mohammed Ali. Ismail gave Egypt railways and irrigation projects and a basically sound economy, but in the process put his country yet deeper in debt to the European banks. He was forced to take out loan after loan, in part simply to pay the usurious interest on earlier loans. The cost of raising the loans often exceeded the portion received by Ismail's government. By 1875, according to some accounts, the government had received only 35-million pounds after paying 29-million pounds in interest and sinking-fund contributions, and still owed 46-million pounds. Over the 15 years of Ismail's reign, Egypt's foreign debt rose from three million pounds to more than a hundred million.[2]

Ismail's predicament was a portent of what was to happen throughout Africa much later, in the post-colonial era, when the independent states found themselves increasingly and often hopelessly in debt to European creditors. That pile of debt remained the biggest single issue of discord between Africa and Europe at the beginning of the 21st century.

Expecting that Egypt's share of the revenue from the Suez Canal would pay off the debt, Ismail began planning to conquer the Sudan beyond Nubia, using the army created by Mohammed Ali, which Said had further Egyptianised by opening the formerly all-white officer corps to the Egyptian elite.

Disguising the operation as a mission to stamp out slavery and bring civilisation to the savage heart of Africa, Ismail recruited as commander of the expedition Sir Samuel Baker. Baker at the time was acting as guide and interpreter for the Prince and Princess of Wales (later King Edward VII and Queen Alexandra) who were visiting Egypt in what appears to have been an effort to take some of the French shine off the formal opening of the Suez Canal.

Baker's brief from Ismail was to annex an area vaguely defined as the Upper Nile. In February 1870 he set off from Khartoum for Gondokoro with two regiments of the Egyptian army and five dismantlable steamboats. It took him seven months to struggle through the Sudd. Reaching Gondokoro at last, Baker renamed it Ismailia and made it the capital of the new Egyptian province of Equatoria.

Fighting off stiff opposition, and with the remarkable Florence always at his side, he 'pacified' most of the Upper Nile, extending Cairo's hegemony from the Mediterranean almost to the Great Lakes. He put down slavery and insurrection with equal diligence, but when his term as governor-general of Equatoria expired in 1873 he had simply driven the slavers into the desert, where they continued to function almost as busily as ever.

To further his imperial plans Ismail now turned to another Briton, the eccentric Charles Gordon. A man of spartan needs and deep yet unorthodox religious conviction, Gordon had served in the Crimea and then made a reputation as a brilliant leader of irregular forces in the second of Britain's opium wars in China.

Gordon's brief from Ismail was to secure the White Nile by building a chain of military posts to the river's source, to annex Buganda, and to get Baker's steamboats operating on Lake Victoria and Lake Albert in order to assert Egyptian sovereignty. He was also to continue suppressing slavery.

Gordon assembled a staff of keen young men – Britons, Italians and restless Americans who had served in their country's Civil War. He began his new function early in 1874, the same year that Livingstone died at Ilala, the same year that Cameron reached the Lualaba on his cross-Africa trek, the same year that Stanley left England for his own trans-continental epic. Finding that corruption among the Egyptian garrison at Ismailia had nullified much of Baker's work, Gordon persuaded Cairo to give him full control of Equatoria, independent of the venal governor-general of the Sudan in Khartoum.

Gordon restored Egyptian control of Bunyoro but was repulsed from Buganda by Mutesa. He got two of the reassembled steamboats up to Lake Albert and circumnavigated it, confirming its link to the Nile. However, the difficulty of portaging the cataracts convinced him that the Nile was not the best route to the lakes. He proposed instead that troops be landed at Mombasa, and marched inland to occupy Buganda, thereby opening a way to the lakes and extending Egyptian influence to the Indian Ocean.

Ismail enthusiastically approved the plan and sent an invasion force in four warships down the Suez Canal to occupy Barawa (in what later became Somaliland), Kismayu and Lamu. Sultan Barghash, however, protested loudly at this invasion of his territory and London intervened, forcing Ismail to call off the operation.

After two and a half years in Equatoria, Gordon resigned. He had failed to annex the lakes firmly to Egypt, but he had established a string of forts reaching almost to the lakes and entrenching Egyptian suzerainty along the whole length of the Nile. With the forts he had imposed peace and order along the river, and he had curbed the slave trade in the region. He had mapped Lake Albert and the upper reaches of the Nile almost to the lakes. What he could not do, he realised, was end the slavery and improve the lot of the common people as long as corruption pervaded Egyptian officialdom.

Gordon returned to England in December 1876 but two months later he was back in Egypt, drawn by an urgent appeal from Ismail and the promise of full control of the whole Sudan as governor-general with full powers to put down the slavery.

Gordon fairly threw himself into his new tasks, frequently dashing off to trouble spots in the long, fast camel rides for which he had become famous. More than once he nipped rebellion in the bud through the sheer power of awe, appearing suddenly out of the desert on his camel, having left his troops far behind, sometimes wearing a gold-embroidered tunic that flashed in the sun, and winning over the malcontents through the force of his personality, enhanced by his blazing, pale-blue eyes.

Meanwhile, however, matters had been going from bad to worse for Ismail. In 1875, desperate for means to pay his debts, he had sold his 45 per cent shareholding in the Suez Canal Company to the British government, giving Britain parity with France in the control of the Canal. Ismail had been about to sell his holdings to French business interests when Benjamin Disraeli, the British prime minister, had got wind of the deal and, with the backing of the Rothschilds bankers, had bought them for his own government.

The proceeds were insufficient, however, for the interest payments on Egypt's loans, and the country was forced to hand control of the debts to a commission formed by the European creditors. Later, control of the government's finances was placed in the hands of a British official responsible for revenue and a French one responsible for expenditure.

Egypt had in effect lost the power fully to govern itself. Colonialism was coming in through the back door, the financial door. Soon it would have control also of the front door, the political one. At the same time Europeans, sensing new opportunities in a romantic Egypt administered by Westerners, began to flock into the country in tens of thousands. Not to settle, though; the politics would never be stable enough for that.

Seeing the goose that was laying their golden eggs falling sick, the European bankers reduced the usurious interest rates that had brought about the crisis. Even so, the siphoning off of a large part of the national income to service the debts kept the government sorely strapped for funds. In February 1879 army officers who had not been paid mutinied. It was a brief rebellion that quickly subsided, but it was a telling portent. Two months later Ismail himself rebelled and attempted to ditch the imposed system of dual control over his finances.

The European powers reacted by simply ditching Ismail. The British and the French, with Germany closely involved in order to look after the investments of its bankers, persuaded the Turkish sultan, the nominal overlord of Egypt, to dismiss Ismail as khedive and replace him with his son, Tewfik, who could be relied on to be compliant. The sultan, being dependent on the British and French to bolster his tottering empire against the Russians, could hardly refuse. Ismail packed his treasures onto his yacht and sailed away to a comfortable if unhappy retirement in Europe.

Gordon, disillusioned by these machinations, resigned again and sailed for England. But he still had a dramatic finale to play out on the Nile.

CHAPTER 11

POWER AND PRETTY STONES

A turn of huge consequence in Africa's history was unwittingly triggered in 1866 when a 15-year-old youth named Erasmus Stephanus Jacobs was sent out on his father's farm in the Hopetown district near the Orange River to look for a straight stick to poke up a blocked water pipe.

In his search he came across a shiny pebble, which he slipped into his pocket and later gave to his young sister as a plaything. He would have been less casual with it had he known that what he had found was a diamond worth a small fortune, and that beneath the region's scrubland was the richest treasure of diamonds the world had known.

A neighbour, Schalk van Niekerk, had a pretty good idea of what the stone might be when he saw Erasmus's sister playing with it. He persuaded the children's mother to give him the pebble and sent it to the nearest town, Colesberg, for assessment.[1]

The stone found its way by way of Grahamstown to London, where it was confirmed as a diamond of 21¼ carats and became famous as the Eureka Diamond.

A few diamonds had been picked up before in the region by wandering Khoi cattlemen, but no-one had ever been able to trace their source. Erasmus was able to point out precisely where he had found his stone, and soon others were discovered along the river. Fortune-hunters rushed in and began to dig eagerly. There were tales of Boer farmers prising diamonds out of the clay plaster on their houses. Tent towns sprang up and were followed by corrugated-iron saloons, shops and hotels.

Many of the Calvinistic Boers believed the diamonds would bring nothing but sorrow, and indeed they did bring trouble. The river diggings lay in an area where the loosely defined boundaries of the Transvaal and Orange Free State more or less came together in territory near that of the Griquas. All claimed ownership. The lieutenant-governor of Natal, RW Keate, was appointed to arbitrate the dispute and in 1871, to no-one's surprise, he awarded the territory to the Griquas, enabling the British to annex it as the new colony of Griqualand West. The Free State's President Brand fought the award for four years until the Cape Supreme Court ruled that the Griquas had no claim to the land. Brand accepted compensation from the British of £90 000, a trifling sum compared with the wealth that would come from the diamond fields.

Soon the focus shifted from the alluvial diggings to new discoveries in dry ground at Dutoitspan and Bultfontein, some hundred kilometres to the north. The richest

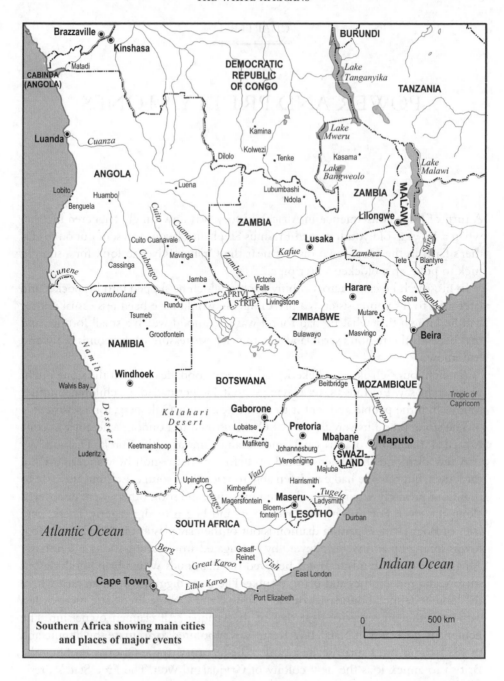

Southern Africa showing main cities
and places of major events

deposits were found on a hill on a farm owned by two brothers De Beer. In a matter
of months the hill had disappeared beneath the urgent picks and shovels of hundreds
of diggers, and was on its way to becoming the largest hand-dug excavation in the
world. The diggings, first called New Rush, were renamed after the colonial secretary,
Lord Kimberley, and became the centre of the world's richest diamond industry.

The rush to the diamond fields developed into one of the more dramatic of the sudden influxes that characterised European migration to Africa in the 19th century. Inevitably, it worked to the disadvantage of the indigenous peoples. At first black diggers staked claims alongside the whites and had substantial holdings – 80 per cent of the licensed claims on the Bultfontein mine, according to one account.[2] However, many white diggers objected to blacks owning claims, either from racism or in the hope of acquiring their claims. There was no question of barring blacks from the diggings altogether, however, since most white diggers could not or would not do without their labour.

The essential racism of the diggers' attitude was expressed by the diggings newspaper, the *Diamond News*, which advocated a policy of 'class legislation, restrictive laws and the holding in check of the native races till by education they are fit to be our equals'.[3]

Richard Southey, appointed lieutenant-governor of Griqualand West, tried to uphold the Africans' rights. He restored confiscated claims, and ended the curfew and the residential segregation that the white diggers had imposed on the blacks. After he had put down an attempted rebellion by white diggers in 1875, more powerful interests prevailed and Cape Town removed him from office. Thereafter the black diggers were squeezed out and then completely sidelined in the amalgamation of interests that resulted in the mining being taken over by companies and eventually monopolised by the De Beers Company.

The man chiefly responsible for engineering that consolidation, Cecil John Rhodes, had arrived in Kimberley in 1871 as a sickly, thin-voiced stripling of 18. Rhodes became rich largely through two visionary decisions. First, when the yellow ground of the diggings gave way to blue ground that seemed to hold no diamonds, he bought up at bargain prices claims that now seemed worthless but turned out to be priceless when deeper digging showed the blue ground to be even richer than the yellow. Second, he led the way in forcing individual diggers and small partnerships to amalgamate into big companies that were more efficient and easier to control, and then manipulated that control largely into his own hands.

Whatever privileges the black diggers still held had little chance in the face of this corporate juggernaut. Some blacks with the wherewithal for agricultural production prospered for a while by selling produce to the diamond fields. But they were largely ousted even from this by a white-dominated society demanding cheap black labour. The blacks mostly ended up as labourers on the diggings, later on the mines, or on white farms.

Not unexpectedly, in this situation, they often participated in IDB – illicit diamond buying, the scourge of the mining companies. A labourer who found a diamond while working in the mine might conceal it in his anus, ear, navel or hair, or swallow it or even push it into a cut made in his body for the purpose. In 1886, by which time the diamond mining was largely controlled by De Beers, a solution was contrived by Francis Thompson, a local farmer.

Because of his knowledge of African peoples, Thompson was recruited by Rhodes specifically to reorganise the workers' quarters in order to curb the rampant IDB. He devised a system for sealing the miners off from the outside world for the duration of their three-month contracts, locking them behind high walls in self-sufficient, prison-like compounds.

At the end of each shift the worker was required to strip naked and undergo a body search. He then had to perform a dance choreographed to relax the sphincter so that any diamonds hidden in the anus would fall out.

In his autobiography Thompson reckons that the compound system turned the diamond mining industry from marginality to large profits.[4] Besides that, it set a pattern for labour relations that would be extended even more widely on the gold mines and would influence attitudes in workplaces elsewhere for generations to come.

Thompson himself seems not to have been a callous man. By the standards of his time he had greater empathy with black people than most whites had, speaking Setswana and Ndebele with some fluency and enjoying good relations with Africans. As one of Rhodes's most trusted lieutenants, he was to play a key role in the creation of Rhodesia.

★ ★ ★ ★

There were others who, like Rhodes, became multi-millionaires on the diamond fields – Barney Barnato, Alfred Beit, Solly Joel, Sammy Marks, JB Robinson – but none of them influenced the course of events in southern Africa as mightily as Rhodes in time did. They and Rhodes all moved to the Transvaal when the gold strikes there proved substantial, and ended up making even more money out of gold than out of diamonds.

The first gold strikes of significant size were found in the eastern Transvaal in 1873. By this time the California gold rush of 1849 had subsided, and output from the strikes in Colorado in 1858 and Idaho in 1861 was dwindling. The Ballarat strike in Australia had peaked, and the strikes of 1896 at Klondike in the Yukon still lay ahead.

Towns such as Pilgrim's Rest, Lydenburg and Barberton sprang up at the eastern Transvaal gold diggings. With these finds, and with diamonds streaming out of Kimberley, South Africa was looking like a new Eldorado – and would seem much more so when the really big gold deposits were found on the Witwatersrand in 1886.

★ ★ ★ ★

The discovery of diamonds and gold in South Africa had a catalytic effect on the politics of the sub-continent. It was as though a powerful new ingredient had been tossed into a cauldron already boiling with conflict over land and nationhood.

Africans and Europeans were fighting with each other and among themselves. National borders were loose, still forming or reforming, as were peoples and nations, after the disruptions caused by the *mfecane* and by European expansion.

The Xhosa, battered by the Frontier Wars and the great cattle killing, were hard pressed by whites' demands on all sides. The Basotho, still in the final stages of forming their young nation, were contesting their western and southern boundaries with both Boers and Britons. The Zulu, their mighty expansion thrown back by the white men's guns, were swirling uncertainly behind the vague borders of their coastal kingdom, while the Europeans pressed covetously from the south. The Matabele had at last halted their plunderous swathe through the interior and were busy subjugating the Shona north of the Limpopo.

The Boers in the Transvaal were scrapping over their new republic's borders with the Zulu and the Swazi in the south-east and with Sekhukhuni's Pedi in the northeast. In 1868 the Volksraad had arbitrarily defined extravagantly ambitious borders stretching eastward to the Indian Ocean, northward into what was to become Rhodesia, westward deep into Bechuanaland and southwards to the Orange River.

They were blocked, however, in the east by the Portuguese and elsewhere by the British, who were especially concerned with keeping open the route from the Cape into central Africa for possible future extension of their own interests.

The British broadly wanted peace and order in the hinterland so that they would not be dragged into expensive conflicts or unwanted annexations. British foreign policy was based on a concept of informal empire rather than conquest and colonisation, of promoting trade as far as possible through special relationships. There was a fear in Britain of over-extending the Empire. The ideal empire was one that would pay for itself rather than draw on the British treasury, while at the same time serving as a market for British manufactures. The European settlements in Canada, Australia, New Zealand and the Cape were being encouraged towards self-government in the hope that they would remain within Britain's sphere of trade and influence while assuming responsibility for their own administration and defence – and their own budget deficits.

The diamond finds gave some urgency to London's ambition for the confederation of the colonies and the republics in order to create a peaceful and stable part of the Empire. When the Transvaal government found itself bankrupted, partly by its unsuccessful efforts to conquer Sekhukhuni's Pedi and to assert a border with the Zulu, Lord Carnarvon, the colonial secretary, saw a chance to promote confederation.

He sent Theophilus Shepstone to Pretoria with an offer the Transvalers couldn't refuse: annexation by Britain in return for getting their treasury out of the red and eliminating the threat from the Pedis and Zulus. The Transvalers blustered and appealed vainly for foreign help, but in the end sullenly accepted Shepstone's proclamation of annexation in April 1877.

Carnarvon reckoned that once the Transvaal was firmly in the British fold the Free State would have no option but to come in too. But first the Zulus had to be dealt with. Though forced north of the Tugela River by the creation of the Natal colony, the Zulus were still well organised and disciplined under King Cetewayo, and posed a potential threat to Natal as well as the Transvaal.

On the pretext of mediating the border dispute between the Transvalers and Zulus, Sir Bartle Frere, governor of the Cape and High Commissioner, offered Cetewayo impossible terms, principally the disbanding of the regiments – the very sinews of Zulu power, the standard-bearers of Zulu pride. And he set an impossible deadline of 30 days for acceptance. Elaborate preparations were made for war in the knowledge that the ultimatum could not be met.

It wasn't, and in January 1879 Lieutenant-General Frederick Thesiger, about to become Lord Chelmsford, invaded Zululand. The Zulus were a formidable force – about thirty regiments strong – but their few obsolete guns were no match for the breech-loading Martini-Henrys of the British troops, who also had a number of Gatlings, the first machine-gun, as well as artillery and rockets.

Twelve days after crossing into Zululand, Chelmsford found himself riding back into Natal in a state of shock, his army shaken by one of the most spectacular defeats in British military history. On 22 January he had left the major part of his main column – about two thousand two hundred men – encamped on the plain beneath the blunt tooth of a mountain named Isandlwana while he went off with a smaller force to find the enemy. Then the Zulu *impis* rose, 20 000 strong, from the nearby valleys where they had been lying in wait, and fell upon the complacent encampment.

Caught in isolated groups, the redcoats fought off the Zulus for a large part of the morning, but by early afternoon none were left alive. It was dark when Chelmsford led his shocked force back to the camp at Isandlwana, now deserted, and his men lay uneasily for the night among the dead. He led them out again just before dawn, wanting to spare them the awful sights the sun would reveal.

Chelmsford left his dead where they had fallen, lying in their red coats in the grass like windfall fruit. Not for another four months would the British be in a position to return and bury the bird-picked remains. The official death toll in the end was 1 329 officers and men.

On the day that Isandlwana was written into British history as a humiliating defeat, another action took place that has become synonymous with heroism. Cetewayo's headstrong brother, Dubulamanzi, had been ordered to hold his force of about four thousand men in reserve. He grew impatient and, ignoring the king's orders not to enter Natal, crossed the Buffalo River, the border, to attack the British position at Rorke's Drift.

The little mission station at the drift had been turned into an advance stores depot and hospital for Chelmsford's army. When two refugees from Isandlwana galloped up and warned of the approach of Dubulamanzi's force, the mission station was hastily fortified with mealie bags and biscuit boxes.

The Zulus began hurling themselves at the improvised fort in the late afternoon. The redcoats fired until their rifle barrels burned their hands. They wrapped their hands in socks and rags and kept firing. Behind them the chaplain walked, passing out ammunition and shouting Biblical exhortations. The sun went down, and it is said that in the dark some of the redcoats' rifle barrels glowed faintly, almost red hot from continuous firing. Not until the dawn did the Zulus break off and retreat as Chelmsford's force approached on its retreat from Isandlwana.

The defenders of Rorke's Drift counted only 17 of their 84 able-bodied defenders dead and six wounded. The Zulus left some five hundred dead.

Chelmsford's right column had meanwhile fought its way to Eshowe. At the Inyezane River the Gatling gun was used for what may have been its first firing in action by the British army. In this and subsequent engagements the Gatling, when it didn't jam, was effective, drilling great gaps in the Zulu ranks with its cluster of ten barrels, fired in rotation with a hand crank. But it was not enough to stop the column being besieged at Eshowe.

Chelmsford's left column under Colonel Evelyn Wood, the Asante veteran, ran into even stronger opposition, losing 123 men in two battles. Again the Gatlings, the artillery and the volleys of rifle fire decimated the attackers. As the Zulus retreated they were pursued and cut down by the cavalry, now shouting 'Remember Isandlwana'.

Repeated offers by Cetewayo of peace talks were spurned by Chelmsford, now obsessed with restoring British pride and his own reputation. He took a strong column out to relieve Eshowe. At Gingindhlovu it was attacked by about twelve thousand Zulus. Again the attack withered under British firepower, and the Zulus' retreat was turned by the cavalry into a rout.

Told that he was being replaced by Wolseley, Chelmsford resolved to save what he could of his good name by finishing the Zulu campaign before Wolseley could reach the front. He launched a second invasion, cutting straight to Ulundi, Cetewayo's capital.

Cetewayo, though still seeking peace, was able to muster about twenty thousand men. The two armies met for the showdown on a plain outside Ulundi. Chelmsford formed his 5 000 men into the hollow square that had served the British military so well before, the front rank kneeling and the rear one standing to form a bristling hedge of rifles. The cavalry waited inside the square.

Again the Zulu spearmen charged to their deaths in the storm of shot from the square.* Again, when the attack broke, Isandlwana was 'avenged' on the points of the lances – as if vengeance was appropriate against a people who had merely been defending their own land against invasion.

Chelmsford went home a hero for the moment but with further career ruined. Wolseley was given overall supervision of Natal, Zululand and the Transvaal. After more than three years of turmoil among rival factions in Zululand, Britain annexed the territory and in 1897 it was joined to Natal. Six years later it was opened up to European settlement, and large chunks were allocated to whites, who turned its rolling hills into vast sugar estates.

While the last Zulu resistance was being put down, Wolseley had led a force of British and Swazi troops against Sekhukhuni's Pedis and defeated them.

Virtually the whole of South Africa except the Free State was now under British control. Carnarvon's dream of confederation remained distant, however, for the Afrikaner republics were more than ever convinced that Britain was far too big and ambitious a bedfellow for them.

---

*Neither the Zulus nor the Mahdists nor any of the native armies that sent spearmen charging against the British square did so by choice. Having only a few outmoded firearms, and little ammunition for them anyway, they could not fight the British at long range, as the Boers later did. They had either to charge the square with their spears or meekly surrender.

CHAPTER 12

THIS MAGNIFICENT CAKE

In the last two decades of the 19th century Africa at last lay open to the Europeans – and not only in a geographic sense.

The obstacles that had kept them largely at a distance for four centuries had mostly been removed. Medical advances had curbed the continent's ferocious diseases. Its hinterland geography had been broadly revealed by the explorers. The African entrepreneurs who for so long had resisted European competition could no longer oppose Europe's industrial strength. Neither could Africa's armies stand any more against European military supremacy. There was no indigenous power capable of withstanding any determined European intrusion. The waning of Turkish power on the Nile and the Mediterranean littoral, and the defeat of the Asantes, the Tukolors, the Zulus, the Xhosas and Theodore's Abyssinians, had left no military power of consequence.

Certainly there was none capable of standing up to the lever-action Martini-Henry rifle, to mobile field guns firing shells with smokeless charges enabling gunners to shoot faster and more accurately, and to the improved Gatling machine-gun. Already the Gatling was being superseded by the even better Maxim. As Hilaire Belloc put it in his couplet in 1898:

Whatever happens, we have got
The Maxim Gun, and they have not.

From now on most of the serious confrontations in Africa would be among the Europeans themselves as they competed for its land and its riches.

A glimpse of the mineral riches had been given by the early diamond and gold discoveries in South Africa, but European merchants still looked to the rest of Africa for trade, chiefly for ivory and agricultural commodities such as palm oil and cotton (and later rubber) in exchange for the manufactures spewing from their factories. As late as 1876 the traders were still mostly based at the coast but were now beginning to look seriously at penetrating the hinterland.

It was not a trader but a king who took the most dramatic initiative. Leopold II, King of the Belgians, was a monarch in his demeanour but not in his soul. A sharp businessman, he had expanded his inherited fortune with clever investments. He remained a fundamentally greedy person who would let no moral nuisance frustrate his compulsive acquisitiveness.

Besides the accumulation of wealth, he had another and more regal passion: he wanted a foreign empire. Belgium's parliament refused to have anything to do with his imperial dreams but Leopold was willing to go it alone, devoting his own fortune to the cause. He made inquiries with the Spanish, the Portuguese and the British about acquiring territory but was politely rebuffed by them all.

Then in January 1876 he saw a newspaper report of Verney Cameron's journey across Africa and Cameron's estimate of the 'unspeakable richness' of Africa's interior. Leopold saw opportunity opening like a lotus, and he devised a cunning scheme to seize it. He invited Cameron and other leading explorers and geographers, Grant and Baker among them, to Brussels for a conference. There he proposed an international crusade to end the slavery that still flourished in east and middle Africa, and to employ European science and technology in bringing civilisation to Africa.

The ploy worked. The Brussels conference formed an International Africa Association, with branches in member countries but with Leopold presiding over the international executive. The king's hidden motive was disclosed only confidentially in a letter to his ambassador in London: 'I do not want to miss a good chance of getting us a slice of this magnificent African cake.'[1]

In the mean time, Leopold waited impatiently for Stanley to complete his epic journey across Africa. If Stanley proved that the Lualaba was the Congo and that the latter was navigable, his information would be even more useful than Cameron's.

As a colonialist, Leopold was ahead of his time. While European mercantilists were beginning to take a closer interest in Africa's commercial promise, their governments were still wary of political involvement in the continent. Sir William Mackinnon, operator of a steamship service round the Indian coast and founder of the first mail service between Britain, India and Zanzibar, had been looking into the building of a road from the coast to Lake Nyasa to open up that part of the hinterland to trade. The year after the Brussels conference he proposed that he and his associates administer the whole area between the coast and Lake Victoria in the name of the Sultan of Zanzibar. Sultan Barghash agreed to give him trading rights but Mackinnon was blocked by the foreign secretary, Lord Salisbury, who, like Gladstone, was afraid the scheme might drag Britain into unwanted responsibility and expense in East Africa.

Competition between the European powers was not then strong enough to override such fears. Eleven years later, however, it was, and Mackinnon's idea was revived with the formation of the Imperial British East Africa Company as one of the companies given royal charters to operate in Africa. By then royal charters were being seen as a good way to keep competitors out of possibly desirable areas without the expense of official colonisation.

On the other side of Africa another future knight of the marketplace, George Goldie Taubman, was beginning the business venture that would widely influence both commerce and politics in West Africa. Taubman, scion of a wealthy Isle of Man family, came to Africa when the family in 1875 bought out an ailing West African trading company. George (who later dropped the Taubman and become known only as Goldie) was put in charge. Realising that too many companies were competing for the palm oil, he talked the four British companies into combining as the United Africa Company (later the National African Company). He cut costs by bypassing the black middlemen, using gunboats to silence those who objected, and began buying direct from the producers up-river. Then he began a price war with the French companies, forcing them to sell out to his company in 1884.

Goldie's efforts to get a royal charter to govern the whole of the lower and middle Niger were at first rejected by the British government for the same reasons that it had dismissed Mackinnon's. Whitehall's thinking was changed, however, by fears of the French expanding southwards from their tacitly recognised sphere of interest on the upper Niger. The British had become alert to French plans for a railway link between the Senegal and the Niger, and another from Algeria across the Sahara to the Niger.

Faideherbe's conquests were now being extended by an equally tough French soldier, Lieutenant-Colonel Gustave Desbordes, who in 1883 had completed a chain of forts from the coast of Senegal to Bamako on the Niger. The British became concerned when in the same year the French revived an old protectorate over Porto Novo in Dahomey. A French presence there would block any hope of the British establishing control of an unbroken stretch of coastline from the Gold Coast to Lagos.

British concerns were heightened when a French agent, Antoine Mattei, tried to negotiate treaties with the chiefs of Bonny on the lower Niger. Though they may have been exaggerated, all these fears gave impetus to the Scramble when it began in 1884. They contributed to the British government's decision to declare a protectorate over the lower Niger in 1886 and give Goldie's company a charter to govern it. Goldie then changed the company's name to the Royal Niger Company.

If the traders were the point-men for the advance of European colonialism, the missionaries might be regarded as the scouts, even if unwitting ones. Their evangelisation cut the path for colonialism almost as surely as did trade. Even before the European businessmen had begun seriously eyeing the hinterland, the missionaries had established presences that in a number of cases were later to be linked with the colonialism of their mother countries. Notable among these were the British missions in Uganda and the German ones in Tanganyika, Togo, Cameroon and South West Africa.

For all the activities of the missionaries and traders, however, Africa was still only peripherally occupied by the Europeans in the last quarter of the 19th century. In 1876 the British had tenuous footholds in the Gold Coast, Lagos and Sierra Leone. They and the Boers occupied most of South Africa. The French were established in Algeria, Tunisia (indirectly still), Senegal and Gabon. The Portuguese held sway in large parts of what were to become Angola and Mozambique. Spain claimed a stretch of the north-west coast.

Apart from the Turkish holdings along the Nile and the Mediterranean, the rest of Africa's huge bulk was occupied by indigenous kingdoms relatively undeveloped in terms of European sophistication, or by ethnic groups living in a politically unstable state. A number of these states were young, and many had tenuous borders and even uncertain identities. None stood out as being especially powerful.

As the Europeans began advancing into the interior the gulf between their technology and Africa's was at its widest. Since the first white men had landed on sub-Saharan shores, European technology had made giant leaps while Africa's had stood still, borrowing only marginally from the Europeans. When Europe's mills were casting and forging huge shafts in steel and milling intricate gears, African metalworkers could not make anything much larger than an axe blade, and then only in simple iron. Africa possessed the raw materials for making steel but not the technology.

Even the use of the wheel was rudimentary in most of Africa, unknown even in many parts, whereas Europeans and Americans were travelling swiftly across continents on railways. For motive power, Africans relied on draught animals when the Europeans had steam engines and electric motors. In the late eighties, African sailors still hugged their coastlines in canoes and small sailboats – although some crossed from East Africa to Arabian and Indian ports in Arab-style dhows – while Europeans crossed the oceans in big, motorised cargo vessels and even bigger liners on which passengers dined and danced to the music of orchestras. Where most Africans, having no script, relied on oral records, Europeans were beginning to use typewriters.* When the first undersea telegraph cable from the Cape to England was opened in 1880, African societies still communicated at long range by drums or runners.

Faced with this technological superiority, Africa's states, even the oldest and strongest, were ripe for the plucking.

★ ★ ★ ★

Only a few months after Leopold's Brussels conference, Stanley staggered out of the Congo jungle with the news that the Belgian king had been hoping for: the Lualaba and the Congo were the same river, and it was navigable for much of its inner length. Stanley, confident of interesting the British government in a Congo protectorate, brushed aside Leopold's first overtures. But when Whitehall rejected his protectorate proposal, a disillusioned Stanley in 1878 signed a five-year contract to establish 'scientific stations and hospitals' for the IAA along the lower Congo from Stanley Pool.

In order to bypass the rapids that blocked boat passage between the sea and the Pool, where the river became navigable again, Stanley began to build a road to link his river stations. It was a brutally hard task, made heavier by lugging along two prefabricated steamers that would be launched on the Pool.

Stanley and others had begun to suspect Leopold of using the IAA to make the Congo a Belgian colony. Paris for its part revised its opposition to Brazza's proposals for a French presence on the Congo. The French had been more interested in extending their presence on the upper Niger against the British competition they

---

*The first were made in 1873 in America by Remington, the gunsmiths.

saw expanding up from the lower Niger. But in 1880 Paris agreed to back Brazza in an expedition that would follow his earlier route up the Ogowe and then go on to establish a French presence on the Congo by concluding treaties with the relevant chiefs. Ostensibly he was to set up stations for the French chapter of the IAA between the Ogowe and the Congo, but in effect it meant his racing Stanley to secure first rights at Stanley Pool, the key to trade on the Congo and its vast basin.

Setting out four months after Stanley, Brazza quickly traversed the Ogowe, establishing a station at Franceville, then crossed the watershed and followed the Alima to the Congo. When he reached the great river in August 1880, Stanley was still battering his road through 300 kilometres downstream from the Pool. Brazza travelled down to the Pool and concluded a protectorate treaty with the paramount chief of the Makoko on the north bank. He hoisted the Tricolor at Ncuna (which later became Brazzaville) then left for France, leaving behind a party to assert France's prior right against Stanley.

When Stanley reached the Pool many weeks later he met with hostility from Brazza's Makoko friends, but renewed the acquaintance he had made with Chief Ngaliema in 1877. He built his fourth and largest station at Ngaliema's capital, Ntamo (later to become Leopoldville and then Kinshasa) across the Pool from Ncuna. His steamers at last launched, he began to travel up-river to collect treaty signatures from chiefs.

The French government, still nervous of becoming over-extended in Africa, dithered over recognition of Brazza's Makoko treaty. Public opinion began to swing officialdom round, however, and the balance was tipped when Stanley angered the French with a crude attack on Brazza during a debate between them in Paris in 1882. The Makoko treaty was ratified soon afterwards.

★ ★ ★ ★

Despite Wolseley's conquest of the Asante in 1874, Britain's suzerainty over the Gold Coast remained tenuous. In 1896 the British found themselves again marching on Kumase. The colonial secretary, Joseph Chamberlain, had again become worried that the French, busily extending their presence along the Senegal River, would come down from the north and befriend the still-recalcitrant Asante. Colonel Sir Francis Scott, a veteran of Wolseley's campaign, led an army of British and West Indian troops to the Asante capital. There, Scott and the colonial governor, William Maxwell, sat on chairs while King Agyemon Prempe and the queen mother were made to kneel before them and embrace their legs in a gesture of submission.

Prempe was exiled to the Seychelles islands in the Indian Ocean, while British firms began exploiting gold mining, rubber and timber concessions.

Asante resistance still smouldered, however. The golden stool that was the symbol of Asante royalty and nationhood was kept carefully hidden from constant British searches. Meanwhile, the Asante quietly collected guns for an uprising.

The revolt began in 1900 when the governor, Sir Frederick Hodgson, summoned Asante leaders to the fort he had built in Kumase and demanded the surrender of the golden stool. 'Why am I not sitting on the golden stool at this moment?' he demanded to know, clearly unaware of the sacrilege that in Asante eyes would be committed by contact between his alien posterior and the sacred relic.

Far from handing over the stool, the Asante presented a list of demands, the chief of which were that King Prempe be brought home and the British quit the country. Their demands rejected, the Asante besieged Hodgson in his fort. An attempt to storm the fort was beaten off by the Maxim guns.

The governor's telegraphed pleas for British reinforcements were ignored by a British government more concerned with getting Tommies to South Africa to stop the humiliating reverses being inflicted by the scruffy Boers. Black troops were sent, however, from Nigeria and Sierra Leone.

To stop these reinforcements, the Asante built elaborate log-and-earth defences on all the approaches to Kumase. Meanwhile, food in the besieged fort ran out. After eating their horses, the defenders were down to consuming rats and snakes. They always had water, though, the Asante allowing them to come out of the fort to draw water from a nearby stream.

Hodgson decided to make a break for the coast, leaving a small force to hold the fort. As the defenders poured artillery and machine-gun fire at the besiegers, Hodgson led his party – some twenty whites, six hundred Hausa soldiers and about eight hundred African civilians – out of the fort. The white women were carried in litters.

Incredibly, Hodgson chose to take all his furniture and household goods, which had to be lugged by 106 starving and staggering porters. Lady Hodgson afterwards told of seeing a porter collapse and die under his load. She did not say whether it was part of her household effects.

The column fought its way through Asante attacks to safety. After repeated Asante attacks on the fort had been beaten off, the siege was broken by a strong relief force.

Asante resistance continued, however, prompting the British to resort to tactics that in modern times might have raised questions about war crimes. Untrained levies, informally known as 'locusts', were formed for the purpose of breaking public morale.[2] Following behind the troops, the 'locusts' looted and destroyed villages and burned crops, at times raping women and taking them and their children into forced labour.

The British in the end subdued the Asante but did not consider it prudent to allow King Prempe to return until 1924. When he died seven years later the British felt secure enough to install his successor, Prempe II, as Asantehene, king of the Asante, for that office was now only one of tradition, not of power.

CHAPTER 13

BEST FOR THE SUBJECT RACE

Alien invasion was nothing new in the history of the Egyptians. Over some ten centuries the lower Nile had been occupied by Assyrians and Persians, by Alexander's Greeks and by Romans, by Caliphate Arabs from across the Red Sea, by Mamluks and Ottoman Turks, by the French and by the British.

In the case of the latter two powers it was more a matter of financial and economic hegemony than military conquest, but still it irked the people of the Nile. It was bad enough having to put up with the foreign control of key aspects of their government through the caretaker administrative system constructed by the British and the French. On top of that there had been a massive influx of Europeans who had begun buying up property. By the eighties, tens of thousands of Europeans were living in Egypt, attracted by its ancient glamour, its sunshine and the economic opportunities and security seemingly offered by virtual European administration.

Resentment boiled up in 1882 in a military coup led by Colonel Urabi Pasha, one of the Egyptians whom Khedive Ismail had admitted to the officer ranks of the army. As head of what amounted to a national government, Urabi dictated terms to Khedive Tewfik.

Ismail's sale of his Suez Canal shares to the British had not solved Egypt's financial problems, and in 1881 its debt to the European banks was more than seven times greater than its average annual exports.[1] Most Egyptians saw Tewfik as a weak stooge of Britain and France, and Urabi manifestly agreed with that assessment.

The two powers responded to Urabi's coup with a joint Note demanding his resignation, and backed it by placing a joint British-French fleet off Alexandria. Urabi's government saw no alternative but to resign, but was immediately reinstated by popular demand. Hatred of Europeans was expressed so vehemently in the streets that many began to leave. In a matter of weeks about fourteen thousand had fled by way of the European warships.

The European banks, shaken by the coup, were even more shaken when the anti-European sentiment erupted in rioting in Alexandria and 40 foreigners were killed. Though Urabi's troops restored order, there were demands in Europe for intervention as Egyptian stocks dropped on European markets. British efforts to work out a joint plan of action with the French were rejected by the French parliament.

Urabi meanwhile attempted to strengthen his hand against the Europeans by upgrading the coastal batteries at Alexandria with modern German artillery pieces. The

A caravel of the kind that enabled Portuguese maritime explorers to open the world to European penetration.

Cape Town, the 'Tavern of the Seas', became a busy port of call for sailing vessels of many nations once the Dutch had settled there. *(National Archives)*

A street scene in British-occupied Cape Town is depicted accurately if somewhat stylistically in this contemporary drawing of Dutch burghers going to church.
(Charles D'Oyly; William Fehr Collection)

Going to the Protestant Church.

Settlement on the Cape Colony's wild frontier took all the courage the British settlers of 1820 could muster after they had been landed on the beach at Algoa Bay, as shown in this contemporary painting.
(C van der Berg; William Fehr Collection)

The discomforts of sailing to the Cape on an East Indiaman could be severe – though never as dramatic as suggested in this cartoon by George Cruikshank.
(William Fehr Collection)

Xhosa attacks like this assault on a waggon were a frequent danger faced by the British settlers in the eastern Cape.
(*Library of Parliament*)

British dragoons charge Xhosa warriors in an action on the Gwanga during the Frontier Wars. In most of the set-piece battles the Xhosa lost against the superior firepower and mobility of the British troops and the settlers.
(*William Fehr Collection*)

Travel was often a difficult and dangerous business, as illustrated in this contemporary painting of a waggon crossing a river during a thunderstorm.
(*Edward Austen; William Fehr Collection*)

As long as they were on their horses or behind laagered waggons, the whites, armed with rifles, enjoyed a formidable advantage in clashes with indigenous armies armesd mainly with spears. The balance was tipped further by even a small cannon such as this one used by the Voortrekkers – who called it Ou Grietjie – in the Battle of Blood River.
(*Library of Parliament*)

Unbridged rivers were only a temporary obstacle to European armies as they spread their dominance inland into Africa. In this 1852 painting, British and colonial troops are shown fording the Orange River.
(*H Martens; Library of Parliament*)

Besides the hazards of unknown Africa, David Livingstone had to face the wrath of his mother-in-law, Mary Moffatt, for taking his wife and children on his first journey of exploration, during which he found Lake Ngami, depicted here in a contemporary engraving in the British illustrated periodical *The Graphic*. (*Library of Parliament*)

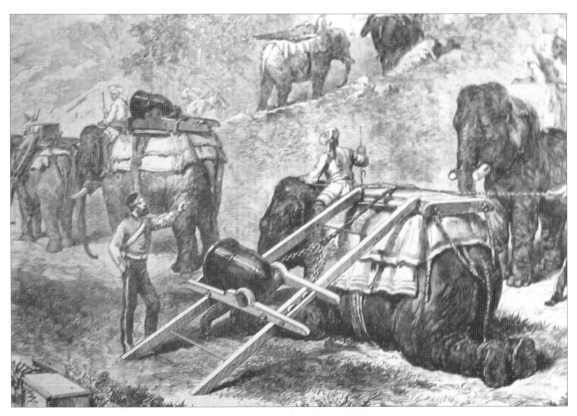

For General Robert Napier's expedition against Emperor Theodore, the heavy guns are loaded onto Indian elephants to be carried up into the roadless Abyssinian mountains. (*Illustrated London News*)

British troops of the Black Watch, having changed their customary Scottish kilts for tropical trousers, form a two-way firing line to fight off an ambush by Asante soldiers during Wolseley's march on Kumase in 1873.
(*Illustrated London News; Library of Parliament*)

The British army's fighting square proved its effectiveness in Africa against poorly armed indigenous forces.

With one rank standing, another kneeling, and sometimes a third lying prone, and each rank firing in repeated sequence, the square could pour out unbroken fire against attack from all sides.
(*Illustrated London News*)

Henry Morton Stanley pictured in the bow of his dismantlable boat, the *Lady Alice*, on his epic exploration of the Congo River.
(*Illustrated London News; Library of Parliament*)

The Battle of Abu Klea was a brief but bloody incident in General Garnet Wolseley's painstaking advance up the Nile to rescue General Charles Gordon. For once, a British square was broken, even if briefly. (*Illustrated London News*)

The advance guard of the Pioneer Corps crosses the Tuli River from Bechuanaland to begin Cecil Rhodes's seizure of Mashonaland. (*Illustrated London News; Library of Parliament*)

Although Rhodes's Pioneers ostensibly occupied Mashonaland with Lobengula's consent, they nevertheless deemed it necessary to form a defensive laager at night against the possibility of attack by his impis. This photograph shows the first laager at Tuli River. (*W Ellerton Fry Portfolio; Library of Parliament*)

Africa's hinterlands were opened to massive European penetration by the railways, sometimes laid at speed through virgin bush in order to meet a political imperative. Here a crew lays the first line into Rhodesia. (*Books of Zimbabwe*)

For some Africans, the colonisation of their countries by Europeans made little difference to their way of life. But for others, such as these ragged and heavily chained prisoners in German South West Africa, it brought misery. (*Namibia Archives*)

People needing relatively quick passage in southern Africa relied on stage coaches drawn by horses or mules, until these were supplanted by the railways. Here the last coach on the run to Johannesburg leaves Pretoria. (*National Archives*)

Many of the Boers of South Africa were unsophisticated farming people, close to the earth, like the family pictured here; which led the colonial British in South Africa to view them generally as inferiors. (*Museum Africa*)

Urban Boers of the late 19th century, such as this group, were generally more sophisticated than their country cousins but were no less resistant to British designs on their republics. (*Museum Africa*)

The men who developed the Rand gold mines and their supply services were overwhelmingly foreigners, predominantly British, and usually adventurous and enterprising individuals, not overly concerned with the history and sensitivities of the Boers. (*Museum Africa*)

As South Africa's underground wealth was uncovered, power politics seemed to swirl centrifugally around Kimberley's Big Hole and the Rand gold mines. In this early photograph the Big Hole is already deep, as shown by the buildings on its rim. (*National Archives*)

British ambitions of consolidation in South Africa were lampooned in a cartoon showing the Colonial Secretary, 'Pushful Joe' Chamberlain, trying to glue together a piece of chinaware representing the British colonies and the Boer republics. (*Library of Parliament*)

British soldiers disembark at Cape Town to reinforce the troops that had suffered defeats in the early part of the Boer War. (*National Archives*)

The Boers who fought Queen Victoria's armies were almost all civilians who went into battle in their everyday clothing. Typical is this group photographed outside their tent (with biltong drying in the background).
(*National Archives*)

Before and during the Boer War, public sentiment in Britain was both influenced and expressed by propagandistic cartoons such as this one, titled A Boer's Cheek, showing a whip-wielding Boer trampling blacks and kicking British soldiers. (*T Merry; Library of Parliament*)

When, after heavy fighting, the Gordon Highlanders charged the Boer positions at Elandslaagte with fixed bayonets, the Boers leaped on their horses and fled – all except one artilleryman who stood, wounded and unarmed but defiant. He was taken prisoner. (*Illustrated London News; South African National Museum of Military History, Johannesburg*)

Life in the colonies could be hard for Europeans who missed the bright lights of home. But it had its compensations, as these Germans found in South West Africa. Colonel Victor Franke, the military commander, holds a pet cheetah on a chain while he and a fellow officer are served wine by an orderly. (*Namibian Archives*)

With colonialism came tourism – but only in the safer parts of Africa. Shepheard's Hotel in Cairo became an internationally famous watering hole as Europeans came in thousands to savour the ancient fascination of the Nile. (*Thomas Cook Archives*)

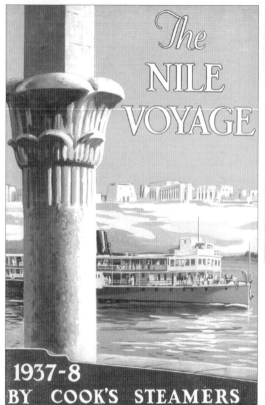

South African troops cross the Ruaha River in East Africa in their pursuit of the elusive German commander, Colonel Paul von Lettow-Vorbeck, during the First World War. (*South African National Museum of Military History, Johannesburg*)

Travel posters such as this one advertising sNile cruises drew Europeans in numbers to Africa in the period between the world wars. (*Thomas Cook Archives*)

Only white and Coloured South Africans bore arms in the First World War but all were volunteers and many died in Africa, the Middle East and Europe. Here infantrymen of the Transvaal Scottish Regiment rest by the roadside after action on the Western Front. (*South African National Museum of Military History, Johannesburg*)

British demanded that he dismantle the batteries; Urabi refused, and the Royal Navy destroyed them with a massive bombardment. Urabi withdrew his troops inland and remained defiant. Fearing that he would sabotage the Suez Canal, the British parliament approved the landing of a protective force. Again the French declined to participate, leaving the field to the British – a decision that was to end any further hope of French influence in Egypt.

While British warships occupied the Suez Canal, Wolseley came ashore in August with an invasion force of 31 000 troops and set up a base at Ismailia, half-way along the Canal's length. He did more than protect the Canal: in a dawn attack, he overwhelmed Urabi's smaller force at Tel el-Kebir on the railway line from Ismailia to Cairo. Then he sent his cavalry dashing 100 kilometres to seize the capital. Within days Tewfik was back in charge, and the European bankers' investments were being protected by a British garrison. Urabi was exiled to Ceylon.

The occupation was fiercely criticised in Britain, where many saw it essentially as a move to protect the interests of Egypt's creditors in Britain. Lord Randolph Churchill condemned what he called this 'bondholders' war' as a departure from the English tradition of not interfering in the affairs of other countries on account of debts owed to private interests in Britain.

Gladstone had promised only a brief intervention, but his government declared Tewfik's regime to be so ineffective that the British had to stay on in order to keep the country on an even keel. In doing so they arbitrarily ended the dual control with the French. The British ended up ruling Egypt as a *de facto* colony, even though it was supposed to be an independent state owing allegiance to the Sultan of Turkey. Not until the outbreak of the First World War would the farce be ended with Egypt being declared a British protectorate. The occupation begun by Wolseley was to last in various forms for 70 years, ending only with the nationalisation of the Suez Canal in 1952.

Sir Evelyn Baring (later Lord Cromer), who had been Britain's man on the joint-control team, was appointed as British consul-general in Egypt. In effect he ran the show and Tewfik did what he was told.

Baring's appointment was a major step in the progression of British presence in Africa from trade to colonial rule. There had been nothing quite like it since the appointment of the British governors in the Cape. Political imperatives aside, it reflected the British vision of themselves as a superior race with not only an opportunity but also a moral obligation to govern and uplift less civilised races, especially those in Africa. Cromer expressed a basic element of the ethos in a commentary on the Egyptian masses: 'We need not always enquire too closely what these people – who are all, nationally speaking, more or less *in statu pupillari* – themselves think is in their own interests … it is essential that each special issue should be decided mainly with reference to what, by the light of Western knowledge and experience … we conscientiously think is best for the subject race.'

British garrisons were left in Cairo and Alexandria. The Egyptian army was placed under Sir Evelyn Wood of Asante and Zululand fame. Wolseley, a hero once more, returned to England, but not for long; the Nile was still in his destiny.

★ ★ ★ ★

Baring had barely settled into his new job in Cairo when he found himself with a war on his hands. It was not seen as a war at first, just a bit of insubordination by some Islamic zealot down in the Sudan, something that had sprung up at about the same time as Urabi was staging his revolt in Cairo.

Life had changed unpleasantly for most of the Sudanese after Gordon had departed in a huff at the deposing of Khedive Ismail. Egyptian officials had quickly revived the corruption and oppression stamped out by Gordon. The Sudanese perhaps hated the Egyptians even more than the Egyptians hated the Europeans.

It required only a leader to transform the resentment into insurrection, and one duly arose: Mohammed Ahmed Ibn el-Sayyid Abdullah, an apprentice boatbuilder of Abba island on the Nile, who convinced himself and his followers that he was the Mahdi, divinely ordained to lead Islam to cover the world. A man of great personal magnetism and moving oratory, the Mahdi soon collected a following and took them into the desert to begin a holy war against the Egyptians.

While Wolseley was defeating Urabi at Tel el-Kebir, the Mahdi was besieging an Egyptian garrison at El Obeid. The British had not considered the threat serious enough to divert Wolseley to lift the siege. But when the Mahdi captured the town early in 1883 Cairo sent 8 000 Egyptian troops under Colonel William Hicks, a retired Indian Army officer, to put down the revolt. Hicks got his force lost in the desert, and it was annihilated by the Mahdi.

Fanned by this victory, the Mahdi's cause swept like a desert storm across the Sudan, isolating most of the Egyptian garrisons. Among these were the outposts still manned by the European officials appointed by Gordon. In Darfur, far out in the desert to the west, was Rudolph Carl von Slatin, who had come to Gordon after serving in the Austrian army. In Bahr al-Ghazal, further south, was Frank Lupton, a former seaman from England. South of that, cut off in Equatoria, was the extraordinary Emin Pasha, formerly a German doctor named Eduard Schnitzer who had embraced Islam and an Arab name.

Hopelessly cut off, Slatin and Lupton surrendered and became Muslims to avoid execution. Emin retreated with his garrison up the Nile deep into Equatoria.

The Mahdi now had a huge following, despite – or perhaps because of – the cruelty with which he imposed his will.

Both Gladstone and Baring were in favour of abandoning the Sudan, but that would have meant also abandoning the Egyptian garrisons. There was a parallel fear that if left unchallenged the Mahdi might conquer Egypt, or that Tewfik would call in Turkish troops to fight him off.

Among the British public there were strong feelings for the restoration of what Gordon had created in the Sudan. A campaign was begun to have him sent back to conquer the Mahdi, avenge Hicks, and restore justice and good governance.

Gordon had been at something of a loose end since leaving Khartoum, a major-general without a command, an odd-job-man of imperialism. In January 1884 he accepted an offer from King Leopold to help Stanley run the Congo, but almost immediately was persuaded by Lord Granville, the foreign secretary, to go to the Sudan instead. The tragedy that was to overtake Gordon was already beginning in

London with indecision about what he was supposed to do in the Sudan – report on the situation in general, report on the modalities of evacuating the Egyptian garrisons, or conduct an actual evacuation.

After Gordon had taken office in Khartoum in February as governor-general of the Sudan, the Mahdi besieged the town. Gladstone refused to budge from his policy of 'disengagement and disinvolvement' in the Sudan despite protests by both Baring and Queen Victoria. Gladstone was convinced that Gordon was capable of evacuating the Khartoum garrison in his steamboats. He suspected that Gordon, rather than leave the Sudanese to the Mahdi's tyranny, was trying to trick the cabinet into reoccupying the country. His suspicions may not have been far wrong but he was hopelessly out in his appreciation of the danger Gordon was in.

Debate over whether a relief expedition should be sent to Khartoum raged in Britain. Public rallies demanding that Gordon be rescued were ignored by the prime minister, even though he was now being jeered in the streets. Only when his minister for war, Lord Hartington, threatened to resign did Gladstone agree to send a relief expedition.

Wolseley was appointed to command the 7 000-man force. Between Cairo and Khartoum lay 2 400 kilometres of desert. Wolseley decided to take his force up the Nile all the way rather than cut in from the Red Sea. He ordered the building of 800 whalers in which the infantrymen and some of the supplies would be towed or rowed up the Nile while the cavalry and the camel corps rode up the banks. Draught camels would carry much of the supplies. Nile steamers based between the cataracts would carry some of the men and supplies.

There were echoes of Magdala in the situation. But in this instance the expedition was doomed from the start by mistakes, first by Gladstone's delays, then by further delays on the march because of a failure to provide enough camels and enough coal for the steamers.

While Wolseley's force was painfully hauling its whalers up through the cataracts, Gordon attempted to evacuate Stewart and the few remaining Europeans on a steamer, but it ran aground and all on board were caught and executed.

At Korti, where the Nile completes a huge loop, Wolseley sent Brigadier-General Sir Herbert Stewart on a 300-kilometre dash across the land enclosed by the loop, to rejoin the Nile at Metemmeh. Nearing the wells at Abu Klea, Stewart's column of 1 200 men found the way barred by the main Mahdist force, 10 000 strong.

It was here that Wolseley's men had their first sight of the opponent they would come to respect, the fighting man they commonly (though erroneously) called the dervish, a lean, barefooted warrior armed with sword and spear if not gun, and wearing a white calf-length *jellabah* on which were sewn large coloured squares of cloth.

As Stewart's thirsty men advanced under fire in a loosely formed hollow square towards the wells, the Mahdists charged and broke into the disorganised square. In desperation, the opposite side of the square was turned round and fired volleys into the melee of flashing swords, darting bayonets, shouting men, bellowing camels and billowing dust and smoke. The volleys killed some of the British troops caught in the melee, but the Mahdists were forced to retreat. Among the British dead was the second-in-command, Colonel Burnaby.

The battle of Abu Klea on 17 January 1885 lasted less than an hour but found a special place in British military annals. It inspired the poem by Sir Henry Newbolt that came to epitomise one of the Victorian era's special characteristics, the belief that the Empire was made on the sportsfields of the elite schools:

> The sand of the desert is sodden red, –
> Red with the wreck of a square that broke; –
> The Gatling's jammed and the Colonel dead,
> And the regiment blind with dust and smoke.
> The river of death had brimmed its banks,
> And England's far, and Honour a name,
> But the voice of a schoolboy rallies the ranks:
> 'Play up! Play up! And play the game!'

Rudyard Kipling viewed the breaking of the square from a different perspective, that of the common soldier, paying tribute to the bravery of the 'dervishes', whom some called 'fuzzy-wuzzies' because of their bushy hair:

> So 'ere's to you, Fuzzy-Wuzzy, at your 'ome in the Soudan;
> You're a pore benighted 'eathen but a first-class fightin' man;
> An' 'ere's to you, Fuzzy-Wuzzy, with your 'ayrick 'ead of 'air –
> You big black boundin' beggar – for you broke a British square!

Though briefly broken at Abu Klea, the British square was extremely effective in the Sudan – as elsewhere – because the Mahdists obligingly persisted in charging it. Sometimes with a first rank lying prone, always with a second rank kneeling and a third standing, and each rank firing in repeated sequence, the square was able to throw out a virtually unbroken hail of bullets.

In another attack near Metemmeh the formidable square again prevailed, but now the commander, Herbert Stewart, was among the dead. The command passed down to Sir Charles Wilson. Instead of sailing immediately with a relief force on steamers sent down to Metemmeh by Gordon, Wilson wasted three days with a reconnaissance up the river.

Meanwhile, the Mahdists stormed Khartoum and began to massacre those within. Gordon was killed on the steps of his palace, and his head was cut off and presented to the Mahdi.

Wilson's steamers reached Khartoum two days later and turned back under heavy fire from the Mahdist forces now lining the ramparts.

Wolseley wept when the news reached him at Korti. Britain was stunned. A distraught Queen Victoria blamed Gladstone. The prime minister, however, blamed those who had insisted on Gordon going to Khartoum in the first place. He narrowly survived a motion of censure in Parliament, but his public esteem was irreversibly damaged.

Wolseley retreated to Cairo to regroup and resupply. Now, however, London's thinking was changed by a Russian incursion into Afghanistan. Fearing that Britain might soon be obliged to go to war against Russia to protect the northern approaches to India, the government ordered the withdrawal of all the troops to Egypt, leaving the Sudan to the Mahdi.

Lupton died while labouring in the Mahdi's boatyards at Khartoum, but Slatin escaped to Cairo and joined the Egyptian army. Messages were got to Emin at Wadelai on the upper Nile urging him to try to evacuate his garrison community to the coast, but he replied that he lacked the necessary transport and supplies. He stayed on, growing crops and keeping his steamers on Lake Albert in working order.

Only when one of the Europeans trapped with him, Dr Junker, a German explorer, managed to make his way out to the coast in 1886 did Emin come to anyone's mind again. Now, suddenly, there was another story for the British papers, another interesting castaway to be rescued.

Mackinnon, the shipping magnate, saw a rescue mission opening up new trading opportunities in the interior. Under his auspices, a large sum of money was collected for an expedition to bring out Emin and his people. And to lead it, who better than HM Stanley?

Stanley was nominally committed to Leopold, but the king released him for the expedition for he saw in it a chance to add Equatoria to his Congo domain. Leopold enjoined him accordingly, while Mackinnon commissioned him to establish a trade route to Buganda and clear the way for a British East Africa Company. Emin was to be offered the choice of opening a trading station on Lake Victoria for the company or governing Equatoria for Leopold.

Leopold's imperatives perhaps explain why Stanley chose a hugely circuitous route instead of heading straight for Emin from the east coast. Starting in Zanzibar in February 1887, he obtained Sultan Barghash's approval of Mackinnon's trading plans. Having sailed on round the Cape, Stanley disembarked at the Congo mouth, and headed upriver with Tippu Tib, more than six hundred porters and a number of European assistants.

Stanley's journey up the Congo was as tormented and bloody as his first one down it. When the ragged remnants of his party met Emin on the shore of Lake Albert in April 1888, Stanley was flabbergasted to learn from an elegantly white-suited Emin that he refused to be rescued unless adequate arrangements were made for the welfare of his charges. He refused Leopold's job offer and hesitated over Mackinnon's. He decided to go out with Stanley, however, when he learned that Mahdist forces were at last approaching.

Emin, far from being grateful for his rescue, led a German expedition aimed at grabbing possession for Germany of Buganda and other territory around Lake Victoria before the British could put their own claims beyond dispute. Britain's claims were in fact recognised by Germany while Emin was still trekking into the interior. Repeatedly ignoring orders to return, he marched blindly on like a sick animal seeking death until, deep in the Congo, his throat was cut by Arab slavers.

Though Emin's rescue had been largely pointless, Stanley's efforts helped establish Mackinnon and Britain in dominant positions in what became Uganda and Kenya. He settled in England, married, entered Parliament, was knighted in 1899, and died in his bed five years later.

Stanley had become a hero at the end, but never a loved one. There was an element of hypocrisy in the diffidence with which Europeans honoured him at his graveside, pointing to the blood on his hands from so roughly unveiling the last of hidden Africa – the continent they were themselves now busy raping.

CHAPTER 14

THE GATE-CRASHER

The dividing up of what Leopold had called the 'magnificent African cake' was a fairly leisurely business at first. Only when Otto von Bismarck came barging in did it become a scramble.

Before that, the division of the newly opened African heartland had been a relatively restrained affair. It was a superficially polite tea party at which two of the older members of the colonial club, Britain and France, helped themselves to another slice or two of the huge cake from their respective sides of the table. The founder member, Portugal, was still having trouble digesting her early mouthfuls and was wondering whether she should have some more. And the newcomer, Leopold, wondered how big a chunk he could sneak without the others noticing.

When Bismarck, the German chancellor, gate-crashed the party in 1884 and grabbed three biggish slices that Britain had been eyeing, the cake suddenly began to look rather small, and acquiring some of what remained became a matter of urgency.

The British had been less inclined to colonial adventure than the French, who were looking to restore the pride lost in the Franco-Prussian War and in Egypt. Some envisaged France creating a 'second India in Africa'. The thrust was on the Mediterranean littoral, the Senegal and the Niger. Some in Paris envisioned the presence on the Niger being extended to Lake Chad and even all the way to the Nile, gaining control of its headwaters and blocking Britain's back door to Egypt. There were also ambitions to open links southward to Ivory Coast and Dahomey.

Both the French and the Germans were aware of the financial vulnerability that Britain had acquired with her control of Egypt. Alone, the British could ill afford to govern Egypt and to service its debts; they needed the cooperation of the other powers in backing the necessary loans. That handicap was a major element in the initiation of the Scramble, forcing Britain into actions it might not otherwise have taken even while at the same time limiting its options. Although Britain was the greatest imperial and naval power, no longer was it the unchallenged industrial giant of the world: its industrial production was being overtaken by Germany and the United States, both of whom had made big advances in technology.

Besides the Egyptian burden, Gladstone's government was preoccupied with Gordon's entrapment in the Sudan and with the troublesome Boers in South Africa. New commitments in Africa were to be avoided. Sentiment in Whitehall generally favoured a situation that would leave the British in control of most of the lower half of the Bulge, and the French dominating everything to the north.

This line of thought was abandoned, however, when the French became increasingly acquisitive in the lower Bulge. Paris had revived the Porto Novo protectorate, Mattei was wooing the Oil Rivers chiefs, and Brazza was up to something similar in the Congo. Whitehall's reaction was to send the British consul in West Africa, Edward Hewett, on an impromptu expedition in 1884 to sign treaties with chiefs that would give Britain a protectorate over the coast from Lagos to Cameroon.

It was not a step lightly undertaken, for it meant that Whitehall would have to abandon its 'informal empire' policy. This strategy had allowed British traders to operate independently wherever there were prospects of African commodities being exchanged for British manufactures. Only if necessary would the government send a gunboat to protect the trade. The royal charter, such as the one that would be given to Goldie's company in 1886, was an extension of the policy. There was no time for anything like that when Hewett was sent off, however; this was something of an emergency, and not even Goldie's company was in a position to administer all of the territory in question.

At the same time, London wanted to guard against being squeezed out of the vast and possibly rich Congo basin. Turning to their old friends, the Portuguese, the British proposed a treaty affirming Portugal's right to control trade on both banks of the Congo from the sea up to Matadi. That would allow the corking of the bottleneck through which French trade must flow from the basin to the sea. The British, of course, would have a right of free passage. The treaty was duly signed in May 1884. But London had reckoned without those master manipulators, Leopold and Bismarck.

At the time Germany was seen in Whitehall as not much more of a serious competitor in Africa than Italy, which seemed neither willing nor able to join the Scramble. Unified only relatively recently by Garibaldi, the Italians were just beginning to develop colonial ambitions. Their flag, too, would follow trade, had in fact already been compelled to begin doing so when in 1882 the Italian state had taken over the assets of the Rubattino Navigation Company at Assab in Eritrea. The Italians were still novices at colonialism, however.

As for Berlin, it appeared to have no colonial ambitions at all. Though Germany in 1884 was the strongest military power in continental Europe, it had no navy capable of challenging Britain's fleet or even those of France or Italy, and so seemed ill-equipped for colonial competition. Bismarck had intimated a belief that the costs of maintaining colonies outweighed any advantages. Change was in the offing, however, arising partly from the fear shared by Bismarck and other Germans about their country lying vulnerably, as in a vice, between France and Russia.

Bismarck's fear was not entirely eased by Germany's new industrial and military strength or by non-aggression treaties signed with Russia, Austria and Italy. Other Germans, however, began to think of their country as a world power with a foreign empire. German banking interests in particular developed an interest in Africa. Societies promoting colonialism began to form.

One of these was the Company for German Colonisation, founded by Dr Carl Peters. This weedy academic seemed an unlikely pioneer. Behind his steel-rimmed spectacles, however, was a single-mindedness that tolerated no obstacles. He landed in East Africa in 1884 on a private expedition to sign colonial treaties, ignoring warnings that they would not be recognised by Berlin. That remained the official position when Peters emerged from the interior a few months later, tattered and starved but clutching a sheaf of treaties.

Bismarck now perceived that colonies in Africa might help in his preoccupation with keeping Germany safe from her neighbours. He was uncomfortably aware of the hostility to Germany that simmered dangerously in France over her defeat in 1871. He looked to distract the French from this preoccupation by fomenting rivalry between them and the British. One way of doing that, he figured, would be to stir up colonial competition in Africa by acquiring a colony or two of his own.

Bismarck appears at the same time to have begun to see some commercial benefit in colonies, especially if international free trade were to be blocked by what seemed to be a rising protectionist sentiment in Europe. The protectionist bogey was already scaring German traders in West Africa, notably in Togo and Cameroon, who saw themselves being shut out by Hewett's treaty-signing expedition and the Anglo-Portuguese agreement on the Congo mouth. They began to urge Bismarck to acquire territory in Africa before it was all seized by the other powers. Public sentiment seemed to give them some backing.

Opportunities had already been opened by German traders – and missionaries, too – and not only in West Africa. In South West Africa an unofficial German foothold had been established in 1882 at Angra Pequena (now Lüderitz in Namibia) by Adolf Lüderitz, a Bremen trader exploiting the rich guano deposits in the rocky inlet. Bismarck had refused a request by Lüderitz for a protectorate, figuring it pointless when the only viable harbour on that long, desert coast, Walfisch Bay (now Walvis Bay), had already been annexed by Britain in 1878.

Having changed his mind about colonies, Bismarck made his move in May 1884, the same month in which Britain and Portugal signed their Congo agreement. He sent the German explorer Gustav Nachtigal off in a gunboat on the pretext of investigating trade prospects, but with secret orders to annex Togo, Cameroon and Angra Pequena. Behind the latter annexation were two purposes: first, to block out any other European power from South West Africa, and second, to use it as a beachhead for expanding German possession into central Africa. In the words of Bismarck's private secretary, Heinrich von Kusserow, 'The aim is to secure a route to the Upper Congo and Zambezi.'[1]

Before making the move, Bismarck had cautiously sounded out London about its interest in Angra Pequena, which sufficiently alerted Whitehall to now ask the Cape government to annex all of the territory from the Orange River up to Walvis Bay, including Angra Pequena. To counter that initiative, Bismarck pulled the Egyptian string, threatening to withhold Germany's backing for a new British loan for Egypt.

While Whitehall dithered in bewilderment over Bismarck's sudden colonial interest, the Chancellor planted his flags – in Togo and Cameroon in July 1884, and at Angra Pequena in August, with a couple of gunboats hanging about to under-score the point. A few weeks later Bismarck proclaimed the annexation of the entire coast between the Orange and Cunene Rivers, from South Africa to Portuguese Angola, leaving Walvis Bay as a British enclave. When Hewett arrived at Cameroon with his parcel of treaties late in July the German flag was already flapping above the palms.

Bismarck's next move was of the same pattern, but more closely camouflaged. Noting the opposition by other parties to the Anglo-Portuguese treaty on the Con-go, Bismarck persuaded the French to join him in proposing that the issue of trade and navigation on the river be resolved at an international conference to be held in Berlin. The French were happy to oblige. Jules Ferry, the prime minister, believed he had already protected Frances's own position on the Congo by obtaining from Leopold a first option on the interests of the International Association of the Con-go if these should ever be sold. Leopold, knowing he would never sell them, had been happy to grant the option in return for the French government's agreeing not to interfere with the association's activities.

Leopold had at the same time persuaded President Chester Arthur of the Unit-ed States and the US Senate formally to recognise the IAC. He sold it to them as a body aiming not to profit from the Congo but to develop it into a democratic and stable free state (or states), open for trade with all other nations. Once the state became economically and politically viable, Leopold's association would withdraw and be disbanded, and the state would become independent, a beacon of civilisation and open trade in Africa. It would be the greatest instrument yet devised for taking to primitive Africa the 'three Cs': Commerce, Christianity and Civilisation.

With Germany and France also recognising his Congo state, Leopold was in a strong position when Bismarck's conference opened in Berlin in November 1884. The United States was present as an observer. Britain had no choice but to at-tend, since Parliament had refused to ratify the Anglo-Portuguese Congo treaty, and France and Germany refused to recognise it. Bismarck persuaded London to recog-nise Leopold's Congo Free State by again jerking the Egyptian loan string.

The Portuguese, under pressure from Bismarck, found themselves giving Leopold the north bank of the Congo at the mouth, in return for being allowed to retain the coastal enclave of Cabinda to the north of that.

From the conference came the Berlin Act of 1885, guaranteeing freedom of nav-igation on the Congo and free trade in its vast basin. Looking beyond the Congo, the conference also agreed that the powers should prove effective occupation be-fore annexing any more territory in Africa. This was intended to nullify Portugal's vague claims to large stretches of the African coastline, but its greater effect was to force the other powers to define clearly their own claims – and in effect to quickly get some if they didn't already have any.

In this sense the conference set rules of a sort for how the Scramble should be conducted. It did not complete the division of the African cake. That process was completed later, over a longer period, mostly by fixing boundaries where the powers' field men bumped noses.

All the leading powers recognised the Congo Free State during or after the conference, in effect handing Leopold administrative control of the whole Congo basin. The Belgian king had pulled off one of the biggest confidence tricks in history.

★ ★ ★ ★

While Leopold gloated over his covert triumph, Bismarck pursued his own imperial skulduggery.

The Berlin Conference was barely over when Bismarck widened his African land-grab by declaring a German protectorate where Peters had obtained his treaties in East Africa. The chancellor had in fact secretly signed Peters's charter while the conference was still in session. The declaration came like a starting gun for the most hectic period of the Scramble.

Sultan Barghash of Zanzibar angrily protested against Berlin's trespass on his preserves, but was silenced when German warships dropped anchor off Zanzibar and trained their guns on his palace. Even the British, his nominal allies, were forced into silence by their vulnerability in Egypt and by their fear of pushing the Germans into an alliance with the French in the contest for the still-unsecured pieces of West Africa. Not for another three years would Baring get the Egyptian albatross off Britannia's neck by wiping out Cairo's debts. By then Africa had largely been parcelled out.

This situation led to Britain and Germany agreeing in 1886 on a division of the East African territories. The border of what became Kenya and Tanganyika was set along a line running north-west from Usambara on the coast to Lake Victoria, with a dog-leg that placed Mount Kilimanjaro, Africa's highest mountain, just inside German territory. The division gave Germany the cool highlands around Kilimanjaro but it gave Britain the larger highlands near Mount Kenya, Africa's other peak of permanent snow. The German colony's southern border with Portuguese East Africa (now Mozambique) was fixed with the Portuguese at the Rovuma River.

The demarcation left undefined the area beyond Lake Victoria, what is now Uganda. Peters and Mackinnon began a race to claim it at the time Junker came out with the news of Emin's situation in 1886. As a backup to Stanley's expedition, Mackinnon despatched another, led by a white hunter, Frederick Jackson, who was to link up with Emin at Wadelai in case Stanley did not make it coming up the Congo River.

Bismarck, now ostensibly cooperating with Salisbury in the division of Africa, placed Africa out of bounds to Peters's private expedition. When he arrived at Zanzibar in June 1889 most of his arms and trade goods were confiscated. Undeterred, he landed secretly on the mainland near Lamu with a few askaris and porters, and headed inland.

On finding that Stanley had taken Emin out of Equatoria, Jackson went off to hunt elephants, leaving Peters to secure an informal agreement with Kabaka Mwanga giving Germany a protectorate over his territory. But events were conspiring against Peters.

In 1889 Bismarck proposed to London an exchange of some African territory for the tiny island of Heligoland off Germany's North Sea coast. A British possession since the Napoleonic Wars, the island would allow Britain if it so wished to interdict shipping in the Kiel Canal, which had been cut between the Baltic and the North Sea to enable German shipping to avoid the narrow passages between the Danish islands. The following year the young Kaiser Wilhelm II, only two years on the throne, threw German politics into confusion by firing Bismarck and replacing him with Count Georg von Caprivi. Wilhelm nullified the assurance given by Bismarck that Germany had no interest in Buganda. Emin was sent heading back to Equatoria in an apparent effort to secure it for the Kaiser.

Now Salisbury played the Heligoland ace. He offered the island to Germany in exchange for a final settlement of the German and British colonial boundaries in Africa. Besides Uganda, Britain got affirmation of its colonial title to Zanzibar, Kenya, Uganda and Nyasaland. Germany got recognition of its claims to Tanganyika, Togo and Cameroon, some other small concessions in West Africa, and the strip of land, only 80 kilometres wide and 500 kilometres long, extending South West Africa to the Zambezi. This outlandish protuberance was named after Caprivi but it had been conceived in Bismarck's time as a means of gaining access to the centre of the continent, perhaps even to the Congo River's headwaters. A second motive may have been to block Cecil Rhodes's suspected ambition to make the whole sub-continent British territory and to extend it unbroken all the way to Cairo.

The Heligoland deal left both Peters and Emin stranded. Emin, unable to accept it, marched on to his death in the Congo. Peters came to terms with it and spent the rest of his life administering German territory and exploring Africa.

★ ★ ★ ★

The Scramble was not essentially about colonisation for its own rewards. In both its causes and style it extended European politics eccentrically into Africa. This accounted for the strange sense of unreality that prevailed at Berlin, as indeed in the Scramble as a whole, what some historians have called a mood of international hysteria. To some extent this mood was created by economic as well as political factors. Europe's industrialised powers had begun ruthless competition at a time of economic depression. The African land-grab was precautionary rather than predatory, motivated not so much by the expectation of great profits as by a desire for insurance against possible protectionist trading in Africa by European rivals as the competition for markets became tougher.

Thus, while the free-trade stipulation of the Berlin Conference was ostensibly aimed against protectionism, the powers took the precaution of grabbing as much of Africa as possible just in case that stipulation came to be ignored. It was a matter of protecting their interests without putting the peace in Europe at risk.

It was essentially about insurance, but each power wanted to keep the cost of the insurance as low as possible. Thus the powers ended up possessing territories they were as reluctant to develop as they were to part with. The rule became long-range government on the cheap.

Like all other aspects of the European experience in Africa, colonisation came late to the continent. By the time of the Scramble, the European powers had staked claims to almost every other colonisable piece of the world, even remote Pacific islands. Africa, it seems, had been just too big and forbidding, disadvantages that had outweighed any advantages discernible to the Europeans.

While the Scramble was going on, Africa was the subject of intense interest, examination, discussion and competition, all conducted in an atmosphere of unreality. Once it had all been divided up reality returned, the interest waned, and the continent lapsed into relative quietude for the next six decades.

African colonies in many cases were of no great benefit to their conquerors, certainly not in the beginning and in some cases never. Once having acquired them, the powers were in some cases not quite sure what to do with them. In the end some of them abandoned their colonies almost as precipitately as they had acquired them, happy to get rid of the burden.

Since it took twenty to thirty years to make a colony self-supporting, most of the territories won in the Scramble were a liability to their possessors for a large part of their tenure. Few colonies produced rich profits for either foreign governments or entrepreneurs, and some colonies never even became self-supporting.

Colonialism was less a matter of exploitation than of trying to make colonies pay for themselves and not become a burden on the colonial power's exchequer. The Europeans took the attitude that the conquered must not only submit to subordination but must pay for it as well, through taxes or unpaid labour. This taxing of the indigent amounted to nothing less than forced labour, but was widely practised by all the colonial powers and was prevalent as late as 1960 in the Portuguese colonies. White settlement was of limited value in generating taxable wages since whites were careful about where they traded and even more choosy about where they settled.

Modern historians generally have rejected the Marxist theory of the Scramble being driven by capitalist exploitation, although that certainly was a contributory factor and colonialism was, of course, fundamentally exploitive. No power went into it for philanthropic motives. In the beginning, certainly, the flag tended to follow trade more than the other way round, but the primary motives of the Scramble itself, the brief and frenzied carve-up, were as much political and expedient as economic or ideological. The foreign interests of Europe's governments were often interlocked with those of its traders. If capitalism was not the engine of colonialism, it certainly provided the fuel.

CHAPTER 15

THE IMPERIAL SUPERMAN

Among famous last words, those spoken in 1880 by Sir Owen Lanyon, the British administrator of the annexed Transvaal, must rate fairly high. 'I don't believe,' he said, 'that those cowardly Boers have it in them to fight.'

Three months later, some ten thousand Boers gathered at Paardekraal near Krugersdorp and proclaimed the restoration of the Transvaal republic that Lanyon's predecessor, Shepstone, had annexed for Britain. The Boers set up a temporary capital at Heidelberg, and besieged the British garrisons in Pretoria and six other towns. A British regiment marching from Lydenburg to relieve Pretoria was ambushed at Bronkhorstspruit and shot to pieces.

British reinforcements coming up from Natal were twice beaten back by the Boers. Thinking to command the heights, the British commander, Major-General Sir George Pomeroy Colley, led half his force to the top of a high hill called Majuba, leaving behind their machine-guns. As the Boers climbed up the hill to attack the British positions there was sporadic fighting, but nothing serious enough to prevent the weary Colley from taking a nap. He was woken by rifle fire and saw his troops in rapid retreat as Boers stormed over the crest. Colley was shot in the head, becoming one of the 92 of his force killed in the attack. Another 50 were captured by the Boers, whose own losses were one man dead.

The Battle of Majuba was a blow to Whitehall's aim to confederate the colonies and republics, an aspiration that had been strengthened not only by the discovery of diamonds in South Africa but by the hints of gold wealth as well. The ambition had already been undermined in an ironic way by Chelmsford's defeat of the Zulus, for it had removed one of the chief reasons for the Transvalers having accepted annexation. They had become even less amenable when Gladstone, though he had campaigned against the annexation during the British general election of 1880, refused to terminate it when he won the poll.

Encouraged by their brethren in the Orange Free State, the Transvalers had stepped up their demands for an end to British rule. When Lanyon had uttered his famous last words, the tension was close to snapping, and it did so only a few weeks later at Paardekraal.

Majuba shocked the British and forced them to revise their opinion of the Boer's military prowess. The fighting farmers had whipped the redcoats in four successive engagements. These men were different from the Zulus, the Asante and others the British had encountered in Africa; they had modern rapid-fire, long-range rifles, and they could use them even better than the British. These were farmers and hunters, accustomed to shooting for the pot, and for them shooting stationary British soldiers, whether in bright red jackets or the later khaki, was a doddle. As for charging a British square, that made no sense when you could pick off its ranks from 400 yards while sheltering from their fire behind a rock.

Sir Evelyn Wood, taking over from Colley, negotiated a settlement granting independence to the Transvaal but with a vaguely defined British 'suzerainty' and a British say in native affairs. The British troops marched out to Natal. They would be back, though, for the fighting with the Boers had barely begun.

★ ★ ★ ★

Brass buttons glistening, moustache bristling, General Sir Charles Warren rode stiff-backed at the head of his mixed force of 5 000 British and colonial mounted infantry. Close behind him, slouched in the saddle, rode Cecil Rhodes, diamond magnate and Cape parliamentarian, wearing his customary shapeless hat, crumpled jacket, stained trousers and old tennis shoes.

It was December 1884 and Warren was taking his force from the Cape up to establish British authority in the territory between the Transvaal republic on the east and the newly proclaimed German protectorate on the west, whose eastern border was still not precisely defined.* Through that corridor ran the road to the north, the Missionary Road, the route from the Cape Colony to the large and possibly rich territory in central Africa that had not yet been claimed by any of the European powers.

The immediate problem arose from the presence in the corridor of the two mini-republics of Stellaland and Goshen, formed in 1882 by Boers spilling over from the Transvaal. Their dubious title to the land had been acquired by aiding or duping various feuding Baralong chiefs. Now the little states sat athwart the corridor like a double cork in a bottle, and the feuding continued to fizz around them, bothering the authorities in both the Transvaal and the Cape. Ostensibly to bring order to the situation, President Kruger had declared a protectorate embracing Goshen that would effectively extend the Transvaal's border into the corridor.

Alarm had immediately been aroused among those in Whitehall who feared the corridor being blocked by either a westward extension of the Transvaal or an eastward extension of the German protectorate, or both. Either would put paid to the British Cape-to-Cairo dream, which Rhodes in particular nursed. And a direct link between German territory and the Transvaal would give both Kruger's republic and the Orange Free State an outlet for escape from the British sphere of influence. (Colonialists in Berlin were indeed proposing that the northern part of German South West Africa be extended eastwards all the way to Portuguese East Africa through what is now northern Botswana and Zimbabwe.[1])

The Transvaal's western border had already shifted several times as Kruger's young

---

* The border of the German territory was not formally fixed until the Anglo-German agreement of 1890.

republic sought to define its boundaries. With the London Convention of 1884 the British had persuaded him to accept a line falling short of Stellaland and Goshen and to agree not to extend the Transvaal's boundaries either to the west or to the east without British permission.

Kruger had accordingly made his Goshen-embracing protectorate subject to Britain's approval. That did not allay suspicions in London that he was trying to link up with the Germans, closer cultural kin of the Boers than the British were. Whitehall was uncomfortably aware that Kruger, after signing the London Convention, had stopped off in Berlin and been given warm assurances of friendship and support by Bismarck.

To add to British suspicions, the Germans had begun surveys for a railway running eastwards from Lüderitzbucht (Angra Pequena) into the hinterland desert. For what strange purpose? They were known at the same time to be investigating the acquisition of St Lucia on the east coast, which was perceived to have potentially the best harbour between Durban (formerly Port Natal) and Delagoa Bay (later Lourenço Marques). At the same time Boers from the Transvaal had obtained land from Dinizulu, Cetewayo's successor, on which they had declared the intention of founding the Republic of Vryheid. To Whitehall this looked suspiciously like a ploy by the Transvaal to gain access to the sea. If all these suspected moves came off there would be a German-Boer band across the sub-continent, isolating the Cape and Natal from the rest of Africa.

The British lost no time in preemptively annexing St Lucia and then Pondoland as well, just in case the Germans got ideas of establishing a foothold south of Durban. That left still vulnerable the Missionary Road, what Rhodes, looking ahead, had called 'the Suez Canal' of British trade to the north.

Rhodes had in 1884 been able to persuade Stellaland – though not Goshen – to accept incorporation into the relatively prosperous Cape Colony rather than to merge with the poverty-stricken Transvaal. While the Cape government dithered over whether to accept Stellaland, Kruger had declared his protectorate in and around Goshen, the northernmost of the two mini-states. London had immediately sent Warren to intervene. Kruger in turn had immediately cancelled his protectorate declaration. By then, however, Warren was on the march and not much inclined to turn back.

Warren and his officers were less concerned with resolving territorial disputes than with having a go at the Boers to avenge the humiliation of Majuba. Rhodes, accompanying the expedition in his capacity as Commissioner for Bechuanaland, was concerned with trying to avoid another Majuba, which might lead to a wider conflict, and with securing the corridor for Britain.

It was a delicate situation. The Transvalers resented London's persistent efforts to cut them off from the sea and confine them in a British bailiwick. And, having thrashed the redcoats at Bronkhorstspruit and Majuba, they were not in awe of them. It seemed, furthermore, that they could count on political if not also military support from Bismarck. Whitehall and Rhodes guessed, however, that the Transvaal, its treasury nearly empty, would not risk a wider conflict.

They guessed right. When Warren occupied Stellaland, the Boers in Goshen re-treated into the Transvaal and Kruger suggested that both mini-republics be an-nexed to the Cape Colony.[2] The British went one better and absorbed both into a Crown colony embracing the whole of Bechuanaland south of the Molopo River. A British protectorate was declared in the northern part (where King Kgama of the Ngwato had sought protection from the Matabele) effectively blocking Ger-man ambitions to link to Portuguese East Africa as well as the Transvaal's hopes of a westward expansion.*

Warren's settlement under force of arms and the obstruction of Transvaal expan-sion caused undoubtedly rancour that would remain when the Boers were called to fight against the British four years later.

Rhodes, of course, was relieved. The road to the north had been secured for the time being. The way was open to the territory beyond, to Matabeleland, where Mzilikazi's son, Lobengula, held sway, and to Mashonaland and the ancient king-dom of Monomotapa from where the Arabs and Portuguese had for centuries ob-tained gold, and where hunter-prospectors had more recently found other evidence of gold.

Rhodes's imperialistic ambitions had begun to develop along with the fortune he was making on the diamond fields. They were strongly influenced by his time at Oxford University, where he studied intermittently while becoming a diamond magnate. He was impressed by John Ruskin's exhortations to his countrymen to make Britain 'a source of light, a centre of peace' for the whole world through ag-gressive colonisation.

In Ruskin's vision, Britain needed to acquire colonies in order to survive, foreign trade being the islands' lifeblood. At the same time it had a moral duty to spread prosperity and peace in those colonies. That concept of a synthesis of material need and moral obligation, each one supporting, justifying and nourishing the other, was a fundament of Victorian social philosophy, and it was injected into the running of the colonies. The material aspect, however, almost always outweighed the moral.

For Rhodes, paradoxically, the moral one was an end whose attainment justified any means. It was not greed for money that drove Rhodes. He sought wealth and power not so much for their own sake as for the means they gave him to further his imperial ambitions, which in turn he viewed as vehicles for benefiting human-kind in general.

In the Confession of Faith that the young Rhodes wrote while at Oxford, he set out the credo that was to guide his future actions: 'I contend that we are the fin-est race in the world and that the more of the world we inhabit the better it is for the human race.' Later he would add a religious element: 'Within the white race, English-speaking man, whether British, American, Australian or South African, has proved himself to be the most likely instrument of the Divine Plan to spread Jus-tice, Liberty and Peace … over the widest possible area of the planet.' He spoke of 'bringing the whole uncivilised world under British rule', even of drawing the

---

*The Crown colony was eventually absorbed by the Cape, and the northern protectorate of Bechuanaland much later gained independence as Botswana.

United States back into the British fold and 'making the Anglo-Saxon race but one Empire'. It was an outlandish concept, but a narrower form of it was shared by many Britons of the time.

In Rhodes's vision of a world made better by being Anglicised there was no time scale for the black man to achieve equality; it was a possibility so distant as to be irrelevant in his own time. Rhodes's great granite memorial on the slopes of Table Mountain was built to commemorate his vision, his strength and his remarkable achievements as seen by European admirers of his own time. These were not seen in the same light by the black Africans, however.

When the flow of stirring events has subsided and those who rode the currents have been deposited on the mudbanks of history, they invariably seem less imposing than in the monuments put up by their contemporaries. So it is with Cecil Rhodes. In time his memorial may come to be regarded – and tolerated – as a monument not to his perceived greatness but as an historical relic, a reminder of the peculiar mindset that enabled the Europeans of his time, with neither question nor guilt, to allocate to their black contemporaries a lesser humanity in the world and a lower station in their own land.

Rhodes, who suffered from a heart complaint, did not live long enough to attempt to apply his philosophy beyond Africa, but he did it with a huge impact within that continent. He had barely begun his imperial entrepreneuring when the Scramble got under way, but once he got going he wasted no time. Fewer than ten years elapsed between his entry into politics – his election to the Cape parliament in 1881 as a member for Barkly West – and his climactic political achievement, the founding of the Rhodesias. They were hectic, swashbuckling years that make one of the most dramatic episodes in the European conquest of Africa, though not one of the most honourable.

Preoccupied with his affairs in Kimberley and Cape Town, Rhodes came late to the Witwatersrand gold finds but still ended up heading one of the biggest companies, Consolidated Goldfields. For Rhodes that became a launching pad for his ambitions to the north.

★ ★ ★ ★

Other than European settlement in general, no happening has had a wider and more radical impact on the course of events in southern Africa – and, indeed, much further afield – than the Witwatersrand gold discoveries of 1886. The gold, while plentiful, was mostly in low-grade reefs running kilometres below the surface. Only big companies could finance the cost of mining the reefs.

For these reasons the discoveries did not attract a diggers' rush like those of California and the Klondike, or even those at Lydenburg and Barberton in South Africa. Still, as the gold reefs were traced and worked for kilometres along the Witwatersrand (which came to be known as the Rand for short) there was enough wealth to be had to bring a different kind of rush, a flood of suppliers and service providers of all kinds, from butchers to bankers, prelates to prostitutes.

Gold mining sucked foreign exchange into the country and attracted an influx of Europeans who often were skilled and enterprising. From the gold mining, as from the diamond mining, prosperity spread throughout South Africa. It was not, of course, evenly distributed, but it made life better for most of the white people and for some of the black ones. For most of the latter, however, the mineral wealth compounded the problems that had come with the Europeans, problems arising from the whites' racial antipathy, their demand for labour, and their fear of the black majority competing with them on equal terms.

The inferior status imposed on the indigenous people of South Africa by slavery, land competition, extensive agriculture and the diamonds was sealed by the discovery of the gold wealth. In part this was a consequence of the high cost of mining the gold. Because cheap labour was seen as essential to profitability, political measures were taken to ensure that there would always be a plentiful supply of blacks seeking work on the mines, and that their wages would be kept as low as possible – measures such as the refinement of the native reserve and migrant labour systems, and strictures on black trade unions.

If the initiative for these measures was not directly attributable to the mining companies, the imperatives may be found in the symbiotic relationship between the mining houses and the politicians.

Besides further hardening white attitudes to blacks, the Witwatersrand gold discoveries had another negative effect in that they provoked the biggest and most vicious conflict between Europeans that Africa had ever known. The knowledge of the vast riches lying below the Witwatersrand gave the British incentive to enter the Boer War and to fight it to the bitter end, at huge human and material cost to themselves and to the Boers.

The Witwatersrand gold mines were still relatively shallow shafts when Cecil Rhodes began to extend his dream to the north, using the lure of gold and of land as the motive power.

The rumours of gold wealth beyond the Limpopo had already sent a number of Europeans to Lobengula's capital, Gubulawayo, seeking prospecting and mining concessions. None dared search without his sanction, for his military society held ruthless sway from the Kalahari's edge almost to the Portuguese territory in the east. Lobengula rebuffed all of the concession-seekers, but allowed them to hang about the outskirts of his capital, calling them his 'white dogs'.

The situation changed dramatically in 1887 when Kruger obtained a treaty from Lobengula giving Transvalers exclusive hunting and trading rights in Matabeleland. Rhodes suspected that Kruger, like himself, was actually after Lobengula's territory. He immediately despatched to Gubulawayo his own agent, John Moffat, son of the missionary Robert and brother-in-law of Livingstone.

Moffat got Lobengula to repudiate Kruger's treaty and accept instead a treaty of friendship with Queen Victoria that barred dealings with any other power. It was ratified by London two months later.

The Moffat treaty was an inadequate vehicle for Rhodes's ambitions, however. A mining concession was needed to secure an effective presence in Lobengula's land

and to use the bait of gold to lure white settlers who would make it British territory. To get such a concession Rhodes sent Charles Dunell Rudd, his friend and partner in the Goldfields company, to Gubulawayo. Rudd's party included Frank Thompson, designer of the Kimberley mine compounds, now acting as interpreter.

Fighting off fierce competition from the 'white dogs' at Gubulawayo, Rudd got Lobengula to cede exclusive mining rights to his group in October 1888. His trump card was a letter provided by Rhodes's ally, Sir Hercules Robinson, High Commissioner in the Cape, which was falsely put forward as coming from Queen Victoria herself. Charles Helm, a missionary trusted by Lobengula, interpreted the concession document drafted by Rudd. But the document to which Lobengula put his mark omitted his stipulation that the mining should be carried out by no more than ten men, and only in designated places.

In return for the concession Lobengula was to be given 1 000 Martini-Henry rifles with ammunition and £100 a month, and, eccentrically, a gunboat on the Zambezi River.

Armed with the concession document, Rhodes proceeded to seek a royal charter to give formal British cover to his operations – but without disclosing the part about the rifles.

Rhodes often referred to 'squaring' persons who stood in the way of his schemes, and a great deal of squaring was now undertaken. Helm, Robinson and many others received favours from Rhodes in serving his purposes.

Cape law prohibited the supply of guns to Africans, but the rifles were smuggled through Bechuanaland. They reached Gubulawayo in the care of Leander Starr Jameson, the medical doctor who had been Rhodes's physician, close friend and business partner since the early Kimberley days, and who now began to direct Rhodes's machinations across the Limpopo.

Before formally accepting the guns, Lobengula sent two of his *indunas* to London to ask Queen Victoria whether Rudd was truly her representative. In the interim he provisionally repudiated the Rudd treaty in a letter to Queen Victoria that was intercepted by Rhodes's cohorts.

The arrival of the *indunas* in London sparked an upsurge of opposition to Rhodes's plans among the 'Exeter Hall element'. The queen denied that any of the whites at Gubulawayo represented her. Rhodes and his associates, however, arranged for the *indunas,* who, though illiterate, had memorised the queen's message, to be sent home on a ship taking a long route by way of South America.

Rhodes in the mean time squared his principal rivals in Matabeleland and South Africa, ending their competition, then went to England and set about squaring the opposition there. In meeting after meeting he won over his critics, even some of the most ardent of the Exeter Hallers, with his remarkable gifts of charm and persuasion – and equally remarkable gifts of cash and shares in his proposed chartered company.

The granting of the royal charter in October 1889 was almost a formality. It did not much matter now if Lobengula cancelled the concession, for the charter would not be withdrawn; none of its influential backers could afford to be seen to have been wrong – or duped.

The charter's terms were sweeping, allowing the company to conduct mining, farming and commercial enterprises, to establish settlements, to build railways and to maintain peace and order with its own police force, all under its own flag.

When the *indunas* at last reached Gubulawayo with the queen's message there was uproar among the Matabeles. Lobengula's own position was under threat, for his power ultimately rested on the support of the *indunas*. To save himself he put the blame on his chief minister and had him and his family, some three hundred in all, killed.

He and the *indunas* appear to have been mollified, however, by Jameson's explanation that the concession did not deprive him of any of his land or power, that he was only giving the Europeans the right to dig for gold. The clincher may have been the morphine that Jameson was supplying Lobengula to ease the pain of his gout. According to some accounts, he soon had the king addicted and easily influenced.[2]

To implement his charter Rhodes formed the British South Africa Company, more commonly known as the Chartered Company, whose one million one-pound shares were soon eagerly sought on the market.

The weight of the known facts suggests that Rhodes and his cohorts had no intention of abiding by the terms of the concession as Lobengula understood them. Instead, there was a cynical acceptance that he would have to be got out of the way of Rhodes's plans. It was decided to bypass him for the time being and send a well-armed force to skirt Matabeleland and occupy Mashonaland in his rear.

Besides being generously paid, the members of the force would each receive 3 000 acres of land and 15 mining claims once the company's flag had been planted in Mashonaland.

With only 220 men, the occupying force was astonishingly small considering that it might have to take on the 15 000 Matabele warriors whom Lobengula was only with difficulty restraining from burying their spears in the white intruders. The column's strength was not in its numbers, however, but in its weapons: Martini-Henry rifles, Maxim machine-guns, nine-pounder field guns, rockets and mines – even a searchlight borrowed from the Royal Navy, its electricity generator powered by steam from a wood-fired boiler.

The uniformed force, known as the Pioneer Column, set out from Macloutsie in Bechuanaland on 26 June 1890, flying the Chartered Company's flag, the Union Jack centred with a lion grasping an elephant tusk. Behind the Pioneers rode a separate force of 500 men assembled by Sir Henry Loch, the new Bechuanaland Commissioner, with the apparent intention of ensuring that Rhodes promoted Britain's interests as well as his own. Behind them came 117 waggons and about a thousand black servants.

When Lobengula sent a deputation of *indunas* to query the presence of so large a force in his territory, Jameson gave a demonstration of its power, felling trees with the machine-guns and artillery. The *indunas* got the message, and the column was not impeded.

On reaching the highlands of Mashonaland without opposition from any Shonas, the column arbitrarily defined a border with Matabeleland, then founded Salisbury, named after the British prime minister, as the capital of Rhodes's first foreign possession. Then the Pioneers dispersed to claim their land and look for their gold. Few found any, for what Rhodes had called 'probably the richest goldfield in the world' was nowhere to be found in Mashonaland. The settlers turned instead to farming. The Shonas, having been broken into small groups by the Matabele, had no power to resist either the taking of their land or being forced to provide labour for the white farmers. Whenever there was resistance the Maxims and the nine-pounders made it short-lived.

Rhodes next attempted to extend his territory – now known as Rhodesia – eastwards to the Indian Ocean. Portuguese forces attempting to intervene were faced down by Rhodes's firepower. His troopers were working their way down the Pungwe River, at whose mouth is the port of Beira, and steam launches were running guns upriver from the sea for buying concessions, when Whitehall pulled the rug from under him.

Rhodes's advances had so infuriated the Portuguese that there was public clamour in Portugal for war with Britain. Warships were sent to blockade the Mozambican coast against Rhodes's gun-running. In Lisbon students formed a 'suicide corps' to fight the British. Salisbury's government, however, had no intention of risking hostilities with Portugal. In June 1891 Britain signed an agreement with Portugal that gave Rhodesia the high land along the escarpment and Portugal the coastal plain below. Rhodes offered to purchase the port at Delagoa Bay (later Lourenço Marques, now Maputo) but was rebuffed.

★ ★ ★ ★

Having acquired Mashonaland and outflanked Lobengula in Matabeleland, Rhodes pursued his drive to the north, into the land beyond the Zambezi. In 1890 he obtained a mining and trading concession in Barotseland, but when his agents sought a similar concession from the Katangese ruler, Msiri, Rhodes found himself in a race with Leopold for the copper-rich territory. Although the region lay within the Congo borders claimed by Leopold, he had not clinched his claim by establishing the 'effective occupation' specified in the Berlin Act. Rhodes hoped to beat him to it.

His agents, however, were rebuffed by Msiri. So, too, were Leopold's agents, but they solved that problem by simply shooting Msiri dead and raising Leopold's flag. Leopold's claim was formally recognised by Germany, and Portugal and Britain had no option but to follow suit, and Rhodes no alternative but to accept it all.

The eastern and western boundaries of Rhodes's adjoining territory were settled by negotiation with the Germans and the Portuguese respectively, and it was named Northern Rhodesia. Before the Company could assert its claim it had to put down resistance by the Bemba and Lunda peoples, an exercise in which the Maxim gun again proved devastatingly decisive.

Ironically, Rhodes never learned that deep below the surface of the territory, alongside Katanga, were equally rich deposits of copper. He had been dead for two decades before these were discovered.

Rhodes next attempted to incorporate the land west of Lake Nyasa that had been largely Christianised by the Scottish missionaries who had followed Livingstone. The British government, however, had other ideas, and in 1891 declared the territory the protectorate of Nyasaland (now Malawi). Still, the declaration furthered Rhodes's Cape-to-Cairo dream.

★ ★ ★ ★

One major loose end remained: getting Lobengula out of the way. This became urgent when the Chartered Company's shares tumbled in value with the realisation that there was not enough gold in Mashonaland to create a New Rand. That trend might be reversed by the acquisition of cattle country – and perhaps even gold – in Matabeleland. But with Lobengula keeping his warriors on the leash in Gubulawayo, an excuse was needed for an attack on his capital.

The excuse was perceived in 1893 when Lobengula sent *impis* to punish a Shona chief whose people had stolen wire from a telegraph line. He expressly forbade the *impis* to attack the Europeans, and advised Jameson accordingly. Among the Shonas killed by the *impis*, however, were a number working for white settlers, some of whose livestock was driven off with the cattle of the Shonas. The settlers, believing they were in danger of being attacked by the Matabele, sought sanctuary at Fort Victoria.

Equipped now with his pretext, Jameson assembled a force of 650 white troopers for an attack on Gubulawayo, promising each recruit 6 000 acres in Matabeleland, 20 gold claims and a share of the loot from Lobengula's capital.

In an apparent attempt to soften up public opinion in Britain, the Chartered Company spread reports that Lobengula was preparing to attack the white settlers. Some historians contend that Jameson was in fact forced into war by Lobengula's aggressive actions. Others assert that he was desperately trying to avert war, that he sent a letter to Queen Victoria pleading for her intervention but it was intercepted. Loch in any event authorised Jameson to take appropriate measures against Lobengula. Rhodes meanwhile secluded himself in a camp in the bush near Salisbury to await the result of Jameson's attack.

Lobengula made one last attempt to stop the invasion, sending emissaries with a message to Loch. The emissaries were stopped by Loch's police force. Only then did Lobengula unleash his warriors.

The first attack on Jameson's force was made by about six thousand Matabeles while it was laagered on the Shangani River. The Maxim had by now been developed into an efficient weapon that fired three .45-calibre bullets every second, and seldom jammed. Jameson's seven machine-guns, together with the 600 rifles and the artillery, dropped the Matabele in lifeless heaps.

A second attack was made as the invaders were laagered on the Bembesi River, only about thirty kilometres from Gubulawayo. Here the crack Ndebele regiments were virtually wiped out. Jameson's force entered the ashes of Gubulawayo on 4 November 1893, Lobengula having set fire to his capital before retreating to the north.

In a despairing last effort to halt Rhodes's pursuing troops, the king sent a bag of gold sovereigns with a message to Jameson pleading for peace. However, both the gold and the message were intercepted and stolen by white troopers.

Lobengula halted his flight some fifty kilometres from the Zambezi, swallowed poison and died. His followers sealed his body in a cave, whose location has since been lost.

Rhodes had meanwhile arrived in Gubulawayo and jubilantly begun marking out the streets of his own town, its name Anglicised to Bulawayo. He told his assembled troops that the country was theirs by right of conquest, and its future must not be left to 'the negrophilists of Exeter Hall'. In a speech oddly prescient of the Unilateral Declaration of Independence by the Rhodesian government 72 years later, Rhodes warned that if they met with interference from London the Rhodesian pioneers might follow the example of the American colonists and break with Britain.

They need not have worried. Thanks in part to careful propagandising, the conquest of Matabeleland was generally accepted in Britain as a necessary reaction to Matabele aggression. Within a year Whitehall had confirmed the Chartered Company's jurisdiction and the boundaries of the new, expanded Rhodesia.

When the scattered remnants of the Matabele nation returned to their homes they found that much of their land had been allocated to white settlers and their cattle shared out as booty. Like the Shonas and the Africans south of the Limpopo, the Matabele would be herded into reserves or made to labour for their white conquerors.

Some of the most telling comments on the conquest came from among the participants. Moffat declared that Lobengula had been 'foully sinned against by Jameson and his gang'. Helm saw the Matabele war as so 'unrighteous' as to justify an inquiry. Thompson in his autobiography relates how in 1904, while standing on the railway platform at Figtree in Matabeleland, he was approached by one of Lobengula's surviving indunas.[4] 'Hau, Tomason,' the old man said, 'how have you treated us, after all your promises, which we believed?' And Thompson recalls: 'I had no answer.'

★ ★ ★ ★

Rhodes used his wealth to send imperial tentacles elsewhere into Africa, buying shares in a number of the companies formed to reap benefits from the Scramble. Believing that the lack of an alternative port to Walvis Bay would persuade the Germans to relinquish South West Africa, he acquired substantial interests in mining and land companies there. He is said also to have acquired land interests in southern Angola.[5] Beyond the Rhodesias, however, his imperial hopes ran dry.

CHAPTER 16

MAKING THE MAP

The African cake was pretty well all shared out as the 19th century drew to its end. The biggest pieces had been taken, and it was largely a matter of grabbing the crumbs and of tidying up, of asserting title and defining boundaries.

Acquiring the crumbs was in some cases no easier than it had been to get the slices. It was a complex business requiring a delicate balancing of the interests of the respective powers, of confrontation and negotiation, of secret deals and open horse-trading.

The major division of the cake had been done with virtually no actual fighting. With threats, yes, and with bluster and bluff, but not with gunfire. The European powers never went to war over the cake, though they came close a few times. None – except perhaps for the British over South Africa – wanted African possessions badly enough to fight another power for them and thereby risk sparking a bigger war in Europe.

Where it was considered necessary they fought campaigns against the natives, but they did not fight one another. The carving up was done not so much at the frontiers of confrontation in Africa itself as at civil servants' desks in the capitals of Europe. Where convenient, physical features – a river, a mountain range, a lake – were accepted as the borders between two colonies. Very often though, especially where there was no handy natural feature (or where the civil servants in Europe didn't know of one), the boundary was fixed along a line of latitude or longitude, visible on a map in London, Paris or Berlin but invisible on the ground in Africa unless marked by a fence.

These straight lines make up nearly forty per cent of the borders of present-day Africa, evidence of the mostly peaceful manner in which they were decided. The consequences were not always as neat or peaceful, however. Sometimes slicing arbitrarily through tribes and kingdoms, the boundaries created a number of new states that were either geographic freaks, demographic monstrosities or economic cripples – or all three of these things. Thus the map of Africa today has bizarre shapes like the Caprivi Strip, knifing weirdly from Namibia to the distant Zambezi; the Pedicle that pokes a predatory proboscis from Zaire into Zambia's copperbelt; and the banana-shaped state of Gambia, geographically not much more than the widened banks of the Gambia river and protruding deep into Senegal.

While the artificial states seemed workable as colonies, some, fraught with eth-

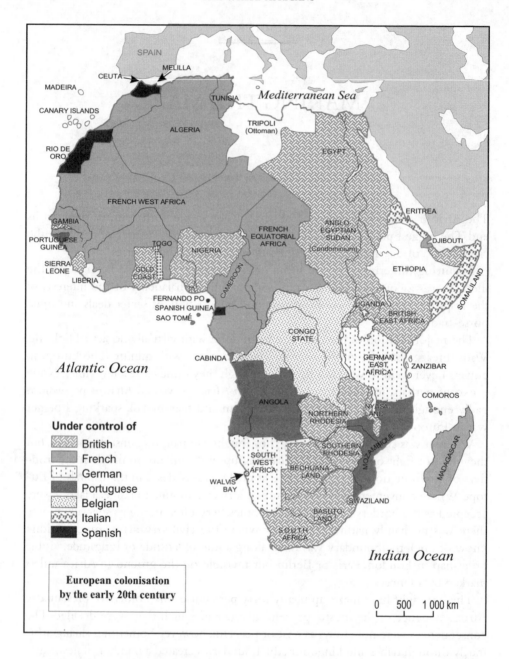

Under control of

British
French
German
Portuguese
Belgian
Italian
Spanish

**European colonisation
by the early 20th century**

0   500   1 000 km

SPAIN

MADEIRA

CANARY ISLANDS

CEUTA
MELILLA

TUNISIA

Mediterranean Sea

TRIPOLI
(Ottoman)

RIO DE
ORO

ALGERIA

EGYPT

FRENCH WEST AFRICA

ERITREA

GAMBIA

PORTUGUESE
GUINEA

TOGO

FRENCH
EQUATORIAL
AFRICA

ANGLO-
EGYPTIAN
SUDAN
(Condominium)

DJIBOUTI

SIERRA
LEONE

GOLD
COAST

NIGERIA

SOMALILAND

LIBERIA

ETHIOPIA

FERNANDO PO
SPANISH GUINEA
SAO TOMÉ

CAMEROON

UGANDA

BRITISH
EAST AFRICA

Atlantic Ocean

CABINDA

CONGO
STATE

GERMAN
EAST
AFRICA

ZANZIBAR

COMOROS

ANGOLA

NORTHERN
RHODESIA

NYASA-
LAND

MOZAMBIQUE

MADAGASCAR

SOUTH-
WEST
AFRICA

SOUTHERN
RHODESIA

WALVIS
BAY

BECHUANA-
LAND

SWAZILAND

BASUTO-
LAND

SOUTH
AFRICA

Indian Ocean

nic rivalry and economically unviable, had not much more than hope to keep them from falling apart once the bands of colonial rule were removed. Some products of the Scramble imprisoned rival ethnic groups within common borders, works of social engineering comparable in their effects if not their intentions to the old colonial amusement of sealing two scorpions in a bottle to see them fight. And fight the ethnic rivals in some cases did once the colonial constraints were removed with independence, spreading destruction and bitterness in Nigeria, Zaire, Angola and

124

other states.

All the powers had at one time or another and with varying degrees of determination pursued the ambition of acquiring a swathe of territory across Africa, from coast to coast. Besides facilitating administration, transport and communications, such strips might create bases for expansion while at the same time blocking rivals. The British Cape-to-Cairo concept was the only one envisaged on a longitudinal basis. The other powers, not being entrenched at these extremities, thought in latitudinal terms. The French aspired to stretch a belt from Senegal across to the Red Sea. The Germans for a while pursued a *mittelafrika* dream, linking South West Africa with Tanganyika along the Zimbabwe. The Portuguese attempted to follow a *contracosta* policy, linking Angola and Mozambique. King Leopold gave serious thought to extending his operations from the Congo to the Red Sea.

None of these visions was realised except the Cape-to-Cairo one, and then the British had to wait until the end of the First World War before they could acquire Tanganyika from the Germans to close the gap in the middle. The French ambition crashed in the famous showdown with the British at Fashoda on the Nile. The *mittelafrika* dream was abandoned with the Anglo-German Treaty of 1890, in which Berlin settled for access to the Zambezi along the Caprivi Strip. The *contracosta* ambition withered with the Anglo-Portuguese Treaty of 1891, which left Portugal with only the right to a telegraphic bridge between its coastal colonies.

In the tidying-up that followed the main Scramble, the powers were concerned with two main issues. All of them saw special advantage in controlling the upper Nile and its headwaters. Then there was the large question of defining borders in the broad swathe of the Sudan, from the Niger to the Nile, where British, French and German interests collided or overlapped. An important side issue was the need to define the boundaries of Leopold's great land-grab in the Congo basin.

Some saw great strategic significance in the Nile headwaters, believing that whoever controlled the headwaters would be able to blackmail those lower down by threatening either to shut off the flow with dams or send down destructive floods. The strategic keys were seen to be Uganda and the southern Sudanese provinces of Equatoria and Bahr al-Ghazal. Uganda was in addition given an economic value because of its high rainfall and fertility.

It was Uganda's commercial possibilities that interested Mackinnon's Imperial British East Africa Company when it sent Frederick Lugard there in 1890 to exercise its royal charter. The IBEAC had bet its fortunes on the completion of its railway from Mombasa to Lake Victoria. First, however, Kabaka Mwanga had to be persuaded to accept the Anglo-German agreement recognising Britain's special interest in Uganda. Lugard was given the job. Tough and resolute, he welcomed adversity and challenge, not just for their own sake but because they helped distract him from the incessant hurt of having been jilted by the woman to whom he had lost his heart (or his head, depending on the degree of cynicism with which one views these things). With a small force of askaris and two old Maxims, he 'persuaded' Mwanga to sign a treaty and, for good measure, halted the disruptive feuding between the Protestant, Catholic and Muslim factions.

But the IBEAC went broke nonetheless, still unable to attract sufficient share investment. Lugard was recalled to England, where he led a successful campaign to have the British government annex Uganda, which it did in 1892. At least that part of the Nile headwaters now seemed secure.

Leopold's ambitions on the Nile were pursued as an extension of his efforts to impose his Congo Free State in the part of the eastern Congo basin still occupied by Arab traders and slavers. The first objective was accomplished in a series of bloody campaigns ostensibly carried out in the cause of putting down slavery. That they did, but at horrific cost in the numbers killed and in the cannibalism that accompanied the fighting. A number of Leopold's European agents ended up as especially rare comestibles.

The French made a bid for the upper Nile in 1894, sending an expedition under Commandant Paul Monteil from the Ubangi, heading for the Bahr al-Ghazal. To block the French move, the British secretly gave Leopold a lease on Equatoria and Bahr al-Ghazal. In return Leopold would give Britain a corridor west of German East Africa that would link Uganda with Lake Tanganyika and provide the missing link in the British Cape-to-Cairo vision. When the deal was exposed, the French and Germans were irate. London quietly nullified it, but issued a veiled threat of hostilities should Monteil try to establish a presence on the Nile.

Monteil was recalled, but behind the scenes hard-line French officials and their civilian supporters planned a new expedition to the Nile, to be led by Jean-Baptiste Marchand. Ostensibly the purpose was to establish a presence in Bahr al-Ghazal, but the secret intention was that he would march to Fashoda with 160 Senegalese *tirailleurs* (askaris) and seize it for France.

At the same time as they were competing for the Nile, the major powers were engaged in a restrained but determined contest for those parts of West Africa and the Sudan belt whose ownership was still uncertain or disputed. Boundaries there were generally open to dispute and negotiation, for the 'effective occupation' part of the Berlin Act applied specifically to coastal areas, and its application inland was uncertain.

London and Paris had broadly agreed in 1890 that France should have the Sahara and part of the savannah below it, but they had not precisely defined where these territories should meet with the British territories of West Africa. As the French expanded their holdings westward from Senegal and down the Niger, they bumped into the northward expansion of the British. The Germans, too, were tentatively pushing north from Cameroon.

Louis Mizon in 1892 tried to claim for France the territory south of the Benue, the Niger's main tributary, but was scuppered by allegations of collaboration with slavers, enabling Britain and Germany to split the territory between Nigeria and Cameroon.

Lugard popped up on the Niger in 1894 as an agent of Goldie's company, competing with a number of French expeditions. Three of these set out overland from Dahomey, and a fourth cheekily sailed up the Niger, accompanied by a French gunboat.

In April 1897 the French occupied Bussa on the middle Niger, in effect putting to the test the inland extension of the Berlin Act's 'effective occupation'. Quickly they established outposts throughout the Borgu region to the west, ignoring the treaties previously obtained by Lugard but never exploited by Goldie's Niger Company. Lacking the means to assert his claims, Goldie turned to the colonial secretary, Joseph Chamberlain.

Chamberlain, whose family had got rich from making screws in Birmingham, typified the middle-class invasion of Britain's halls of power. Affecting the role of the dandy with his monocle and a fresh orchid always in his lapel, Chamberlain was in reality a tough and ruthless politician, earning the sobriquet of 'Pushful Joe'.

Early in 1898, Chamberlain persuaded the British cabinet to buy out the Niger Company and to send Lugard with a 3 000-strong West African Frontier Force to challenge the French in Borgu. He was to plant the Union Jack wherever the Tricolor had been planted and try to stare the French down. It was a dangerous move, risking war between the two powers.

While the two negotiated over the dispute, Lugard sailed up the Niger and began to run up his flags within shouting distance of the French outposts. Those beneath the respective flags treated each other courteously but with fingers nervously on triggers until word came that agreement had been reached in the negotiations. Under the Niger Convention signed in June the French conceded Bussa, Sokoto and most of Borgu to the British in return for a piece of Borgu as an extension of Dahomey and navigational rights on the lower Niger.

The British occupation of the lower Niger had been completed in 1897 with the conquest of Benin. Ibo resistance was smashed in 1901 after Chamberlain had informally enunciated policy in these terms: 'You cannot have omelettes without breaking eggs; you cannot destroy the practices of barbarism, of slavery and superstition which for centuries have desolated the interior of Africa, without the use of force.'

★ ★ ★ ★

In the final stages of European colonisation, clear differences had emerged between the two major colonisers in both their motives and their methods.

For the British, a cramped nation depending on foreign trade to be able to live a life larger than the size of its islands alone would allow, the imperative of colonisation was always commercial. More than just Napoleon's 'nation of shopkeepers', the British were of necessity a nation of foreign merchants, a race dependent more than most others on the outside world for prosperity; parasitical, perhaps, but in a creative way that arguably gave more than it took from the world. The Briton was the essential seafarer, a buccaneer if necessary, a conqueror by need as much as choice; a driven imperialist whose chauvinism was born of necessity as much as of pride, whose foreign conquests were often for strategic reasons but of a strategy always commercially based; conquering where possible by guile rather than force, by the insidious expansion of the treaty rather than the blast of the cannon; a careful book-

127

keeper who colonised for profit rather than pride, and watched the pennies, crafty at making even the strategic conquests pay their way, cunning at making those he conquered serve his cause, even on the battlefield. It is not surprising that the British were reluctant entrants into the Scramble, nor that they nevertheless came out of it with some of the best pieces of Africa.

The French, preoccupied with the Americas and Asia, neglected their little African foothold in Senegal until fairly late in the game, with the result that they ended up with a lot of what Salisbury called 'light soil' besides their few choice properties. Their major expansion in Africa in the late 19th century was driven by impulses that were emotional as well as economic. Having been evicted by the British from India and Canada, humiliated in Europe by the Prussians in 1871 and then outwitted by the British in Egypt in 1882, the French, and especially the military, were looking aggressively to restore prestige when the Scramble began. There was a tendency to acquire territory for the sake of possession rather than material benefit. The expansion into West Africa was led by soldiers rather than merchants, soldiers who often acted independently of the politicians and officials in Paris, giving scant regard to economic considerations.

CHAPTER 17

CRESCENDO

The European conquest of Africa came to an explosive climax in the last five years of the 19th century, a violent crescendo of events somewhat like the culmination of a fireworks display.

There were four big bangs at the end and a number of smaller ones, all helping to fix the final form of white domination. First, Dr Jameson set off in 1895 on the infamous raid into the Transvaal that virtually destroyed his mentor, Cecil Rhodes, probably hastened the Boer War, and in any case aroused hatred and resentment that would poison the sub-continent for generations. Jameson's escapade was followed immediately by the Matabele and Shona rebellions in Rhodesia, whose bloody suppression sealed white supremacy in the region for the next eight decades.

Then came the battle of Adowa in which European forces (Italian in this case) suffered their biggest defeat in Africa, leaving the Abyssinians / Ethiopians and the Liberians as the only African nations not conquered and dominated by whites.

In the same year, Kitchener launched the campaign on the Nile that was to give the British control of the river from mouth to source and destroy the last Muslim power, putting nominally Christian powers in control of the entire continent.

And lastly there was the Boer War itself, the final and the greatest conflict, the biggest of the bangs, in which the whites at last fought each other for what had turned out to be by far the richest part of the cake.

The lesser explosions came as African nations resisted the arbitrary imposition of European colonialism. These were smaller because no indigenous society other than those in Abyssinia and the Sudan had the military power to stand against Europeans abundantly armed with modern weapons. The rebellions crackled across Africa, in Senegal, Nigeria, the Gold Coast, Sierra Leone, Gambia, Uganda, Kenya, German East Africa, Rhodesia and Nyasaland. Some ran on into the 20th century, and others began in the early years of the century, among them the Herero revolt in German South West Africa, the Maji-Maji uprising in German East Africa, and the Bambata rebellion in Zululand. All were quickly suppressed, and by the second decade of the century native resistance had been put down everywhere except in Abyssinia, and the white man ruled all of the rest of the world's second-largest continent.

The first of the climactic bangs, Jameson's raid, was not greatly explosive in itself so much as in its repercussions. It was revolutionary in its intention: to overthrow

Kruger's government and force the Transvaal republic into docile membership of the British Empire. Cecil Rhodes, who envisaged both Boer republics as self-governing colonies within a British South African federation, secretly planned and directed the raid. Prominent Britons in Cape Town actively supported it. Rand gold barons who stood to benefit financially from it (including Rhodes) helped finance it. And the British colonial secretary, 'Pushful Joe' Chamberlain, connived in it.

Some of those backing the operation envisaged the Transvaal and Orange Free State in a British colonial conglomerate stretching from the Cape north to the Congo, embracing the Rhodesias and Nyasaland, in fact the entire sub-continent except for the German and Portuguese colonies. In Britain there was even talk of an African equivalent of the United States of America, a laughable notion now but one that gives an insight into the thinking of the time.

Without the Rand gold, the conquest of the Transvaal would have been desirable in order to enlarge and secure the Cape-Cairo strip. With the gold it became essential, in the view of certain influential Britons, to ensure that it enriched Britain and not some other power, especially not Germany, which was becoming disturbingly intrusive in the sub-continent. By antagonising and uniting the Boers in both Transvaal and Orange Free State and making sympathisers of many in the Cape, the Jameson Raid sealed the inevitability of war.

The excuse for the raid was found in the grievances of the foreigners, the Uitlanders, mostly British, who had flocked to the Rand goldfields and threatened to outnumber the male Boers in the republic. The grievances were a mixture of justifiable complaint – notably the prime grouse that they were denied the vote despite contributing most of the Transvaal's tax revenue – and expediency. They knew as well as Kruger that equal franchise would have seen the Boers politically overpowered in their own country by people they regarded as foreigners who were there only for the gold and who would in any case overwhelm the language, customs and culture of the Afrikaners with the sheer weight of their own. Kruger, well aware that the gold mining had rescued his republic from bankruptcy, tried to mollify the foreigners with concessions.

But there was more to it than Uitlander grievances. London was more concerned with the possibility of the Transvaal slipping out of Britain's sphere of influence. Diligently implementing their policy of encirclement, the British had foiled the landlocked republic's efforts to acquire Swaziland as a stepping-stone to the sea. The Transvaal, however, had obtained an indirect outlet with the building of the railway to Lourenço Marques on Delagoa Bay, completed in 1894, two years after the line from the Cape reached the Rand. No longer could the republic be brought to heel by the threat of being cut off from the Cape railways and ports. On top of that, Berlin had assiduously been promoting relations with Pretoria. German investment in the Transvaal mining industry was substantial, exceeding 300-million marks in 1890.[1]

Whitehall was painfully aware that the gold wealth was transferring the political centre of gravity in the sub-continent from Cape Town to Johannesburg. Whereas Rhodes's predictions of gold riches north of the Limpopo had proved baseless, the

Rand's gold reserves had been shown to be good for at least a hundred years. The Transvaal was clearly going to be the richest region in the sub-continent and therefore the most powerful in local terms. Yet its government adamantly refused to be drawn into a customs union or any form of common market that might bring them under British influence.

As the centre of the international gold trade, Britain had a strong interest in controlling the world's chief source of gold. The gold price, however, was fixed on the world market, preventing the mainly British mining companies from covering the increasing costs of ever-deeper mining through price increases. The only solution lay in cutting costs. Reducing the wages of the black miners was only a partial solution. Besides greater technical efficiency, an obvious remedy lay in a reduction in government taxes, which Kruger's government refused to consider, believing they were keeping the Transvaal afloat. Rhodes became convinced that the Kruger government must be replaced by an administration more understanding of the mining industry's problems.

Ignoring the lessons of Bronkhorstspruit and Majuba, Rhodes turned to the expedient of an Uitlander uprising supported by a British force invading from the Bechuanaland Protectorate. Not all of the Uitlanders were in favour of redressing their grievances through violence, and neither were all the mining companies, especially those which, unlike Rhodes's, had not yet had to engage in expensive deep-level mining. Rhodes therefore set about working up both the Uitlanders and the British public to support a popular uprising.

The military force that was needed to back it would be provided by the paramilitary British South Africa Police, under Rhodes's control in Rhodesia. For a base and jumping-off point there was the strip of Bechuanaland Protectorate running alongside the Transvaal border that the Chartered Company had been promised by Whitehall for the extension of the railway from Kimberley to Bulawayo. Rhodes now called in the promise and was given the strip by Chamberlain, by coincidence at the same time as relations between London and Pretoria went into crisis over rail tariffs.

The Cape Colony, afraid of losing Rand-bound traffic to the new railway from Delagoa Bay, had cut its tariffs up to the Vaal River border. Pretoria responded by tripling the tariffs from the Vaal to the Rand. The Cape railway then evaded the tariffs by offloading goods at the Vaal and taking them on to the Rand by ox-waggon. Kruger riposted by closing the drifts (fords) where the waggons crossed the river. Whitehall, declaring that his action violated the London Convention, demanded that he reopen the drifts and threateningly diverted India-bound troopships to the Cape. Kruger saw no option but to comply.

The planning of the Uitlander uprising meanwhile went ahead. Sir Hercules Robinson was briefed to stand by in Cape Town, ready to entrain for Johannesburg to put a formal stamp on the new dispensation in the Transvaal.

Chamberlain's role in the plot remains disputed but there is little doubt that he knew all about it and did nothing to stop it, until it was too late. Not all the meticulous planning could save the Raid from going wrong, however. At the last minute the conspirators in Johannesburg postponed their rising. Jameson, sitting at the end of the telegraph line at Pitsani, was bombarded with contradictory instructions and advice. On the prearranged date, 29 December 1896, he rode for Johannesburg. His reasons remain unclear, but the immediate effects were electric.

The news that Jameson was riding bombshelled around the world. Rhodes went into an attitude of despair yet made no attempt to turn Jameson back. It has been strongly suspected that he secretly hoped Jameson would carry off the escapade.

In Cape Town and London there was a rush for the lifeboats. Sir Hercules Robinson sent a messenger from Bechuanaland with instructions to Jameson to turn back, and further covered his back by writing a letter to Rhodes repudiating Jameson's action. Chamberlain sent a telegram to Robinson threatening to cancel Rhodes's Rhodesian charter if the reports of the raid proved true.[2]

The rapidly mustered Boer commandos neutralised Jameson's machine-guns and artillery by steering his force into a blocked valley near Krugersdorp, where they began to cut it to pieces from the cover of the hills. Jameson was forced to surrender.

With Jameson and his survivors sitting in jail in Pretoria, Kaiser Wilhelm of Germany sent Kruger a telegram congratulating him on suppressing the rebellion 'without having to invoke the help of friendly powers'. The French government presented him with a sword whose hilt depicted the British lion being strangled by a Boer. Both acts caused fury in Britain.

Kruger magnanimously allowed Jameson and his officers to be tried by the British in London. Jameson was sentenced to 15 months' imprisonment but was released after only four. In Pretoria, the four ringleaders of the planned uprising were sentenced to death for treason, but the sentences were commuted to imprisonment or fines, all of which were paid by Rhodes and his associates.

Rhodes 'squared' Chamberlain with a veiled threat to disclose telegrams proving his complicity, and Chamberlain in turn used his influence to ensure that a parliamentary inquiry came to a bland finding. Chamberlain's own involvement was whitewashed, and his political career continued to flourish. That of Rhodes was shattered, but he was able to fend off efforts to strip him of his Rhodesian charter. Jameson became a respected politician and ended up as prime minister of the Cape Colony.

The raid's net effect in the Transvaal was to convince Kruger of the need to safeguard the republic's independence by resisting all British ties.

In Rhodesia, only three years had elapsed since Lobengula had been toppled, and resentment was still boiling among the Matabele. Realising that the country had virtually been denuded of policemen for Jameson's raid, Lobengula's warriors retrieved their hidden weapons and rose in revolt on 23 March 1895. Within a few days 140 whites – men, women and children – had been killed. Some whites managed to flee to Bulawayo and Gwelo, which were hastily fortified. The British government sent troops from the Cape while Rhodes assembled a relief force in Salisbury, leaving some white families in Mashonaland defenceless without their menfolk. While the combined forces were pushing the Matabele back into the hills, the Shonas rose and began killing the now-vulnerable white families.

In an act of great courage, Rhodes rode with three white companions into the Matopo hills to negotiate a peace agreement with the 10 000 Matabele warriors holed up there. The Shona rebellion sputtered on for a further year before it was finally extinguished with ruthless use of the Maxims.

Rhodesia ended up divided into a patchwork of lands separately reserved for whites and blacks respectively, with much of the best land set aside for whites. Political and economic power remained in white hands.

★ ★ ★ ★

It was a battle that almost did not happen, but when it did the conflict at Adowa resulted in the greatest defeat of a European army by indigenous forces in Africa. More died than at Isandlwana, and the political consequences were as wide.

The Italian and Abyssinian armies had been facing each other for weeks at Adowa on the border of Abyssinia and Italian-occupied Eritrea. Each had waited for the other to attack or withdraw. General Oreste Baratieri, governor of Eritrea, knowing his invading force was outnumbered by the Abyssinians, hoped they would charge his position and expose themselves to his machine-guns and artillery. Menelik II, the Abyssinian emperor, had no intention of charging the entrenched Italian guns.

So the two commanders sat, figuratively staring each other down. Both began to run out of food. And then both blinked. Menelik decided to pack up his starving army and withdraw. Baratieri, not knowing this, but given a virtual ultimatum by pompous politicians in Rome to attack, prepared to do so.

Baratieri's plan was to advance his four brigades at night and then dig in and await an Abyssinian charge. However, in the darkness his force became split. When Menelik responded by charging the Italian positions on 1 March 1896, his troops, though decimated by the Italian fire, were able to drive between the isolated Italian flanks and overwhelm them. More than six thousand Italians and four thousand African askaris were killed or missing at the end of the battle. Menelik had lost even more – about seven thousand dead and ten thousand wounded – but he had won the day.

Menelik's victory halted Rome's colonial ambitions. The Italians, despite being just across the water from Africa, had come late to its colonisation. It was only about a decade before the Scramble began that the ancient peoples of the Italian peninsula were united in a modern nation by Victor Emmanuel. And then they were blocked from crossing the Mediterranean by the greater military strength of the British, French and Turks.

Fresh opportunities were opened along the Red Sea by the opening of the Suez Canal. In 1882 the Italian government acquired Assab, just north of French Somaliland, from the Rubattino Navigation Company. Rome saw an even better opportunity when the British in 1885 abandoned the Egyptian outpost of Massawa on the Eritrean coast, a relic of Ismail's imperial ambitions. Ownership was at first assumed by Emperor Yohannes, the Tigrean leader who had seized the Abyssinian throne after the death of Theodore. The British, however, were anxious to prevent Massawa falling into the hands of the French, and so secretly donated it to Italy in return for a promise not to interfere in the Nile valley.

In that same year, Italian troops were landed at Massawa and at Assab. Yohannes resisted the occupation for a while but was himself killed in 1889 while defending his Coptic Christian empire against the Mahdists. He was succeeded by Menelik, with whom the Italians had established friendly relations. In exchange for several thousand modern rifles, Menelik granted Eritrea to Italy under the treaty of Wichale (Ucciali).

The Italians took the treaty to give them an effective protectorate over Menelik's entire territory. In Rome it was seen as an opportunity to link Eritrea across the Horn with the strip of Somaliland that Italy had been given by the British. When Menelik began to deal directly with the French and Russians, the Italians asserted the protectorate claim, citing not only the Wichale treaty but also the Berlin Act. Britain and Germany accepted Italy's stance but France, Russia and Turkey did not.

Thus encouraged, Menelik abrogated the Wichale treaty. In response the Italians extended their Eritrean foothold, whereupon Menelik marched against them with some eighty thousand troops, mostly armed with modern rifles supplied not only by the Italians themselves but also by the French and Russians. After initial successes, Menelik opened negotiations but these reached stalemate.

It was against this background that Menelik clashed with Baratieri at Adowa. After the battle Menelik, having insufficient food to press the attack, withdrew his hungry survivors to his capital at Addis Ababa. In subsequent peace negotiations he signed the Treaty of Addis Ababa, which recognised his country's sovereignty, abrogated the Wichale treaty and fixed Eritrea's boundary along the Mareb River.

★ ★ ★ ★

While the Italians were seeking to expand their foothold in the east, King Leopold was advancing his interests from the west, flush with profits from the soaring demand for rubber (thanks to John Dunlop's invention of the pneumatic tyre). After the French had torpedoed the British plan to lease him the whole of the Bahr al-Ghazal and Equatoria in 1894, London had given him a lease on the Lado Enclave, the strip of Equatoria linking the Congo with the Nile. In 1896 Leopold sent two expeditions from the Congo to Lado. One marched openly with the ostensible purpose of ousting the Mahdists from Lado so that his company would be ready to begin trading on the Nile once Britain had removed them from the rest of the river. The second marched furtively through the Ituri forest with secret orders to take possession of the upper Nile from Lado all the way down to Khartoum. Leopold's ridiculous hope was that the British and French would then accept his presence on the Nile as a *fait accompli*.

The covert expedition failed when its troops mutinied, but the overt one chased the astonished Mahdists out of Lado and took possession. Emboldened by this improbable success, Leopold tried to lease Eritrea from the Italians in the hope of extending his holdings to the Red Sea. But now more powerful interests began vying for the Nile, prompting the British to shoo Leopold out of the Lado Enclave and away from the Nile.

The Italian defeat at Adowa had changed the power balances in the region. It now seemed to the British that Menelik might chase the Italians out of Eritrea altogether and form an alliance with the Mahdists in the Sudan. The Abyssinians and the Mahdists were the only sizeable African powers still resisting European conquest. Though their religious rivalry made an alliance seem unlikely, it was not impossible. The Khalifa's ambition to conquer the whole Nile had been set back in 1889 when his invading forces had been routed by the British-officered Egyptian army at Toski, 100 kilometres inside Egypt, and an alliance with Menelik must have been tempting.

These factors and the evident French designs on the Nile persuaded Lord Salisbury's cabinet in March 1896 to authorise an advance by Egyptian troops up the Nile to Dongola as a first step to recapturing the Sudan. The expedition would be led by the commander-in-chief of the Egyptian army, General Sir Herbert Kitchener.

In reaction, Paris ordered Marchand to speed up his march to Fashoda and began plotting a division of the upper Nile between France and Abyssinia. The French suggested that Menelik seize the Sudanese territory up to the east bank of the White Nile, opposite Fashoda, which Marchand would hopefully soon occupy for France.

Meanwhile, two French expeditions marched to the Nile from the Red Sea in support of Marchand. Both set out from French Somaliland in mid-1897 but, hampered by heavy rains, malaria and supply problems, both failed.

Menelik in the meantime had indeed made overtures to the Khalifa for an alliance against the British, offering the Khalifa some of his ample stock of rifles. Menelik was allowed to make a reconnaissance in strength to the White Nile, accompanied by a small party of Frenchmen. They reached the Nile shortly before March and planted the Tricolor on its marshy banks, only to have it sink out of sight after their departure.

Once it became clear that the various French and Belgian expeditions were heading for Fashoda, Kitchener's brief was dramatically enlarged. He was ordered to go beyond Dongola all the way to Khartoum to smash the Khalifa, avenge Gordon, and establish British suzerainty over the upper Nile and the Sudan.

As an alternative, tentative plans were made for an advance down the river from Uganda, with supplies coming up from Mombasa on Mackinnon's railway. That advance would hopefully occupy Fashoda and then go on to join with Kitchener and establish an unbroken British swathe from Mombasa to Cairo. Construction of the Mombasa railway was painfully slow, however, held up among other things by lions in the Tsavo region that evidently developed a taste for the labourers brought out from India to build the line.

As an emergency measure, Salisbury sent a column of troops from Uganda under

Lugard's successor, Major James MacDonald, to march posthaste to Fashoda and occupy it before Marchand could get there. MacDonald, however, was forced to turn
back when his Sudanese askaris mutinied. Taking advantage of MacDonald's absence, Mwanga and Kabarega joined forces in a rebellion in Uganda. So it had to be
Kitchener coming upriver who must take Fashoda and secure the Nile for Britain.

Kitchener began a crash project to build his own railway, a 640-kilometre line
knifing from Wadi Halfa across the bend of the Nile to rejoin it at Abu Hamid,
avoiding three of the cataracts. When completed it would enable him to move
troops and supplies from Cairo to Berber in as little as two weeks.

In April 1898 Kitchener's army, now reinforced with British troops, bombarded
and then stormed the Mahdist zeribas at Atbara. Afterwards, Kitchener, blue eyes
glaring fixedly above his luxuriant moustache, rode past the British infantry and
they raised their helmets on bloody bayonets and cheered.

Reaching Omdurman on 1 September 1898, Kitchener positioned his forces
against the Nile. Next day the Khalifa's army, 50 000 strong, advanced against the
infidels. Kitchener sent a message down his lines: 'Remember Gordon.' What followed was a clash of the medieval with the modern, the Khalifa's army, armed
mainly with spears, swords and obsolete rifles, charging the Maxims and magazine-
fed rifles of Kitchener's tight formations, backed by field artillery and the heavier
guns of eight Royal Naval gunboats on the river.

Winston Churchill, then a young lieutenant with the 21st Lancers, was scout-
ing with his patrol ahead of the British positions. From a rise he watched the 'dervishes' advancing across the plain in a front about six kilometres wide, 'a deadened
roar coming up to us in waves', their 'ordered ranks bright with glittering weapons,
and above them dance a multitude of gorgeous flags. We saw for ourselves what the
Crusaders saw.'[3]

The Crusaders, of course, had never seen anything like the storm of shells and
high-velocity bullets that now smashed into the dervish forces and sent the survivors reeling into retreat.

Kitchener's casualties had been negligible until the 21st Lancers charged over a
rise and into a mass of enemies concealed beyond. It was one of the few occasions
in the conquest of Africa when the superior weapons of the Europeans gave them
no advantage over the primitive arms of the Africans, when the fighting was hand-
to-hand. In about three minutes the regiment lost nearly a quarter of its strength.

Two more attacks in strength were beaten off by the British, leaving about ten
thousand dervishes dead on the battlefield and about sixteen thousand lying wounded. Kitchener left them to die on the arid plain, and marched on to Omdurman as
the Khalifa fled into the desert. Kitchener had the Mahdi's remains dug up from his
shell-damaged tomb and thrown into the Nile. He sent the skull down to Cairo as
some kind of trophy. News of this caused an outcry in England, and Baring quietly
took possession of the skull and had it decently buried in the Muslim cemetery at
Wadi Halfa.

In Khartoum, Kitchener attended a memorial service for Gordon at the ruins of
his palace. Hymns were sung, and the gunboats fired a salute from the river. Kitch-

ener for once lost his control, turning away with shaking shoulders and leaving an officer to dismiss the parade. The victory was wildly celebrated in England, and Gordon was much remembered.

It had taken Kitchener two years to advance from Cairo to Khartoum. Now he opened sealed orders he had been given earlier and learned that he was to go on to Fashoda and occupy it.

Kitchener learned from captives that some foreigners were at Fashoda and had beaten off an attack by Mahdists in a couple of Gordon's old steamers. He piled British and Sudanese troops on five gunboats and sailed off to investigate. The foreigners turned out to be Marchand and his little force.

After a two-year march across Africa, Marchand had arrived at Fashoda six weeks earlier and claimed it for France. Incredibly, he had lugged the pieces of a small steamer all the way from Brazzaville, assembled it on the Nile and sailed it down to Fashoda. Having decisively repulsed the Mahdist attack he awaited reinforcements from the Red Sea. Instead, there came Kitchener with his greatly superior force, announcing that he had come to reclaim Fashoda for the khedive. Marchand declared he would fight to defend his right of first possession.

Clearly the buck could not stop at Fashoda. Over glasses of whisky and soda on Kitchener's gunboat, it was agreed that both the French and Egyptian flags would fly at Fashoda until the matter had been resolved by Paris and London. Then Kitchener sailed away, leaving a small force to watch over British interests.

The stand-off at Fashoda aroused indignant turmoil in Paris and a steely resolve in London. Britain and France edged closer each day to war. In France, Fashoda shared the headlines with another big story, the agonising row over the imprisonment of Alfred Dreyfus, the Jewish army officer wrongly accused by the military of passing secrets to Germany.

In the end Paris, recognising that France's comparative naval weakness made war with Britain impossible, yielded. The decision was announced on 4 November to cheers in London. Five weeks later a devastated Marchand hauled down the Tricolor and sadly decamped. In an agreement signed in March 1899, France formally abandoned any claim to the Nile, while Britain recognised French title west of the Nile-Congo watershed.

It took the British more than a year to track the Khalifa down and defeat his remaining army at Jebel Gedir, in the wild country south-west of Khartoum.

The conqueror, elevated to the peerage as Lord Kitchener of Khartoum, became governor-general of the Sudan. Though supposedly ruled jointly by Britain and Egypt, it was now effectively part of the British Empire. One more war, the biggest of all, had still to be fought to define that Empire in Africa, and by the time of the Khalifa's death it had already begun in the Transvaal.

CHAPTER 18

WAR OF THE WHITES

When the whites fought each other in what is commonly known as the Boer War it was, not surprisingly, the greatest struggle Africa had yet known in respect of numbers of men deployed, weapons used and money spent.

For this war pitted the strongest European power against what was arguably the strongest African power, the Afrikaner by now being truly indigenous, even though still maintaining some links with Europe. While they could not come near to matching Britain's military strength, the Boer commandos possibly had better resources and arms and were more effective in battle than any other existing force native to Africa, except perhaps the Abyssinians who had beaten the Italians at Adowa.

In essence the Boer War was the latest episode in a history of resistance to European colonisation by people rooted in Africa. It was different only in that this time the skins were white on both sides – white Africans resisting domination by white Europeans – and the Boers were sufficiently well armed and skilful to force the British to exert their full strength to win. It was a big war even in European experience, the biggest since Crimea, and bigger than Crimea in cost and casualties. More than half a million men took the field, probably more than in any other war previously fought on African soil.

The conflict was over the land – as native soil for the Boers, as strategic territory for the British – and, for both, over its riches. It was essentially a white man's war in its causes, its conduct and its objectives, although thousands of black men took an active part in it. At least ten thousand and perhaps as many as thirty thousand bore arms for the British, usually in a guard rather than a combat capacity, and a few carried arms for the Boers. Others were pulled in by both sides as labourers, servants, horse grooms, transport drivers and so on – about a hundred thousand for the British and substantially fewer for the Boers.

Many other black people indirectly suffered hardship and even death; they were the grass that in the African adage gets trampled when the elephants fight. The great majority of the blacks, however, were sidelined, dispassionately watching their conquerors locked in desperate combat – except towards the end, when some began to attack the Boers on their own account. The war was not about the black people, however, and in the end they were left no better off than before, and in some ways much worse off.

In its causes and purposes the Boer War was in several ways an extension of the Jameson Raid on a larger scale. Besides gaining control of the Transvaal and its gold mines, however, Salisbury's government had other reasons for going into the war. It was seen to be vital that Britain defend its status as a global power against challenges from Germany, France and Russia, not only in Africa but also in the Far East where it had vital trading interests. To allow the Transvaal to escape from the British to the German sphere of influence in southern Africa would have been seen as a sign of weakness to be exploited by its competitors. In the Great Power rivalry, it was important not only to have power but also to manifest the will to use it.

In the Boer War, Britain showed that it had the will, but the limits of its power were embarrassingly exposed by the commandos. The difficulty which Britain's best professional soldiers had in defeating the amateur Boers was humiliating for the nation that only two years before the war had staged extravagant demonstrations of power and grandeur in the celebration of Queen Victoria's diamond jubilee.

In that year, 1897, the nation had appeared set in an upward spiral of power and prestige. From its islands in the Atlantic stretched the sinews and symbols of the greatest empire of all, reaching every continent and ocean, every climate, almost every people, touching somewhere on the globe almost every line of longitude and latitude. Britain's wealth seemed dazzling, her achievements inspiring, her industrial and naval strength paramount, her people by and large the most fortunate in human experience.

There could hardly have been a Briton – even the beggars on the streets – who did not feel proud as the haughty old queen, dumpy and unbeautiful yet symbolically revered, led the grand procession from Buckingham Palace to St Paul's Cathedral, a parade representative of her subjects around the globe, perhaps the most varied and brilliant assemblage of races and uniforms ever brought together.

The *Times* of London declared Britain and her domains to be 'the mightiest and most beneficial Empire ever known in the annals of mankind'. Other European and American commentators tended to agree, at least with the first adjective. The accuracy of the second one was and still is arguable. But even the first one was beginning to come into question, for the glitter and gladness of the jubilee hid the harsher truth that Britain's star was, if not waning, certainly finding it hard to keep shining.

Britain's industrial, technological, commercial and naval supremacy was being overtaken by Germany, France and the United States. Its economy was being weakened by a decline in its vital exports. The 'splendid isolation' which its politicians had deliberately cultivated now seemed less advantageous as it surveyed a jealous world in which it had no firm alliances, and no friends, apart from the white Dominions and, in a rather cold-blooded sense, America.

Given all this, Britain could hardly afford to be bested in the Transvaal, not with German troops patrolling the very borders of the Cape Colony and the Bechuanaland Protectorate. There was besides a fear that the Cape and Natal, both self-governing colonies, might be drawn into a closer association with a wealthy Transvaal than with Britain. Domination of the sub-continent was essential for Britain to protect its wider interests, and it could hardly be dominant when the economic and political nucleus had moved from the Cape Colony to the Transvaal republic.

Besides the political imperatives for going to war, some historians have seen economic ones, such as a British need to control the world's prime source of gold in order to protect its own central bank reserves once gold had been adopted as the international monetary standard of value. In London's financial district an opinion was held by some that the Kruger government was incapable of facilitating the creation of capital at the rate required by the gold mining industry, not because it was deliberately anti-capitalist but because, as a farming nation, it lacked the skills. Not all the gold barons, the Randlords, were in favour of ousting Kruger, however. They stood to lose from the disruption of their industry by war, and eventually did when the mines mostly remained closed from the start of hostilities until 1901. Some of them in any case had no objection to Kruger retaining power provided he took a more sympathetic view of their own difficulties and requirements.

Besides control of the mining industry, the prime motive behind Britain's actions remains the perceived need to assert hegemony over southern Africa – much the same motive as that which prompted the powers into the Scramble, only in the case of the Boer War it was in response to a more cogent and urgent imperative.

Despite all those pressures, the Boer War, like so many others, was tragically avoidable. The Boers remained open to negotiation to the very end, and Salisbury's own government was not hell-bent on war. Even Chamberlain preferred a victory through political coercion, although he failed dismally to keep the issue on this track and steer it away from war. In seeking the villains of the tragedy, historians look at Chamberlain but more pointedly at Sir Alfred Milner.

Chamberlain had appointed Milner, a fellow imperialist, as High Commissioner in 1897 in order to maintain pressure on the Transvaal to become part of the Empire. Milner took that pressure to outright warmongering, being convinced that Britain's interests could best be served by the military conquest of the Transvaal. Even more assertive and arrogant than Pushful Joe himself, Milner soon took the bit between his teeth, and Chamberlain found himself being pulled behind his protege towards war with Kruger.

Milner had started out as a lawyer, but his arithmetical inclinations had led to his becoming Britain's chief tax-collector. As high commissioner he brought the simplistic efficiency of the bean-counter to bear on a political situation volatile with human pride, passion and greed. The influence he wielded in Whitehall through his reputation, intellect and personality enabled him to discourage negotiation with Kruger and to steer matters towards war. To this end he propagated the fallacy that the Boers were unable or unwilling to change their agrarian ways to meet the needs of the industrial economy arising from the mines. In fact, the reality was different: the Transvaal was well on the way to developing an efficient administration, fashioned and run by qualified men from the Netherlands and the Cape. It was rapidly improving communications, had expanded food production to meet the needs of the Witwatersrand, and had enacted effective mining legislation.

The rise of Afrikaner nationalism, accelerated by the Jameson Raid, made it impossible for Milner to deal with the Transvaal as a separate entity. Fight the Transvaal Boers and you risked fighting those in the Free State as well, and even sparking a rebellion in the Cape Colony, where Afrikaners still outnumbered their British conquerors. One sign of this new unity was the decision by the brilliant young Cambridge-educated lawyer, Jan Christiaan Smuts, to move from the Cape to the Transvaal in 1896 out of disgust at the Jameson Raid. He became the Transvaal's State Attorney in 1898, the year before the war began, and went on to become an able commando leader in the war.

Despite a fairly large number of Britishers having the vote in the Free State, that republic had in 1897 concluded a political alliance with the Transvaal which, among other things, had the effect of a military assistance pact. Other than a few artillery units, however, neither republic had a standing army at the outbreak of war.

When Chamberlain proposed talks in London, Kruger, guessing it would mean accepting interference in his country's internal affairs, refused. Chamberlain then found another means of interference, using the London Convention of 1884 as an excuse for attempting to dictate Transvaal foreign policy and for challenging the treatment of the Uitlanders.

The Kruger government temporised and compromised, trying to maintain the Transvaal's independence without going to war with Britain. Substantial concessions were made to the mining industry, and the government cracked down on corruption within its own ranks. Neither move did much to lessen the tension. Kruger was being depicted by Chamberlain's political caravan as a boorish yokel, unable to govern his own country properly, determined to suppress and exploit the Uitlanders, and hampering the efficiency of the gold mining industry. Yet the record of his long exchanges with the British shows Kruger to have been flexible and accommodating almost to a fault, nearly always giving ground in order to reach a settlement and avoid hostilities.

In an effort to ease the rising tension, President Steyn of the Free State and Prime Minister Schreiner of the Cape arranged a meeting between Kruger and Milner in Bloemfontein in May 1899. Milner was not interested in compromise, however, and broke off the talks. He needed the Uitlander vote issue as an instrument to force war, and he could not afford to negotiate it away. Kruger implicitly accused him of having a hidden agenda, crying: 'It is my country that you want!'

The situation was being funnelled inexorably into war. Troop reinforcements were being sent from Britain to the Cape and Natal. Still the Transvalers offered concessions. While Chamberlain still hoped to manoeuvre them into submission within a British colony without war, Milner appeared set on doing it through war. The end of the road was reached when Smuts, in confidential negotiations, agreed to meet Milner's conditions provided Britain undertook to abstain from further interference in the Transvaal, and Whitehall refused.

The British were preparing to deliver an ultimatum to the Transvaal but were pleasantly surprised when the Boers beat them to it. Convinced now that Britain was bent on war, Kruger and Steyn decided to bring matters to a head before the British could ship in more troop reinforcements. On 9 October 1899 the Transvaal and Free State presented a joint ultimatum, giving the British two days to begin withdrawing the troops stationed on their borders and to recall the reinforcements being sent.

'They've done it!' Chamberlain exclaimed jubilantly when he received the Boer ultimatum. Salisbury declared that it had 'liberated us from the necessity of explaining ... why we are at war.' Ignoring the ultimatum was for the British a formality.

Opposition to the war was expressed from the start among British intellectuals and liberal politicians, and it increased as the war progressed, especially when the British conduct of it took on shamefully cruel aspects. The general public, however, gave the war effort their enthusiastic support, unable to see beyond the propaganda and the jingoistic newspaper commentaries.

Most South Africans of British descent, mainly in the Cape and Natal, sided with Britain and many joined colonial units. Some, however, were strongly opposed to the war. Most of the Afrikaners in the Cape and Natal remained at least neutral if not openly loyal to the Crown, but more than thirteen thousand fought on the British side.

Whatever hopes the Boers had of practical help from Britain's rivals among the European powers soon ran dry. Moral support was abundant, even material support of certain kinds, but no power was prepared to intervene directly in the war, not even Germany for all the Kaiser's earlier bluster. Expectations of intervention that had been raised by his telegram after the Jameson Raid had been popped like a balloon when at the outbreak of the war he had congratulated the British on the efficiency of their mobilisation. But then he was Queen Victoria's nephew, after all.

In 1899 the British had not forgotten Majuba, in fact many were looking forward to avenging it, and the humiliation of Jameson's raid as well. They were not expecting anything like a repetition of 1881, being better prepared now and having stronger forces in South Africa – 12 000 at the outbreak of hostilities. At first, though, it was Majuba all over again.

With war now upon them, the Boers mobilised with characteristic speed. Within weeks the two republics had more than thirty thousand men under arms.

Except for the few artillerymen, all the Boers were civilians who fought in their civilian clothes, even the generals. Joining his local commando with his own horse, rifle and bedroll, the Boer was the instant soldier, a complete fighter. The effectiveness of the commandos lay in their marksmanship, mobility and tactical skill. They could live hard, travel light, and move fast and far without losing cohesion.

Although the Boers briefly used trenches with great success, they mostly fought as mounted infantry, moving swiftly over wide fronts and whenever possible shooting from behind cover. In this kind of warfare the machine-gun that had proved so deadly against mass charges elsewhere in Africa was less effective, as even was artillery to some extent. Because it was a war of mobility, the principle weapon on both sides was the small-calibre, high-velocity, long-range, repeating rifle firing smokeless ammunition. Not until the trench warfare of the First World War did the machine-gun again come into its own.

Riding into Natal, the Boers routed a British force at Talana near Dundee, then inflicted a heavy defeat on another outside Ladysmith and laid siege to the town. On the Cape front they besieged Mafeking and Kimberley.

By late November the new commander-in-chief in South Africa, Sir Redvers Buller, was sending the first of his 50 000 reinforcements up the railways from the ports. He sent an infantry division under Lieutenant-General Lord Methuen to relieve Kimberley. Smaller forces under lieutenant-generals French and Gatacre marched to the north-east to head off Boer commandos that had crossed into the Cape from the Free State. Buller himself took one and a half divisions up from Durban to relieve Ladysmith.

More shocks lay ahead for the British, however: three disastrous defeats in six days that became known in Britain as 'Black Week'. General Gatacre was thrown back with heavy losses at Stormberg, well inside the Cape. General Methuen also suffered heavy losses, first from Boers dug in along the Modder River and then at their trenches and barbed-wire entanglements at Magersfontein. Five days later Buller, trying to cross the Tugela River at Colenso, was thrown back by heavy fire from trenches tiered up the hillsides.

Then, at Spion Kop, 30 kilometres south-west of Ladysmith, a British force blundered into a trap on top of the hill and was decimated by Boer fire from higher ground.

A stunned and bewildered British public was now facing the painful realisation that, man for man, the civilian-suited Boers were at least as good at fighting as their own uniformed troops, even when holding fixed positions, and so far had proved even better than the Tommies.

The situation in the besieged towns became desperate as food supplies ran low. The black inhabitants were made to suffer worse than the whites, many dying of privation and disease.

The Boers hoped that the British would return to negotiating, but the very severity of the defeats made it imperative that the British win a convincing victory to restore national pride and international respect. Every resource was marshalled to the British side. More infantry divisions were mobilised, volunteers were recruited for a 10 000-strong yeomanry force, and a call went out to the Dominions for help.

Volunteer forces were raised by the governments of Australia, New Zealand and Canada, the latter after initial opposition from French Canadians, who saw uncomfortable similarities between themselves and the Boers. It was the first time the Dominions had been asked to fight overseas for Britannia but, as they did again in the two world wars, they responded willingly to the call to the blood, even though most of them had never been to England. A New Zealand poet expressed it thus:

> The signal had flashed oe'r the water,
> The word that old England wants help;
> The Mother has cried to her daughter;
> The lion has roared to its whelp.
> Cast away any dread that appals ye,

Any doubts to the sea winds toss —
'Tis the Old, Old Country that calls ye,
Ye sons of the Southern Cross.

More than eighty-two thousand colonial troops – almost as many as the 87 000 Boers in the republican forces – fought in the war. It did not matter to the Dominion contingents that they would be fighting in Africa against other white men, whites outnumbered by the indigenous blacks. This was a war between whites who were of British extraction and whites who were not.

White the Afrikaner might be, with roots as deep in Europe, but he would always be an ethnic oddity among the British communities of the Empire, long after he had been drawn into that Empire by the outcome of the war. Like the French Canadian, he was never more than a half-brother of foreign parentage, speaking a different language, having a different culture and antecedents, and he could never really be British – in fact didn't want it. It is a distinction that is still drawn today, especially when the rivalry is continued in rugby and cricket matches pitting South Africa against Australia and New Zealand.

Supporters rallied from overseas to the Boer cause, too, though in much smaller numbers, only some two thousand volunteers from Holland, Germany, France, Russia, Ireland and the Scandinavian countries. In their desire to give practical effect to their libertarian ideals, they set a precedent for those non-Iberians who later rallied in numbers to the anti-Fascist cause in the Spanish Civil War.

By the end of January 1900, British numbers were beginning to prevail. Lord Roberts, who had succeeded Buller as commander-in-chief, was rolling inexorably north with 43 000 men. His juggernaut rumbled into the Boer republics, through Bloemfontein and on to Johannesburg. Pretoria was entered in June as Kruger rode bitterly down the railway to Lourenço Marques and exile in Holland. Both the Free State and Transvaal were formally annexed to the British Crown.

The Boers were far from beaten, however. The conflict now entered a hide-and-seek phase, with the comparatively ponderous British columns trying to trap the elusive commandos as they flitted around both the former republics, inflicting heavy losses. President Steyn of the Free State rode with his men in the field, once galloping off in his nightclothes when British troops raided the village where he was stopping.

Unable to contain the commandos, Roberts now introduced the scorched earth tactic that was to bring the British army into its greatest disrepute. The man known affectionately to the British public as 'Bobs' was about to become a war criminal – but one whose own people were unable or unwilling to see him as such. Farms whose owners were fighting with the commandos were destroyed, the crops torched, and homes and outbuildings dynamited. The women and children were left destitute among the ruins. When their numbers grew and their plight worsened, the British felt compelled to gather them into tented camps, the notorious concentration camps.

The Boer forces were suffering heavily from the attrition of the war. Nearly fourteen thousand, or about forty per cent of the original Boer strength, surrendered and took the oath of neutrality demanded by the British. A growing proportion of the Boer forces were lost to capture by the British.

Roberts, convinced that the war was virtually finished, sailed for England in December 1900. Large numbers of British troops were sent home. Kitchener was left to tidy up with the remaining forces. But it was far from over.

The death of Queen Victoria in January 1901 plunged the British into mourning, not so much for the loss of the person as of the certainty and stability she had symbolised. But the war must carry on, even though Britons were becoming weary of it. The imperatives remained unchanged, the goal of supremacy as vital as ever, but the methods were open to revision.

In the month after Victoria's death, Kitchener initiated a meeting with Botha at Middelburg in the Transvaal in an attempt to negotiate peace terms. The negotiations broke down, largely on Chamberlain's insistence on the vote being extended to the black and coloured people in the two republics. Kitchener then stepped up the scorched earth tactics originated by Roberts. But now the number of women and children in the concentration camps exceeded the will or the ability of the British to give any of them adequate care.

In all, some 116 000 Afrikaners were herded into 40 camps, where they died in large numbers from disease, exposure and starvation. Children as well as adults in many cases were reduced to living skeletons of a kind not seen again until the Nazi Germans refined the concentration camp concept in the Second World War. One of every five Boer children in Kitchener's camps died. By the end of the war 26 251 women and children, and 1 676 mostly elderly men, had perished in the camps, four times as many as the Boer fighting men killed in battle and about six per cent of the total Boer population of the republics. The bitterness permeated South African society and festers to this day.

Black people, too, were brought in from the farms, partly to prevent them from producing food that could be raided by the commandos, and partly to provide labour for the British war machine. About 115 000 all told were forced into 66 camps whose conditions were even worse than in the white camps. Some twenty thousand black inmates – almost one in six – died. Most were women and children.

When word of the horrors of the camps reached Britain there was outrage among liberals. The camps were removed from Kitchener's control and placed under the efficient Milner, who effected improvements that drastically cut the death rates.

In March 1901 Kitchener decided after all that the Boers' families would be a greater hindrance to them if left on the farms, and he stopped the intake into the camps. More decisive in bringing the war to an end, however, was his decision to turn the main theatre into a gigantic spiderweb by dotting 8 000 blockhouses around the central plateau and linking them with 6 000 kilometres of barbed-wire fences. He also staged drives and sweeps in which troops advanced in close order over a wide front.

Worn down in the field, their people painfully divided, the Boers were further concerned that the war was again lifting the blacks into competition with the whites.

Talks were opened in April 1902 in Pretoria, and continued there and at Vereeniging on the Vaal River. Milner, anxious to gain complete control of the republics, demanded unconditional surrender but was overruled by Kitchener. On 31 May a peace treaty was signed in Pretoria.

The republics became Crown colonies under Milner but were promised self-government within the Empire as soon as possible. The British agreed to contribute three million pounds towards repairing the war damage. Perhaps the most significant clause as far as the future of South Africa was concerned was the one, adroitly engineered by Smuts, that affected the rights of the blacks. In the first draft, the franchise would 'not be given to natives until after the introduction of self-government'. In other words, the franchise would in time be given. Smuts amended it to read that 'the question of granting the franchise to natives will not be decided until after the introduction of self-government.'[1] In other words, whether the franchise would be given at all was still undecided.

At £200-million the war had been expensive to the British treasury. To the Boer republics it had been ruinous. The cost in lives had also been onerous: 22 000 Britons, 34 000 Boers, and more than fourteen thousand black people. To win the war the British had had to put nearly 450 000 troops in the field, of whom nearly a quarter were killed, captured or seriously wounded.

The invisible costs of the war were profound and long-lasting. Britain's appetite for war and for empire-building was blunted. While the British had won the contest of arms they had effectively lost the peace by uniting the Afrikaners, despite a campaign by Milner to Anglicise them. The black-white racial imbalance was significantly widened and accelerated by the losses in the field and in the concentration camps, which amounted to a sizeable proportion of the white population of South Africa. This in turn increased white fears of being swamped and, consequently, strengthened their perceived imperative of black subjugation.

CHAPTER 19

THE POLITICALLY DEAD

The Boer War in a sense wound up the Scramble by putting the Transvaal, the last major territory in dispute, beyond the reach of Germany, the only power besides Britain that had any prospect of enfolding it politically.

Black resistance to external European domination continued for a while longer. A fierce ripple of opposition, a last heave of defiance, surged across Africa. By the end of the 20th century's first decade, however, Africa's colonial fate had been fairly comprehensively sealed. The last holdouts had given up, except for some in Morocco who were in any case destined to fail. The European powers were able to settle down to what was to be six decades of mostly peaceful – even if enforced – colonialism, two generations of foreign rule covering almost the entire continent.

African resistance to European colonialism was overcome largely because of the superiority of European weaponry. Even when the Africans acquired guns the Europeans were always a technological step ahead of them once the industrial revolution got under way. There was parity of a sort in West Africa while both sides had only muzzle-loading, flintlock muskets. This was ended when the Europeans introduced cap-fired rifles. When the Africans got those the Europeans had advanced to breech-loading, single-shot rifles, and by the time the Africans acquired these the white man had progressed to long-range, rapid-fire, magazine-fed rifles.

The ultimate weapons of colonialism were the Maxim gun and the field gun firing canister shot or shells capable of breaching mud and log forts. Africans at times besieged Europeans in their forts, but the Europeans never had to besiege an African fortress; they simply blasted its walls down. By the time the bomb-dropping, machine-gunning aircraft was added to the European arsenal there was virtually no African resistance left against which to use it. Aircraft were used a few times, though, notably when Smuts sent planes to bomb the rebellious Bondelswarts in South West Africa in 1922 (he was not necessarily racist in this; he also bombed white strikers in Johannesburg in the same year). A few African leaders acquired artillery but never in quantities or calibres sufficient to affect the outcome of their struggles. The same was the case with the machine-guns used by Menelik, the Mahdists and the Moroccan rebel, Abd el-Krim. None appear to have got hold of aircraft except for Abd el-Krim, who acquired three planes while fighting the French in the 1920s but never sent them into action.

Nowhere was resistance stamped out more ruthlessly than in South West Africa,

147

where the Germans resorted to outright genocide to assert their dominance and take over the indigenous peoples' best lands. Indecision about whether to keep the territory or dump it was ended when settlers began to join the initial handful of officials, traders and missionaries. In 1891 there were only 310 Germans in the territory; twelve years later there were 3 000, and another 1 600 Europeans of other nationalities, mainly British.

The best parts of South West Africa were the grasslands already occupied by indigenous peoples. To acquire these lands, the Germans resorted to fomenting the traditional enmity between the indigenous peoples and then acquiring their land in return for 'protection' against their enemies. Both Hereros and Namas were coerced into service through means such as luring them into debt and then demanding impossible terms of repayment.

Resentment among the indigenous peoples was exacerbated by ill-treatment. Flogging and rape were commonplace. Even murder was at times excused on the grounds that the white culprit had been seized by 'tropical frenzy', a fictional condition invented to cover a variety of misdemeanours.[1]

Rebellion sputtering periodically among the indigenous peoples was fairly easily put down until the Hereros rose with determination in January 1904, killing more than a hundred German men – but sparing their women and children. Berlin rushed in troop reinforcements. Demands in Germany for the annihilation of the Hereros were opposed by the commissioner, Major Theodor Leutwein. He pointed out that it would be difficult to exterminate 70 000 people, and in any case the Hereros were needed as labourers. 'It will be quite sufficient,' he said,' if they are politically dead …'[2]

Berlin evidently disagreed, for the military command was transferred to Lieutenant-General Lothar von Trotha, who had demonstrated his ruthlessness in helping to put down the Hehe rising in East Africa in 1896 and the Boxer Rebellion in China in 1901. Von Trotha chased the Herero rebels and their families – about twenty-four thousand people all told – into the Omaheke sandveld, a western extension of the Kalahari desert, then posted a 250-km cordon to prevent them breaking back. About five thousand of the fugitives managed to trek the 300 kilometres to Bechuanaland; a few slipped back through the cordon, but the others perished.

When Berlin countermanded an order by Von Trotha for the extermination of the surviving Hereros he put them in concentration camps which were used as labour pools.

Then the Namas rose in revolt and fought a long-running guerilla war from hideouts in the hills and the desert before being subdued.

Herero and Nama numbers had been hugely reduced in the fighting and especially in the concentration camps, where nearly half of the 17 000 inmates died.[3]

According to a census taken in 1911, the Hereros, once numbering about eighty thousand, had been brought down to just over fifteen thousand, an 80 per cent reduction. The Nama population had been halved – from twenty thousand to just under ten thousand.

Many of the surviving Hereros and Namas were forced into labour for the whites

148

by the same methods that had proved successful elsewhere in Africa. Designated areas were proclaimed as native reserves. By barring Africans from owning land and cattle outside the reserves the Germans ensured that many could never become self-sufficient, and would have to work for the colonists. Movements were controlled and identities monitored through the issuing of passes. From May 1904 indigenous people were required to hang numbered brass tokens from their necks signifying permission to work or live in a designated district. Anyone not working outside the reserves was prosecuted for vagrancy.

In German East Africa, resentment of foreign rule sputtered from the first occupation in 1887. The Hehe fought the Germans for seven years from 1891. A shorter but more violent conflict was the Maji Maji rebellion that erupted in July 1905, taking its name from the potion claimed by its dispenser, the prophet Kinjikitile, to stop bullets. The Germans put the rising down with scorched earth tactics, burning villages and crops as they drove the rebels before them. Thousands of rebels fell to the German guns, but many more – some estimates put it as high as three hundred thousand – died of starvation and exposure in the torched countryside.

The British were not above some scorched-earthing of their own. In Kenya, for instance, the burning of villages and crops was resorted to as late as 1905 in an effort to bring to heel the rebellious Nandis in the western highlands bordering Uganda.

Long-running Nandi resistance to European intrusion was stepped up when the railway being pushed up from the Indian Ocean to Lake Victoria reached Nandi country. Work on the line came to a halt. The British authorities decided in 1905 to move the Nandis into a reserve away from the railway, to keep the line safe from further attacks and at the same time make land available for European settlement.

The Nandis were flushed out in an operation similar to a game drive, with troops advancing in a cordon 60 kilometres long. Behind the cordon all huts and crops were burned and the country generally laid waste, to make it impossible for the Nandis to return. A ring of army posts was formed around the Nandi reserve, and patrols were sent into the evacuated area with orders to shoot on sight any Nandi found there.

Some of the most stubborn resistance to European domination was put up in West Africa, notably by the Asante but also in Sierra Leone, where the indigenous peoples resented the creole 'aristocracy' formed by the freed slaves who had been settled in 1787. The indigenous Temne people rose in rebellion in 1898 and fought the British from loopholed stockades in the forest, and the revolt was later joined by the Mende. It took the British a year to quell the rebellions.

When Lugard was appointed high commissioner for northern Nigeria he found himself struggling to subjugate the vast territory he had ostensibly inherited from Goldie. The slave-trading Muslim emirates of the north were especially intractable, but Lugard was not averse to ruthless measures to get his job done. In 1902, with Kano still resisting subjugation, Lugard blasted the walls down with his field guns and sprayed the defenders with his Maxims, killing more than a thousand.

Sokoto's defenders, having no weapons to counter Lugard's modern arms, wisely capitulated. When Muslims in nearby Satiru rose in revolt in 1906, Lugard sent in his machine-guns. The rebels, mostly armed with nothing more than agricultural implements, were mown down by the hundred. Those captured alive were beheaded and their heads displayed on stakes.

Winston Churchill, then colonial under-secretary, was dismayed at the news of the massacre. He wanted to know how, when Lugard was 'butchering' Nigerians, the Colonial Office could chastise Natal's colonial rulers for executing 12 rebellious Zulus.

The executions that aroused Churchill's concern came at a time when whites in South Africa had been made especially uneasy by the Herero revolt in South West Africa, the Maji Maji rebellion in Tanganyika and, closer to home, the rise of what were called the Ethiopian churches. The Ethiopian Movement, started among black Christians in South Africa with the encouragement of black churches in the United States, expressed black rejection of the establishment churches for what was seen as their collaboration in white domination in Africa. There was a cross-pollination with the 'Africa for the Africans' philosophy that also had some backing in America. The Movement's philosophy spread to South West Africa where it was thought by some Germans to have influenced the Namas to rebel.

In February 1906, whites in Natal were alerted to mounting opposition among the Zulus to the poll tax. There was discontent among the Zulus over land issues as well, more than a third of Zululand having been taken for white plantations. When two white policemen were killed in the Richmond district, panicky authorities declared a state of emergency, summarily tried the alleged killers, convicted 12 and had them executed by firing squad.

Two months later Bambata, chief of the Zondi clan, sparked an uprising that spread widely. By the time it was brought to an end more than three thousand five hundred Zulus and 30 white soldiers and civilians had been killed. The deposed Zulu king, Dinizulu, who had returned from his two years of exile on St Helena after the Zulu wars, was implicated in the rebellion, convicted of treason and jailed.

Though never a threat to white supremacy, the Bambata rebellion stirred the white South Africans' primal fear of being overwhelmed by the black majority. That majority was much less then than it became later, for the black population increased much faster than the white. Still, the rebellion brought home to the whites their vulnerability when split among two colonies and two republics. By emphasising the value of joint defence, the Bambata rebellion helped persuade the Afrikaners and the British South Africans to join forces in the Union of South Africa in 1910.

★ ★ ★ ★

For all the determination they showed in acquiring and holding their African possessions, there was at times an element of extraordinary casualness in the way the colonial powers treated both their colonies and their indigenous inhabitants.

The British Colonial Office, for instance, was quite careless of how the natives might feel about it when in 1903 it offered Uganda to the Zionist movement as a possible Jewish homeland instead of Palestine. As late as 1939 the governor of Kenya was asked by Whitehall for his views on settling large numbers of Jewish refugees from Germany in the colony. He opposed the idea, but not out of consideration for the views of the indigenous peoples.

Like all collectors, the colonial powers sometimes swapped their acquisitions, such as when the Germans exchanged pieces of East Africa for Heligoland. There were also occasions when the powers traded interests in territories. A notable instance was France's surrender of its long-asserted interest in Egypt in exchange for Britain's abandoning any interest in Morocco.

That exchange was typical of the under-the-counter deals that tidied up the Scramble. It was secretly signed by France and Britain in April 1904, Whitehall having been moved to heal the breach with France by the realisation that it must end Britain's 'splendid isolation' and form friendships in Europe in view of the volatile political situation developing there.

The deal was made possible by the Sultan of Morocco having got his country deeply in debt with the European banks, like his counterparts in Egypt and Tunisia. France, Britain and Germany were all alert to the possibility of one of them exploiting the debt crisis to gain control of the country. The French asserted a prime interest in that they had had a presence of sorts there since 1844 and that the instability in Morocco threatened their hold on neighbouring Algeria. Once assured by the British of a free hand in Morocco, the French withdrew their interest in the Caisse that controlled Egypt's debts, thereby at last giving Baring (now Lord Cromer) his own free hand to assert British authority in Egypt.

Kaiser Wilhelm objected to the deal but was sidestepped when the issue was made the subject of an international conference at Algeciras in Spain in 1906. France and Britain were supported by Russia, needing allies herself after having had her navy and much of her status as a power sunk by Japan in the Battle of Tsushima in 1905. These three were joined by Italy, looking for backing for her territorial ambitions in Africa.

Outvoted, the Germans agreed to recognise the paramountcy of French interests in north-west Africa provided Germany had free access to trade in Morocco. As a further sop the French ceded a portion of their West African territory to allow Germany's colony of Cameroon to extend up to Lake Chad.

In 1907 the killing by Berbers of Frenchmen working on a railway gave France an excuse to widen its 'interests' into formal occupation of eastern Morocco and Casablanca. Five years later the cash-strapped sultan was forced to grant France a 'protectorate' over the whole country. France ceded the northern strip of the territory to Spain. It took the French and Spanish another 22 years, however, to put down native resistance to their rule, the toughest opposition coming from the redoubtable Abd el-Krim between 1921 and 1926. He was defeated only when a Franco-Spanish army 250 000 strong was sent against him. After that France, which had ruled its part of Morocco indirectly, instituted direct administration from Paris.

Italy's involvement in the horse-trading over Morocco was aimed at expanding Rome's colonial opportunities in Africa, which by the end of the Scramble were limited. Italy appeared to have been left with only crumbs of the great cake, nothing more than little Eritrea and a piece of Somalia. And the defeat at Adowa still rankled. Italians began to eye the only substantial territory that still seemed up for grabs, the huge stretch lying between Egypt and Tunisia. Apart from the reasonably fertile but narrow coastal strip it was largely semi-desert or outright desert, governed by Turkey as the provinces of Cyrenaica and Tripolitania. South of these was the Fezzan desert, whose inhabitants had for centuries made a living by taxing or robbing the trans-Saharan caravans, and who paid scant regard to anyone's claims of suzerainty.

Having taken the eastern and western extremities of the Mediterranean coast, the Great Powers could see little strategic or commercial value in the barren centre. Still, it seemed better than nothing to Rome, even worth going to war with Turkey. On 28 September 1911 Italy gave Turkey 24 hours to give satisfaction over its 'interests' in Cyrenaica and Tripolitania. The Turks, perhaps finding it hard to discern those interests, ignored the ultimatum and found themselves at war with Italy. It took some hard fighting to seize Tripolitania, but when Italian troops made big advances in Cyrenaica the Turks ceded sovereignty in the aptly named Treaty of Ouchy.

The Italians were no more successful – or interested – than the Romans had been in occupying Fezzan, whose inhabitants carried on pretty well as they had before. When the First World War broke out in 1914 the Turks, fighting on Germany's side, called on Muslims in Turkish possessions to rise against the Allies. The Italians, preoccupied with supporting the Allies in Europe, were driven back to the coast.

After the war General Rodolfo Graziani led Italian troops in a ruthless campaign to recover the territories. Tripolitania was not subdued until 1923, Fezzan more or less subdued in 1929, and Cyrenaica only in 1932. Two years later the two provinces were joined to form a colony the Italians called Libya, borrowing the ancient Greek name for the whole of north Africa. Fezzan, always troublesome and difficult to administer, was made a military district adjoining the colony.

In the two decades of fighting the Italians are estimated to have killed as many as one third of the indigenous inhabitants of the territory. Having established mastery, the Italians poured emigrants and money into Libya, building towns and roads and waterworks. However, they were destined not to keep it for much longer, for the Second World War lay only a few years ahead.

★ ★ ★ ★

A bizarre effect of the Scramble was that one of the biggest and richest pieces of the African cake was held not by a European power but in effect by an individual, King Leopold. He had won it through the skilful advancing of his greedy ambitions, but it was his greed that would lose it to him in the end.

Having gained control of most of the Congo Basin under the guise of opening it to international free trade and Western civilising influences, Leopold had begun to exploit it to expand his wealth and ego. Initially he had lost rather than made money from the Congo Free State. But when rubber came into demand with the proliferation of the pneumatic tyre, Leopold hit the jackpot, for rubber trees grew in wild profusion in his Congo jungles.

The extraction of the rubber was done both by the CFS and by private Belgian companies under concessions awarded by Leopold, and he hauled in fine profits from both. The method of collecting the rubber was simple and cheap: arbitrary quotas were imposed on each village, so heavy that the villagers had little time to produce food for themselves. Some died of starvation, others of exposure and disease. No payment was made for the rubber – the only reward was the privilege of being allowed to stay alive. The penalty for failing to meet the quotas was death, mutilation or enslavement. The soldiers charged with enforcement of the quotas brought back the severed hands of their victims, sometimes by the basketful, as proof of their diligence.

Leopold was able to stifle persistent rumours of the atrocities until 1900, when the lid was lifted by Edmonde Morel, a clerk in the Liverpool headquarters of the Elder Dempster shipping line that had the contract to bring the rubber from the Congo. Morel deduced from discrepancies in the figures for the trade that the natives were not being paid for gathering the rubber.

He began a campaign that led to efforts in Britain to invoke the Berlin Act's requirements of free trade and upliftment of the Africans. The Foreign Office, however, turned a blind eye, afraid of antagonising the Belgians and pushing them into alliance with Germany, whose growing military strength and assertiveness were beginning to worry Whitehall.

Mounting public agitation led in 1903 to an investigation by the British consul in the Congo Free State, Roger Casement. His damning report caused a sensation in Britain but still the government refrained from acting on it. Morel took his campaign to America, and to counter it Leopold hired a lobbyist, Harry Kowalski.

In Belgium, the king made the mistake of appointing an independent-minded judge, Emile Janssens, to conduct another inquiry. To Leopold's discomfort, Janssens's report broadly corroborated Casement's findings, as now did the once-fearful Congo missionaries.

In 1905 Morel's Congo Reform Association began pressing the Berlin Act signatories to demand that the Belgian state take over the CFS from the king. Two more years passed, however, before the Belgian parliament supported the demand.

Leopold, with his back now to the wall, made another mistake: he fired Kowalski, who retaliated by exposing his former employer's involvement in the atrocities. President Roosevelt and the US Senate joined the demand for Belgian annexation of the CFS. In January 1908 Britain and the United States made a joint demarche demanding the restoration of free trade and missionary activity in the Congo and 'humane treatment of natives'.

Leopold appeared at last to give in, agreeing to hand over the CFS to the Belgian state in return for handsome compensation. But the Treaty of Cession left largely intact the old administrative infrastructure. The concession companies and their ruthless officials still controlled the rubber-harvesting, and Leopold could, if he wished, still pull the strings. It was a situation that none of the powers wished to confront, with Belgium ever more precariously balanced as Europe began to slide into the First World War.

Leopold solved the problem himself on 14 December 1909 by dying after a stomach operation. He was given the obligatory state funeral but the mourning was muted. Even the Belgians were beginning to realise that the monarch they had once respected would take a place in history as one of humankind's monsters.

Leopold's monstrosities tended to overshadow another reign of atrocity on the other side of the Congo River, where French entrepreneurs had imitated his enforced rubber-gathering. At first they had been blocked by Brazza, the governor-general, but in 1898 they succeeded in having him replaced by the more amenable Emile Gentil. However, growing disclosure of the atrocities obliged the Colonial Ministry to appoint a commission of inquiry. Brazza, though sick, agreed to lead it.

The ministry, however, merely intended Brazza's mission as a cover. In Gabon and Brazzaville, he found himself officially blocked at every turn. He was able nonetheless to gather evidence of cruelties but then became seriously ill. While returning home he died at Dakar in September 1905. The government gave him a state funeral in France but suppressed his half-finished report. The gist of it was made public by his assistant on the mission, Felicien Challaye, but no official action was taken against the iniquities of the concessionaires, which continued more or less unchecked for another two decades.

CHAPTER 20

A MARRIAGE OF CONVENIENCE

The memories were still bitter and the wounds still hurt when those who had fought each other in the Boer War joined together in forming the Union of South Africa in 1910, only eight years after the war's end. It was a marriage of incompatibles if ever there was one, and widely recognised as such. Yet it was as widely praised as a remarkable act of reconciliation between Boer and Briton.

It was a pragmatic rather than a noble accommodation, however, a matter of self-interest on both sides. By melding the Transvaal and Orange Free State with the original two colonies in a union within the Empire, the British could expect less trouble from their Afrikaner populations than if the two former republics had remained conquered colonies, albeit self-governing ones. The important thing was to pull them into the club alongside Australia, New Zealand and Canada (where a large French section mostly resigned to loyalty might serve as a model for the Afrikaners). While union might lessen Britain's ability to protect her vital interests in the Cape sea route and the mineral wealth, those interests could probably be served as well and more cheaply by an independent dominion within the Empire.

The Boers, for their part, could have expected worse than a union with their conquerors on more or less equal terms. Although they had lost their independence, they had gained a measure of protection against their greatest fear: being engulfed by the black majority.

While the Vereeniging peace pact had been a matter between the British government and the Boers, in the creation of the Union there was a third party very much involved: the English-speaking South Africans. They, too, now saw this part of Africa as their home – not as Africans, though, but as Europeans, as Britons living in extra-territorial Britain, in a white part of the Empire, like Australia and New Zealand and Canada.

Most of the British South Africans shared the Afrikaner's fear of black domination. They were as well aware that the union, besides joining the white groups, was a coercive impounding, with inferior status, of coloured and Indian communities and a number of disparate African nations which together outnumbered the whites four to one.

The main body of the whites believed that only by uniting and keeping the blacks perpetually subordinate could they imitate the white supremacy that had already been entrenched in Australia, New Zealand, Canada and the United States.

They could never duplicate it because the native peoples in their country were far more numerous than those in the other white-dominated countries. They could only try to match it through continued suppression of the natives.

When the constitution of the Union came to be negotiated in 1908 there was some opposition in Britain to the continued subjugation of the black people, but it was not strong enough to overcome the demand for white supremacy. Black rights had been shelved during the peace negotiations in 1902 because the *bittereinders* had still been fighting and would certainly have continued to fight had racial equality been introduced into the terms. Even the *hensoppers** would have objected. At that time, too, the British public, afflicted in pocket, energy and conscience by the war, had been in no mood to have it drag on. As far as the British government was concerned, control of the gold mines, a prime reason for fighting the war, had pretty well been assured. Now the blacks would be required to provide the cheap labour necessary to maximise profits.

Attitudes had not changed much by 1908. London was now concerned that equal rights for blacks in South Africa might spark demands for full franchise and other rights from peoples elsewhere in the Empire. Could full political rights be given to black people in South Africa and not to those in Rhodesia, Kenya, Nigeria, the Gold Coast, or, heaven forbid, India? The South African issue epitomised the fundamental British dilemma throughout the Empire: the moral desire to uplift the conquered natives conflicting with both the commercial imperative to exploit them and the political one to subjugate them.

The white unity forged in South Africa in 1910, the unity in dominating the blacks, was to be shaken by friction, dispute and occasional violence, but it would hold fast for 84 years. The fear would hold it together even when the world eventually turned against the whites' racism and made them outcasts. White supremacy would be abandoned only when it was seen to have become hopeless and self-defeating. But for three generations the fear glued the incompatible Boers and Britons together in South Africa as nothing else could have done.

Their unity was maintained despite Milner's efforts to forcefully Anglicise the Afrikaners and swamp them with immigrant Britons. Rather than weakening the Afrikaners' sense of identity, Milner's efforts undoubtedly strengthened it. It is unlikely, however, that the attitude of the whites in general to black rights would have been much different had Milner achieved his British majority.

Milner himself was no supporter of Exeter Hall, and pleased most of the Boers and English-speakers in the Transvaal by maintaining and even extending its restrictions on the blacks. Milner departed in 1905 and was succeeded by Lord Selborne, who took the former republics to self-government in 1907. By then the Afrikaners had formed the *Het Volk* party in the Transvaal and the *Orangia Unie* in the Orange Free State, and each won office in the first elections.

Het Volk's victory dismayed those in Whitehall who, like Milner, had been banking on the gold mines attracting enough British immigrants to the Transvaal to out-

---

*The *bittereinders* were the Boers determined to fight to the bitter end; and the *hensoppers*, the 'hands-uppers', were those who surrendered.

vote the Afrikaners. This had not come about because the mines, squeezed between high costs and fixed price, had not brought sufficient prosperity to attract immigrants in large numbers. To prosper, the mines needed cheap labour, which was not always readily available, not even from the areas where poverty had been entrenched by factors such as the restrictive socialism of tribal tradition and the taxation by the white government at levels above what rural communities could afford.

Bowing to the demands of the Chamber of Mines, the government sanctioned the recruitment of mineworkers from China but, while it was a commercial success, the move provoked political opposition that brought it to an end.

Coercion of black labour was common not only on the mines but in agriculture and other industries as they developed. In Natal, however, it failed to meet the demands of the labour-intensive sugar estates, and Indians were brought out from 1860 as indentured labourers. Unlike the Chinese miners, the Indian cane-cutters posed no threat to white workers and were allowed to remain when their contracts ended. By 1886 they numbered nearly thirty thousand, and in the year of union 150 000.

A second influx came in the form of 'passenger Indians', who paid their own way to South Africa and who, unlike the Hindu indentured workers, were mostly Muslim traders. In neither case were they granted political rights.

Most of the indentured labourers quit cutting cane as soon as they could and took up other occupations. The government, now seeing the Indians as an incipient threat to white hegemony, squeezed off the flow from India and introduced measures to persuade those in South Africa to go back to India. Hardly any did so.

Despite forming nearly eighty per cent of the population by 1904, the blacks remained hamstrung by the 1902 agreement to shelve the question of their political rights in the Transvaal and Free State. In Natal the strict conditions imposed on blacks ensured that only an insignificant handful had the right to vote. Even in the Cape, with its more liberal tradition, the voting restrictions had resulted in coloureds forming only ten per cent of the registered voters and blacks making up fewer than five per cent.

Finding themselves marginalised in the land of their ancestors, the black people began to create their own political organisations, as did the coloureds and Asians.

Among the white South Africans, the fear of the black majority was so fundamental and widespread that it was a barely acknowledged element in shaping white attitudes as they prepared to take control of the country in the infant Union. Alongside the fear was an unquestioned conviction of black inferiority, an old growth rooted deep in European experience in Africa as traders, slavers, explorers, hunters, missionaries, colonialists and settlers; a disrespect seeded early in unfavourable comparisons of African civilisation and culture with those of Europe.

Even Jan Smuts, who in his time was the South African most widely admired in the world before Mandela, deviated from that conviction only in the belief that Africans might in time catch up to European standards. But he never envisaged a conjoined society, rather a perpetually separate though parallel existence of black and white societies. In a speech in 1895, Smuts said democracy as understood and practised in Europe and America was inapplicable to the coloured races of Africa. He warned that the African must be elevated otherwise he would drag the white man down with him. But rights should be granted 'only in proportion as duties are learnt'. He argued that the whites should try persuasively to discipline the native 'into something worthy of our civilisation and his humanity'.

The racial issue was always for Smuts a ball of thorns that he touched only gingerly. In 1906 he wrote:'I sympathise profoundly with the native races of South Africa, whose land it was long before we came here to force a policy of dispossession on them.' Sympathy, however, was a far cry from solution.'I feel inclined,' he added, 'to shift the intolerable burden of solving the problem on the ampler shoulders … of the future.' In the meantime, he supported segregation.

Eleven years later Smuts was advocating some kind of separate development, which was later to become the basis of the apartheid policy of his political opponents, the National Party. At a dinner given in his honour in London in May 1917 on his appointment to the Empire War Cabinet, he noted that 'unlike other British Dominions, our future as a white civilisation is not assured.' While deriding as 'arrant nonsense' the rise in Germany of the doctrine of pure race, for South Africa he endorsed the principle of 'no intermixture of blood between the two colours'. It was possible, he said, that the race problem in South Africa might be solved by 'giving the natives their own separate institutions on parallel lines with institutions for whites'.

Smuts's ideas were relatively liberal compared with some of those held by delegates to the National Convention that began sitting in 1908 to devise a constitution in response to the swelling move for unification. Black leaders had already begun to make their case for their rights to be recognised in the constitution. At a meeting in Queenstown in 1907, black and coloured representatives called for the Cape's qualified black franchise to be adopted in a federation (rather than a union) of the four colonies. That they did not demand equal rights appears surprising now, but they probably were acting from an appreciation of the prevailing political realities. There was no possibility that the all-white National Convention would extend the full franchise to the black majority. Better to go for the lesser possibility than the larger impossibility.

Two months before the National Convention had its final sitting in Bloemfontein, black leaders from around the country met there as the South African Native Convention (which in 1912 would become the South African Native National Congress and later the African National Congress, destined to take power with the advent of democracy in 1994). The Native Convention opposed all the clauses of the draft constitution that limited black rights, and drew up a petition demanding that black rights be recognised.

The (all white) Cape delegates to the constitutional convention argued for the general adoption of the Cape's common role with qualified franchise, but were outvoted by the other delegations. The final draft recognised only the limited voting rights existing in the Cape and denied them to Africans, coloureds and Indians elsewhere.

The Cape premier, WP Schreiner, led a deputation of black and coloured leaders to London in an effort to persuade Parliament to reject the constitution. Mahatma Gandhi, too, went with a deputation of Indians. Louis Botha, the Boer War general and now leader of Het Volk, had with Smuts beaten them to it, however, and won strong support at Westminster. Besides, British politicians were then infatuated with the philosophy of 'social Darwinism', which applied Darwin's theories of natural selection and survival-fitness to society, to the disadvantage of Africans.

Apart from its racial provisions, the political system devised by the National Convention broadly followed European patterns, with a bicameral parliament and a constitution protectively interpreted by the courts. Afrikaans and English were given equal status as official languages. No other African language was recognised. Delegates advocating a federal system had been outvoted by those demanding a unitary one, a decision that was later to ease the way for the institution of autocratic racism under the name of apartheid. Extended even later into the post-apartheid constitution, it left open the possibility, even though seemingly remote, of a one-party state in a supposedly democratic South Africa.

The Union was formally instituted in South Africa on 31 May 1910. By the king's seal the non-white peoples of South Africa had been consigned indefinitely to inferior status because in the end almost all the whites, on both sides of the ocean, had been afraid or mistrustful of the black majority – or had wanted to continue exploiting its members.

Among later generations of whites some would rue the action for making it more difficult and costly for them eventually to accept black majority rule when its inevitability overwhelmed its opposition. Among other things, it blocked the continued rise of the black middle class that was already emerging, and which, some whites now believe, could have taken South Africa relatively peacefully into a dispensation more stable and prosperous than it was when majority rule was at last accepted in 1994.

Perhaps more than any other society, white South Africa reflected both of the fundamental forms of racism: the one offensive or proactive, the other defensive or reactive. The proactive form comes from a gratuitous antipathy to persons of another complexion or from a desire to exploit them, sometimes from both. It is the kind of racism found among white majorities such as in Europe, the United States and Australia, where the people of colour pose no serious social, economic or political threat to the predominant whites. Reactive racism, on the other hand, grows mainly among minorities who have a real fear of losing their jobs, lifestyles or identities to the majority. South Africa was distinctive in that it was one of the few countries dominated by an ethnic minority, which practised reactive racism as a means of defence against the subjugated majority, and proactive racism to exploit it. Colonialism, too, induced both proactive racism in the interests of exploiting the colonised peoples, and reactive racism as a means of defence against their greater numbers. Apartheid in South Africa was different, however, in that it was carried out on home ground, in a domestic rather than a foreign milieu. Colonialism was an impermanent thing that could be scrapped with little or no risk, but apartheid was home-grown, socially intertwined and impossible to unravel without extreme trauma.

In 1910, however, it was the proactive more than the reactive racism that dominated white thinking and set the course of events for the next eight decades.

CHAPTER 21

TRICKLING IN

Around the time the Scramble for Africa was ending, Europeans were emigrating in millions to the Americas and Australasia. Few went to Africa, despite the opportunities ostensibly opened there by the Scramble.

Africa was fascinating, romantic even, but only from a comfortable distance. Europeans considered it no place to make home, except, of course, for the temperate extremities and central highlands. The rest of it was still a place for the exceptionally hardy and adventurous – hunters, missionaries, explorers, traders.

Well over twenty million Europeans sought a new life in the new worlds in the last half of the 19th century and the first decade of the 20th. Most went to the United States: six million Italians, two million Germans, a million each of Irish, Scandinavians and Austro-Hungarians, together with tens of thousands of Hollanders, Belgians, Greeks, Turks, Rumanians and other nationalities. More than seven million Britons emigrated – to Canada, the United States and Australasia, with a relatively small proportion going to South Africa. About four million Spaniards went to South America, as did two million Portuguese and thousands of Germans, Hungarians and French.[1]

The Europeans emigrating to Africa, however, were numbered not in millions but in tens of thousands. For much the same reasons for which they had delayed their exploration and conquest of Africa, the Europeans now hesitated to settle there.

They especially avoided the interior, for, although it had been penetrated and broadly mapped by explorers such as Brazza, Stanley and Cameron, it remained mysterious and forbidding. Few white men, still fewer white families, would seek a new life in gloomy, saturated jungles where they believed fierce gorillas lived and the natives often ate each other. Europeans would settle in relatively small numbers on the continent's Mediterranean coast, and they would go to the sunny highlands of East Africa and Rhodesia and even more readily to South Africa, where white people had for generations been engaging in activities as European as growing apples and making wine, where the natives had been subdued, where the world's richest goldfields were being worked, and where some parts had snow in winter.

The rest of the continent was left largely to traders willing to suffer for profit, to misfits and miscreants hounded out of European society, to hunters and missionaries, and to colonial officials forsaking civilisation for the sake of careers or an eccentric fondness for lonely and savage places.

Colonialism was not necessarily the same as colonisation; it was not primarily about white settlement. For all the colonialising of Africa, there was not much colonising in the sense of white settlement. The Americas and Australasia remained much more attractive to European emigrants, for these lands had long been widely settled by their kind. When the Scramble for Africa began, the Europeans had been established for five generations or more in the eastern United States, and had driven the Indians out of almost all of the prairies and the western mountains and coastal plains. The first transcontinental railway had been completed to San Francisco, already a sizeable city. Europeans were as well established in South America, too; Brazil, Argentina, Chile and Peru had all existed as independent states for more than sixty years before the European powers began to grab at Africa. Whites had settled at the Cape much earlier than in Australia, yet all the Australian states had capitals, constitutions and governments in place before the Berlin Conference of 1884 triggered the territorial equivalent of a bargain basement sale in the rest of Africa.

White emigration to the two main points of settlement in the continent – South Africa and Algeria – was substantial in itself and proportionately quite heavy. Before the Scramble began, each had about two hundred and fifty thousand whites, and when it ended these numbers had more than quadrupled in South Africa's case and nearly trebled in the case of Algeria. By 1910 South Africa had something over one and a quarter million whites (22 per cent of the national total) and Algeria about seven hundred and fifty thousand (about 14 per cent of the total).[2]

Still, the increases were a trickle compared to the flood into the United States (whose population rose from 50-million in 1880 to 92-million by 1910), and much less even than the flow to Argentina. Despite the lure of the gold mines, European emigration to South Africa was less than to Australia, whose gold deposits were turning out to be nowhere near as rich as the Witwatersrand's. What Australia had that South Africa didn't have was a small indigenous population easily subjugated by the immigrant whites.

One of the strongest deterrents to European settlement in Africa was the presence almost everywhere of indigenous populations too large for extermination and whose subjugation, where it was seriously undertaken, invariably required the use of armies of professional soldiers. It was no work for white settlers except for large, cohesive, well-armed bodies such as the Voortrekkers.

Unlike America, there was no central government independent of Europe to support white expansion into territory occupied by indigenous peoples and to back it with soldiers. The nearest thing to the US Cavalry were British or French troops who might or might not be sent out by a government which was not always sympathetic to white expansion, certainly not if it was going to involve expenditure of dubious value. Genocide of the indigenous population was easier in an America whose government turned a blind eye than it was in a British colony subject even at long range to Exeter Hall scrutiny. The Exeter Hall syndrome never reached as strongly to distant, self-governing Australian territories as it did to Africa.

The relatively few whites who went to Africa to settle were generally somewhat more affluent than the 'huddled masses' who went to the United States. There were no boatloads of indigent Irish and penniless Poles stepping ashore in worn shoes, no equivalent of Ellis Island to funnel in immigrants by the thousand. Most white immigrants to southern and central Africa were fairly well skilled or educated, and many had some capital with which to go farming or start a business. It had to be that way because there was no informal safety net for them in most of Africa, no swiftly expanding economy sucking in workers, artisans and clerks, no large communities of Italians, Jews, Poles, Germans, Norwegians and Irish to take in and help others of their kind coming in from the motherland. The immigrants to Africa were pretty much thrown on their own resources from the moment they came down the gangplank.

There were few assisted emigration schemes because the relatively small economies of white Africa could not absorb mass immigration. And not many Europeans were willing to try their luck on their own in Africa when they could do so in more settled places with a more certain future.

Of the high-lying, temperate regions, only Abyssinia (Ethiopia) was never settled by Europeans, primarily because its people were relatively powerful militarily and its terrain mountainous and lacking minerals.

The limited immigration and the strength of the indigenous populations meant that the Europeans were always outnumbered wherever they settled in Africa. As late as 1939, South Africa, South West Africa, Algeria and Libya were the only African countries whose whites exceeded ten per cent of the national population (which in Libya was indigenously small in any case). In only two other countries, Southern Rhodesia and Tunisia, was the white population more than five per cent of the total; only in Angola and the Spanish possessions was it as much as five per cent. Elsewhere, including Kenya, it was less than one per cent. In contrast to the millions of Germans who had gone to North and South America, Germany's African colonies attracted a relative handful of immigrants. The largest German population, that in South West Africa, was only 14 000 in 1914, thirty years after Bismarck had grabbed the territory.

The reason is plain. Like the other powers with most of their acquisitions, Germany had seized its African colonies not because they were rich or especially suitable for white settlement, but mainly because they were there and available and Berlin perceived a need to acquire them for reasons of politics and prestige, to take them before some other power did, to hold them as insurance.

When the European Powers quit Africa they left little of themselves behind apart from some social structures and their languages, French, English and Portuguese having perforce become the *linguae francae* of the disparate peoples tossed together in the artificial states. The only exceptions were the relatively large white communities in South Africa – where the whites were in any case well established before the Scramble began – and in Zimbabwe and Namibia.

The whites' attempts to put down roots in Algeria, and to some extent Kenya, failed because they were never strong enough to avoid being swept out by indigenous nationalism and the later politics of their European motherlands. The Algerian settlers had the numbers, but neither they nor the relatively few Kenyans (a hundred and fifty thousand at most) and Rhodesians (never more than three hundred thousand) had the economic muscle to defy both indigenous nationalism and European moral politics. The Algerian settlers fought a long and bloody war to retain possession, but in the end found themselves powerless to resist the will of the majority of their countrymen that Algeria should be returned to its indigenous people. Once Britain had similarly pulled its colonial rug from beneath the Kenyans and the Rhodesians, both were obliged to bow to majority rule. The Portuguese in Angola, Mozambique and Portuguese Guinea were in a similar situation, and suffered a similar fate.

Only the South Africans, more numerous, longer established and blessed with a mineral bonanza, had the ability to stay and grow, to withstand both pressure from Europe and the numerical power of the indigenous majority – and later the moral force of the international community. In the end, though, even they succumbed and now, like the whites in Zimbabwe and Namibia, they find themselves living increasingly at the mercy of the indigenous people.

Because European settlement was so sparse, colonialism displaced very few Africans outside South Africa, South West Africa, the Rhodesias, East Africa and Algeria. Most Africans remained where they had been before the Europeans arrived. More disruptive than European settlement was the arbitrary definition of new boundaries. Since most African communities were relatively small, this had the effect not so much of splitting ethnic groups as of pulling numbers of them together within artificial frontiers in what has been described as 'a ruthless act of political amalgamation'.[3] In not all cases, however, were those thrown together compatible in language and customs, and the result, once the colonial masters had withdrawn, was some of the most horrific conflicts of the 20th century.

After the First World War, European migration to Africa picked up quite sharply but was never as heavy as it continued to be to America. When the Germans were displaced from East and South West Africa their places were largely taken by whites from countries in the Allied camp who were eager to take advantage of the infrastructure established by the Germans. Nothing was returned to the original inhabitants. There was a fairly large post-war settlement of Belgians in the Congo, mostly tied to copper mining in Katanga or trading in Leopoldville. Most of the immigration, however, went to the existing white communities in Algeria, Kenya, the Rhodesias and South Africa.

Except for the Mediterranean territories, there was relatively little white migration to France's African possessions before or after the war. What there was went mainly to steamy Côte d'Ivoire to exploit the territory's potential for tropical agriculture. By the end of the thirties whites owned a third of the acreage under coffee, and all of the banana plantations and the timber industry. They were still vastly outnumbered by the indigenous people, however.

Just before the start of the Second World War, the Italians began the biggest single white settlement of Africa, a massive operation that within a year would place more than thirty thousand Italians in Tripolitania and Cyrenaica and see Libya incorporated into metropolitan Italy.

That war would radically change attitudes in both Europe and Africa and start the demand for freedom that would see the colonial powers decamping almost in a body. Yet even at the start of the war few Europeans doubted that those in Africa and their descendants would hold their settled lands forever. In 1935, only four years before Hitler's blitzkrieg hit Poland, the then colonial secretary, Leopold Amery, was able to declare that 'no plans for the ultimate future of East Africa will be soundly based that do not face the fact that in the course of the next century there will be a more or less continuous white population from the Cape to the borders of Abyssinia forming, in all probability, part of a single political entity'.

It took only about twenty years for the essential fallacy of Amery's words to be demonstrated. In the mean time, however, the Europeans kept coming into Africa in the belief that their hegemony would last forever, as they had believed since the beginning of white settlement.

CHAPTER 22

THE THIN WHITE LINE

Deep in the African bush, a district officer is sitting alone outside his tent on a canvas chair at a folding table lit by an oil lamp and the light from a large fire. From time to time the firelight reflects from the eyes of wild animals staring in from the dark. An African servant wearing a long white robe and a red tarboosh is serving dinner to the white man, who is wearing evening dress, the same black tie and starched shirt in which he used to dine in London before coming out to Africa.

It is a scene so bizarre that it may belong only in colonial mythology. It is reputed, however, to have been enacted more or less as described above. While British colonial officials regularly 'dressed for dinner' at the main administrative centres, doing it while out on safari was odd behaviour even among the sometimes eccentric men who served in Africa's far-flung places. Nonetheless, a few are said to have done it, at least occasionally and perhaps regularly.

Even if mythical, the scene symbolically illustrates the attitudes and values that British colonial officials brought to the task of administering vast and isolated districts that to them appeared primitive and savage. Maintaining the standards of their own culture became an essential defence against the powerful alien environment. The more isolated the posting, the more important maintaining those standards became. Rather than evening dress, however, a district officer encamped on safari would more typically have been wearing khakis – but with his fire nevertheless suitably distant from those of his black staff.

Styles of colonial government varied markedly between the British, the French, the Germans and the Portuguese, shaped partly by the differing attitudes to race.

The British, ruled by an upper class that considered Africans lower even than their own lowest classes, adopted a patronising attitude verging on condescension, but diluted with the sense of *noblesse oblige* with which the British aristocracy bolstered its claim to supremacy. Their African subjects were to be ruled with all necessary firmness but with as little harshness as possible. They were to be encouraged to advance from their lower civilisation to the higher form already attained by their colonial masters, and if they ever reached it they might perhaps be considered equal but they would jolly well have to prove themselves first. In the mean time they were to be kept at a distance, separate socially, politically and, as a sometimes incidental consequence, economically as well. Benevolent segregation was the theme, with integration as the ultimate but not necessarily inevitable end.

The British relied on a form of indirect rule – heavy reliance on existing ethnic authorities to administer colonial districts. The official rationale for the policy was that Britain could not afford large expenditure on running its African colonies. A truer reason, probably, was that the colonies were not considered worth large expenditure unless they had some economic worth, which was not always the case.

Indirect rule was in any case made possible by the fact that often the indigenous communities pretty well carried on as they had before the British informed them that they had been colonised. Their objection to the material disadvantages of colonialism, such as paying taxes and providing labour, tended to be offset by the relative certainty of order and stability, of having the askaris available for defence against rivals or enemies. The knowledge that larger military forces with Maxims were on call if necessary was one of the factors that made it possible for the district officer backed by a few askaris to maintain control over an area too large to cross in a week's march.

Informally, the governing style was sometimes referred to as the 'thin white line'. In Nigeria after the First World War there was one white official for every 54 000 Africans, and in Uganda the ratio was 1 : 49 000. In the Belgian Congo it was only 1 : 34 000 and in French West Africa 1 : 27 000. Kenya, with the largest white settler population (and therefore relatively more social displacement, disruption and resentment) had the most administrative officials, the ratio being 1 : 22 000.

Kenya came closer than the other colonies to the rigorous labour exploitation practised in South Africa and the Rhodesias. The larger the white settlement the greater the demand for black labour, the tougher the regulations for its provision, and the larger the official staff required to enforce them. In Kenya's areas of white settlement, African men aged between 15 and 40 were required to register and to carry a pass containing their employment record.

Since the native peoples in British colonies were not to be integrated in the foreseeable future, the emphasis was on 'civilising' them rather than Anglicising them. Native customs and languages were left untouched as long as they seemed unthreatening to the administration and not overly offensive to British moral codes. Polygamy was allowed, for instance, but not the Muslim severing of hands to punish theft.

The colonial era spanned less than a hundred years but it was long enough for the creation of a distinctive service to which men – and a few women – were happy to devote their lives. Many were lured into the British Colonial Service by the prospect of adventure, sunshine and an outdoor life, or by a desire to exercise authority. For some, especially for ill-paid army officers without private means to maintain the lifestyle expected of them, it was a means of getting out of debt. Once having joined it, few left the service and many came to be professionally absorbed in and devoted to it as a calling. Service in the colonies became a tradition in some families. Even marriages tended to be effected within the service.

In the earlier days, colonial officers were often drawn from military or para-military forces outside Britain, such as the Indian Army and the British South Africa Police. Later they came mostly from the British universities, prepared for colonial service by special courses of instruction, initially conducted at the Imperial Institute in London and later moved to Oxford and Cambridge universities.

Almost always the recruits came from the British upper classes, jealously guarding privileges of birth with the powers these conferred. Thus even Cecil Rhodes's BSAP, pioneering a new colony in virgin Africa, advertised in the *Times* inviting applications from 'the sons of gentlemen who can ride and shoot and are fond of an open-air life'.

Rather than the rigid British class system being relaxed in the colonies, it seems to have been considered necessary to raise the social barriers a little, or at least to maintain them more fiercely, the threats to class distinction being greater in the uncertain foreign world. In Africa, as in India and elsewhere in the Empire, the accents tended to get plummier, the snobbery exaggerated. Impostors were sniffed out and snobbed out. In the upper echelons, neckties were generally old school or regimental. Polo, cricket and bridge were the games to play, and almost always in clubs, but not always in the same clubs.

There was one kind of club for the more senior officials and the better-connected settlers, its memberships tending to reflect Debrett's Peerage, even if only distantly. There was another kind for those whose genealogy was less illustrious or whose station in life lower. Officialdom was generally divided into A and B classes, and there were even A and B classes of governor, depending on the size or other importance of the incumbent's colony.

In larger colonies there might be a third grade of club, informally existing in a bar or restaurant, catering to those from the cloth-cap class, the artisans, mechanics and foremen who came out on short-term contracts for specific projects. Their sports might be dominos, darts and soccer rather than tennis and bridge, their drink beer rather than pink gin or scotch.

A fascinating insight into the life of the colonial servant has been given in interviews with more than fifty of them conducted for the BBC by Charles Allen and Helen Fry, and later published in book form.[1]

Allen and Fry note that when a colonial official was given his first posting, his immediate task was to get himself kitted out by one of a number of specialist firms. His purchases, when crated, might be enough to fill a dray or, in later times, a lorry. Besides clothing and equipment it might, in the case of an isolated posting, have to include enough canned food for a year. A specimen list supplied by Walters and Company for clients going to Tanganyika in 1925 included, besides basic camping gear, two sporting guns, tropical weight evening dress, a blue blazer (with wire college crest), grey and white flannel trousers, khaki clothing, a cholera belt, cord breeches, leather leggings, tropical puttees, one pair of bush boots, two pairs of mosquito boots, spine pads and two pith helmets, one white and one khaki, with metal carrying cases.

The spine pads (thick felt strips buttoned to the back of the shirt) and helmets (otherwise known as solar topees) were regarded as essential to ward off sunstroke. Juniors who went out in the sun without a helmet were likely to be sternly reprimanded by their seniors. It was considered acceptable for a man attending a daytime social function to go out into the garden to urinate discreetly on the lawn provided he first put on his topee to keep the sun off his head. Only during the Second World War, when British soldiers by the hundred went out hatless and suffered no ill effects, was it realised that sunlight on the cranium was not necessarily harmful. In fact, it was surmised that those who in the old days supposedly had been afflicted by sunstroke had most likely suffered from heatstroke as a result of wearing a heavy pith helmet!

Having kitted himself out with an advance from the Colonial Office (to be deducted gradually from salary) the colonial officer embarked with it on a steamship, invariably of the Elder Dempster Line. Cabin accommodation, dinner-table seating and social activity were all dictated by rank and social status.

Once ashore, the officer might find himself having to march for several weeks into the interior to reach his station, with porters carrying his gear. In Nigeria, the allowance was 80 porters for each officer going to a new station.

The greatest danger faced by the officer at an isolated posting was illness, for medical help could seldom be reached in time. Besides malaria and the other dread diseases, he might encounter a variety of ailments that, while not necessarily fatal, could be extremely unpleasant. For instance, there were in West Africa the filaria worm and the guinea worm, both of which travelled about the body and were usually extracted with a pin or straw when they emerged on the eyeball or the skin.

At all tropical stations the daily routine of swallowing quinine against malaria was as strictly enforced as the wearing of helmets. The quinine tablets were customarily served with the sundowners so that they would not be forgotten. Anyone who did forget and caught malaria was likely to have his salary docked while he was incapacitated.

Official and social life revolved around the Civil Service List, which contained the personal details of every member of the service: his age, schooling, salary, service record and decorations. It was the colonial hostess's bible, guiding vital matters such as the seating at dinner parties.

Women were few, however, where there were no settlers, and children even fewer. Marriage was at first forbidden, and later discouraged, by both colonial authorities and trading companies, for the life was considered too rough for women, and looking after them would distract the husbands from their work. When medical and other facilities improved, wives were permitted. Those who became pregnant, however, usually sailed back home in good time for the birth, and sometimes remained there during the child's infancy. Young children who did live in the colonies were usually shipped back home to boarding school or to live with relatives when they reached school-going age. Part of the price of empire was the traumatic parting of parents and young children that in many cases made them forever strangers to one another but which, like all traumas, had to be faced with the mask of the British ruling classes: the stiff upper lip.

Colonial communities were often dichotomous, with traders balancing or even outnumbering the officials, especially in West Africa. The traders, however, were usually runged lower down the social ladder than the Colonial Service staff. Where the climate encouraged white residence, settlers made up the third element of the white community. The social rules remained much the same, however.

Besides mosquitoes, colonial wives had to guard against other household invaders: snakes, spiders, scorpions, bats, ants, lizards, all of which could be especially worrisome at an outlying station where not only was there no flush toilet but its function was performed by an outdoor pit privy.

Those women tough enough to survive the initial shock and adapt to the hardships often came to like the life, especially those who accompanied their husbands on safari. They learned to shake their boots for scorpions before putting them on, to relish bread baked by the cook in a mud oven, and to drink Ovaltine made with camel's milk. They discovered the value of devices such as the portable lavatory seat (basically a folding stool with appropriate aperture).

Special qualities were required for a European to tolerate colonial life in Africa, especially in remote postings. Not only wives but also male officers in some cases cracked in face of the loneliness and returned home. Some took to drink, and a few committed suicide. A much larger number, however, joined the white settler communities rather than leave the continent to which they had become emotionally captive.

The French, having long sidelined their aristocracy in favour of liberty, equality and fraternity, were prepared to regard the Africans as fellow humans, even as fellow French, but initially as subjects of a 'civilising mission'. The French protocol offered a surer prospect of equality than that of the British. At first the French tried to follow a policy of 'assimilation', a top-down form of integration beginning with the creation of a black elite. The colonies would be treated as overseas departments of metropolitan France and would send representatives to the French parliament and other institutions, though in restricted numbers. Economically, they would be integrated with the wider French economy. The assimilation policy was applied first in Senegal, the oldest of the French possessions, where the natives of the four communes were given full French citizenship and all its rights.

There were problems, however, in extending the policy to the newer territories, for a number of reasons. Firstly, it was more difficult for the colonial administrators to maintain control of their subjects. Secondly, the colonies didn't produce enough revenue to give their inhabitants the same educational and other facilities as those enjoyed by the French back home, and Paris was not inclined to make up the difference. Equality was one thing, expensively subsidised equality was another. Thirdly, there was the problem of cultural difference. Besides not speaking French, the peoples of the African territories were either Muslim or animist, whereas France was Christian. They practised polygamy, whereas France legitimised only monogamy. And their customary laws were quite different from the statutes of France.

In the face of these difficulties, Paris abandoned the assimilation policy outside the four Senegalese communes and replaced it with a modified version known as 'association'. The inhabitants of the French territories became subjects rather than citizens of France. Though this gave them lesser rights, it afforded them a closer relationship with France than the peoples of the British colonies had with Britain.

They were nonetheless subject to the disadvantages of colonisation, including taxation that few could afford and, in lieu thereof, forced labour at low rates of pay or conscription into the African regiments of the French army.

French-style direct rule meant that the powers of the indigenous chiefs had to be reduced, which the chiefs, not surprisingly, resisted. Thus was created an ironic situation in which the French system, though ostensibly more democratic, had to be imposed more forcefully and at greater expense.

The Portuguese for their part prized their African colonies as adjuncts enhancing the small size and relative poverty of their own country. Their African territories came to be regarded officially not as colonies but as integral parts of Portugal. The Portuguese believed they had gone even further than the French in assimilating the natives in the African 'provinces'. Intermarriage, though not common, was socially acceptable, and Africans were fairly common in the clerical and ecclesiastical fields.

Yet cultural assimilation touched only a small proportion of the indigenous populations. They were more strongly affected by the deliberate exploitation of the Africans that ran parallel with the liberalism. After having reluctantly abandoned slavery, the Portuguese in 1878 enacted laws effectively providing for compulsory labour. Adult Africans had to be able to provide proof that they were employed at least six months of every year.

Despite their ancient presence in Africa, the Portuguese held to a policy of slow and gradual advancement of the indigenous peoples to European standards of civilisation. It was not something that could be done quickly, in the Portuguese view. The labour laws were thus enforced in the guise of 'civilising' the natives. The goal was for them to attain the status of a *civilizado* or *assimilado*, giving them recognised equality with the Portuguese. The assimilation, however, was permissive rather than proactive; it was more a case of the indigenous people having to seek it than of the colonialists promoting it. Those native peoples not officially assimilated were subjected not to the Portuguese common law but to a separate system, the *regime do indigenato*, replacing tribal law and custom with a form of paternalism shaped in and directed from Lisbon.

As late as 1954, when the ferment of independence was beginning to bubble throughout colonial Africa, a Portuguese statute defined the *indigenas* as 'individuals of the black race ... who do not yet possess the enlightenment and the personal and social habits ... of Portuguese citizens'. To progress to *assimilado* the *indigena* was required to speak Portuguese, be capable of sustaining himself with a trade or skill, be of good reputation, and have fulfilled his obligation for military service. By 1950 only 0,75 per cent of the native Angolan population and 0,08 per cent of the Mozambican had been granted *assimilado* certificates. Perhaps the truest measure of the *assimilado* policy's sincerity – certainly of its effectiveness – is the fact that the native populations of all the Portuguese territories fought long and bitter wars to throw off Lisbon's rule and assert their Africanism.

The Germans, for their part, had their own distinctive ideas about how to run foreign possessions. In the relatively short time that Germany was a colonial power,

German attitudes to colonial administration were much simpler and more straight-forward than those of the French, British or Portuguese. Aside from the work of the German missionary organisations, there was no question of integration and lit-tle of upliftment of the natives. The colonial territories and their indigenous popu-lations were to be exploited for the benefit of Germany and the Germans. Should the natives refuse to cooperate in this they were to be coerced, and if they got in the way they were to be removed, terminally if need be. The colonies were not and would never be seen as parts of Germany, and the natives would never ever be seen as Germans. If European colonialism is to be viewed as regenerative plunder, then the German system was the most extreme form of it.

★ ★ ★ ★

As a sometimes incidental companion of colonialism, the Christian churches had a powerful influence in defining the nature and style of the European presence in Af-rica – for better or worse. Christian missionary endeavour changed the lives of mil-lions of sub-Saharan Africans and often influenced official policy.

European religion impacted on Africa almost from the arrival of the Portuguese – and then paradoxically. The interpretation of Christianity that prevailed in Eu-rope at the time allowed the Portuguese to seek converts to Christianity at the same time as they busily sent other Africans into slavery in Portugal and its island colo-nies in the Atlantic. Both evangelisation and slavery probably firmed the European perception of African inferiority, in the first case because the Africans were not al-ready Christians and in the second because they and not whites were selected for slavery.

Like their commercial dealings, the evangelical activities of the Portuguese were for a long time confined largely to the coast. They had mixed success, partly because the church condoned slavery – some of its priests practised it themselves. On the east coast the Portuguese church made little headway against entrenched Islam.

From the early European contacts with sub-Saharan Africa the continent became an alluring field for Christians driven by a need to spread their faith and implement its injunctions. Ostensibly the church (viewed as a single element) was the most benign of the four major vehicles of European intrusion into Africa. It was by its nature more concerned with the wellbeing of the native peoples than either com-merce, colonial administration or settlement. The church, however, often viewed the gospel from a European perspective, and in some instances aligned itself more firmly with colonial or settler establishments than with the indigenous people.

The Dutch, English and French made tentative missionary efforts in West Africa during the 17th century, but the rise of slavery all along the west coast stifled any serious Christian endeavour. European slavers couldn't afford to have their business threatened by Christian morality, and Africans couldn't reconcile it with slavery, so it lost out on both counts.

Where Islam had become entrenched – in most of the northern third of the continent – Christianity made little headway. The Scramble slowed the spread of

Islam, however. The colonial powers, although professedly Christian, tended to discourage Christian competition where Islam was established. Peace and profitability were placed above proselytisation in the colonial order of priorities, even though Christian missionaries almost always outnumbered colonial officials. There often was greater competition between the Roman Catholic and Protestant creeds than between Christianity and Islam.

The pioneering Christian missions usually welcomed colonial authority when it caught up with them because it brought stability and good order, which made their own job easier and safer. They did not always sacrifice the principles of their faith to colonial expediency, however. On the contrary, the activities of the churches often encouraged opposition to colonial rule, even if inadvertently, through both moral preaching and basic education. An African with a Cambridge School Certificate was obviously going to be less in awe of European authority and better equipped to challenge it than one without a European-style education. Church membership was boosted when Africans realised that the education provided by the churches made them eligible for the best jobs. They were happy to embrace the cross to reach the better lifestyle beyond it. While the churches promoted education primarily as an instrument of proselytisation and evangelism, it also became an instrument of politicisation, demonstrating that Africans if given the opportunity and means could run their own affairs.

There was a steady increase in Christian church membership throughout the colonial period. By 1970, barely eight decades after the start of the Scramble, the membership was estimated at 97-million, roughly equal to the number of Muslims in Africa after centuries of Islamic influence in the continent. Christian missions had of course been functioning long before the Scramble, but it seems that Christianity in black Africa rose largely with the tide of colonialism that followed it. This would bring a touch of irony to the fact that, later on, in both West Africa and South Africa, resistance to European rule developed strongly among mission school graduates.

It was usually only when a colony was becoming self-sufficient that serious efforts were made by the authorities to provide education and health services, but even then they were happy to leave as much as possible to the missionary organisations. Often the missions, being relatively flush with feel-good donations from their mother churches' parishioners back in Europe and America, had more money to spend on schools and hospitals than colonial governors could wheedle out of their home governments.

For much of the 19th century European attitudes had been shaped largely by the 'three Cs' concept – the exporting to Africa of Christianity, commerce and civilisation in the interests of uplifting the indigenous population from barbarity. But when Europeans began to settle in Africa, upliftment became awkwardly entangled with exploitation, separatism and supremacy.

The churches then became deeply involved in the polemic over whether Europeans had any permanent rights or future in Africa. At one extreme were those, mostly settlers, officials and business people, who believed that large parts of Africa would become increasingly white until there were virtually no blacks left in them except on sufferance. Some in this camp believed all of Africa would in any case be forever dominated by whites with the blacks perpetually subservient in one way or another. At the other extreme were those, principally in the churches, who saw European domination, even European occupation, as a temporary phenomenon leading to the emergence of self-governing black states in most if not all of Africa.

The quandary over reconciling Christian principles with white supremacy was resolved to some extent in places like Kenya by segregation, enabling settlers to go to a church in a white area on Sunday while promoting subjugation of the blacks for the rest of the week. In South Africa, this had been the practice for generations. In the Afrikaans churches in particular, segregation had been a matter of principle, even of dogma.

But that dogma inevitably gave way to the African realities, to inexorable black majority rule. Outside the mainstream churches, the religion of Europe is being modified and transformed to suit African needs and customs. Indigenous religions are emerging, based on what was brought by the Europeans but far removed from the dictates of Rome and Canterbury.

How strong these new churches will become is uncertain. But, like almost everything else the Europeans brought to sub-Saharan Africa, Christianity is likely to take on an increasingly distinctive African character.

CHAPTER 23

EUROPE'S DRUMS

At the Imperial Conference in 1911 all the Dominions agreed that they were bound to side with Britain if it became involved in war. The South African prime minister, Louis Botha, declared that his country would immediately invade German South West Africa.

This seemed rash to some, given that only nine years had passed since the end of the Boer War and that many Afrikaners were more sympathetic to Germany than to Britain. But Botha considered his country now bound to British loyalty by the treaty ending the Boer War and by membership of the British Empire. Besides, he expected that if South Africa seized South West Africa for Britain the territory would in gratitude be handed over to the Union as a fifth province.

On the day war was declared in 1914, Botha invited Britain to withdraw its garrison in South Africa for service in Europe, leaving the Union to defend herself with her own forces. London accepted the offer and went further – would South Africa please seize the wireless station at Windhoek?

This request was inspired by the knowledge that roving German fleets were positioned to attack British shipping in the southern and central Atlantic, and were communicating with Berlin through wireless transmitters at Luderitzbucht, Swakopmund and Windhoek. The coastal transmitters could be shelled from the sea, but the main station at Windhoek was deep in the interior.

Not only the South African parliament but Botha's cabinet as well was deeply split over entering the war for Britain. Botha claimed that the Germans planned to invade South Africa from South West Africa. The Germans in fact had too few troops for that. They did, however, hope to encourage an Afrikaner uprising that might require British troops to be diverted from elsewhere in Africa and from Europe to put it down. And if Germany won the war South Africa might be opened to massive German immigration.

The South African parliament approved the entry to war on 10 September 1914, but with the opposing votes of General Hertzog's newly-formed National Party manifesting the split among the Afrikaners. Within days one South African force invaded across the Orange River. Another went ashore at Lüderitzbucht in the first seaborne invasion by South African forces.

But then the invasion came to a halt as 10 000 dissident Afrikaners did as the Germans had hoped – they rose in rebellion, led by a number of the hero generals of the Boer War. All were against the government's decision to fight for Britain, and some saw a chance to take back their old republics while the British were preoccupied with fighting the Germans. Botha's government called up loyalist commandos, and soon Afrikaners were fighting Afrikaners in an uprising that would take more lives than would the conquest of South West Africa.

The fighting flared viciously across the Transvaal and the Orange Free State. Families were divided, and men found themselves fighting their brothers. A German contingent supported the rebels in an unsuccessful attack on the town of Upington in January 1915. In their only other invasion of South Africa in strength, the Germans on their own attacked the border town of Kakamas but were repulsed there as well.

Gradually the rebellion was put down. The surviving rebel leaders were sentenced to relatively short jail terms, the government being sensitive to Afrikaner sentiment. The casualties had been light, fewer than four hundred dead on both sides. But the social scars would ache for generations. During the fighting Jopie Fourie, an officer in the Union Defence Force who had joined the rebels, was captured and executed for treason, and he was subsequently given martyr status by Afrikaner nationalists.

The rebellion over, Botha's government returned its attention to South West Africa. It was an extraordinary force that went off to continue the invasion. There were several infantry and mounted regiments made up of English-speakers anxious to fight for Britain. But the majority of the force consisted of the same Afrikaner commandos that had fought the British in the Boer War and then had fought their own brethren in the rebellion. Now they went off, again as volunteers, to fight the Germans on behalf of the British.

Though outnumbered and cut off from reinforcements, the Germans hoped to hold out until their armies won in Europe, where the war was going well for them. As well as advancing from Lüderitzbucht, the South Africans attacked from three other directions. One force marched north from Upington and another advanced from the east, crossing the Kalahari desert from Kuruman. A second seaborne force, including a Rhodesian contingent, landed at Walvis Bay and advanced up the coast to seize Swakopmund, where the wireless station had already been destroyed by Royal Navy gunfire. Then, with Botha in command, it headed inland to capture Windhoek and the main radio station.

Botha sent his mounted regiments on wide sweeps round the German flanks while the infantry advanced up the centre, forcing the enemy always to abandon his prepared defences and retreat along the railways. The Germans came to the end of the line at Tsumeb in the north of the territory, and surrendered on 9 July 1915.

Casualties in the campaign, the only one of the First World War planned and executed entirely by one of the British dominions, were kept down by the nature of the fighting. Of the 50 000 men who served in the South African forces, all but 266 came home. The Germans lost only 103 men.

The South African forces had hardly returned home before they were being asked to volunteer for service in German East Africa, where troops commanded by Colonel Paul von Lettow-Vorbeck had crossed into British East Africa. Chasing Von Lettow back into his own territory and then bottling him up with a blockade would have been the cheaper option, but strong views in favour of invasion and conquest were held in both London and Pretoria. Some, including Smuts, believed it necessary to seize the territory to neutralise the German *mittelafrika* concept. There were even fears that the Germans might march south, brush aside the Portuguese in Mozambique, and attack South Africa.

After two attempts to land Indian troops had been defeated, the British switched to a landward strategy, advancing along a spur line built for the purpose from the Mombasa-Uganda railway at Voi towards the nearby German border. The aim was to link up at Moshi, beneath Mount Kilimanjaro, with the German railway running from there down to Tanga.

To reinforce the British forces, South Africa in December 1915 sent two mounted and two infantry brigades and five artillery regiments. A large proportion were raw and hastily-trained, and all came under the command of an unusually inept set of British officers.

In their first two engagements the South Africans were sent on suicidal frontal assaults on the German machine-guns and were thrown back with heavy losses. Smuts was asked to take over command and replaced all three of the top British generals with South African veterans of South West Africa. The South Africans, though undergoing fearful hardships, failed in repeated efforts to encircle the extraordinarily elusive Von Lettow.

Rejecting the advice of his staff officers to wait out the impending rainy season, Smuts launched his forces – African, Indian, British and Rhodesian as well as South African – into atrocious conditions: heavy rains in disease-ridden and difficult country, largely unknown and unmapped, with few roads. Opposing him was a well-supplied enemy retreating with scorched earth tactics that denuded the country of food and fodder, destroying bridges and railways, falling back on prepared defences.

Smuts pushed his army ahead of his ability to keep it supplied, and his men suffered accordingly. More than eighty per cent went down with malaria. By the time he had seized most of the German colony, nullifying Von Lettow as a threat, public anger was rising in South Africa at the high casualties. Botha intervened and, in what appears to have been a diplomatic attempt to ease Smuts aside, asked him to represent South Africa at the Imperial War Conference in London.

Many of the battered South African units were withdrawn from German East Africa with Smuts. Colonel Jacob van Deventer, a veteran of the Boer War and of South West Africa, assumed overall command of the army, now reinforced with fresh troops from England and Nigeria. The supply lines were improved. Von Lettow, however, held out for almost two more years, resupplied by ships that successfully ran the Royal Navy's blockade. When the war ended he had been chased into Northern Rhodesia but was still fighting. In Berlin, Von Lettow was feted as a hero. With never more than fifteen thousand men he had for four years held off much larger forces – over the duration of the campaign South Africa alone sent a total of

110 000 men to German East Africa.

With Von Lettow fielding twelve thousand askaris, and with several thousand men of the Nigeria Regiment and the King's African Rifles serving with the British forces, the campaign was in effect the biggest conflict between African soldiers fighting for their colonial masters.

After the war, Smuts played an important part in the formation of the League of Nations. His hopes of acquiring South West Africa were blocked, however, by opposition in Britain and the United States. South Africa received only a mandate to administer the territory. Smuts succeeded, though, in blocking an Indian effort to acquire the mandate for German East Africa, which some in New Delhi hoped to develop for Indian settlement. The mandate for the bulk of that territory was assigned to Britain, which changed the name to Tanganyika and became almost as open in treating it as a colony as Pretoria was with South West Africa. The remainder of the former German colony, the ancient kingdoms of Rwanda and Burundi, was assigned to Belgium, which administered them jointly as Ruanda-Burundi until they became independent in 1962.

Togo and Cameroon, lightly garrisoned, had fallen to British, French and Belgian forces within weeks of war being declared. In both territories, the League of Nations awarded split mandates to Britain and France.

★ ★ ★ ★

While Smuts was chasing the Germans in East Africa, other South African troops had fought in Egypt against a rebellion by the Senussi Arabs threatening the Suez Canal. Going on to France, the 1st South African Infantry Brigade suffered heavy casualties in the trenches of the Western Front, notably at Delville Wood and the adjoining village of Longueval. In six days of repeated German assaults and heavy artillery bombardments, the brigade was virtually destroyed. When it was relieved, only 720 of the brigade's 3 155 officers and men were still operative. But it had held the line. When the remnants of the brigade paraded again, the commanding officer wept when he saw how few remained.

Reformed with more volunteers from South Africa, the brigade went back into the trenches, fighting at Butte de Warlencourt, at Arras, Fampoux, Ypres, Menin Road and Passchendaele, through gas attacks at Gauche Wood and Chapel Hill. At Marrieres Wood, the South Africans crucially delayed the German advance.

Defending Messines Ridge, the SAI lost nearly half its strength but saved its section of the front from collapsing. Again reformed, the brigade secured a crossing of the Selle River at a point that had been considered impregnable, an achievement described by the XIII Corps headquarters as 'one of the most outstanding feats of the war'.

The SAI on the Western Front never numbered more than half of those in the South African contingent in East Africa, yet some five thousand died in action, more than half of the total of 8 550 white South Africans who died in all theatres of the war. The brigade's casualties of 15 000 were three times its original strength.

South African volunteer forces fought also in Palestine, and in Russia with the British forces supporting the White Russians against the Bolsheviks. Besides those in the Union forces, a comparatively large number served in the uniforms of the Royal Navy and Royal Flying Corps.

★ ★ ★ ★

At the outbreak of the First World War the South African Native National Congress, affirming its 'absolute loyalty' to the Union, offered 'any assistance or sacrifice' from its members. 'We fully realise that our lot is one with that of white South Africans,' the organisation said. Despite being segregated and exploited, the black people were still espousing brotherhood rather than confrontation. And again the hand of friendship was slapped aside by a white government fearful that arming and training members of the darker majority might encourage them to revolt, or at least demand the vote.

In 1915 Botha's government, urgently needing troops for the war, decided to form coloured combat units. The all-volunteer Cape Corps served in German East Africa and Palestine, losing more than four hundred and fifty officers and men.

About 33 500 African and coloured men served in the South West African campaign, and 15 000 in German East Africa. More than 20 000 members of the South African Native Labour Contingent served in France and Belgium as drivers, stretcher bearers and labourers. Nearly four thousand black and coloured servicemen died of illness and accidents – 616 when the troop transport *Mendi* collided with a British freighter in fog in the English Channel. The British War Medal, awarded to all who served with the British in the war, was given to members of the labour battalions from other countries, as well as the white officers of the SANLC, but was denied to its black members by white South African politicians obsessed with prejudice and fear.

★ ★ ★ ★

For all the South African government's refusal to arm black soldiers, the First World War changed black perceptions and attitudes in South Africa. The fact that black soldiers had been used against white ones, in both Europe and Africa, eroded the tradition of white inviolability that had assiduously been fostered by the European colonialists. It had already been undermined by Kitchener when he put black troops up against the Boers in the South African War. Members of the black non-combatant units from South Africa lost some of their awe of whites when in England they saw white labourers doing the kind of menial work reserved for blacks back home. Though none of this radically changed black attitudes, it set minds and clocks ticking. It would take another world war, however, to turn the black peoples from resentment to resistance.

CHAPTER 24

PARADISE PRECARIOUS

In her famous memoir, *The Flame Trees of Thika*, Elspeth Huxley describes how, when she was six, her parents went to their new home in Africa with her mother riding on an ox-cart loaded with the family's possessions, the pile topped with 'a sewing-machine, a crate of five speckled Sussex pullets and a lavatory seat'.[1]

At first the Huxleys lived in tents pitched in the bush as Elspeth's father struggled to make a farm from his 500 acres of wilderness in the British East Africa Protectorate.

Later the Huxleys moved into a house made of grass and reeds tied to poles. It was true pioneering stuff – except that this was the 20th century. It was 1913, and in Europe and America (and parts of Africa, too) aircraft were flying about the skies. Motor vehicles were fast displacing horse-drawn ones, and people were listening to radio programmes and going to the cinema to watch Mack Sennett in the silent movies.

Knowing that they would be leaving all that behind, the Huxleys apparently were determined at least to have the luxury of a lavatory seat, even if it was to be over a pit in a little grass hut visited by snakes.

It was a far cry from the Huxleys' earlier existence in the upper reaches of the British aristocracy, like many of their fellow settlers. Contrary to her account in her memoir, Elspeth did not join her parents until a year later. That liberty aside, her book gives an accurate account of white settlement in what later became Kenya Colony.

The Huxleys made their trek midway through the European settlement of the territory, the last of the major white migrations into Africa before the two world wars, apart from the brief Italian effort in Libya. The Kenyan influx came much later than those in the north and south of the continent, for the reason that even in the early 20th century middle Africa was still considered primitive by Europeans and offered no sure prospect of mineral wealth.

Organised settlement in the East African Protectorate began only in 1902 under Whitehall's scheme for settling European and Asian farmers along the railway from Mombasa. Asians were already living in the territory; some had been trading on the coast, and others had come to build and work on the railway.* The few Europeans already living in the Protectorate were mostly transient British officials, traders and hunters.

---

*Other than those who were brought out as indentured labourers, the Asians who came to Africa were generally entrepreneurs, representing what some Africans saw as a form of colonialism that was accordingly resented, a sentiment that led to excesses like Idi Amin's expulsion of the Asians from Uganda and the massacre of Asians by Zulus in Durban in the late 1940s.

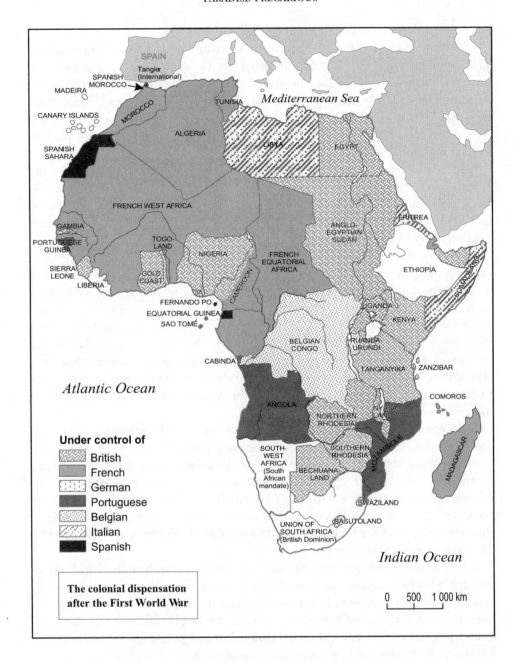

Under control of

▨	British
▨	French
⋯	German
■	Portuguese
▨	Belgian
⫽	Italian
■	Spanish

The colonial dispensation after the First World War

0   500   1 000 km

Previous to the white settlement the social pattern in Kenya had been shaped and reshaped by migrations and settlements typical of tribal movements that had occurred across Africa, most recently the arrival of the Nilo–Hamitic Masai from the north in the 18th century. The Masai had shouldered their way in between the powerful Wahehe in what became Tanganyika, the equally warlike Nandi on the western Rift Valley escarpment, and the vigorous Kikuyus in and around the forested Aberdare Mountains and Mount Kenya.

Like those in the south of the continent, the white settlers found large tracts of land seemingly unoccupied by African people. It was again a deceptive appearance, however, for these lands had long been used on a seasonal or occasional basis by the Africans. The settlers began to move in at a time when the indigenous social structures had been disrupted by epidemic diseases among the Masai and Kikuyu and their cattle, and by tribal feuding. The Kikuyu had withdrawn into only a portion of their traditional land.

Native land rights in any case seem not to have been much respected by the British government. The second commissioner for the Protectorate, Sir Charles Elliot, clearly did not see indigenous land claims as an obstacle to white settlement. In 1905 he declared that 'East Africa will probably become in a short time a white man's country, in which native questions will present but little interest'.

In essence the European land occupation in Kenya was only slightly different from the seizures of land that had characterised African expansion and migration for centuries. Like peoples everywhere else in the world, including modern Europe, Africans who wanted land occupied by others and had the power to seize it generally went ahead and did so. The main difference in this case was that the whites were not Africans, had greater land-seizing power than any African had ever had, and used it at a time when the practice was being made questionable by their own ethical development and its extension around the world. Their own morality – or that of their kin in Britain – in the end became an obstacle to the fulfilment of their conquest.

Land was offered for European settlement by the British authorities as early as 1897, two years after work had begun on the railway from Mombasa, but there were few takers. Attitudes had changed by the time the railway reached Kisumu on Lake Victoria in 1901. In that year Elliot became commissioner and directed the offer of settlement land specifically to South Africans. This time there was an immediate response; a number of Afrikaners trekked up and settled, mainly around Eldoret in the northern part of the highlands. The British began to follow in numbers, and by 1916 there were 8 000 whites in the Protectorate.

It had for the British government been serendipitous that the railway had to pass through what became known as the White Highlands in order to reach Lake Victoria. It could not have been better country for attracting white settlers. Straddling the equator at elevations of between six thousand and eight thousand feet, the highlands had a climate that was seldom less than exhilarating. Rolling, well-watered, often misty, the terrain was in parts reminiscent of the Scottish highlands.

Beyond granting the settlers 999-year leases on their allotments, the British government gave them little if any assistance, with the result that many were from the British middle and upper classes, people who could afford the large expenses of pioneering European-style farming in virgin Africa. Many had been officers in the army, which at that time was the exclusive preserve of members of the social upper crust. Kenya ended up with perhaps more of the British aristocracy to the square kilometre than anywhere else outside Britain itself.

Most of the settlers put enormous effort, capital and enterprise into making their wild lands productive. They developed a love of the country that would continue for a few generations and be heartbreaking to those who were eventually forced out by African nationalism and European politics. It was inevitable, though, that when land taken by force was no longer held by force, its return would be demanded by the previous owners.

Although the early Kenya settlers never allowed themselves to be absorbed into their African environment, they adapted to it, often with great panache, implanting their own lifestyle – chintz-covered lounge suites, rose gardens, cocktail and tennis parties and bridge evenings, polo clubs and fox-hunting.

To all of this the settlers added the special luxury of colonial Africa: numerous black domestic servants. The Kenyan natives were on the whole unwilling, however, to work as farm labourers for the white man, so the settlers resorted to the instruments of coercion already well-proven in South Africa and Rhodesia: hut and poll taxes which obliged the natives to work for the Europeans to get the money to pay the taxes. Protests in Britain forced the authorities after the First World War to forbid compulsory labour. The settlers then borrowed more refined ways from 'down south', such as the enforcement from 1918 of a measure barring Africans from living in areas set aside for Europeans unless they worked there. In 1920 labourers were required to register and carry the equivalent of the South African pass, known in Kenya as the *kipande*. Africans were barred from economic competition with Europeans by measures forbidding them to grow coffee, which was then emerging as the mainstay of the territory's economy, and cotton.

From first settlement to the post-independence exodus, the white experience in Kenya was a conflict between the demands of the settlers and the vacillating policies of successive British governments in regard to the indigenous peoples. The settlers demanded more land, more labour and, eventually, more autonomy. British governments dithered between keeping the settlers happy and fulfilling their moral duty to the natives.

In 1907 the British authorities, responding to settler pressure, formed an Executive Council, but with only two nominated members representing the settlers against six official members. The settlers' demand for the right to elect their own members to the council was not granted until 1919.

After the First World War, Whitehall encouraged settlement by ex-soldiers. Predictably, the response came from officers rather than other ranks, and Kenya became more than ever what has been described as 'a natural sanctuary for Blimps'.[2] By 1919 the white population of the Protectorate had risen to 10 000 and their influence in Whitehall had increased correspondingly, despite their still being outnumbered by the 23 000 Indians. Whitehall's ambivalent attitude continued, however, even after the Protectorate had in 1920 become the colony of Kenya.

In 1922 settler irritation flared into a crack-brained plot to kidnap the governor and install Lord Delamere, the settlers' leader, in his place. The colonial secretary, the Duke of Devonshire, tried to clarify matters by declaring in 1923 that 'primarily Kenya is an African territory' in which 'the interests of the natives must be paramount', although minorities (the Europeans and Asians) would not lose their rights.

The Asians had begun their own campaign for equal rights, but not until 1927 did they, too, get their own seats in the legislature. By that time they had largely been squeezed off their land allotments by settler-inspired pressures such as the Crown Lands Ordnance of 1915, which gave the commissioner powers to reserve land for whites and thus protected the exclusivity of the White Highlands. Most of the Asians became artisans and traders.

Devonshire's declaration did nothing to clarify the matter of rights and political power. It simply extended and formalised the ambivalence of official policy. It was a classic manifestation of the British dilemma in Africa, the conflict between two irreconcilable imperatives. On the one hand were the economic and political demands of survival as an island race, which required that the British acquire foreign sources of raw materials and foreign markets for their products, which usually in turn required that they dominate and exploit foreign peoples. On the other hand were the ethics dictated by the national religion, which in their very nature held that the rights recognised for Britons should be extended to their foreign subject peoples.

The first set of imperatives had led to the British occupation of the territory and its settlement with Britons; from the second had emerged Whitehall's protective, though patronising, attitude to the native peoples. Having placed the settlers among an indigenous majority whom even the British government considered backward and inferior, the government could not and did not expect the settlers to accept the natives as equals. Yet at the same time it recognised the paramountcy of the natives' rights. It was an impossible situation, and sooner or later something had to give; in the end it was the settlers, or rather their descendants.

Whitehall's contradictory stance can only be explained in terms of the British belief that in time the Africans would evolve to the same 'levels of civilisation' as the Europeans, when both would enjoy equal rights. For the present, however, Devonshire's decree resolved nothing. Friction between settlers and Africans continued, peaking in the Mau Mau rebellion of 1952, which put the crack in the dyke of white supremacy. Already in 1921 political resistance was being organised among the Kikuyu with the formation of the Young Kikuyu Association, renamed the Kikuyu Central Association (KCA) in 1927.

Kenya's white population had grown to 12 000 by 1929, still outnumbered by the Asians but still having more members on the Legislative Council (where the Africans were represented by a solitary white missionary). In that eventful year, however, a British commission of inquiry dashed settler ambitions for self-government along the lines of that granted to Rhodesia in 1923. The Hilton Young Commission recommended instead that appointed British officials continue to outnumber the settler representatives in the Legislative Council until the indigenous people were ready to share the council seats equally with the whites. The commission's views were endorsed by the new colonial secretary, Lord Passfield, who in addition lifted the restrictions placed by the council on meetings and fund-raising by the KCA.

He appears to have recognised that it was unrealistic to withhold political parity from the Africans until they had achieved parity of 'civilisation' with the settlers; that might take generations, and the Africans might in any case not want to become imitation Europeans.

The writing was now on the wall for white supremacy, though few of the whites could read it. Even the least optimistic thought there would at least be some kind of racial partnership that would protect their interests and their holdings forever.

Not all the whites who settled in Kenya went there as pioneers. Some were more like refugees, rich refugees fleeing from intolerable social constraints in Britain and seeking a life of liberties that ordinary Britons considered licentious. Like mercury, a number of these volatile spirits gravitated together in a part of the White Highlands informally known as Happy Valley.

There the pursuit of outrageous conduct for its own sake (or perhaps as principled rebellion against conformity) was conducted with a panache and dedication that appears for its adherents to have taken decadence beyond sin and into art. Their amoral, sybaritic mode of living, a reckless existence fuelled by alcohol and drugs, of wife-swapping and sexual orgies, was eccentric even in a colony known for the eccentricity of its white settlers.

A kind of frontier spirit pervaded all of white-occupied East Africa, for it was indeed a frontier between indigenous Africa and invasive Europe, between the customs and rights of black people and the demands of white ones, between disparate civilisations, between an old order and a new in Africa. The frontier syndrome was more sharply etched there than elsewhere in Africa because the white invasion came relatively late and suddenly. Kenya and Tanzania did not experience anything like the slow, generations-long seepage of the whites into South Africa. The Europeans came into East Africa abruptly and in numbers, and within a few years were making it their own – or thought they were.

★ ★ ★ ★

Life tended to be harder for the white settlers in Southern Rhodesia than for those in Kenya's White Highlands. There were fewer titles and less money among the Rhodesian settlers. And breaking new farmland was even tougher in their drier bushlands than in the moist White Highlands.

By the start of the 20th century, with the indigenous tribes subdued, the best farmland taken and adequate labour supplies secured, life had become somewhat easier for the whites than it had been for Rhodes's pioneers. Some settler farmers began to prosper, but there was also white poverty on a scale unknown in Kenya.

Since their territory was governed by the Chartered Company, the Rhodesians were shielded from the kind of Colonial Office interference that the Kenyan settlers found so irksome. When a Legislative Council was set up in 1898 the settlers were allowed four elected members. The Company still had control with its five nominated members and the Company Administrator as chairman with casting vote. The British government's representative, the Resident Commissioner, had no vote, only a seat on the council.

The indigenous people had no representation. Their governance was left to their traditional chiefs but under the strict control of the white government. Whitehall saw this arrangement as a prelude to a 'future self-government', but one dominated by the white minority, as in the Cape and Natal. It was envisaged in London that Southern Rhodesia would in due course join a South African federation. Northern Rhodesia, though also governed by the Chartered Company, was viewed separately.

By 1900 there were 11 000 Europeans in Southern Rhodesia, and they began to demand greater autonomy. In 1911, a year after union in South Africa, they were given a majority in the Legislative Council of seven elected members against the Company's five nominees, though with the Administrator retaining the chair and having a casting vote. By 1912 the white population had risen to 24 000 but was still outnumbered by the 750 000 Africans. Despite this huge disparity the Colonial Office was still envisaging Southern Rhodesia being merged with South Africa.

General Smuts's government was in favour of incorporating Southern Rhodesia even though this would increase the disparity between blacks and whites. He was still confident of the white minority's ability to remain dominant, and believed incorporation would improve the economic prospects of both countries.

The Chartered Company was itself not averse to incorporation, for it still had not paid any dividends to its shareholders despite having spent large sums on railway and other development. Smuts was willing to compensate the Company handsomely for giving up its rights. Many in Rhodesia, however, favoured self-government as a British colony. London put the issue to the vote in a referendum in 1922. Union with South Africa as the fifth province was rejected by 8 744 votes to 5 989.

Years later Ian Smith, who as prime minister led the abortive Unilateral Declaration of Independence, would describe the vote against union as a great mistake, one that changed the whole course of history in the sub-continent. In his book *The Great Betrayal*, published in 1997, three years after white South Africa had followed Rhodesia into black majority rule, Smith argues that had the 1922 vote gone the other way, Smuts would not have lost the 1948 election that put the architects of apartheid into power.[3] The Rhodesian vote would have gone overwhelmingly to Smuts, denying the inflexibly segregationist National Party their narrow victory. Under Smuts's white immigration policy, the white population of South Africa would have more than doubled, and the coloureds and Indians would not have become alienated from the whites. Faced with a much smaller black majority, white South Africa would have adopted more liberal policies instead of 'falling into the apartheid trap'. South West Africa would have become part of South Africa. If it is accepted that the more than eighty thousand whites in Rhodesia in 1948 would have given it more than seven constituencies, Smith's scenario holds up. Most white Rhodesians would probably have voted for Smuts's party, negating the seven-seat victory of his opponents. And certainly increased white immigration would have resulted from a Smuts victory. Dr Malan's victorious Nationalists did indeed shut off the flow from Europe for fear that it would dilute Afrikanerdom and that an influx of Anglicans and Catholics would weaken the influence of Afrikaner Calvinism. In the same period there was a massive post-war influx of Europeans into Rhodesia that more than doubled the white population, taking it from 80 000 in 1945 to 200 000 by 1955, and something similar, even if not proportionately as large, could probably have been expected in South Africa.

There is no question that Malan's stifling of European immigration had the ironic effect of weakening white political power, which in turn made the Nationalists more intransigent in their segregationist policies. There can be far less certainty, however, about the Africans' willingness amicably to 'evolve' into some sort of partnership with the minority whites. That concept had more substance in white hopes than in black acceptance. The wave of liberation from colonialism after the Second World War would have swamped acceptance by any blacks of an evolutionary approach.

As a result of the referendum, Southern Rhodesia became a self-governing colony the following year. Britain retained control of foreign affairs and the right to veto any legislation discriminating against the indigenous peoples. The vote, however, was made conditional on property qualifications, which excluded most Africans on account of their communal lifestyle and the restrictions on their land ownership. The colony's constitution barred whites from owning or occupying land in the native reserves, but allowed blacks to own land anywhere.

In 1924 Whitehall's remaining powers over the colony were shifted from the Colonial Office to the newly formed Dominions Office, strengthening the belief among the whites that the limited self-government would be expanded to full dominion status.

By 1930 the whites had edged closer to something resembling apartheid by formalising a 'parallel development' policy, also known as the 'two pyramids' policy. Its cornerstone was the Land Apportionment Act, which set aside a large proportion of the country for exclusive white ownership, while reserving the remainder exclusively for blacks. The proportion was amended from time to time and ended up in 1970 with 44-million acres reserved for just under 4-million blacks, and 36-million for the 275 000 whites, with six million open to either race. Slightly more than half of the soil classed as 'high-fertility' was in the areas reserved for Africans, and half of the African area fell into the area of relatively high rainfall.[4] However, the population density was enormously higher in the African areas. Not only did the comparatively few whites have nearly half of the best land, but it was mostly situated on either side of the railways. Little of the African areas was close to rail links.

Southern Rhodesia's hopes for full dominion status were based on the granting of similar status to other former colonies settled by whites, such as New Zealand, which had got it in 1907. However, they overlooked the crucial fact that all the dominions had been settled for much longer, and the proportion of whites to indigenous peoples was far greater than in Rhodesia, which had only 35 000 whites in 1923, compared with nearly one million Africans. When Canada, Australia and New Zealand had attained dominion status the position of the indigenous peoples had not been of overriding concern to Whitehall since they did not outnumber the

whites, as they did in Rhodesia. Though no such policy was ever openly enunciated, it seems that a large white population, if not a white majority, was essential for
dominion status. And Southern Rhodesia's white population was never enough to
qualify. It was one thing for Britain to impose dominion status on indigenous minorities in Australia and New Zealand, whether they liked it or not, but quite another to do the same to the huge indigenous majority in Southern Rhodesia.

As fast as it increased, Rhodesia's white population always lagged behind the
political and ethical evolution in Britain that led to the dissolution of the Empire.
Dominion status had eluded them by the time London began granting independence to its African colonies. And then the whites in Rhodesia were still too greatly
outnumbered to be given their own way. In other words, there were never enough
of them to save them from being seen by the British government as expendable, at
least in terms of political power.

White settlement was even slower in Northern Rhodesia, even after the railway
was pushed through from Bulawayo to just across the northern border in 1909 to
serve the copper mines of Katanga in the Belgian Congo. In 1911 the white population was estimated at fifteen hundred. White settlement was largely along the
line of rail until the growing demand for copper from the world's booming electri-
cal and automobile industries led to the discovery in the late twenties of huge but
deep-lying copper deposits in Northern Rhodesia adjoining the Belgian Congo.

By this time the Chartered Company, having abandoned hope of getting rich
from the meagre surface deposits of copper in the territory, had handed control to
the Colonial Office, which ran it as two separate protectorates before merging them
as Northern Rhodesia. From the copper discoveries emerged one of the biggest
copper mining complexes in the world, bringing an influx of whites into what became known as the Copperbelt. When copper mining was about to begin in 1924
there were 4 000 Europeans in the territory. The white population thereafter leaped
to about fifteen thousand in 1940, to 37 000 in 1950, to 65 000 in 1956, and 75 000
in 1960. More than half of these lived on the Copperbelt.

Blacks were also drawn in large numbers to the Copperbelt, but only as workers
on the mines. Using the migrant labour and compound systems, the mining companies and the British authorities discouraged blacks from settling in the towns that
grew up beside the mines.

★ ★ ★ ★

Between the wars, the South African government consolidated its hold in South
West Africa. While the First World War was still being fought in Europe, South African troops occupied Ovamboland south of the Cunene River, killing the Ovambo chief and 100 of his followers when they resisted. Immediately after assuming
the League of Nations mandate Pretoria began deporting the German civil servants and soldiers. Businessmen and farmers were allowed to remain to sustain the
economy. South Africans were encouraged to settle, and hundreds did, frequently
displacing Germans.

More land was taken from the indigenous peoples for white settlement. Pretoria rejected requests from the Hereros for the return of the land taken from them by the Germans, and instead gave them 800 000 hectares of the barren Omaheke sandveld.

By 1928 most of the best farmland was in white hands and the white population had reached 28 000, double the figure at the start of the world war. Laws were in place restricting the free movement of black people and prescribing penalties for 'offences' such as deserting from a white employer. Indigenous resistance to South African domination was forcefully put down, notably when the Bondelswart Namas in 1922 rose in rebellion again measures designed to force them into labour on white farms. Smuts sent troops and aircraft against them. Cornered on a hilltop, the Bondelswarts were machine-gunned from the ground and bombed from the air, and some one hundred and fifteen, women and children among them, were killed before the survivors surrendered.

★ ★ ★ ★

After the First World War Smuts pursued an ambition to combine South Africa, South West Africa, Southern Rhodesia, the southern half of Mozambique and the British protectorates of Bechuanaland, Basutoland and Swaziland. This would make a white-dominated country comprising about a quarter of the African continent. South West Africa would be incorporated by right of conquest from the Germans. Mozambique south of the Zambezi River would be acquired from Portugal in exchange for Tanganyika. The protectorates would be handed over by Britain in the interests of having a single friendly government controlling the whole of southern Africa.

This grandiose scheme was based on the belief that the black people who over-whelmingly outnumbered the whites in the region would accept Smuts's vision of their subjugation for generations to come while they gradually advanced to what was deemed a level of civilisation equal to that of the whites. It came to naught in the end. Britain would not countenance the Tanganyika-Mozambique exchange, and the 1922 referendum put Southern Rhodesia beyond reach. Both Smuts's and succeeding National Party governments still tried to incorporate the protectorates, but were foiled by a clause in the South African Act of Union that allowed incorporation only with the consent of the indigenous inhabitants. Their leaders consistently rejected ingestion by South Africa, and all three territories eventually achieved independence (Bechuanaland as Botswana, Basutoland as Lesotho). South West Africa was denied to South Africa through the intervention of the United Nations and also became independent. That concept in any case had more substance in white hopes than in black acceptance.

CHAPTER 25

THE HUNTERS

The camp would always be ready, a welcoming home from home, when the white hunter and his clients drove in from the day's shooting. Pitched perhaps beneath spreading acacia trees, the clients' tents would be next to the bigger tent that served as dining and living room when it rained. The white hunter's tent would be a short distance away, far enough for privacy but close enough for comfort.

The campfire logs would have burned into red coals and clean flames so that the clients would not be bothered much by smoke. Beside the fire the folding chairs would be drawn up, and beside them a table carrying the materials for the sun-downers. From a second fire some distance away, near the service trucks, among the servants' bedrolls and the safari baggage and the kitchen tent, hot water would be steaming in large pots ready to be carried on command to canvas baths in the clients' tents.

The clients might have a quick drink to unparch the throat before going off to wash away the day's dust. No blood, probably, only dust, for their killing that day would likely have been distant, and if the client had botched the job the white hunter would have finished it off (a part of the story unlikely to be disclosed when the client later displayed the stuffed head in his home in Europe or America). For the second drink the clients would be bathed and changed into clean clothes and would be sitting, long trousers tucked into mosquito boots, at the fire. The sun might be going down, and if the combination of dust, cloud and sun angle was right it would leave the sky ablaze for a while with the same colours that were visible in miniscule in the fire.

Then the dark would flood in, and in the clean sky the stars would be spread with a denseness astonishing to European city-dwellers, seeming closer to earth and brighter than back home, blazing rather than twinkling.

From the other fire, the cook's fire, would come smells of roasting and baking, of venison on the spit and perhaps a liver from one of the day's kills being blended skilfully with herbs; smells of bread rolls being baked with wondrous art in an oven made from an old four-gallon paraffin tin.

From the bush beyond the firelight would come the smells of sun-baked dust and vegetation cooling in the night and receiving the dew. There might be reflecting eyes looking in from the dark. There would certainly be the sounds of the bush as it stirred from the afternoon's somnolence into the quick and furtive perils of the night. Jackals would begin howling and yapping, hyenas cackling and giggling. Something, perhaps the scent of a leopard, might make impalas sound the alarm with their blend of grunt and snort, and zebras with their odd, equine bark. If they were near a river, the clients might hear the grunting riffs of hippos. And if they were especially lucky they would hear close by a male lion's roar, seeming to shake the hairs on a person's head, or at least to make them stand up, three or four base-baritone blasts descending into a cascade of deep coughs, leaving everything and everyone, the animals in the bush, the clients at their fire and the servants at theirs, silent for a while in respect.

If the clients were perspicacious enough they would be aware of the privilege that had come to them, the rare experience of going on safari in Africa, an experience in its truest form shared by only a relative handful of people and which can no longer be known by anyone except in pale imitation of what it once was. If they had gone out on the East African savannah in the twenties and thirties, the clients would have known the heyday of the African safari, the summit of the era of the white hunter, when there was still enough of unspoiled Africa and its wild life to enjoy; when technology, principally in medicines, steamships and motor vehicles, was sufficiently advanced to make it relatively easy and comfortable but had not yet begun to destroy what it had made available, and population growth had not spoiled most of the wilderness with human dross.

The white hunter was a refined form of the professional hunter who for two centuries or more had gone into wild Africa to make a living from hunting elephants for their ivory and, as a sideline, other animals for their skins and horns. So thoroughly did they and the part-time and occasional hunters kill that when the white hunter came into his own with the advent of tourism in Africa, wild animals were already becoming scarce.

The insatiable demand for ivory had sent hunters ever deeper into Africa, slaughtering on a vast scale. As many as thirty thousand elephants were killed each year in the 1850s in what became Kenya, Uganda and Tanganyika, and by 1880 the toll was up to seventy thousand a year.[1] In the last decade of the 19th century, the tusks of 185 000 elephants were sold on the Antwerp ivory market.

The notion that any species among Africa's teeming wild life might be shot out of existence came slowly to the Europeans and Americans, even to the hunters. It hit with something of a jolt when the world's last quagga died in a zoo in Amsterdam in 1883. Seven years later an International Conference for the Protection of Wild Animals, the first of its kind, was held in London, adopting the first – and typically ineffectual – measures aimed at curbing the slaughter of the elephants.

Most of South Africa had been denuded of game by the turn of the century. The timely creation of the Sabi Game Reserve in 1898 led to its transformation in 1926 into the Kruger Park.

The realisation of urgency in conservation came quite late in East Africa, whose famous Tsavo game reserve was established only in 1948. Controls on hunting had been introduced by the authorities before then, however. A safari hunter's bag (two each of elephant, rhino and hippo per hunter) had been restricted by the time US president Theodore Roosevelt took his mammoth safari into East Africa in 1909. In a matter of weeks, however, Roosevelt's party shot more than five hundred big game and thousands of lesser game.

For those who could not afford the real thing, Hollywood provided the vicarious version with a succession of movies that brought cinema audiences in America and Europe face-to-face with the big five while sitting eating popcorn. As a film theme the hunting safari subsequently became somewhat passe in itself but also outdated, for the slaughter had led to hunting being banned in Tanganyika in 1973 and in Kenya in 1977. Tourists still went on safari, but with cameras substituted for guns.

Though it was very special and in a sense self-contained, the era of the safari and the white hunter was part of a general opening-up of Africa in a decade on either side of the First World War. It was a time in which not only did the flow of European immigration swell considerably, but also Europeans began going out to Africa for fun, as tourists and adventure-seekers. Europeans began to experience the realities of Africa in numbers. Previously, their perceptions of the continent had been shaped by the accounts of the missionaries and explorers, and then by romantic but unrealistic novels such as H Rider Haggard's *King Solomon's Mines*, published in 1885, and *She*, two years later. That view was reinforced, though in a lighter and ridiculous way, when in 1914 the American-made hero Tarzan came swinging and yodelling out of Africa as envisioned by Edgar Rice Burroughs, and subsequently by Hollywood.

After the First World War, Western perceptions of Africa had become more enlightened and more realistic. Africa seemed much safer in the twenties than it had at the turn of the century, some of it quite civilised by European standards. The powers had had 30 years to put their stamp on their colonies. Transport and other infrastructures were improving, as were health services and facilities such as telegraphic communication and hotel accommodation.

Getting to and from Africa had become much quicker and cheaper than when the early steamships had to carry so much coal for propelling themselves that there was little room for cargo or passengers. The mailship run from England to Cape Town, which had taken about forty-five days when steamships still carried backup sails towards the end of the 19th century, had been shortened by the development of more efficient engines. By 1919 (by which time the *Titanic* had been on the seabed for seven years) multi-funnelled liners of 18 000 tons or more were making the run to Cape Town in just over two weeks with more than a thousand passengers. Accommodation in first class was as luxurious as in the trans-Atlantic liners. Union-Castle Line advertisements exclaimed 'It's Fun to Travel!' and 'Sail in Comfort!' and the Europeans duly obliged.

Ports visited by the ocean liners were linked to the interior by railways and by the improved roads that had been made necessary by the almost explosive replacement of the animal-drawn vehicle by the automobile. The airplane, also developing exponentially, would not be far behind the automobile. The first flight from England to South Africa was made by two South Africans, Quentin Brand and Pierre van Ryneveld, in 1919, little more than four decades after Stanley had completed the last of the great journeys of African exploration. Rickety-looking aircraft were already making short flights within the continent, but more than a generation would elapse before the airliner put the ocean liner out of business on scheduled runs between Europe and Africa.

Both tourism and white settlement remained negligible outside the temperate regions, however. Disease and discomfort still kept Africa's interior beyond the interest and the ken of most European and American tourists. Most of them were interested only in visiting the parts they considered reasonably safe and sophisticated besides being picturesque – in effect, where whites had elected to put down roots: South Africa, Southern Rhodesia, Kenya and Tanganyika, besides the Mediterranean littoral.

★ ★ ★ ★

The motor vehicle opened up parts of Africa that previously had been accessible only on foot, carrying white settlement and tourism deep into the more temperate parts of the interior. But in a large continent with few navigable rivers – only the Nile, the Niger, the Congo, the Gambia and the Zambezi, and these only in part – the railway was the instrument that opened the hinterland to commercial and industrial development and to colonial advancement. European intrusion came in the beginning at the pace of the head porter, the horse and the ox. Once the interior had been mapped and the commercial possibilities assessed, once exploration turned to exploitation, it went at the speed of the railway train. Africa's great distances were conquered by lengths of steel rail shipped over from Europe and by the steam locomotive fuelled with wood from the local trees, swiftly transporting imports and exports and the means of colonial domination.

Some of the ancient trading systems in the Sudan belt were ruined by the railways, but then new opportunities were opened for commercial production of groundnuts and other crops.

A few of the railway lines were built for short-term military purposes, such as Kitchener's 640-kilometre short cut across the Nile's big bend, but more often they were built to open territory to commercial development. Railways moved the produce of both settlers and the indigenous population to markets, helping to produce profits and wages that could be taxed.

The absence of navigable rivers made development more costly, it being more expensive to build, run and maintain railways than simply to put boats on a river. It meant that economic development had to pay for the railway built to serve it before it could make profits. Where rivers were navigable only on inland stretches, these stretches were linked with railways. It helped if a railway built to serve, say, an inland mine could promote commercial agriculture alongside its length. Thus it was that almost everywhere a railway was built in the temperate parts of colonial Africa, the land through which it ran was set aside for European settlement.

The 1 000-kilometre railway from Mombasa to Lake Victoria was built largely to make viable the growing of cotton and coffee in Uganda (as well to give Britain a strategic back door to the Nile). When Mackinnon's Imperial British East Africa Company gave way to British control of the East African Protectorate in 1895, the government looked for ways to ensure the line's economic viability. From 1902 it encouraged settlement by granting 6 500 square kilometres of land along the line of rail to Europeans and Indians, who were considered more likely than the natives to produce revenue-earning products.

In Tanganyika, the Germans built a railway from the port of Tanga to the highlands around Mount Kilimanjaro to enable German settlers to develop coffee plantations. Later they built a second line from Dar es Salaam to Tabora, to encourage agricultural production by the natives but also to facilitate the development of sisal and other plantations by Germans. The Tabora line was later extended to Kigoma on Lake Tanganyika.

In South West Africa, German settlement crept inland along the railway from Swakopmund on the Atlantic to Windhoek in the central highlands, displacing the Herero pastoralists. The settlement then spread along the next stage of the railway, which ran like a spine from north to south down the full centre of the territory, linked to the original line from Lüderitzbucht on the coast.

In the Rhodesias, railways were built to serve white settlement and mining. Rhodes had pushed the railway up from the Cape, first to Kimberley to serve the diamond mines. Once he had gained control of Rhodesia, he extended the line through Bechuanaland, bypassing the Transvaal, to Bulawayo. From there he ran a line to Salisbury and linked that with Beira port in Portuguese East Africa. Here, too, the land alongside the railways was given to Europeans.

Rhodes hoped the railways would encourage development and attract British settlers, who were vital for securing Rhodesia as a permanent British possession and a major link in his envisaged Cape-to-Cairo chain. His next extension was in fact to the north, taking the line from Bulawayo to the mines in Northern Rhodesia and the Belgian Congo. The land alongside the line in Northern Rhodesian was opened to white settlement.

In North Africa there were railways along the coast in both Algeria and Tunisia, with spur lines running inland. The only other railways in Africa in 1914 were the stretches covering most of the length of the Nile up to and some distance beyond Khartoum, the single line from Lagos to Kano in northern Nigeria, the line linking the Senegal River with the upper Niger River, short stretches inland from the coasts of Angola, the Belgian Congo, Cameroon, Dahomey, Togo and the Gold Coast, and another from Dakar. There were no other railways anywhere in Africa.

Cecil Rhodes dreamed of travelling in the same train from Cape Town to Cairo, but that was impossible for two reasons: there were three major rail gauges, and the gap in the middle – southern Sudan and northern Uganda – has never been closed by any one of them. In southern Africa the railways copied the 3 feet 6 inch (1,067m) 'Cape gauge' that had been preferred in South Africa to the wider European gauges because it was cheaper to build. In Tanganyika and Kenya the railways were built to the slightly narrower one-metre gauge. In the Sudan the railway reverted to the Cape gauge, but in Egypt it went over to the standard European gauge of 4 feet 8½ inch (1,67m).

Mining almost everywhere became the principal colonial industry because of Africa's comparatively low agricultural potential – no sweeping wheatlands such as those of the American prairies, and the deadly tsetse fly prohibiting cattle ranching on the scale of the Argentinian pampas. Most of the foreign investment in Africa went into mining. Of an estimated £1 222-million invested in sub-Saharan Africa by 1938, nearly half (£555-million) went to South Africa, mainly for mining. The copper mines received most of the £143-million invested in the Belgian Congo, and £102-million went to the Rhodesias, again mostly for mining. Only £422-million was invested elsewhere, mostly on railways.[2]

Not all white settlement was along the line of rail, but it is illustrative that much of the early railway construction in Africa was in areas suitable for white settlement.

By 1914 South Africa had a rail network so comprehensive that few new lines would be needed in the future. The South African system was linked to Lourenço Marques and to the line running into the Rhodesias and the Belgian Congo and the extension to Beira.

CHAPTER 26

IN THE SWEAT OF THY FACE

Race relations in South Africa were often somewhat like a theatre of the bizarre, most often within the context of the conflicting imperatives of the whites – wanting the blacks to serve them but at the same time not to be among them.

As the country became more industrialised the paradoxes multiplied. For instance, the Labour Party, formed in the year of Union, 1910, was a workers' party for whites only, advocating territorial and job segregation on racial lines. It favoured sending the Indians back to India and barring coloureds from having sex with whites.

And when white miners went on strike on the Witwatersrand in 1922 they saw nothing incongruous in marching with a banner exhorting 'workers of the world' to 'unite for a white South Africa'. Neither did the right-wing National Party have insuperable difficulty in joining the Communist Party in backing the strikers.

An especially incongruous element was introduced into the social structure when the discovery of gold brought members of the European working classes in large numbers into the country. The skills of deep-level mining that the white miners brought from the coal and tin mines of Britain, and from the gold and coal mines of Australia, gave them bargaining power. Trade unionism had arrived – but in aberrant forms.

The British miners fitted somewhat eccentrically into the system of white domination. They had brought with them to Africa something of the ethos of the British working class, the spirit of the struggle for workers' rights that had begun in the late industrial revolution, mixed with influences such as the ideals of the Tolpuddle Martyrs and as much as suited them of Keir Hardie's labour politics. They had, however, also brought the conviction of white superiority that was common in Britain. Hardie had found little support among the Rand's white miners when, on a visit to South Africa, he had spoken out for African rights as they were being swept under the carpet of Union in 1909.

The white miners went on strike for the first time in 1897, after the mine owners had lowered black mineworkers' wages and tried to do the same with the whites. The owners gave in and restored the wage cuts – but only for the whites. The blacks dared not go on strike for they had no skills and no bargaining power.

As more whites learned mining skills union membership was opened to all whites, the qualification being switched from skill to race. At the same time unions began to enter politics, supporting the South African Labour Party and the Afrikaner National Party in return for those parties' efforts to protect the interests of white workers. Workers had become an influential new constituent in white politics.

White miners downed tools over cost-cutting measures in 1902 and again in 1907. When they went on strike again in 1913 violence erupted over the use of 'scab' labour. The government called on troops from the British garrison to maintain order. Mobs set fire to the main railway station and the premises of *The Star* newspaper, the mouthpiece of the mine owners. The troops foiled attempts to do the same to the Corner House, headquarters of the newspaper's owners, and to the Rand Club, the mine owners' exclusive watering hole. Firing into the crowds, the soldiers killed 21 white people. Botha and Smuts negotiated a settlement.

Declining profits persuaded the Chamber of Mines in December 1921 to cut the wages of white miners and open semi-skilled work formerly reserved for whites to blacks at lower pay. Within days 20 000 white miners had downed tools. Control of the strike slipped into the hands of a militant group that included members of the newly formed Communist Party of South Africa. Members of non-mining unions joined the strike and supported a resolution accusing the government of 'backing the employers in their attack on white workers', and demanding the installation of a new government 'calculated to protect the interests of the white race in South Africa'.

Early in 1922 the action became violent as strikers tried to free arrested fellows. By March strike had become revolt, spreading across the Rand as the strikers formed well-armed commandos, many of whose members had seen military service in the First World War. The commandos derailed trains, seized a police station and burned down another. About thirty mine officials besieged in their offices at a Brakpan mine were overwhelmed when they ran out of ammunition, and a number were clubbed to death as they lay wounded.

With all the East Rand towns in rebel hands, the government declared martial law and called up the Active Citizen Force. Strike commandos fought open battles with police and troops. Smuts, who had taken over the premiership after Botha's death in 1919, used artillery and aircraft to bombard the rebel defences. Troops stormed the strikers' positions and the revolt was crushed. At least two hundred and ten people had been killed and eight hundred wounded on both sides. About five thousand strikers were arrested and 18 sentenced to death, but only four were executed.

Some saw the revolt as a treasonable attempt to form an Afrikaner republic, and others as a Bolshevik plot to seize power. A commission of inquiry found evidence of both aspirations, but in time the strike came to be seen primarily as a collision between the interests of mine owners and white union leaders, coloured by and played out in the context of white racism. Racial equality was anathema both to the British miners who led the strike and to the Afrikaners who made up the majority of the strikers, their people having increasingly found employment on the mines as they were driven from the farms by the Boer War farm burnings, drought and cattle disease – notably the great rinderpest epidemic that devastated South Africa's cattle population from 1897.

Essentially the revolt was symptomatic of the strains being imposed on the social fabric of the new Union by the old tensions about land, labour and white fear. The labour issue was more volatile in the mining industry than any other. The mining companies, represented collectively by the Chamber of Mines, were the most powerful economic force of the time, generating and distributing greater wealth and creating more white employment than any other sector of the economy. Gold mining nonetheless recorded a profit retention of only 2,1 per cent between 1887 and 1914, and with miners' wages making up more than half the production costs, suppressing wages became a prime concern.

The mining houses would happily have employed only blacks, believing they could acquire the same skills as the whites if allowed and still accept lower wages. White politics and white trade unions stood in the way, however. The government had no problem with black wages being suppressed but did have difficulty with blacks replacing whites in the workplace.

The mines found it difficult to recruit enough blacks for the basic pick-and-shovel work, for it was arduous, unpleasant and dangerous labour that blacks avoided if possible. In 1901 the mining houses formed the Witwatersrand Native Labour Association (Wenela) to widen the recruitment of black mineworkers throughout the sub-continent. Still the mines continued to find it difficult to recruit enough labour at wages low enough to offset the fixed gold price.*

In order to increase the supply of labour within South Africa, the mining interests collaborated with agriculture, the other main employer, in promoting legislation aimed at ensuring that black communities would continue to provide workers, and cheaply. The laws they initiated added heavy layers to the strata of prejudice and protectionism that had been formed over more than two centuries by the Europeans' experience in South Africa, by their need to acquire the indigenous people's land and labour while protecting themselves against their greater numbers. Each stratum was nothing more than the thin sediment of its time, but together they formed a deep aggregation whose base had become bedrock.

At no time, not even in the more liberal Cape with its black franchise, did any white community seriously contemplate, let alone attempt to achieve, a non-racial, egalitarian society. One of the reasons, perhaps, was that few whites believed that blacks were capable of good governance; or that they would not, if dominant, practise racism against the whites.

While taxation and poverty in the reserves were broadly effectual in coercing blacks into working for white employers, their effect was limited in that as soon as the worker had earned enough to pay his taxes – usually after about six months – he went home to be with his family. To overcome this problem a contract system was introduced that bound the migrant worker to his employer for up to eighteen months.

---

*The effective price of gold did not change until South Africa went off the gold standard in 1933, when the price shot up by 65 per cent. The formal price, however, remained fixed at $35 an ounce until 1970, when a second-tier free market was created, and profits increased hugely.

The rising demand for labour towards the end of the 19th century turned the attention of white employers to the relatively large proportion of black farmers whose self-sufficiency enabled them to pay their taxes and so remain outside the labour net. Most of the black farmers operated outside the 'native reserves' as share-croppers – commonly known as squatters – on the white farms that comprised the major proportion of South Africa. In Natal in the 1870s, for instance, about one-third of the black population was squatting on white-owned land, and about a tenth on Crown land.[1] Productive these black farmers might be, and helping to feed the mining towns, but the mining industry needed their muscles more than it needed their mealies.

In 1895 the Transvaal government moved to reduce the number of black share-croppers and force their men to work for longer terms for white employers. The chosen instrument was a law permitting no more than five black families to squat on a white man's farm. From the five families the farmer would obtain his labour; any excess or any subsequent increases through marriage would have to find work on other farms or in the mines or factories.

A government commission found that African men had insufficient incentive to work for white employers when they still were largely able, despite the hut and poll taxes, to meet their simple needs in the reserves, in whose subsistence and barter economies they had relatively little use for money. The commission, however, rejected proposals that Africans be forced into migrant labour through interference with prevailing tribal or land tenure structures. To do so, it said, would create huge social problems.

Instead, the government allowed the Chamber of Mines to recruit mine workers in China from 1904. That backfired when many of the mainly British miners, fearful of losing their jobs to the industrious Chinese, supported Het Volk in the 1907 self-government election, thereby helping to put the Transvaal under the political control of Afrikaners only five years after the latter had lost the war. The recruitment of Chinese mineworkers was stopped in 1908 after an outcry in Britain against 'Chinese slavery' on the mines.

Five years later the government tried another tack, enacting the Native Land Act of 1913, a momentous measure increasing the size of the reserves and banning sharecropper squatting in order to make available more labour for the mines and factories. Just over seven per cent of the country was set aside for black occupation. There was provision for the reserves to be enlarged later if this proved necessary to ensure an adequate flow of black labour. Africans and whites were barred from acquiring land in each other's areas.

Achieving the aims of the Act required striking a fairly delicate balance between making the reserves large enough to provide sufficient manpower but small enough to keep them poor and overcrowded, so that the young men would be forced into migrant labour.

Iniquitous though the Act was, there was little white opposition to it, although the generally conservative Anglican church demanded that the Act be repealed. The Dutch Reformed Church, for its part, had affirmed its stance on the race question in general by obtaining government approval in 1911 for barring black people from its churches in the Transvaal and Orange Free State.

Although much of the reserves was good farmland, population pressures and ignorance of conservation practices led to overgrazing, overcropping and soil erosion. Thus the overall productive capacity of the reserves tended to diminish rather than increase while their populations grew.

With the reserves reduced to little more than labour pools with subsistence economies and meagre cash flows, their social structures deteriorated. Since most of the men were away much of the time, women dominated the home scene; children grew up hardly knowing their fathers, and, in the prevailing poverty and under-development, with inadequate schooling. The effect of the laws was to turn the reserves into something approaching human-farming.

Tribal and family structures that had given the black nations their virility were crippled. At the same time the blacks were blocked from transferring to the white-dominated social structure. An inevitable result was a heightening of political protest among blacks and an increase in crime.

The black man who sought a wider life and opportunities was trapped between the white man's system of passes and contracts, and the authority of his traditional chief, who invariably cooperated with the white authorities since they had the power to depose him if he didn't. Without a pass and a good labour record, such a man was condemned to what the whites liked to regard as his 'traditional way of life' in the reserves, which was now an incarcerated existence barring him from progressing through education and economic enterprise. In the reserves he was shackled to his past and shut off from the advancing outer world.

Even with a pass there was not much the black man could enjoy in the white man's world. If he worked on the mines, it was an especially hard life of confinement and discomfort in the compounds, and of danger underground. In barracks with minimal facilities the mineworkers lived for the duration of their contracts without their women or children, sleeping on narrow concrete bunks, side-by-side like boxed fruit, and having to cope with theft, violence and sodomy.

Down the mine there were rockfalls and other lethal hazards. But the greatest killer was disease, principally pneumonia, brought on by the living and working conditions. Of the 5 022 deaths among black mineworkers in 1903 (a death rate of 112 per thousand), only a little more than four per cent were from mining accidents.[2]

The mine hospitals were in effect little more than sorting stations, sorting those who could be returned to work from those too ill or crippled to be of further use.

CHAPTER 27

THE END BEGINS

Church bells and sirens had summoned the people of Rome, and now tens of thousands waited outside the Palazzo Venezia on a moonlit night in May 1936. Applause erupted as Benito Mussolini appeared in the glare of spotlights on a balcony, striking his familiar posture: hands on hips, jackbooted legs wide apart, massive jaw thrust out as far as it would go.

The outsize jowl and the theatrical stance might be manna to cartoonists in other countries, but for millions of Italians they were respected characteristics of the man who held their faith, *il Duce del Fascismo,* who was transforming their country, lifting them from poverty to promise, making Italy a power in Europe and giving it the prestige of foreign possessions.

Mussolini's operatic voice boomed out through the loudspeakers: 'The destiny of Abyssinia has been sealed today in the fourteenth year of the Fascist era ... Italy has her empire ...'[1] Waves of applause beat against the palazzo, and *il Duce's* chin could go no higher.

Yes, Italy had her empire (Libya, Eritrea and Italian Somaliland being the others) but the possession would be brief.

Italy had staked an imperial claim of sorts in Ethiopia in 1906. With Menelik seeming to be close to death, Italy, France and Britain had declared 'spheres of interest' (the imperial version of a first option) in the region – the Italian one adjacent to Ethiopia and Italian Somaliland, the French one inland from their Somaliland Protectorate, and the British one in the Blue Nile region.

Menelik in fact didn't die until 1913, when he was succeeded first by his grandson, then his daughter, with Ras Tafari, son of Ras Makonnen, as regent. A weedy little man but with an imperial bearing, Tafari became the effective ruler. Dedicated to unifying and modernising his nation, he won it membership of the League of Nations in 1923.

Mussolini coveted Abyssinia to avenge Adowa, obtain more space for Italy's crowded population, and create an Italian swathe across the Horn of Africa, from Somaliland to Eritrea. Having signed a treaty of friendship with Tafari in 1928, Mussolini went ahead with his plans of conquest. The excuse to invade came in 1934, when he rejected an Abyssinian proposal of arbitration of a minor border dispute. Ras Tafari, who had become emperor in 1930 and taken the name Haile Selassie, appealed to the League of Nations for help.

The League, however, was dominated by the European powers, who made sure that its interests never superseded their own. Britain and France wanted to avoid driving Italy out of its association with their countries and into an alliance with Adolph Hitler, who was rearming Germany and exhibiting territorial ambitions in Europe. They proposed an arms blockade on both Abyssinia and Italy, and the League duly obliged. That suited Mussolini fine, for Italy could make her own arms whereas Abyssinia couldn't.

Publicly, Britain and France vowed to oppose any unprovoked aggression by Italy. Their private intentions were the opposite. The British foreign secretary, Sir Samuel Hoare, was worried that Italy's troop strength in Libya might threaten the Suez Canal. He secretly agreed with prime minister Pierre Laval of France that if necessary, in order to placate Mussolini, they would oblige Abyssinia to surrender much of its territory to Italy.

Mussolini didn't bother to declare war before launching a two-pronged invasion in October 1935 from his Eritrean and Somalian colonies with tanks, bombers, artillery and 400 000 troops. Haile Selassie again appealed to the League, which condemned the aggression and imposed economic sanctions on Italy. Britain and France ensured, however, that the sanctions excluded petrol, without which the Italian forces would have been paralysed. Hoare kept the Suez Canal open to Italian shipments of both petrol and munitions.

When the French press broke the story of the Hoare-Laval pact, Hoare was forced to resign. But Mussolini's military supplies continued to pass down the Canal, and his armies rolled back the poorly armed Abyssinian forces. Where fleeing troops and civilians retreated into the mountain ravines, Mussolini's aircraft dropped mustard gas on them.

Haile Selassie went himself to Geneva in May 1936 to make an urgent plea to the League of Nations. Three days later the Italian army occupied his capital. The League went through the motions of hearing Selassie's plea, then lifted the Italian sanctions, with only South Africa and New Zealand dissenting.

In that same year the Spanish Civil War broke out, leading to thousands of Europeans and Americans fighting with the International Brigades against the fascists. There was no International Brigade to help the Abyssinians, however, for they were Africans, not Europeans.

The Abyssinian debacle was so abject that the League's authority collapsed completely. Both the League and Abyssinia had been sacrificed by Britain and France in the interests of averting war with Italy, but the sacrifice was in vain. Emasculated by its creators, the League watched in helpless silence as Hitler, soon joined by Mussolini, took Europe into the Second World War.

Haile Selassie went into exile in England, but disgust spread through Africa at what was seen as Britain's sacrifice of Africans to European expediency. The anger deepened when in 1938 Britain, followed by Australia and Canada, formally recognised the Italian conquest, and when some in Britain suggested that the rampant Hitler be pacified by the return of Germany's former colonies. For Africans to be seen as nothing more than pawns of European politics was nourishment for the seeds of nationalism in their continent.

★ ★ ★ ★

The conquest of Abyssinia was the last fling of European colonisation in Africa. It was something of an aberration, coming when the other powers were beginning to look beyond acquisition to the responsibilities, even the disadvantages, that colonialism had brought; and when some Africans, encouraged by the disposition of the former German and Turkish possessions after the First World War, were beginning to look ahead to a European withdrawal from the continent. By agreeing to account to the League of Nations for their administration of the territories, and by accepting that these would eventually 'stand on their own feet in the arduous conditions of the modern world', the executors of the mandates had implicitly accepted the territories' right to eventual self-determination. That right had implicitly become applicable to other African possessions as well. The die had thus been cast for decolonisation, though not everyone could see it.

The trustee mandates had been demanded by the United States, which thereby signalled its emergence from isolationism into the role of international power broker. Isolationist sentiment had made Washington refuse to join the League of Nations, but when it emerged from the war as the world's strongest nation it found that an interventionist role had been thrust on it.

When President Woodrow Wilson in February 1918 made his famous 'self-determination' speech, declaring that 'people may now be dominated and governed only by their own consent', his words were heard in Africa and set minds thinking, especially when five months later he added that the principle of self-determination should guide 'the settlement of every question, whether of territory, of sovereignty ... or of political relationship'.

American repugnance of colonialism doomed South Africa's hopes of absorbing South West Africa, which had taken a symbolic place in African nationalist politics when the League of Nations had in 1933 refused a formal South African request for incorporation. The territory had then come to represent for many Africans the possibility of independence for all of Africa.

In the thirties the major colonial powers had in any case largely accepted that, having acquired African colonies for political reasons, and having sought to exploit them for economic reasons, they had an obligation to promote the interests of the indigenous peoples for moral reasons. Besides that, keeping the subject peoples happy made good economic and political sense.

In the years between the wars even those Europeans who envisaged a more democratic dispensation beyond colonialism did not anticipate it emerging for many decades. Concepts of the form it might take were vague, and tended not to extend to self-determination. The French, Portuguese, Belgians and Italians were thinking more of eventual assimilation of the conquered Africans into their own citizenship.

For the British, there was never any question of assimilation. British policy was seen vaguely as an extension of the civilising mission into some form of loose association within the Empire; never as members of the Empire alongside the Dominions, though. Smuts was pretty well expressing the views not only of white South Africans regarding their own country but of most Britons for Africa as a whole when in 1930 he envisaged in South Africa 'a slow, gradual schooling of peoples who have slumbered and stagnated since the dawn of time' and said 'only an ever-present, settled European order can achieve that high end.'[2]

The thinking among whites in general was that Africans did not have it within them to rise on their own to European levels of civil and technical sophistication. If they were even capable of achieving parity, they needed the whites to haul them up to it. For some it was a self-serving philosophy, justifying continued white domination and segregation. For others it was honestly held belief.

Certain of their dominance in Africa through the assumed superiority of their race and the undeniable power of their motherland, Britons continued between the wars to emigrate in substantial numbers to South Africa, the Rhodesias and Kenya, with Whitehall's encouragement. The French continued to settle in Algeria, and the Portuguese in Angola and Portuguese East Africa (Mozambique).

Where white settler communities had grown too large to be easily controlled from Europe, the powers considered it expedient to grant them various degrees of autonomy. Effective autonomy had been given to the whites of Algeria in 1905, and to those in Southern Rhodesia in 1923. Full autonomy, and with it full control of the black majority, had been obtained by South Africa's whites with the creation of the Union in 1910.

In Kenya the whites had not become numerous enough to be able to demand autonomy with any hope of success. But not even London's declaration of African paramountcy in East Africa in 1923 (when there were only about twelve thousand whites in Kenya) stopped them from demanding, if not white domination, at least control of their own destiny.

In Northern Rhodesia, too, the white population never became large enough to cock a snook at Whitehall. It was only about five thousand when in 1930 the African paramountcy policy declared for Kenya was extended to Northern Rhodesia as well, over the loud protests of the whites there.

It was not only the British settlers in Kenya and Northern Rhodesia whose survival as a dominant minority depended on protection by their motherland. The French and Portuguese settlers also found it impossible to resist African nationalism when they lost the backing of Paris and Lisbon respectively. White South Africans alone could hold out on their own, but, as it was to turn out, only for a limited time.

★ ★ ★ ★

Though it transformed Africa, the colonial era was relatively brief, lasting little more than a century and its heyday half that. Its decline began imperceptibly, just when it seemed at its strongest, in the period between the two world wars.

The imperatives that had driven colonialism and white settlement had begun to wane even at the turn of the century. The decline was not widely discerned at the time, and was least obvious in the colonies themselves, where the powers were spending more than ever before on administration and development.

To some extent this expenditure was inspired by the burgeoning concept of obligation, but it was also made possible by the fact that, after more than twenty years of European administration and funding, some colonies were showing a profit, producing more revenue than was required for the priority of maintaining domination. More funds were becoming available for roads, harbours, power supplies, schools and hospitals. There was something of an infrastructural boom in colonial Africa until over-production in America spread the Great Depression across the world in 1930.

Even without that particular catastrophe, however, there was endemic decay behind the orderly fronts of colonialism. France had entered an era of political instability, with governments sprouting and dying like mushrooms, and her economic growth was consequently hampered. Britain, her economy and manpower drained by the war, and deeply in debt to the United States, was a waning power, even if few Britons were aware of it.

The very expansion of Britain's Empire had masked the decline in her economy in relation to the other Powers, a decline that had begun in the last decade of the 19th century if not before, and been hastened by the war.

The Empire itself was beginning to come apart at the seams. At the start of the twenties, nearly a third of the English-speaking whites outside America lived in the Dominions, and their dependence on Britain was fast diminishing. At the same time there was a growing sentiment in the colonies for independence.

In Africa, a crucial phenomenon was the emergence in substantial numbers of Africans educated in the colonies as well as in Europe – Africans equipped with the academic and technical knowledge of Europe and exposed to its social mores, Africans capable of bringing a new sophistication to the old resentment of colonial domination and a new confidence in their ability to challenge it on its own terms.

The significance of this development came rudely to light in Egypt when in 1919 the British foreign secretary, Lord Curzon, brusquely rebuffed requests for independence put forward by a group of Egyptian politicians and business and professional leaders known as the Wafd. Riots and strikes erupted. The British, determined to protect the Suez Canal, responded harshly, killing about fifteen hundred Egyptians, some bombed and machine-gunned from the air.

The Wafd went on to become the country's leading political organisation, supported by the peasantry as well as the upper classes – but not by King Fuad, who sided with the British. A number of conferences were held with the Wafd over the next few years, but the British had twice to station warships off Alexandria, with their implied threat of bombardment, and to land troops and parade them through Cairo in order to discourage further uprisings. In 1936, alarmed by Mussolini's expansionism, the British signed the Anglo-Egyptian Treaty, giving Egypt full independence but allowing Britain to retain its garrison and air and naval bases.

From the Imperial Conference in London in 1926 emerged the 1931 Statute of Westminster, recognising the equality of the British and Dominion parliaments and barring Britain from interfering with the Dominions' governance.

★ ★ ★ ★

The Statute of Westminster put beyond legal challenge the ability of the Pretoria government to order the lives of the country's black majority. Challenge was growing within the country, however. The South African Native National Congress, formed in 1912, had sent a delegation under Sol Plaatje to London in 1919 to present a memorial of grievances to the British government. Black workers on the Witwatersrand demonstrated against the pass laws, and large numbers of black and coloured workers joined the newly formed Industrial and Commercial Union (ICU).

Students burned buildings at the South African Native College at Fort Hare, the country's first tertiary institution for blacks. Black miners went on strike in 1920, and blacks rioted in Port Elizabeth after the local ICU leader had been arrested for inciting strike action.

Smuts, who had tightened the pass laws in 1919, responded to the agitation with the Native Affairs Act of 1920, creating an all-white Native Affairs Commission that liased with a Native Conference supposedly representing black leaders. But segregation and supremacy remained the watchwords. In 1923 the government passed the Natives (Urban Areas) Act, a landmark measure confining urban blacks to separate townships on the outskirts of white towns.

Through all this, General Hertzog's Pact Government was energetically pursuing Afrikaner interests, even sovereignty, albeit within the Empire for the time being. His zeal was partly restrained by the largely English-speaking Labour Party, with which his National Party had made a marriage of convenience to defeat Smuts's South African Party in the general election of 1924. Those restraints did not, however, stop Hertzog from making a quixotic appeal to London for the restoration of the Boer republics.

Using the Pact government as a vehicle, Afrikaners accelerated their own advancement, promoting Afrikaner membership of the civil service and widening the Afrikaner base in commerce and industry.

The delicate matter of unifying the whites who had fought each other in the Boer War inevitably produced friction over the symbols of identity and authority. After years of acrimonious controversy, a new national flag incorporating the Union Jack and the flags of the Boer republics in miniature was adopted in 1928.

Hertzog attempted to reduce the indirect black representation in parliament and slightly extend the reserves as labour pools, but was unable to get the necessary two-thirds majority in parliament. As an interim measure he devalued the black voting power in the Cape by abolishing the 'civilisation' requirement for white men in that province and by extending the vote to white women throughout the country in 1930.

Soon, however, Hertzog and Smuts had together to duck for cover from the economic fallout from the Great Depression, from Britain's departure from the gold standard in 1931 and from the worst drought in living memory. Obstinately remaining on the gold standard (with the support of the Chamber of Mines), Hertzog saw the Labour Party desert the Pact Government and South Africa's currency become so over-valued that foreign trade became almost impossible. In desperation, Hertzog formed a coalition with Smuts's party and abandoned the gold standard, allowing South Africa to return to prosperity.

In the general election of 1933 the coalition won support so overwhelming that the two parties the next year fused to form a new one, the United Party, with Hertzog as leader and Smuts his deputy. Right-wingers in Hertzog's old party hived off to form a Purified National Party under the dour leadership of the former Dutch Reformed Church minister, Dr DF Malan, who would in time become the midwife of classic apartheid. Equally dissatisfied English-speakers formed the Dominion Party under FC Stallard.

The fusion enabled Hertzog in 1936 to get the two-thirds majority for his 'native bills', but now watered down. There would now be four African representatives in the Senate, while Cape Africans would be put on a separate roll to vote for three whites who would represent them in the House of Assembly. Outside parliament, a Natives' Representative Council was created to 'advise' the government. To the 8,3-million hectares set aside for 'native reserves' in 1913 were added another 5,8-million hectares, to be purchased by the state.

The vulnerability of the whites to the effects of their own policies was emphasised by the census of 1937, which showed that 55 per cent of the black population lived outside the reserves, working on farms or in the factories and mines. In the Transvaal, now the country's industrial hub, blacks comprised 53 per cent of the urban population. On the Witwatersrand, the very centre of that hub, they outnumbered the whites by a ratio of 1,5:1. The United Party government reacted with legislation to tighten the controls on blacks' access to white areas and on where they lived there.

Thus by 1937 the basic structure of what would come to be known as apartheid was firmly in place, with the approval of the overwhelming majority of white South Africans, English-speakers as well as Afrikaners.

Opposition to Hertzog's 'native bills' had been led by an All African Convention, a newly formed umbrella organisation representing African political groups across the spectrum, from the moderate Cape Native Voters' Convention to the SA Communist Party.* Meeting in Bloemfontein in 1935, the delegates accepted the principle of the vote being tied to a civilisation test. They agreed that political rights in a democratic state should be exercised by those possessing 'a reasonable meas-

---

*With anti-black sentiment still running strong among its members, the Communist Party supported the alliance between Hertzog's National Party and the Labour Party in the 1924 election in which they defeated Smuts's South African Party and formed the Pact government. Subsequently, however, the Communist Party began to attract black members and – with strong encouragement from Moscow – came to see its 'main revolutionary task among the natives'. Leading white members who preferred to promote the party's future among the white working class were expelled. Thereafter the party eschewed racism.

ure of education and (making) a material contribution to the economic welfare of the country'. At the same time, they rejected any criterion of race or colour in the granting of the vote.

This black endorsement of a qualified vote could radically have altered the subsequent history of the country had it been accepted by the Hertzog government. Demographically, the timing might have been advantageous for the whites, for the black majority was smaller then than it was later to become. Politically, however, it was a non-starter, for conditional suffrage would have disqualified many whites, mainly Afrikaners, who at that time could not have met even limited educational or property qualifications.

By 1937 the AAC had accepted into membership the whites representing blacks in the Parliament. The AAC, however, soon disappeared as the African National Congress (renamed in 1923 from the SANNC) consolidated its position as the leading black political organisation – but still opposing racial differentiation.

★ ★ ★ ★

The failure of South Africa's white leaders to embrace the black elite in 1935 was echoed by a similar development at the other end of the continent. In Algeria, white settlers successfully opposed a move to grant French citizenship to Muslims with certain qualifications, making inevitable the war that subsequently engulfed the country and lost it to France.

The proposal was put before the French parliament in 1936 in a bill sponsored by the Socialist prime minister, Leon Blum, and his Minister for Algerian Affairs, Maurice Viollette. Arabs in Algeria formed a Muslim Congress broadly sympathetic to the Viollette reforms. Blum and Viollette responded with a bill giving French citizenship to Algeria's Muslims without prejudice to the status of their faith but with the vote restricted to elected officials, high-school graduates and Muslims who had served in the French armed forces. Though the vote would initially be exercised by only about thirty thousand of the six million Algerian Muslims, the bill was acceptable to the Congress. It was bitterly opposed, however, by most of the whites in Algeria. Almost all the mayors threatened to resign. White settlers formed armed militias, and threatened civil war if the measure should be approved.

While the opposing camps disputed, Blum was ousted from office and the bill died. Conceding defeat in 1939, Viollette told the Assembly: 'These (Muslim) men have no political nation. They do not even demand their religious nation. All they ask is to be admitted into yours. If you refuse this, beware that they do not soon create one for themselves.'

His warning was prophetically accurate; after the Second World War, the Arabs rose in revolt and forced the French to abandon Algeria.

The whites in Algeria and South Africa refused to grant equality to their indigenous elites for the same basic reason: fear that it would insert a wedge into their hegemony that would inexorably widen until they were squeezed into submission to a majority whose culture was alien to and therefore incompatible with their own.

Not that the South Africans gave much thought to that as the Great Depression faded into the past. Their country was becoming Africa's superpower, the industrial giant of the continent. By the mid-thirties South Africa had more than half of the international trade of sub-Saharan Africa. This prosperity came at a price, though, the price of having large numbers of black people living within the areas reserved for whites in order to provide labour.

Few whites realised that the black locations were ticking bombs on their doorstep.

CHAPTER 28

UNDER FREEDOM'S FLAG

Europe's war clouds again cast long shadows across Africa in the late thirties. Again people of Africa, white and black, became involved, through the links of settlement and colonialism, in a war of the Europeans. Now, however, both had a closer interest in that both were threatened by European totalitarianism, even if only indirectly or distantly.

Not all the whites in South Africa saw it that way, for some Afrikaners sympathised with Hitler's Naziism. The ghosts of 1914 rose again, and rebellion and civil war brewed.

Malan's National Party had gained enough support for it to hijack the cultural organisations formed under Hertzog's auspices, the *Afrikaner Broederbond* and the *Federasie van Afrikaanse Kultuurvereenigings (FAK)*, and to politicise both. Parallel with the desire for political power was the imperative of fostering Afrikaans culture and identity. To these ends it was seen to be necessary to reshape and politicise history. The Great Trek was seized on as a catalyst for uniting Afrikaners and bringing all within the doctrinal fold. The Trek was refashioned as a kind of Passover of Afrikanerdom. Sympathetic academics promoted the idea, exaggerating the scope and significance of the migration.

The fortuitous arrival of the Trek's centenary offered a rare opportunity for further promotion. A commemorative ox-waggon trek was conducted in 1938 from Cape Town to Pretoria. The waggon crews and their attendant outriders all wore Voortrekker dress, and all along the route they were cheered by crowds of whites in similar garb, flying the flags of the old Boer republics.

Crowds clamoured to touch the waggons, to bond with the ideal. Some wept as they touched. The journey ended at a hilltop outside Pretoria where the foundation stone was laid of a great granite memorial to the Voortrekkers – and, in another sense, a totem of the Afrikaner renaissance.

The rise of the new Afrikaner nationalism was emotionally manifested in the reception given the trek party all along their way. For a people buffeted by the adverse swirls of history, their very identity threatened by the demands of other and very different peoples, it was like a spring welling up in the desert, a clear stream of purpose and hope.

Inevitably, it was channelled by the extremists, who were often hard to distinguish in all the cultural bubbling of the renaissance. In that glad stream was spawned a new organisation, the *Ossewabrandwag* (literally translated as Oxwagon Sentinel), ostensibly another cultural body but in its operations increasingly militaristic, its members the musclemen of the renaissance.

Extremists attempted to identify Afrikaner nationalism with German Naziism. On the Witwatersrand, Afrikaners sympathetic to Hitler began appearing in dark shirts with swastika armbands, parading in the streets and giving stiff-armed salutes, and holding meetings at which Nazi ideas were espoused.

Moderate Afrikaners were distressed by these activities. Even more so were English-speakers loyal to their British roots, and there were violent clashes between them and the brownshirts.

As the Trek centenary waggons crossed the Great Karoo, the British and French prime ministers met Hitler and Mussolini in Munich in their bid to avert war. By the time the waggons reached Pretoria in December, white South Africa was in a state of ferment, with right-wingers openly expressing hopes that if war came Britain would be defeated and the old Boer republics restored by a friendly Germany.

South African whites were perilously divided when the war broke out. In Parliament, Hertzog moved that South Africa remain neutral. Smuts moved an amendment to the contrary and offered the assurance that this time South African forces would not serve outside Africa.* The amendment carried by 80 votes to 67. Hertzog demanded a new general election but the anglophone governor-general, Sir Patrick Duncan, refused. Hertzog resigned, and Smuts formed a new government.

Had the vote gone the other way, South Africa might have faced another civil war, for its armed forces were as divided as its parliament. Manie Maritz, the rebel of 1914, and other right-wingers were again plotting rebellion, while many English-speakers were determined to fight for Britain. Reservists in the Active Citizen Force had already begun travelling to the cities to join the war. Anticipating this, Hertzogites at Defence Headquarters in Pretoria had removed the ammunition from the ACF depots. In Johannesburg, senior officers had nonetheless made contingency plans to take their men in a sudden dash into English-speaking Natal. In Pretoria, pilots of the air force had likewise surreptitiously planned to fly their aircraft to Rhodesia.[1]

As in the First World War, the country's ethnic politics made conscription impossible, and again all in the armed forces were volunteers. Young men flocked to the recruiting offices, among them many Afrikaners – by the end of the war sixty per cent of the volunteers would be Afrikaners.

From its abundant resources of coal and iron ore, South Africa had been making its own steel since 1928, and now it was turned into guns and armoured cars. Motor vehicle assembly plants were converted to make army trucks. Factories that had made explosives for the mines churned out munitions.

Lacking sufficient troops, Smuts had to send police armed with machine-guns to quash an incipient revolt by Hitler Youth members among the Germans in

---

*Privately, Smuts believed that both the Nazi Germans and the Italian Fascists had designs on all of temperate Africa and especially on South Africa's mineral riches.

South West Africa. There and in South Africa suspected Nazi sympathisers were put in internment camps, including BJ Vorster, the future prime minister. Still, their womenfolk marched several thousand strong to the Union Buildings to urge the government to come to terms with Germany.

Nazi supporters sabotaged power lines and government buildings. There were melees in the streets between soldiers and *Ossewabrandwag* toughs. The *Ossewabrandwag* spawned a military wing, the *Stormjaers,* somewhat similar to the Nazi SS. In Germany, the South African Olympic heavyweight boxer Robey Leibbrandt was being trained for a mission to conduct sabotage in his homeland, assassinate Smuts and incite rebellion. Leibbrandt had met and been enthralled by Hitler at the Berlin Olympics in 1936, and had returned to Germany as an ardent disciple.*

In Rhodesia, most of the sizeable Afrikaner population accepted conscription into the armed forces, but a number refused and were lightly punished

★ ★ ★ ★

After the fall of Paris in June 1940 French officials in Morocco, Algeria, French West Africa, French Somaliland and Madagascar sided with the Vichy government. Only French Equatorial Africa – Chad, Cameroon and French Congo – declared for De Gaulle's Free French.

Fearful that French warships would fall into the hands of the Germans, the British attacked and destroyed the great French Atlantic Fleet moored at Mers-el-Kebir in Algeria. That left the strong French fleet at Dakar in Senegal which, with the ports on the Atlantic coast of Morocco, became important for the control of the eastern Atlantic. Hitler was in fact contemplating taking control of all the French ports of Atlantic Africa if the Vichy government seemed unable to defend them.

A joint British and Free French force sailed for Dakar, hoping to disembark De Gaulle without resistance and hoist the Free French flag. Efforts would then be made to rally the French in North Africa to his cause. De Gaulle, however, had grossly under-estimated the strength of Vichy support in Dakar, and the Allied landing attempt was strongly resisted. After three days of furious gun battles and an unsuccessful attempt to land Royal Marines, the attackers withdrew, leaving heavy damage on both sides.

★ ★ ★ ★

Italy's entry into the war cut off its powerful forces in the Horn of Africa from further supplies through the Suez Canal. The Horn armies were seen, however, as the lower half of a nutcracker, with those in Libya as the upper half, still receiving supplies across the Mediterranean. Egypt, defended by smaller British forces, was the nut between. Closing of the nutcracker would give the Italians control of the Suez

---

*In June 1941 Leibbrandt was landed on the coast of South West Africa. Recruiting followers, he carried out sabotage across South Africa for six months before being arrested. He was sentenced to death in 1943, but the sentence was never carried out and he was freed when Malan's National Party took power in the 1948 election.

Canal, threaten Britain's northern links with India, and open the way for an assault on the Middle Eastern oilfields on which Britain was dependent. The British forces in the Sudan would be isolated, and the Italians positioned to drive westward and southward into Africa.

While Hitler's planned invasion of Britain was being thwarted by the battle in its skies, Italian forces invaded the Sudan from Abyssinia. The British (including the 1st Rhodesian Regiment) were chased out of British Somaliland, enabling the Italians to link up with the Vichy troops in French Somaliland.

At the same time the nutcracker's upper jaw began to close on Egypt with a massive offensive by the Italian forces in Libya that advanced 100 kilometres into Egypt. A British counter-attack drove the Italians back into Libya, however.

The lower jaw of the Italian nutcracker was likewise about to be prised loose by a combined force of mainly African troops, supported by Indian units and under overall British command. Among the African units were white and black South Africans, but only the whites bore arms.

As in 1914, the white South Africans, nursing their old fear, had begun the war with only white combat units. Since South Africa's white population could produce no more than three combat divisions, the Union Defence Force had been obliged to recruit coloured men and then Indians, too. In 1940 it was decided to recruit black men as well for the service units, and in the first year 30 000 joined. By 1941 the 'non-whites' formed the backbone of the transport and supply services of the South African forces. In contravention of the Defence Act, coloured soldiers fought in artillery and machine-gun units, and others manned coastal defence guns, as did a number of Zulus who had surreptitiously received artillery training.[2] Their actions were kept secret by the Smuts government throughout the war.

At the battlefront the white South African soldiers came to rely increasingly on the black service units. The stretcher-bearers and ambulance and truck drivers, sharing the dangers and hardships with the white soldiers, earned their respect. The white infantrymen also found themselves fighting alongside troops from India and black riflemen from Nigeria, the Gold Coast and East Africa, with whom they are said to have formed 'a bond of comradeship'.[3]

In counter-attacking against the Italian 'lower jaw' in the Horn, the British forces were activating a nutcracker of sorts of their own, attacking from the Sudan in the north and from Kenya in the south. The northern force turned back the Italian drive on Khartoum and invaded Abyssinia.

The southern attack from Kenya is generally called a British offensive, but it was in reality an African one, conducted by African-born fighting men from Kenya, Tanganyika, Uganda, Nyasaland, Nigeria, the Gold Coast, South Africa and Rhodesia, waged largely with weaponry, transport, food and equipment provided by South Africa and with the aircraft and artillery mostly operated by South Africans. The white South Africans formed the core of the assault against the Italians in both East Africa and the Horn.

The southern offensive was a two-pronged drive, one heading north into Abyssinia, the other north-east into Somaliland. There were intense air battles, which largely negated the Italians' superior air strength. The eastern prong swept through Somaliland then turned west into mountainous Abyssinia. The Italians doggedly contested every peak and pass, but Addis Ababa was captured in April 1941, enabling Haile Selassie to return to his capital.

To the north, the British freed Eritrea and pursued the Italians into Abyssinia. They made their last stand at Amba Alagi, high in a mountain wilderness bristling with defences. The Allied forces fought their way up, past Magdala where the Emperor Tewodros had met his fate 73 years earlier, to the last lofty dugout. On 18 May the Italians surrendered to the South Africans, who with their African allies had fought their way from the Kenyan border over four thousand kilometres of desert and mountains in only 100 days.

The victory was a severe blow to the Axis fortunes and had an important influence on the course of the war. It probably would not have been possible had the vote in the South African parliament gone the other way in 1939.

★ ★ ★ ★

From the misty peaks of Abyssinia the South Africans were switched to the endless desert plains and dunes of North Africa, where tactics became as fluid as in naval combat. It was ping-pong warfare, with rival armies repeatedly advancing and retreating across the bare tabletop of the Western Desert.

When the South Africans arrived in Egypt in May 1941, three of the seven great offensives that were fought across the Mediterranean littoral were over. First, there had been the Italian invasion of Egypt in 1940. Then the British had chased the Italians back to El Agheila in the Tripolitanian half of Libya. The Germans had then moved in to stop the rot, and General Erwin Rommel's Afrika Korps had driven the British back from El Agheila all the way through Cyrenaica to Sollum on the Egyptian border, leaving only the besieged garrison of Tobruk port still in British hands in Libya.

With the arrival of the 2nd South African Division in October there were 100 000 South Africans of all races, including white nurses and women's auxiliary forces, in North Africa. The 2nd Division was put to work constructing fortifications along a 65-kilometre rearward defensive line on the hard ground between the sea and the salt marshes of the Quattara Depression. It was tedious work but it was to help save Egypt for the Allies.

The two South African divisions joined British, Australian, Indian, New Zealand and Free French troops in the Eighth Army. The fighter and bomber squadrons of the SAAF operated alongside the RAF. The South Africans were to fly 32 808 sorties, shooting down more than four hundred enemy aircraft, before the campaign in the Western Desert ended 14 months later.

In November 1941 the Eighth Army launched the fourth of the great offensives, driving the Axis forces back almost to Tobruk. Rommel made a two-pronged counter-attack that if successful would probably have opened Egypt to his panzers. It was stopped largely by the 5th South African Brigade at Sidi Rezegh, south-east of Tobruk, but at the cost of the brigade being virtually wiped out. Rommel's tank losses in this assault forced him to retreat to El Agheila as the Tobruk garrison broke out to join the Eighth Army.

Rommel struck back in January 1942, capturing Benghazi and then sending the Eighth Army again into full retreat in what has become known as the 'Gazala Gallop'. By July it was back at the El Alamein defences, having seen Tobruk and its garrison surrendered to the Germans.

The loss of Tobruk was a psychological as much as a strategic blow to the Allies, with 25 000 men being taken prisoner, among them two brigades of the 2nd South African Division. The blame for the disaster was placed by the British on Major-General HB Klopper, commander of the South African Division and of the garrison, despite Klopper having later been cleared of blame by an official inquiry.

The British retreat came to a halt at the defence line prepared by the 2nd South African Division at El Alamein. Rommel's Panzers launched repeated attacks on the northern sector held by the 1st South African Division. Thrown back each time, they hit further south at the British sector and broke through but were then repulsed.

In August General Bernard Montgomery took over command of the Eighth Army. Rommel launched a second attack on the El Alamein line on 31 August, breaking through a minefield in the south. He was held by the British forces Montgomery had waiting for him in the rear at Alam Halfa, and after an eight-day battle the Germans remained stalled. Rommel had shot his bolt in Africa, losing his last chance to seize Egypt and the Suez Canal.

Montgomery went on the offensive on the night of 23 October with one of the most famous of artillery barrages, opening the second battle of Alamein. Through the gap thus blasted in the German defences poured British, Australian, New Zealand, South African and Rhodesian troops.

Rommel was now caught between the Eighth Army and the American troops coming ashore on the Atlantic coast of Morocco, and British forces landing at Oran and Algiers. The Vichy forces accepted a cease-fire, and Rommel retreated from his eastern front.

Soon afterwards, the South African and Australian divisions were withdrawn from the Eighth Army for a rest. Montgomery's forces, still including the South African air force, sappers and transport units, pushed westward until they met the British–American forces under General Dwight Eisenhower advancing from the opposite direction. The last German forces surrendered on 13 May 1943.

The fighting in Africa was not yet over for the South African forces. They had still to complete the defeat of the Vichy forces in Madagascar, which had been invaded in April 1942 in order to prevent the Vichy French from handing over to the Japanese the main French Indian Ocean naval base at Diego Suarez at the northern tip of the island. While the invasion fleet was being assembled, South African bombers based for the purpose at Lindi on the Tanganyikan coast flew over Diego Suarez to photograph the Vichy defences.

The invasion was opened by a British force that left Durban in the biggest war fleet ever to sail from a sub-Saharan port – almost forty vessels in all. It was the first amphibious assault since the British landing at Gallipoli in 1915, and it tested techniques and landing craft that were to be refined in the later landings in Europe and the Pacific.

Diego Suarez was captured, but Vichy resistance continued in the south. Most of the British troops went off to India while South African, Northern Rhodesian and East African forces took their place in Madagascar. The SAAF took over the chief responsibility for air operations, and South African armoured cars led the ground campaign.

Seaborne landings at Majunga and Tamatave cleared the way for the capture of Antananarivo, the capital. Governor Annet, commonly known as 'Annie' to the South Africans, retreated further south. Another seaborne landing at Tulear on the south coast left Annet surrounded at Ihosy, and he surrendered, taking the salute as South African armoured cars entered the town in formation, their crews singing 'Annie Doesn't Live Here Any More'.

★ ★ ★ ★

The oath confining service to Africa having been superseded by a parliamentary vote allowing service outside Africa, the South African forces moved to Italy.

With the volunteer pool largely having been sucked dry, the South African forces were formed into a single division of armour and motorised infantry, the 6th South African Armoured Division.

The 6th Division entered the Italian campaign after the Allies had seized Sicily, landed on the mainland and twice leapfrogged up the coast with seaborne landings at Salerno and Anzio. In May 1944, as part of the British Eighth Army, the South Africans were thrown into the assaults on the Gustav Line that the Germans had thrown across Italy in an effort to stop the Allied advance on Rome. After the Gustav Line had been breached, the division became one of the spearheads of the Allied advance, operating on the right flank of the American Fifth Army.

SAAF fighter squadrons operated in close support of the ground troops throughout the Italian campaign. They won respect, not least from the Polish, when at heavy cost in men and aircraft they dropped supplies to the Poles in Warsaw who in June 1944 had risen in unavailing revolt against their German conquerors.

In Italy, the Germans made their first real stand west of the Tiber River at Viterbo, but it was broken by the 6th Division armour, which then raced on, becoming the first Allied troops to enter Florence.

In September the 6th Division was transferred to the American Fifth Army, whose assault on the Germans' mountainous Gothic Line was at first foiled by the onset of winter. In the spring offensive the South African infantry was given the key task of capturing the heavily defended twin peaks of Monte Sole and Monte Caprara. Reunited thereafter with their tanks, the South Africans captured Treviso as the Allied forces entered Venice. Switched 300 kilometres to the west to help quell the last German resistance, the 6th Division was approaching Milan when the

Germans surrendered in Italy.

The South African Air Force had one more job to do before going home: joining the British and American airmen in the great Berlin Airlift, flying vital supplies over the ground blockade thrown by Stalin around the German capital in an effort to seize it for the Soviets.

While the ground and air forces were operating to the north, the South African Navy had operated mainly in South African waters in anti-submarine, minesweeping and escort duties, and intercepting Vichy convoys heading to and from Madagascar.

More than ten thousand Rhodesians[4] served in their own or in the British armed forces – a comparatively large proportion of a white population that during the war never much exceeded the 1939 figure of 67 000. Most of the 15 153 black men recruited served in non-combat capacities, and only 1 505 served outside the colony.

Aside from those in the air and armoured car units, most of the Rhodesians served as officers and NCOs in the Nigerian, Gold Coast and East African regiments, fighting in the Horn of Africa and in Burma, or were attached to British regiments in North Africa and then to the South African 6th Division in Italy. Numbers joined the Royal Navy, and other Rhodesians were sprinkled through almost every British unit, including the famed Long Range Desert Group and Orde Wingate's Chindits.

The more mobile nature of the fighting in the Second World War meant that casualties were relatively less than the carnage in the trenches of the First World War. South Africa's toll of 7 200 whites dead, and Southern Rhodesia's 916, were nevertheless substantial proportions of the white populations and proportionally more than those of any of the other Allied partners.

At the end of the war South African and Rhodesian contingents marched in the great Victory Parade in London. For a while the memory of the black and the white Africans who had died in the two world wars was honoured in Europe. But as apartheid grew in South Africa and international disgust rose against it, it became politically incorrect to honour the whites from Africa whose bones lay in war graves from Flanders to Florence and unmarked on the beds of all the seas. Their deaths and the contributions of South Africa and Rhodesia to the Allied war effort were simply wiped from the slate – together with the memory of the 2 300 black South Africans who died serving alongside them.

All that was remembered of the whites was that their country had a long history of racism. What was forgotten was that in most respects it was not much different from the anti-black racism that had been commonplace in all other white-dominated countries up to the end of the war. The war dead were going to dust by the time apartheid emerged as a distinctive evil.

CHAPTER 29

SHIFTING WINDS, RISING TIDES

When the smoke and thunder of the Second World War died away, Africa seemed largely unchanged apart from the freeing of Abyssinia and the tank hulks strewing the Western Desert. The war, however, had set change brewing like yeast among both colonisers and colonised. The continent now experienced a political transformation, with consequences as profound as those of the Scramble.

In a few years the artificial colonial structure created by the Scramble was stripped of its foreign autocracy. On the remaining framework were hastily hung the appurtenances of democracy – many so flimsy they soon began to fall off.

Only where the whites were rooted in large numbers was it different. All except those in South Africa tried to preserve white hegemony under the skirts of their European motherlands. The *colons* in Algeria clung to France. The Portuguese fastened to the pretence that their colonies were extensions of metropolitan Portugal. The Southern Rhodesians sought Britain's patronage as an independent Dominion.

South Africa's whites, their ties to Europe more tenuous and their loyalties divided, pursued a destiny of their own making. The war had brought the racial issue in South Africa to a climactic point that demanded either democracy or more structured repression of blacks by whites. The former being unacceptable to most of the whites, it was the latter that prevailed. To the surprise of most and the dismay of many, they found themselves under the control of the ideologues of apartheid.

That the war was the beginning of the end for colonialism was not immediately apparent to everyone, least of all to the European powers themselves. Some saw a European presence in Africa continuing indefinitely but in a different form, at least some kind of partnership with the colonised. Even those who discerned the inevitability of independence did not see it happening for the best part of another half-century.

For many of the white people born in Africa or who had made it their home, democracy loomed as a catastrophe, for they could not envisage a life for themselves under black rule and they strove to avert it. For the black people decolonisation opened welcome opportunities, but also presented challenges and hazards for which they were ill-prepared, either by their pre-colonial experience or by colonial rule. So freedom in many cases came painfully to Africa, sometimes causing greater trauma than had the hard hand of colonial rule.

Before the war, Britain and France had kept their colonies not so much for any intrinsic gain, of which there was little in some cases, but rather in perpetuation of the reasons of strategy and status for which they had acquired them. Some of the colonies had become profitable, however, and their raw materials valued. After the war, the productive colonies were seen by Britain and France as a means of paying off their crippling war debts and rebuilding their own battered economies. It was not possible, however, to keep only the profitable colonies and dump the rest by granting them independence. Give freedom to some, and the others would demand it too.

The general intention therefore was to maintain something like the pre-war situation. Britain would gradually lead its colonies into a civilisation fitting them for partnership in the Commonwealth. France would continue to absorb its colonies and turn their peoples into French citizens. At a conference of France's African governors convened by De Gaulle at Brazzaville in 1944, it was firmly stated that the 'the task of civilisation' in the French colonies ruled out any idea of autonomy or self-government.

Of the colonial powers only Portugal, remaining neutral, had gone relatively unscathed through the war. Britain, once the greatest imperial power, had been shown during the war not to have the wherewithal to defend its empire.* Fighting the Axis powers had cost Britain two-thirds of its export markets and a quarter of its foreign currency stocks. It had been left effectively bankrupt, embarrassingly indebted financially to its dominions and excruciatingly so to the United States. Britain still posed as a great power on the strength of its still-powerful navy and its still-visible empire, but it was a façade that was transparent to the Americans and they acted accordingly.

France had been economically ravaged – it had lost all its foreign stocks, its national income had been halved, and inflation was out of control. Its industrial and other infrastructures remained largely functional, however, and the French were able to begin a relatively rapid return to great power status.

The United States had been the only power to get richer rather than poorer from the war. Its gross national product had increased by 50 per cent, largely through war production, much of it sold or leased to its allies. The conversion of its vast industrial capacity for wartime production had left an even bigger structure for easy conversion back to peacetime production.

Like Woodrow Wilson at the end of the previous war, Franklin Roosevelt took a strong stand against the perpetuation of colonialism. It was easier to do that than to right the wrongs still being inflicted on his black and Indian countrymen. Churchill, hamstrung by economic and military dependence on America, had been unable to resist Roosevelt's pressure in 1941 to accept the Atlantic Charter and its affirmation of 'the right of all people to choose the form of government under which they live'. That declaration rang loudly in the colonies despite Churchill's later efforts to pretend that it was 'primarily intended to apply to Europe'.

Attitudes among Africans had been changed in other ways, too, by the war. The

---

*This was one of the reasons Chamberlain temporised with Hitler at Munich.

Europeans, having fought against totalitarianism in the name of freedom and democracy, and having recruited their colonial subjects to fight with them in that
cause, had opened the subjects' eyes to its ideals. The same freedom and democracy
could hardly be denied to them after the cause had been won with their help.

Furthermore, the respect for European might that had previously helped the colonial powers to keep Africans and Asians in subjugation had been eroded by the
spectacle of the British being kicked out of imperial strongholds by the Japanese
they had despised. The white bwana and his gadgetry and weaponry could never be
as awesome as before, certainly not after black colonial troops had fought against or
alongside white soldiers.

Roosevelt died in the last year of the war, but his policies were carried on by
Harry Truman. There would be no return to isolationism; the United States would
take up the leadership role that its exclusive wealth and power mandated amid the
worldwide wreckage of war. Democratic Party libertarianism was applied to the
formation of the United Nations Organisation, and was largely instrumental in
having the old League of Nations mandates converted to trusteeships supervised by
the UN Trusteeship Council, thus making the imperial powers accountable to international opinion.

When the drafting of the UN Charter began in 1945, with the war still going on
in the Pacific, its first article borrowed from the Atlantic Charter a clause enshrining
'respect for the principle of equal rights and self-determination of peoples'. Smuts,
now a field marshal, and highly respected internationally as soldier, statesman and
philosopher, played a main role in the drafting of the UN charter but was unable
or unwilling to block this clause, which was later to be exploited in the colonised
peoples' struggle for independence and, indeed, the struggle of the black people in
his own country.

If there was irony in America's support for the human rights clauses, much the
same applied to Canada and its sidelined Indians and Eskimos; to Australia, where
the aboriginal people had been pushed into a socio-political vacuum; and to New
Zealand, whose Maoris' protests against the alienation of land and culture were
largely being ignored by the dominant whites.

America's eagerness to prod its wartime allies into decolonisation was tempered
by its own experience in the Philippines. Bloodily conquered by the US in 1902
in a spinoff of the Spanish-American War, the Philippines was not given independence until 1946. Washington had considered that it needed what Roosevelt called 'a
period of preparation', firstly through education and social and economic development, and secondly through the evolution of self-governing institutions. Roosevelt
saw the need for a similar process in Africa.

American pressure for decolonisation would nonetheless have been stronger had
it not been for the ominous presence of the mighty military machine built by the
Soviet Union – with Western help – during the war. When Moscow began using
this muscle to become increasingly assertive in world affairs – and even belliger-
ent once it had acquired its own nuclear weaponry – it was realised in Washington
that Britain and France were necessary partners in resisting the Kremlin's efforts to

extend its ideology and influence in the world. Against this overwhelming imperative, the colonised peoples' rights subsided in Washington's order of priorities. They
tended to be brought to the top only whenever the Soviets forced it by intruding
on the colonial turf as agitator for independence – independence under Moscow's
wing.

By driving a Soviet wedge into the colonial cohesion of the European powers,
the Cold War made them vulnerable at last to African nationalism. Not since the
late 19th century had Europeans been challenged by their own kind for hegemony
in Africa.

In the confrontation between the superpowers, the UN inevitably became a centre for both public contest and covert manoeuvre. The UN's General Assembly and
committees and its prolific documentation gave venue and voice to the concepts
of national independence that were rising around the world. These became a major phenomenon of the post-war years, exceeded in scope and impact only by the
Cold War itself and, indeed, frequently being dragged into its ambit. The Cold War
turned the UN into a hot-house for the propagation of ideas of self-determination
and freedom from alien rule. Eager to embrace the new champion of decolonisation, the Soviet Union, the colonised peoples were blind to Moscow's own form
of imperialism and colonisation in Eastern Europe, blinkered to the horrors behind
the Iron Curtain.

As the world ostensibly marched to freedom and democracy, the whites in Africa chose to stand aside. To join the parade would mean abandoning their hegemony and nowhere were they prepared to do that, for it seemed suicidal. In Algeria,
Angola, Mozambique, Kenya, Rhodesia and South Africa they chose to stay with
white supremacy.

The great international lurch in morals and policies brought about by the war
had left most white South Africans, even Smuts, perceptually stranded. Smuts still
entertained his grand, Rhodes-like visions of an expansion and consolidation of
white hegemony in the southern sub-continent, a political amalgamation reaching
from South Africa to Tanzania; all of this within a Commonwealth that would accept his concept of black political evolution under white guidance. When the General Assembly in 1946 rejected his request for incorporation of South West Africa
he declared himself 'dazed and amazed' by the rebuff.

The UN that he had helped create was turning into something of a Frankenstein
monster for Smuts. What he had envisaged as an instrument for world harmony and
rational resolving of disputes had become what he called a 'cockpit of emotion, passion and ignorance' about his racial policies.

Smuts was strangely blind to the irreversible displacement of European colonialism by African independence and to the world's rejection of white supremacy. Even
his perception of human rights was obsolete in terms of the standards gaining currency after the war. In his opinion, the fundamental human rights enshrined in the
UN Charter that he had helped draft did not include 'political rights and freedoms'.
To argue the contrary, he said, was 'tantamount to saying that the most progressive
races should be retarded by the less progressive if the latter were in a majority'. In

Smuts's view, 'equality in fundamental rights and freedoms could be assured in a multiracial state only by a measure of discrimination in respect of non-fundamental rights'.

While declaring a love for all humanity, Smuts saw South Africa as 'a little epic of European civilisation on a dark continent' and himself as 'a Westerner' rather than an African. Rather than being typical of the Afrikaners, his thinking was closer to that of those whites who regarded themselves not as Africans but as Europeans in Africa.

In that respect he differed from Dr Malan's Nationalists, who were sensationally to oust him from power in 1948. They, too, cherished their European culture but, much more than Smuts, it seemed, they identified with Africa. When they first came to power the Nationalists' ideas were rooted in white *baasskap* (domination) in a single country, and it was only later that they evolved the concept of territorial separation under their bantustan policy, of dividing the land, even though unequally. For them that was a means of asserting both their Europeanness and their Africanness. Even as he first won power, Malan openly accepted South Africa's inseparability from the rest of Africa.

'We are a part of Africa,' he declared, 'and our actions here in South Africa are largely influenced by what takes place in the rest of Africa.' He made it clear, however, that he perceived the whites' role in Africa as one of leadership rather than partnership. Malan expressed a set of values and ambitions in a proposed 'African Charter' that he first mentioned as early as 1945 while still in opposition in parliament. The charter's five aims were: to preserve Africa for the Africans, to protect it from Asian domination, to promote a Western Christian ethos throughout the continent, to bar communism, and to prevent militarism. In the first two ideals was a clear identification with Africa: the Afrikaners were Africans and the Asians were not and should not ever be. It seemed that 'Africa for the Africans' was a catchphrase with which Malan, the segregationist and white supremacist, was entirely comfortable.

CHAPTER 30

CLOSING THE LAAGER

Throughout their relatively long time in South Africa the white people had the choice of abandoning white supremacy. At a number of points the circumstances became especially propitious for it. Always, however, they clung on, for supremacy was both their faith and their shield. Always the reasons for maintaining hegemony seemed far stronger than for giving it up.

An especially propitious opportunity came as the whites were preparing for union in 1909, but it was brushed aside in the prevailing obsession with furthering white privilege and interests (including those of the British establishment). A similar opportunity arose after the Second World War, when whites and blacks returned from serving together in Africa and Europe, when Europe's colonies began to receive their freedom and black people in South Africa began to demand it too. Again the chance was passed over.

With the benefit of hindsight, it might now be argued that had the whites accepted democracy for everyone then (or, indeed, at any of the other points) they would have saved themselves the castigation and guilt of the pariah years, the violence and trauma of the black freedom struggle, and the bitter cost of the wars in Angola and Namibia. They might have been better off than they are today, more secure in a more stable and prosperous society.

A converse argument is that in the late forties the blacks were not as well prepared to assume political power as they were 50 years later, when more of them had been exposed, through the freedom struggle, to foreign influences, examples and education, and when they had as precedents to avoid the disasters suffered after independence by so many African countries through dictatorship, corruption and misgovernance.

At any rate, at the end of the Second World War hardly any whites could envisage democracy for all in their country. For the whites, yes, of course; it had always been their privilege. But never for whites and blacks together. A few whites favoured some sort of compromise, something along the lines of Smuts's idea of separate equality. The great majority, however, were adamantly opposed to abandoning racial discrimination, either because of their fears for themselves, their culture and their values, or because of sheer prejudice, or because they doubted that the blacks could manage democracy and free enterprise and that extending it to them would wreck the country for everyone, blacks as well as whites.

Most whites did not see themselves as unjustly privileged over the blacks. They regarded their better incomes, houses, cars and lifestyle as a natural reflection of the civilisation, sophistication, culture and technology they had inherited from their European origins, just like the whites elsewhere in the world. The blacks were seen to live on a lower scale because of their intrinsic backwardness, the relative primitiveness they in turn had inherited from their own past. Some whites might have recognised that their own benefits were due at least in part to the exploitation of cheap black labour, but they would not have thought that even without it they would have been any worse off than the whites in, say, Australia or New Zealand.

The Cold War spilling into Africa was the clincher for white intransigence. The Africans' acceptance of Soviet backing for their freedom struggle, and their seeming embrace of Marxism, raised a spectre of communist domination that was enough to make almost every white close the shutters on liberal thinking.

Rather than open their society to democracy after the war, the white electorate went the other way and put into power the party that was to institutionalise racism as apartheid and become likened to the Nazis.

The astounding National Party victory in the general election of 1948 has been attributed by some historians largely to the self-determination clauses of the Atlantic and UN Charters. It goes wider than that, however. The African National Congress was indeed prompted by the Atlantic Charter to abandon its wartime freeze on political activity and in 1943 to demand full rights for blacks. And this no doubt raised whites' fears. But the two charters merely encouraged a demand for black freedom that was already rising and would have continued to rise without them. The charters affected only the timing and vehemence of the demand.

Even during the war, domestic factors were radicalising black politics. There were bus boycotts, strikes and demonstrations against the passes. Young blacks, impatient with their elders' moderation, formed the ANC Youth League, which galvanised black activism. The Natives' Representative Council became derided as a 'toy telephone'.

Thus, while the international climate was conducive to embracing democracy in the post-war years, the reasons for maintaining hegemony were for many whites stronger than ever. The greater the pressure, the greater the fear. There was a reciprocating escalation: suppression provoking militancy and militancy provoking stronger suppression. For compromise there was little incentive.

Smuts's United Party government did in fact try to temporise. Its left wing proposed reforms, but they were not enough for the blacks and too much for those whites who feared they would lead to white job losses and social integration.

In the wartime election of 1943 the United Party had won 110 seats against the 43 of Malan's National Party. By 1948, however, the UP's ideology had become stretched too thin between its two wings for practical politicking. Malan's party offered a narrow policy answering white needs and fears. It retained enough of Hertzog's principles to allow an election alliance with NC Havenga's more moderate Afrikaner Party.

In the 1948 election the UP won only 65 seats. Even with the Labour Party's six seats it was not enough to retain power, for the National Party won 70 seats and the Afrikaner Party nine, giving the alliance a majority of eight.

The alliance had won some votes from English-speakers – ex-servicemen dissatisfied with their treatment by the UP government, and war-weary civilians fed up with issues such as the lack of jobs and housing. But Malan owed his victory more to an accident of delimitation, which had loaded rural votes in order to offset the logistical advantages enjoyed by urban voters. Since the rural communities were largely Afrikaans, the consequence was to load the Afrikaner vote, which went largely to the alliance. Malan won power despite receiving less than forty per cent of the vote, a smaller percentage than the UP.

The irony did not trouble Malan and his followers. What mattered to them was that for the first time Afrikaner Nationalists were in power in the whole of South Africa. As Malan put it: 'In the past we felt like strangers in our own country, but today South Africa belongs to us once more.' It was sweet vengeance, in a way; not only had the Afrikaners in effect regained the old Boer republics, but they had won ultimate control of the old British colonies of the Cape and Natal as well.

Malan's Nationalists energetically set about replacing English-speakers with Afrikaners wherever possible in government ranks. The civil service and the police became something of an Afrikaner preserve. There was an outright purge in the army and air force. Out went the senior officers who had served with distinction in the war, and in came Afrikaners from the lower ranks or wherever they could be found, even among the Nazi-sympathisers who had been interned during the war. Uniforms, insignia and even some regimental names were changed in order to fumigate the armed forces of English taint.

Smuts continued in politics as leader of the opposition but he was a sad and declining figure, seemingly bemused by the turn domestic politics had taken while he had been distracted by international affairs. After his death in 1950 the United Party was led by a succession of mediocre politicians and eventually fragmented.

For a while idealism remaining from the wartime years provided opposition, sometimes dramatic, to what was becoming a National Party juggernaut. In 1951 a War Veterans Action Committee was formed by ex-servicemen disgusted at the rise in their own country of something like the totalitarianism they had fought against in the war. Holding rallies and marching at night with flaming torches, the veterans called their movement the Torch Commando. After a year it claimed a membership of 120 000. In 1951 it joined the United and Labour parties to form the United Democratic Front.

In politics, however, the Torch Commando came up against the fundamental quandary of the middle mass of the whites, the dilemma seemingly posing morality against survival of identity, in this case: should it admit coloured ex-servicemen to its ranks? Even for the white ex-servicemen that was the thin end of a wedge whose thicker body they feared to accept as their country became beleaguered in the world. So the old soldiers of the Torch just faded away, and by 1954 the organisation had been disbanded.

In the 1953 election the United Party again won more votes than the Nationalists, but Malan was again able to exploit the delimitation dodge to increase his majority in the house to 29. He had gerrymandered six additional seats in 1950 by giving South West Africa representation in the South African parliament and extending the franchise to the Germans there.

Still seeking the two-thirds majority that would enable it to tailor the constitution, the National Party in 1958 lowered the voting age to 18 in the belief that it would get the support of most people in that age group. A youthful Afrikaner electorate now emerging brainwashed from the Afrikaans schools helped to give his party for the first time more votes than the UP. Working assiduously towards the two-thirds goal, the party turned the growing international pressure against apartheid into a weapon of its own, promoting among whites the concept of a small but brave community fighting for its existence and its Christian beliefs against a world deluded by communist and Afro–Asian propaganda.

The United Party was as much a prisoner of white South Africa's past as the National Party was. Much as the UP and its constituents disliked what the Nationalists were doing, they could find no alternative, no workable compromise between apartheid and black majority rule that would satisfy the majority of the white electorate. Though the black political organisations continued to espouse non-racial democracy, the whites knew that meant only one thing: black majority rule, and they weren't ready to trust themselves to it.

There was something Canute-like in the politics of the whites as they strove to control the rising black tide. At the outbreak of the war, when blacks outnumbered whites by five to one, 55 per cent of the blacks already lived in white areas. While most were on white farms, they were numerous enough in the main industrial region of the Transvaal to comprise 53 per cent of the urban population. After the war the imbalance became much greater as blacks fled the poverty in the reserves and flocked to the jobs increasingly available in the white towns. The urban black population doubled in a decade, becoming the defining factor in white politics.

The whites were finding themselves hoist by their own petard, so to speak. They had tried to create a labour pool by confining the blacks' social structure to reserves that were kept poor and backward. However, the poverty there had become so severe and the external demand for labour so great that the pool had overflowed into the white towns, bringing to the whites' very doorsteps the old nightmare of being swamped. In order to control the flow better, the government constructed a large and sometimes merciless bureaucracy.

A torrent of racist legislation poured through parliament as the ruling party went ruthlessly about separating the races and protecting white supremacy. Separation, however, was never divorced from exploitation, for the white society had been built on black labour and could not function without it.

Had black labour been dispensable the Nationalists would no doubt have moved all the blacks to the reserves and sealed them off, leaving them to make the best of things on their own, even to become independent states if they wished, while the whites went their own way in the rest of the country, like the whites of Australia, New Zealand and Canada. However, through exploiting black labour in the past,

In both world wars, General Smuts appealed to his countrymen to enlist on the side of Britain. His efforts were satirised in this cartoon by Boonzaier in *Die Burger*, a play on the famous recruitment poster of the first war showing Kitchener pointing a demanding finger at the young men of Britain. (*Library of Parliament*)

At a Durban dockside, South African soldiers crowd a troopship taking them to fight for the Allies in the Second World War. One of them has lowered his helmet on a rope for the girl below to receive – or to send? – a last message. (*Museum Africa*)

Drought and depression between the wars sent thousands of white South Africans to the soup kitchens and the government work projects. The widespread poverty among whites is illustrated by this Cape Town family. (*National Library*)

After defeating the Italians in Abyssinia, South African troops march into the liberated capital, Addis Ababa, soon to be reoccupied by the exiled Emperor Haile Selassie. Within a few years Abyssinia, now known as Ethiopia, would lead campaigning in the United Nations against South African apartheid. (*South African National Museum of Military History, Johannesburg*)

The race track at Monza is normally occupied by speeding racing cars, but in this picture the Axis forces have been defeated in Italy and tanks of the 6th South African Armoured Division stage a victory parade down the main straight. (*South African National Museum of Military History, Johannesburg*)

After flying 77 missions against the Germans, a South African Air Force Liberator bomber is retired, and crew members pose for a farewell photograph.
(*South African National Museum of Military History, Johannesburg*)

Sherman tanks of the 6th South African Armoured Division cross the Arno River in their advance against the Germans in Italy.
(*South African National Museum of Military History, Johannesburg*)

After sensationally winning the 1948 South African parliamentary election, Dr DF Malan flashes a rare grin as he boards a train to take up the premiership. Soon his country will have little to smile about as he begins imposing apartheid. (*Cape Times, National Library*)

Women of the Black Sash movement stand in silent protest in Cape Town against the enforcement of apartheid in South Africa. (*Cape Argus; Trace Images*)

Despite apartheid, South Africa had not yet become an international pariah when the Korean War broke out in 1950, and South African Air Force pilots fought with the United Nations forces there. Some are shown here with their propeller-driven Mustang fighter-bombers. Later they switched to Sabre jets. (*South African National Museum of Military History, Johannesburg*)

Mau Mau suspects awaiting interrogation at a special camp near Nairobi are forced by British colonial police to squat in a queue. Mau Mau's resistance, however, marked the beginning of colonialism's end. (*East African News; Trace Images*)

In the seventies, colonialism was being resisted by liberation movements in much of Africa. Here Portuguese troops leap from a vehicle to take cover during clashes with the MPLA movement in Angola. (*Argus Africa News Service; Trace Images*)

Afrikaners from South Africa were among the first whites to settle in Kenya, mostly at Eldoret. At independence, however, their descendants began to return to South Africa. Now the last thirty members of the once-strong congregation gather outside the town's Dutch Reformed Church, which soon will be closed and sold. (*Argus Africa News Service; Trace Images*)

After Ian Smith's government unilaterally declared Rhodesia independent in 1965, the British had the governor, Sir Humphrey Gibbs, remain at his post, defiantly flying the Union Jack at his official residence.
(*Argus Africa News Service; Trace Images*)

The military coup in Lisbon in 1974 sent thousands of Portuguese fleeing from black rule in the colonies. Former residents of Angola are shown here forming a convoy on the Namibian border before making a risky dash down the Skeleton Coast to Windhoek. (*Cape Argus; Trace Images*)

Farmers like Rob Long, shown here with his family, armed themselves and their wives and fortified their farmhouses as insurgent attacks in Rhodesia mounted. (*Trace Images*)

Rhodesian premier Ian Smith (right) was summoned to Pretoria by Prime Minister BJ Vorster of South Africa and 'persuaded' to accept a version of majority rule. (*Cape Argus; Trace Images*)

South African President PW Botha was criticised for not announcing far-reaching reforms in his 1985 'Rubicon' speech, yet buried in his defensive verbiage were quite radical proposals.
(*Trace Images*)

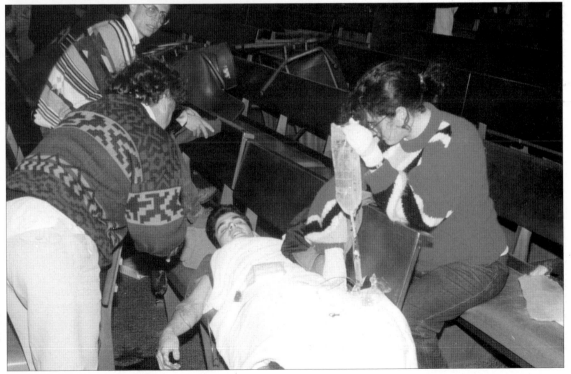

Wounded churchgoers at St James' Church in Kenilworth, Cape Town, are helped by other parishioners after PAC terrorists in 1993 attacked their service with automatic rifles and hand grenades, killing eleven worshippers.
(*Trace Images*)

Armoured vehicles are designed primarily for warfare in open county, but the fighting between South African / Unita and MPLA / Cuban forces in Angola was often in thick bush, limiting visibility. A South African Ratel is pictured in action in 1988. (*South African National Museum of Military History, Johannesburg*)

Having a longer range than any other artillery piece then in existence, the South Africans' G5 gun gave them a significant advantage in the fighting in Angola. (*South African National Museum of Military History, Johannesburg*)

An emotional President FW de Klerk stands with hand on heart as the South African flag is lowered for the last time in Namibia at the independence celebrations in Windhoek. Swapo leader Sam Nujoma, Namibia's first president, grins with pleasure.
(*Argus Africa News Service; Trace Images*)

AWB gunmen lie dead in Bophuthatswana, shot during a bloody but abortive attempt in 1994 to stop the bantustan from being reincorporated in South Africa. Symbolically, the segregationist aspirations of white right-wingers lie dead in the dust with them.
(*Louise Gubb; Trace Images*)

History is made with happiness as whites line up with blacks to vote in South Africa's first democratic election in 1994, ending centuries of white supremacy.
(*Trace Images*)

Vasco da Gama

Mungo Park

Richard Lander

Andries Pretorius

Paul Kruger

Queen Victoria

David Livingstone

General Garnet Wolseley

Henry Morton Stanley

Cecil Rhodes

Dr Leander Starr Jameson

Louis Botha

BJ Vorster

PW Botha

JBM Hertzog

After unsuccessfully re-forming itself as the New National Party, the former party of apartheid suffered the ultimate humiliation of seeking survival in an alliance with its former arch-enemy, the ANC, in 2004. The irony of it was captured by the cartoonist Dr Jack. (© *Dr Jack / Independent Newspaper Group*)

the South African whites had become dependent on it, unlike the whites in the other Dominions. They had become cheap-labour junkies, and that was to be their undoing, for it was impossible to maintain the addiction and its requisite domination in the face of rising domestic resistance and international protest.

The National Party sought to solve the land-labour problem by giving the blacks a semblance of political autonomy, initially by scrapping the old Natives' Representative Council, the 'toy telephone' derided by blacks, in 1951 and creating a system of territorial authorities in the 'native reserves'. Blacks long-resident and employed in white urban areas were given the right to remain. The territorial authorities were at first denied full autonomy, but within eight years the government, bowing to the domestic and international pressures, offered the promise of full autonomy to eight (later nine) territories defined as the 'homelands' of specific ethnic groups. Few had any illusions that these 'bantustans' could ever become anything more than dependencies of the white-controlled state.

Efforts were made by the government to encourage white immigration, and there was a strong influx after the war. The purpose, however, was not to replace black labour but to strengthen white hegemony. And yet large numbers of white immigrants were lost through the government's blocking of Roman Catholics lest they weaken Afrikaner Calvinism.

The National Party faithful, mostly deeply religious Afrikaners, could not easily see evil in apartheid when their churches found divine purpose in it. The concept of black inferiority was ingrained in Afrikaner history and culture, as was competition with black people and fear of them and, indeed, exploitation of them, and these had all become entwined with a theology fashioned in the harsh realities of an African frontier.

Neither as Dutch Reformed Church minister nor as prime minister did Dr Malan have any moral problems with his party's chosen means of racial segregation. He was, after all, only extending a structure solidly established on foundations laid nearly three centuries previously, and doing so with the blessing of his church. His successors in the premiership trod the same path, succoured by the same theology and assurance of righteousness.

Early in the process of institutionalising segregation, the National Party bumped into the special problem of the people who were neither black nor white but of mixed race, the coloured people. Unlike the blacks, who could generally be identified with tribal areas and in theory be segregated there, the coloureds had been intermixed with the whites from the very beginning, residentially as well as genetically.

The party jibbed at treating coloureds as whites because many coloureds were much darker than lighter, which made it difficult to draw a line between coloured and black. But the line had to be drawn somewhere. The coloureds were a link, a genetic bridge, between white and black and therefore the bridge must be gated at some point along its length – preferably closer to the white side than the black – in order to preserve the separation of identity. Not surprisingly, considering its potential advantages, 'trying for white' had long been commonplace among persons of mixed race who might pass as 'Europeans'. Identifying those who might pass through the gate to the white side became the function of a Race Classification Board, whose officials became in effect the gene-police.

Lacking DNA technology or, indeed, any other means of identification, these inexpert arbiters based their verdicts on skin colour, nose and lip shape and hair conformation. They employed mechanisms as primitive as the pencil test – if a pencil thrust into the hair did not fall out it was proof of negroid ancestry. Their judgments were made on such arcane criteria as fingernail conformation, a large or purplish half-moon at the base signifying black lineage.

In their omnipotence, the gene-police on occasion separated families, leaving parents and children, brothers and sisters, on opposite sides of the gate simply because they looked different. The injustice and absurdity of it all was compounded by the strong suspicion that a number of National Party politicians or their wives concealed dark-skinned ancestry.

There was still the risk, of course, that a coloured person might jump the gate by marrying a white, or even that a white might leap it in the other direction to marry a 'non-white'. So the government fenced around the gate with legislation forbidding mixed marriages. In order further to preserve the purity of the Caucasian gene, even sexual intercourse between whites and 'non-whites' was prohibited. No jumping the gate, no copulation through the gate.

Having cordoned off the coloureds, the government attempted to cordon off their parliamentary vote by putting them on a separate roll. When the United Party had the move declared unconstitutional by the Appeal Court, the government simply doubled the number of senators in the upper house and judges on the court, and packed both with stooges. Legislation for the coloureds to elect four whites to represent them in parliament was duly approved by both sets of lackeys.

As the juggernaut rolled on there was little its opponents could do besides protesting. Some of the bravest protest came from the Black Sash, a group of white women who took to standing silently in public places, carrying placards and wearing white dresses with black sashes of mourning for the violation of the constitution.

Government policy was formally termed not apartheid but separate development, but the emphasis was overwhelmingly on separation rather than development of the 'non-white' peoples. A cornerstone of the apartheid structure was the Group Areas Act of 1950, providing for the demarcation of separate residential areas for whites, blacks, coloureds and Asians. Together with the Natives Resettlement Act and the Prevention of Illegal Squatting Act, it legalised the mass removal of communities that was one of the cruellest aspects of the cruel policy of apartheid.

It was not only because of what it stood for that apartheid became despised around the world, but also for the always callous and sometimes brutal way in which it was implemented.

Major new elements were added to the apartheid structure in the fifties. One law provided for the racial segregation of public buildings, transport and amenities, effectively preserving the sanctity of white buses and trains, railway station platforms, restaurants, theatres, beaches, public lavatories and park benches. Another law barred blacks from working as artisans in white areas. Other measures tightened the pass regulations and imposed a night curfew.

Hendrik Verwoerd, then Minister of Native Affairs, explained government policy thus: 'There is no place for the black man in the European community above the level of certain forms of labour. ... It is of no avail for him to receive a training which has as its aim absorption in the European community.'

With one of its most infamous laws, the Bantu Education Act, the government sought to ensure that blacks would receive a lesser education that would keep them inferior to the whites. Government black schools were to work to a syllabus different from that in the white ones. Government funding would be denied to private schools that refused to cooperate. Separate universities would be created for blacks, who were barred from the white ones.

Awkwardly seeking to give balance to its policy, the government created special councils that ostensibly gave urban blacks a form of representation. Rural blacks were similarly provided for by the creation of a Bantu Authority in each of the reserves, the homelands.

Malan retired and was succeeded by JG Strijdom, a flinty-eyed lawyer from the ultra-conservative northern Transvaal. He died and was in turn succeeded by Verwoerd, a deeply religious academic who could implement heartless social engineering with fervent conviction and smiling sincerity.

Verwoerd found himself put in something of a bind by the findings of Prof. FR Tomlinson, whom he had appointed to head an inquiry into development in the reserves. Tomlinson's commission found that while separate development was necessary to avoid racial friction, it could succeed only if the reserves were adequately developed.

The idea of spending large amounts of the white taxpayer's money on developing the black homelands did not sit well with the government or its conservative constituents. Some government funding was provided, but it was grossly inadequate for implementing Tomlinson's recommendations. At the same time whites were prohibited from investing privately in the reserves for fear it would undermine apartheid.

That these policies were inherently self-defeating was not perceived by the National Party. By persisting with them the government hastened the doom of white supremacy, for separate development could never have become politically viable while economically imbalanced. Heavy infusions of government and private investment and expertise into the black homelands might not have satisfied black aspirations, but they would have offered a better hope for a separate white existence than apartheid ever did. Later the government established white industrial areas on the borders of the homelands, hoping to get the best of both worlds – ample black labour on the white doorstep. The effort offered no solution to the wider racial problem, however, because it perpetuated inequality and lack of opportunity.

In the wake of the National Party juggernaut, white opposition staggered ineffectually. In 1953 the Liberal Party, a multi-racial party advocating universal suffrage, was formed, represented in parliament by Margaret Ballinger, one of the whites standing in for the blacks there, and outside parliament by Alan Paton, author of *Cry, the Beloved Country.* When the government banned mixed-race parties in 1968, the Liberal Party disbanded rather than bow to the government dictate.

In 1959 the tight-stretched fabric of the United Party ripped, 12 left-wingers breaking away to form the Progressive Party, advocating multi-racial government but a qualified franchise. Even that was too much for the white electorate, and in the 1961 election all lost their seats except Helen Suzman. The Progressives accepted the whites-only dictate of 1968, figuring it could better oppose the government with only whites in parliament – even only one – than with nobody there at all.

CHAPTER 31

INFLUX AND EXODUS

In the decade after the Second World War European immigrants streamed into Africa as never before. Most of them might be considered refugees of a sort, fleeing now not from war but from its harsh aftermath, escaping from Europe's bombed cities and ravaged economies, from the rationing and the shortages and socialist regimentation, seeking freedom and opportunity and a new home in Africa's sun and space.

Their vision of Africa was in many cases mythical and unrealistic. But they came with the same assurance with which generations of Europeans had come to Africa before them, confident of transplanting their values and lifestyles, their assumed superiority, into Africa and keeping it all safe there through dominance of the natives.

Well over three hundred thousand Europeans came in the first seven years after the war. It was numerically, though not proportionately, the largest influx of Europeans into Africa. About a hundred thousand, mostly French, went to Algeria, and smaller numbers to Tunisia and Morocco. A proportionately significant number of Portuguese went to Angola and Mozambique. Most of the rest came from Britain.

South Africa alone received more than a hundred thousand new white faces. Proportionately, however, the biggest influx was into the British territories of white settlement. Between 1946 and 1955 the white population of Southern Rhodesia shot from 80 000 to more than two hundred thousand. Northern Rhodesia's exploded from 5 000 to more than sixty thousand, and the 12 000 in Kenya leaped to more than fifty thousand.[1] Some of the immigrants into Southern Rhodesia came from South Africa and therefore shifted rather than swelled the continent's white population, but this detracted only slightly from the magnitude of the overall influx.

The migration was again small compared to the surge into the Americas and Australasia, but the numbers were offset by the strong impact they were able to exert through having more knowledge, skills and capital than most Africans. Any European in Africa could have greater political and economic influence than almost any African. The Africans, having been technologically backward when the Europeans first came, and having then been kept that way by slavery and colonialism, could assert themselves only through their numbers.

As a result of the European influx there were at the beginning of the sixties probably more than five million whites living in Africa, the largest number ever to in-habit the continent.

And then, rather suddenly, the flow slowed as colonialism began to be supplanted by indigenous majority rule. In some cases the flow stopped and even reversed, the influx becoming an outflow and then an exodus. By 1962 white *colons* were depart-ing in hundreds of thousands from an Algeria now in the hands of the indigenous Berbers they called Arabs. A year later white settlers were fleeing in similar propor-tions from a Kenya they had failed to make their own. Not only had the Africans begun to fight for freedom from foreign domination, but they had begun to win, essentially because the colonial powers no longer considered it worthwhile to resist. Many of the colonies were still economically unprofitable. And, in the Cold War, strategic interests were better protected by giving them independence as friends than making them enemies by suppressing their demands for freedom. The colonial powers were beginning to pull out of Africa, and the white settlers they had planted there were becoming unimportant in the European scheme of things.

In the early sixties, whatever incentives remained for the powers to stay in Afri-ca were eclipsed by the pressures to quit. It was the beginning of the end of white supremacy in Africa, for without the backing of their European motherlands the smaller white communities could not hope to maintain hegemony over the black majorities. The larger ones in South Africa, Southern Rhodesia and Algeria could hold out somewhat longer, but even their time was limited.

Oddly, however, colonialism did not simply go into reverse. For the British and, to a lesser extent, the French, it became a curious two-way stream, anomalous counter-currents of occupation and evacuation. At the same time as the British were preparing to withdraw from the continent, they were reinforcing their pres-ence on the ground. And even when they began to pull out, relatively large num-bers of their citizens were still migrating there as settlers, unaware that they would soon have to choose between scuttling back with their departing government or being left stranded in an Africa governed by people they had either patronised or despised.

Even as the prospect of decolonisation loomed larger in the official perspectives of London and Paris, so too did the perception of a need to retain some kind of hold on the colonies. At first the motive was to milk the colonies in order to help repair the war damage to their own economies. Later, as their economies recovered, the motive became one of making the colonies as self-sufficient as possible before independence so that they would not afterwards be financially encumbrant. Devel-opment and decolonisation thus became incongruously overlapped.

As early as 1940 the British had instituted the first of a series of Colonial De-velopment and Welfare Acts which pumped millions of pounds into the colonies. Yet at the same time, larger sums generated by some colonies from their burgeon-ing wartime and post-war exports were retained in Britain in order to strengthen its depleted sterling reserves.

France from 1946 poured large sums into developing its colonies through its FIDES organisation, though more in pursuance of the policy of absorption and

Frankenisation than of exploitation.

Conjoined exploitation and development required a large increase in the number of British officials in the colonies. Some were involved in ambitious development projects that were monumentally impractical, such as the great scheme to grow groundnuts in a part of Tanganyika that was unfriendly to the peanut. And the plan to turn the Gambia, which had never been noted for poultry production, into a giant egg farm.

By the end of the fifties the powers were more than happy to quit those colonies for which they had little real use – which was most of them. They just found themselves doing so sooner than they had expected, and once one colony had gone the rest inevitably followed. The first one pulled the plug. Then the evacuation became almost as precipitate as the occupation had been in the Scramble, and in some cases even quicker.

The French, engrossed with the 'France Overseas' concept of an egalitarian Francophone community encompassing the colonies, found it harder to envisage them becoming independent than did the British with their non-integrationist colonial policy. Only later did it become appreciated in Paris that the Frankenisation policy would inevitably result in the whites of the 'one and indivisible' French Empire being vastly outnumbered by those who were not white. And that the Africans, for their part, would inevitably be more African than French.

It took a number of years for the French to accept that neither the Indo-Chinese nor the Africans could be forced to become French if they didn't want to, and that most of them didn't. Friends, yes, partners, perhaps, linked by a common language of convenience but never by the same culture. The 'France Overseas' concept collapsed at Dien Bien Phu in 1954 and was history by the time Morocco and Tunisia became independent in 1958.

For Britain the writing was appearing on the wall as early as 1945, when a Pan-African Congress was held in Manchester by delegates from Africa and the Caribbean. The congress issued a declaration calling on all colonies to fight 'by all means at their disposal' for self-government and freedom from foreign control. Among those attending were three men who would go on to lead their countries' struggles for independence: Kwame Nkrumah of the Gold Coast (later Ghana), Jomo Kenyatta of Kenya, and Kamuzu Hastings Banda of Nyasaland (later Malawi).

In 1947 a committee appointed to chart a 'new approach' in British policy on Africa concluded that 'perhaps within a generation' many of the principal colonies would have attained or be nearing full responsibility for their own affairs. It was therefore necessary to arrange for a smooth transfer of power to an educated local elite and to speed up development so that each colony could be given self-government as a viable state within the British Commonwealth.

In Colonial Office thinking, self-government within the Commonwealth was preferable to independence since it might give Britain the best of both worlds – friendly countries giving preference to British trade but not requiring British upkeep or protection. If, however, independence was unavoidable then it, too, should if possible be attained within the Commonwealth, as India had chosen (and Burma had not) in 1948. In that year the governors of Britain's African colonies were instructed to prepare them for self-government within the foreseeable future.

Looming decolonisation and the rise of nationalism were not always apparent to the migrants from Britain, or, if they were, failed to disabuse them of the notion that there was a future for them as settlers in Africa, not as Africans but as Europeans, as beneficiaries of the best of both worlds. It mattered not to them that in the late fifties the whites were grossly outnumbered in the favoured countries of settlement: 5:1 in South Africa, 13:1 in Southern Rhodesia, 30:1 in Northern Rhodesia and 90:1 in Kenya. They thought the dyke of European superiority would hold against the black majority. They failed to realise, though, that the dyke was embedded not in Africa but in Europe, and there only as firmly as political expediency dictated. When that dictate became decolonisation the dyke became mud.

European settlement in Africa had always had a curiously contradictory nature: motivated in part by a desire for independence from Europe but characterised by dependence on Europe. It worked well enough when European governments wanted to maintain a colonial presence; then, white settlers were a useful tool in developing the colonies and keeping them orderly, and they could rely on the motherland to protect them and promote their interests. But when decolonisation became the order of the day the settlers became something of a problem, an embarrassment even. What to do about them became an increasingly tricky question in both Whitehall and the Quay d'Orsay.

In France the shaping of African colonial policy had been contested after the war between the Communists and the Socialists on the one hand, and the French equivalent of Christian Democrats on the other, with the former courting the African delegates in the national assembly and the latter more attentive to the settler lobby. While the left-wingers favoured faster advancement of the African *evoluees* to full and equal citizenship, the settlers were more interested in advancing their own special interests over those of the indigenous populations. Thus the relative handful of settlers in the Cameroon petitioned Paris in 1945 for assisted European immigration and greater control over black labour.

The *colons* in Algeria, while demanding integration with France, were less than supportive of the corollary of the indigenous people's right to eventual equality that was intrinsic to French policy.

There were enough Europeans in French North Africa in the early fifties theoretically to be capable of operating a powerful lobby in Paris had they been able to act together. With close to a million in Algeria, 325 000 in Morocco and 250 000 in Tunisia, they numbered well over a million and a half altogether. There was, however, never any effective coordination between them in resisting decolonisation when it began.

Coordinated resistance among the British settler communities was largely confined to those in the two Rhodesias, and even that collaboration was short-lived.

The colonial powers had to balance the demands of the white settlers not only against those of the indigenous peoples but also against the exigencies of the Cold War. It became imperative to keep the Soviet Union from intruding into the colonies by taking advantage of and ostensibly supporting their peoples' demands for independence.

The Kremlin's ulterior motive was always plain enough. As early as 1949 Moscow was demanding bases of its own in Libya, where America had its big Wheelus air base. With long-range nuclear bombers now calling the tune in world politics, both Britain and America valued airfields in Libya and the Suez Canal Zone, not only for posing the threat of possible strikes against Russia but also to protect the Middle Eastern oilfields against Soviet encroachment. Suez may have lost its initial strategic importance to Britain after India became independent, but it had assumed a new value as a springboard into the volatile region where Europe and Asia met above subterranean seas of oil. Indirectly, therefore, Suez continued to influence British colonial policy elsewhere in Africa.

When Turkey gained membership of the North Atlantic Treaty Organisation in 1951 and offered the United States air bases on its territory, bases in North Africa lost importance to Washington. Not so, however, to Britain, whose claim to big power status now rested largely on its ability to drop nuclear bombs on distant targets. Well aware of the Suez base's vulnerability to Egyptian nationalist politics, the British tried first to establish an alternative in Libya (Cyrenaica) and then for the same purpose clung desperately to Cyprus, despite violent Cypriot opposition.

A British base in Cyrenaica seemed possible immediately after the war, since the British had driven the Italians out of this territory as well as out of the Horn. Britain then controlled virtually the whole of north-eastern Africa, a crescent running from the Indian Ocean to the Mediterranean. The British proposed a three-way split on the Mediterranean littoral, with themselves administering Cyrenaica, the Italians taking over Tripolitania, and the French governing the Fezzan, which was bordered by other French territories. The future of the former Italian colonies was now subject to the decision of the United Nations, however, and the General Assembly in 1949 rejected the three-way split in favour of independence as a unitary state, to be known as Libya.

This decision hammered a big nail in colonialism's coffin, demonstrating the potential power of the world body to override the colonial powers. The state of Libya came into being in 1951 as an artificial paste-up of three disparate regions under an imposed monarchy (Sayyid Muhammad Idris, leader of the region's most powerful group, the Senussis of Cyrenaica, was declared king). Nonetheless, as an independent state and a member of the United Nations it stood as an example for the ambitions of other territories still under colonial rule. Only four other African states – South Africa, Egypt, Ethiopia and Liberia – were UN members.

Of the other territories occupied by the British in the war, Abyssinia posed no problem, Haile Selassie being restored to the throne of what was now called Ethiopia. The Somali territories were a problem. The British proposal for unification was blocked by the United States, influenced by American oil interests suspecting there was oil there, and by the Soviet Union, which saw advantage in fragmentation of the Somalis. Italian Somaliland was temporarily placed under a ten-year Italian trusteeship by the General Assembly. The Ogaden was awarded to Ethiopia, which later got Eritrea as well, making inevitable the later wars for independence in both territories.*

Decolonisation was now on a roll. It had been given impetus by the General Assembly's adoption of the Universal Declaration of Human Rights in 1948. Rioting the same year in Accra frightened Attlee's government into hastening the whole self-determination timetable.

South Africa, however, was still a special case in Africa, as was shown when in 1948 Pretoria protested against Seretse Khama, the heir to the paramount chieftainship of the Bamangwato of Bechuanaland, marrying a white woman, Ruth Williams, whom he had met while studying in England. Malan threatened economic or other reprisals against Bechuanaland if Seretse was allowed to return there with his white bride. There were also strong warnings from Smuts and from Sir Godfrey Huggins in Rhodesia, both of whom shared Malan's fear of the race-mingling precedent that might be set by the couple's presence just across their borders. The Bamangwato tribal leaders, too, were opposed at first to his marriage. Seretse was allowed to return home with his white wife only in 1956, and then only after surrendering his claims to the Bamangwato chieftainship. (He nonetheless ended up as president of his country, now Botswana, and with a knighthood bestowed by Britain.)

The outbreak of the Korean War in 1950 gave urgency to European imperatives that the colonies became independent within the Western and not the communist camp. South Africa's standing was still good enough for the UN to accept a South African Air Force squadron among its forces fighting against the communist north. The airmen who volunteered for Korea believed they were defending the same freedom and democracy they had fought for in the Second World War. Pretoria, however, sent them to Korea not so much to defend democracy, which it did not practise itself, as to oppose the spread of communism, which it saw as the greatest threat to its own apartheid ideology. Besides that, however, participation in the UN operations would boost South Africa's standing in the world body and the Commonwealth, and give its forces access to and experience with the latest weaponry. It would hopefully also promote Pretoria's acceptance in a major Western alliance, among the advantages of which might be a closer Western committal to the defence of Africa.

Informally known as the 'Flying Cheetahs' from its cheetah mascots, the squadron was attached to 18 Fighter-Bomber Wing of the US Air Force, and fought for the remainder of the Korean war. Of the 209 South African pilots who served in Korea, 34 were killed in action, a casualty rate of more than one in six. The high regard the Americans formed for the Cheetahs is reflected in the honours awarded them: a Presidential Citation for the squadron, two Silver Stars, three Legions of Merit, 55 Distinguished Flying Crosses, 40 Bronze Stars and 176 Air Medals. At the end of the hostilities 18 Fighter-Bomber Wing resolved that all its retreat ceremonies would in future be preceded by the playing of the introductory bars of the

---

*The modern state of Somalia did not come into being until 1960, formed from the British and Italian territories.

236

South African national anthem.

The kudos that the Flying Cheetahs earned for their country was soon obliter-ated by the opposition to Pretoria's burgeoning apartheid policies. In the three years the squadron had been fighting in Korea there had been significant changes in Afri-ca. In the same year that Libya had gained independence, Kwame Nkrumah's Con-gress People's Party had won a landslide victory in the Gold Coast colony's election for 'semi-responsible' government. A year later Churchill's Tory government, newly returned to power, had agreed to make Nkrumah prime minister, irrevocably set-ting the Gold Coast on the road to becoming the first British colony in Africa to become independent. Churchill felt obliged to inform Malan that the decisions 'are the consequences of what was done before we became responsible'.[2]

On the Nile, Britain had waived its claim to sovereignty over the Sudan in or-der to appease King Farouk, but then Farouk was ousted in 1952 in an army coup master-minded by Colonel Gamal Abd al-Nasser. There was growing resistance to French rule in Tunisia, Morocco and Algeria. And in Kenya armed resistance to white domination had broken out among the Kikuyu through the movement known as Mau Mau.

CHAPTER 32

PANGAS IN PARADISE

Kenya became an epicentre of white shock when Kikuyus began to kill settler farmers and their wives and children in 1952. The accounts of Europeans being hacked, dismembered, decapitated or disembowelled were both horrifying and terrifying to the settlers. From Kenya the shock spread in diminishing ripples, descending to trepidation among the whites in the Rhodesias and then to unease in South Africa.

For all of them, it was the whites' worst nightmare coming true, still a distant one for those to the south but holding ominous portents nonetheless. From the beginning, white domination everywhere in Africa had been underlain by the fear of the subjugated black majorities rising in vengeful revolt. There had been other rebellions before, but those were in the past, before the natives had been 'pacified'. White domination was now supposed to be absolute as far as the Africans were concerned, and, as far as the whites in Kenya, the Rhodesias and Algeria were concerned, vulnerable only to the politicians in Europe.

Most of the Kikuyu were in fact opposed to the methods of the rebellion but not necessarily to its aims. Crowded ever more densely by population growth in the reserves demarcated by the Europeans, the Kikuyu looked covetously and resentfully at the 'stolen' White Highlands.

Most of the white farmers for their part felt they had fair title to their lands, firstly because of the 999-year leases given by the colonial authorities, and secondly because they had through hard work and capital investment developed the land, converting 'wilderness' into productive farms.

The settlers had in fact been left in a hopeless situation, a veritable fool's paradise, by ambivalent British government policy. The Devonshire Declaration of 1923 affirming Kenya as 'primarily African territory' was fundamentally incompatible with the granting of leases long enough to span several generations. One or the other had to give way, and inevitably it was the settlers' assumed rights. The ambivalence of British policy had been repeated in 1929 when London, reacting to settler demands for greater security and autonomy, had confirmed the Europeans' exclusive right to the White Highlands, excluding not only the Africans but also the Asians who outnumbered the whites by more than three to one. At the same time, however, the government had reaffirmed African paramountcy and rejected any possibility of white self-government.

238

So now the settlers found themselves in a paradoxical paradise in which they had title – a 999-year lease being as good as title – but not right and not the political power to protect their privilege. They had assumed that the British Empire would always be there to protect them. But when Britain no longer had an interest in their being in Kenya, they were left only with the options of going back to England or taking their chances under majority rule.

The settlers sought another option: the creation of an East African Dominion embracing Tanganyika and Uganda – an idea supported as recently as 1953 by the colonial secretary, Oliver Lyttelton. Some in Kenya envisaged this union going on to join up with the Rhodesias, Nyasaland and South Africa to create a huge, white-dominated dominion stretching from the Cape to the Nile.

But, as always for the Europeans in Africa, the numbers were against it. There just weren't enough whites to pull it off. In any case, the United Nations, which had inherited control of the trusteeship, in 1954 firmly opposed a multi-racial constitution for Tanganyika and declared that the territory, 'though multiracial in population, is primarily an African country and must be developed as such'. And in Uganda the dominant Baganda kingdom had specifically rejected federation with the other two territories.

Besides the seizure of their land, Kikuyu resented the subjugation of tribal authority to European forms of governance and the attempt to transform their people into a labour pool for the whites. The Kikuyu Central Association began campaigning for direct representation on the Legislative Council and the removal of the ban on Africans growing coffee and cotton. In 1929 it sent Jomo Kenyatta to Britain to lobby for its cause. He went on to study in Moscow and join the Comintern, and to campaign for Kikuyu independence.

When the Second World War broke out, the KCA was proscribed and its leaders banned on security grounds. It reappeared in 1944 as the Kenya African Union, demanding access by Africans to land ownership in the White Highlands. In 1946 the authorities detected the first signs of the Mau Mau movement, and linked it with the KAU. Mau Mau's influence was substantial when Kenyatta, his reputation now high, returned to Kenya in 1948 as president of the KAU and head of a college being established at Githunguri to offer the Kikuyu an education alternative to that provided by the European church schools. Githunguri, however, was perceived by the colonial authorities as the nursery of Kikuyu disaffection.

Mau Mau was a liberation movement in its aims but a terrorist one in its methods. It sought to frighten the whites into abandoning Kenya – or at least the traditional Kikuyu lands – by killing them, their families, their livestock and their farmworkers as horrifyingly as possible. Vastly more Kikuyus were killed than whites (13 000 as against 32) before the rebellion was put down.

To enforce loyalty among the Kikuyu, the Mau Mau turned the Kikuyus' traditional oathing rituals into ceremonies so bestial and degrading as to ensure that those oathed could owe allegiance thereafter only to the Mau Mau. Oath-takers operated at night, enforcing oaths on pain of death. Large numbers of Kikuyus nevertheless collaborated with the authorities, and for the Kikuyu it became a civil war.

Mau Mau was proscribed in 1950 and in response began limited insurgency, leading to the declaration of a state of emergency in October 1952. Within days, 11 whites were hacked to death on outlying farms. The government flew in British troops and called up local whites for service with the security forces. Still the killings continued. Farmers in the White Highlands fortified their homes and armed their wives. Whites there and in Nairobi carried guns and locked their servants out at night.

Nairobi needed to identify Mau Mau's leaders in order to decapitate the movement, and suspicion pointed conveniently to Kenyatta. In 1953 he was put on trial, convicted of 'managing Mau Mau', and sentenced to seven years' imprisonment. The college at Githunguri was closed. Outside the British establishment, the trial was seen as a travesty of justice, a cynical move to weaken Mau Mau and satisfy a settler community threatening to take the law into its own hands.

Still the rebellion continued. Security force sweeps drove the insurgents into the dense forests of Mount Kenya and the Aberdare range. They were still supplied, however, by sympathisers in the villages. A stream of suspects was moved through government 'screening' centres notorious for brutal interrogation. Thousands were put into detention camps. Scores were executed.

Whole communities were moved into fortified villages in order to separate the insurgents from their sympathisers and to protect the loyalists. The Aberdares were sealed off with barbed wire along a deep ditch kilometres long and filled with sharp stakes and dotted with fortified posts.

In the forests, insurgents armed mainly with machetes and traditional swords fought security forces armed with modern weapons and backed by aircraft. Possessing few real guns, the insurgents made their own contraptions that tended to blow up in their faces.

Having penned the insurgents into the forests, the security forces had to go in after them on foot. Mau Mau groups were infiltrated by pseudo gangs made up of captured or surrendered insurgents accompanied with great bravery by Kenyan-born, Kikuyu-speaking whites with blackened hands and faces.

Gradually the forest bands were whittled down to a scattered few. Their leader, Dedan Kimathi, was isolated, hunted down, wounded and captured. For nearly five years this extraordinary man had survived in the forest, eluding the most intensive manhunt of the rebellion and continuing to direct Mau Mau operations from his hideouts. Charged with 182 murders, he was convicted and hanged in November 1957.

The state of emergency was continued for another three precautionary years but Kimathi's capture was the end of it for the Mau Mau – and the beginning of the end for the white settlers. Britain could no longer defend their special status, and speeded up the granting of majority rule. White exclusivity in the Highlands was doomed when in 1959 African access to the region was accepted in principle by London.

In that same year the government declared that neither Kenya, Uganda nor Tanganyika would attain independence before 1975. Within two years, however, Tan-

ganyika was independent. Uganda followed suit a year later. Kenya's relatively large
white community obliged London to go through the longer formalities of negotiation before they could formally be abandoned in Africa. The process was begun
in 1960 with a constitutional conference at Lancaster House in London. There, the
Conservative Party, returned to power in 1959 under Harold Macmillan, presented a draft constitution effectively giving power to Kenya's indigenous majority. As
most of the whites saw it, they were being thrown to the wolves while the British
sled of state sped safely on out of colonialism.

The Kenyan whites had gone to Lancaster House angrily split between die-hard
segregationists and moderates led by Sir Michael Blundell. After long and often-bit-
ter negotiations, Blundell reluctantly accepted the terms. On his return to Kenya he
was derided as a traitor and pelted in the streets.

Two more conferences were held at Lancaster House – in 1962 and 1963 – but
the purpose was just to tie up the loose ends left from the first one. In a pre-inde-
pendence election, conducted in January 1961 on a common voters' roll, Africans
won all but one of the 33 unreserved seats (ten Europeans, eight Asians and two
Arabs got the reserved ones). Kenyatta was freed and assumed the leadership of the
KAU, now renamed the Kenya African National Union. He became prime minister
after KANU won the first election of self-government in May 1963.

Kenya was rushed from self-government to independence in less than a year. Independence was formalised in a rain-soaked ceremony in the Uhuru Stadium in
Nairobi on 12 December 1963, presided over by Kenyatta, now president, and the
Duke of Edinburgh, representing Britain. As the Union Jack was lowered for the
last time and the new flag of Kenya raised in its place, Africans packing the stadium
cheered in delight. Some of the Europeans seated in a small, sad group near the podium quietly wept. It was a moment of crackling emotion. Perhaps it was in order
to relieve the tension that the Duke leaned over to Kenyatta and asked: 'Are you
sure you don't want to change your mind?'

Lancaster House today stands as a kind of cenotaph for British settlement in Africa. The conferences there in the sixties doomed the Kenyan settlers to an essentially unprotected minority status. Nineteen years later, at the same venerable venue,
another Conservative Party government would engineer a settlement in Rhodesia
enabling the British to shed that burdensome responsibility as well.

Despite his treatment by the British, Kenyatta urged the settlers not to leave Kenya. They had begun to leave as early as 1959, however, and by 1965 some twenty
thousand had gone, leaving fewer than forty thousand still willing to take a chance
under African rule. Some saw no option but to leave when their farms were expropriated for black settlement. More than one million acres of the White Highlands
were purchased at economic prices with funds from the Commonwealth Development Corporation and the World Bank.

Those whose farms were taken over may have got out in most cases without financial loss, but they left in most cases with deep emotional pain. Those born in
Kenya but who chose to leave it went to an England that was almost a foreign
country to them. Settling in Britain was in some ways as formidable a change and

challenge for them as emigrating to Kenya had been for their forefathers.

As the indigenous farmers moved into the White Highlands the things of Europe that had been transplanted there began crumbling into Africa. 'Happy Valley', where the wayward aristocracy of Europe had expensively disported, became a place of hand-hoed peasant plots. The little country inns and pubs closed. Many of the wide-verandahed bungalows that once had smelled of furniture polish and flowers became permeated with the odours of open fires and goats.

★ ★ ★ ★

Though white domination had proved an impossible dream in Kenya, it was still pursued with faith and zeal further south. The whites there took courage from their greater numbers and, in the case of Southern Rhodesia, from the relative freedom from interference from London that their limited self-governing status gave them.

Some of the mostly British communities of whites in the two Rhodesias looked to amalgamation as a means of weakening London's supervision. They envisaged forming themselves into a Dominion, possibly incorporating Nyasaland.

It would be an odd fellowship, however. While Northern Rhodesia had also been founded and brought into the British fold by Rhodes, it had been governed not by the Chartered Company but directly by London, as had Nyasaland. Whatever powers the whites of these two territories exercised were entirely at the discretion of Whitehall. Southern Rhodesia, however, was a creature not of London but of South Africa, of Cecil Rhodes's Cape Colony. It had from the start been governed by his Chartered Company. The settlers had been given representation in the Legislative Council in 1900, and when the company's hold had been relinquished in 1923 the territory had been granted limited self-government with a racially qualified franchise that ensured white domination. Britain had retained the final say on matters affecting the indigenous peoples and kept control of foreign relations, but in most other respects, including matters of defence, the territory had autonomy. The limited control retained by London was exercised not through the Colonial Office, as with the other two territories, but through the Dominions Office, emphasising Southern Rhodesia's quasi-dominion status. The prime minister attended the meetings of the Dominion prime ministers.

Churchill's Conservative government was prepared to consider a three-way federation, believing it might create a strong and prosperous dominion, attracting foreign investment in which the British would be dominant. But it was not willing to give the whites a free hand with 'native policy'.

Some in Whitehall had still hoped to bring Southern Rhodesia into South Africa as a fifth province despite the rejection of the idea in the referendum of 1922, but that hope had died with the accession to power of Malan's segregationist, Anglophobic Afrikaners in 1948. The hope had been replaced by fears that the whites in the two Rhodesias might form an alliance with South Africa.[1] That possibility might be lessened by federation with Nyasaland. And the black populations, though initially subservient, would benefit from the prosperity and, hopefully, gradually ad-

242

vance in social status and political rights.

The fact that the black populations objected to federation, seeing it as an extension of white settler domination, was not enough to forestall it. However, the British government retained final control of 'native affairs' and gave the Africans seats – a minority, though – in the federal parliament. None of this pleased the whites but they accepted it as the best that could be got.

The Central African Federation's constitution was hammered out in 18 months of negotiation dominated by the Southern Rhodesian prime minister, Sir Godfrey Huggins, and the leader of the Northern Rhodesian Legislative Council, Roy Welensky, and without any African participation. Both Huggins and Welensky accepted the eventual equality of the blacks with the whites. But Huggins did not expect it in 'the foreseeable future', and Welensky thought it would take at least a century.

The Federation formally came into being on 1 August 1953, with Welensky, now knighted, as premier. It was a string-and-wire thing in which three unequal and incompatible entities were tied together under a parliament and government with limited powers of rule, two of its partners being subject to external control that was not applicable to the third. Even more than Kenya, the CAF reflected the dilemma faced by Britain in reconciling its perceived moral obligations to the colonised indigenous peoples with the demands of the kin the colonisation had deposited in temperate Africa.

Economically, the Federation looked healthy, with investment coming in briskly and the Kariba Dam on the Zambezi creating one of the world's largest man-made lakes. Politically, however, it was cracking over the matter of African rights and representation. This issue brought to prominence three men who were to become heroes – at least for a while – of African liberation: Kenneth Kaunda of Northern Rhodesia, Joshua Nkomo of Southern Rhodesia, and Banda of Nyasaland. Their demands for the dissolution of the Federation and the independence of their respective countries led to each being jailed.

Banda began pressing the point after returning to Nyasaland from England in 1958 to assume the leadership of the Malawi Congress Party. His agitation led to his arrest the next year and the declaration of a state of emergency. Rioting ensued and was put down by troop and police reinforcements rushed in from Southern Rhodesia. The Tory government sent a judge, Sir Patrick Devlin, to inquire. He found widespread opposition to federation. A few months later Lord Monckton, appointed by Macmillan to examine the wider issue of the future of the Federation, confirmed that it was detested by the black people of all three territories. He recommended constitutional changes providing equal representation for blacks in the Federal Assembly and a black majority in the Northern Rhodesian legislature. Any member of the Federation that wanted to secede should be free to do so.

Monckton's report infuriated the settler leaders, who had been assured that he would not address the question of secession. They cried treachery and hinted at an American-style revolution to throw off British authority and seize independence. The battle raged on in the British parliament and in a succession of constitutional conferences.

It was now becoming increasingly clear that white privilege in Africa could no longer be supported by any British government. If it was to survive it would have to do so by its own devices. Welensky and Huggins turned to a strategy of writing off Nyasaland and forming a smaller, tighter union of the two Rhodesias. But that became impossible when Kaunda demanded majority rule in Northern Rhodesia and threatened insurgency. Welensky in turn threatened to put that down with Rhodesian troops, but his words rang hollowly against Britain's determination to leave no colonial coat-tails in Africa.

The Central African Federation was disbanded at a conference at Victoria Falls on 4 July 1963, only ten years after its formation. Within a year Nyasaland became independent as Malawi under Banda, and Northern Rhodesia as Zambia under Kaunda. Britain denied the same privilege to Southern Rhodesia since its whites still rejected immediate majority rule, while the African nationalists, led by Nkomo and Rev. Ndabaningi Sithole, were demanding it.

The scenario was fixed for a continuing struggle that would torment British governments and the African sub-continent for another 17 years and see the repeated threat of white rebellion at last carried out.

CHAPTER 33

MAYHEM ON THE MAGHREB

Mau Mau introduced terrorism to the African freedom struggle; the Algerian insurgents made it more sophisticated and took it into urban areas. The French responded in kind, and the result was the most vicious of the wars against colonialism.

When the bombs began to go off in the sidewalk cafes the French may not at first have realised what they portended. Organised, sustained terrorism against civilian targets was a new refinement of guerilla warfare, and the urban variety was especially unfamiliar. In Algeria its effectiveness on a large scale against conventional police and military operations was demonstrated for the first time. Ruthlessly and successfully used there by the indigenous Arabs, it later became a favoured Arab weapon throughout the Middle East, notably in the Israeli–Palestinian conflict.

At first the French were confident of being able to stamp out the Algerian insurgency with their superior military power. If necessary they would match insurgent terrorism with government terrorism. But, as they learned, in a contest of that kind an occupying power is at a disadvantage against an insurgent force backed by an indigenous population – or prepared to intimidate it. While France was not seen as an occupying power by the *colons* and those Arabs who embraced the Algeria-as-France concept, most of the indigenous people probably did, and that was enough to make insurgency a viable proposition.

With hindsight it might be said that Algeria-as-France was never a viable concept, given the cultural and religious differences between the French and the indigenous Berber-Arab people. That and the special status accorded the territory by France made a violent confrontation highly likely if not inevitable. The other African territories might without much conviction be declared parts of France, but Algeria's one million European settlers put numbers as well as conviction behind the concept. Besides having the largest offshore French population, Algeria held a special significance for the French army, it having motivated the initial conquest and sealed France's claim to possession with the blood of many of its soldiers. Paris could abandon the protectorates of Morocco and Tunisia with less compunction, despite their relatively large European populations: nearly 400 000 in Morocco and 250 000 in Tunisia.

The concept of Algeria as an extension of France might have been more realistic had the territory, like Corsica, been an island off the French coast. But it was geographically part of Africa, and a huge chunk at that. And the white residents who

245

considered it part of France were outnumbered eight to one by indigenous people who mostly thought otherwise. They did not necessarily think of it as part of Africa, but they certainly didn't see it as any part of Europe, French or otherwise.

The indigenous people might have accepted Frankenisation had they not been expected to do so as second-class Frenchmen. In the beginning they had not had a strong sense of their own nationality; for generations they had identified with their Berber-Arab culture and their Muslim faith but not with any concept of Algerian nationality. A number of the Arabs were indeed willing to be embraced by France, but for most of them that was ruled out by the law that denied them French citizenship as long as they held to their Muslim faith, which few if any were prepared to abandon. This meant that the vast majority had little or no say in their own governance and were made aliens in their own land. There was furthermore a deep sense of grievance over Paris having allowed the European settlers to seize most of the best land along the coast, leaving the Arabs struggling to survive on the edge of the Sahara desert.

For these reasons, and for the reason that the French had defined territorial boundaries, a sense of Algerian nationalism did, in fact, develop. Like the Arabism that spread throughout the Middle East and North Africa after the Second World War, it had as much to do with Islam as it had to do with ethnicity (the Arabs and the Berbers in Algeria in fact continued to fight each other while they fought the French).

Still, the Algerian nationalism was not fundamentally Francophobe. After the Allies had seized the territory from the Germans towards the end of the Second World War, indigenous leaders presented them with a request for the creation of an autonomous Algerian republic federated with France. The request was passed to De Gaulle as leader of the Free French but he, perhaps unwilling then to grasp the nettle of settler-Arab relations, responded only with vague promises of voting concessions.

Algerian nationalism was firming up, however, and some of its adherents had devised an unofficial national flag incorporating the Islamic crescent. As the end of the war in Europe was being celebrated in 1945, some of these flags were hoisted in the town of Setif. When police hauled them down rioting broke out in which 88 Frenchmen were killed. The authorities responded so fiercely that, by the official version, 1 800 Arabs were killed. The locals claimed a count of 8 000.

The massacres spurred the French government to reform. A Statute for Algeria established an Algerian Assembly of 120 members, half elected equally by the European voters and the few Algerians with French citizenship, and half elected by the Muslims. They also gained greater access to employment opportunities in France, and within a few years 350 000 Algerians were working there.

The concessions kept Algeria quiet for the time being, but in the mean time insurrection broke out in Morocco and Tunisia, where, too, indigenous grievances had festered around the occupation of the best land by white settlers.

In both these territories resistance to French rule had been galvanised by the creation of an independent Libya. The unrest in Morocco prompted the French to depose Sultan Muhammad Ben Yussuf in 1953 and replace him with the elderly and pliant Ben Arafa. But Yussuf, exiled to Madagascar, became a martyr and in 1955 young nationalists invoked his repute in forming a liberation army in the Rif mountains, covertly supplied by the Spanish in their protectorate in the north of the territory.

In Tunisia the faltering Destour Party had been revitalised as the Neo-Destour under the Paris-educated lawyer Habib Bourguiba. Arrested twice before the war, Bourguiba, like the Algerians, had found his appeals for autonomy rejected by the Free French after the war. For five years he campaigned abroad for his cause, and after his return to Tunisia he was again arrested, together with the other Neo-Destour leaders. In reaction, armed groups formed in the mountains and insurgency broke out in the settled areas.

These were anxious and bewildering times for France, with insurrection in Morocco and Tunisia and defeat looming in Indo-China. Into this volatile situation stepped Pierre Mendes-France, newly elected as Radical Socialist premier of France and bent on extricating his country from the colonial wars that he believed were draining its exchequer to no good purpose and preventing it from taking full advantage of the Marshall Plan to rebound economically.

France did indeed soon enter a period of economic prosperity at home. Like Britain, it was already turning its old outward concentration on the colonies inward back to Europe, the Europe that would soon form the Common Market and have little use for fractious colonies. Military strategists, too, were beginning to frown on the wasting on colonial wars of funds that would be better spent on keeping France competitive in the fast-developing technology of the nuclear age.

Having extricated France from the Vietnamese morass in 1954, Mendes-France turned his attention to the Maghreb. He saw Morocco and Tunisia as protectorates but Algeria as part of France. Thus his governor-general, Jacques Soustelle, told the Algerian Assembly: 'France will no more evacuate from Algeria than it will from Provence or Brittany.' And François Mitterrand, minister of the interior (later president of France), declared: 'War is the only negotiation.'

As quickly as he had pulled out of Indo-China, Mendes-France moved to cut loose the encumbrances of Tunisia and Morocco, the better to deal with the insurrection now again rising in Algeria. He paid a price, however. For opening negotiations on self-government with the two protectorates he was later ousted from office by a parliamentary coalition opposed to withdrawal from the Maghreb. But already, while nipping the insurrection in the protectorates in the bud, he had made irrevocable their advance to self-determination. Under his successor, Edgar Faure, Morocco attained independence in March 1958 as a kingdom under Ben Yussuf as King Muhammad V. Spain immediately handed over Tangier and the northern protectorate, retaining only the enclaves of Ifni, Ceuta and Melilla. Tunisia became independent 18 days after Morocco, with Bourguiba as prime minister (later president).

Inevitably, the independence of the flanking territories intensified nationalist sentiment in Algeria. But that in turn strengthened the resolve of the white settlers

247

to remain part of France. Whereas in Tunisia the French had been outnumbered 14:1 by the Arabs and in Morocco by 22:1, in Algeria the ratio was at most 9:1, and the one million *colons* there fully exploited their numbers and also the support they enjoyed in the French bureaucracy, armed forces and parliament.

Arab resistance led by a clandestine wing of the *Mouvement pour le Triomphe des Libertes Democratiques* (MTLD) was too slow-paced for the young Ahmad Ben Bella, a much-decorated former NCO in the French army. In November 1954 he and his contemporaries attempted armed uprising but it was premature, ill-planned and quickly put down. It did, however, publicise the militants' cause. Within 18 months they had united most of the indigenous leaders of note in a new organisation, the Front of National Liberation (FLN). Six months after that the FLN was operating a guerilla force of about twenty thousand and taking control of an increasing number of remote areas.

When the authorities declared a state of emergency in 1955 the FLN in response called for country-wide insurrection and warned that no mercy would be shown to anyone who sided with the French. The FLN sought to bind adherents to obedience through criminality. An FLN initiate was required to kill a policeman, a *colon* or an Arab marked as a traitor. On this first murder mission the initiate would be accompanied by a 'shadow' whose function was to execute him if he tried to pull out of his assignment.

The method of execution favoured by the movement was slitting the throat, a practice dubbed *le grand sourire* (the broad smile) by French troops. If it was not already so, the war became locked into atrocity when on 20 August 1955 the FLN attacked the town of Philipville and killed 71 Europeans and 52 Arabs in horrifying fashion. Pregnant women had their bellies slashed open, children were beheaded, people had limbs hacked off and skulls smashed in. In an outraged hunt for the perpetrators the security forces killed more than twelve hundred Arabs (the FLN put the toll ten times higher). The authorities now for the first time allowed the *colons* to arm themselves for their own defence.

But now the FLN had found an effective weapon of its own – the bomb. Normal life became impossible as the bombs sprayed public places in Algiers and other cities with shrapnel and human tissue. FLN terrorism cells operated at first from hideouts in the tortuous warrens of the Casbah, Algiers's ancient Arab quarter. The French countered by sealing off the Casbah and patrolling it minutely, by handsomely paying informers, and by torturing FLN associates for information. The bombings continued in Algiers nonetheless, and were taken even to mainland France. In Algeria they were supplemented by sabotage and workers' strikes.

While the Algerian conflict was primarily an urban one, the battleground was in fact virtually the whole of Algeria, four times bigger than France. The FLN functioned more widely still, basing as many as forty thousand guerillas in Morocco and Tunisia. The organisation also received moral and material support from Nasser's government in Egypt and from Arabs elsewhere, as the notion of Arab solidarity grew among the emerging states of the Middle East.

In 1958 the military in Algeria, without authority from Paris, sent French planes to bomb Sakiet in Tunisia. The bombing was widely condemned in France, and brought about the downfall of yet another French government. Coming after Ben Bella and other Algerian rebel leaders had in 1956 been kidnapped while travelling in a chartered plane outside French territory, the Sakiet bombing heightened international criticism of France and support for the FLN.

In an effort to seal the borders with Morocco and Tunisia, the French lined them with electrified fences backed by minefields, machine-gun posts, searchlights and motorised patrols. More and more French troops were dragged into the conflict until half a million were deployed against the insurgents and Paris was forced to put on hold the plans for diverting resources from colonial wars to domestic development.

In an effort to separate the insurgents from their non-combative support base, about two million people were moved into huge camps supervised by the military. The camps were widely criticised internationally, giving the FLN useful material for propaganda. But even better material was about to be offered them in the abortive Anglo-French attempt to oust Nasser from power in Egypt.

★ ★ ★ ★

In November 1956 the governments of Britain and France stood in the world with egg on their faces, splattered there by the ignominious failure of their attempt to replace Nasser's Egyptian government with a friendlier regime. The operation ranks as one of the most inept exercises ever undertaken by the European powers in Africa. It weakened the positions elsewhere in Africa of the two major colonial powers. Decolonisation was speeded up in consequence. And the whites living in Africa were brought closer to their respective moments of truth.

The operation was undertaken under the cover of securing international rights of passage through the Suez Canal. Sir Anthony Eden, who had succeeded Churchill as prime minister, saw it as a means of halting the decline of Britain's influence in the Middle East, in which Nasser was seen as a major villain. The French for their part regarded Nasser as the key figure promoting Arab nationalism in general, and particularly in raising support for the FLN in Algeria. With him out of the way, France might buy time to resolve the Algerian problem. Both powers were worried about Nasser's role as middleman in obtaining arms from the communist countries for the FLN.

By 1956 British influence in the Middle East had slumped sharply from the position in 1945, when Britain had held sway in Egypt, Jordan, Iraq, Iran and the Persian Gulf sheikdoms, and had military bases in these countries and in Malta, Cyprus, Haifa, Libya and Aden. In 1951 Mohammed Mussadiq had seized control in Iran, nationalised its oil and forced the British into abject withdrawal. It was the first sign that Britain, for all its nuclear bombers and navy, might no longer have the wherewithal to assert itself on the ground.

In the same year the Wafdist premier of Egypt, Al-Nahas, revoked the 1936 Anglo-Egyptian Treaty allowing the British to occupy the Suez Canal Zone. The British reaction was to place the Canal Zone under military government and begin to disarm the Egyptian forces therein. The garrison at Ismailia resisted and 50 were killed. Rioting ensued in Cairo. Mobs burned down the famous Shepheard's Hotel and other landmarks of British presence, and killed numbers of Britons.

King Farouk, ever anxious to placate the British, sacked Al-Nahas but six months later was himself deposed by General Neguib, with General Nasser pulling the strings. With the United States having opened new air bases in Turkey, and with the Suez Canal treaty only two years from its legal termination, Anthony Eden, then foreign secretary, accepted that there was no point in Britain hanging on in Egypt provided the Canal could be kept secure and open. He agreed to a British withdrawal from the zone by 1956 in return for Egypt entering a defence agreement that would give Britain the use of the Suez base in the event of a war in the Middle East. At the same time he negotiated independence for the Sudan for the same year (prime minister Nasser having accepted that with the Sudanese-born Neguib as Egyptian head of state he could keep the Sudan within Cairo's sphere of influence).

Eden became prime minister in 1955 when Churchill retired. By now Nasser had deposed Neguib and taken over the Egyptian presidency. Eden and Nasser were heading for a crucial clash of wills.

Having written off Egypt (though not the Suez Canal), Eden had pinned his Middle Eastern hopes on the Baghdad Pact, to which Britain had recruited Turkey, Iraq, Iran and Pakistan. But Nasser, who saw the pact as a threat to his vision of Arab solidarity, not only refused to join but persuaded Syria, Saudi Arabia, Yemen, Lebanon and Jordan also to spurn membership. Nasser's focus was rather on the efforts then being made to form what became known as the Non-Aligned Movement, ostensibly sympathetic to neither the West nor the Soviet Bloc. At the same time, however, he was looking to the West to finance the planned Aswan High Dam on the Nile, which he hoped would boost his country's economy and his own group's political support in Egypt.

Alarmed by the Israeli raid across the 1948 cease-fire line into Egypt in 1955, Nasser approached both the West and the Soviet Bloc for arms for defence. In this he leaned towards the Soviets, for, besides his dislike of the Baghdad Pact, he had a deep hatred of British domination and carried a grudge against France for supplying arms to Israel in retaliation for Cairo's support for Arab nationalism in the Maghreb. The United States was wary for strategic reasons of arming Egypt, and was made even more cautious by the strong opposition of the powerful pro-Israeli Jewish lobby in America. So it was hardly surprising that in the end Nasser plumped for Czechoslovakian and Soviet military aid.

American displeasure at this was compounded when Nasser joined an anti-Israeli military alliance with Saudi Arabia, Syria and Yemen, and then switched Egypt's diplomatic recognition from Taiwan to Communist China. That was too much for secretary of state John Foster Dulles, and in 1956 he curtly rejected Nasser's request for finance for the Aswan dam.

Both Dulles and Eden were surprised by Nasser's reaction. Within days he had nationalised the Suez Canal in order to use its profits to finance the dam. It was a legitimate action as long as he compensated the Canal company's shareholders, but to Eden it was like an Egyptian tongue stuck out at him. Eden was already smarting from the successive setbacks suffered by once-mighty Britain since the war: obliged to leave India; seeing the rest of the Empire coming apart; even the Dominions growing uppity and independent; indebted to and militarily dependent on America, and browbeaten accordingly by Washington; snubbed in Syria, Iraq and Jordan; having to put down rebellions in Kenya, Malaya and Cyprus, and so on and so on. Besides, Eden was feeling rather small-footed in Churchill's large shoes, and perceived a need for, as it were, some assertive inner soles.

Furthermore, the British withdrawal from Egypt in 1954 had been roundly condemned by the Tory right wing, and Eden felt it necessary to give them some reassurance that he was not abdicating altogether in the Middle East.

There are conflicting accounts of whether the Suez plot was conceived by Britain, France or Israel. Whatever its genesis, the plan was that Israel, claiming it was reacting to Egyptian raids across the armistice line, would attack in strength. Britain and France would demand a cessation of hostilities and Anglo–French protection of the Canal. Nasser would, of course, refuse, and Britain and France would then intervene, ostensibly to secure the Canal but actually to topple Nasser and install a friendly government. The plot was sealed at a secret meeting at Sevres between Eden and the French premier, Guy Mollet, with the Israeli military commander, Moshe Dayan of the eye-patch, in close attendance.

The Israelis attacked on 29 October 1956. The British and French issued their ultimatum. Nasser duly rejected it, and Anglo–French air forces began bombing strategic targets in Egypt while the joint invasion fleet sailed from Malta (the nearer Cyprus base having been found to be inadequate). It took the fleet six days to reach Egypt, by which time Nasser had rallied international support and raised the ante by blocking the Canal with sunken ships. Both powers were now forced to revert to the longer Cape route for some of their oil and other major imports. The first splatters of egg had landed on the French and British faces.

Washington was aghast at the operation, seeing it as undermining its policy of persuading rather than forcing Middle Eastern states to side with the West rather than the Soviet Bloc. The United States accordingly sponsored a motion of censure in the Security Council. Britain and France were obliged to use their vetoes to block it. The US turned to the General Assembly, where there are no veto powers, and pushed through a resolution questioning whether the invasion was justified and calling for a truce. In the meantime it moved to seal off alternative oil supplies to the invading powers.

It was high-stakes poker, and Eden has misread the hands. He had not foreseen the strength of the reaction, not only in the United States but also at home in Britain, where there was uproar in parliament, press and public. Crucially, Eden had overlooked the possibility that the invasion might provoke a run on the pound and a consequent sterling crisis. It did just that, and the Chancellor of the Exchequer, Harold Macmillan, was obliged to fly cap-in-hand to Washington to seek American support for the pound. Washington played its ace: unless the invasion was called off, sterling would be allowed to collapse. Eden threw in his cards. The French were furious but had to do the same. The invasion force was halted while still fighting its way southward down the Canal.

Britain had been defeated by its own economic weakness, specifically its indebtedness to the United States, and by international opinion, which through the United Nations was becoming a new force in the world. The debacle had shown that Britain, too poor now to be a big power in its own right, could successfully be challenged, perhaps even by its unwilling colonial subjects. British prestige in the Middle East and in Africa was severely damaged. Eden was obliged to resign, and was succeeded by Macmillan.

★ ★ ★ ★

The Suez Canal debacle added to the opprobrium that was already attaching to France from the harsh measures taken against the Algerian insurgency. This and the other costs of the war began to tell. French families were losing sons in defence of a white population that was only half French. There was growing dissatisfaction with the expenditure on an unworthy conflict of resources much needed domestically. Rapid and unsettling changes of government in France, and two decades of unending war at home and in Asia and Africa, had left the French nation weary and disillusioned and ready to abandon Algeria.

These sentiments were not shared, however, by the more extreme of the Algerian whites, the *pieds noir*, and the majority of the army officers. After Dien Bien Phu and Suez the officers were in no mood to accept further humiliation. As talk of a negotiated settlement was heard in Paris, the right-wing '*Ultras*' among the Algerian settlers rose in indignation in May 1958. Reaffirming the principle of Algeria's oneness with France, they organised militant Committees of Public Safety and called for the return of General de Gaulle to power. The army commanders backed them. French paratroops invaded Corsica and threatened to go on to the mainland to stage a coup. In June the National Assembly voted to install De Gaulle as head of government, thereby terminating the Fourth Republic.

The *Ultras'* expectations of De Gaulle turned out to have been misplaced, however. His vision for restoring the glory of France did not embrace an Algerian limb perpetually inflamed with agitation by its Arab majority. He immediately granted French citizenship rights to Muslim Algerians and introduced a reform programme that included measures to bring more Muslims into the civil service. The settler-military alliance was dismayed. But worse was to come. In a speech to the UN General Assembly in September 1959, De Gaulle undercut the Algeria-as-France principle by recognised the right of the Algerians to self-determination. Outraged *colons* attempted another uprising three months later, but De Gaulle's stature deterred the army officers from giving it their support and it quickly collapsed. De Gaulle made it clear that decolonisation was essential if France was to exploit the possibilities arising from the new European Common Market.

When negotiations on Algerian independence appeared imminent there was another attempt at a white uprising in Algeria, led this time by General Challe, with the intention of staging an army coup that would force De Gaulle to keep Algeria French.

France took a dangerous lurch towards civil war, for Challe was supported by about eight thousand French troops. The rebels made plans for paratroops to be dropped in France to back their demands, but they failed to get the support of the majority in the army and also of the French air force and navy. Naval vessels berthed at Mers-el-Kebir opened fire on a parachute battalion as it marched on the port. When the air force was asked to join the uprising its pilots either flew their planes back to France or refused to fly them at all. Challe was left with no option but to surrender, and the troops that had supported him were put in detention camps.

Negotiations were opened in secret with the provisional government that had been set up by the FLN in Cairo and backed by the other Arab states. When word of the talks leaked out, right-wing whites turned to terrorism, forming an *Organisation Armée Secrète* (OAS) in a desperate effort to block the negotiations. The talks continued nonetheless, and openly now. On 19 March 1962 at Evian agreement was reached on holding a referendum on independence for Algeria. If the vote was in favour, those whites who chose to remain in Algeria would have three years to choose between French or Algerian nationality. Those who chose to retain French citizenship would have their rights protected by a Court of Guarantees.

The Evian agreement provoked a renewed outburst of terrorism from the OAS, but the referendum went ahead nonetheless on 1 July 1962. The vote was overwhelmingly in favour: almost six million against 16 478.

The vote ended a war that had ravaged Algeria and scarified France. At least a quarter of a million Muslims had been killed. Scores of villages had been destroyed, and about two million of their inhabitants uprooted. About three hundred thousand had been sent into exile. On the French side, 17 656 soldiers had been killed and 66 000 wounded, and 10 000 civilians killed or wounded.

Algerian Arabs wildly celebrated the referendum result, but among the Europeans there was dismay and consternation. Algeria came close to anarchy, with revenge killings and lawlessness everywhere. Panicky whites began to flee the country at the rate of several thousand a day. More than eight hundred thousand left in less than three months, among them most of the administrators and technicians whose skills had underpinned governance and the economy. By the time Ben Bella's appointment as premier was ratified by the National Assembly on 25 September, there were only about a hundred thousand whites left in the country.

This had been the greatest exodus of Europeans Africa had known. While Algeria under the French had ostensibly been a multi-racial society, that status had been so heavily qualified that for the Arabs it had in practice been a society dominated by European privilege. The writing was now clearly on the wall for white separatism and white domination everywhere in Africa, though those in the southern quarter of the continent either could not or would not see it.

For the whites in southern Africa, two important truths were emphasised by the

Algerian experience. The first was that neither freedom nor democracy could be qualified. They were not a privilege but a right. People could not evolve to democracy. Freedom of choice could not be stratified, or extended only to an elite, only to those Africans judged to have risen to a level of civilisation equal to that claimed by Europeans. There was no such thing as half-democracy; it was an all-or-nothing right and had to be accorded to the peasants, to the masses, as well as the elite, or it was not freedom. France eventually recognised and applied this principle to its sub-Saharan colonies. It was rejected by the Rhodesian whites as they proceeded tortuously with a qualified franchise for the black majority.

The second truth was an obvious one, but one that had been and would still be widely overlooked. It was that democracy was a great deal more difficult to install in a society of marked ethnic and cultural differences than it was in a uniform one.

Acknowledgement of both truths was in fact implicit in the South African government's apartheid policy, which through segregation sought security, and, less earnestly, democracy. In its ultimate rationale, National Party policy reckoned that only by separating the white society from the black one could the whites allow democracy in both and still protect themselves from domination by the black majority. But that would entail dividing the country into at least two separate portions. The party did, in fact, make a half-hearted attempt at that when it gave ostensible independence to the tribal regions that became known as bantustans. But the exercise was doomed from the start because the division was unrealistic in demographic, moral or any other terms, and because Pretoria would not or could not do whatever was necessary in other ways to give the bantustans the economic self-sufficiency essential for effective independence.

Perhaps it seemed to the National Party to be a catch-22 situation: without the black labour in the bantustans, white South Africa would find it difficult to sustain a level of prosperity sufficient to subsidise the development of the bantustans to a state of economic viability, but if the black states were to continue to supply the labour for the white state they would have to be kept poor, undeveloped and dependent, since economic viability of the bantustans would jeopardise the labour supply.

The essential fallacy of this view became apparent only after apartheid had given way to democracy. The general economy did not collapse when employers were forced to negotiate wage levels with black trade unions (or when the governmental levers of the economy were placed in black hands). The former bantustans did not immediately become prosperous, of course, for their poverty had been caused by factors that could not quickly be removed or rectified.

The problems inherited by democracy from apartheid would have been lesser had the whites at a relatively early stage made an equitable division of the country, and had they been willing to make the sacrifices necessary to subsidise the development of the black states and make them viable. The majority of the whites, however, could not bring themselves to do this, and they ended up paying the price: domination by the blacks. The epitaph of the conservative white might well be that he placed greed above a separate existence.

CHAPTER 34

WIND RISING

The South Africa parliament had experienced dramatic moments before, but never one quite like this. Here was the British head of government, and a Conservative one at that, standing in the lion's den of apartheid and telling its leaders that they had better change their wrong ways and get in step with the new world.

Harold Macmillan's address to the South African parliament in February 1960 is remembered not because it was especially stirring or because he was the first British prime minister to visit the continent in two centuries of British presence. What seized his audience was the message: that the remaining whites should bow to the 'wind of change' blowing through Africa, the wind of black freedom from white domination.

Macmillan's message rang loud but somewhat differently for all of the dominant whites in the sub-continent. It was discomforting for the Portuguese, still confident in their 'assimilative' racial policies, but chilling for the Rhodesians, knowing their vulnerability to British pressures. For the ruling South Africans, for whom it was primarily intended, it was somewhat offensive, but also disturbing in the confirmation that they could no longer expect support even from a Conservative Party government, not even in the Cold War.

The speech sharply emphasised South Africa's beleaguerment in the world – only two weeks after Prime Minister Verwoerd had announced a referendum on whether South Africa should become a republic rather than a Dominion within the British ambit.

Macmillan hung his address on the thesis that Africa, like Asia before it and Europe before that, was undergoing the ancient process of the emergence of independent nations, with different races and civilisations pressing their claims to an independent national life.

'The wind of change is blowing through the continent,' he said, 'and whether we like it or not this growth of national consciousness is a political fact ... and our national policies must take account of it.'

Affirming his own government's acceptance of the inevitability of African independence, Macmillan was urging the ruling whites in the sub-continent to find ways to come to terms with it. Far from acknowledging South Africa's strategic importance in the Cold War, he was giving an oblique warning to Pretoria: Asia and Africa were crucially balanced between falling into the Western or the Soviet sphere, and the Commonwealth might have a crucial influence in deciding which way they fell. The implication was that Pretoria's race policies might tip them into the Soviet camp – especially if South Africa remained a member of the Commonwealth without renouncing apartheid.

Verwoerd's followers might if they wished have extracted from Macmillan's speech an ironic though unintended endorsement of the South African government's separate development policies. After all, were these policies not all about 'different races and civilisations pressing their claims to an independent national life'? In particular, was that not what Verwoerd was trying to achieve for his own white people?

In his brief response Verwoerd did indeed declare that his government's policies were 'in the fullest accord' with 'the new direction in Africa'. They would not be abandoned, however, if it jeopardised the survival of the white race in southern Africa. Justice must be done not only to the black man in South Africa, he said, but to the white man as well. 'This is our only motherland,' he reminded Macmillan. 'We have nowhere else to go.'

Here were two philosophies bumping head-on in the same chamber. On the one hand, the British ethic – comfortably founded in a prosperous, mono-ethnic society – of respect for democratic rights; and, on the other, the white Africans' fear of being overwhelmed in every way by the culturally different and rapidly growing black majority.

A generous interpretation of Macmillan's words was that he was suggesting that the white South Africans devise a more equitable form of separation. To most of his audience, however, it seemed that he was advocating that they take a chance under black rule. Verwoerd for his part was refusing to budge from a separate white existence ensured by white supremacy. He was not going to experiment with any kind of partnership that compromised separateness, and certainly none that involved ethnic mingling. Neither was he about to give up the material advantages and privileges that apartheid gave the whites, the exploitive aspects that deprived his 'separate development' policies of their professed morality.

In pointing out that the South African whites had nowhere else to go, Verwoerd was reminding Macmillan that they were a special case; they could not be regarded in the same light as those in Kenya, Rhodesia and Algeria who had European motherlands to return to if they could not accept indigenous domination in Africa. The older South African roots were deeper in Africa, and long sundered from Europe. The South Africans must maintain their separate existence or be submerged in the black majority.

Verwoerd was talking against the wind, however. The Western powers did not believe that the whites would necessarily suffer by bowing to black rule. The powers did not in any case attach paramount importance to that aspect. What they wanted in southern Africa was political stability to protect their own special interests and Western interests in general, which in part meant keeping out the Soviets. And if the whites had to make painful sacrifices to that end so be it.

The European powers saw no reason to believe that the Africans might be as racist as the Europeans if the positions were reversed. That possibility had not yet been put to the test anywhere in Africa, and so it remained theoretical. But they were willing to put it to the test in the interests of ensuring that the sub-continent did not become a cockpit of racial strife that might harm their own concerns. Perceiving this, many of the white Africans became convinced that they were considered expendable in the larger European interest.

The whites attempted to make 1960 a year of celebration to mark the 50th anniversary of the formation of the Union, the formal beginning of their nationhood. There was little unity to celebrate, however, for resistance to white domination was surging among the African, coloured and Indian people, and the whites themselves were divided over the apartheid policies.

International opposition to apartheid was sharpening, too, notably in the United Nations, which had been transformed by worldwide decolonisation from European predominance into an organisation numerically dominated by African and Asian states. Only through their vetoes in the Security Council could the former colonial powers dictate decisions, and even there they were often countered by the Soviet Union's veto. Since India had hauled the apartheid issue into the UN arena in 1948, the Afro-Asian bloc had put the all-white South African delegation increasingly on the defensive.

In 1960 South Africa's trusteeship of South West Africa was challenged in the International Court of Justice (the World Court) by the two oldest African members of the UN, Ethiopia and Liberia. In the same year was formed the South West Africa People's Organisation (Swapo), which would go on to launch an armed struggle against Pretoria's administration.

★ ★ ★ ★

Macmillan's speech had drawn attention to the external pressures against white supremacy; the internal pressures exploded on 21 March the same year in the dusty little black township of Sharpeville near Vereeniging. A crowd of black people, heeding a call by the Pan-Africanist Congress to protest against the pass laws, surrounded the Sharpeville police station. As the excited crowd pressed against the surrounding wire mesh fence, frightened young policemen, perhaps aware that a few weeks previously nine policemen had been killed by a mob in Durban, panicked and opened fire, and then kept firing, killing 69 and wounding 180. Many of these were shot in the back as they fled.

Before Sharpeville the rising resistance to apartheid had brought demonstrations, strikes, an organised campaign of civil disobedience, including the public burning of passes, and a mass march on the Union Buildings by some ten thousand women protesting against the pass laws. Every new direction taken by apartheid's opponents had been countered by further repressive legislation. Still the Africans had eschewed violence. In 1955 a Congress of the People had been held at Kliptown near Johannesburg and a Freedom Charter adopted, calling for a non-racial, democratic state. Far from heeding that call, the government the next year had charged 156 accused, including the young Nelson Mandela, with treason in a trial that was to ramble on, past Sharpeville, until all were acquitted in 1961. The judiciary, at least, was still largely independent of government control.

In the weeks after Sharpeville the government declared a state of emergency, arrested more than eleven thousand people, including 224 white opponents of apartheid, and outlawed both the ANC and the Pan-Africanist Congress. The PAC had been formed the previous year by militants who found the Freedom Charter too mild and favoured an exclusive African nationalism. Under Robert Sobukwe's leadership it had begun its own campaign of civil disobedience.

On being banned, both organisations went underground and began to see violence as the only option to the peaceful protest that had brought only tougher government suppression.

White opposition to apartheid had now been largely emasculated by the pervasive fear of black rule and of imprisonment or banning under the government's draconian new laws. It was expressed in a necessarily muted way in the English-language churches, newspapers and academia, by organisations such as the Black Sash or through clandestine support for the ANC. One man, a white farmer named David Pratt, made his own protest a few weeks after Sharpeville, shooting and wounding Verwoerd while he was opening the Rand Easter Show in Johannesburg. Verwoerd recovered; Pratt was officially declared mentally ill and locked up for life, which, intentionally or not, left no risk of Pretoria's policies being questioned in a highly publicised court trial.

Sharpeville intensified international opposition to apartheid, but also increased the white fears that had already been exacerbated by Mau Mau and were heightened by the massacre of whites in the Belgian Congo only three months after Sharpeville. Many whites believed they were on their own in a world that did not understand their fears. They turned for security to the laager offered by Verwoerd's government.

When the government asked them to vote for republican status in the referendum on 9 October 1960, enough did so to give it a narrow majority: 850 458 for and 775 878 against. It was illustrative of the strange twists taking place in the white society that many Afrikaners voted against a republic but many English-speakers voted in favour. On 31 May the next year South Africa became a republic and the government pulled out of the Commonwealth, knowing that the country would be expelled if it didn't.

In the same year, 1961, the ANC abandoned its adherence to non-violence, having seen every peaceful protest countered by force by the government. The government had, in Nelson Mandela's words, 'left us with no other choice'. A militant wing, Umkhonto we Sizwe (Spear of the Nation), commonly known as MK, was formed under Mandela's leadership to launch a campaign of sabotage but avoiding human targets. Elements within the PAC set up a similar organisation named Poqo, but which, unlike MK, targeted people rather than installations.

Huge resources were flung by the government into countering this new dimension of the struggle. MK's effectiveness was largely blocked by efficient government counter-measures, but it gained prestige with audacious attacks on state-owned targets, forcing the government to take costly protective measures.

After generations of largely undisputed hegemony over the black people, of only isolated black resistance, of easily getting their own way, the whites were now for the first time on the defensive across the whole country. They were increasingly beleaguered internationally as well. In 1960 South Africa had found itself casting the only vote in the UN General Assembly against a motion condemning its policies. Only reluctant British vetoes saved it from worse in the Security Council. African and Asian countries formed a militant and vociferous bloc at the UN. The Organisation of African Unity, formed in 1963, cranked up the tempo in the UN and elsewhere.

MK planned an ambitious campaign of insurrection, code-named Operation Mayibuye, beginning with the infiltration of nucleus groups of insurgents who would establish secret bases, train new recruits and widen support among the black population. Then a major assault would be launched on state targets in four selected areas which, it was hoped, would elicit strong international support and lead to the fall of the white government. The operation was ill-planned and premature, however, and against the strengths, skills and ruthlessness of the government machine it barely got off the ground. Many of the operation's leaders were arrested.

Mandela became a hunted man, dubbed the 'Black Pimpernel' as he travelled South Africa and between times slipped abroad to organise opposition to apartheid. The police at last caught up with him in 1962 on the main highway through Natal. The next year Operation Mayibuye was dealt a fatal blow with the seizure of most of the rest of the MK high command at their hideout at Rivonia near Johannesburg. Charged with high treason, a capital offence, Mandela and the others were convicted only of sabotage and sentenced to life imprisonment.

From the dock Mandela made another of Africa's famous speeches, a defiant but principled oration that rang round the world, succinctly expressing the ethos of the moderate black struggle. He spoke for all black people when he recalled how he had spent 30 years patiently knocking at 'a closed and barred door'. Moderation, however, had brought only greater restriction.

'I have fought against white domination and I have fought against black domination,' Mandela said. 'I have cherished the ideal of a democratic and free society in which all persons live together in harmony and with equal opportunities. It is an ideal which I hope to live for and to achieve. But if needs be it is an ideal for which I am prepared to die.'

Basic though they were, the wants and rights listed by Mandela were unacceptable to a government locked into the fear that granting them would jeopardise not only white identity but also white privilege. Mandela's vision was ephemeral against the rock-set protocols of a government that could formally decree that 'the Bantu are only temporarily resident in the European areas of the Republic for as long as they offer their labour there. As soon as they become, for one reason or another, no longer fit to work or superfluous in the labour market, they are expected to return to their country of origin or the territory of the national unit where they fit ethnically …' This was a government that could officially consign to the homelands 'the aged, the unfit, widows, women with dependent children ... Bantu on European farms who become superfluous as a result of age or disability ... Bantu squatters from mission stations and black spots which are being cleared up ... doctors, attorneys, traders, industrialists, etc. who are not regarded as essential for the European labour market.' *

There were whites as well as blacks among the accused in the Rivonia trial. Numbers of whites were jailed for their opposition to apartheid.

A growing number of blacks fled from South Africa to join the struggle abroad or simply to escape apartheid and seek a normal life under democracy. The Justice Ministry estimated in 1964 that as many as five thousand might be receiving military training overseas. The government countered with tougher repression domestically, with tighter border patrols and hot-pursuit raids into the neighbouring High Commission territories.

Partly because it gave South Africa a more respectable appearance in the world, the rampant Nationalist Party government tolerated the white opposition parties. South Africa's partial democracy was more partial than ever, even more contradictory in terms. It had never been a democracy for the blacks, and now only the thin remnants of white democracy – constitution, parliament, elections and semi-independent judiciary – differentiated it from a one-party police state for the whites.

As the sixties drew to a close, the structure of apartheid was virtually complete. Segregation had been enforced in terms of residence, employment, trade, education, marriage, sexual intercourse, social life, politics and sport. At the same time, black labour was available for white industries, offices and homes. And the extremist Afrikaners who dominated government had at last attained their republic.

Verwoerd was dead, stabbed by an apparently insane parliamentary messenger, Dimitri Tsafendas, in the House of Assembly on 6 September 1966, but his place had been taken by Balthazar Johannes Vorster, a former general in the *Ossewabrandwag* and one of the suspected Nazi sympathisers interned by the Smuts government during the war. Subversion had been restricted by an efficient secret police and tough action from a strong uniformed force, and by new laws allowing the government to detain opponents indefinitely without trial.

Even the English-speaking whites were beginning to come on board, helping to give the government an additional 21 parliamentary seats in the 1966 election. The economy was growing well, and despite the increasing international opposition to apartheid there had been a significant increase in white immigration.

White exclusivity and privilege seemed safe for now. But the price had been grievous. South Africa had become a pariah in the world, cast out of the Commonwealth, beleaguered in the United Nations, and barred from the Olympic Games and the OAU. Besides these formal setbacks, South Africa was under informal but growing attack by the anti-apartheid movements that were forming throughout Europe and elsewhere in the world. An OAU ban on flying over member states had forced South African Airways to make a 1 400-kilometre detour out to sea and

---

*It was one of South Africa's political oddities that the Afrikaners, despite having adopted an African identity, should still use the term 'European' to refer to the whites in official pronouncements.

round the 'bulge' of Africa in order to reach Europe.

South Africa had virtually no friends of consequence in the world, and those who gave support did so out of perceived strategic need and with great embarrassment. It was a sad tumble for a country that only two decades earlier had had an honoured place in international councils, a respected voice in world affairs.

A UN group appointed to find solutions to the South African issue (but which was denied visas to enter the Republic) reported in 1964 that 'what is now at issue is not the final outcome but the question of whether on the way the people of South Africa are to go through a long ordeal of blood and hate.'

By the end of the decade the majority of the whites were committed to enduring that very ordeal, fearing that the alternative would be worse.

★ ★ ★ ★

Within months of his address to the South African parliament in 1960, the wind of change perceived by Macmillan had become a gale, a libertarian blast that blew 17 African colonies into independence before the year was out, and most of the rest within the decade.

The wind had been fanned by riots in the Gold Coast, Mau Mau, the Algerian war and the Suez crisis. The independence of Libya in 1951 and then of Sudan, Morocco and Tunisia in 1956, followed by Ghana the next year, had made it difficult for the European powers to retain colonies. The two principal powers, France and Britain, now had little interest in doing so anyway. Both De Gaulle and Macmillan had perceived the obsolescence of imperialism. They became the undertakers of colonialism.

By 1954 the immediate post-war idea of a 30-year stroll to independence for the colonies was but a memory. Now it was a sprint with the wind behind. By 1968 there wasn't a British colony left in Africa except the self-governing one of Rhodesia.

It had taken two centuries to build the British Empire; it took less than two decades to demolish it. Nearly all the British colonies in the Far East and the West Indies as well as those in Africa became independent in the 15 years that followed Suez, Britain's last effort to retain power in Africa through the barrel of the gun.

Sierra Leone and Tanganyika got their independence in 1961, Uganda in 1962, Zanzibar (later being enfolded in Tanganyika to form Tanzania) and Kenya in 1963, Nyasaland (as Malawi) and Northern Rhodesia (as Zambia) in 1964, Gambia in 1965, Bechuanaland (as Botswana) and Basutoland (as Lesotho) in 1966, Mauritius and Swaziland in 1968.

Macmillan was able to cut the British colonies loose without much trouble not only because the Empire had lost its value to Britain but also because Britons had lost interest in the Empire. A confidential study commissioned by his government in 1957 had found that Britain would suffer no serious loss through giving up its colonies.[1] On the contrary, Britain, in trying to maintain its old Commonwealth markets, was losing out in other world markets and especially in the growing European markets, where France was cashing in. Economically, the Empire/Commonwealth was becoming less valuable to Britain, and the old imperial preference agreements would soon be overtaken by the advantages of European Common Market membership. No British jobs were lost because of decolonisation, no factories closed, no business sacrificed.

The loss of the British colonies was mourned only by the old guard of Conservatism, represented by ageing bureaucrats, a furiously protesting League of Empire Loyalists, and right-wing parliamentarians.

The Empire had lost its importance not only in Whitehall but also in the Main Streets of the counties. The British public, which had been enchanted by the Livingstonian epic, which had been thrilled by Stanley's explorations, which had cheered Victoria as monarch of the greatest empire in history, which had mourned the death of Gordon as of a favourite son, which had celebrated the relief of Mafeking with parties in the streets, which had felt its national rhythm in the poems of Kipling, was now less interested in this sort of thing than in the latest fashions in clothes, music and hairstyles.

Since the Empire was now unnecessary there was no longer any need for the kind of propaganda that had whipped public emotions into the febrile froth of the Victorian heyday. Besides, the public had other interests and outlets now. Who would want to watch military parades and listen to brass bands in the parks and hear patriotic speeches at the monuments when they could be transported by *Coronation Street* on the telly?

Macmillan cleverly exploited the rising standards of living in Britain to gain public acceptance of the divesture of the colonies, most of which to the average Briton were now little more than names, in some cases not even that. Macmillan could retain power in the 1959 election on the strength of constant assurances to the voters that 'You've never had it so good'. They believed him, the man promoted by the Tories as Supermac, as they believed that granting independence to the colonies was the right thing to do. Soon the past pride in the glories of empire would be largely replaced by a growing sense of guilt, even of shame at what the Empire had done to other peoples' systems, beliefs and customs in the name of imposing a supposedly higher civilisation. And that would be followed by a lessening of respect for authority, a rise of antagonism against 'the establishment', and the emergence of the social rebel as hero.

Against all these factors, the whites who would not or could not leave Africa were impotent. They had become redundant to the needs of modern Britain; an embarrassment, even. Those among them who treasured the links with home were left waving sadly from the beach as Britannia sailed remorselessly away into the colonial sunset. The others shrugged their shoulders and strengthened their stockades against the natives.

★ ★ ★ ★

The French, like the British, had never settled in large numbers in tropical Africa, and after the North African territories had gained independence only relatively small pockets of French citizens had remained in the continent and its associated islands. Almost all the whites left behind by the European withdrawal were in former British territories, and most of the others remaining in Africa were in the Portuguese territories.

Preoccupied with their own 'Economic Miracle' of the fifties and sixties, the French had been able to cut loose their sub-Saharan colonies with as little trauma as the newly prosperous British. And, again like the British, they begrudged any colonial expenditure that might better be diverted to keeping France in step with the post-war technological revolution.

The French withdrawal from tropical Africa was comprehensive and synchronous. The process had begun at the Brazzaville conference of 1944, which had led to the 1946 constitution providing for direct representation of the African territories in the French parliament as well as in the quasi-federal and local authorities of French West and French Equatorial Africa. In 1956 the parliament had passed the *Loi Cadre*, offering responsible government to individual territories rather than federations.

Two years later De Gaulle's new constitution had abolished the concept of the indivisibility of France and its overseas territories and replaced the French Union with the French Community, in which member states could opt for internal self-government but with Paris retaining control of foreign affairs, defence and economic policy. When the issue was put to a referendum in 1958 all the African territories except Guinea chose independence within the Community rather than outside it. Guinea thus automatically became independent immediately. All but one of the others – Cameroon, Togo, Mali, Senegal, Madagascar, Dahomey (later Benin), Niger, Upper Volta (later Burkina Faso), Ivory Coast, Chad, the Central African Republic (formerly Oubangui Chari), Congo (Brazzaville), Gabon and Mauretania – attained formal independence in 1960, and now with no French control over their affairs. The exception was Algeria, which for a while was still regarded as part of France and had therefore to suffer another two years of bloody turmoil.

Most of the former French territories retained close economic and other ties with France. The arrangements meant that in general the parting was no great loss to France and was unmourned except by a minority of imperialists in the metropole and the relative handful of Europeans living in the newly independent states.

★ ★ ★ ★

The Belgians were slower than the British and French to perceive the inevitability of African independence, but when they at last agreed to grant it to their Congo its accession was both fast and furious, marked by bloodshed more than celebration.

The territory was an unnatural creation, like most of the European colonies, but made more freakish by its huge size, pulling together in unwilling union numbers of culturally different peoples who over the centuries had dispersed themselves more or less harmoniously across the great basin of the river from which the country got its name.

After the government had taken over the Congo from Leopold, the indigenous people had been given only indirect representation, through white civil servants and missionaries, on a consultative body. Later elected councils were allowed in the main urban areas.

Complacency was shattered in January 1959 when Bakongo in the Belgian territory grew envious of the independence coming to the Bakongo across the river in the French Congo. Some two hundred people were killed when police dispersed a demonstration by a supposed cultural organisation led by Joseph Kasavubu. Brussels panicked and decided to grant independence in only six months.

There was, however, no indigenous structure capable of taking over governance, for Africans had deliberately been confined to the lower ranks of the civil service and armed forces. Brussels decided to leave the old colonial framework of administration in place until the indigenous people were able to take it over. Belgians would continue to run the civil service and armed forces for the time being. To give the administration an indigenous façade, however, Africans were appointed to the cabinet. The obvious candidates were formerly low-ranked civil servants who had been elected to parliament.

It was more than the army NCOs could stand to see clerks jumped up to ministerial status with big salaries and flashy cars while they remained stuck where they were, bullied by a hated Belgian commanding officer. Five days after the proclamation of independence on 30 June 1960, the armed forces mutinied. Kasavubu, now president, and Patrice Lumumba, the leftist prime minister, responded by making some of the NCOs officers and appointing one of the three sergeants-major, Joseph-Desire Mobutu, as commanding officer of the army with the rank of colonel. The mutiny spread, however, and when Belgian civilians were attacked and white women raped the Belgians, including the white army officers, began to flee the country. Brussels despatched Belgian troops to protect its nationals, and Belgian warships bombarded mutineers in Matadi port.

In the uproar, the copper-rich provinces of Katanga (now Shaba) and South Kasai attempted to secede, with the connivance of Belgian commercial interests. Lumumba and Kasavubu called for help from the United Nations. Then Kasavubu tried to dismiss Lumumba and Mobutu intervened, setting up a government of academics. Lumumba and his followers set up a rival government in Stanleyville, but Lumumba was captured, ostensibly by Mobutu's troops but actually by Belgian officials. Soon afterwards he was murdered in Katanga with the connivance of the Belgian officials if not at their own hands.

According to evidence presented to a United States Senate select committee, Lumumba was killed at the instigation of the CIA, which feared that he would create 'another Cuba' in the Congo. President Eisenhower was alleged to have approved the assassination. The British government is said to have backed the decision. A Belgian parliamentary inquiry in 2001 implicated Belgian government ministers in the killing, and Brussels subsequently issued a formal apology.

In his brief time of prominence Lumumba had inspired Africanists and left-wingers internationally, and his death caused widespread anger. It helped persuade the Security Council to take a tough stance in support of Congolese unity and against the Katanga secessionists led by Moise Tshombe.

With 15 000 'black gendarmes' under his command, supported by a strong body of French, Belgian, Rhodesian and South African mercenaries, Tshombe had formidable forces, which soon clashed with the peacekeeping forces deployed by the UN. The UN secretary-general, Dag Hammarskjold, flew to negotiate with Tshombe but was killed when his plane crashed on the Northern Rhodesian border in mysterious circumstances.

The Congo debacle continued on its tortuous and tortured path for a few more years. Tshombe was defeated and exiled. The Lumumbists and the Leopoldville government were uneasily reconciled, then began fighting again. Tshombe returned from exile, was appointed prime minister and reassembled his mercenaries. With weaponry provided by the United States, they pushed back the Lumumbist forces. In November 1964 the Lumumbists attempted to halt the advance by taking Europeans in Stanleyville hostage, then began executing them as the advance continued. Belgian paratroopers were dropped into the city from American planes to save the Europeans. They encountered scenes of blood-soaked horror, of whites hacked, tortured and shot.

The accounts of the slaughter and rape of Europeans, even nuns, in the Congo sent shock through white communities elsewhere in Africa, and hardened the resolve of those in the south to resist majority rule.

At the same time, the images of whites on the run from the blacks they had long ruled were deeply imprinted in the minds of Africans across the continent, adding to the perceptions that had emerged from Kenya and Algeria of whites being on the defensive. There was not much left now of the awe with which the white bwana had been regarded in imperialism's purple times.

The continuing rivalry between Kasavubu and Tshombe prompted Mobutu to seize power in a coup in November 1965. He went on to consolidate his power to the point of absolute dictatorship, ruling – and ruining – the country for more than three decades. Besides trading and continuing to run the copper mines that were the mainstay of the country's economy, the Europeans played no further role other than in the form of the mercenaries, who took part in a number of actions before the last of them were expelled in 1967.

CHAPTER 35

THE FRONT LINE

Independence rolling southward through Africa came to a halt at the end of the sixties at the white stronghold in the continent's lower quarter. Here in their fastness those whites who still held domination made their stand against black rule.

Kenya and Algeria were gone but they had been distant places, separate struggles. Now the white communities were side by side, sharing common borders and an unbroken frontier, running from sea to sea.* In the centre was Rhodesia. On the flanks were the Portuguese possessions, Mozambique on the right and Angola on the left. In the rear was South Africa, the economic and military giant (relatively speaking, of course), and its hostage-by-mandate, South West Africa.

Within that frontier were slightly more than four million white people, fewer than the continent-wide total of a decade earlier largely because the massive outflow from Algeria had not been fully offset by the immigration to South Africa and Rhodesia and by population growth. Though hugely outnumbered by the indigenous people, the whites held sway by virtue of strong police forces and small but efficient standing armies backed, in South Africa and Rhodesia, by well-trained civilian reserves. They saw more reason to resist black empowerment than had the colonial powers. And they had substantial means with which to do it, the countries of the white fortress possessing the greatest concentration of wealth and skills in the continent.

The economy of South Africa alone was by any measure greater than those of the rest of the continent combined. It had by far the largest manufacturing, mining and agricultural output, the biggest gross national product, the biggest stock exchange, the busiest ports, the biggest merchant navy, the largest national airline. It had more railways and tarred roads, more telephones and motor vehicles, than the rest of Africa. It had the most universities and was far more advanced in medical care and research, in electronic and nuclear technology, in management skills.

Rhodesia and South West Africa were also relatively well endowed with these assets. Angola and Mozambique, though lagging behind the other white communities, were nevertheless better equipped with expertise and capital than many of the

---

*Elsewhere on the main continent Europeans were still dominant only in Portugal's other colony, Portuguese Guinea (later Guinea Bissau) on Africa's Bulge; in the little French territory of Djibouti on the Red Sea; and in the equally small Spanish enclaves of Ceuta and Melilla in Morocco. Of the Indian Ocean islands, only in the Seychelles might whites be said to be dominant.

black states.

The white fortress was threatened not only from outside, however, but also from within. For all their resources, the whites had been unable to prevent black resistance to their rule from rising in their midst, most aggressively in the Portuguese territories.

Political opposition to Portuguese rule had become organised in Angola in 1957 with the formation in Luanda of the *Movimento Popular de Libertacao de Angola* (MPLA), led first by Mario Pinto de Andrade and then by Agostinho Neto. The first shots had been fired in March 1961, when a group led by Holden Roberto rebelled in the northern Uige region, killing about seven hundred whites. Government troops had killed an estimated twenty thousand blacks in quelling the insurrection.

The next year, Holden Roberto had formed the *Frente Nacional de Libertacao de Angola* (FNLA) and declared it the provisional government of an Angolan republic. A third movement, the *Uniao Nacional para a Independencia Total de Angola* (UNITA), had been formed in 1963 when one of Roberto's lieutenants, Jonas Savimbi, had broken away.

In Portuguese Guinea the *Partido Africano da Independencia da Guine e Cabo Verde* (PAIGC) of Amilcar Cabral and Aristides Pereira had begun armed resistance in 1962.

Mozambican dissidents had found a sanctuary in newly independent Tanganyika and formed the *Frente de Libertacao de Mocambique* (Frelimo), in 1962, with Eduardo Mondlane as leader. Two years later 250 well-armed Frelimo insurgents trained in Algeria infiltrated Mozambique from Tanzania and opened their armed struggle.

The era of the Kalashnikov had begun. The Russian semi-automatic assault rifle formally known as the AK47 was to change the nature of African politics after its emergence in 1951. Named after its inventor, the Kalashnikov was simple in design, cheap to make and tough, virtually trouble-free even after atrocious mishandling. It was the ideal weapon for guerilla warfare, especially in the bush. Since the Soviet Union and its satellite states were happy to supply the gun and its ammunition at low cost to any nationalist movement not aligned to the West, the AK became the basic instrument of insurgency.

The AK dramatically lessened the advantage of superior firepower that for centuries had enabled the Europeans to conquer and dominate large African communities. Now the Africans could shoot back. Now they had plentiful supplies of a weapon that could double as a rifle or a light machine-gun and was as good in its class as anything possessed by their white overlords. The AK was the equaliser. The days of black spearmen charging against the white man's Maxims were over. And no longer would Africans have to fight with obsolete guns against whites armed with the latest and best.

The guerillas naturally used hit-and-run tactics, waging a war of attrition rather than set-piece battles. Armour and aircraft were of limited value against guerillas operating elusively in bush or rough terrain. It was a matter of extending and wearing down the enemy, forcing him to stretch his manpower and supplies, hopefully to a point where he would consider the purpose not worth the cost, and negotiate terms or quit the contest – which is more or less what happened in the end in the Portuguese colonies and Rhodesia.

The insurgents' chief handicaps were logistical. They could live largely off the land, fed by sympathetic or intimidated villagers, but, lacking vehicles or pack animals, they had to carry all their weapons and supplies on their backs. Their munitions were brought in on long and hazardous marches from bases in neighbouring countries, and when these supplies ran out they had to walk back to get more. Many of them never made it back through the gauntlet of government security forces possessing helicopters, spotter and ground-strafing aircraft and bombers and, on the ground, armoured vehicles, motor-cycles, horses and tracker dogs. Against these, the guerillas' losses were proportionately high, for they had no means of evacuating their wounded.

Thanks to the Soviets and the Chinese, the insurgents had a few other weapons besides the AK. They had no artillery – a weapon of limited use in guerilla warfare – other than a few mortars. But they did have the rocket-propelled grenade (RPG), which, fired from the shoulder, could stop a tank. Later the insurgents acquired shoulder-fired ground-to-air missiles. And always they had land mines, the liberal use of which killed or maimed far more civilians than combatants.

A major factor in the rise of the freedom struggles was the post-war emergence of the Soviet Union and China as major powers able and willing to challenge the former colonial powers of Europe. For the first time, Africans seeking to throw off colonialism were able to get foreign assistance, both financially and in the form of weapons and military advisers.

External assistance came also from newly-independent African states able to provide safe bases for liberation movements, an advantage denied to any resistance movement that might have been formed while all of Africa was under European colonial control. Thus the Mau Mau, besides being confined mainly to only one ethnic group, had never had the advantage of either the AK or of foreign sanctuaries. The Algerian insurgents were more successful because they had modern guns and were able to operate from bases in Tunisia and Morocco.

In the early years of the struggle against Portuguese rule, Frelimo operated from bases in Tanzania, the MPLA from Congo (Brazzaville), and the FNLA from Zaire. Algeria, and later Libya, provided military training and acted as conduits for the supply of Soviet-made weaponry and for the Chinese imitations that also became available as China involved itself in the African liberation struggle in competition with the Soviets.

A third source of external assistance was the new international organisations. Through the United Nations, the Organisation of African Unity and the Non-Aligned Movement, the liberation movements received encouragement, advice and coordinated political support, especially highly effective propaganda.

It was a situation tailor-made for Moscow's expansionist ambitions. The Soviets found Africa wide open to new ideologies and alliances in the vacuum left by the colonial withdrawal. Whatever benefits colonialism might have brought, it had been enforced and therefore resented, even after it had ended. At independence the tendency was to turn away from it and from its trappings, a major one of which was capitalism. Socialism, dangled enticingly by Soviet propagandists, was an attractive alternative to Africans left by colonialism to run poor and largely undeveloped states. The colonialists had indeed brought capitalism to their conquered territories, but for themselves rather than for their subjects; little or no effort had been made to promote it as ideology or to encourage its application by the indigenous peoples.

When communism arose as an option at independence it had an attractive appearance. Not only did it offer a radical departure from colonialist capitalism but it seemed to offer the means to redress the resultant inequalities and hardships.

Moscow was happy to encourage any shift to the left. Though hard-pressed to find the wherewithal to improve the lot of its own people, the Kremlin saw advantage in countering the Western power, which it did in part by arming and training the emerging African states' armies. Moscow also opened embassies and consulates in African capitals to promote Marxist policies and systems, and to lure the host countries from the Western into the Soviet ambit.

After the Soviets had been denied an air base in Cyrenaica, another window in Africa had been opened by the invasion of the Suez Canal in 1956 and Nasser's turn towards the Soviets for aid in fostering Egypt's sovereignty and economy. Moscow's influence poured unremittingly through that window thereafter, and spread. Less than two decades after the advent of African independence, communist or socialist regimes had emerged in the Congo, Guinea, Mali, Benin, Madagascar, Tanzania and other states.

Both the MPLA in Angola and Frelimo in Mozambique embraced communism early in their existence. Generously supplied with Soviet and Chinese weaponry, and later with Soviet Bloc military advisers, the two movements forced the Portuguese on the defensive in their respective territories.

Their successes, seeming to thrust Red pincers towards the white south, worried Washington and London, which still attached strategic importance to the Cape sea route and to the minerals of the hinterland. About sixty per cent of Europe's oil supplies and as much as twenty-five per cent of its imported food were passing round the Cape, together with about twenty per cent of America's oil imports. The importance attached by Moscow to the minerals was reflected as late as 1977 when the then Soviet leader, Leonid Brezhnev, expressed his government's ambition to acquire control of 'the two great treasure houses of the world': the fuel of the Middle East and the minerals of southern Africa.

The Western powers, and America in particular, were caught somewhat in the middle in the new situation. They discouraged military solutions to local conflicts and sought political ones, if possible through bilateral negotiation, otherwise through the UN. Moscow, however, was not averse to backing conflict in Africa as a means of ideological proselytisation. As the dominant Western power, Washington had spurred the decolonisation process quietly from the rear. But Moscow's extension of the Cold War into Africa forced the US to take a more forward role. Hence the formation of a Bureau of African Affairs in the State Department in 1957, and the indirect involvement in the Congo debacle in 1960.

While it was politically damaging for the US and the other Western powers to be seen to be supporting white racism in the sub-continent, they were reluctant to undermine the white fortress in southern Africa when it was providing a bastion against Soviet expansionism. Thus they were less enthusiastic than they might otherwise have been about supporting coercive action in the UN against apartheid or against the colonialism of Portugal, a fellow member of Nato (and which, incidentally, used Nato weapons against the Mozambican and Angolan insurgents).

The non-mandatory ban on arms sales to South Africa that was imposed by the General Assembly in 1963 was ignored in various degrees by the Western powers. France had earlier become a major arms supplier with the delivery of helicopters in 1961. Before being forced to lower the boom (but even then not all the way) by the mandatory Security Council embargo of 1977, it provided jet fighters, armoured cars, submarines and other armaments.

South Africa, which had always been the major economic power in Africa, was now becoming also the military power, its strength matched only by Egypt.* But Egypt was dependent on Soviet weaponry, and lacked the arms-production capacity that South Africa was rapidly developing in anticipation of, and later in response to, the arms embargoes. These resources would eventually give apartheid South Africa a self-sufficiency and efficiency that in the end, when the showdown came in Angola, could be countered only by enormous supplies of modern Soviet armaments, by large numbers of Soviet military advisers, and by a copious insertion of Cuban soldiers and airmen into the conflict.

Whatever incentives the South African government might have had to abandon apartheid were offset in the early sixties by economic boom. Foreign investors, seemingly seeing the apartheid state as impregnable, poured capital into the country regardless of UN and other strictures. Thus the economy grew at more than seven per cent between 1963 and 1965. There was something of a boom even in trade with black African states, imports from Africa rising almost fifty per cent and exports to Africa by more than that.

★ ★ ★ ★

The insurgency in the Portuguese colonies was slightly puzzling to those in Lisbon who believed in the equity of a policy that offered equal rights to Africans who were deemed to have reached a suitably civilised state. They overlooked the fact that most of the African people did not regard themselves as Portuguese even after 500 years of Portuguese presence and a century of formal efforts to stamp out indigenous culture and replace it with a Portuguese one. Only a small proportion of the indigenous population had achieved *assimilado* status – by 1950 according to the census of that year, only 0,75 per cent of those in Angola and only 0,08 per cent of those in Mozambique, and ten years later the number was estimated at no more than one per cent in any of the territories.

---

*South Africa's defence expenditure increased from 7 per cent of the national budget in 1959 to 17 per cent in 1966. The armed forces grew from 11 500 men in 1960 to 42 000 in 1967 – mostly conscripts.

Proponents of the policy argued that many more were eligible for *assimilado* status but had not applied for it; also that a large proportion of the indigenous population was well on the way to achieving it, having reached the first stage of detribalisation.

Since the policy of assimilation was overshadowed by one of exploitation, few of the Africans perceived much benefit to themselves. So poor were the job opportunities in Angola and Mozambique that some two million Africans born in these territories lived and worked more or less permanently in other countries at the time the insurgency began.[1]

Lisbon was unable to countenance parting with the African colonies for a number of reasons: the patriotic one of the international status derived from their possession, the sentimental one of the long presence in Africa, and the economic one of Portuguese dependence on the territories. Not only did Portugal's industries rely on the colonies for vital raw materials but, from the 1940s, the colonies had begun showing surpluses that compensated for deficits in the metropolitan budgets. Marcello Caetano, successor to Antonio Salazar as dictator of Portugal, believed that 'without Africa we would be a small nation; with Africa we are a big power'. But as the country with the lowest per capita income and the lowest literacy rate in Western Europe, Portugal could afford neither to develop nor abandon the African possessions. For all these reasons the insurgency was seen in official quarters in Lisbon not as a struggle for the right of freedom but as treasonous rebellion, and was dealt with accordingly.

Insurrection continued to grow nonetheless. By 1967 the efforts to stamp out the insurgency in Africa were consuming nearly half of Portugal's national budget, with 130 000 troops in the field (60 000 in Mozambique, 50 000 in Angola and 20 000 in Guinea). By 1970 the deployment had risen to 150 000 troops, 60 000 of them in Angola.

Even while fighting against the common enemy of Portugal, the Angolan liberation movements were exhibiting the rivalry that was to inflict far more damage on their country in two decades than Portuguese colonialism had in five centuries. Not only did the movements challenge one another for power, but their members fought for it within their own ranks. As was so often the case with African liberation struggles, the ideal of freedom very quickly gave way to the ideal of power, even before either had been won.

Portugal was handicapped in combating the rebellions in Africa by the insurgents' use of neighbouring territories as safe bases. Lisbon refrained from attacking these bases for fear of aggravating the growing disapproval of its African wars among the Western powers. Cross-border attacks would in addition give more material to the OAU and the Afro-Asian bloc at the UN for their vocal support of the liberation movements. Lisbon was able, however, to discourage Zambia by threatening to close the Benguela railway to the copper exports that were the mainstay of Zambia's economy.

Another impediment was the attitude of the conscripts who made up most of the Portuguese army, serving four-year terms. Many were reluctant to fight for a cause

– African colonialism – that they did not consider worth risking their lives for. The lower levels of Portuguese society from which the cannon fodder was drawn for the African wars did not fully share the historic pride and economic interest of the upper classes, notably the 'great families' that dominated those classes and Portuguese politics.

Even the Portuguese settlers were in large part reluctant to fight for their stake in the colonies despite their numbers having grown by 1974 to about 335 000 in Angola and 200 000 in Mozambique. Many of them had taken the opportunity of government assistance to go to Africa with the intention of making some money and then getting back to Portugal as soon as possible. Their hearts were never in Africa.

To some extent this drawback was countered by the recruitment of large numbers of Africans into the Portuguese forces. In Mozambique they comprised about sixty per cent of the forces, and in Angola about forty per cent. Blacks joined the Portuguese forces for much the same reasons as they had always enlisted in the white man's armies everywhere in Africa, mainly because it offered employment in a job-scarce society, or in response to manipulation of tribal rivalries by the ruling whites.[*]

For all their difficulties, the Portuguese after a decade of fighting insurrection were able to claim that they had frustrated it in Mozambique and Guinea and might even crush it in Angola. They would soon discover, however, that the African freedom struggles were not to be decided on the battlefield but behind the lines, in the ability of the whites to sustain the will and the means to keep on fighting for supremacy.

★ ★ ★ ★

In the sixties, in a world now largely cleared of colonialism and overt foreign domination, the continuing white supremacy in southern Africa stood out like the proverbial sore thumb – stark, ugly and infuriating.

With internal dissent still firmly suppressed in South Africa, South West Africa, Rhodesia and the Portuguese territories, international organisations became the channels of the outrage, the major instruments of resistance to white supremacy. Chief among them was the United Nations, now the megaphone of the aggrieved, of the dispossessed and of the powerless.

Opposition to white hegemony became something of a growth industry in the UN. It was nothing less than an obsession with the Afro-Asian bloc, taking precedence over the economic and political woes that progressively beset the Afri-

---

[*]There has hardly been a war waged by the whites in Africa in which they were not able to recruit large numbers of black soldiers to their forces. Indigenous soldiers were used from the beginning of European hegemony. Not even the struggles for freedom from white domination had unanimous indigenous support; Rhodesia and even apartheid South Africa were also able to make extensive use of black volunteers to fight insurgency. For many Africans, the immediate imperative of betterment, if not of survival itself, was more important than the broader ideals of freedom. It was often left to those fortunate enough to have some education and income to begin resistance.

can states after independence. Through more than fifty coups, through civil wars, through spreading dictatorship and one-party rule, through economic regression across the continent, the cause of freedom from white domination remained the prime issue with the Africans in the world body.

Even more widely, white racism in southern Africa became a coconut shy around the world for former colonial subjects appreciative of a target against which to vent lingering resentment at their own past humiliation by the white people from Europe. Apartheid was an affront to all people of colour, all those still smarting from past European domination. Among them had developed an informal brotherhood, growing not only from the commonality of dark complexion but also from the shared experience of hegemony and exploitation. Every act of apartheid was an express insult not only to blacks in South Africa but to every African, and indeed to every Indian, Arab, Indonesian, Chinese and Polynesian, to everyone who was not of the pale Caucasian breed.

The antagonism of the Western nations to residual white supremacy in Africa was different to that of the once-colonised. They shared a common concept of morality, but among the former the ethos was the righteousness of the reformed, whereas among the latter it was the bitterness of the scarred.

Both, however, viewed white racism in southern Africa differently from white racism elsewhere. No outrage was voiced in the UN at the fact that in the United States, for instance, negroes were still being hanged from trees by white lynch mobs in the fifties and sixties. According to one account, 21 black civil rights activists were murdered in the American south between 1961 and 1965 without any white perpetrator being punished – or any protest being voiced in the UN.[2] It went without remark in the UN that in Australia thousands of Aboriginal children were torn from their families between the fifties and seventies and placed in the care of whites in an exercise that might be called benevolent genocide since it was aimed at having the indigenous people die out as a definable ethnic group.

The principles of the UN charter were not deemed relevant to the plight of indigenous peoples who had been consigned to the social shadows in other countries occupied by Europeans, from Auckland to Santiago, from Hudson Bay to Tierra del Fuego. There was no place on UN agendas for any of this dispossession and exploitation, even less for the caste discrimination and oppression in India.

Southern Africa, however, was a different matter, for there the indigenous peoples remained in the majority and there the minority's racism was defined, institutionalised and defended, and therefore was especially unacceptable and especially targetable. Apartheid in South Africa, being the ultimate refinement of racism, was particularly odious. Besides, it was a safe target – there was no political risk in attacking apartheid, for it had no friends to offend; the world was unanimous in damning it, and even the Western powers could safely do so as long as they covertly protected their strategic interests.

Their condemnation, however, rang hollow against their use of the veto in the Security Council to protect their South African interests. Among these were not only the strategic concerns but commercial ones as well. Western nations, notably Britain, the United States and Germany, fostered trade with South Africa, where apartheid's cheap labour helped provide excellent returns on investments. The British between 1960 and 1967 got bigger returns from their capital investment in South Africa than from any other country. American investment rose from R459-million in 1959 to R741-million by 1969. The following year the South African investments of 260 American companies were reported by the *Wall Street Journal* to be their most profitable outside the US itself. The Germans pushed up their investment from R70-million in 1965 to more than R1 000-million in 1970.

Japanese investment increased almost as much, from R180-million in 1967 to more than R1 000-million in 1973. Pretoria showed its appreciation by excepting Japanese citizens from the apartheid restrictions on 'Asiatics' and treating them as honorary whites in South Africa. Under the criteria ruthlessly applied to South Africans by the Race Classification Board, the Japanese would have been classified as non-whites and therefore ineligible for admission to white society. But even apartheid's steely gauleiters could find room for expediency when perceiving benefit without threat to themselves.

From the ferment over southern Africa there grew in the UN an exceptionally elaborate structure, combining General Assembly committees with a branch of the secretariat devoted almost exclusively to the African freedom struggle. The issue commanded an extraordinary amount of the assembly's time during its four-month-long annual sessions, and much of the time of the standing committees in between. In 1972, for example, 19 of the 51 sessions of the assembly's Special Political Committee were devoted to the situation in South Africa. In various forms it arose perennially in the Security Council. Though blocked by Western vetoes from effective action there, the Afro-Asians pursued their cause with single-mindedness and great skill in the rest of the world body, probing and exploiting every weakness.

By the mid-sixties the opponents of white supremacy had built up in the UN a formidable body of institutions, declarations and resolutions. Key instruments included the Convention on the Elimination of Racial Discrimination and the Declaration on the Granting of Independence to Colonial Countries and Peoples. A Special Committee on Apartheid had been created in 1962 solely to keep tabs on the infamous policy and recommend action against it. It was fed with information and ammunition by a Unit on Apartheid whose shrewd and industrious director, an Indian, had never been to South Africa yet knew more about its politics than most South Africans.

The UN became an important lobbying ground for the African liberation movements. Some, principally the ANC and PAC of South Africa, appointed full-time representatives at the world body. Given semi-official accreditation by the UN, and subsidised by Soviet and other benefactors, the representatives of the ANC and PAC assiduously worked the committee rooms, corridors, lounges, dining halls and cocktail parties of the UN. They were active participants in the deliberations of the UN bodies concerned with their causes, and they had open admission to the

274

seats reserved for non-participating delegates in the General Assembly and Security Council chambers.

Foiled in the Security Council by Western power vetoes, the Afro-Asians concentrated their efforts in the General Assembly and its committees. In 1962 they got together enough votes to have the Assembly ask member states to implement a diplomatic and trade boycott of South Africa and to bar its ships and aircraft. The next year they did achieve success in the Security Council with an arms embargo, but only a non-mandatory one.

Both the Smuts and the National Party governments tried to block UN intervention in South Africa on the grounds that it contravened the fundamental Charter provision barring interference in the internal affairs of member states. Their protests were ignored, legalities being of less concern to the Afro-Asians than practicalities. In 1955 South Africa withdrew from the UN Educational, Scientific and Cultural Organisation (UNESCO) in protest against its endless sniping at apartheid. The next year Verwoerd's government came close to pulling out of the UN altogether, and for a while it maintained what the aggressive foreign minister, Eric Louw, called a token representation in the world body.

In the end, however, it was decided to continue membership. Louw's successor, Hilgard Muller, explained that the UN, for all the hostility, remained 'the best, the largest international forum where we can state our case in a positive and business-like way'. This was an optimistic view, however, for although the South African delegates were able to speak in the General Assembly and its committees they were resentfully received there. When Muller exercised his right to address the General Assembly itself in 1969, most of the other delegations pointedly boycotted the meeting, leaving Muller addressing a largely empty chamber.

★ ★ ★ ★

In the vast, vaulted General Assembly chamber, delegations cast their votes by pressing one of three buttons at their desks: green for yes, red for no, yellow for abstain. Their votes are reflected in lights of the same colour opposite their country's names on large display boards flanking the podium. No delegation followed the voting with closer attention than Pretoria's during the apartheid era, for the voting was a measure of standing and support in the world. South Africa was the subject of more resolutions than any other state. By 1974 the South African delegation had grown used to seeing the green lights sweep across the voting boards on motions of condemnation, the reds and yellows as sparse as baubles on an orphanage Christmas tree.

One issue focused their attention more than all others: the annual challenge to the credentials of Pretoria's delegation. Each delegation's credentials were examined in committee each year, and in most cases automatically approved. But those of the South African delegation had come to be challenged by the Afro-Asians on the grounds that it was not representative of all of the people of South Africa, only of the white minority. In response, Pretoria had by 1974 included a number of blacks among its delegation but to no good effect, for they were dismissed as Uncle Toms, South African style.

In the early seventies the credentials committee had routinely rejected the South African credentials but had always been overruled in the Assembly by Western or otherwise sympathetic presidents upholding the view of UN legal counsel that the rejection was unconstitutional in terms of the UN charter. In 1974, however, it was Africa's turn to provide the assembly president, and the man chosen was Abdelaziz Bouteflika, Algeria's foreign minister (later to be that country's president). Ignoring both legal opinion and the South Africans' protests, Bouteflika ruled the credentials challenge effective. The ruling set off unprecedented jubilation on the Assembly floor, and apartheid's delegates filed silently out of the chamber for the last time. South Africa's seats would remain empty and its voting lights dead until Nelson Mandela's democratic government took office 20 years later.

Whether the UN was damaged more by apartheid South Africa's membership than by the flouting of the charter in its exclusion from the General Assembly was a talking point of the time. Apartheid's defenders had long accused the UN of selective morality in focusing on Pretoria's racial policies while ignoring practices among other member states that were as heinous if not more so in the trampling of human rights and the wholesale killing of dissidents. Privately, if not often publicly, Pretoria's delegates argued that the crimes of apartheid were minor in scale, if not in evil, compared with those committed behind the Iron Curtain. They asked why the campaign against apartheid took up so much of the UN's time and resources when the world body essentially ignored the repression and atrocities in the Soviet Union, China and the Latin American and African dictatorships. Why, they asked, was the oppression of blacks by whites considered a greater crime than the oppression of blacks by blacks, which was not uncommon in Africa?

Certainly the obsession in the UN with white supremacy in southern Africa was an extraordinary phenomenon of the time. Part at least of the reason is that for a large proportion of the UN's members, apartheid was emblematic of the whole of white racial discrimination over the centuries. In stamping on present-day apartheid, Africans and Asians were stamping also on European colonialism and the slavery of the Americas. Though these evils had ended, their effects were still painfully felt. Thus the governments of Barbados and Jamaica had no difficulty in joining with the Afro-Asians in devising ways to attack apartheid in preference to castigating the human rights violations of totalitarian communism.

Representivity was South Africa's Achilles heel in the UN, the one area where it could effectively, even if illegally, be attacked in the General Assembly. It did not matter that many of the UN members had no more claim than Pretoria to have democratically elected governments. Moral culpability was a less effective weapon, open to the charge of double standards – not that that was often more than a selective consideration in the UN. Some of Pretoria's accusers had more blood on their hands than apartheid's executives did.

A year before Pretoria's ousting from the General Assembly, the military coup in Chile had seen opponents of the junta herded in droves into the national stadium to await execution or torture. Over the next 17 years, General August Pinochet's regime murdered some four thousand people, tortured an estimated fifty thousand, and imprisoned or exiled hundreds of thousands – a record as appalling statistically as apartheid's. Yet the Pinochet regime was never subjected to the same castigation in the UN as Pretoria, quite deservedly, experienced.

Neither did the UN condemn the Argentinian dictatorship that between 1976 and 1983 killed thousands of political dissidents (accounts vary from nine thousand to thirty thousand) and tortured thousands of others.* The Peruvian regime, which in two decades from 1980 caused the 'disappearance' of more than sixty-nine thousand citizens, likewise escaped serious censure in the UN. Not even the death of some two million Cambodians from 1975 to 1979 in Pol Pot's 'killing fields' regime was as energetically castigated as apartheid's evils.

Bouteflika's judgment was a significant marker of the passage of the UN from being a body designed by the West to serve its concepts of democracy and world order (but Western interests above all) to a body dominated by the Afro-Asian and Soviet blocs and serving those blocs' visions and concerns, restricted only by the Western vetoes in the Security Council.

After South Africa's exclusion from the General Assembly, neither the ANC nor PAC could in terms of the charter be invited to take the South African seats, but they increased the scope and level of their activities in the world body. The apartheid state for its part, though barred from the General Assembly and its committees, was still entitled to retain its UN membership, and resolved to do so rather than resign in dudgeon. Afro-Asian efforts in the Security Council to kick the Pretoria government out of the UN altogether were blocked by the Western powers. Pretoria reduced its contribution to the UN budget, refusing to pay for facilities it had been denied in the General Assembly, but its permanent representative and his staff continued to use all the other UN amenities and facilities, including occasional addresses to the Security Council when they could wangle an invitation from one of the Western permanent members.

A major factor in Pretoria's decision to hang on to its UN membership was the fear that withdrawal might open opportunities for opponents to challenge South Africa's sovereign status and perhaps even to give the South African seat in the General Assembly to a government-in-exile. While any attempt at that would have been complicated by the rivalry between the ANC and PAC, Pretoria did not entirely discount it.

Though not an outcast, South Africa was now a pariah in the organisation it had helped found, its representatives living a half-life on the fringes of the UN. Prior to its exclusion from the General Assembly, South Africa had been expelled from the International Labour Organisation, UNESCO, and a number of other UN subsidiary bodies. The General Assembly expulsion set the seal on white South Africa's exclusion from almost all of formal international life. Its forced departure from the Commonwealth had been followed by its banning from the Tokyo Olympic Games

---

*The Argentinian junta pioneered the technique, later copied by Pretoria's agents in Namibia, of drugging dissidents and then pushing them out of aircraft over the sea.

in 1964.

The government had attempted to regain admission to the Mexico Olympics of 1968 by agreeing to send a mixed-race team – but chosen after separate trials for blacks and whites to obviate their competing against each other in South Africa. That compromise had been rejected, and all South African athletes, black and white, had been forced to watch the Olympics from the distant sidelines until 1992, when the imminent dismantling of apartheid allowed their readmission at the Barcelona games.

After a while not even Australia and New Zealand would play against South Africa's national cricket and rugby teams. A South African rugby team touring New Zealand was fiercely harassed by demonstrators. For a games-loving society, the sporting isolation hurt more than any other.

The Pretoria government's conviction that the way back to international acceptance lay through Africa remained unfulfilled. South Africa had been denied membership of the OAU and squeezed out of the pan-African trade and scientific bodies it had once belonged to. It had been forced to close its consulates in Cairo and Nairobi, and been denied overflying rights for its national airline.

The UN's dealings on white domination in southern Africa often became a confrontation between the Western powers on the one hand and the overlapping groupings of Afro-Asians, Non-Aligned States and the Soviet Bloc on the other. Moscow, however, was wary of strong enforcement powers being given to the UN. Hammarskjold's independent initiatives, especially in the Congo, had strengthened Moscow's desire that the world body and its executive officer be kept under the control of the Big Powers. Moscow preferred a UN that functioned primarily as a political forum, with the secretary-general's powers limited accordingly. In such an environment Moscow could more easily present itself as the champion of the former and present colonial subjects, as it did, for example, in 1962 when Britain was faced with an Afro-Asian move to have Southern Rhodesia declared a non-self-governing territory under Chapter Eleven of the UN Charter, which in effect gives the UN oversight over the interests of the peoples of non-self-governing territories.

A Chapter Eleven classification would have given the General Assembly the right to intervene in the dispute over the country's constitutional disposition. The British argued, however, that Southern Rhodesia had been a self-governing colony since 1923 and therefore couldn't possibly fall under Chapter Eleven. By the same token, they added, Britain could neither intervene in Rhodesia's internal affairs nor change its constitution without the consent of the government in Salisbury. Political advantage usually overrode legality in the Assembly, however, and the Afro-Asians went ahead and had the Assembly declare the territory to be a Chapter Eleven case. The British treated the declaration with much the same sort of contempt that Pretoria had applied to objectionable General Assembly decisions – they ignored it.

Three years later, however, the situation changed when the Rhodesians unilaterally declared independence and the Wilson government decided it now had a legal right to intervene in Rhodesia. Wilson, however, being unwilling or unable to send troops in to put down what he considered a rebellion, could see no option but to ask the Security Council to impose economic sanctions, thereby bringing the issue within the UN's bailiwick after all. True, it was the Security Council's and not the General Assembly's bailiwick, but the upshot was that Rhodesia had formally been made a UN matter in the end.

Unlike the South Africans, the white Rhodesians had no defences within the UN itself against the furious attacks made against them there. They had to rely on an unofficial representative stationed in New York whose office functioned as a listening and lobbying post outside the UN premises. He reported to an equally informal office that was maintained in Washington for the same purposes. Always conscious of their vulnerability, both the Washington and New York representatives kept a low profile, hovering on the fringes of the cocktail party circuit but operating more heavily through expensive lunching and other private lobbying.

CHAPTER 36

PARADISE IMPERILLED

It was a good life the whites lived in Rhodesia, good enough to make them fight for it with passion when it seemed threatened by black majority rule.

What they liked to refer to as 'the Rhodesian way of life' was a rare and satisfying existence made possible by an equable climate, largely beautiful scenery, good farming country, relatively rich mineral resources, plenty of cheap labour, and superb recreational amenities.

There was, of course, poverty among the whites, but proportionally there was less of it than in Europe. Few white families did not possess a car. White households without at least one black servant were rare; in 1951 the average Rhodesian household employed two. Private swimming pools were fairly common in most white suburbs.

The Rhodesians had imported from Britain the cultural elements they prized: posh private schools as well as good government ones (for whites only at first), sports clubs, lending libraries and amateur dramatic and dance companies. They had created an efficient civil service and police force, both largely free of corruption and backed by a healthy exchequer. There was an honest and impartial (for the whites, anyway) judicial system. Crime was a relatively minor problem. There were excellent hospitals and other medical services, and well-ordered municipal governments sustained by sound rates bases. In the cities there were immaculate, colour-splashed parks, modern high-rise buildings on wide streets lined with flowering trees, and department stores offering imported staples and luxuries. An efficient and dependable airline with reassuringly white pilots (few whites had much faith in the ability of a black man to fly an airliner) linked the major cities and the outside world.

With all this, the whites might well feel they had the best of both worlds: the best of Africa and the best of Europe. They tended accordingly to be thankful, if not also proud, to be Rhodesians.

Defining a Rhodesian was problematical, however, since most of those who called themselves Rhodesians had come from elsewhere. Rhodesian-born whites were a minority even among the white minority – in 1969 only 40 per cent of them. The rest had come from other countries (almost twenty-three per cent from Britain, twenty-two per cent from South Africa or South West Africa, and five per cent from Northern Rhodesia or Kenya). More than half of the whites could claim non-Rhodesian citizenship, and many if not most of these held foreign passports,

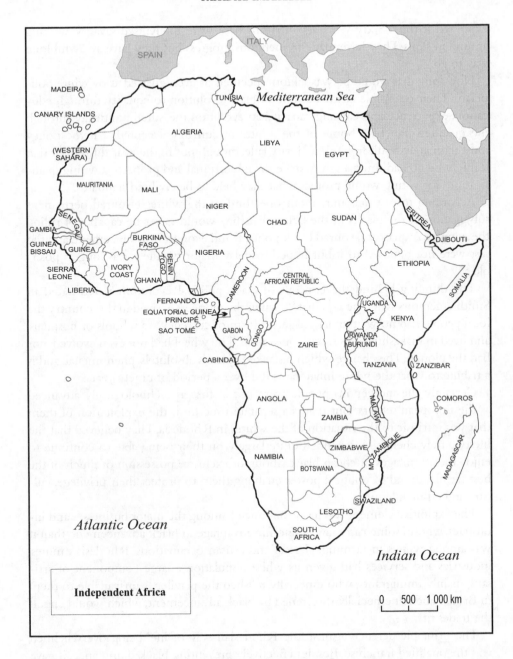

Independent Africa

0   500   1 000 km

suggesting an ambivalent loyalty and identity; and almost one-third of those born outside Rhodesia had been in the country for less than ten years.[1]

Few of the whites, it appears, doubted that their way of life would seriously deteriorate, if not perish, under immediate black rule. This view was to a large extent based on the belief that too few blacks were yet qualified through education and experience to be able to govern effectively if blacks as a whole obtained political power in a democracy. At an election meeting in 1970 Prime Minister Ian Smith expressed it thus: 'Sixty years ago Africans here were uncivilised savages, walking around in skins. They have made tremendous progress but they have an awful long way to go.'

How long that would be was seldom specified or even guessed at by white politicians. Their ostensible ethos was one of black evolution to equality through education, experience and earning capacity, an evolution measured politically through the qualified franchise. Some of the whites presumably accepted that the policy must ultimately result in black majority rule, though not in the near future, but that it might be no bad thing anyway since the educational and property-owning qualifications for voting would protect what they held to be civilised standards.

According to one account, about one-third of the whites favoured permanent subjugation of the blacks in the belief that they would never be capable of ruling the country. A quarter favoured black political and economic advancement, and the rest were not opposed to it but hoped to delay majority rule for as long as possible.[2]

The thinking behind the concept of black political evolution is illustrated in Smith's memoirs when he says that '... when the pioneers arrived in this country the local people had no written language, no form of currency, no schools or hospitals, and lived in makeshift houses with grass roofs. The wheel had not even evolved, nor had the plough. The change which has taken place is absolutely phenomenal, and is a tribute to what the white inhabitants did over a period of ninety years.'[3]

Certainly the indigenous people were not at first as technologically advanced as the European settlers. But that is a separate issue from the exploitation of them that was intrinsic to the situation of the whites in Rhodesia. They believed that the lifestyle they cherished depended quite largely on their being able to continue to enjoy the advantages of cheap black labour, of exclusive possession of much of the best farmland, and of political power enabling them to protect their privilege, culture and ethnic identity.

The exploitive element was less pronounced among the major businesses and industries, who in some cases saw economic advantage in black advancement, than it was among whites in farming, clerical and artisan occupations. Rhodesia's mines, industries and services had given its white population a large component of artisans, mainly immigrants, who especially relished the privileges unavailable to them in Britain and felt especially threatened by black advancement, which would engulf the trades first.

The principle defence against 'the Rhodesian way of life' being overwhelmed was the qualified franchise. Besides effectively preventing black dominance, it gave the barrier a semblance of morality. It made it ostensibly temporary, to be scrapped when the blacks eventually achieved parity in sophistication. In the meantime it allowed for blacks to be paid lower wages than whites and, for many years, barred from the appurtenances of sophistication: white schools, hospitals, shops, bars, restaurants, cinemas and municipal swimming pools.

The system not only defined a racial divide but hampered efforts to reach either way across it, stifling communication. Thus through its muffling of black protest and demand it contributed to the widespread belief, frequently enunciated by Ian Smith, that Rhodesia had 'the happiest blacks in the world'. That it was some of these happiest of blacks who began armed resistance against white rule was nothing more than an aberration to Smith's ruling Rhodesian Front. To the RF the insurgents were communists or Kremlin-inspired opportunists seeking personal gain through political power, and quite unrepresentative of the happy majority. That majority's views and aspirations were seen to be expressed through the traditional chiefs.

The chieftainship structure and traditions had from Rhodes's time been adapted to white governance. The chiefs had been given white pith helmets and other symbols of office, and organised in councils to form an arm of government. To the extent that they administered to the people in their charge they performed an essential and beneficial function. But to those among their charges who were impatient at the slow pace of black political advancement, or who rejected white rule outright, the chiefs became an obstructive and intolerable anachronism, stooges of white domination.

Inevitably the chiefs came into confrontation with that phenomenon of post-colonial Africa, the black politician. Under colonial rule, dissident or politically innovative blacks had seldom been allowed to establish a platform. They had generally been regarded as subversives, threatening the authority of the chiefs who, throughout most of colonial Africa, had been used as satraps of European rule, their ancient allegiance to the tribe preserved but subverted to a higher allegiance to the foreign crown. Only with the groundswell of independence, when the decamping colonialists had to find an authority to take over the power, had the native dissidents been given freedom to thump tubs, to mount platforms and espouse policies, unpalatable though these might be to the colonialists.

Throughout colonial Africa, efforts to transfer the power to the chiefs as independence neared were resisted by the young men who had been given a new vision by the local mission schools, or in Europe by the universities and trade union movements. Challenge to the chiefs became acceptable. Thus one of colonialism's major legacies, the supplanting of traditional African democracy by European democracy, became established.* Not firmly so, however, for European-style democracy never flourished in post-colonial Africa. Neither, for that matter, did traditional democracy, for often neither style was acceptable to the new breed of black politician, but that is another story.

In Rhodesia the conflict between the chiefs and the black politicians began in earnest in 1957 when Joshua Nkomo revived the moribund African National Congress, prompting the government to ban it two years later. Nkomo and his followers were hugely encouraged, however, by the success of their neighbours in collapsing the Central African Federation and forming independent Zambia and Malawi. The whites in Rhodesia would now be brought sharply up against the refusal of many

---

*Before colonialism, African societies tended to practise a form of democracy through consensus. Whether inheriting or being appointed to the position, chiefs often ruled at the discretion of their subjects, and were expected to consult them directly or through their sub-chiefs or headmen, and to carry out the expressed wishes of their people or be replaced.

blacks in their own country to accept gradual evolution to full rights.

Most of the Rhodesian whites, however, still believed – or perhaps now only hoped – that despite being outnumbered about twenty to one they could continue to impose political evolution on the blacks through the qualified franchise. Inherited from the Cape in Rhodes's time, the qualified franchise had at Whitehall's insistence been maintained even after apartheid had replaced it in the Cape with indirect representation in parliament by whites. It seems likely that the Rhodesians would have done the same if given the choice. In 1945 Godfrey Huggins's governing United Party, foreseeing the eventual probability of a black majority in the Assembly, considered withdrawing the franchise from even the few hundred blacks who had it and giving them indirect representation in the Assembly. The idea was vetoed, however, by Whitehall.

The qualified franchise itself was an academic matter for most of the black people. While it was superficially fair in that the same tests were applied to both whites and blacks, the disparities in education and earning capacity had the effect of entrenching white hegemony for the foreseeable future.*

In 1947 a white group calling themselves the Liberal Party proposed a segregationist policy: dividing the country roughly equally between blacks and whites, with separate parliaments. The idea got little support, however. Three years later the same group, its name changed to the Rhodesia Party, proposed that the country seek full self-government without the controls that London held over its foreign and native affairs (including the qualified franchise). A Select Committee was appointed to look into the matter, but its deliberations were overtaken by the move to create the Central African Federation.

As long as Whitehall had the final say in black rights, the whites could never dismiss their fears of being swamped. This unease was one of the driving impulses behind the growing demand for independence for Rhodesia.

The racial issue aside, independence was not regarded by the Rhodesians as a gift to be bestowed by Britain but a right long established, one that could not indefinitely be denied. That right was based on three major components. First, the country's long-established self-governing, quasi-dominion status. Second, the perception that Britain had promised them independence and that this would be granted with the evolutionary system left intact and not on the basis of majority rule. Third, the sacrifices that the white Rhodesians had made for Britain in the two world wars.

International events had moved on, however, introducing new factors into the issue. The Afro-Asian bloc at the United Nations had achieved a unity and vocality that the British government could not ignore, especially with the Soviet Union courting the bloc and siding with it in the UN, using its Security Council veto to extend by proxy the power they had as a voting block in the General Assembly. The Commonwealth itself had been changed by the flood of independence from the cozy white club it had been at its formation in 1931 to a body most of whose

---

*When the voters' roll came to be split in two in 1963, only 570 whites failed to qualify for the higher-level A roll and were placed on the B roll, while 88 256 whites qualified for the A roll. There were only 2 251 blacks on the A roll (as well as 1 275 coloureds and 1 193 Asians) but 10 214 blacks on the B roll (and 166 coloureds and 107 Asians.

members were not white.

British attitudes had been changed by other influences as well. Besides the economic vulnerability to American pressures and the shifting of the commercial focus from the Empire to Europe, public opinion in Britain had become more liberal. Anything smacking of racial discrimination or white privilege was politically difficult to defend. No Labour government wanted to do it, and a Tory one couldn't even if it wanted to.

The Rhodesian whites had been left stranded in what was essentially a colonial situation, holding the mores and values thereof, when Britain and the rest of Europe had moved on to different values and imperatives.

The most liberal of the prime ministers, New Zealand-born RS Garfield Todd, a former missionary, was forced out of office in 1958 when his views became too liberal for his United Federal Party. Some of his supporters joined him in forming the Central African Party but he was ejected from that, too, when he proposed that the constitution be made more democratic and forcefully imposed by Britain. His successor as premier, Sir Edgar Whitehead, also ran into trouble with his constituents when he began to remove the apartheid-style restrictions on black access to white amenities.

Whitehead had strong white support, however, for pursuing the efforts to shuck off London's stranglehold on changes to the constitution and to black rights. These efforts led in 1960 to a series of conferences convened by the British government, which reached agreement on changes to the 1923 constitution. Whitehead assured Rhodesians that the changes, among other things, did away with London's discretionary powers and guaranteed Rhodesian independence in the event of the Federation collapsing. In a referendum in July 1961, a large majority accepted the proposals, apparently in the belief that they would give Rhodesia independence, though without Dominion status for the present. However, when the proposals were tabled as a Bill in the House of Commons it was found that clauses had been inserted that retained London's veto powers. Perfidious Albion had done it again, it seemed.

The new constitution retained the qualified franchise but extended political rights by splitting the qualifications into two categories based on property, income and education, and dividing the voters' rolls accordingly. Those on the A roll, the better qualified, would elect 50 of the 65 Legislative Assembly members, while those on the B roll would elect only 15. However, the lower qualifications of the B roll opened the vote to many blacks who had not previously qualified. Furthermore, blacks could for the first time sit in the Assembly. There was now to be a Bill of Rights protecting both blacks and whites from racially discriminatory legislation, and a Constitutional Council with powers of review over legislature.

Though the right-wing Rhodesians represented in the opposition Dominion Party disliked the 1961 constitution, saying it introduced racism into Rhodesian politics, they accepted that it had been approved (except for the inserted clauses) by a majority of the voters in the referendum.

Joshua Nkomo and his supporters, who now included Rev. Ndabaningi Sithole, a Congregationalist minister, began campaigning against the bill, enforcing their views by harsh intimidation of those who supported it, notably the traditional chiefs and those loyal to them. Whitehead banned Nkomo's National Democratic Party (NDP), but it was promptly renamed the Zimbabwe African Peoples' Union (ZAPU) and the intimidation continued. It went on even after ZAPU had in turn been banned in September 1962.

Whitehead was defeated in a general election in 1962 by the Rhodesian Front, newly formed from the Dominion Party and UFP dissidents. Led by a British-born tobacco farmer, Winston Field, the Rhodesian Front had campaigned on a policy of amending the 1961 constitution, saying it would bring about dominance by Africans before most of them were qualified to rule. The RF also opposed compulsory (but not voluntary) racial integration, and favoured separate schools and other amenities for blacks and whites, for the present at least. It rejected 'subordination' to the British government.

When Macmillan's government called the 1963 Victoria Falls conference for the purpose of dissolving the Federation, Field threatened to torpedo the meeting by refusing to attend unless he got guarantees of independence for his country at the same time as the other two. But the Northern Rhodesian African leaders, Harry Nkumbula and Kenneth Kaunda, threatened to boycott the conference themselves if Southern Rhodesia were to be promised independence on anything other than a one-man-one-vote basis. Their stance was given additional weight by the backing of the OAU and the African groups in the UN and the Commonwealth. Coordination of African opposition to white domination through these bodies was becoming increasingly effective; it had already put Pretoria on the defensive over apartheid and its administration of South West Africa.

White political leaders were adamant that at Victoria Falls the British representative, secretary of state Rab Butler, had given the Rhodesians a clear verbal undertaking that if they cooperated in dismantling the Federation, Rhodesia would get its independence, and no later than the other two members of the Federation. Butler later denied this and the dispute enhanced the growing bitterness among the Rhodesians at what was seen to be British government perfidy.

Duncan Sandys, the Commonwealth Secretary, tried a new tack in 1963, proposing that the Rhodesian issue be discussed at a special conference of selected Commonwealth leaders, including President Julius Nyerere of Tanzania. There was outrage in Salisbury at the attempt to involve the Commonwealth in a matter considered to be strictly between Britain and Rhodesia and to bring in, of all people, an outsider dedicated to the unconditional removal of white rule.

Sandys, however, figured that the issue had expanded beyond British and Rhodesian boundaries whether anyone liked it or not. Independence for Rhodesia on Salisbury's terms, he said, would mean the country being denied membership of the Commonwealth. More important, African and Asian members might quit the Commonwealth in protest, seriously demeaning its importance if not threatening its very existence. It would make no difference even if an independent Rhodesia were to forego Commonwealth membership, which Field indicated a willingness to do if necessary.

In a sense, Sandys's attitude suggested that Britain had become hostage to nations it had once ruled as parts of its empire. Or, expressed metaphorically, that Britannia, stripped of the rich robes of Empire, had only the thin cloth of the Commonwealth to hide her shrunken form, and no British government was going to allow that covering to be rent for the sake of a few thousand whites in Rhodesia, British stock or not.

Macmillan's successor, Alec Douglas-Home, for his part feared that meeting Salisbury's terms might lead to insurrection in Rhodesia along Kenyan and Algerian lines.

Insurrection was indeed already brewing. In 1963, Sithole had broken with Nkomo and formed a rival movement, the Zimbabwe African National Union (Zanu), with Robert Mugabe, an avowed Marxist, like Nkomo, as his second-in-command. Both organisations used intimidation and terrorism as weapons against each others' supporters, further establishing violence as a major instrument of black politics. Though their aims were basically the same – to end white hegemony and reclaim the land taken by the whites – ZAPU and Zanu reflected and perpetuated the ancient tribal rivalry, with ZAPU allied to the Ndebele (Matabele) and Zanu with the Shona. They also mirrored the rivalry between the major communist powers, ZAPU being backed by the Soviet Union and the Warsaw Pact governments, and Zanu by China. Members of both organisations slipped out of Rhodesia to receive military training in one or other of Tanzania, Ghana, Algeria and later North Korea.

★ ★ ★ ★

It had taken a while for the unpalatable truth to sink in, but by 1964 the Rhodesian Front and its supporters had accepted that they could not rely on Britain for salvation from black domination.

That a Tory minister could think of referring their fate to the decision of the Commonwealth was more than a straw in the wind – it was a haybale in a gale.

The RF government was beginning to think seriously about cutting free from a perfidious Britain that seemed to have disowned them – more than that, a Britain that seemed resolved to sacrifice them to appease the Commonwealth. A unilateral declaration of independence was not a new idea. It had been informally discussed and even threatened, by previous Rhodesian government leaders and by Welensky too. But now it began to appear to conservative whites as the only alternative to a rush to majority rule.

Impatient with Field's temporising with London, the RF caucus fired him in April 1964 and replaced him with Ian Douglas Smith, who had been Treasury Minister in Field's cabinet. Smith was a Rhodesian-born farmer who had flown fighter planes and been wounded in combat for Britain during the war. He carried the scars proudly, for he was passionately loyal to Britain. His mindset was almost Victorian in this and in his professed belief in the moral codes and social ideals that had prevailed in the old imperial Britain.

Smith has said he would have preferred a negotiated independence agreement and saw a unilateral declaration as a last resort. The negotiating, however, dragged on through 1964, hung up mainly on how African views should be ascertained. Broadly, London and the black politicians favoured a straight referendum while the RF, mindful of past intimidation – and perhaps of their hold over the chiefs – wanted the chiefs to be given a special role.

In October the Tories were defeated by Harold Wilson's Labour Party in the British general election. There was dismay in the RF. Among the Tories they had discerned some sympathy for the white Rhodesians, a strong respect for the bonds of kinship, for all Macmillan's desire to scrap the Empire. The Labourites, however, appeared to see the white Rhodesians as racists stuck in a wrong past, claiming rights long invalidated.

The RF believed its gradualist approach was accepted by most of the blacks, notably the chiefs who were seen to be the best judges and articulators of black opinion. ZAPU and Zanu were considered to represent only an extremist minority, bent on winning power through terrorism, and who had won support in the UN, the Commonwealth and the OAU largely because that suited the aims of the Kremlin and of anti-white racists in the former colonies.

Smith appears to have believed sincerely in the moral rectitude of his party's policies but to have been blinkered by a contrived history. He shared the belief of most white Rhodesians that their settler forebears had acquired their disproportionate share of the land fairly and legally. Though this view of history may well have been held honestly by his generation, it appears as a convenient fabrication by the original settlers when measured against evidence of indigenous occupation of the country long before the white settlers arrived. Smith and the other Rhodesians of his belief might have been on firmer ground had they argued that almost everyone in southern Africa was descended from settlers and/or conquerors, the only difference (apart from complexion) being how far back the settlement/conquest took place. Rhodes's Pioneers would then be seen simply as the most recent settlers, and their conquest perhaps no more wrongful or ruthless than any earlier ones.

Smith obviously got a first-hand account of the early days from his father, who had arrived in Rhodesia in 1898, but by then the conquest had been made, the settlement effected, the subjugation completed, and the histories aligned with the beliefs, prejudices and ambitions of Victorianism. And it was this version that entered the curricula of the schools and moulded the attitudes of Smith's and succeeding generations.

British governments regarded the white Rhodesians' gradualist approach to majority rule as politically impracticable, if not morally indefensible. To the black nationalists, it was plain anathema. At the same time, their espousal of non-racial democracy was essentially expedient, since a universal franchise could only result in the black majority having complete power without guarantees that it would not turn against the whites. (As it turned out in the end, Smith's fears were largely borne out, for under the autocratic rule of Mugabe the whites were left politically impotent and increasingly vilified and threatened.)

Wilson hung his Rhodesia policy on the five principles that had emerged from the earlier negotiations with the Tory government and had been amended by his own: unimpeded progress to majority rule, no retrogressive amendments to the constitution, immediate improvements in the blacks' political status, progress towards ending racial discrimination, and any independence formula to be acceptable to the people of Rhodesia as a whole.

The Rhodesian problem had become an albatross that Wilson's government wanted cut from the British neck as soon as possible. The white Rhodesians were prepared, however regretfully, to do the cutting themselves if necessary, through a UDI. The Labour government knew, however, that even if it was prepared to accept a UDI it would not be allowed to get away with it by the black politicians in Rhodesia and by their backers in the OAU and the UN. For these the ideal was immediate majority rule, if necessary imposed by British arms.

Wilson did indeed consider military intervention as an option but rejected it. The British chiefs of staff advised against it, pointing out that it would require a long and costly build-up in Zambia, and that the Rhodesians might well fight back. There was concern that some British soldiers and airmen would refuse to fight against other Britons. Ken Flower, head of the Rhodesian Central Intelligence Organisation, says the CIO was convinced that the British military commanders would obey orders to intervene in Rhodesia and that the Rhodesian commanders would not resist such an intervention.[4] But Smith had satisfied himself, through soundings by his High Commissioner in London, Brigadier Andrew Skeen, that there would be strong resistance among the British forces to an invasion of Rhodesia.

Even slight resistance to British military intervention would have caused deep emotional and political trauma in Britain. Since most Rhodesians either had British passports or recent British parentage, and professed loyalty to the Crown, a British invasion would have been civil war of sorts, one fought outside Britain but kin against kin nonetheless, the first conflict of this kind since the American War of Independence.

The political agitation of the black militants prompted Smith in August 1964 to ban Zanu and detain Sithole and Mugabe, and to rusticate the ZAPU leadership in a wilderness area.

In the same year Smith canvassed popular opinion of independence on the basis of the 1961 constitution. Majority support came from the mainly white electorate in a referendum, and from the chiefs at a special conference. When he called a general election in May 1965 his RF made a clean sweep of all the A roll seats.

UDI suddenly assumed alarming proximity for Wilson, and in October 1965 he flew to Salisbury in an effort to avert it. Wilson insisted on a settlement he could sell to the OAU, and Smith insisted the dispute was only between Britain and Rhodesia. Wilson held out for the blacks to be given a 'blocking third' of the parliamentary seats, for the Land Apportionment Act to be phased out, and for the settlement to be endorsed by 'the people of Rhodesia as a whole'.

While UDI was initially opposed by all of Smith's prime ministerial predecessors, the great majority of the whites clearly believed they were being given no tolerable option. All that Wilson appeared to be offering was an unacceptably rapid advance to black dominance, which would plunge the country into the same chaos that independence had brought in most of the rest of Africa: one-party rule or one-man dictatorship, inept and corrupt governance, disintegration of the economy, infrastructure and services, and oppression of minorities.

From the start the odds were against UDI succeeding. In international law and practice, Rhodesia's independence would not be recognised in the world until endorsed by Britain. But no British government was going to grant independence or recognise a unilateral declaration of it that was opposed by the OAU and the Commonwealth. And oppose it these bodies would, even if Salisbury was able to crush the insurgency – and perhaps especially so in that case.

Just over two weeks after Wilson's visit the Rhodesian cabinet decided unanimously to take the fateful plunge into UDI. The government announced the decision on 11 November, Armistice Day, a ploy to remind Britons of Rhodesia's wartime sacrifices under the Union Jack. As a further spin, the declaration imitated the American independence declaration in the hope that it would be seen to have equal validity. These gimmicks did not work, however; the UDI was denounced around the world. London declared it illegal.

Even South Africa refrained from giving its endorsement. Vorster's government had privately tried to dissuade the RF government from UDI.[5]

Since Rhodesia seemed unwilling to imitate South Africa's policy of a territorial and political separation of blacks and whites, the next-best thing in Pretoria's view would have been immediate majority rule with constitutional protection of white rights. But the illegal UDI undermined that, creating instability in the subcontinent, establishing a precedent for economic sanctions and jeopardising Pretoria's efforts to gain acceptance in Africa (and elsewhere) by forcing it to seem to be supporting Smith.

Vorster was unwilling to condemn UDI, however, for fear of antagonising right-wing whites in South Africa and jeopardising white solidarity in the sub-continent. The defenders of the fortress must stand together. Vorster tackled the dilemma by giving the UDI government de facto but not de jure recognition. In keeping with his policy of non-interference in the affairs of other countries (which he hoped would be reciprocated) he declared the Rhodesian issue to be a matter between Salisbury and London.

Vorster nonetheless felt compelled to give Salisbury material support in order to preclude the creation of a precedent dangerous to South Africa: the defeat of a white state by either sanctions or black nationalism, and with it the removal of the buffer between South Africa and a black Africa backing insurgency against white rule. When sanctions were imposed against Rhodesia by the UN, Vorster refused to respect them under the policy of non-interference. But his government went beyond maintaining normal trade – it encouraged an increase to take advantage of the situation, even building a direct railway link over the Limpopo at Beit Bridge, short-cutting the vulnerable rail route through Botswana.

Immediately after UDI, Pretoria joined Portugal as the only two countries voting against a General Assembly resolution condemning the move and demanding Security Council action. Britain and France abstained. The British wanted to avoid being forced to use their veto in the Security Council, which would have them depicted by the Soviet Bloc as protecting their British kin in Rhodesia at the expense of the Africans. When the matter duly went to the Security Council the British were able to steer it away from action under the UN Charter's booby-trapped Chapter Seven.*

When, two years after UDI, a majority in the Security Council voted for sanctions against South Africa and Portugal for their assistance to Rhodesia, both Britain and the United States vetoed the resolution.

The Salisbury government insisted that UDI complied with the principle of unimpeded progress to majority rule that had been endorsed by the British government. It appears, however, that Wilson's government was already moving towards – and may already have adopted – the new position it subsequently announced of 'no independence before majority African rule', famously acronymed as NIBMAR, and denounced by the RF as an abrogation of the previous agreement.

UDI continued to have overwhelming support from whites fed up with what was seen as cynical British government manipulation of their rights for its own political ends. Most whites evidently endorsed the RF's view that the 1961 constitution had the support of the majority of blacks as well as whites, and that the British government therefore had no good or lawful reason to deny Rhodesia independence. They largely agreed with Smith that ZAPU and Zanu were extremists representing a minority.

As with Smith, their consciences were clear about their treatment of the black population, which had increased more than tenfold in only three generations. Most of the discriminatory measures had been scrapped, beginning in Whitehead's term. All urban public places, including railways, parks, cinemas and churches, were now open to all races, as was the country's only university. Hospitals were segregated, as were primary and secondary schools, but providing the same education as the white schools. (A 1964 UNESCO report had given Rhodesia proportionately the highest per capita school attendance in all of Africa and Latin America.) And Africans had seats in parliament, even if only a few.

Some four million acres of the land reserved for Africans had been set aside for purchase by black farmers to enable them to escape from the traditional communal ownership that gave black farmers no collateral for raising loans for expansion, pre-

---

*Chapter Seven is the ultimate weapon in the UN's limited arsenal. It provides for an issue to be declared a threat to world peace and theoretically obliges UN members to accept and perhaps even join in the economic sanctions, military intervention or other action decided on. No member state can be forced against its wishes to take the prescribed action. But the significance of a Chapter Seven resolution is that it gives any bloc of Big Powers the authority – or excuse, as the case may be – to take the action in the name of the UN. It legitimises intervention. Hence Chapter Seven proposals were often vetoed by one or other of the Security's Council's five Permanent Members – but usually at the expense of being made out to be the villain. The ploy was used to good effect by the Soviet Union during the Cold War in order to embarrass the Western powers and to promote itself as the champion of the Third World. Thus, throughout the struggle against white domination in southern Africa, the Western powers were often forced to do an egg-dance behind the scenes at the UN to prevent the Soviets invoking Chapter Seven at their expense over Rhodesia, the Portuguese colonies, South West Africa or South Africa.

venting them from progressing from subsistence farming to wealth-generation.

There were still similarities with apartheid South Africa, though. Large numbers of Africans were still barred from voting. The towns were effectively reserved for whites, and blacks lived there on sufferance, forced to carry passes. The Land Apportionment Act had resulted in the Africans occupying only 44-million acres of land against the 36-million occupied by the white minority. True, more than half of the country's 'high fertility' soil and highest rainfall regions were in the black areas. But the population disparity and the fact that most whites lived in the towns meant that there was a glaring difference between the small agricultural holdings in crowded African areas and the huge farms owned by a relatively few whites, a number of whom had more than one farm – or didn't even live in Rhodesia.

The government spent more per capita on educational and other basic services for whites than for blacks, and justified it on the grounds that whites paid far more in taxes. It seems not to have been considered that these disparities might be seen as unflattering indices of the extent to which the whites were willing to make sacrifices in order to bring the blacks to economic and political parity. There evidently was no thought that if white security lay in black evolution it would make sense for that evolution to be accelerated, to be made urgent rather than deliberate. The RF government considered that UDI was forced on it by the British government and by outside interests. There was no room for the converse argument that that situation would not have arisen had the white minority acted to stay ahead of events rather than be overtaken by them.

At Wilson's request, the governor, Sir Humphrey Gibbs, remained in Government House to manifest the illegality of UDI. The RF, however, maintained that it was Gibbs who had been made illegal by UDI. It appointed Clifford Dupont as Officer Administering the Government – in effect replacing Gibbs.

So Rhodesia now had two figureheads, both professing loyalty to the same queen and to the same flag but neither of them recognising the other. The military commanders and senior civil servants professed an equally bizarre dual loyalty to both the RF government and the Queen. Wilson had asked the public servants to stay at their posts, for anything else would have dropped Rhodesia into ungoverned chaos. Rhodesia House in London continued to function, as did the British High Commission in Salisbury.

Wilson rejected the Afro-Asian bloc's demands for British military intervention in Rhodesia, but persuaded Zambia to request British forces to protect the Kariba Dam installations on its side from Rhodesian interference. His real motive is thought by some to have been preventing the Soviets from exploiting the opportunity to gain a foothold in the centre of Africa, perhaps under the aegis of the UN. A squadron of Javelin jets was sent to Lusaka, and troops of the RAF Regiment posted near the border with Rhodesia.

Far from being willing to fight the Rhodesians, the RAF pilots are said to have toasted Ian Smith in their Officers' Mess on New Year's Eve. And the ground troops are reported to have taken to crossing the border to enjoy the hospitality of the Rhodesian army and police messes until London put a stop to it.

CHAPTER 37

GUNFIRE GROWING

By the late sixties, the embattled whites in southern Africa were becoming worried as much by the growing insurgency within their fortress as by the political campaigns outside it.

In 1964 Frelimo began its armed struggle in Mozambique, and the next year Swapo followed suit in South West Africa. By 1966 the black rights struggle in Rhodesia had broken into armed insurgency on a scale large enough to make it a war. Insurgency, termed terrorism by the governments, was now being conducted in all the white-ruled countries.

The guerilla attacks in Rhodesia brought a sense of urgency to the efforts to find a settlement there. In December 1966 Wilson and Smith met for talks on board a British cruiser, HMS *Tiger*, off Gibraltar. Wilson made sufficient concessions – in essence ensuring minority rule into the 21st century – for a tentative settlement to be reached. The agreement collapsed, however, over Smith's refusal to give London unlimited control over the implementation of the proposed new constitution. Fourteen years later, Smith's government would find itself accepting a settlement on far less favourable terms, a settlement that would hand control of the country to his worst enemy, Robert Mugabe.

Wilson responded to Smith's intransigence by getting the Security Council to impose mandatory economic sanctions, principally on oil imports, and by adopting his NIBMAR stance.

In August 1967 the ANC of South Africa and ZAPU of Rhodesia infiltrated a joint force into Rhodesia, but most were killed or captured.* Pretoria reacted by sending a para-military police force to Rhodesia, ignoring the protests of a British government that saw this as an intrusion into its own area of responsibility.

Parallel with the growing insurgency, the political war against white supremacy intensified in the international organisations. The formation of the OAU in 1963 provided a new instrument for coordinating African opposition. The UN, however, remained the principle body of opposition, even though it was more symbolic than effective. The arms ban that the General Assembly imposed on South Africa in 1963, for instance, was largely ignored in Europe.

Pretoria's administration of South West Africa had unsuccessfully been chal-

---

*The ANC's collaboration with ZAPU reflected their joint alliance with the Soviet Union, as distinct from the ties that Zanu and the PAC developed with China and therefore with each other.

lenged in the World Court, which, with Western judges predominating, had repeatedly found in South Africa's favour in advisory opinions delivered in 1950, 1955 and 1956. Its major finding was that while the UN had inherited supervisory powers from the League of Nations, South Africa was not obliged to place the territory under the UN trusteeship system. The complaint in 1960 by former League members Liberia and Ethiopia that South Africa had violated its mandate collapsed with a ruling six years later that the complainants had no legal right or interest in the matter.

Turning in frustration to the General Assembly, the Afro-Asians got it to do what they had failed to get the court to do: declare that South Africa had in fact misused its mandate and oppressed the people. By 114 votes to two (South Africa and Portugal), with Britain and France abstaining, the Assembly decided to revoke the mandate and strip South Africa of its authority over the territory and place it under the administration of a Special Committee. South Africa ignored the resolution and blocked a subsequent attempt by the Special Committee to send a take-over team to Windhoek – an exercise so impractical as to verge on comedy.

By now, however, Swapo's guerilla incursions had grown to a point that prompted Pretoria to jail the movement's internal leaders and send troops in to defend the territory rather than leave it to the para-military police. With combat forces in both Rhodesia and South West Africa, the apartheid government was for the first time having to go beyond South Africa's borders to defend its policies and ambitions.

The military activity was part of a two-pronged policy now being pursued in Africa by Pretoria, the other prong being a diplomatic one. The military side included covert military supplies to the Portuguese forces fighting Frelimo in Mozambique. At home, it had introduced compulsory military service for whites. At the same time it was building up the strength of its armaments.

The diplomatic prong was a major initiative launched by President John Vorster with the aim of persuading African states to accept the invincibility of white supremacy in South Africa and by extension Pretoria's policy of dividing the country into a large white republic and a number of small, independent black ones.

Pretoria had arrogantly rebuffed offers of diplomatic relations from Nigeria in 1962 and from Zambia in 1964. Afterwards, however, came the realisation that, as Hilgard Muller put it in 1968, 'our relations with the rest of the world are largely dependent on our relations with the African states'. Under an overall 'outward policy' aimed at widening diplomatic and trade links, special emphasis was placed on Africa, and the southern sub-continent in particular. The initiative was largely fruitless, however, since it implied acceptance of apartheid and of a dominant role by Pretoria. Trade increased, but mainly on a clandestine basis that did not really suit Pretoria's diplomatic purposes. The government therefore switched its general 'outward' policy to a more specific one of dialogue with key states and leaders.

'We are the only white people that are of Africa,' Vorster declared. '... No-one understands the soul of Africa better than we do.'

Again the response was meagre. The prime minister of newly-independent Lesotho, Leabua Jonathan, visited South Africa in 1967, and diplomatic relations were established with Malawi. By 1968 Vorster was corresponding secretly with President Kaunda of Zambia, and Muller was openly claiming regular private contacts with other African leaders.

In what appears to have been an effort to deflect Pretoria's dialogue initiative, and perhaps turn it into channels considered more appropriate, Kaunda and President Julius Nyerere of Tanzania initiated a meeting in Lusaka in April 1969 at which 14 heads of state signed the Lusaka Manifesto. The 24-point document in effect offered the whites in the sub-continent protection against reverse racism if they surrendered to majority rule.

'We are not hostile to the administrations of [South Africa, Rhodesia, Mozambique and Angola] because they are manned and controlled by white people,' the manifesto declared, but 'because they are systems of minority control ... based on the doctrine of human inequality. Our stand towards southern Africa thus involves a rejection of racialism, not a reversal of the existing racial domination. We believe that all peoples who have made their homes in the countries of Southern Africa are Africans, regardless of the colour of their skins, and we would oppose a racialist majority government which adopted a philosophy of deliberate and permanent discrimination between its citizens on the grounds of racial origin.'

Here were African heads of state extending to the whole sub-continent the principle of equal and democratic rights regardless of colour that had been set out in the Freedom Charter adopted by black South Africans at Kliptown in 1955. And now again the olive branch was rejected by the whites, again out of fear, mistrust and reluctance to give up their privileges. They were being given assurances but not guarantees that they if they surrendered to morality they would not be subjected to black racism and would not see everything their forebears had created sink into the degeneration, corruption, despotism and tribal strife that had afflicted most of the rest of Africa after independence.

(As it turned out their fears were borne out in Zimbabwe, and soon after the turn of the century similar unease arose in Namibia from anti-white sentiments expressed by President Sam Nujoma, a close ally of Zimbabwe's Mugabe.)

Perhaps, it was not so much the privileges as good governance and true, multi-party democracy that many of the whites wanted. Not the radical right-wingers, of course, but perhaps the large body of moderates, or incipient moderates, whose views remained unsought and unheard, to some extent even unformed, in the clamour and alarums of the contest between the extremists.

In the Lusaka Manifesto the African presidents expressed a preference 'to negotiate rather than destroy, to talk rather than kill', but they vowed to continue supporting the freedom struggle as long as these preferences were blocked by the white administrations. For their part, these administrations, all run by extremists, were not interested in negotiation with what they regarded as communist-backed terrorist organisations.

Vorster's attempted dialogue with black Africa was aimed at getting it to accept Pretoria's concept of separate development as the equivalent of decolonisation. His attitude to the blacks within his country was reflected in his statement in 1969 that, for peace to be assured, 'the development must not be towards each other but away from each other'. There was an odd, even ironic, reflection of this in the attitude of the emerging black consciousness movement, whose prime ideologue, Steve Biko, believed that blacks must develop their own identity and institutions in order to be able to deal with the whites on a basis of mutual respect.

Vorster's dialogue initiative did succeed in getting tentative responses from a number of moderate African leaders, notably President Felix Houphouet-Boigny of the Ivory Coast. Relations with Malawi were taken further with a formal visit by Vorster in 1970. These developments were sufficiently disturbing to the more hard-line African leaders to get them to persuade the OAU at its summit in Khartoum in 1971 to adopt a declaration banning dialogue with South Africa unless directed specifically at installing democracy and involving the liberation movements. This was followed by the Mogadishu Declaration in which the East and Central African States averred that white supremacy could be ended only by force.

Despite these setbacks, it seemed for a while that dialogue was expanding, with further promising exchanges with the leaders of Ivory Coast, Senegal and Liberia. Pretoria's hopes appeared illusory, however, when it became clear that none of the African leaders saw dialogue as an acceptance of white supremacy in South Africa but only as a means of achieving acceptable change there.

In Rhodesia meanwhile the guerilla war had steadily been escalating despite the limited portal of infiltration through Zambia. It was still fairly easily containable by the Rhodesian security forces, however, when in November 1968 Wilson and Smith met again on another British warship, HMS *Fearless*, in Gibraltar harbour. Wilson, putting aside his NIBMAR principle, proposed that Smith form a broad-based, multi-racial government pending elections. Progress to majority rule would be ensured by empowering a quarter of the MPs to block contrary legislation. In addition, any such legislation would be subject to approval by the British Privy Council. It was on this provision that the *Fearless* talks collapsed. Again Smith's mis-trust of perfidious Albion had scuppered a settlement. Besides that, Smith regarded Privy Council approval as a negation of the very concept of independence.

On his return home, Smith said in a radio broadcast to the nation that it had be-come clear that '[the British government] are prepared to accept that the white man in Rhodesia is expendable.'

Despite sanctions, the Rhodesia economy was prospering. Inventive measures had been devised to breach the sanctions, and enforced import substitution had created new domestic industries. Sanctions could never be fully effective as long as South Africa and Portugal refused to observe them, and Pretoria was not going to support a coercive mechanism that might later be turned against it by the en-emies of apartheid. From the first imposition of selective mandatory sanctions by the UN in 1966, Pretoria had stood firm on a policy of opposing sanctions against any country and of continuing to do normal trade with any country. Lisbon had taken a similar line.

After an initial panicky exodus at UDI, the white population of Rhodesia had re-sumed its growth through immigration. Thousands of Britons (and others) seemed willing to make a new life in Rhodesia, even if going there meant doing compulsory military service in the bush war. The biggest influx came between 1967 and 1973, when 39 000 whites entered the country. After that, as the attrition of the guerilla conflict began to take effect, it slowed but was still not exceeded by emigration.

Despairing of reconciling their loyalty to the Crown with their mistrust of British politicians, the RF in 1969 held a referendum on whether Rhodesia should become a republic. The vote was overwhelmingly in favour: 81 per cent of the (mostly white) electorate. A republican constitution was duly instituted in March 1970 and the new green-and-white-striped flag raised in place of the Union Jack. In a general election a few weeks later the RF retained all 50 of the A roll seats. Gibbs no longer saw any purpose in staying on in Government House, and vacated it to make way for Dupont, now proclaimed President of Rhodesia.

The Tories having been returned to office under Edward Heath in 1970, Home, now foreign secretary, reached agreement with the Smith government in November 1971. Essentially, the agreement accepted the RF policy of gradual progress to majority rule while granting an immediate increase in black representation in parliament.

Both sides agreed that the new proposals must be shown to have popular acceptance, and the job of assessing this was given to a commission under a British judge, Lord Pearce. Having made its own soundings of black opinion through the chiefs, the RF government was confident that most blacks accepted the new settlement proposals.

However, an intensive campaign against the proposals was now launched by a new black organisation, the African National Council, led by the Methodist bishop Abel Muzorewa. In response, the RF government detained some black opponents of the settlement proposals, and even two prominent white ones, the former premier, Sir Garfield Todd, and his daughter, Judith.

The Pearce Commission's finding in 1972 that the settlement proposals did not have majority black support came as a shock to the RF. The party complained that Pearce had given undue weight to the views of the minority represented by the militants, and too little to those of the majority as expressed by the chiefs.

In the same year, Frelimo's growing strength in Mozambique had enabled Zanu to open bases north of the Zambezi for cross-border operations into Rhodesia. With insurgents infiltrating also from Zambia, the RF government in 1973 attempted to dissuade Lusaka from hosting the guerillas by closing the border, cutting off Zambia's main routes to the sea and to the supplies of Rhodesian coal and coke for the Zambian mines. The South Africans, however, were much annoyed, for the closure imperilled their new 'railway diplomacy', which aimed to exploit the rail links to the South African ports and industries as a means of improving relations with the black states to the north. Some arm-twisting by Pretoria persuaded Smith to reopen the border.

But then Kaunda tried to up the ante by refusing to reopen the Zambian side, believing the international community would come to his rescue with economic aid. With the Tazara railway to Dar es Salaam not complete, Zambia was forced to rely on the Benguela line through Angola and on truck traffic to the Tanzanian ports over dirt roads impassable in the rains. Neither route was adequate. A special fund set up by the UN to compensate Zambia for its sacrifice brought paltry donations. Zambia's economy was badly damaged in consequence.

The Afro-Asians could claim advances, however, on the issue of South West Africa, which since 1968 had officially become known in the UN as Namibia. In 1970, having got the World Court staffed with a majority of judges hostile to white supremacy, they had prevailed on the Security Council to request yet another advisory opinion on South Africa's administration. The court had duly advised a year later that the administration was illegal, thereby opening new avenues for challenge to Pretoria's rule.

Pretoria was encouraged when in 1972 the Austrian Kurt Waldheim became UN secretary-general in succession to U Thant, the Burmese adamantly opposed to apartheid. Waldheim's wartime service with German forces had not yet become generally known, but he was viewed in Pretoria as being more favourably disposed than his predecessor. Waldheim, however, failed to make progress with his initial attempt to negotiate a solution to the Namibian dispute. At the same time the military conflict escalated, principally with the use of land mines by Swapo guerillas in 1972.

By 1973 the South African Defence Force had begun a substantial increase in its forces in South West Africa, and was beginning to raid into Angola against the Swapo insurgents infiltrating through the Portuguese territory from Zambia.

In that year Swapo had scored an important political advance through the General Assembly having declared it to be the 'only authentic representative' of the people of Namibia. The declaration was intended to counter Pretoria's efforts at doing an independence deal with other Namibian parties, but it inevitably killed at birth another settlement initiative by Waldheim the same year.

Vorster's government could see little reason for compromising on either Namibia or apartheid. The fortress was under wide attack, to be sure, but its defences were holding. The Rhodesians were containing the guerilla incursions without serious difficulty. While the Portuguese had lost some ground to the insurgents in northern Mozambique they were holding their own in the rest of the territory and in Angola. Swapo's incursions into Namibia posed no real threat to the security of the administration.

In South Africa itself the ANC and PAC appeared to be effectively hobbled by harsh laws and tough police action. The economy had been boosted by foreign investment and then further strengthened by the decision in 1971 to abandon the fixed gold price of $35 an ounce and allow it to float. Four years later it had shot up to $168, bringing in an unprecedented flow of foreign exchange.

The seesaw effect of rising protest and the suppression of it were nonetheless pumping up tension within South Africa. The government found itself having to crack down on white as well as black opposition to its oppressive policies, and not only from the white political parties. Protest bubbled with varying degrees of earnestness in the churches, newspapers and student organisations – but only the English-language ones. Led by the Dutch Reformed churches to which most Afrikaners belonged, the Afrikaans newspapers and student bodies dutifully rallied behind apartheid as the shield of their ethnicity and culture. Separated by religion, language and history, the two white communities faced the forces of change in different ways, though with some cross-over, but united in the fundamental desire for survival – survival of their societies if not their privileges as well.

The newspaper owners, faced with the threat of direct censorship, had in 1962 collaborated in the establishment of a Press Board of Reference to deal with government complaints of inaccurate or harmful reporting. Still the government sought to cow the troublesome newspapers through harassment and threatened and actual prosecution of editors and reporters. These efforts were only partly successful, however, leaving the English-language newspapers as one of the most effective opponents of apartheid within the country.

The English churches, having a higher affinity and a more protective constituency, were a more difficult proposition. But even they were not considered immune from official harassment, such as the (ultimately unsuccessful) prosecution of the Anglican Dean of Johannesburg on charges of possessing subversive material and inciting violence.

Both the Christian Institute and the National Union of South African Students were denied foreign funding by a new law applying to 'affected' organisations.

Vorster's government viewed any white protest as a threat to white solidarity, and in 1968 had moved to counter it with the Prohibition of Political Interference Act barring inter-racial political activities. Informal white opposition continued, nonetheless, though it had been made a dangerous business by the maze of restrictive laws and by the efficiency and ruthlessness of the police Special Branch.

Vorster's policies were denounced not only by apartheid's opponents but also by its more extreme supporters. His own party had been split in 1969 when the right wing had hived off to form the *Herstigte Nasionale Party* (HNP) under the leadership of Dr Albert Hertzog. The HNP's support was so small, however, that Vorster was able to emasculate it by calling an early election in 1970 in which Hertzog's group won not a single seat.

Vorster marched ahead on his chosen path, continuing his policies of strengthening apartheid domestically and of seeking international acceptance of separate development. In spite of the OAU's opposition, Pretoria made some gains with its dialogue initiative, though the dealings with black states remained largely covert. The gains were offset to some extent by the formation of a Front Line States group dedicated to opposing dialogue with Pretoria and to supporting the liberation movements. Initiated in the mid-seventies by Presidents Kaunda of Zambia, Nyerere of Tanzania and Seretse Khama of Botswana, the group operated on an informal, ad hoc basis.

The Front Line group took their title both from their geographic position on the line of the white fortress and from their leading role in opposing white supremacy. In both respects the lines of battle were indeed now drawn taught across the sub-continent.

★ ★ ★ ★

There would be no quick victories over white supremacy in southern Africa. The strength of the white fortress lay not only in its own formidable defences but also in related interests of the Western powers.

Neither the United States, Britain nor France was eager to see white rule fall to black rule lest that threaten their own special concerns, principally their fear of Soviet expansionism. Their readiness to exercise their vetoes in the Security Council was a shield which, though not primarily intended to protect white privilege, had that continuing effect – one of the spinoffs of the Cold War.

The Western powers may have been willing to write off the African whites in a moral sense but not in a political sense, not as long as they still had a use in the Cold War. So, in a perverse way, the Cold War was good for white hegemony in Africa. In the interests of solidarity in Nato against the Soviet Bloc, Portugal was given no serious problems by its fellow Nato members with its continued colonialism. Indeed, it was given armaments, not specifically for the defence of that colonialism but which were used for that purpose anyway.

In the case of South Africa and Rhodesia, the Western powers, Britain especially, were guided by their obsession with fending off Soviet competition over the Cape sea route and the sub-continent's minerals. There appears to have been an unexpressed but common conclusion that this was best done by keeping both sea route and minerals in the hands of the white minority rather than seeing them transferred to a black majority suspected to be more sympathetic to communism and the Soviet Bloc than to capitalism and the West.

France, though accepting the importance of keeping southern Africa out of Soviet hands, was more preoccupied with its special interests in Francophone Africa, where more than 320 000 French citizens were living in pursuit of commerce and as many as fifteen thousand French troops were stationed to protect French interests. What was good for France was good for the West, was the unspoken philosophy.

It was American rather than European concerns that ultimately dictated Western group policy, the United States having prime influence over both the economic and strategic interests of the West. Any doubts about Washington's determination to assert itself in the company of the British and French had been dispelled back in 1956 when America had forcefully signalled its disapproval of the invasion of Egypt, first by sending the United States Sixth Fleet on a course right through the Anglo-French invasion fleet, and then by the economic arm-twisting that forced Britain to back out of the exercise.

Washington, still holding some strings to the underpinnings of the British economy, could whistle Britain into line on major issues. France, though economically freer and obstinately independent of mind, had to consider the realities of the time, principally the magnitude of the power that Washington could wield if it chose. Not only did the US provide the principal shield against Soviet nuclear aggression but, more than ever before, it was the economic mover and shaker of the world.

Throughout the West, alongside the old fear of a worldwide economic depression was the new fear of nuclear holocaust, signified by the fallout shelters burrowed into suburban backyards from Southampton to Seattle. A mole syndrome pervaded communal psyches. Europeans had lived through the damage done to their cities by the bombing raids of the Second World War, but it was a different matter living with the knowledge that the Soviets could and indeed might send nuclear fireballs to consume entire cities. Fear of oblivion was perhaps stronger now than at any other time in human experience, and it created a dichotomy in world politics: the new morality existing parallel with the imperatives of survival. Television, now a prime shaper of perceptions, had brought into Western living rooms images of bigger and better fireballs, and of Nikita Khrushchev, the man who could trigger the Soviet ones, demonstrating his belligerence by removing his shoe to pound the Soviet desk in the General Assembly. Nuclear war phobia accelerated with the Cuban missile crisis.

The shadows of the eagle and the bear extended wide across Africa. The United States and Russia had attended the 1884 Berlin Conference on the carving up of Africa but had stayed out of the Scramble. Now they had been pulled by the Cold War into the Scramble's aftermath – the post-colonial redispensation.

Moscow, desperately conscious of America's economic, technological and military superiority, played something of a spoiling game in Africa, as elsewhere. Special opportunities existed in Africa, where the sudden exodus of colonialism had left the newly independent states teetering on flimsy ideological underpinnings and inclined to seek firmer footing in socialism rather than free enterprise, which had unpleasant associations with their former masters. Africa, abandoned by Europe and of no direct interest to America, was something of a vacuum which the Kremlin was eager to fill.

Both ideological proselytisation and political advantage could be and were promoted with zeal, but only as far as allowed by Moscow's severely limited resources. Aside from the big spending in Egypt on weapons and the Aswan High Dam, the thrust was at first mainly in fostering the growth of indigenous socialist parties and arming insurgents receptive to Soviet ideology.

American policy on Africa in the post-war years tended to be tentative and haphazard. It has been aptly said to have varied between 'benign neglect and romantic embrace, corresponding with the range of Soviet inaction or action.'[1] The basic motive, though, was to avoid deep involvement in either white or black interests in Africa, leaving it to the former colonial powers to do the dirty work of protecting Western concerns. The prime functions of the State Department's Africa Bureau were observational rather than interventionist. Only when it seemed that the Europeans were not up to the job did the Americans intervene substantially in the late seventies.

Insofar as American policy was neglectful, it was especially so under the Kennedy and Johnson presidencies, preoccupied as they were with the Vietnam war. Richard Nixon, though equally involved with Vietnam, had a wider international vision, and he took time out from the Vietnam concern to endorse a policy on white Africa formulated in 1969 by his then security adviser, Henry Kissinger, and famously set out in National Security Study Memorandum (NSSM) 39.

The memorandum actually put forward five policy options, all based on assessments of 'the depth and permanence' of black resolve to obtain a military victory over white dominance in southern Africa. None of the options is known to have received formal adoption. It is generally accepted, however, that Nixon administration policy was based on Option Two, dubbed by the State Department the 'Tar Baby Option' because of the difficulty that would be experienced in getting unstuck from it once it had been embraced. Option Two postulated thus: 'The whites are here to stay and the only way that constructive change can come is through them. There is no hope for the blacks to gain the political rights they seek through violence ... which will only lead to chaos and increased opportunities for the communists.

'We can, through selective relaxation of our stance toward the white regimes, encourage some modification of their current racial and colonial policies ... Our tangible interests form a basis for our contacts in the region, and these can be maintained at an acceptable political cost.'

It was from this perspective that Washington kept an eye on Africa and on Soviet Bloc activities therein, although the State Department's perceptions of American interests did not, of course, always match those of the CIA.

President Johnson took only a distant interest in the southern African issues but was moved to take a major role in the UN's imposition of the arms ban on South Africa in 1963. Pretoria did nothing to improve relations by imposing the colour bar on black seamen who went ashore from American warships visiting Cape Town, and protesting at mixed-race cocktail parties being held at the US embassy in Pretoria.

When Richard Nixon took over the White House in 1968 he took a closer interest in the sub-continent but espoused a policy of what he called 'constructive influence' in southern Africa, based on the hope that economic imperatives would undermine apartheid. Changing political realities were to overtake that view, however, and when Ronald Reagan restored the Republicans to the White House after Jimmy Carter's defeat, his assistant secretary of state for Africa, Chester Crocker, would find it advisable to extend the old Nixon policy to the more interventionist and therefore more controversial one of 'constructive engagement'.

Cold War competition also brought the Cubans into direct involvement in the Congo, essentially from ideological commitment on Havana's part but necessarily as Moscow's surrogates. As it was to be later in Angola, it was a chicken-or-the-egg question whether they came to counter CIA intervention or whether it was the other way round. By 1965 the legendary Che Guevara was leading a group of Cuban military instructors in an unsuccessful effort to rally the beleaguered Lumumbist forces. In the same year Guevara sent a similar group to help the MPLA resistance movement against the Portuguese in Angola, opening the door to what would in time become a major Cuban military intervention there, the biggest postwar insertion of foreign troops in Africa, leading to the biggest battles on that continent since the world war.

It was not only the Soviet Bloc that the Western powers felt a need to watch;

Communist China, the backward but fast-developing giant, was also asserting itself in Africa. Peking (as it was still being called outside China) had several motives: a wish to assert itself on the world stage, a concern with protecting its future interests, and an ideological desire to counter the spread of what it considered to be Soviet imperialism in the guise of socialism. While strongly supporting the African liberation movements with military aid, Peking also sought avenues for development assistance. Its big chance came when Western nations rejected requests by landlocked Zambia for help in building a railway to Dar es Salaam to provide an outlet to the sea that would end Zambia's dependence on the roads and rails through South African and Portuguese territory.

Peking, eager to match Moscow's financing of the Aswan dam, poured money, materials and men into what became variously known as the Uhuru Railway, the Great Freedom Railway and the Tanzam or Tazara Line. Measured in man-hours, it was one of the biggest engineering projects ever undertaken in Africa. Besides the 50 000 African labourers employed, Peking sent a veritable army of Chinese, 20 000 strong, to work on the line. From the start in 1969, it took seven years to complete the 2 000-kilometre line. It was seldom efficiently run, however, and never diverted all of the traffic from the South African routes throughout the remainder of the freedom struggle in the sub-continent.

Big power influence in Africa was exerted by proxy rather than directly. Broadly, the Western powers saw their strategic interests best served for the time being by preservation of the status quo in the white-dominated south, while the Soviet Bloc took an opportunistic interest in the liberation movements. Partly because of this backing, the movements were becoming forces to be reckoned with by the white supremacists. The freedom struggle had made significant progress since the early sixties, when the liberation movements had begun to take up arms against white rule and to establish presences abroad to gather political and material support. In those seminal years the movements had sprung up independently, essentially without collaboration or even communication, sensing and responding to the wind of change.

There had, though, been some inspirational interchange among the founders of the movements in the Portuguese territories. University studies in Lisbon had brought together Agostinho Neto from Angola, Amilcar Cabral from Portuguese Guinea, and Eduardo Mondlane from Mozambique. Their exchanges of ideas had led to each of them opposing Portuguese hegemony and then to Cabral in 1956 founding the *Partido Africano de Independencia da Guine e Cabo Verde* (PAIGC) to challenge the Portuguese in Guinea. And to Neto taking over the leadership of the exiled MPLA from Mario Pinto de Andrade in 1962; and to Mondlane co-founding and heading Frelimo in the same year.

Elsewhere the liberation movements had influenced one another more by distant example than by direct contact. Swapo's formation in South West Africa in 1960, and its establishment of a headquarters in Dar es Salaam in Tanzania in 1961, were essentially autonomous and separate from the parallel developments in South Africa: the ANC and PAC establishing their respective armed wings, *Umkhonto we*

Sizwe and *Poqo*, and the ANC setting up a foreign presence in London. In 1963 Jonas Savimbi formed UNITA, the third of the Angolan liberation movements that were to help end Portuguese domination, and in Rhodesia Sithole broke away from Nkomo's ZAPU to form Zanu. Each of these growths had had a separate genesis, however.

CHAPTER 38

THE FIRST DOMINO

After more than four centuries of it in Africa, the bottom fell out of Portuguese colonialism virtually overnight when on 25 April 1974 leftist military officers toppled Marcelo Caetano's dictatorship in a bloodless coup.

The leftists being opposed to the African wars, Portugal's ancient presence in Africa immediately became untenable. Within months Lisbon had abandoned the colonies, the territories that for Portugal had made the difference between assumed grandeur and relative nugacity. Astonished liberation movements found themselves stepping unopposed into the offices of political power for which they had been fighting for a decade. Almost half a million Portuguese began fleeing from the colonies, leaving behind their homes, businesses, lands and other possessions, in one of the greatest of the white exoduses from Africa.

The coup spun consequences far beyond Portugal and its colonies. The political situation in southern Africa was profoundly affected in a number of ways:

• An opportunity was opened for the Soviet Union to intervene directly in the sub-continent, which in turn prompted a sharper American interest in the region. Whether it was Moscow acting to counter expected American intervention or the other way round, southern Africa became an active theatre of the Cold War, with both superpowers represented on the ground by surrogates.

• With the eastern and western bastions of the white fortress fallen, Rhodesia was left as a salient jutting deep into a hostile, black-ruled Africa, linked to protective South Africa only by the short stretch of border along the Limpopo. Rhodesia's entire eastern border, more than twelve hundred kilometres long, was now exposed to infiltration by guerillas sheltered in Mozambique by a friendly black government. And the country's access to its natural ports of Beira and Lourenço Marques was severed, making Smith's government more than ever dependent on Pretoria. South Africa for its part was brought face to face with the forces of black liberation, both on its own border with Mozambique and on Namibia's border with Angola. The enemy was at Pretoria's very gate.

• For white supremacy's opponents in South Africa and Rhodesia, the collapse of the Portuguese colonial regime came as heartening confirmation that armed struggle could succeed; the fortress was not impregnable after all.

• The coup came as a great stroke of good fortune for the liberation movements in Angola and Mozambique, if not also in Portuguese Guinea, handing them a victory they had not been able to win on the battlefield. In Portuguese Guinea, Cabral's PAIGC had by 1972 liberated enough of the country to hold elections. The next year the movement had made its own unilateral declaration of independence, calling the country Guinea Bissau, and it had soon been recognised by more than sixty governments. The Portuguese, however, remained in command of the main urban centres and of fortified camps elsewhere. And they were still in control of most of Angola and Mozambique when the coup came.

While the coup in a sense gave the liberation movements victory by default, they could nonetheless claim that the victory was verily theirs, for it was their sustained guerilla campaigns that had worn down the Portuguese national will to continue with the wars and had precipitated the coup.

Those at the core of the Caetano autocracy were still for continuing the wars, as were some in the powerful families that dominated Portuguese commerce and politics, and the officers on the right wing of the military. But the larger body of the population, the source of the (white) cannon fodder for the wars, had become embittered by having to send their sons to die in African colonies they could see no great benefit in retaining. Likewise the leftist officers and others in the military who had either moral, political or practical objections to the maintenance of colonialism by force of arms, to the fiction of Portugal-in-Africa, to the subjugation of indigenous peoples who objected to it strongly enough to have fought for their freedom for year after bloody year.

The Caetano regime, successor to the Salazar regime, had continued to resist African nationalism in the colonies partly for reasons of national and historical pride, which was already scarred from India's seizure of the ancient enclave of Goa in 1961. Besides that, the colonies had become economically useful: surpluses generated there had helped offset deficits in the Portuguese balance of payments in the 1940s and 1950s.

The wars, however, had taken an increasingly heavy economic and social toll. At the time of the coup a quarter of Portugal's adult males were serving in the armed forces (even though about half of the troops in the government forces were locally recruited blacks) and the average term of conscription was four years. The Portuguese economy had prospered in the 1960s and early 1970s, profiting from a spillover of the boom elsewhere in Europe. But the African wars, besides taxing Portugal's resources (consuming nearly half the national budget), were distracting the country from joining the other European nations in their exploitation of the growing market on their own continent. And even the military leaders, after seeing more than seven thousand Portuguese die in the fourteen years of conflict, were coming to realise that while the insurgents could not win a military victory in any of the colonies, neither could the Portuguese. It was a stalemate.

What the politicians and generals perhaps did not clearly see was that the social toll of the wars was more telling than the economic one. After more than a decade of having their heirs and their taxes expended on distant African battlefields, most Portuguese had had enough. They had not only had enough of war but they had also had enough of Africa. Many of the thousands of Portuguese settled in the colonies by their government were not committed settlers; they were there only in the hope of making enough money to return as soon as possible to a better life back home. Portuguese who went in search of a better life elsewhere than their homeland tended to go not to Africa but to the Americas or even other parts of Europe. Thus, at the time of the coup in 1974 the half a million Portuguese in Angola and Mozambique were outnumbered by the estimated one million working in the Americas and an equal number working elsewhere in Europe.[1] Naturally, those in Africa were remitting less money to their motherland than those in the Americas and Europe.

By 1974 growing dissatisfaction with the war and the Caetano regime had led to large-scale emigration, to the emergence of left-wing groups, to incidents of sabotage, to draft-dodging and mounting discontent in the armed forces, and to open questioning of the retention of the African territories. In 1972 General Antonio de Spinola, the open-minded military commander in Guinea, recommended negotiations with the PAIGC. Caetano, however, was reluctant to choose sides between the opposing political factions of the armed forces – the reformers represented by Spinola and General Costa Gomes, the leftist chief of staff, and right-wingers such as General Arriaga, the aggressive military commander in Mozambique. In February 1974 Spinola, now deputy commander of the army, went public with his opposition in a book, *Portugal and the Future*. He declared that the colonial wars could not be won, were hampering the country's economic development and causing growing international hostility. Portugal, he said, was threatened with 'revolutionary disintegration'. For his pains Spinola was cashiered, together with Costa Gomes.

Two months later middle-ranking officers in a political movement that had formed in the army, the *Movimento das Forcas Armadas* (MFA), rose in rebellion, ostensibly over pay and promotion grievances, but asking Spinola to take over the presidency. Senior officers, seeing which way the wind was blowing, sided with the coup, and the lower ranks were happy to do likewise. Caetano accepted the inevitable and exited the stage. Spinola agreed to take his place, hoping to keep the colonies in some form of Lusophone federation. But he found himself in charge of an administration and society that had gone into neutral gear. The troops confined themselves to barracks, and the public disregarded the MFA's authority. Civil servants were left in limbo.

It was worse in the colonies, where the whole administrative system collapsed, despite efforts by Arriaga to restore the old order in Mozambique. Without an obedient army to enforce a central will, and with wide public disillusionment with colonialism in general, the ancient empire began to fall apart. The liberation movements quickly seized the initiative, Frelimo advancing south of the Zambezi in Mozambique and all three Angolan movements establishing a presence in Luanda.

The dramatic turn of events caused dismay in Pretoria and Salisbury, whose governments, seeing the advances made by Frelimo, had considered forming, with Portugal, a Zambezi Defence Line, abandoning northern Mozambique to the insurgents but consolidating the defences of the white fortress. Caetano's government, however, had insisted there was no need for any such move. Unconvinced,

Pretoria had begun making contingency plans for dealing with a Portuguese collapse and the likely consequence of either a black government or a white UDI in Mozambique.[2]

Pretoria's worst fears were realised when, under pressure from the increasingly assertive leftists in the MFA, the colonial disintegration became official at the end of July, with Spinola announcing immediate negotiations for the transfer of power to the respective liberation movements, beginning with Guinea. Six weeks later, Guinea's earlier declaration of independence was formally recognised by Lisbon. And three weeks after that, Spinola, unable to control the rampant MFA leftists, resigned.

Amid the near-anarchy in Mozambique, right-wing whites, supported by a smaller number of blacks and mulattoes, formed a Movement for a Free Mozambique and in September tried to stage a counter-coup aimed at seizing power and, presumably, declaring independence. There was a brief flurry of something close to civil war as the troops were deployed to put down the insurrection. In a week of fighting, vandalism and looting, 86 people (27 of them whites) were killed. The rebellion fizzled, and Frelimo assumed power in a transitional government.

According to Ian Smith,[3] 'powerful' military and civilian forces in Mozambique had after the coup in Lisbon sought his collaboration in a plan to seize southern Mozambique and form some kind of association with Rhodesia and South Africa. Smith says he favoured the idea but that Vorster, after giving it some thought, rejected it on the grounds that it would now be unfavourably received in the rest of the world. The real reason, Smith believed, was that it would have conflicted with Vorster's dialogue exercise.

As it became clear to the whites in Angola and Mozambique that Lisbon was abandoning them to black rule, they began to swarm out to safety. Few whites were prepared to take a chance on being fairly treated by the indigenous people after centuries of subjugation, and by the liberation movements after years of vicious war. Many could not accept Marxist government. The great majority of the half-million Portuguese in the two territories fled in a matter of months. Some boarded ships and planes and small boats with whatever they could carry. Others loaded as much as they could in cars and trucks, and drove into South Africa from Mozambique or into Namibia, Zambia and Zaire from Angola. The docksides became littered with crates of goods that the refugees had hoped to ship to Portugal but in the end abandoned.

With the social structure and the economy in collapse, there was no market for possessions, fixed or movable. Few blacks could afford to buy them, or could see any reason to do so, and few whites were remaining to buy. So the refugees abandoned houses, flats, furniture, vehicles. Factories were left with their plant and machinery, offices with their equipment, shops with their stock, farms with their livestock and crops. Beachfront holiday homes were left for the taking, as were yachts at their moorings.

Those who could do so got their money out of the country, in cash, in coins and jewellery, in bank transfers, any way they could. Most of the refugees made their way back to Portugal. A large number, mostly from Mozambique, settled in South

Africa, perhaps hoping to be able to return one day to Mozambique. In South Africa they were certain of a welcome from the Pretoria government (which now had come to value any white skin, even if it covered a Catholic) and from the relatively large Portuguese community already established there.

Overnight, in historical terms of time, Angola and Mozambique had been drained of skills and capital, for one of the effects of colonialism, deliberate or incidental, was that the indigenous people had little of either. Factories and businesses were left without managers, whole industries left rudderless. The boilers and the engines shut down. It was a case of last one out switching off the lights – or leaving them on; who cared? Some plants were deliberately sabotaged. Whole government departments were stripped of administrators. Hospitals had few doctors and nurses. Schools lacked teachers. The police service, courts and other structures of governance were gutted of personnel. Both central and commercial banks were left with meagre holdings, and those of questionable value anyway as the victors prepared for independence with their own new currency.

Though the liberation movements had won, their victories in Angola and Mozambique were pyrrhic in the sense that they had won empty countries, by no means empty of indigenous people but sucked almost clean of finance and expertise, states whose governmental and productive infrastructure stood mainly intact but largely unmanned, ghost states, in a sense. Into these empty structures the liberation movements moved joyously, noisily and incompetently, largely lacking the means of governance, having to learn and invent from scratch in many areas.

Lisbon did indeed make efforts to hold elections in order to establish governments to which it could formally hand over power. But it was on this issue that the freedom struggle ran off the rails. For the liberation movements, freedom meant power rather than democracy. Only the PAIGC in Guinea Bissau made any serious effort to establish elected government. This was relatively easy since there was little organised opposition to speak of. Elections conducted by the PAIGC resulted in the movement taking power virtually unopposed.

In Mozambique, Samora Machel's Marxist-oriented Frelimo refused to tolerate any form of opposition. With only token resistance from Lisbon, it brushed off Portuguese efforts to arrange elections, shouldered aside the minor political groups and installed itself in office in Lourenço Marques. That it did not have the support of all Mozambicans would become distressingly clear later when civil war broke out, exploited and fanned by the white governments in Rhodesia and South Africa for their own purposes.

Nothing as simple as Frelimo's assumption of authority was possible in Angola, where there were three liberation movements – the MPLA, the FNLA and UNITA – strong enough to contend for power, and none much inclined to give up the bullet for the ballot. Lisbon tried to steer the three into a coalition government pending elections. In January 1975 at Alvor in Portugal all three movements signed an agreement to hold elections for a constituent assembly in October, with independence set for 11 November.

A prime objective was to weld the three movements' armed forces, together with a like number of Portuguese troops, into a joint national force that would make further factional fighting difficult. But, having fought the Portuguese for power, none of the movements was willing to risk losing it through the ballot now that it was within reach. They were as willing to fight one another as they had been to fight the Portuguese. Angola was being tossed from the frying pan of colonial exploitation into the fire of indigenous political opportunism. It was being thrown from foreign control that had been relatively constructive even if oppressive into the hands of indigenous politicians who placed party and personal advantage above the welfare of the country and the people, and who would go on to drag the potentially prosperous country into civil war, corruption, starvation, disease, degradation, decay and human misery the like of which has seldom, if ever, been known on the African continent.

Policy differences were not a major factor in the collapse of the transitional government set up under the Alvor agreement. All three parties were agreed on virtually all major issues except the crucial one: the disposition of power. The MPLA's Agostinho Neto had no intention of going through elections, knowing he did not have enough popular support outside the cities to win by ballot. And the FNLA's Holden Roberto, vain, power-hungry and hating Neto, could never have accepted being defeated by him in an election. Savimbi and his fledgling UNITA appeared willing at first to respect an election result but later came to realise that it was an all-or-nothing struggle in which there could be only one winner and the losers would be wiped out. There was to be no second place, no loyal opposition. Only untrammelled power to the victor.

The MPLA, besides being the best organised in the capital, started with a big advantage in that its planned seizure of power was fully backed by the new governor-general appointed by the MFA, Vice-Admiral Rosa Coutinho, widely known as the Red Admiral for his radically leftist views. Much later, in 1984, Coutinho, who had been in charge of the Alvor agreement, confirmed that he had never expected it to lead to elections, describing the very idea as 'a kind of fantasy'. He had favoured Lisbon simply transferring power to the MPLA.[4]

Inevitably, the Cold War flooded into the power vacuum left by the Portuguese in Angola. The sequence of the Big Powers' entry is another chicken-or-egg matter, its definition seemingly dependent on the political sympathies of the definer. Certainly a primary factor was the leftist orientation of the MFA in Portugal and the matching sympathies of the MPLA. Although officially rejecting the Marxist tag attached to it by its opponents, the MPLA was much more inclined to the Soviet Bloc than to the West, which in any case had been tainted by its support of Portugal through Nato. It was from the Soviet Bloc that the MPLA had obtained weaponry for the struggle against Portuguese colonialism, and it was on Moscow that the MPLA again relied for arms to turn against its rival liberation movements. By late 1974 Moscow had sent the MPLA $6-million worth of heavy armaments and had trained large numbers of its officers in Russia.

Fidel Castro, burning with revolutionary fervour in Havana, needed no urging by Moscow, only Soviet weapons and funds, to rally to the cause. Cuba had provided military training to the MPLA – and a bodyguard for Neto – since 1966. By the end of 1974 the numbers of Cuban military advisers and instructors in Luanda had been substantially increased.

The FNLA for its part initially found support in a mainland China ever ready to counter Moscow. However, it did not receive enough military backing to tip the balance against the MPLA before Peking thought better of being drawn into an African brawl and quietly withdrew. Roberto's ally, Mobutu Sese Seko of Zaire, at one stage sent some troops and armoured cars, but again not enough to change the course of events.

Washington viewed the upheaval in Angola with unease. At the height of the Cold War the US still attached a high strategic value to the mineral wealth of southern and middle Africa. There was an associated concern that Moscow was seeking the use of African ports in pursuing its ambition to establish a blue-water naval capability and aimed to take control of the Cape sea route and other 'choke points' of international maritime traffic. The CIA therefore had no difficulty in extending its interests from Zaire to Angola.

A US grant was covertly made to the FNLA in January 1975. American intervention in Angola had in any case been invited by both Zaire and Zambia, whose president, Kaunda, had described the Soviet Union and the liberation movements it supported as 'a plundering tiger with its deadly cubs'. The prospect of the MPLA seizing power worried other African leaders as well, notably those in Ivory Coast, Senegal and Zambia, and if they did not explicitly request American involvement they implicitly endorsed it. In June 1975 the US National Security Council's 'Forty Committee' began to extend aid to both the FNLA and UNITA, channelling it through the CIA.

The MPLA was making its own pleas for help from the Soviet Bloc, and in October Cuba, responding to an appeal from Neto, sent three ships carrying between a thousand and fifteen hundred troops. Their function remained instruction rather than combat, but their very presence, like the US intervention, nudged Angola closer to all-out civil war.

Fighting had already broken out between the Angolan movements early in 1975. In May the Portuguese high commissioner, General Antonio Silva Cardoso, accused the MPLA of working to a deliberate plan to seize power by force of arms. In an effort to halt the slide into civil war, Lisbon persuaded the leaders of the movements to reaffirm the Alvor accord at a meeting at Nakuru, Kenya, in June but it was a fingers-crossed ceremony and the fighting resumed almost immediately. The MPLA, reinforced with more Soviet armaments, and reportedly with the active help of some Portuguese troops, was able to chase both its rivals out of the capital in July. The FNLA was pushed to Ambriz in the north, and UNITA to Silva Porto in the south. The Portuguese government, like most of its troops, appeared to have lost interest in Angola and seemed resigned to leaving the Angolans to fight it out among themselves. Lisbon announced that it would withdraw its forces before Angola became independent on 11 November.

CHAPTER 39

THE BRIDGE TO NOWHERE

In August 1975 a railway carriage was parked in the middle of the bridge across the deep chasm through which the Zambezi River roars after its plunge over the Victoria Falls.

In this way was a neutral venue contrived for negotiations that Prime Minister Vorster of South Africa and President Kaunda of Zambia had engineered between the Rhodesian nationalists and the RF government: a South African Railways carriage with one half in Zambia and the other half in Rhodesia, a mobile conference room figuratively and literally straddling the divide between white-ruled and independent black Africa.

Up on that lonely bridge, Smith may have realised how vulnerable he had been made by the Portuguese coup, which had exposed the intrinsic weakness of the white Rhodesians' situation. They had long been regarded by the British government as expendable; now it seemed they were expendable to Pretoria as well, but for different reasons. Whereas Whitehall was obsessed with getting shot of the vexed Rhodesian problem, Pretoria's concern was that the white Rhodesians' defence of their particular interests should not jeopardise the white South Africans' defence of theirs. Ian Smith clearly thought the two sets of interests overlapped but Vorster evidently disagreed.

As Vorster's government saw it, the Portuguese coup had left it with two choices. One, it could commit its armed forces fully to the defence of a front line along the Zambezi, treating Rhodesia virtually as part of South Africa (which might have meant eventually incorporating it). Or, two, it could pin its hopes on the emergence of a moderate black movement able to form an alliance with the whites that would be strong enough to resist ZAPU and Zanu The latter might then be neutralised through the forging of détente with Mozambique and the other Front Line states.

The first option would be acceptable to most white Rhodesians. And it might have appealed to those South African generals who believed in fighting black nationalism on a front as far as possible from South Africa's own borders in order to lengthen the lines of guerilla infiltration into the Republic. But it would mean committing South Africa to a long and costly conflict against Rhodesian liberation movements that had time on their side and were assured of unending supplies of weaponry and relatively secure bases in friendly black countries. South Africa's resources would be painfully stretched, and international hostility heightened.

Option two would premise that UDI was unsustainable and would require Smith's RF government to be persuaded to accept majority rule with safeguards for the whites. Even with safeguards there was a risk that the whites might become politically dominated and emasculated by the blacks, but it was a risk that Pretoria evidently was prepared to accept as the lesser of the evils on choice. Vorster's government in effect was willing to risk sacrificing the whites in Rhodesia in the interests of saving those in South Africa. If necessary, the 40 000 Afrikaners in Rhodesia could always come to South Africa.

Subsequent events have confirmed that there never was much of a possibility that the white minority in Rhodesia could retain any significant political influence in a country controlled by black leaders obsessed with and competing for power on personal, tribal and, to a lesser extent, ideological lines. Looking back, Vorster's hope that the sacrifice would save his own whites from his own black majority appears astonishingly naive (but then, so does the whole apartheid vision).

Vorster's thinking had been changed by the coup in Lisbon. Previously, he had conducted his dialogue initiative as a long-range exercise, directed at the independent black states in the northern half of the continent. The nearer ones in the sub-continent had been leapfrogged, they being considered already tied to South Africa's ports and economy whether they liked it or not, and therefore manipulable. The coup and the consequent emergence of Mozambique and Angola as bases for cross-border insurgency into South Africa and Namibia altered all that. Pretoria's focus dropped down closer to home. The promotion of dialogue with the distant states became less important than the promotion of détente with the neighbours. Détente became the buzzword. Détente with the north, too, if possible, but first and foremost with the south.

Not much could be done with Angola as it reeled into catastrophe. Mozambique was different, open to pragmatic dealing. The Frelimo government had good reason to avoid confrontation with Pretoria: the repatriated earnings of Mozambicans on the South African mines and the revenue from South African trade passing through Lourenço Marques port formed a large part of Mozambique's revenue. Vorster made it known that Pretoria was not concerned with Frelimo's ideology, only that it should provide stable governance and uninterrupted trade, and refrain from backing ANC insurgency. In return, Pretoria would respect Mozambique's sovereignty. Frelimo's leader, Samora Machel, who would become president with independence in June 1975, was essentially a pragmatist and responded positively to Vorster's intimations.

As far as Zambia was concerned, some groundwork had already been done in private exchanges with Kaunda, beginning in October 1974. Pretoria and Lusaka were agreed on the urgency of a settlement in Rhodesia. Vorster offered to withdraw the South African police (now 2 000 strong) from Rhodesia if Kaunda would stop the Zambian-based ANC insurgents from crossing Zambia's borders in efforts to reach South Africa. The next step would be a ceasefire in Rhodesia and negotiations for majority rule, phased in over five years, with safeguards for the whites. Vorster would persuade Smith to release the detained dissident leaders, and Kaunda would deliver them to the negotiating table. Vorster would likewise deliver Smith.

Vorster's détente initiative had been built partly on the expectation that the Rhodesian government would accept a settlement on the basis of a timetable for the eventual sharing of power between whites and blacks. He believed he had an assurance of this from Smith, and is said to have been badly shaken when at a meeting in Cape Town in February 1975 Smith reversed himself and said he was not prepared to accept even parity, let alone eventual majority rule.[1] Smith's version is that he suggested, by way of testing Vorster's sincerity, that Rhodesia emulate South Africa's apartheid policy. This 'would have destroyed the main plank of détente: the imminence of black government in Rhodesia that was being dangled before Kaunda and Nyerere'.[2] Relations between Vorster and Smith are said to have deteriorated markedly after that meeting.

Vorster and Kaunda attended the opening of the Victoria Falls bridge talks but then retired to another carriage for private talks. Vorster had delivered Ian Smith to the talks by withholding some of the supplies, notably fuel and ammunition, that were vital to the RF government's survival. Smith had duly been persuaded to accept a cease-fire and to free the insurgent leaders, who had then been flown to Lusaka to become Kaunda's responsibility. Vorster had pulled his para-military police out of Rhodesia – though that was a mainly symbolic act, for he had left behind much more effective forces in the shape of helicopters with their air and ground crews.

Smith attended the conference with deep scepticism. He was now growing increasingly embittered, seeing white Rhodesia betrayed not only by London but now also by Pretoria. His own highly efficient military forces were easily containing the insurgency and could, he believed, defeat it if given the wherewithal by Pretoria. He had no faith in either the willingness or the ability of the dissident leaders to negotiate a settlement. As he had expected, the cease-fire that was supposed to have taken effect with the release of the dissidents had been breached almost immediately by their forces with the murder of four South African policemen after they had been persuaded to lay down their arms in a gesture of peace. Smith realised, however, that his dependence on Pretoria gave him little room for independent manoeuvre.

Kaunda had been able to deliver the dissident leaders to the talks by persuading them that they depended on his continued backing not only for their bases in Zambia but also for their international support.

Leading the horses to the water was far from making them drink, however. The liberation movements insisted on presenting demands outside the agreed agenda, which was to discuss arrangements for substantive negotiations, and the RF refused to cooperate. Journalists, cameramen and observers jostled at the ends of the bridge but in the end they had nothing to report but atmosphere. The meeting came to naught, largely because both Vorster and Kaunda had misread the situation on the ground.

Vorster had misjudged the mood of the RF and its supporters, who still believed they could impose their will on Rhodesia. Kaunda for his part had failed to understand that the nationalists were too divided to agree on settlement terms. In Zambia they had been riven by internecine rivalry, even assassinations. Earlier in the year the Zanu military cadres had withdrawn (or been pushed by an exasperated Kaunda) into Mozambique, leaving the Zambian field to Nkomo and his ZAPU. Sithole, though he led the Zanu delegation at the bridge talks, had effectively been supplanted by Robert Mugabe as leader of the movement. Mugabe, ruthlessly climbing to the top of the Zanu pile, had become the key figure, and in reality there was little point in Kaunda getting Nkomo to the conference if he could not deliver Mugabe as well. But Mugabe was no longer beholden to Kaunda and had not bothered to attend. While Sithole vaguely talked peace on the bridge, Mugabe was in Mozambique single-mindedly preparing to escalate the war.

★ ★ ★ ★

Hardly had the journalists and observers departed from the Victoria Falls than they were on their way to yet another meeting over another of the sub-continent's flashpoints: Namibia. In Windhoek's old German drill hall, the Turnhalle, Pretoria had gathered the territory's political groups in the hope of negotiating a constitution that would end, or at least fend off, the increasingly hostile challenge to its administration.

Namibia was the other fly in Vorster's détente ointment after Rhodesia. The two issues had to be resolved in tandem if Pretoria was to hope to get the world off its back.

By 1975 Vorster's government, while still treating Namibia as a province of South Africa, giving it representation in the South African parliament and a form of provincial council to take care of domestic legislation, had abandoned any realistic hope of incorporating Namibia in the face of the growing domestic and international pressure for its independence as a unitary state. Pretoria was now aiming to engineer some form of independence that would retain strong ties with South Africa and preserve the separate existence of the territory's white community. That could be achieved only if the other ethnic communities accepted a similar separation for themselves, probably through some form of federation. A straight handover to Swapo was out of the question, given that organisation's resort to insurgency and its close links with Moscow and the red-hued MPLA.

Vorster's thinking was influenced by his awareness that his own Nationalist constituency in South Africa was far less prepared to see Namibia's mostly Afrikaans whites sacrificed to international pressures than it was to accept the same for those in Rhodesia.

Vorster's first plan had been to tackle the Namibian problem by exploiting the ethnic differences between the indigenous peoples, bantustan-style. Each ethnic group, given its own homeland, would be allowed to decide whether it wanted to become independent or to join the other homelands in a confederation, or to submerge its identity in a unitary state as demanded by the UN. The unstated assumption was that the whites, for whom most of Namibia had been designated as homeland, would opt for independence for their outsize area and form some sort of relationship with South Africa.

The first indigenous homeland, that of the Ovambos (comprising about half of Namibia's population), had been given self-government in April 1973. The next month the same status had been conferred on the neighbouring ethnic region, Kavango.

Vorster attempted to give a further semblance of self-determination in 1973 by forming a multi-racial Advisory Council that supposedly would inform the authorities in Windhoek and Pretoria of the indigenous peoples' wishes. The council was boycotted, however, by both Swapo and the other major political organisation, the South West Africa National Union (Swanu). Vorster's government then came up with the Turnhalle idea.

Unlike the Victoria Falls meeting, which was essentially a one-day stand about talks over talks, the Turnhalle Conference was a long-term project to conduct substantive negotiations over the actual form of independence. At the opening session in September 1975 the conference adopted a Declaration of Intent to produce a constitution within three years.

The concept of ethnic differentiation was broadly supported by the black delegations, which tended to reflect tribal distinctions and to favour ethnic autonomy within some kind of federation. That, however, clashed diametrically with the concept of a unitary state that Swapo, dominated by the majority Ovambo, had successfully sold to the OAU and the UN. A cynical view would be that Swapo's leaders wanted total power in the territory as a whole for the Ovambo majority; a more charitable one that it believed a federal system would not work.

Swapo's leadership in any event refused to attend the Turnhalle conference, leaving the exercise in much the same situation as the Victoria Falls talks: without the key liberation movement.

Even among the indigenous groups that did participate there were squabbles over representation. And both internally and in the outside world there were suspicions that Pretoria intended to use the conference as a divide-and-rule ploy to reduce the non-white groups to puppets of the Namibian whites and of Pretoria. Such fears were hardly surprising when the dominant figure at the Turnhalle was Dirk Mudge, leader of the territory's National Party, which, far from being a strictly Namibian entity, was a branch of Vorster's own National Party in South Africa. And no less surprising when Pretoria continued to implement the segregationist Odendaal Plan, giving bantustan-style independence to the Rehoboth Gebied early in 1976, for instance, while the Turnhalle Conference supposedly was still negotiating basic constitutional forms.

But it was not at the Turnhalle that Namibia's destiny was to be decided. That would be shaped across the border in Angola. Something of a nightmare was growing there for Vorster's government.

★ ★ ★ ★

While the politicians were negotiating at the Victoria Falls and in the Turnhalle, events were spinning ominously faster around the vacuum created in Angola by the Portuguese withdrawal. South Africa was being sucked into the vortex, together with the United States, the Soviet Union, Cuba and the neighbouring states.

The MPLA's seizure of Luanda had raised fears in Pretoria of the MPLA defeating the rival liberation movements and establishing a communist government, a puppet of Moscow. Then Swapo, with MPLA and Soviet backing and with Angolan bases secure from South African attack, would be able to lock South Africa into a long and draining war over Namibia. And, with both Angola and Mozambique lost to communism, Zambia, Malawi and Rhodesia could go the same way, and if Namibia went too South Africa would be left as the last domino.

The Western powers, the United States in particular, were for their part concerned at what seemed to be a dangerous extension of Soviet intrusion into Africa.

It has since come to be fairly widely accepted that neither Moscow nor Havana had any real interest at that time in establishing a permanent presence in Africa, but that was not apparent then in Washington or Pretoria. Moscow was primarily concerned with defending the Soviet Union – its political, economic and strategic interests as well as its ideological values – against the greater powers possessed by the US and its capitalist allies. It was in this light that the Kremlin aspired to gain indirect control of southern Africa's minerals and of strategic 'choke points' such as the Suez Canal, the Red Sea and the Cape. Anything that might help to inconvenience the Western allies or throw them off balance was to be welcomed and exploited. The spreading of Marxism-Leninism was also desirable but less imperative.

The Cubans, far more than the Soviets, were driven by a missionary zeal for Marxist proselytisation. But once they had accomplished this objective in Angola and seen the MPLA firmly in power, Havana would be happy to withdraw.

Washington, not knowing or accepting these verities, was concerned at the prospect of the Soviets establishing in Angola a dominant presence and perhaps military bases, theoretically enabling Moscow to interdict shipping around the Cape; and to support revolution elsewhere in the sub-continent, especially in South Africa, installing friendly governments that would give the Soviets favoured access to the region's minerals; perhaps even to extend its influence northwards through Africa.

The enactment of even a small part of this scenario would have been a major Cold War victory for the regime that Ronald Reagan was later to dub the 'Evil Empire'. The psychological and political consequences would have extended far beyond Africa. Not much credence was given to the worst scenario by Henry Kissinger, the Ford administration's secretary of state, but he was sufficiently concerned to contemplate some kind of intervention. To Kissinger, Africa up to now had been not much more than a shape on the world map, as unimportant as it was large. Now he saw the Soviet-Cuban intervention in Africa as an extension of the Cold War, a new theatre of the rivalry with Russia. For Kissinger, the Angolan intervention was an unwelcome replication of the Soviet intrusion in the Horn of Africa, which he saw as an effort to outflank the US in the Middle East.

Soviet influence in the Horn had greatly increased after the coup in Somalia in 1969 had put the avowedly socialist regime of Siad Barre in power. The Soviets had been giving Somalia substantial military aid since 1962, and in 1975 concluded an arms deal that made Somalia one of the best-armed countries in black Africa. In Washington this was seen as a challenge to US influence in neighbouring Ethiopia, with which the US had had close ties since 1953. In the fifties and sixties, under Haile Selassie, Ethiopia had been the largest recipient of American military and civil aid in Africa. It was partly to counter the growing Soviet influence in Somalia that the aid to Ethiopia had been maintained even after Selassie had been ousted in September 1974 by the military council, the Dergue, and a socialist state proclaimed.

As far as southern Africa was concerned, Kissinger's thinking was initially shaped by the 'Tar Baby' view of continuing white domination in southern Africa and how this related to Soviet ambitions in Africa. Angola had an importance of its own by reason of its oil wealth, which was being tapped by the American oil company, Gulf, and because of its other resources, notably reflected in its prospective status as one of the world's major producers of diamonds and coffee. Ford tended to the view, as he expressed more clearly in 1978, after he had vacated the White House, that the Soviets were 'waging an undeclared war in Africa' for the continent's resources and raw materials, which were 'essential to Western society, especially the United States'.

However, both Ford and Kissinger shrank from any thought of direct American intervention in Angola. Apart from anything else, the US was still trying to come to terms with the traumas of Vietnam and Watergate. Kissinger clearly thought, though, that the Soviets should be countered in Angola in some way, in the interests of curbing the expansionist enthusiasm of the Soviet leader, Leonid Brezhnev. The question was, how to do it?

There had already been some indirect American intervention by that loose cannon of the United States establishment, the CIA, as an extension of its clandestine operations in the Congo. Without the official knowledge of either the Ford administration or Congress, the CIA had begun covertly supplying weaponry to the FNLA in 1974, only three months after the Lisbon coup, according to the former head of the CIA operations in Angola, John Stockwell. The CIA hoped that Roberto's movement would either defeat the MPLA or force it into some form of democratic compromise with its rivals. (The FNLA had also received military assistance from Zaire, Romania and China, though Peking later stopped its aid when it saw Angola becoming a theatre of US-Soviet rivalry and the pariah South Africans becoming involved.)

The CIA may have been reacting to the Soviets' arming of the MPLA, which, according to Kissinger's testimony to a Congressional committee, had begun at about the same time if not a year earlier, in 1973. In January 1975, immediately after the signing of the Alvor accord, the Forty Committee had given the FNLA $300 000 to be used for 'political action'. It had followed this up in July by initiating a $31-million programme of 'para-military' aid to both the FNLA and UNITA, seemingly in response to an increase in Soviet arms supplies to the MPLA.

So by early 1975 the Soviets and Americans were engaged in a tit-for-tat process of boosting the arsenals of the rival Angolan movements. Exactly who began
it is a question that is overshadowed in significance by their mutual willingness to
continue it. Angola was now tragically infected by the leprous touch of the Cold
War, deeply exacerbating the primary infection of internecine party rivalry. Even
after Congress later cut off American aid to the MPLA's rivals, Angola remained in
the grip of a seemingly incurable affliction that would bleed and rot the country
for decades.

The entry of the Cubans in some strength in 1975 added a volatile new dimension to the situation. Havana claimed it had entered the conflict to help the MPLA
repel a South African military invasion in support of the other parties. The South
Africans claimed they had deployed troops to aid the other parties only after the
Cubans appeared on the scene. While the issue is yet another chicken-or-egg question, there is no doubt that Fidel Castro sent his troops to Angola to ensure that it
was the MPLA and not either of the other movements that won power there. It is
also clear that the Cubans were present in a military capacity in the Angolan civil
war before the South Africans became involved in it.

Initially, besides some non-military help, Cuba provided only instructors for the
MPLA forces. Cuban combat troops began arriving in Luanda in August 1975,
according to the then US assistant secretary of state for Africa, Nathaniel Davis.
By September, according to another account, between fifteen hundred and three
thousand Cuban infantrymen with 20 troop carriers, 50 tanks and multiple rocket
launchers were encamped at Porto Amboit, south of Luanda.[3] This was before the
South African Defence Force sent troops against the MPLA, and even before South
Africa began supplying arms to the FNLA and weapons and instructors to UNITA
in late September 1975.

Prior to August, the SADF had, with the consent of the Portuguese, made shallow incursions into Angola to attack Swapo targets. Then on 9 August the SADF
had stationed a small contingent at the Calueque Dam, which had been left un-
guarded by the withdrawing Portuguese. The dam, just across the border on the
Cunene River, formed part of the costly Ruacana project that was being developed
jointly with Portugal to provide water and hydro power for northern Namibia, and
Pretoria did not want to see it left unprotected and vulnerable to Swapo attack.

In the beginning Pretoria was concerned primarily with keeping the MPLA and
Swapo away from the Namibian border, and it was to this end that it had begun
aiding the FNLA and UNITA. Later it apparently extended its interventionist policy to securing the Ovimbundu territory in the south for UNITA, which drew its
support largely from this region. To this end, according to one authority,[4] the SADF
had by late September begun making contingency plans for occupying the whole
area to the Cuanza River, securing the Benguela railway, clearing Swapo from a
militarised belt along the border and, if possible, helping the FNLA in the north.
At a meeting in Pretoria on 23 September, the Rhodesian intelligence chief, Ken
Flower, was told by his South African counterpart, General HJ van den Bergh, that
he was 'planning for the South Africans to participate in an anti-communist group-

ing against MPLA in Angola …'.[5]

In the south-western segment of Africa, in Angola and Namibia, was now about to be played out the last and the greatest of the repercussions of the Cold War's intrusion into the continent. The coming upheaval would be the ultimate consequence of the overlapping of Western decolonisation and Soviet expansionism. This was to be the penultimate heave of the African liberation struggle; victory would leave still to be taken only the greatest prize of all, South Africa.

CHAPTER 40

INVISIBLE SUPPORT

For all its sound and fury, war is a furtive business, and secrecy and deception may be as vital as weaponry. Even after the fighting is over, the obfuscation tends still to shroud perceptions of what happened on the battlefield and what motivated the decisions of the generals and the politicians. The anecdotal camouflage of the conflict may become its history.

So it is with crucial elements of South Africa's intervention in the Angolan conflict, beginning with the question of whether Pretoria had furtive foreign backing for its first invasion in 1975.

The decision to launch the invasion was, of course, essentially a South African one. But there is strong evidence of American and some African encouragement. Pretoria intimated afterwards that it would not otherwise have undertaken the operation.

South Africa, it seems, provided the answer to Kissinger's search for some form of non-American intervention against the Soviets and Cubans. From Washington's perspective, South Africa looked good for that. It had a direct interest in what happened in Angola, and above all a real fear of an MPLA victory there. Despite the non-mandatory UN arms embargo of 1963 – in some ways because of it – South Africa was developing its military strength, and its domestic armaments industry was already producing sophisticated weaponry besides rifles and machine-guns. The SADF was emplaced along the entire 1 680 km of Namibia's border with Angola in order to block Swapo incursions. It would have relatively short lines of communication and supply into Angola.

Pretoria believed that, besides the US backing, its incursion into Angola had the support, clearly even if covertly stated, of a number of influential African governments, notably Ivory Coast, Zambia and Zaire, which were worried about Soviet expansionism in Africa. Some in Pretoria thought the efforts at détente with black Africa might be imperilled if South Africa failed to act strongly against the Soviet danger.

Before August, officialdom in Pretoria had been divided over further involvement in Angola beyond the incursions against Swapo and the guarding of the Calueque Dam. The Department of Foreign Affairs was opposed to any military intervention at all. Some at least of the army generals, supported by Defence Minister PW Botha, were in favour of larger cross-border operations to crush Swapo in Angola.

They reckoned Pretoria would then be free to pursue its own leisurely agenda for Namibian independence.* There was at an early stage support in the military for a positive response to the pleas from the FNLA and UNITA for weapons and instructors. Prime Minister Vorster, however, was reluctant to heed these pleas, and later reluctant to extend direct intervention beyond Calueque.

Both the military and politicians in South Africa wanted to avoid clashes with the MPLA if possible. However, as that movement gained the upper hand over its rivals, fears grew in Pretoria that with the MPLA in power the limited war against Swapo would intensify and spill ever more strongly over the border into Namibia. South Africa would then have no option but to strike at Swapo in Angola on a large scale, which would necessarily mean striking against the MPLA as well. Rather do it now than later from a weaker position, some of the generals argued. Rather keep the MPLA (and therefore Swapo) out of southern Angola, away from the border. But if this had to be done with SADF help, that aspect should remain clandestine.

Thus when SADF instructors were sent to UNITA headquarters at Nova Lisboa they were ordered to speak English rather than what was in most cases their native Afrikaans in order to create the impression that they were hired mercenaries.**

The incremental nature of war was already coming into effect, however. When MPLA forces struck southwards in September and threatened Nova Lisboa, UNITA was reckoned not strong enough on its own to hold back the advance. Pretoria, deciding that the defence of Nova Lisboa was imperative, ordered the SADF to take appropriate action. From the 19 instructors at Nova Lisboa and a battalion of UNITA troops, the SADF hastily formed what was rather grandiosely named Battle Group Foxbat. Among the instructors were six armour specialists sent to teach UNITA to operate the three old French Panhard armoured cars that were the movement's only armoured vehicles. There were also three Entac anti-tank missile launchers mounted on Land Rovers.

Foxbat and the advancing MPLA forces clashed at Norton de Matos on October 5, and the advancing MPLA columns were stopped.

This action might perhaps be taken as the beginning of Pretoria's war against the MPLA-Cuban-Soviet alliance in Angola, except that it was a reflexive response to an emergency rather than part of the strategically planned offensive that was launched later, code-named Operation Savannah. Either way, however, Pretoria had pretty well accepted the risk of conflict with the MPLA, although it still hoped to limit it and to keep South Africa's role covert, to this end making as much use as possible of FNLA and UNITA troops.

Pretoria hoped that with a little help these forces would be able to drive the MPLA from as much as possible of southern Angola before the formal advent of independence on 11 November. If they could seize the Benguela railway and occupy the ports and major towns in the southern half of the country, UNITA and/ or the FNLA could advance a stronger claim than the MPLA to the leadership of

---

*While Pretoria had now accepted the inevitability of Namibian independence, it hoped to arrange it on its own terms, without Swapo in power and with the country still functioning within South Africa's ambit.
**SADF instructors had also been sent to help the FNLA at two camps in southern Angola in September 1975.

Angola at independence.[1]

The thinking was influenced by the knowledge that international support for the various Angolan liberation movements was then sharply divided, notably in the OAU, where there was strong opposition to Soviet intervention through the MPLA.

The MPLA for its part probably felt it could not allow the FNLA and UNITA time to become established in the north and the south respectively without risking prolonged conflict or the dismemberment of Angola among the three movements. So, bristling with Russian weaponry, it launched offensives in both directions from Luanda. It might not have been expected in Luanda that South Africa would intervene, but Moscow was perhaps happy to see it do so and get sucked into a war it could not win as long as the Soviets kept sending arms and Cuba troops to support the MPLA.

With the independence deadline only weeks away, the South Africans had to move quickly. Operation Savannah was to be spearheaded by a battle group named Taskforce Zulu, which was hastily thrown together from a battalion of 'Bushmen' recruited on both sides of the border, three companies of half-trained soldiers from the Chipenda faction of the FNLA and a handful of SADF officers. So hurriedly was the operation pulled together that there was insufficient transport, and the troops set out from Namibia on 14 October in vegetable trucks and furniture vans commandeered from Portuguese civilians fleeing Angola. All the men, including the South Africans, wore FNLA uniforms.

Ten days later, the column was strengthened by more white troops – some infantry, a mortar group and a squadron of armoured cars, Eland-90s, the former Panhards that had been extensively modified by the SADF and were to become the highly effective work-horses of the war. Foxbat, still in Angola, had also been reinforced with a squadron of Elands two weeks after the action at Norton de Matos.

Pretoria was still confident of American support when Taskforce Zulu crossed the border at Cuangar on 14 October. In quick succession it seized Pereira d'Eca, Villa Rocades, Joao de Almeida, Sa da Bandeira and then, on 27 October, entered the port of Mocamedes, about eight hundred kilometres from its departure point. In the next ten days, fighting off increasingly strong MPLA/Cuban resistance, Zulu advanced about five hundred kilometres, taking Benguela, the terminal port of the railway serving the Zairean and Zambian copper mines, and then Lobito port further north.

While Zulu was dashing up the coast, Foxbat advanced further inland, also encountering strong resistance. By early November the two columns had virtually accomplished their mission, seizing control of most of southern Angola before the independence deadline. Savimbi was content to negotiate the future dispensation from this position of strength. Not so the FNLA's Roberto, who became obsessed with a vainglorious plan to seize Luanda itself, rejecting the urgings of his SADF and CIA advisers that he sit tight and negotiate with the beleaguered MPLA.

Evidently seeing that Roberto was not to be deterred from his foolhardy assault, Pretoria flew in three 5,5-inch guns with crews to give the FNLA at least some artillery. It also agreed to support the assault with a bombing run by SAAF Canberra jet bombers.

Roberto launched his attack on 9 November along a narrow strip between the sea and inland marshes, a suicidal route exposing the attackers to the MPLA's massed artillery. The SADF artillery duly laid down a barrage on the MPLA and Cuban positions. The Canberras, having flown 1 200 km from the base at Rundu in Namibia, dropped their bombs on time – though largely without effect, having been ordered to remain at high altitude to avoid any of them being shot down and South Africa's participation thus revealed (as if anyone other than the South Africans could have conducted such an air raid!). But the ground attack, having been delayed by Roberto to allow him to have a leisurely breakfast, was launched long after the defenders had had time to recover from the bombardment. Their artillery blasted the FNLA troops off the narrow approach route, and the attack failed dismally.

Although the FNLA continued to operate sporadically thereafter, and made its own declaration of independence in the north, it was effectively finished as a military and political force, and Roberto along with it. The MPLA and UNITA were left to fight it out for domination of the country.

The debacle at Luanda left the SADF artillerymen trapped deep inside Angola. The CIA unit that had undertaken to help extricate them if necessary had absconded from what was now seen in Washington as a lost cause. Withdrawing to Ambriz on the northern coast, the gunners radioed for help from home. Eighteen days after the battle they were rescued in a hazardous operation by the SA Navy, being taken off at night in the boats and the helicopter of the frigate SAS *President Steyn* while it stood close inshore. The guns were taken out through Zaire.

Operation Savannah ended with the South Africans at Novo Redondo, within striking distance of Luanda itself, but halted for the present by blown bridges across the rivers. Some military officers and politicians asserted afterwards that the SADF could, if so ordered, have gone on to take Luanda and install UNITA there. Pretoria would have been hard put, however, to ensure that UNITA's occupation became permanent.

Operation Savannah had so far achieved rather more than its planners had originally envisaged. Having travelled more than three thousand kilometres in its advances and fought more than fifty actions in just 33 days, it had driven the MPLA-Cuban forces north of the Benguela railway. By mid-December a newly-formed combat group, code-named X-Ray, had seized the railway as far as Luso in eastern Angola and another, called Orange, had thrust up the centre in an unsuccessful effort to find river crossings that would open a way to Luanda. UNITA could not hold the captured territory, however, without substantial Western and African support, neither of which appeared forthcoming.

American aid to UNITA and the FNLA was in fact specifically prohibited when on 19 December the US Senate, fearful of getting into another Vietnam, voted for an amendment initiated by Democratic senator Dick Clark.

The senator was either unaware or unconcerned that the measure would enable the MPLA-Cuban-Soviet alliance to seize the military initiative and effectively end prospects of a negotiated, political solution in Angola. Kissinger has claimed that after the adoption of the Clark Amendment Cuba more than doubled its forces in Angola and Moscow greatly increased the scale of its military aid.

The South Africans now began preparations for a phased withdrawal, but held off to see which way the OAU would vote at its long-postponed meeting on the Angolan issue. Operation Savannah had perversely changed the situation, however, especially when four SADF soldiers captured in Angola were paraded at the OAU conference in Nigeria. The key state, Nigeria, formally recognised the MPLA on 6 December.

Despite this, the OAU was split down the middle when it voted on 18 January. With the help of strong American lobbying, a Senegalese proposal for a cease-fire, foreign troop withdrawal and government of national unity won 22 votes. But a Nigerian motion for recognition of only the MPLA got the same number of votes. The South African invasion and the Clark Amendment were together swinging the issue the MPLA's way. Some African states had been angered by the disclosure of the South African invasion, and now saw South Africa as a greater danger than the Soviet Union. The Clark Amendment having seemingly ended any prospect of Western support for the FNLA or UNITA, African governments began to accept what they saw as the reality of unchallenged Soviet power in Angola. One after the other, they recognised the MPLA government and it became a landslide.

With the African support vanishing, with the US publicly recoiling from any involvement, and with Cuban troops and Soviet weaponry still pouring in, the SADF began its gradual withdrawal on 23 January, with the MPLA/Cuban forces moving in behind them as they pulled out. The last SADF troops crossed into Namibia on 27 March. A few days later the first MPLA troops arrived at the border, and the South Africans negotiated an agreement with them for the protection and continued working of the Calueque Dam project.

★ ★ ★ ★

Operation Savannah's soldiers were hailed as victors when they pulled back into Namibia, with the minister of defence and military brass saluting from a dais hastily erected on the banks of the Cunene. They had indeed won all their battles and done more than had been expected of them. But in the end it had all been in vain, for, as is often the lot of the soldier, their triumph on the field of battle had been turned to defeat on the field of politics.

Both strategically and politically, the Angolan invasion had been a failure and Pretoria's worst fears had been realised. What Operation Savannah had attempted to prevent had in fact come about. The 'Marxist' MPLA was installed in Luanda and ensconced all the way down to the Namibian border. An estimated twelve thousand Cuban troops were stationed in Angola. The MPLA had widely been recognised as the government of Angola, and as such accepted as a member of the OAU. It would soon be admitted to the UN.

The FNLA was fading away and UNITA had been chased into the wilderness of the south-east. Swapo was now free to strike into Namibia from bases just inside Angola. Pretoria's hopes for détente with black Africa had been severely set back, if not ruined. And America's backing for South African military support of the anti-communist movements in Angola had vanished.

Washington denied that it had ever supported Operation Savannah. Pretoria openly insisted the backing had been given, seemingly tearing off the veil in anger after being left out on a limb in the glare of the world's spotlights. Both Vorster and PW Botha later spoke bitterly about being left in the lurch by Washington after being encouraged to go ahead with the invasion. Kissinger, however, denied it under oath before a Congressional committee.

Had South Africa not launched Operation Savannah the result would have been the same in strategic terms: the MPLA-Cuban forces would have reached the Namibian border and isolated UNITA in the south-east. But the Clark Amendment might not have been adopted, and the Senegalese motion might have prevailed in the OAU, putting pressure on the MPLA to accept negotiations for a political solution and obstructing the Havana-Moscow ambition of putting their protégé in power through the gun.

Swapo might, of course, in the mean time have begun striking into Namibia from more secure bases in southern Angola, prompting SADF cross-border retaliation and, inevitably, clashes with MPLA-Cuban forces. But Pretoria would have been operating from a sounder political base, even if the clashes had escalated into something approaching the all-out war that later erupted in southern Angola.

As it was, the MPLA-Cuban-Soviet alliance was able to wage unrestrained war against UNITA, a war in which South Africa became ever more deeply and unavailingly embroiled, and which it had to fight alone against heavy Cuban and Soviet involvement on the MPLA side.

Besides losing support in black Africa, the Vorster government had seen its standing among white South Africans damaged through its efforts to keep the invasion secret from its own electorate. Determined efforts were made to keep the South African public ignorant of their country's very participation in the fighting in Angola, let alone of any details of it. It had been a furtive slide into war, leaving many of the electorate unable to support or oppose it with much conviction.

For much of the operation, young white soldiers – conscripts this time, not volunteers – fought and some died deep inside Angola, and neither their mothers nor the rest of the public knew they were there. The men were known to be serving in a theatre of conflict vaguely and euphemistically described by the government and the SADF as 'the border'.

Most of the public at first presumed the men were guarding the Namibian border against Swapo 'terrorists' infiltrating from Angola. The parents did not know that their boys were hundreds of kilometres deep in Angola, fighting not Swapo insurgents but Angolan and Cuban troops. Or that they were rapidly being outnumbered by more Cuban troops, rushed into Angola by the thousand in a massive sea and air lift, and that the Soviet Union was arming the MPLA and Cuban forces with planeloads and shiploads of its latest weaponry.

The 'border war' was the first in which the South African government had been forced to resort to conscription rather than the voluntary recruitment of the world wars and Korea. Consequently, it was the first in which military service had been refused by young whites – on a relatively small scale but enough to make the government deal harshly with offenders. A number fled the country as conscientious objectors, and some of these joined the exiled wing of the ANC.

Had the whites known the true situation in 1975 they might have been less acquiescent than they were of the commitment to this war, despite the fears that had made them increasingly support the government in the more recent general elections. Those fears had deliberately been fanned by the right-wing Afrikaners who now ruled the country through the semi-secret *Broederbond* organisation, which both fashioned and operated the levers of power within the National Party and government.

With extraordinary determination and astuteness, the Afrikaners had burrowed their way up through the layers of Anglican domination imposed after the Boer War and had taken over as the major political force. The National Party's victory in 1948 had opened an aperture of opportunity through which conservative Afrikaners had resolutely poured. The party had Afrikanerised all government departments and state services. The employment thus offered had helped to reduce the poor white problem – a largely Afrikaner phenomenon – to a point where it was no longer a social crisis. The government had furthermore stimulated the creation of Afrikaner commercial and industrial institutions – from banks to fertilizer factories – that had become major influences in the economy. Afrikaners had become big players in the stock market, and prominent among the country's wealthiest citizens.

So now the Afrikaners had more to lose than ever before, and therefore more to fight for. But so, for that matter, did the English-speakers, whose standard of living was also higher in general than it had ever been. Most of them perceived the same threats to their way of life as did the Afrikaners, and were as willing to defend it.

In nearly three decades of National Party rule, the perceptions of white rights, especially among younger people, had largely been influenced by the education and information systems shaped by the government. Young whites mostly accepted without question that their kind had an inalienable right to the lands held by their race and to the wealth they believed had been created by their race. These beliefs, inculcated in school, had been reinforced by the monolithic state radio services.

Until 1976, television had been denied to South Africans by a government fearful that it would open blacks' minds to the outside world and make them more difficult to dominate. Then, realising the power of the medium, the government had created a monopolistic state TV system and made it a propaganda instrument even more effective than radio.

Broederbond-controlled newspapers also helped influence Afrikaner thinking. The English-language newspapers remained a problem, even though their character and content was controlled by editors who traditionally had never been much more liberal in their thinking than Jan Smuts, and who in any case had to take care not to think too far ahead of the mass of the white readers – and, more important, not to jeopardise the interests of the mining and other business concerns which owned the newspapers.

The English-language press was nevertheless enough of a nuisance for the government to impose restrictions, backed by harsh penalties, on reportage and comment. Broadly, the restrictions covered almost all aspects of opposition to apartheid and government efforts to curb it, as well as almost all military and much police activity. Though there was never direct censorship, the threat of it persuaded the newspaper owners to do a deal with the government that amounted to editors having to accept a large measure of self-censorship. Editors were left uncertain how far they could go in testing the boundaries of their freedom. One of them is reputed to have likened it to walking blindfold on a tightrope over a minefield.

By the time South Africa launched Operation Savannah, the whites in general had come to believe that their way of life was gravely threatened, not only by communist forces intent on imposing a totalitarian system but also by a non-communist world more concerned with its own moral perceptions than with the cultural survival of the African whites, a world baying for sanctions and other coercive measures against apartheid regardless of the consequences.

And so, for weeks, as the SADF columns raced ever deeper into Angola, Pretoria remained silent about the operation. The news media were barred from reporting or commenting on it, even when soon after the start it became clear from reports from Europe what was happening. While the rest of the world was given daily accounts of the progress of 'the South African force', the South African public was kept in the dark. The state-controlled radio meekly complied with the censorship, but the privately owned newspapers resorted to innuendo and suggestion, sailing as close to the legal wind as they dared in order to pass on the information they were receiving from foreign news reports and, in the case of the Argus group, from the reporters its own Africa Service had operating in Angola.

In the beginning the government had good enough reason for keeping the Angolan venture under wraps. None of the covert support of the US and African states could be maintained if it became known that the armies of apartheid were fighting a black 'liberation movement' in an African country about to become independent. And exposure would kill off any hope of extending détente.

Once the cat was out of the bag, however, the need for secrecy beyond basic military needs fell away. Yet Pretoria persisted in maintaining it within South Africa, to a point where it became ludicrous and self-damaging.

Few, if any, in Pretoria appreciated in the beginning what South Africa was getting into with its Angolan intervention. It was supposed to be a quick incursion that would have the SADF forces out in a few weeks at most. Those weeks, however, stretched into months and then years. The involvement in Angola was to run, intermittently, for 13 years, longer than the two world wars together. If the Angolan campaign is taken as an extension of the conflict against Swapo in Namibia then it was much longer – 22 years from the beginning of Swapo's insurgency in 1966 to the signing in 1988 of the New York Accords under which South Africa withdrew from Angola. Either way, it was to be the longest war fought by white South Africa, the only one fought against another African state, against a fellow member of the UN and against a member of the OAU. Most significantly, it would be the last war for white supremacy in Africa – and one that would be lost.

The war would force white South Africans to overcome their ancient fear of arming the blacks and to admit them to an ever-greater degree into its armed forces, eroding one of the prime underpinnings of apartheid. The country would escalate its extraordinary development of an armaments industry, one capable eventually of making jet fighters and an uncommonly effective attack helicopter, of producing the word's deadliest artillery and of making intermediate-range rocket missiles with a potential nuclear capability. From that armaments base would spin off a wider industrial technology creating new job opportunities for all races.

The political consequences of the conflict would be seismic, leading to Pretoria having to abandon Namibia to a UN-supervised independence. The collapse of white supremacy in Rhodesia would be hastened, reducing the white fortress to South Africa alone, and soon that, too, would succumb to black rule.

CHAPTER 41

TIME RUNNING OUT

Ten weeks after withdrawing from Angola, the apartheid government found itself confronting an eruption in its own domain that was possibly even more dangerous than the one over the border.

What the government had sowed, it began to reap when on 16 June 1976 the most serious riots South Africa had known broke out as high school pupils took to the streets of Soweto township.

The spark for the demonstrations had come from an official attempt to make Afrikaans a medium of instruction on an equal basis with English, evidently in the belief that this would strengthen the cultural power of Afrikaans. The students, however, saw it only as a reinforcement of apartheid. Their rioting was not only a rejection of the Afrikaans edict but also of all of the injustices and indignities of apartheid and, indeed, of what they saw as the timidity of their fathers in bowing to white oppression, however resentfully.

Harsh police action failed to stop the Soweto rioting from spreading to almost every black township in South Africa and to coloured townships as well. By the time the violence ended in October 1977, some seven hundred people, many of them secondary school pupils, had been killed by government security forces.

It had quickly become clear to the more perceptive whites that things would never be the same again in South Africa. White supremacy simply could not be maintained in peace when white prosperity depended on huge numbers of blacks working and making their homes in the white areas, blacks who bitterly resented their enforced inferiority and restricted opportunities. In these circumstances, blacks had no option but to grow increasingly militant in their protests and more violent in their opposition.

To most of the blacks, the bantustan concept of separate development was a sham. If, indeed, any blacks did accept its basic premise they could not but regard it as woefully inadequate for creating a fair political and economic dispensation. The government had only two realistic options: either impose segregation on an equitable basis or abandon it, and it was not prepared to do either. Most blacks for their part were not prepared to accept the former, out of mistrust if for no other reason.

While the ANC was strengthening its underground activities within the country and extending its organisation and support abroad, black political expression was taking new forms within the country, notably in the growth of the black conscious-

ness movement. In essence, the movement rejected the paternalism and exploitation intrinsic to the apartheid policies and affirmed black pride and independence.
When attempts were made to formalise the movement in a Black People's Convention the government tried to block it by jailing the movement's leaders in 1974.
The ethos lived strongly on, however.

At the same time, the government's efforts to satisfy the political aspirations of
the coloured and Indian communities without giving them too much power were
achieving only limited success, and protest continued to simmer in both groups.

The ruling Afrikaners were themselves divided even in their dominance, split
now between the right-wing extremists of the breakaway *Herstigte Nationale Party*
and the more moderate adherents of the governing party. The right-wingers' demands for unadulterated apartheid were forcing the premier to take more conservative positions than he might have preferred in order to protect his own support
among the electorate. At the same time the international pressures against those
stances were eroding the economy, and trade and budget deficits were developing.

There was some light for Vorster in the gloom. Despite an Opec ban on supplies
of oil to South Africa, oil was still being provided by Iran in return for technical
aid. South Africa was building up huge stockpiles and at the same time expanding
its domestic production through its world lead in the technology of extracting oil
from coal.

Perhaps because of the opposition in some foreign quarters to the sanctions and
because of the exaggerated importance given by Pretoria to the cries of support it
heard from right-wingers in the West, Vorster's cabinet was still labouring under the
delusion that its policy was simply misunderstood by governments and critics in
Europe and America. The critics, it was thought, failed to distinguish between racism and apartheid's concept of egalitarianism within separation, of a vertical partition of different peoples, each free to embrace democracy among its own kind. If
only Pretoria could break through the misconceptions among the Western press,
politicos and public, its policy might yet be seen to be fair, practical and desirable.
And the opposition to apartheid would be seen to be driven largely by self-serving
black politicians, sentimental Western liberals and communist-bloc zealots.

There evidently was growing within Vorster's government a perception that its
policies of egalitarian segregation were being confused in the West with the qualified franchise policies of Smith's government in Rhodesia, which were seen to be
intended to extend white supremacy as long as possible. Apartheid, in contrast, was
supposedly not about supremacy but about separation. It was not about a qualified
franchise, it was about one-man-one-vote, but in separate ethnic territories. Pretoria believed the interests of the whites in South Africa were increasingly being jeopardised by the refusal of those in Rhodesia to accept majority rule.

The Rhodesians might see themselves as allies of the South Africans in the defence of the white fortress, but in Pretoria they were increasingly being perceived
as a liability. Besides aspects of political strategy, some influential Afrikaner politicos
could not forget the Rhodesian connection with the Jameson Raid, and that the
Rhodesians had in 1922 rejected union with the Afrikaners in South Africa. The

40 000 Afrikaners in Rhodesia could always find a home in South Africa if Rhodesia fell to majority rule. But even if they had to be sacrificed to save the 75 000 Afrikaners in Namibia, so be it.

Even after seeing his détente ambitions snuffed out in Angola, Vorster still believed South Africa's interests were being compromised by Smith's intransigence. Vorster appears still to have hoped that by cooperating with the Western powers, by persuading Smith to accept majority rule with guarantees for the whites, Pretoria might get the West to accept a different dispensation in South Africa, namely, separate territories for different races. Not that he appears to have received any encouragement from Washington or London to cherish that hope. It may be that he believed it might at least buy time for Pretoria to adapt its own policies closer to something that would get the rest of the world off its back. Vorster may also have hoped for something along the same lines for Namibia, despite Swapo's support in the OAU and UN. And, perhaps, if that hope died, Namibia, whites and all, would at least remain a bargaining counter for acceptance of a separate existence for the whites in South Africa.

Any such expectations were in fact unrealistic, given that an outside world now largely following black Africa's lead was not going to favour any special dispensation for the South African whites that formed part of the exploitive bantustan concept. Vorster's government, however, blinkered by its obsession with a separate existence for the whites, was oblivious of the realities and the need for radical change.

The Smith government, for its part, was reluctant to accept majority rule in any form that would destroy white privilege. And Smith himself was growing increasingly bitter at what he saw as Pretoria's betrayal of the joint interests of the whites in the sub-continent.

Vorster, however, was well aware of how Smith's position was steadily worsening. As the SADF was completing its withdrawal from Angola, Mozambique had closed its border with Rhodesia (on 3 March 1976), cutting the UDI state off from the ports of Beira and Maputo and initiating a sharp escalation in the scope and intensity of the insurgent war. On 19 March Nkomo had formally ended his bilateral settlement talks with Smith. Nkomo's chief backer, Kaunda, had called for an intensification of the armed struggle. Three days later the foreign secretary, James Callaghan, set out his independence proposals and committed Wilson's Labour government to the NIBMAR policy on Rhodesia. Rhodesian forces, retaliating against stepped-up guerilla incursions across the borders, had by now turned increasingly to raids into Mozambique and Zambia against insurgent bases there, further internationalising the conflict.

Vorster was himself now feeling a new sense of vulnerability. Not only was he coming under stronger pressure externally but his policies were being resisted with growing determination domestically as well. Externally, the policy of dialogue and détente on which he had embarked in the confidence of his economic and military strength had been blown away by the events in Angola. His dream of a friendly Africa accepting a benign separation of the races in South Africa had dissipated with the battlesmoke of Savannah. From now on the few African governments willing to deal with him would feel obliged to do so in secret. As would later become apparent, it did not help much for Pretoria to announce that it had covert trade and other associations with a number of African states when it was barred from all open discourse. For those black states still having truck with South Africa it was like dealing through the back gate of a leper colony in the dead of night.

To no avail would Pretoria with much fanfare make the Transkei the first of the bantustans to advance from 'self-government' to 'independence' in 1976; no state other than South Africa would recognise it. There was by the same token to be no recognition of the other half of the bantustan policy, a separate white state, for that concept had become intolerable to black Africa and therefore unacceptable to Europe and America.

Black Africa and the West each pursued its own vision of democracy in South Africa for its own reasons. The Africans wanted to end the insult of white hegemony (perhaps in some cases even the affront of whites wanting a separate existence from blacks) and to ensure that all of South Africa came under majority rule. The Western powers wanted to remove white supremacy as an element of Cold War competition, and perhaps also to expunge the residual guilt of slavery and colonialism.

A peripheral aspect of the Western attitude was the inability, or unwillingness, to see the whites in South Africa as Africans. Although they had been abandoned by Europe as kin they were still regarded as Europeans living in Africa. Thus the Western nations could ignore black hegemony over other blacks elsewhere in Africa, such as the Nigerian government's refusal to let the Ibos break free of Lagos's control, while denouncing white hegemony in South Africa. Apartheid was seen by the Europeans not as an African thing but as a continuation of their own past racism and colonialism.

If ever there had been any willingness to make a distinction between the two, however, it was made impossible by the exploitiveness basic to the apartheid policy. Both Africa and the West were unanimous in seeing Pretoria's vision of a white state within the bantustan concept for what it was: a realignment of the political structure that retained the old white privileges.

The self-serving expediency of the bantustan plan was plainly manifest in its geography. Not only did the bantustans amount to a very small proportion of the country as a whole, but few of them were a whole piece, the rest comprising a number of parts separated by white territory. The 'independent' state of Bophuthatswana was an especially ludicrous scattering of six widely spaced bits, one of them 250 kilometres away from the nearest other bit. Apartheid's social engineers might have envisaged a more rational consolidation of the fragmented bantustans at a later stage, when white opinion might be more amenable to the large interspersing areas of white-owned land being given to the blacks. But on the face of it, in the seventies the bantustan map looked to the world at large more like a hoax than a serious concept.

It is unlikely that black South Africans would as late as the seventies have accepted an alternative division of South Africa to ensure the continuance of a separate white state. To win acceptance it would have had to be a radical division, requiring huge sacrifices of land, possessions and power by the whites. It is difficult to envisage the whites giving up the gold mines of the Transvaal, the sugar estates of Natal, the horizon-to-horizon maize fields of the Free State, the cattle ranches and timber plantations and the cities and ports that had been established in areas once occupied by blacks. It is equally difficult, however, to envisage a viable division without the sacrifice of a large part of these assets.

Most of the whites simply could not countenance an equitable division of the land, not only out of selfishness or greed but also because they had been brought up to believe that they had a right to what they held and that black people had no right to it, only to the land that they, the blacks, now held. In 1974 a poll conducted by two German academic institutions showed that a large majority of the whites, 84 per cent, were opposed even to a suggestion that South Africa be divided equally between the blacks and the whites, let alone on a basis proportional to the respective populations, which would more or less have reversed the proportionality of the land holding.[1] Two years later, a similar poll by the same institutions revealed that the opposition to an equal split had come down to 63 per cent. Even then it was probably too late for any such division to have much chance of acceptance. Though debated academically, the concept was never raised as a serious proposition in political circles.

When the whites eventually surrendered power to the majority, the more extreme among them were left only with the pathetic option of trying to set up a tiny white state called Orania in the dry north-west of the country, an attempt so unrealistic that it was essentially ignored by the black-dominated government. Orania could at most be little more than a white town and perhaps a few farms. That was what grand apartheid, the Verwoerdian dream, had come down to. There was a certain apt pathos in the fact that Orania's most prominent citizen was Betsie Verwoerd, widow of apartheid's grandmaster.

Seeing a need for the political support of the coloureds, the Afrikaners had begun to see them as *bruin Afrikaners* (brown Afrikaners) but few of the white Afrikaners would welcome the brown ones into their perceived 'chosen race', not as equal citizens of the white state. Or into their church, not in the same pews and certainly not in the front ones and, God forbid, never in the pulpit.

Demographic acrobatics aside, the outside world's rejection of segregation in South Africa was matched by the determination of the majority of the whites to retain it. And the National Party government was caught in the trap of its own arrogance. Its blinkered intransigence having forced the blacks in South Africa and their supporters to take extreme measures against apartheid, any concessions now made by Pretoria would perforce have to be equally extreme, and therefore more unpalatable to the white electorate.

In the mid-seventies, while the apartheid government was pleading for the outside world to give it time to bring its vision to completion, it was giving the world no reason or substance to believe that its intentions were either realistic or honourable.

★ ★ ★ ★

Henry Kissinger blazed onto the African scene in 1976 somewhat like a comet in a dark sky – but one with a waning tail. The secretary of state came to Africa as the *wundermensch* of Washington, a luminary who outshone his drab president, Gerald Ford, appropriating to the State Department much of the glitter that normally emanated from the White House.

Kissinger had dazzled the international scene with his wit, intellect and social glitz. More practical prestige was attached, though, to his peacemaking skills; he had been awarded the Nobel Peace Prize for his work in ending the Vietnam war, and high hopes were held for his intervention in the Arab–Israeli conflict.

As he jetted into Dar es Salaam, African leaders waited for the wizard to work his magic on what they and most of the rest of the world saw as the continent's most serious problem – not the degeneration and dictatorship in independent Africa but the protraction of white hegemony in the south. Black Africa, knowing his conservative views and perhaps suspecting his involvement in Angola, was sceptical but not without hope. What the Africans did not yet know was that Kissinger's thinking had been turned around by the events in Angola. At the turn of the decade, having focused his famous intellect for the first time, and probably superficially, on the African continent, he had concurred with the 'Tar Baby' Option.

This view had been reversed, however, by the unexpectedly vigorous entry of the Cubans and Russians into the Angolan theatre. If Kissinger did indeed back the SADF invasion of Angola, as is now widely accepted, he probably expected that it would result in no more than the FNLA and UNITA occupying enough territory to firm up their considerable support in black Africa and force the MPLA to accept a joint interim government. He had very likely been surprised by Havana's eagerness to intervene in strength and Moscow's willingness to arm that intervention to the hilt.

These actions had posed a challenge at which the American superpower, wounded by Vietnam, had quailed. While the deployment of American troops in Angola to counter the communist inroads had never been an option, the Clark Amendment had made it plain that even the supply of American arms to a Pretoria–UNITA alliance would be blocked by Congress. The American legislative arm, if not the executive, was willing to leave the field to the communists. Kissinger was not going to get himself stuck out on a limb with the South Africans, and he quickly retreated from it, leaving them exposed and angry there.

The withdrawal of the South Africans from Angola had emphasised that Pretoria was neither willing nor able to take on the MPLA–Cuba–Soviet alliance alone. And Moscow, having established that the US was unwilling to become directly involved in hostilities against that alliance, could for its part now extend its foothold in southern Africa without fear of military interference. America was in a quandary: it could not easily block communist imperialism in southern Africa if at the same time it meant defending white supremacy, and the Kremlin was happy to exploit Washington's dilemma.

Savannah was a triple setback for Washington: the Soviets and their Cuban allies were now more firmly emplaced in Africa than ever before, the moderate states in the OAU had lost ground to those sympathetic to Moscow, and the southern white fortress had been shown to be vulnerable to a determined assault backed by Moscow. The whites had therefore lost their value to Washington. In fact, they had become an embarrassment in a situation in which US interests now demanded not a military but a political solution. Tar Baby had suddenly become an unwanted child.

Kissinger, having decided that the US must counter the Soviets in Africa politically, figured that the best way to do it was to win the support of African leaders by reversing policy, abandoning Tar Baby and endorsing the aim of majority rule in all of southern Africa. To this end the US must cooperate closely with the Front Line presidents and also, of course, with the British on Rhodesia, where they still held nominal responsibility. It also became apparent to the secretary of state that the Rhodesian and Namibian issues were linked through Pretoria, which on the one hand could bring Ian Smith to heel by crimping his fuel and arms supplies, and on the other was itself becoming more vulnerable to pressure to grant Namibia a form of independence acceptable to the OAU and the UN.

Apart from the strategic imperatives, Kissinger personally needed a political success to restore the gloss taken off his image by Savannah. And he needed to get it in the few months left before the American presidential election in November, which might see him replaced in the State Department by a Democratic Party appointment. He resolved to go himself to Africa to apply his powers of mediation to the flashpoint. The way was opened for him when Callaghan set NIBMAR in stone and proposed that the Smith government hold elections within two years for an assembly that would negotiate a majority-rule constitution. The foreign office followed this up by emphasising that it expected more from Smith than just an acceptance of the principle of majority rule; he must agree also to 'a rapid and orderly transfer of power'. It was up against the wall with Smith.

Kissinger's proposed venture immediately received the blessing of Callaghan, who was no doubt more than happy to let the Americans have a go at the vexed problem that for so long had defied all British attempts at solution. An invitation from President Nyerere, the chairman of the Front Line presidents, was as quick in coming.

At his meeting with Nyerere early in April 1976 Kissinger was pleased to learn that the Front Line presidents shared his view that Pretoria held the key to both the Rhodesian and Namibian issues. Resolving the latter, he no doubt appreciated, would require an accommodation between Pretoria and Swapo, and this in turn would require some sort of concord in Angola since Swapo's insurgents were operating from there. While the Frontliners wanted to tackle the Namibian issue first, Kissinger believed Rhodesia offered the best chance of success since the Soviets and Cubans were not directly involved there.

Rather than increasing Vorster's leverage, the key position perceived for him made him a target of American pressure. It was essential that he be forced into line and the first step would be to demonstrate that Washington was now aligned with black Africa against him. At his next stop, Lusaka, Kissinger dropped his bombshell, publicly stating that the United States was now committed to achieving majority rule in Rhodesia and Namibia and even in South Africa. Tar Baby was not just being abandoned but sacrificially executed.

Kissinger was the most eminent Western politician to visit Africa since Harold Macmillan in 1960, and his Lusaka statement was even more significant than the British premier's 'wind of change' address in Cape Town. Whereas Macmillan had been warning of what might happen, Kissinger was using American power to make it happen. His new stance was received with delight by the Front Line presidents.

The new US policy was especially significant in the light of a decision by the Front Line presidents at Quelimane in February that the intransigence of the Salisbury government made a peaceful solution in Rhodesia impossible, and that white supremacy could be eliminated only by armed struggle. The Quelimane decision undermined Ian Smith's efforts to negotiate a deal with Nkomo, and strengthened Mugabe in his commitment to armed struggle rather than negotiation. It also encouraged the resistance movements waging insurgency in Namibia and those planning it in South Africa. Kissinger's statement, coming only a few weeks later, indirectly shored up the Front Line stand.

The secretary of state's next move was to invite the South African premier to a meeting in the neutral territory of West Germany early in June – two days after the eruption of the Soweto riots. No details of the talks were disclosed, but it was obviously made plain to Vorster what Washington now expected of him. It was agreed to meet again in Zurich in September.

Kissinger gave some background to his new thinking in an address in Philadelphia on 31 August when he described Africa as 'one of the compelling concerns of our time' and said the escalating violence there posed the risk of foreign (i.e. Soviet) intervention. The best guarantee against that was for Africans themselves to be encouraged to 'defend their own independence and unity'. The 'white population of Rhodesia and Namibia must now recognise that majority rule is inevitable. The only issue is what form it will take and how it will come about ...'. Significantly, he excepted South Africa from this declaration. Whether he had given Vorster reason to think that the South African whites were regarded differently is not known, but it seems unlikely.

When he met Vorster again in Zurich early in September, Kissinger hinted that the US might support mandatory economic sanctions against South Africa. It might not do so, however, if he would force Ian Smith to accept the demands made by Callaghan in March. Vorster, who had already made public his government's support for majority rule in Rhodesia, agreed to put pressure on Smith to accept it in return for US moves to improve the gold price – or, more accurately, to desist from forcing down the price as a means of putting pressure on Pretoria.[*]

Smith was duly summoned to Pretoria on 13 September and given the Anglo-American proposals with, according to Ken Flower, who was there, a 'last chance' warning from Vorster. Flower was told by Van den Bergh that it was not so much a matter of Smith being put under pressure as of Vorster having his arm twisted by

---

[*]Washington in fact not only continued to manipulate the gold price but at the same time also manipulated the credit market to deny Pretoria the loans made necessary by the falling gold price – a double squeeze.[2]

Kissinger.[3]

The secretary of state was meanwhile flying out to Africa from Washington, having told a news conference that the situation in the sub-continent posed a 'very severe' risk to world peace, a danger of outside intervention that could lead to Africa becoming 'an arena for superpower conflicts'. After stopping in Dar es Salaam for a talk with Nyerere and in Lusaka for a word with Kaunda, Kissinger arrived on 17 September in South Africa – with police gunfire rattling again in Soweto as fresh riots broke out – and was told by Vorster over dinner that Smith was ready to 'offer the necessary concessions'.[4]

The next few days were pure pain for Ian Smith, though he could not know that it would get even worse, that this was the beginning of the end for his Rhodesian dream. Kissinger and Vorster separately and jointly impressed on him that Rhodesia could not long resist the growing guerilla incursions if it lost the support of a South Africa that in turn had lost the support of the US. Smith needed no reminding that if South Africa cut off his supplies he would be dead in the water. Pretoria had already given a pointer to its interests not only by crimping those supply lines but also by cooperating with the Mozambican government at the very time that it was helping Mugabe's forces to wage insurgency in Rhodesia.

The Callaghan-Kissinger plan called for the UDI government to make way for an interim government headed by a Council of State with equal black and white membership but with a white in the chair. There would also be a Council of Ministers with a black majority. Smith would publicly accept majority rule within two years. These concessions would be softened by the establishment by the Western powers of a large fund to help Rhodesia over the transition to majority rule. At Smith's insistence it was agreed that the key posts of Defence and Law and Order in the ministerial council would be held by whites.

Smith returned to Salisbury to put the plan to his cabinet while Kissinger flew to Dar es Salaam to brief Nyerere on behalf of the Front Line presidents. Smith was under the impression that Kissinger had undertaken to let him know whether the Front Line group accepted the plan, especially the key proviso that the security ministries remain in white hands, before he publicly accepted it on behalf of the Salisbury government. Without that Front Line acceptance he could not expect his cabinet to accept the plan. While discussing the plan with his cabinet, Smith received a message from Kissinger to the effect that the Frontliners would accept all the proposals in the plan. With that assurance, Smith in a broadcast to the nation on 22 September announced acceptance of the British-American plan and the principle of majority rule within two years.

To the outside world it was a sensational breakthrough – the UDI government at last accepting majority rule with a visible deadline. But Smith in his broadcast made it clear that the acceptance was unwilling, and had been forced on his government by the two Western powers. He added a personal qualification that majority rule must be responsible rule, which was Smithspeak for the old qualified franchise.

In this light, it was perhaps not surprising that when the Front Line presidents met in Lusaka four days later they rejected the plan as being tantamount to 'legalising the colonialist and racist structures of power'. The equal representation of whites with blacks in the government was seen by the Frontliners to give the whites the power to block majority rule, a power backed by the white command of the security forces. So, for all Kissinger's sleight of hand, the problem had been thrown by the Front Line leaders back to its basic element: the seeming impossibility of reconciling white fears with black ambitions. The Frontliners called on Britain to convene a conference of 'the authentic and legitimate representatives of the people' (i.e. the black liberation movements) to decide the structure and functions of the transitional government.

Whether Kissinger thought he was justified or honest in telling Smith the Frontliners had accept the plan remains unclear. The upshot of the exercise, however, was that Kissinger's initiative had achieved little more than an acceptance by the Salisbury government, heavily qualified by Smith, of majority rule within two years. The secretary of state had, however, ratcheted the settlement process forward to a point from which it would be difficult for the whites to retreat.

The *wundermensch's* foray into Africa had indeed been comet-like in that it had been spectacular and brief. Ford's defeat by Carter in the presidential election soon thereafter bumped the Kissinger comet out into the comparative darkness of academia, commerce and the lecture circuit. He did, however, leave a lasting trail behind him, a trail of partial accomplishment that sufficiently changed the political firmament in southern Africa for a settlement to be reached soon in Rhodesia – although most of the whites there would come to see it more as a disaster.

CHAPTER 42

'STRANGULATION WITH FINESSE'

Jimmy Carter's victory in the 1976 American presidential election considerably darkened the outlook from the battlements of the southern African white fortress.

Though Kissinger had switched Ford's support from Tar Baby to majority rule, the Republicans had not approached that ideal with the same urgency and emotionalism as did Carter and his secretary of state, Cyrus Vance. It became clear that the Ford-Kissinger pursuit of short-term realpolitik was to be replaced by Carter's overriding concern for human rights.

In his election campaign Carter had promised 'unequivocal and concrete support for majority rule in South Africa' – and, by implication, in Rhodesia as well. Vance followed up by declaring that the new administration's 'deep belief in human rights … means making our best efforts peacefully to promote racial justice in southern Africa'. Peacefully was better than belligerently, but the southern whites knew that the end result would be the same: black domination.

Somewhat at the expense of his own deputy for African affairs, Richard Moose, Vance allowed much of the running on the southern African issues to be made by the US chief representative at the UN, Andrew Young, a youthful, black, former Baptist minister whose fight against segregation in the American south had taken him into Congress on the Democratic ticket. Young was less concerned with global strategies and East-West rivalry than with human rights, which he naturally perceived from a black American perspective – and a UN perspective. He viewed the southern African questions as human rights concerns rather than political or strategic issues, and he approached them with a glib, shoot-from-the-hip style. He put Pretoria's back up by calling the South African government an illegitimate and racist regime. Even worse, in Pretoria's eyes, he described the Cubans in Angola as a stabilising force, and said the US was willing to work with Marxist governments.

Soon after taking office, the Carter administration presented to Vorster a 'Declaration on Southern Africa' calling for apartheid to be replaced by a policy of equal rights for all in South Africa, for Pretoria to end its illegal occupation of Namibia, and to comply with UN sanctions on Rhodesia. Pretoria's relations with Washington, already stretched taught by these developments, vibrated with tension when Vice-President Walter Mondale summoned Vorster to a meeting in Vienna in May 1977 and in hectoring tones told him that even if South Africa cooperated in resolving the Rhodesian and Namibian problems, the pressure to end apartheid would not be relaxed. Vorster stiffly replied that in that case Pretoria would not co-operate.

Undeterred, Mondale at a subsequent news conference twisted the knife, saying the US 'cannot accept, let alone defend, governments that reject the basic princi-ples of full human rights'. Every citizen, he said, should have the right to vote, and every vote should be equal. Vorster might have responded that that was precisely what grand apartheid was all about, except that the votes would be exercised in separate black and white states. He would have had a hard time, though, in justify-ing the racial antipathy, the cruelty and the exploitation with which that separation was being implemented. What he did say before leaving Vienna was that the whites were not prepared to share power in their own territory, for to share power would be to lose it.

Back home, Vorster warned that the course adopted by the US would lead to regional anarchy. Rather than the 'death by brute force' of Marxist revolution, the Carter policy was 'strangulation with finesse'. Foreign minister Roelof 'Pik' Botha followed up with a protest that the US was demanding human rights in South Af-rica at the cost of depriving the whites of their own right to govern themselves and to be themselves.

Vorster also made the point that the US was mistakenly equating the blacks in South Africa with those in America, and was ignoring the fact that the black Amer-icans had lost their ancestral languages and cultures whereas those in South Africa still had theirs, making South Africa a multicultural and multinational country, un-like monocultural and mononational America.

Nothing the Carter administration said stopped the Pretoria government from pushing ahead with its grand apartheid plans, granting self-government to the Zu-luland bantustan as kwaZulu and full 'independence' to Bophuthatswana.

In the mean time, black resistance to Pretoria's plans was ruthlessly suppressed by the government's secret police. The suppression backfired when in September 1977 the black consciousness leader, Steve Biko, was 'interrogated' to death by the police in Port Elizabeth. Biko was one of the most charismatic, visionary and respected of the new generation of black resistance leaders. He was widely recognised as one who would play a powerful role in whatever happened in the future. There was a storm of outrage and condemnation from both within and without the country. It was further inflamed when the minister of justice, James Kruger, said Biko's death 'leaves me cold', thereby creating for himself a specially noisome niche in apart-heid's foul history and imbuing in blacks a cold fury that was to boost the black struggle to a degree unforeseen by the myopic minister. At the same time Kruger's words ripped like buckshot through whatever sympathy South Africa still enjoyed abroad.

These events and the continuing detention without trial of opponents of apart-heid persuaded the Western powers in November 1977 to withhold their Security Council vetoes in order to make the voluntary arms embargo of 1963 mandatory. The Western powers were still blocking Afro-Asian efforts to impose general eco-nomic sanctions, but the South African economy had nonetheless been hurt by a

decline in investor confidence and by the disinvestment campaigns being enthusiastically pursued in Europe and America.

Britain had in 1974 introduced a Code of Practice aimed at using economic
contacts to promote reform in South Africa, and in 1977 persuaded the European
Community to accept a similar Code of Conduct. In that year the UN reported
that foreign firms' reinvestment of earnings in South Africa had already been halved
as a result of the disinvestment pressures. In 1978 there was an informal adoption in
America of guidelines proposed by an activist churchman, the Rev. Leon Sullivan,
for US companies operating in America. While not banning trade and investment,
the 'Sullivan Principles' required signatory companies to eschew racial discrimination in their South African operations.

Both America and Europe held back from full economic sanctions for fear of
harming their own economies and of encouraging hardline attitudes in South Africa. They were in any case sceptical that sanctions would be effective. Britain, with
10 per cent of its foreign investment in South Africa (against 1,5 per cent for the
US), was especially wary of mandatory sanctions, as was West Germany, with an
11,1 per cent investment. And both America and Europe were still heavily dependent on imports of essential minerals from South Africa and Rhodesia. So reliant was the US on Rhodesian chrome that Congress had in 1971 adopted the
Byrd Amendment exempting chrome from the ban on imports from Rhodesia. The
Carter administration succeeded in having the amendment repealed in 1977, making South Africa even more important as a source of supply. By 1978 South Africa
was supplying 48 per cent of America's chrome, as well as 70 per cent of Britain's
and half of the EEC countries' needs.

In reaction to the arms embargo, Pretoria stepped up the activities of Armscor, the arms production corporation jointly operated by the state and private enterprise. Armscor soon became one of the largest industrial organisations in the
country, making foreign arms under licence (including Mirage aircraft, armoured
vehicles and missiles under permits continued by France because they had been issued prior to the embargo), by secretively acquiring foreign technology, and increasingly by developing its own technology. A naval shipbuilding industry was
established in Durban. Armscor went on to become an exporter of arms – and then
to become the country's largest exporter of manufactured goods.

The apartheid government made concessions to its critics, but always these were
dismissed as being too little and too late. In 1976, for example, Pretoria allowed
sporting contacts between clubs of different races (but not mixed teams), but in
the same year South Africa's membership in the international athletics and foot-
ball bodies was suspended. And the next year Commonwealth members undertook
through the Gleneagles Agreement to discourage sporting contacts with South Africa.

The idea that South Africa was the target of a wide, if not coordinated, 'onslaught'
from abroad was firming up in official minds by 1977 and in that year a white paper on defence expressed the concept of a Total National Strategy to counter the
onslaught.

One of the immediately worrying aspects of the perceived onslaught was the increase in Swapo infiltration into Namibia from the bases it had set up in southern Angola after the MPLA had filled the vacuum left there after Savannah. Zambia, too, had allowed Swapo to establish bases on its territory, and from there raids were being made into the Caprivi Strip.

Faced with Swapo's wide international support, Vorster had abandoned his firm stand against negotiations with the movement. Thus encouraged, the Carter administration initiated the formation of a 'Contact Group' of the five Western nations who were then members of the Security Council: the US, Britain, France, Canada and West Germany. Led by Andrew Young's deputy at the UN, Don McHenry, the group began negotiations with South Africa, Swapo and the Front Line leaders.

The group's first settlement proposals were neither accepted nor rejected by Vorster, but a month later, in June 1977, his government made its own dramatic move towards independence for Namibia. It abolished the Namibian whites' representation in the South African parliament and placed the territory under the rule of an administrator general, effectively ending the Turnhalle exercise. These moves were pragmatically accepted by the Contact Group despite Swapo's objections that it undermined the UN's right to administer the territory until independence. The group's negotiations became snagged, however, on Swapo's insistence that all SADF troops leave the territory before independence elections, and on Pretoria's refusal to reduce the troop level below four thousand.

While Pretoria could no longer hope to retain full control of Namibia it was still holding out for a settlement that would at least leave South Africa with political and economic influence. To achieve that objective it was pinning its hopes on a constitutional division of power among the different ethnic groups, some kind of federal system that would prevent the UN from handing the territory on a plate to the Ovambo-dominated Swapo (and its Soviet backers) at the expense of the many Namibians who rejected Swapo hegemony (especially, of course, the whites). Vorster at the same time was acutely aware of the need to resist any concessions that would offend the conservative rump of his party and send them in droves over to the HNP.

While Pretoria's diplomats continued the negotiations with the Contact Group, the generals began to urge tougher action against Swapo's escalating hostilities. Since 1966 the insurgents' mortar bombardments and infiltrations from Angola and Zambia had killed 88 members of the security forces. That was still a relatively small toll, but if the numbers of Citizen Force soldiers killed on 'the border' were to increase significantly the psychological impact on the South African public, let alone the political and economic repercussions, could become severe.

★ ★ ★ ★

In the peaceful atmosphere of Vorster's holiday cottage at Oubos on the Cape coast, South Africa's military leaders in December 1977 took a fateful decision that would help tip the limited 'border war' into the biggest military conflict fought in Africa since the Second World War.

The Oubos meeting was called to discuss what should be done to prevent the internal settlement efforts in Namibia from being jeopardised by Swapo's growing insurgency. Vorster, though still smarting from Savannah, was persuaded by his generals and his defence minister to accept a change of tactics.

No longer would the SADF confine itself to blocking the Swapo incursions at the border, to making hot-pursuit raids into Angola and shallow incursions into Angola to attack camps of Swapo's armed wing, the People's Liberation Army of Namibia (Plan). Now an effort would be made to nip the insurgency in the bud, striking deep into Angola in force. A major new dimension to the conflict would be opened. Both militarily and politically the risks would be high.

It is doubtful that any of those at the Oubos meeting fully appreciated just how high the risks were, that the new strategy would be a major factor in escalating the intermittent Swapo insurgency into comparatively large-scale warfare against Angolan and Cuban troops heavily armed by the Soviet Union. Neither perhaps did Vorster's cabinet perceive the implications when it immediately approved the Oubos decision.

The new plan was not immediately put into effect, however, while Pretoria waited to assess the latest settlement moves.

In the early part of 1978 the Contact Group arranged negotiations in New York between South Africa and Swapo, but these quickly proved fruitless. Their failure was capped by the Swapo leader, Sam Nujoma, declaring in a television interview that 'we are not fighting even for majority rule; we are fighting to seize power in Namibia for the benefit of the Namibian people.' That was enough to confirm Pretoria's impression that Swapo was not interested in sharing power or accepting a democratic system allowing opposition. Theirs evidently would be the Marxist method of taking power through the barrel of the gun and retaining it the same way.

Suspicions in Pretoria that Swapo was bent on enforcing Ovambo dominance in Namibia were strengthened by the murder in March of Clemens Kapuo, chief of the Hereros and chairman of the Democratic Turnhalle Alliance (DTA), the multiracial party that had grown out of the Turnhalle Conference, aligning Dirk Mudge's National Party with indigenous black organisations. Kapuo was the best-known of a number of non-Ovambo indigenous leaders whose assassination was blamed on Swapo, though never with proof.

Nonetheless, Pretoria accepted the Contact Group's settlement proposals when they were presented in April. Swapo jibbed, however, saying the proposals favoured Pretoria, and then backed off altogether when the SADF in May launched the first of the cross-border operations that had been decided on at Oubos in December.

Code-named Reindeer, the operation was aimed at a Swapo camp at Cassinga, 250 km inside Angola; another at Chetequera, 25 km beyond the border, housing Swapo's forward operational headquarters, and a series of smaller bases about twenty kilometres east of Chetequera, designated Charlie by the SADF. The Cassinga attack was made especially risky by the depth of the target inside Angola, the presence at nearby Techamutete of a Cuban and MPLA armoured force, and the possibility

344

of counter-attack by Cuban MiG 21 aircraft.

Cassinga was first heavily bombed and strafed from the air and then assaulted by a small force of paratroops, who were then evacuated by helicopters operating from a forward post set up inside Angola. The armour at Techamutete attempted to intervene but was held off by air attacks long enough for the last helicopter to take off as the tanks roared up. Chetequera was attacked by a mechanised battle group operating from a forward post on the border. The Charlie camps were hit by motorised infantry of 32 Battalion, the unit formed by the SADF from the remnants of the FNLA forces in southern Angola.

The SADF claimed Reindeer to have been a great success, especially at Cassinga, where it said at least sixteen hundred Swapo combatants were killed. Swapo in turn claimed that the camp was a lightly defended refugee camp and that most of those killed were unarmed women and children. The SADF admitted that women and children were among the dead but said some of the women were uniformed soldiers in Swapo's army, Plan. It insisted that the camp was a heavily defended military target, this being proved by aerial photographs and the strong resistance encountered by the attackers.

National servicemen who had taken part in the Cassinga attack, and who had no political axe to grind, later confirmed that some civilians had been killed while sheltering in the trenches with the Swapo combatants and were therefore difficult to distinguish from the troops in the heat of battle. Swapo nevertheless presented Cassinga as a callous and deliberate massacre of women and children. No explanation was offered as to what Pretoria or the SADF would have gained from the massacre of Namibian women and children. Nonetheless, the Security Council condemned the attack and the General Assembly in a special session demanded South Africa's unconditional withdrawal from Namibia, despite its acceptance of the Western settlement proposals. The attack is still commemorated annually in Swapo-governed Namibia as a massacre.

Behind this shadow-boxing, the settlement efforts continued. In July the Security Council appointed a special representative, Martti Ahtisaari of Finland, to implement the Western proposals. These envisaged a cease-fire, elections for a constituent assembly, a seven-month transitional period with Ahtisaari monitoring the administrator general's administration, and the arrangements for the election. A combined military and civilian Transitional Assistance Group (Untag) would monitor law enforcement by the Namibian police. Discriminatory legislation would be repealed, political prisoners released, and exiles allowed to return. Both armed forces would be restricted to base, and the SADF strength would progressively be reduced to 1 500 troops.

The settlement proposals were formalised in Security Council Resolution 435, but South Africa rejected it as deviating from what had previously been accepted. Pretoria had earlier been angered by the Security Council's adoption of a resolution demanding the early integration of Walvis Bay into Namibia despite that issue having been divorced from the Western proposals. Pretoria considered Walvis Bay's historic status as South African territory to be no less valid than Britain's claim to the

Falklands, Gibraltar or Hong Kong. Pretoria saw the Walvis Bay resolution as UN toadying to Swapo's wishes, and became more convinced than ever of the UN's bias towards the liberation movement.

As a counter to the UN decisions, Vorster announced in September that his government would hold its own elections in Namibia for a constituent assembly that would be free to decide whether to accept the UN plan or devise its own. It was a clever ploy, setting Swapo's seeming power-lust against an ostensibly impartial bid to place the Namibians' future in their own hands, to give them a chance to choose liberation through the ballot rather than the gun. It was never a realistic proposal, however, given the Afro-Asian bloc's commitment to majority rule through Swapo, that movement's apparent ambition for power at all costs, and the general mistrust of Pretoria's intentions and good faith.

With Swapo boycotting the elections, the outcome was predictably a heavy win by Dirk Mudge's DTA: 41 of the 50 seats. Equally predictably, the DTA's victory went unrecognised anywhere except in South Africa.

In the mean time, the hostilities continued. In November, Swapo forces in Zambia, together with Zambian troops, made a heavy rocket and mortar attack on the SADF base at Katima Mulilo in the Caprivi Strip, one missile killing ten SADF soldiers in a bungalow. The SADF immediately retaliated with air and ground attacks into Zambia.

By that time the political situation in South Africa had changed significantly, and so by extension would that in Namibia. A new era had begun with the resignation of Vorster and his replacement as prime minister by PW Botha, the hardliner who as minister of defence had supervised the Angolan invasion and had since given the SADF new muscle and a new pugnacity.

Vorster's resignation in September 1978 had been forced by the exposure of his involvement in what became known as the 'Info Scandal'. Judicial probes into allegations of malpractice had uncovered massive and clandestine use of the taxpayers' money by the Department of Information in efforts to improve South Africa's foreign image. These had included attempts to buy control of English-language newspapers in South Africa and abroad, and the secret use of state funds to launch an English-language newspaper, *The Citizen*.

South Africa's embattled situation in the world had made the Information Department an increasingly important arm of government, domestically and abroad. The worse South Africa's foreign image had grown, the more frenetic and innovative had become the department's spin-doctoring. While it won more right-wing friends for Pretoria in Europe and America, it was largely ineffectual against the growing international abhorrence of apartheid and its methods. No amount of official scrubbing could cleanse the government's dirty linen once it had been hung out by the news media and human rights organisations and seen to be forever fouled by official brutality and heartlessness, by the ruthless enforcement of apartheid policy and the suppression of dissent. Nothing could remove the stains of Sharpeville, of the Soweto riots, the jailing of Mandela and his compatriots, the detentions without trial, the deaths of Biko and others at the hands of the police.

If these were separate blotches on the linen, there had been drawn across it an unbroken smear of infamy from the forced removals policy, the wholesale shifting of black and coloured communities from areas designated for whites. No efforts of the Information Department could wipe out the images that had gone out to the world of black homes bulldozed and their occupants taken in government trucks and dumped with their belongings in distant places – if they were lucky, in match-box houses with minimal services, otherwise in bare veld, sometimes with tents, sometimes not. By the end of the seventies the removals, started in the early six-ties, had torn 3 500 000 people from their chosen habitations and dropped them wherever the government dictated, often far from shops, schools, hospitals and oth-er services – but seldom too far from the white factories that needed their labour, even if travelling between those places of employment and their new slum homes became a daily, grinding ordeal.

Ugly though they were, the stains on the government linen were the stains of truth, of ugly truth, and in trying to bleach them the Information Department's chief laundrymen had hopelessly entangled themselves in the folds. Both the min-ister and the department's director-general had been forced from office, and Vorster along with them.

His departure at a time when the whites believed themselves to be in great peril reflected the strange anomaly characterising South Africa at the time: the existence of democratic principles that could force the resignation of an elected premier on ethical grounds alongside totalitarian practices such as the ruthless suppression of dissent.

Vorster's successor, PW Botha, evidently saw himself as a strong man, a man with no patience for weaklings, and a man entrusted with a duty to take his people safely through the perils facing them. Botha certainly did not see himself as many others saw him, as a vain bully whose sense of self-importance ballooned in the thin air of the highest office. A National Party official by occupation, his sense of mission and overbearing personality had driven him from the party back rooms to elective of-fice. As premier he was a dictatorial chairman who brooked no opposition or criti-cism from his own cabinet.

South Africa's embattled situation had given Botha as defence minister an unu-sual measure of involvement in foreign affairs as well as in formulating the concept of a total strategy to counter a total onslaught. He brought both experiences to the premiership, not only in directing domestic policy but also in the handling of the Namibian and Rhodesian issues. For all his steeliness, Botha had a capacity for see-ing immediate issues realistically, and he attempted – though seldom with much fi-nesse – to deal with them pragmatically. He was fundamentally influenced, however, by his perception that Soviet Bloc support for black rule was aimed primarily at in-stalling Moscow-friendly governments in Rhodesia and South Africa.

In equating majority rule with communism and the suppression of white cul-ture, Botha was at one with the majority of his fellow Afrikaners and with the white electorate in general. Though the 'onslaught' by the Western powers had the osten-sible objective of installing democracy rather than the autocracy threatened by the 'onslaught' of the communists, both seemed equally menacing to the whites. Democracy might mean freedom to the black majority, but to the white minority it meant cultural subjugation, or at least submersion.

To counter both 'onslaughts', Botha involved the security apparatus – the military, police and intelligence services – more closely in governance, from cabinet level down to relatively mundane administrative matters. All government departments were integrated as far as possible in a National Security Management System. The State Security Council (SSC) that had existed relatively blandly since 1972 now became the most powerful and important of the cabinet committees. With Botha in the chair, the SSC sometimes took important decisions without reference to or even without the knowledge of the cabinet itself.

Under Vorster and his predecessors, South Africa had become something close to a police state (though with an elected parliament). Under Botha it moved closer to being a military dictatorship, in which opposition to the government was tolerated only insofar as it did not seriously interfere with the attainment of the government's objectives.

Heavily backed by a white electorate made ever more fearful in direct proportion to the intensification of the opposition to white rule, Botha's government knew it could take extreme measures with little fear of domestic repercussion from its (all white) voters. As for external repercussion, well, that would be handled as pragmatically as circumstances allowed.

CHAPTER 43

ARTIFICE AND SACRIFICE

When the right-wing Rhodesians at last bowed to majority rule it was only a half-bow, an attempt to get the world off their backs while retaining the ability to protect their security if not all their privileges.

If majority rule had to come, the RF reasoned, better to hand it to the more moderate blacks inside Rhodesia who did not support the exiled insurgent movements and who accepted a continuing major role in government for the whites. In other words, more or less the old concept of immediate majority rule with safeguards for the white minority – what Pretoria had been urging for some time.

The Western efforts at negotiation had been making no headway against Mugabe's ambition for personal power. Smith's private negotiations with Nkomo had failed. So, in March 1978 the government concluded an agreement for a new political dispensation with a triumvirate of 'friendly' black leaders: Bishop Abel Muzorewa of the United Methodist Church, Ndabaningi Sithole, and the Shona chief, Jeremiah Chirau. Of the three, Muzorewa was the most influential as leader of the United African National Congress (UANC), which had once been associated with the Patriotic Front but had since been abandoned by it. He could claim a substantial following of churchgoers and black people anxious for peace.

The hope in Salisbury was that the agreement would gain acceptance abroad and undercut the PF. It did, after all, envisage a new constitution providing for majority rule through universal adult suffrage, even if 28 of the 100 parliamentary seats were to be reserved for whites for ten years – 20 elected by white voters and the other eight by voters on the common roll from candidates nominated by a white electoral college. There would be a justiciable Declaration of Rights to protect basic freedoms and property rights, and an independent judiciary. Pending elections, an interim government headed by a Ministerial Council and an Executive Council would rule.

It was all too little and too late, however. The Western powers rejected the internal settlement, considering it pointless without acceptance by the PF and the Front Line group. The outside world in general largely saw it as something like white supremacy in drag.

For different reasons, the settlement was rejected also by the Rhodesian Action Party (RAP), an extreme right-wing group that had broken away from the Rhodesian Front in 1977 to campaign for continued white supremacy.

Meanwhile, the RF government launched new raids against the insurgents' bases in both Zambia and Mozambique. The hope, it seems, was that the raids would either make the internal settlement more viable by weakening the insurgent movements, or would strengthen Salisbury's bargaining position in any further negotiations.

The raids began in October 1978 with an attack on three bases of ZAPU's military force, the Zimbabwe People's Revolutionary Army (Zipra), at Lusaka in Zambia. Besides crippling Zipra, the raid was intended to avenge the shooting down of an Air Rhodesia Viscount airliner by Zipra guerillas in which 38 passengers and crew had died, and ten survivors had been massacred by Zipra insurgents.

Despite the affront of the raids, Kaunda reopened his border with Rhodesia at the end of 1978, for the closure had proved counter-productive. The massive international economic compensation he had expected had simply not materialised, not even when the UN had set up a special fund for the purpose.

Four months after the downing of the first Viscount, another was shot down in the same way, hit by a Russian SAM7 heat-seeking missile soon after taking off from Kariba. None of the 57 passengers and five crew survived. The retaliation in this case was a raid by Canberra jet bombers on Zipra camps in Angola. This time the raid evidently had some South African backing: as the Rhodesian Canberra jet bombers went in, Mirage fighters of the SAAF are said to have stood by (presumably on the Namibian border) to counter any interception by the MPLA's Cuban-piloted MiGs.[1]

In Mozambique, Rhodesian aircraft bombed and destroyed a major Zanla ammunition store at Tete on the upper Zambezi, and kayak-born commandos exploded bombs at a Zanla barracks on the river at Tete.

The Rhodesians had found yet another way to retaliate against the Mozambique government's support for Zanu's military wing, the Zimbabwe National Liberation Army (Zanla). In what might be termed retributive insurgency, the Rhodesian CIO had since about 1976 been actively supporting the movement resisting Frelimo's one-party rule in Mozambique, the *Resistencia Nacional Mocambicana* (Mozambique National Resistance), known outside Mozambique as the MNR or Renamo. Though Renamo was unlikely to seize power, backing it might discourage the Frelimo government from supporting Zanu.

There is some controversy over whether Renamo was founded by the Rhodesians. The weight of evidence points to it having been formed by opponents of Frelimo shortly before being taken over by the Rhodesians. It is unlikely, however, that the movement would have become effective without the Rhodesians, for it had no other likely source of arms and training. At that time, the South African government, which later took over the movement after Rhodesia became independent, had no interest in adopting Renamo. There is no doubt that the Rhodesians set up the Renamo radio station, the 'Voice of Free Africa', to broadcast propaganda into Mozambique.

Salisbury's backing of Renamo failed in its aim of discouraging Frelimo's support for Zanla. Rather, the cross-border insurgency increased, with hits even in urban areas. Notable among these was the attack in December 1978 on the central oil storage depot in Salisbury itself, which set off a conflagration that raged for six days and destroyed 25-million gallons of fuel.

This strictly military operation was in sharp contrast to the terrorist bomb blast in a Salisbury department store in August 1977 that killed 11 people and injured more than seventy, mostly black. The mere threat of urban bombings, however, was enough to force expensive security measures – armed guards, shopping bag and body searches - at all public buildings, shops and restaurants included. It all added to the pressures on the economy and on white morale. Though the war seldom came into the white residential areas – a few houses attacked on the outskirts of Salisbury, a few rockets fired from Mozambique landing in the suburbs of the border town of Umtali – it slowly sapped white spirit and resources.

The attrition reached a point where most whites were prepared to accept some form of majority rule, as they demonstrated by accepting the internal settlement constitution in a referendum early in 1979.

The consequent elections were duly held in April, marking Rhodesia's first concession to universal suffrage. With the PF boycotting the poll, the UANC won 51 of the 72 seats for blacks. Salisbury claimed a 64 per cent poll despite the boycott. On 1 June Muzorewa was installed as prime minister of what was now called Zimbabwe-Rhodesia.

By the end of 1979, however, it was becoming apparent even to the RF that the internal settlement was not going to work. The Muzorewa government had gone unrecognised by any other except that in Pretoria. Salisbury had expected that the election would be rejected by the Front Line presidents, who were still guiding world opinion on Rhodesia. What had not been anticipated was that the Tory 'Iron Lady', Margaret Thatcher, elected to power in Britain in May, would renege on her promise to recognise the result if the election was found to be free and fair, which her man-on-the-spot, Lord Lennox Boyd, had duly certified to be the case. Boyd found that despite the PF boycott the election result 'represented the wish of the majority of the electorate, however calculated'. Thatcher's about-face was influenced at least in part by a Nigerian threat to cut off its trade (principally oil) with Britain if she recognised the Muzorewa government, but that left the white Rhodesians feeling more than ever betrayed by their British kin.

Some analysts have opined that it was not so much Thatcher as her foreign secretary, Lord Carrington, who pulled the rug from under the white Rhodesians by persuading Thatcher to go for an all-party settlement conference rather than recognising the internal settlement, which Carrington believed would never work.

Carrington and his advisers perceived that the internal settlement constitution was 'manifestly designed to keep the main levers of power, including control over the armed forces, police, civil service and judiciary, in the hands of the whites'.[2] This view was shared by the Carter administration, which also disagreed with Lennox Boyd's conclusion, holding that since the referendum and election had been boycotted by the PF, the new constitution had not been voted on by the whole electorate. A further possible reason was that acceptance of the settlement would have put the US in conflict with black Africa, and the White House in conflict with the black caucus in Congress. On top of all that Lord Harlech, sent out to Africa by Thatcher in June 1979 to test opinion there, found that no African government would recognise the Muzorewa government even if Britain did.

So the internal settlement exercise really brought no change other than seeming to put a black mask on the white government. Sanctions were still being maintained, and the PF was continuing its insurgency. Most of Rhodesia outside the main towns was under martial law, and the insurgents were pushing more and more guerillas into the urban areas. Zanla was estimated to have some twenty thousand combatants inside the country and more in training outside. And Zanu was preparing to establish 'liberated zones' in which it would be the effective government – in between sweeps by government forces.

An earlier resurgence of white immigration had faded, and whites were leaving the country in growing numbers – well over a thousand a month by the middle of the year. Those remaining were simply too few to simultaneously man the security forces and maintain the economy. The situation was not much improved by the private armies of ill-disciplined 'auxiliaries' that were formed by Muzorewa and Sithole in order to have some troops of their own to offset the PF's military strength.

Besides conducting the internal settlement election, the RF had tried to strengthen its position by hitting ever harder against the insurgent movements. In a four-month period from April, Zipra's bases in Zambia were attacked in a series of operations that prevented what was thought to be a planned invasion of Rhodesia by Zipra's armour to disrupt the internal settlement election. An attack on the Lusaka base failed in its objective of killing Nkomo. According to Flower, the attack coincided with secret approaches to Nkomo by the CIO 'as part of a last-ditch effort by Ian Smith to make the internal settlement work'.[3] So secret did the intelligence people keep the approaches that they failed to inform the military, and so instead of the military killing Nkomo they killed Smith's secret approaches. One of Zipra's main infiltration routes was cut by the blowing up of the ferry crossing the Zambezi at Kazangula, where the borders of Botswana, Zambia, Rhodesia and Namibia converge. In the most spectacular raid of 1979, the Special Air Service (SAS) in March struck the fuel storage depot in the port of Beira, setting off a mighty conflagration. There were strong suspicions in Maputo that the raiders had been brought in from the sea by the South African navy and evacuated the same way.

The success of these raids could not hide the fact that the Salisbury government was in a desperate situation, the economy declining through sanctions and the more effective attrition of the unwinnable war. Even the UDI hardliners were beginning to see that there was no light at the end of the tunnel.

The negotiations, which had run down after Geneva, were now jump-started by Thatcher and Carrington, who had accepted that there could be no real settlement in Rhodesia without impartially supervised elections and international (especially African) acceptance, and no end to the war without the acceptance of the Patriotic Front.

Thatcher's plan for an all-party conference was endorsed at the Commonwealth Conference in Lusaka in August 1979. Within weeks the warring parties were glowering around the conference table at London's Lancaster House, now about to extend its reputation as the hospice of white hegemony in British Africa. Robert Mugabe, the key player, had jibbed at first, knowing that he might not win an election that was truly free and fair. However, President Samora Machel, apparently having had enough of the war spilling over into his country, is said to have forced Mugabe to the table by threatening otherwise to throw him out of Mozambique.

The war did not stop for the Lancaster House talks. The Rhodesians sent the SAS on raid after raid across the borders. In Mozambique, the commandos' task was to destroy infrastructural targets, mainly bridges, in an apparent effort to persuade Machel to force Mugabe to compromise at Lancaster House. The attacks are said to have had other purposes as well: hampering the growing participation by Frelimo government troops in Zanla's operations in Rhodesia, and reducing the threat of Zanla attacks on the railway from South Africa that was Rhodesia's supply lifeline.[4]

Five days before the Lancaster House talks began on 10 September, aircraft and helicopter-borne troops attacked the key road and rail bridges at Barragem, where the railway from Maputo crossed the Limpopo River on its way to the border, more than two hundred kilometres away, and four other bridges in the area. Soon afterwards, helicopter-borne troops attacked Mapai, further inland on the railway, with the intention of making it unusable by Frelimo and Zanla troops, but were beaten off.

In their deepest cross-border raid, Rhodesian parachute commandos early in October were dropped more than three hundred kilometres inside Zambia to blow up the two long bridges that carried the Tazara railway and the road to Tanzania over the Chambeshi River. Zambia consequently became entirely dependent on the railway lines from South Africa that ran through Rhodesia. Salisbury's hope was that Kaunda might then be persuaded to press Nkomo to make concessions at Lancaster House.

★ ★ ★ ★

A common pattern of events had emerged in Rhodesia and Namibia by the late seventies. Both territories were being subjected to cross-border insurgency by liberation movements backed by Moscow or Peking and conducted from bases in newly independent neighbouring states. The governments of both territories had begun striking back with strong raids across the borders against the insurgents' bases. At the same time, both countries were coming under growing political and economic pressure from outside, directed mainly through the UN and OAU.

Meanwhile, efforts were being made by the Western powers, in collaboration with the UN, to negotiate political settlements requiring the whites to surrender power to the black majorities in both territories. The white rulers of both territories had given up hope of maintaining white hegemony, and were countering the Western initiatives with efforts of their own to achieve internal settlements that would hand nominal power to moderate blacks under constitutions providing safeguards for the whites – and, in Namibia's case, with a bantustan-style territorial division that would preserve a measure of white autonomy and white land ownership.

In both territories internal settlement elections had already put indigenous groups into nominal power. In Namibia, the constituent assembly had been converted into a national assembly with a multi-racial composition and with domestic legislative powers.

President Botha was hoping that with such dispensations in place, Rhodesia and Namibia would join the Constellation of Southern African States he was now intent on forming. Theoretically, the constellation would group Botswana, Lesotho and Swaziland with South Africa in a political and economic union that would preserve white interests in a form acceptable to, or at least unchallengeable by, black Africa, and, therefore, the rest of the world.

★ ★ ★ ★

The British have always been uncommonly good at diplomacy, defined as achieving political objectives at minimal cost, whether it be in money, territory or prestige. The talent was exercised masterfully, even ruthlessly – some said perfidiously – by Margaret Thatcher's Tory government in slipping free of the burden of Rhodesia.

In this case there was no territorial interest at stake for the British, but indirectly there was an economic one in that Whitehall feared Britain's trade elsewhere would suffer if it failed to enforce a settlement in Rhodesia. It was also a matter of prestige, arising essentially from moral obligation – the assumed obligation to protect the rights of the indigenous peoples. If the British had chosen to be morally derelict in other, less conspicuous cases, they could not afford to appear so now when the whole world was looking to majority rule for Rhodesia.

The more conservative Britons perceived an obligation to protect the interests of the white kith and kin whom the motherland had settled there three generations ago or more. But in the balance of contemporary political values this obligation was outweighed by the cause of the indigenous peoples, carrying as it did the full weight of black Africa through the OAU, of the Third World through the Non-Aligned Movement, and of these and just about everyone else through the UN. And it was on those scales that the government of Margaret Thatcher weighed the Rhodesian issue. In the late seventies, Rhodesia was something of an eccentric relic, a hangover from the glory days of imperial expansion. When every former colony of any consequence had been cast off into independence, Rhodesia remained irritatingly attached to the body Britannic, notwithstanding UDI. Irritating to the British, that is, because they had allowed themselves to be left with responsibility for the territory but with no authority. They had become stuck with the problem through the contradictory Victorian imperatives of imperialism and liberalism. The imperial one had dictated attaching Rhodesia to the Empire, first as a concessionary territory and then as a white-dominated, self-governing semi-dominion. The liberal one, however, had mandated that in the process Britain assume an obligation to protect the rights of the indigenous population.

Despite the presence of possibly the largest expatriate British community, Rhodesia had never been of much economic interest to London once it had been ascertained that it did not have gold or diamond resources like South Africa's. Neither did its landlocked geography give it much strategic value once it had served the purpose of blocking territorial expansion by the Transvaal Boers and of keeping open Rhodes's road to the north.

The indigenous peoples' inevitable demand to be given independence and democracy like all the other former imperial territories put Whitehall between the rock of white intransigence and the hard place of the blacks' rightful demands. The compromise offered by the whites in the internal settlement agreement was simply not enough to make for an acceptable solution.

By the time the Conservatives were returned to power in the United Kingdom in 1979 the white Rhodesians were an anachronistic and painfully lonely community, without friends to speak of anywhere in the world, not even among the Tories to any effective extent. Their support on the British right wing, though clamorous, was ineffectual against a Boadicean prime minister and a Machiavellian foreign secretary who were both determined to rid Britain of the Rhodesian problem. And in America it was more vociferous than influential. The white Rhodesians had become a nuisance even to their supposed ally in the white fortress, South Africa.

While most white Rhodesians believed majority rule would mean the end of everything they cherished, the Thatcher government for its part believed it could do no other than to expect the whites to conform to the civil rights norms now more or less standard throughout the world, in ideal if not in practice. True, these were ignored or rejected to various degrees by the majority of OAU and UN member states, notably by the other superpower, the Soviet Union. But since Britain professed to respect these norms it could hardly make an exception in the case of the white Rhodesians. Neither did it dare assume that their rights would not be respected by the black majority under democracy, despite the trampling of the democratic ideal elsewhere in independent Africa.

Though it was prepared to allay white fears with protective clauses in a settlement agreement, the Thatcher government's attitude was based less on conviction than on hope that blacks and whites in Zimbabwe-Rhodesia would form a largely harmonious society in democracy, despite their bloody past. If they did, it would encourage the whites in South Africa to follow their example. If they didn't, well, that was hard luck for the castaway kin. They were free to return to Britain – all 180 000 or so of them, though Whitehall fervently hoped it wouldn't have to cope with that many. Those with no claim to British citizenship could try to flee to wherever their forebears had come from, or take their chances across the Limpopo, in the last refuge of white supremacy.[*]

Whatever party was in power in Britain would see no alternative but to open

---

[*]Rhodesians who fled to South Africa would perceive the fundamental difference in the rationale of white supremacist policy on either side of the Limpopo. In neither country was the policy acknowledged to be one of white supremacy. In Rhodesia it was claimed to be a policy of equality, but only above a horizontal line of qualification. In South Africa, on the other hand, it was proclaimed as one of equality on either side of a vertical line of ethnic distinction. In Rhodesia, the ethos was 'We'll all be the same once the blacks have caught up with us above the line.' In South Africa, it was 'We'll never be the same until and unless the blacks draw level with us on their side of the line.'

Rhodesia to democracy as perceived in the West. What the Rhodesian Front regarded as the protection of civilised standards through the internal settlement was
seen in the outside world as the continuation of white privilege. And white privilege in any form was no longer acceptable or defensible in the modern world. The
only protection the whites could be offered was safeguards written into the constitution – for what that was worth.

Thatcher's government might have accepted the internal settlement had it been
saleable in the outside world. Some in Whitehall had indeed pointed out that Muzorewa had been installed in an election that, for all its shortcomings, was more
democratic than the processes that had put many other governments in office elsewhere in Africa. But those who dictated policy in the OAU (and therefore, on this
issue, in the Commonwealth and the UN) were not prepared to accept the semi-
democracy of Zimbabwe-Rhodesia. Some of them might have had covertly racist motives, using the demand for full democracy as a cover for vengeance against
white domination in their own past, or for the ideal of black power, but if that was
indeed so it could not be distinguished from support for the undeniable right to
real democracy.

The dominant factor in the Thatcher government's settlement exercise, besides
the intimidation that was later to influence the voting, was that the British government, though accepting sole responsibility for fixing the problem, felt obliged
to obtain the approval of the OAU and the Commonwealth for whatever means
were chosen to do so, fearing that if it upset these bodies its trade would suffer. The
more conservative Rhodesian whites consequently felt that the Tory government
was prepared to sacrifice them to appease the OAU, and were accordingly outraged
at what they saw as political fratricide – and not much less heinous at that than the
physical kind.

Going into the Lancaster House negotiations, Carrington perceived that almost
all concerned wanted a settlement, but for different reasons. The white Rhodesians
realised that, since they could not win the war, their best hopes lay in a negotiated
solution. The South Africans felt their own interests would best be served by there
being a hopefully friendly black government in power across the Limpopo. Of the
Front Line leaders, only Nyerere was still demanding Salisbury's unconditional surrender, his country being unaffected by the war or the sanctions. The neighbouring
states, for their part, had had enough of suffering from the Rhodesian raids and the
cost of implementing UN sanctions without adequate recompense from the UN.

Among the insurgents, a settlement would suit Nkomo if it left him free to use
his powerful conventional forces to secure the political position of himself and his
Ndebeles, or even put them in power. Only Mugabe was adamantly opposed to
negotiation, figuring that time was on his side and if he held out long enough the
power would fall into his lap.

Mugabe was something of an unknown quantity, despite having been politically
active for some twenty years. He appeared to have been ruthless in attaining power, having risen to the leadership of Zanu above other more charismatic candidates
commanding greater support. He was reputed to be extraordinarily antipathetic to

whites, and not without with good reason, for he had been detained without trial for ten years for his political activities and not allowed even briefly out of prison to attend the funeral of his only son. Having ostensibly led Zanu to embrace Marxist policies and the seizure of power through the gun, he was viewed by most of the whites as a demonic figure with whom there could be no dealing, no compromise.

Whitehall, too, evidently took a skeptical view of Mugabe's movement. Robin Renwick, head of the Rhodesian Department in the Foreign and Commonwealth Office and one of Carrington's point men in the settlement initiative, felt that even if Zanu won an election 'they did not look likely to be much interested in checks and balances and arrangements to protect minority rights'. Zanu 'was based on the idea that power had to be won, not negotiated for. [Mugabe] was interested only in the moment at which the whites, under the pressure of military necessity, would agree to surrender power.' [5]

This opinion, presumably shared by Carrington, does not make it easy to understand the Thatcher government's acceptance of Mugabe's victory in the subsequent election despite his movement's gross intimidation of voters. It does, however, support the view that it was Mugabe's rather than Ian Smith's intransigence that was the core of the problem faced by Carrington at Lancaster House. Smith had already accepted majority rule, or at least a semblance of it in the Muzorewa government. He and his supporters had now to be persuaded to accept the real thing, with safeguards for the whites. More important, Mugabe had to be similarly persuaded.

Carrington, perhaps wanting to protect the settlement effort from the ingenuous impulses of the Carter administration, insisted that it be an exclusively British operation. To end the war, however, the settlement must not only have international acceptance but also impartially supervised elections. The 'impartial' supervision would also be a function of the British government, but, for what that was worth, with oversight of the Commonwealth and the OAU – and any other body that cared to participate.

★ ★ ★ ★

At Lancaster House, Lord Carrington attempted a strategy that had never been tried before in the years of British negotiations over Rhodesia. It worked in the short term, but the ultimate consequence was perhaps not quite what he had envisioned.

The essence of it was that Britain would act not as a mediator, as it had in all the previous settlement exercises, but as a proactive arbitrator. Robin Renwick says the idea was 'to lay down what Britain would accept and then stick to it'.[6] Any party that prevaricated would, it seems, be bypassed and shown up as a self-obsessed spoiler. Those who hesitated risked missing the bus.

Ian Smith presented a special obstacle in that he dominated the Zimbabwe-Rhodesia delegation ostensibly led by Muzorewa and was still opposed to negotiating with the Patriotic Front 'terrorists'. Carrington got round that by methodically isolating him from his fellow delegates, picturing him as a man who could offer the whites a past but no future, and by emphasising the leadership of Muzorewa. The next step was to persuade Muzorewa to agree to fresh elections, and then to persuade him to step down from the premiership to make way for interim British administration and to level the playing field, as it were, for the election campaign.

To avoid becoming mired in the fruitless squabbles of previous settlement efforts, Carrington reversed the priorities, insisting on first getting agreement on a new constitution. Only then would the conference deal with the modalities of electing the new government. As eventually approved, the constitution assigned 20 of the 100 House of Assembly seats to whites with the right to elect ten whites in a senate of 40 members. This arrangement could not be changed for seven years without the unanimous consent of the lower house. There was similar protection, but in these cases for ten years, for pension rights and private property (this expressly to protect white farmland) except for under-utilised land, and then only with compensation.

The British team recognised that the real power in Rhodesia now lay not with Smith or even Muzorewa but with the commanders of the armed forces, especially General Peter Walls, the army commander who headed the Joint Operational Command of all the security forces, and with Flower, the security chief. Accordingly they did the real negotiating with these officials rather than with the politicians. A notable exception was made of David Smith, who as Rhodesian finance minister was more aware than most of his colleagues of his government's parlous economic position.

David Smith ended up going along with the main settlement proposals and as a consequence being branded by his namesake the prime minister as something of a traitor. Ian Smith for his part ended up flying back to Rhodesia in an unsuccessful effort to get his supporters in parliament to repudiate the draft constitution accepted by Muzorewa and Walls at Lancaster House.

Muzorewa at last agreed to new elections in the firm belief that his party would get more votes than the Patriotic Front, certainly more than Mugabe's Zanu(PF), a belief shared by the white members of his delegation and by the military commanders. That belief was the foundation on which they based their acceptance of the British settlement plan, never suspecting that it would become the tombstone on which they mourned the death of their hopes. They declared afterwards that Carrington had assured them that the whole exercise would be directed at keeping Zanu(PF) from taking power. Ian Smith, for his part, correctly believed that Zanu(PF) would win hands down.

Pursuing his high-risk strategy of limiting the options of the negotiating parties, Carrington announced, more or less arbitrarily, that a British governor would assume responsibility in Rhodesia in the run-up to the election, thus overriding the Patriotic Front's demand for a multi-party council to run the government, which Carrington saw as a formula for disaster. To make way for the governor, but also on the grounds that all parties should be enabled to contest the elections with equal standing, Muzorewa was now openly requested to resign.

It was asking a great deal of him, for if he agreed he would be finished politically.

Even if the British didn't betray him (which they did in a sense by tolerating the intimidation that helped put Mugabe in power) he would lose the respect and support of his black electorate. But if he refused to step down, the conference would collapse. Flower claims to have discovered later that Thatcher's team had made elaborate arrangements to complete the sacrificing of Muzorewa.

'I could only guess then at British double-dealing behind the scenes,' Flower writes in his memoirs. 'It was to be several years before something of the extent of their duplicity emerged, such as the revelation that a senior Foreign Office official was given the job of handling a Foreign Office press campaign to discredit the bishop and push Thatcher towards Mugabe.' [7]

After agonising indecision, Muzorewa agreed to resign in order to save the negotiations. It was a courageous and principled decision but it did indeed seal his doom, for he was for practical purposes wiped out in the independence elections, to some extent, probably, because his supporters saw his abdication as cowardice and desertion.

At Carrington's behest, enabling legislation was rushed through both houses of the British parliament for the implementation of the independence constitution and the holding of the elections, and for allowing the economic sanctions to lapse. At Lancaster House he tabled proposals for a cease-fire, and for the Zanla and Zipra forces already in Zimbabwe to be brought together at special assembly points, monitored by a Commonwealth force, prior to the elections.

While the negotiations went on in London, the hostilities continued in Rhodesia and across its borders, with Zanla and Zipra trying to get as many of their insurgents into the country as possible ahead of the cease-fire and election campaign, and with Salisbury's forces trying to stop them by attacking their bases in the neighbouring countries and the roads and bridges they used to reach the borders.

Special attention was given to the belief that Nkomo would launch his Zambia-based conventional troops (estimated at between eighteen thousand and twenty-five thousand strong) and their armour into Zimbabwe-Rhodesia with the intention of seizing power in the whole country or at least in Matabeleland, alternatively of enabling ZAPU to withstand Zanu dominance and get a fair share of government. To foil these plans, Salisbury ordered a further series of raids into Zambia to cut Zipra's invasion routes. There is some evidence of a second motive on the part of some white politicians and military leaders: keeping Nkomo talking at Lancaster House to give Salisbury time to persuade him to bring ZAPU into an alliance that would make a settlement at Lancaster House unnecessary, and sideline Mugabe and Zanu.

Beginning on 16 November, helicopter-borne commandos in less than a week blew up five road bridges in southern Zambia, effectively preventing a Zipra motorised invasion. In the same period three bridges on the road to Malawi were destroyed and the commandos again hit the remains of the road and rail bridges over the Chambeshi River that had been blown up in October to cut the Tazara railway. To tighten the screws on Kaunda, Salisbury cut the maize exports that had been going to Zambia.

The appointment of Lord Soames, leader of the House of Lords, as governor of Rhodesia was announced in the British parliament in December. Within days Soames was flying off to take up his post in Salisbury, taking a roundabout route via the Azores and Ascension Island since no African country would give his plane clearance until the Patriotic Front had accepted the settlement proposals.

With President Carter formally agreeing to the lifting of the sanctions, Carrington's plan seemed to be going well. The Patriotic Front, however, remained an obdurate obstacle. When the Lancaster House conference formally ended on 15 December neither ZAPU nor Zanu had accepted the settlement proposals, and the British initiative appeared to have ended in stalemate, with Soames out on a limb in Salisbury.

Carrington had not given up, though, and continued to prod for soft spots in the PF intransigence. He broke through when Nkomo, now deprived of his invasion card by the Rhodesian raids into Zambia, was persuaded to agree to sign the terms by being offered an additional assembly point for his troops. (Salisbury's plan for an alliance with Nkomo had got nowhere at this stage, though it had not been abandoned.) But still Mugabe refused to sign.

The British team now played its ace, turning to President Machel of Mozambique to put pressure on Mugabe to sign. Zanu was vitally dependent on Machel's goodwill but that goodwill had been seriously strained by the infrastructural and economic damage done to Mozambique by Rhodesia's commando raids and support for Renamo. A settlement on the Lancaster House terms was looking attractive to the Maputo government, confident as it was that Mugabe would win the election (as it turned out, Maputo was able to predict exactly the outcome of the poll). In response to the British plea, Machel gave Mugabe his second ultimatum: sign or lose Mozambique's support.[8] That did the trick. Mugabe promptly telephoned his agreement to the terms, and on 17 December he and Nkomo formally signed the agreement.

As it turned out, then, the Rhodesians, in attacking infrastructures in Mozambique and Zambia, had undermined their own cause by helping to bring Carrington's plan to fruition.

Muzorewa returned to Rhodesia as just another political party leader, like Ian Smith. Mugabe returned to Maputo, unwilling to run the risk of being assassinated in Rhodesia by the Selous Scouts.[*] The RF government voted itself into dissolution. Dupont descended from head of state to party hack. Soames was installed in Government House, ran up the Union Jack again, and restored *God Save the Queen* as the official anthem. It was heady stuff for the handful of loyal white Rhodesians who gathered to cheer him and wave the old red-white-and-blue, but Soames for his part was painfully aware of how thin was the tightrope he now walked.

The governor, a man of large physical stature and personality despite his pudgy face and reputed fondness for drink, had been as brave in taking on the job as Mu-

---

[*]The Selous Scouts were a shadowy commando unit that, in the words of their commander, Lieutenant-Colonel Ron Reid-Daly, specialised in 'the clandestine elimination of Zanla and Zipra terrorists'. They were suspected of engaging in other clandestine actions as well.

zorewa had been in abdicating his. The difficulties and the risks facing him were enormous, and failure would reflect on him more than on Carrington and Thatcher, who could easily deflect the blame from themselves if the settlement collapsed.

Almost every party to the settlement was at risk. The white Rhodesians, certainly those who feared black rule and especially feared Mugabe, were staking their future and everything they cherished on Muzorewa and his party winning the election. The latter were in turn gambling on retaining power, suspecting (rightly, as it turned out) that if they lost it to Mugabe they might never be given a chance to win it back. The insurgent leaders for their part were well aware that their fighters, when gathered together in their assembly points rather than dispersed in the bush and the tribal lands, would be excruciatingly vulnerable to attack by the Rhodesian forces.

Tricky as the settlement negotiations had been, implementing the agreement was going to be infinitely trickier, involving as it did the bringing together of armed and implacable enemies who, for all the signing of agreements by their leaders in London, deeply distrusted one another and could resume open warfare at the first sound of gunfire, even if accidental. The gamble begun at Lancaster House was only half won.

CHAPTER 44

A VERY WILD THING

Nothing seen before in Africa had ever been quite as bizarre as the spectacle of British bobbies in their helmets of ancient design patrolling under the baobab trees out in the dusty tribal lands of Rhodesia.

But then the Rhodesian election was unlike any other in a number of ways. It was an extraordinary operation mixing democracy with intimidation, liberty with fear, candour with duplicity, idealism with expediency.

Beyond the benign gaze of the bobbies, insurgents who had stayed out of the assembly points brutally intimidated black villagers into supporting their movements. Meanwhile, Rhodesian officials plotted variously to attack the assembly points, to stuff ballot boxes, to assassinate Mugabe before the election, and to stage a coup afterwards if he won.

There was crackling tension at the assembly points as insurgents who had survived by flitting through the bush found themselves gathered into camps excruciatingly vulnerable to attack by government forces. The little bands of Commonwealth troops monitoring the camps felt equally vulnerable, but in their case to the different dangers of being wiped out by jittery insurgents or even by government forces attacking the insurgents now so temptingly concentrated.

As the brittle cease-fire took hold, British and American cargo planes arrived in a brisk shuttle, bringing in 1 160 monitoring troops from Commonwealth countries and the 565 British policemen; as well as vehicles, supplies and equipment for maintaining the monitoring force in the field, and for providing food and shelter for perhaps twenty times that number of insurgents in the assembly camps.

The guerillas, suspicious that it was all a trap, came warily into the assembly points, but most were in before the seven-day deadline. They came in with their weapons, it having been agreed at Lancaster House that this not only would reassure them of having a means of defence if attacked but would provide proof that they were genuine guerillas and not civilian imposters sent in by the PF while the real insurgents remained in the bush to 'influence' the voters or torpedo the election if it went the wrong way for them.

That, as it happened, was exactly what Zanu(PF) did – in the first part, at least. It kept about seven thousand fighters in the bush and sent to the assembly points a like number of imposters – youths and older men armed with rusty and useless weapons. Those in the bush went busily about ensuring a heavy vote for Zanu(PF) by threatening, mutilating or killing any suspected of alternative sympathies.

According to the British, when the deadline for assembly expired there were about twenty-two thousand insurgents in the assembly points. The Zanla component was said to be fourteen thousand – half the number Salisbury estimated to be in Zanu's forces.

The whole election exercise was literally on a hair trigger. Miraculously, the cease-fire held on both sides with only minor breaches.

The fundamental ethnic incompatibility of the Patriotic Front partners was confirmed when Mugabe announced that Zanu would contest the election on its own and not as a partner in the PF. Clearly he was confident that his movement could win enough seats to govern without ZAPU, and there was no need for the Shona to share power with the Ndebele. Partly because Ndabaningi Sithole claimed patent rights on the Zanu title, Mugabe's party campaigned as Zanu(PF).

At the end of the Lancaster House negotiations, Carrington had pledged that 'no party or group could expect to take part in elections if it continued the war or systematically to break the cease-fire and to practise widespread intimidation'. Indeed, if the politicos in London were to achieve their aim of shedding Rhodesia it was essential that the election be declared with a semblance of authority to have been free and fair. As the campaign gathered momentum, however, it began to seem that this quality could be ascribed to it only in that intimidation and obstruction were employed by both sides, by the auxiliaries of Muzorewa and Sithole as well as by the insurgents – but with Zanu(PF) doing it more widely and brutally.

The key to the election outcome lay not in rural Matabeleland, which Mugabe had largely conceded to ZAPU, but in Mashonaland and the towns, where Muzorewa's party was expected by Salisbury to win enough votes to keep Mugabe from taking power. So it was against Muzorewa's supporters that the Zanu(PF) intimidation was mainly directed.

For many of the rural blacks, physical intimidation was unnecessary – it was enough for them to be told that Zanu(PF) had supernatural means of detecting how each voter had marked his ballot, and that those who failed to endorse Mugabe's party would be dreadfully punished.

Zanu(PF)'s most effective tactic, however, was simply to spread the word that if it lost the election it would go back to the bush and resume the war. No-one wanted that, for the war had brought grievous suffering to the rural people. It is more than probable that many in both rural and urban areas, including many of Muzorewa's supporters, voted for Mugabe's party in the conviction that that was the only way to end the war.

The assurances given at Lancaster House that Soames would act against intimidation meant little in the field. There was very little effective action he could take without jeopardising the whole settlement operation, and that was something the Thatcher government simply would not countenance. The albatross must be cut loose whatever the cost. It appears that there simply was no stomach in London for more negotiations or new elections.

For the Governor simply to condemn the Zanu intimidation was, of course, ineffectual. In Zanu(PF) eyes, the beauty of the tactic of threatening to resume the war if they lost the election was that there was nothing Soames or anyone else could do to counter it.

Soames appeared in any case to take the view that intimidation was an inevitable part of any African election. On arriving in Salisbury he had undertaken to do whatever he could to 'minimise' the intimidation but then had added: 'You must remember this is Africa. This isn't Little Puddleton-on-the-Marsh, and they behave differently here. They think nothing of sticking tent poles up each other's whatnot, and doing filthy beastly things to each other. It does happen, I'm afraid. It's a very wild thing, an election.'

By the beginning of February 1980 the intimidation had become so severe that the senior white military commanders, in the form of COMOPS (Combined Operations headquarters), went in a body to Soames to demand that he put a stop to it. Soames prevaricated. Muzorewa for his part was now complaining that the British, having persuaded him to resign in order to facilitate the election, were betraying his trust by taking no action against the intimidation.

Mugabe for his part protested against the continued presence of South African forces in Rhodesia. Soames was reluctant to order the South Africans out for fear that they would also withdraw their material support for the Zimbabwe-Rhodesian security forces, which in turn would have resulted in Salisbury pulling out of the settlement exercise. The number of SADF personnel in the country appears never to have been much more than eight hundred, but some were integrated in Rhodesian security force units.

Some SADF personnel were withdrawn but several hundred remained. Pretoria averred, however, that it had no intention of trying to influence the outcome of the elections. Indeed, Botha's government had informally intimated that it would accept a Patriotic Front government if it won the election, preferably one headed by Nkomo.[1] When Mugabe's movement turned out to be the overwhelming winner there was a fast and comprehensive withdrawal of SADF men and materiel.

The dirty tricks in the election were not all on the Zanu(PF) side. Flower disclosed in his memoirs that certain powers in Salisbury – either COMOPS or CIO, presumably – had arranged to manipulate the election with ballot boxes stuffed with fake Muzorewa votes should the polling appear to have gone too much the wrong way. Flower said the final decision was left to him, but when he realised at the last minute that a Mugabe victory was inevitable and that the substitution would arouse too many suspicions, he aborted it.[2] Another account suggests the plan was squashed by the Commissioner of Police, Peter Allum.[3]

Another plot, code-named Operation Quartz, envisaged simultaneous attacks on the Zanla assembly points and on the Audio Visual Centre in Salisbury, which now housed the Zanla and Zipra leaderships. At the same time Mugabe and his top officials would be assassinated at their new homes in the capital. The Zipra commanders at the Audio Visual Centre would be tipped off in time to escape or surrender under a plan to have Nkomo join a coalition with Smith and Muzorewa.

According to one account, Quartz was intended not to reverse a Mugabe victory in the election but was based rather on the assumption that he would go back to the bush, either because he had lost the election or because the British had annulled the election or proscribed his party because of the intimidation.[4] The strike against Zanu(PF) would then be seen as a legitimate one against an outlaw. Walls countermanded the plan when he realised that Mugabe had won the election and it would be politically impossible and disastrous for the country for the operation to go ahead.

In another 'dirty trick' exercise, generally attributed to rogue Selous Scouts, bombs were detonated outside two churches in the capital with the apparent intention of having Zanu(PF) blamed.

Mugabe, though given a police escort, had escaped a number of attempts on his life since returning to Zimbabwe-Rhodesia. A bomb was remotely detonated as his car passed, and the house in which he was living in Salisbury was attacked with grenades and gunfire, deciding him to retreat to the safety of Maputo.

Despite the intimidation and the demands for the postponement or abrogation of the election, there was before the poll widespread confidence both in Salisbury and Pretoria that the Shona vote would be split between Muzorewa and Mugabe, with Muzorewa's votes and those of the whites giving the anti-Mugabe element a majority in parliament. And if this majority were to be joined in an alliance with Nkomo's ZAPU representatives, Mugabe's Zanu(PF) would be marginalised. Only a few days before the polling began, even the CIO was forecasting that Muzorewa and Mugabe would win about thirty seats each, with Nkomo taking about twenty.

That applied to the 80 seats reserved for the blacks. The whites had already voted – on 14 February – for the 20 seats reserved for them under the Lancaster House constitution. Predictably, the Rhodesian Front had won them all. The whites, it seemed, were not inclined to take risks with new political dispensations, not with the demon Mugabe knocking on the door and Smith and Muzorewa alleging British duplicity. The whites had voted for the only security they knew of, the RF of 'good old Smithy' and the possibility of an alliance with Muzorewa and perhaps even Nkomo that would keep the demon from gaining power.

Before, during and after the voting a number of approaches were made to Soames by leaders and officials of the Salisbury government about the intimidation. At one time or another he was approached separately by Muzorewa, Smith and Walls with complaints about the intimidation or requests for the annulment of the election. Smith cited 'thousands' of affidavits that had been made detailing intimidation.

Soames conceded that there had been intimidation but averred it had not been sufficient to justify postponing or invalidating the election. At one point, according to Smith, Soames told him he was contemplating nullifying the election in the three provinces most affected by intimidation, but later said this had been countermanded by Carrington on the grounds that it would upset the OAU.[5]

General Walls found himself thrust into a crucial political role. As military commander, he was virtually in charge in Zimbabwe-Rhodesia, the local politicos having lost control and Soames having no influence over them. But he was out of his depth and fumbling. Walls may have been a good soldier but he was no politician, and his political naivety made him easy meat for the British.

In the three days of voting from 27 February, nearly 2,7-million black voters cast ballots, and the country founded by Cecil Rhodes had entered a radical transformation that must have had him spinning in his grave up in the Matopos.

★ ★ ★ ★

Between the closing of the polls and the counting of the votes, intimations of doom had begun to spread through the Salisbury establishment.

It became apparent to the CIO that its predictions had been wrong and that Zanu(PF) had won a huge proportion of the votes. Flower persuaded Muzorewa to seek a coalition with Nkomo but the Zanu leader spurned the offer, declaring he was still confident of winning an outright victory on his own.

On 1 March the military commanders in the hottest parts of the 'operational areas' called on Soames to declare that the election had not been free and fair, to abort it and to run the country with an all-party council. Though Soames had before the election said he viewed a victory by Mugabe 'with the greatest possible horror', he found himself unable now to grant Walls's request. Walls in desperation bypassed him and appealed directly to Margaret Thatcher with a message saying the Lancaster House promises of action against intimidation had not been honoured by Soames, and asking her to nullify the election. Thatcher, too, refused.

For the Iron Lady, it seems, there was to be no turning back, especially when her people on the spot had reported favourably on the election and said Zanu(PF) had drawn much bigger crowds than Muzorewa's party in the campaigning (hardly surprising in the light of the intimidation).

Before the results were known, Soames asked the various foreign bodies monitoring the poll to declare whether or not they had found it free and fair. All the official ones, notably those appointed by the Commonwealth and by the British government, reported affirmatively. The British monitors declared that while intimidation was likely to have influenced the voting in some areas, the degree of intimidation in the country as a whole was not so great as to invalidate the overall result, which was a fair reflection of the wishes of the people.

When the results were announced on 4 March white Rhodesians went into shock. Mugabe's party had won 57 of the 80 African seats, giving Zanu(PF) an absolute majority in the National Assembly. There was no possibility of a coalition to keep him from power, for Muzorewa, with only three seats, had virtually been eliminated and Nkomo, though taking all 20 of the Matabeleland seats, had won none elsewhere.

While Mugabe's supporters surged triumphantly through the streets, whites kept out of sight and waited for the worst. White soldiers who had been led to expect to stage a coup if Mugabe won waited in vain for the command to go into action.

While there is evidence of efforts among the military to plan a take-over, it seems never to have been organised at a senior level or effectively at a lower one. Arrangements are said to have been made to shoot down the plane bringing Mugabe and the Zanu(PF) leadership back to Salisbury from Maputo. There had indeed been armoured vehicles placed at strategic points in the capital during the voting, but these evidently were intended to ensure an orderly election. Flower later denied that there had ever been a coup plot. SAS commanders, however, gave one writer details of a coup plan and spoke bitterly about it not having been carried out.[6] Ron Reid-Daly, commander of the Selous Scouts, bluntly accused Flower of having traitorously quashed the coup plot at the last minute.[7]

Walls inevitably became the scapegoat of the whites' frustrations and was accused of selling them out both at Lancaster House and in the election. Immediately after the election results became known, many whites made panic-stricken arrangements to flee the country. Houses were put on the market at give-away prices. Top secret government documents were shredded or rushed to safekeeping in South Africa.

The panic subsided somewhat, however, when Mugabe in a broadcast to the nation promised not revenge but reconciliation, and pledged respect for minority and property rights. He appointed whites to the key finance and agriculture portfolios in his cabinet, gave ZAPU four cabinet posts, offered Nkomo the presidency, kept Walls on to preside over the amalgamation of the formerly hostile armies, and retained Flower as his intelligence chief.

As late as two weeks after the election, according to Smith, efforts were made to have the result formally challenged.[8] The only ones who had the power to do that, however, were the military commanders, Muzorewa having resigned himself to defeat. But the military commanders were in disarray and did nothing.

At midnight on 17 April in Salisbury – soon to be renamed Harare – the Union Jack was lowered and the new flag of Zimbabwe raised for the first time. Prince Charles was there to represent the Queen, as his father had done at that other ceremony in Nairobi 17 years before.

The ceremony was attended by the representatives of more than a hundred foreign governments, but not that of South Africa, which had not been invited, much to its chagrin. Though Pretoria had played the key role in replacing white supremacy with majority rule by choking Salisbury's essential supplies, it was seen to have done so for its own ends. Within its own borders it was still the arch white supremacist, the last remaining objective of the black rights movement. South Africa the country was indeed represented at the ceremony, but by the ANC and the PAC, and Namibia by Swapo.

Also conspicuously absent from the formalities was Ian Smith, refusing to lend his presence to the last act of what he considered to be a 'great betrayal'.

The representatives of the British government felt huge relief. Gone was the albatross. The most unwanted, most adhesive vestige of empire had at last been jettisoned. If the Rhodesian blacks could cry, 'Free at last!', so could the British politicians. Their agents could now jet back to England for the last time, leaving the inhabitants of the new state to sort out their racial and other problems in their own way. Britannia had done her duty. The OAU and the UN were happy.

Most of the white Rhodesians had already accepted the inevitability of majority rule, but what many could not accept – or forgive the Thatcher government for – was the expediency with which it seemed to have dumped a Mugabe government on the country. As some saw it, Thatcher and Carrington, in order to win the acceptance of the OAU, had sacrificed a Muzorewa government with admittedly questionable election credentials for a Zanu(PF) government whose credentials were even more suspect. True, Muzorewa's legitimacy had been compromised in that the Patriotic Front had boycotted the election and the instruments of power had been left in the hands of the whites. Yet Mugabe had been given control of those same instruments of power despite his apparently having won election through intimidation, which made him no more legitimate than Muzorewa.

These factors, however, made no difference in the OAU and the Commonwealth, where Mugabe was the chosen one, and where Whitehall was reluctant to challenge.

The intimidation question will forever shadow the Zimbabwe independence election in history. The issue is now academic, but historians who seek the truth will have to weigh the reports of security force personnel intimately familiar with the people and places against the findings of foreign monitors unfamiliar with these aspects and seeing them from a superficial – and, in some cases, biased – perspective. Soames was relying primarily on the assessment of Sir John Boynton, the election commissioner who, having been appointed by a government anxious to get shot of the issue, could not necessarily be regarded as impartial.

It is extremely unlikely that he or the other foreign monitors could accurately have assessed the effect on the black voters of the intimidation and especially of the Zanu(PF) threat to go back to war if it lost the election. They sought no explanation for the huge discrepancy between Muzorewa's support in the internal settlement election and in the Lancaster House election.

Ian Smith saw Carrington as the arch villain in a British plan of duplicity, he having assured the Zimbabwe-Rhodesia delegates at Lancaster House that Mugabe would not be allowed to take power and then having allowed that very thing to happen in order to avoid confrontation with the Front Line states and OAU.

As the white Rhodesians figuratively watched Lord Soames flying off into the sunset, they were bewildered, angry and apprehensive, feeling lost in the land of their birth, betrayed by their own kin, fearful of what might happen to their families and their lifestyle. In their struggle to defend these, they had been defeated neither on the battlefield nor by sanctions. They had succumbed in the end – allegations of British trickery aside – to their own lack of numbers, which had left them without the manpower to keep waging the war, and to their landlocked situation, which had enabled Pretoria to dictate terms by squeezing their lifelines to the outside world.

The cost of their resistance of the inevitable had been heavy, not so much in material terms – Mugabe's movement inherited an economy and infrastructure that had survived, even flourished in many ways, under the stress of civil war and sanctions – but in human losses. According to COMOPS estimates, about twenty thousand people had died, a total made up of 7 790 black and 468 white civilians, 1 360 members of the security forces (almost half of them white) and 10 450 insurgents. What was less easily measured was the cost in human suffering, mainly in the tribal areas, and in the damage to racial goodwill.

For the whites across the Limpopo – and for their opponents in black Africa – the ceremonies in Salisbury marked the collapse of another bastion of the white fortress. Now only South Africa and Namibia remained, and the struggle against white domination could now be concentrated there.

As the British thankfully departed, Zimbabwe-Rhodesia, now plain Zimbabwe, had ostensibly been given democracy. It would be beyond the power of Thatcher and Carrington – but not perhaps beyond their concern – when Mugabe, after a period of conciliatory and cooperative governance, began ruthlessly to create a virtual one-party dictatorship and, in the process, to ruin the economy. Within a few years he would eliminate opposition in Matabeleland, killing thousands. He would denigrate the whites, frightening more than half of them into leaving the country, and send his supporters out in masses to seize white farms without compensation. He would discourage foreign investment and foreign aid, and condemn his people to unemployment and mass starvation.

Neither Thatcher nor Carrington could have foreseen the worst of Mugabe's excesses, and it remains arguable whether these can be seen entirely as a consequence of the kind of settlement they brought to the country. Both have remained silent on this point, neither of them confronting it in their respective memoirs, both of which were published after Mugabe's bloody suppression of opposition in Matabeleland in 1983, and Thatcher's well into his destructive reign. Neither went beyond the assertion that the level of intimidation had not been sufficient to invalidate Mugabe's victory in the election.

Carrington in his memoirs acknowledged the white Rhodesians' accusations against him, but denied that he was ever indifferent to their interests.[9] Rather, he intimated, it was a matter of his assessment of their interests being 'better than their own'. Rhodesia, he believed, 'could not exist for long without the acceptance of the international community and some sort of *modus vivendi* with the African states' and 'it was no act of friendship to the white Rhodesians to pretend otherwise'. Imperfect though the election results were, he said, they showed that the Patriotic Front really did have the support of the majority of the blacks.

Carrington asserted that to accept Boyd's finding and the Muzorewa government would have led to increased insurgency by Nkomo and Mugabe, with Soviet and Chinese support. It would also have brought down 'embargoes on British goods around the world'.

In that last sentence perhaps lies the key to Carrington's (and also Thatcher's) approach to the Rhodesian problem. The whites in British Africa seem never to have appreciated that, as Lawrence James noted in a different context, British conservatism was 'a flexible and opportunistic creed'.

Thatcher's conclusion was that 'it was sad that Rhodesia/Zimbabwe (sic) finished up with a Marxist government in a continent where there were too many Marxists maladministering their countries' resources. But political and military realities were all too evidently on the side of the guerilla leaders. A government like that of Bishop Muzorewa, without international recognition, could never have brought to the people of Rhodesia the peace that they wanted and needed above all else.' [10]

Thatcher did not comment on whether the people of Rhodesia wanted above all else the kind of peace that Mugabe the dictator imposed on them.

CHAPTER 45

THE CLIMACTERIC

Mugabe's victory in Zimbabwe, the greatest triumph over white domination since Algeria, was celebrated throughout black Africa. For the whites in the sub-continent, however, it was another body blow – the third in seven years.

First there had been the coup in 1974 that had ended Portuguese colonialism and surrendered the flanking bastions of the southern white stronghold to the forces of black liberation. A year later had come the American decision to abandon the Tar Baby option, revealing that Washington had come to figure that its own interests in the region would be safer in the hands of friendly black governments than friendly white ones. Since the white regimes had suddenly been perceived to be vulnerable to international pressures, Washington had reckoned it could best protect its interests – access to the region's mineral wealth and the Cape sea route, and blocking Soviet expansionism – by helping to put suitable black governments in power. The Pretoria government consequently had been obliged to begin thinking less of the whites as a valued adjunct of the West, and more seriously of their being on their own in Africa.

Now Mugabe's election victory had overwhelmed the white stronghold's central bastion, leaving only Namibia and South Africa still in white hands. Besides boosting the morale and determination of the South African and Namibian liberation movements and their supporters, the election outcome had given the South African movements new bases and infiltration routes for insurgency. And Zimbabwe's admission to the UN and the Commonwealth would give them new support there.

The two hundred thousand or so whites in Zimbabwe (their numbers were decreasing by the day as the less optimistic emigrated) were now isolated, cut off from South Africa's support – not that that had turned out to be worth much when the chips were down. The Africanisation of those who remained in Zimbabwe was no longer a matter of choice. Most remained fearful of what it might mean, despite the last-minute revision of Zanu(PF)'s Marxist policies and Mugabe's gestures of reconciliation. It was not, after all, anything like the sharing of power with Muzorewa's 'friendly' blacks that they had expected. For all Mugabe's gestures, they were acutely aware that they had been politically emasculated and left entirely vulnerable to any unwelcome changes in his government's attitude, especially a reversion to his call to his supporters during the bush war: 'Let us rid our home of this settler vermin.'

The whites in South Africa were now more lonely and vulnerable than before.

371

In putting pressure on Salisbury to accept majority rule, Pretoria had expected it to take the form of a Muzorewa-Smith coalition. This would preserve the northern buffer against ANC insurgency, provide a model for Namibia, and encourage acceptance of an amicable separation of whites and blacks in South Africa. But now Mugabe's Zimbabwe stood as a barrier to PW Botha's plans for a South African-dominated constellation of states. Zimbabwe had joined the other southern black states which, with Tanzania, had the previous year formed the Southern African Development Coordination Conference (SADCC), aimed at loosening ties with South Africa and promoting economic collaboration among themselves.

None of the neighbours would now contemplate a close association with Pretoria. The constellation concept had been reduced to a meaningless partnership with the 'independent' bantustans. South Africa ostensibly was isolated not only in the world at large but now also in the sub-continent it supposedly dominated through its economic and military power.

In practice, however, the actions of some of the neighbourhood states were different from their posturing. There was more show than substance to their membership of the SADCC, for most of them had perforce to continue depending heavily on South Africa for trade, transport and other essentials. Three of them, Botswana, Lesotho and Swaziland, remained members of the South African-dominated Southern African Customs Union, which provided the latter two with most of their national revenue. Except for Swaziland, however, it was a reluctant partnership. Swaziland's absolute monarch, King Sobhuza, fostered friendly ties with Pretoria, even signing a secret security pact, but the other two made it plain that their cooperation was unwilling and their sympathies were with the liberation movements.

Though angered by Mugabe's refusal to maintain diplomatic relations, even to deal with South Africa at ministerial level, Pretoria agreed to have relations at trade commission level. It was, after all, simply a cover for full consular relations.

Mugabe's victory was not seen by Pretoria as a blow to white supremacy, for that had long been abandoned as ambition or policy. For Pretoria, the goal was now a form of white separation acceptable to the blacks of South Africa and to the world at large.

The exploitive and dominative concept of the black 'homelands' had undergone a small but significant change. Originally they had been viewed primarily as labour pools for the white state and only secondarily as black states in their own right. Now they were seen primarily as a means of ensuring the survival of the white state as a separate entity. All of Pretoria's manoeuvres appeared now to be aimed at achieving an acceptable separation of the races, and it wanted time to find a way to do so. But time was running out, may already have run out.

When Zanu(PF) won Zimbabwe, white supremacy in Africa was already in its climacteric, if not beyond it. What was now at stake was not the power to call the tune but only separate white survival. Though the biggest battles were still to come, for all their ferocity they were essentially rearguard actions in the whites' retreat from hegemony. While few whites still nurtured the old notions of *baasskap*, many still hoped for a white society existing apart from, even if alongside, the blacks.

It was probably too late for that, however, probably only a matter of getting the best possible deal under black majority rule. For, both in South Africa and abroad, the opposition to white rule had become ineluctible and uncompromising in its insistence on majority rule. Separation was indistinguishable from segregation, which had become a dirty word, fouled first by the events in the American south, and then by apartheid. It mattered not if the First World broadly demanded democracy for South Africa while the Third World specifically demanded black majority rule, for the former would inevitably bring about the latter. Neither world, it seemed, was much interested in considering whether democracy would be ensured by majority rule. Any proposed alternative to majority rule was lumped together with apartheid, and Pretoria's tentative efforts to revise its race policies were largely ignored.

There were really only two choices left to the whites: fight to the death – the Masada option, entertained only by the lunatic fringe on the right – or negotiate with the black majority.

Negotiation, however, was out of the question for Pretoria as long as it believed that the MPLA, the Cubans, Swapo and the ANC were all being used by Moscow as instruments for imposing Soviet hegemony on southern Africa and that South Africa was the main target. In this situation, Pretoria could see no option other than to fight on, if not for acceptance of segregation then for the best of whatever else might be attainable – and opinions in Pretoria appeared to be divided over what that might be.

For the present, the dominant opinion was that of the military. The rise in domestic insurgency, the Rhodesian disaster, the growing threats perceived in Namibia and Angola, PW Botha's rise to power – all these factors had made security aspects paramount in both domestic and regional policy. The military had assumed a direct role in the formulation and execution of both. Even in external matters the SADF's judgments and imperatives tended to outweigh those of the Department of Foreign Affairs. Thus the military view now strongly influenced the government's approach not only to internal dissension and resistance, but also to the settlement of the Namibian issue and to the neighbouring states.

The generals and like-thinking politicians appeared to feel that no solution could be fashioned until the military and insurgent threats to white security – whether they be Soviet, Cuban, Swapo, ANC or PAC – had been defeated or nullified. In regional affairs, the olive branch of the old outward policy was still held out, but now alongside it was a sword. Diplomacy had become coercive as much as persuasive.

As the last of the outer defences, Namibia had a new significance. Pretoria was simply not prepared to see it going the same way as Zimbabwe. It was decided to weaken Swapo by stronger military action so that if it did come to an election, Sam Nujoma would not easily be able to copy Mugabe's tactic of threatening to go back to war if his party did not win. At the same time the internal parties in the DTA would be strengthened so that they could compete with Swapo at the polls.

The old ambition to incorporate South West Africa into South Africa was now as dead as the old policy of *baasskap* in South Africa. Pretoria's imperative now was to ensure that the seemingly Marxist Swapo and its Soviet and Cuban backers would not gain control of Namibia. That would put regimes that were either communist or Moscow-friendly in power on most of South Africa's border – and with them, ANC or PAC bases for insurgency.

'No red flag in Windhoek' became, for the present, Pretoria's motto. The further that flag could be kept from Windhoek the better; anywhere in southern Angola would be getting too close. The ethos was strongly reinforced with the disclosure that the ANC's armed wing, *Umkhonto we Sizwe*, not only had military bases in Angola but also combat units serving with the MPLA government's army, Fapla.

Pretoria at first adopted a policy of continuing to strike at Swapo in Angola while avoiding clashes with Fapla and the Cubans. But since these continued to support Swapo, the SADF felt it necessary to counter them as well. This it sought to do by stepping up its support for UNITA, sending more weaponry, other supplies and instructors to Jonas Savimbi in his stronghold at Jamba in the desolate south-eastern corner of Angola. This indirect backing proved insufficient, however, against the vastly greater flow of Russian arms and advisers and Cuban combatants thrown against Savimbi's movement. Pretoria would soon find itself having to send its own troops to fight alongside UNITA's forces to keep the red flag north of the border.

At the same time the threat from domestic insurgency was mounting as the ANC and PAC military wings became better organised and armed, staging attacks on railway lines, powerline pylons and police stations. The government responded with ever-harsher measures against both domestic political subversion and cross-border insurgency. It sought to counter the latter by attacking suspected ANC bases in neighbouring states and by punitively undermining the economies of those states.

As the urban terrorism escalated and the warfare on 'the border' intensified, whites increasingly perceived the situation less as a legitimate struggle by the blacks for fundamental rights and more as a freedom struggle of the whites against communist dictatorship of the kind that had enslaved the peoples of the Soviet Union and Eastern Europe. The impression was enhanced by the ANC's close ties with Moscow and the movement's embrace of the South African Communist Party. It was further reinforced by the relatively large number of African governments professing to adopt Marxism, a menacing red tide seeming to spread down Africa towards South Africa.

★ ★ ★ ★

Apartheid's enemies called it destabilisation in the cause of white supremacy. Apartheid's practitioners saw it as self-defence against black supremacy. Under either label, destabilisation or defence, it spread killing and destruction through the subcontinent for more than a decade.

'Destabilisation' became a catchword applied indiscriminately to any act by Pretoria in the neighbouring countries, direct or indirect, that was judged nefarious by apartheid's opponents in the Front Line group, the OAU and the UN. It was attached, for instance, not only to South Africa's attacks on its neighbours' infrastructure and economies, but also to strictly military operations such as the SADF raids on Swapo bases in Angola.

Thus, because of its material support of UNITA in Angola and of Renamo in Mozambique, Pretoria was blamed for the entire loss of life and assets in the civil wars in those countries. Botha's government rejected such liability on the grounds that it had created neither Renamo nor UNITA, and that both arguably had a genesis as valid as those of the regimes they opposed. (The fact that neither the Frelimo nor the MPLA government was democratically elected tended to be lost in the hortative heat of the campaigns against destabilisation.)

Pretoria insisted it backed UNITA only as an indirect means of countering MPLA support of Swapo's cross-border insurgency; and that it aided Renamo only to discourage Mozambique from hosting ANC insurgents. Whether either UNITA or Renamo would have been able to continue its resistance without Pretoria's backing is debatable, however. Neither of them of course saw South Africa's support as destabilisation – or cared whether it was or not. Still, the public images of UNITA and Renamo were soiled by the backing of the apartheid state, and the Afro-Asian bloc was happy to fan the odour of it.

There could be no argument, though, about the deliberate destabilisation intended in Pretoria's dirty tricks in Zimbabwe, and no excuse could be found for it in the dubiousness of Zanu(PF)'s accession to power.

Riven as it was by the extension of the old Shona-Ndebele hostility, Zimbabwe was wide open to South African destabilisation. Mugabe took office in an excruciatingly vulnerable position. The merging of the Zanla and Zipra forces in the new national army was still more theoretical than actual. Mugabe's lightly armed former guerillas had nothing to counter the Russian armoured vehicles and artillery Nkomo had kept in reserve in Zambia. Only a token number of these had been handed over to the national army as required in the Lancaster House agreement. Nkomo kept the rest back, to use either for the purpose of seceding Matabeleland from Zimbabwe or for bargaining with Mugabe or even seizing power from him.

In this situation, Mugabe's best defence against his former partner in the freedom struggle turned out, ironically, to be some of the white soldiers and airmen who had once fought his guerillas in the bush and whose units now formed part of the country's defence force. Some five thousand members of the Rhodesian armed forces are said to have crossed the Limpopo to join the SADF when Zanu(PF) won the election, but numbers remained in the Zimbabwean forces.[1] It was to these that Mugabe turned when in February 1981 Nkomo made his bid for independence and/or power.

As Zipra armoured columns advanced on Bulawayo from two directions with the apparent intention of seizing the city, Mugabe's government deployed the air force and white units of the Rhodesian army and police, together with black troops. Jet planes buzzed the advancing armour while sky-shout aircraft warned that the columns would be bombed and strafed if they did not turn back. Realising they had no defence against aerial attack, the Zipra commanders ordered a retreat – but not before some of the leading Zipra armoured cars had been destroyed by the ground troops of the old Rhodesian army. Militarily, Nkomo had shot his bolt.

Had the white airmen and soldiers not been available for this mission or refused it, Zimbabwe would probably have been plunged into a new and highly destructive civil war. As it was, the country was shaken by rebellion. Zipra elements deserted from the army, and Nkomo prepared for a campaign of insurrection, secreting his lighter weapons in arms caches. When the caches began to be uncovered early in 1982 an angry Mugabe fired Nkomo from his cabinet.

It is unlikely that the armoured advance on Bulawayo was initiated by South Africa, but certainly Pretoria had already seen in the internecine rivalry in Zimbabwe an opportunity for discouraging Mugabe's support for the ANC. Besides taking over Renamo, Pretoria soon after the first Zimbabwe election had taken dissident Zipra elements to South Africa and begun forming them into what became informally known as Super-ZAPU. They were deployed extensively as insurgents in Zimbabwe from 1983. In the same year South Africa began clandestine broadcasting of dissident ZAPU radio propaganda into Zimbabwe (parallel with managing Renamo's broadcasts into Mozambique).

Pretoria had professed a desire for peaceful coexistence with Mugabe's Zimbabwe provided it refrained from taking an active part in the campaign against apartheid. That was expecting too much, however, given Zanu(PF)'s long struggle against white supremacy in Rhodesia and the expectations (backed by pressure) among anti-apartheid elements around the world that Zimbabwe would become the new front line in the war against white supremacy in South Africa.

When Mugabe's government duly adopted a hostile attitude, severed diplomatic relations with South Africa and allowed an ANC office in Harare, Pretoria early in 1981 conveyed its displeasure by withdrawing 25 loaned locomotives and restricting Zimbabwe's trade traffic through South Africa on the pretext of railway congestion. Relations were maintained at trade representative level, but Pretoria held over Mugabe's head a threat to scrap the preferential tariffs on the bulk of exports to South Africa, which totalled nearly twenty per cent of Zimbabwe's trade.

Pretoria's hopes of obtaining time to implement a dispensation acceptable to the outside world became progressively slimmer in the face of the mounting pressure from international groupings baying for the blood of the apartheid monster and unwilling to settle for anything less. The Botha government, though not abandoning its hopes, responded with strength. The total onslaught would be met with total resistance, with tougher laws more firmly applied against domestic resistance, and retaliatory strikes against insurgency across the borders – and against its hosts.

In January 1981, Pretoria implemented its year-old threat to Mozambique of direct action if it did not stop ANC insurgents from raiding into South Africa. Commandos drove to Matola near Maputo and attacked three houses targeted as ANC bases, killing 13 of the occupants. The precedent had been set for what would become a bloody practice by Pretoria in the sub-continent.

ANC policy, and Pretoria's reaction to it, were both based on the recognition that the South African security forces were too strong for the ANC to maintain insurgent bases within the country – not even in the black townships. For its insurgency the ANC therefore needed bases in or transit routes through the neighbouring states, the same states with which Pretoria sought economic and political alliance. Hence Pretoria's seemingly ambivalent policy of offering the neighbours aid and trade while at the same time attacking ANC bases in their countries and undermining their economies.

In its attacks inside South Africa the ANC was still avoiding civilian targets, its president, Oliver Tambo, having made it the first insurgent movement to sign the relevant protocol of the Geneva Convention.

In August 1981 the ANC made its most audacious strike, sending a number of rockets into the sprawling SADF headquarters complex at Voortrekkerhoogte on the outskirts of Pretoria. In the same month, the ANC's representative in Harare, Joe Quabi, was assassinated, and suspicion pointed to Pretoria's agents – as it did again two weeks later when the armoury at the Zimbabwe army's Inkomo barracks near Harare was blown up. And again when on 18 December a bomb was exploded on the roof of the Zanu(PF) headquarters in Harare. And yet again when explosive devices were planted on armoured vehicles at the Zimbabwean army headquarters in Harare – but mostly failed to go off.

In this period Pretoria had also raised the stakes against Mozambique's support for the ANC. South African agents working with Renamo helped sabotage the Beira-Mutare railway line and the Pungue River road and rail bridges in October. In November South African seaborne commandos destroyed the marker buoys at the entrance to Beira harbour.

Destabilisation became comic opera when in November 1981 a ragtag band of mercenaries botched an attempt to overthrow President Albert Rene's government in the Seychelles islands in the Indian Ocean, apparently on behalf of former premier James Mancham, and with the secret support of the SADF. The South African involvement might have been seen in Pretoria as a chance to install a friendly regime in an OAU member state, but it would have been quite incidental to the SADF operations on the main continent, where they were viewed by the targets as anything but comic opera.

CHAPTER 46

PUTTING UP WITH THE POLECAT

Six months after Mugabe's victory in Zimbabwe, Jonas Savimbi emerged from his hideaway in south-eastern Angola to capture the strategically important town of Mavinga. UNITA, rejuvenated by South African military aid, was resuming its challenge to the MPLA, and Angola was back into civil war.

Two months after that, Ronald Reagan defeated Jimmy Carter in the American presidential election, putting a conservative Republican administration in the White House.

In the Afro-Asian bloc, these two developments were seen as setbacks to the cause of African liberation. As they perceived it, UNITA's resurgence showed that Pretoria was still bent on intervention in Angola despite the MPLA now being widely recognised in Africa as the legitimate government there. That in turn meant Pretoria remained intransigent over Namibia. As for Reagan's election, there could be no doubt that his administration would be softer on apartheid than Carter's had been.

During his election campaign Reagan had committed himself to 'halting the Soviet advance' in Africa and to getting the Cubans out of Angola. He had pledged support for UNITA in overthrowing the 'illegitimate' MPLA regime, and had labelled Swapo a 'terrorist organisation'.

Reagan had furthermore promised a policy of 'constructive engagement' rather than confrontation with Pretoria and the other parties in the southern African turbulence. He had borrowed the concept from Chester Crocker, head of African Studies at Georgetown University in Washington, whom Reagan was to appoint as his Assistant Secretary of State for African Affairs.

Against this background, Reagan's election came as good news for Pretoria, especially welcome after the disaster in Zimbabwe, a glimmer of hope in a darkening landscape. Pretoria nonetheless remained cautious about its implications for South Africa and Namibia. Reagan's stance was clearly not a return to Tar Baby. His administration still accepted the inevitability of majority rule and the need to accommodate policies to that reality. Reagan at first professed what his opponents decried as an outdated respect for South Africa as a loyal ally in the two world wars. His administrative team took a less sentimental view, however, simply seeing no sense in undermining South Africa's economic and military strength while it remained a present-day ally in the Cold War.

The situation had changed since Kissinger had abandoned Tar Baby on Ford's behalf. The Soviets and their Cuban surrogates had become more deeply involved and entrenched in Angola than anyone in Washington had expected, and were building strong diplomatic presences in southern and Central Africa. As long as PW Botha's government firmly held the power in South Africa it seemed strategically unwise to undermine it when the Russians were pressing in from the north. In this situation, it would be too risky to entrust America's interests to a black government in South Africa that had demonstrated a closer rapport with Russia than with the West.

Botha's government for its part was not in a mood of desperation, beleaguered though it was. Confident of its military and economic strength, it saw no compulsion to give way drastically to the pressures for reform. The gold price had risen as high as $850 an ounce, boosting the economy. And aircraft, armoured vehicles and artillery were rolling off the domestic production lines as never before.

Botha believed he had an extra card up his sleeve in the form of South Africa's nuclear capability. South Africa was known to be able to enrich uranium, and appeared to have exploded a nuclear weapon in an isolated part of the South Atlantic in 1979. Not until 1993 would Pretoria confirm that it had indeed made six or seven nuclear bombs in the late seventies. In the mean time, however, the belief in the West that it had acquired the necessary capability was exploited to the maximum by Pretoria.

As with all nuclear weapon threats, it was a matter of political poker, of the other players estimating the bluff. It never became a major factor in the political manoeuvrings, however, because everyone knew that the weapon would not be fired except in a Masada scenario, and it was extremely unlikely that it would ever come to that. It was perhaps at best a means of keeping the world from forcing the pace of reform, from pushing Pretoria – and especially its military – into desperation.

In this climate, the Botha government's attempts at reform were hardly radical – though his party's right wing thought they were. He appointed a parliamentary select committee to review proposals made by Vorster's government in 1977 for the formation of separate parliaments for whites, coloureds and Indians. On the recommendations of his committee, Botha's cabinet in 1979 scrapped the Senate and set up a President's Council with advisory powers, and to which coloureds and Indians would be appointed. The President's Council was empowered to draw up a new constitution embodying the tri-cameral concept.

These attempts at reform, scornfully rejected by most blacks, did nothing to stem the rise of insurgency, which had prompted Pretoria in February 1980 to threaten action against Mozambique if it did not stop supporting ANC 'terrorism'. The attacks had continued nonetheless, achieving a fiery success in June with the rocketing of the oil-from-coal plant at Secunda in the eastern Transvaal (now Mpumalanga province).

In Namibia, too, the insurgency had escalated. In February 1980 Swapo insurgents had penetrated the white farming area south of Ovamboland and attacked white civilians. Only two whites were killed, but the attacks had a disproportionately larger propaganda effect.

In May Botha came out in favour of home rule for Namibia, and two months later the administration of the territory was transferred to a Council of Ministers – but with Pretoria retaining final control through its administrator-general.

At the same time SADF units had been in Angola on the largest mechanised infantry operation by South African troops since the Second World War. Begun in May 1980 under the code-name Operation Sceptic, it was a relatively shallow but widespread assault on Swapo bases – which now were in some cases being protected by Fapla troops. The five-week operation saw some of the fiercest fighting yet experienced by the SADF in Angola. A month later SADF troops again rode into Angola to attack a Swapo logistical base, only 5 km from the border, in Operation Klipkop.

Pretoria had meanwhile pushed ahead with the deployment of indigenous Namibian units against Swapo's forces in order to ease the burden on the white national service conscripts of the SADF – and to ensure that strong anti-Swapo forces would remain in the territory after most of the SADF forces had been withdrawn in the event of Security Council Resolution 435 being implemented. In August 1980, ethnic units that had operated under the wing of the SADF since 1974 were combined as the South West Africa Territory Force (SWATF), operating alongside but separate from the SADF.

In the early eighties the situation in the southern sub-continent was a tangle of different yet interrelated issues and interests making it extraordinarily complex, volatile and difficult to resolve – a Gordian knot that defied all efforts to untie it, and it seemed there was no Alexander to slash it open with his sword. But now came the man who figured it could be done without a sword.

★ ★ ★ ★

With all the friction and fighting, destruction and destabilisation, southern Africa was truly what Chester Crocker found to be 'a rough neighbourhood' when he took office. And it was to get rougher still.

In 1981, when Reagan entered the White House, a detached stance on the region was not an option much favoured by either Moscow or Washington. Both still attached importance to the strategic value of the southern African minerals and the Cape sea route. As the Reagan administration saw it, the United States, with older and closer relations with most of the regional states – especially South Africa, the regional power – could best protect its insider position by promoting peace in the region. Moscow, on the other hand, was the outsider, and needed to promote instability and turmoil in order to break in.

Crocker did not necessarily share Reagan's evaluation of the minerals and sea route, but he was a realist and he approached the southern African problem with a pragmatism contrasting with the moralistic stance taken by Carter's team. Whereas Carter had in effect demanded unconditional surrender by Pretoria, Crocker sought a 'no losers' solution in which everyone could claim to be a winner. He pursued a negotiated end both to apartheid and to South Africa's occupation of Na-

380

mibia through his 'constructive engagement' concept.

Through much of his term at the State Department, Crocker was portrayed by critics as a conservative unfriendly to the ideals of African liberation, as a closet racist, and even as a secret friend of Pretoria. He was in fact none of those things, but rather a man better able than many politicians to appreciate the truism about politics being the art of the possible.

With his academic background, his round glasses, clipped moustache, precise diction, neat suits and bow ties, Crocker was not a heroic figure in the Alexandrean mould. But he proved to have a facility for unravelling knots.

As Crocker saw it, the Soviet decision to project military power into Africa and Cuba's readiness to act as Moscow's proxy represented 'a geopolitical challenge with potentially global implications'.[1] At issue was not only Soviet-Cuban hegemony in Angola 'but also the opportunity it offered to project Soviet power and influence to other states (such as Namibia) and to guerilla groups such as Swapo and the ANC (both, not coincidentally, based militarily in Angola).'[2]

Crocker could not expect his ideas to be widely shared in the UN, and especially not in respect of the Namibian issue. In that regard the UN's bridges had been burned when the General Assembly had endorsed the Ovambo-dominated Swapo as the 'sole and authentic representative' of all the Namibians. That endorsement ostensibly was intended to deny legitimacy to stooges of Pretoria among the internal parties. But at the same time it arbitrarily dismissed the legitimate claims of other organisations, notably the South West Africa National Union (Swanu), with its strong Herero representation. Smacking of one-party totalitarianism, the endorsement appeared to bear the fingerprints of its Soviet backers in the UN, although it was sponsored and guided through the General Assembly by the African and other ostensibly non-aligned states. Swapo in any event was happy to accept the advantage of the endorsement, and fought off challenges to its exclusivity for as long as it could.

Crocker accepted that the UN was the proper forum for resolving the Namibian issue, but believed its standing had been compromised by the Swapo endorsement. The UN demand for a straight transfer of power to Swapo was hardly conducive to a solution while South Africa remained able and determined to resist. Crocker sought a solution within the UN but outside of the endorsement, with Swapo's support being tested through a free and fair election.

When Crocker and William Clark, the deputy secretary of state, visited South Africa and Namibia in 1981 it was impressed on them that South Africa would not accept an election victory by Swapo that resulted in a Cuban and Soviet presence in Windhoek. The Americans had been thinking in terms of a Namibian settlement encouraging a Cuban withdrawal from Angola, but now they saw a Cuban withdrawal as a necessary part of a settlement in Namibia, if not a necessary precondition.

The MPLA, however, needed the Cubans for defence against Pretoria and UNITA. Luanda therefore could not dispense with Havana's troops while UNITA was resurgent with Pretoria's backing – and as long as the South Africans were striking from Namibia at Swapo in Angola. The South Africans for their part would not want to stop attacking Swapo inside Angola as long as the organisation continued its cross-border insurgency from bases there. And they would not want to halt their aid to UNITA as long as it remained a means of dissuading the MPLA and Cuba from assisting Swapo. It was a revolving conundrum, and it was spinning into ever greater violence.

A Soviet-Cuban military presence in Angola was unwelcome to Washington as well as to Pretoria. The Cubans had shown by their military interventions in the Congo, the Horn and elsewhere that they relished the role of Marxism's storm troopers in Africa. Crocker believed that Luanda, by declaring that the Cubans would leave Angola only after Namibia became independent, had defined the South African presence in Namibia as the ultimate rationale for retaining Castro's troops. He could not take it for granted, however, that the Cubans would leave Angola once there was a settlement in Namibia. All of this meant that if a South African withdrawal from Namibia and a Cuban withdrawal from Angola were to be made mutually conditional then they must happen more or less simultaneously. That was the essence of the linkage policy pursued by Crocker.

The Carter administration had made a Cuban withdrawal a condition of American recognition of the MPLA government, but had not also linked it to a South African pull-out from Namibia. The Reagan administration made the Namibian linkage formal policy early in 1981, and the South Africans quickly endorsed the idea. Although they had not previously associated a Cuban withdrawal with a Namibian settlement, they had raised their concerns about the Cubans with the Carter administration as early as 1977. Crocker believed these fears helped explain why Pretoria had kept stalling on the implementation of Resolution 435.

The linkage concept did not sit well with the other members of the Western Contact Group. France was especially disapproving and eventually quit the group. The others – Britain, West Germany and Canada – remained in the group but left it to the US to take the lead and make what it could of its linkage brainchild.

Certainly no other approach through the UN was making much headway. A UN-organised conference in Geneva in January 1981, attended by Swapo, South Africa and the Namibian internal parties, had failed, partly because some participants were reluctant to make commitments until they saw how the Reagan administration would move.

Meanwhile, the fighting on the ground escalated. MPLA forces tried twice without success to recapture Mavinga from UNITA. Swapo stepped up its cross-border incursions from bases collocated with Angolan and Cuban units for protection against SADF attacks. In order to counter South African air strikes, the Soviets strung a line of radar and missile bases through southern Angola. Unwilling to risk losing its irreplaceable aircraft to the missiles, the SAAF was forced to curtail its air missions but stepped up its ground incursions instead.

In August 1981 the SADF launched Operation Protea, a ten-day raid reaching more than a hundred and fifty kilometres into Angola that disrupted Swapo's military infrastructure over a wide area. More than a thousand Swapo and Fapla troops were claimed killed, and large quantities of Soviet armaments seized. SADF garrisons were left holding the towns of Xangongo and Ngiva – the first prolonged South African occupation relatively deep inside Angola. The operation was universally and angrily condemned in the UN and elsewhere.

For the pariah state, however, UN condemnation was relatively harmless words against the sticks and stones of insurgency. And so the South African attacks continued. In November the SADF again struck deep into southern Angola with Operation Daisy. No Fapla troops were encountered this time, but now the MPLA's MiG-21 jet fighters showed up, supposedly piloted by Cubans. One was shot down in what was the first aerial combat by the SAAF since Korea – but with the SAAF pilots no longer UN heroes; now they were the villains.

The war was taking on a significantly different nature in several respects. Operation Protea had shown that the MPLA government was now prepared to intervene with determination against SADF attacks on Swapo bases. The building of the radar-missile line and the appearance of the MiGs meant not only that South African aircraft could no longer operate with impunity across the border, but also that the Kremlin was ready to go to great lengths to promote its Angolan intervention. By the end of 1981, the Cuban troop strength in Angola had been reinforced to about fifteen thousand, evidently in reaction to Operation Protea and UNITA's growing assertiveness.

In November that year the oil refinery in Luanda was sabotaged in an operation that could only have been carried out by South African seaborne commandos. The purpose presumably was to curb the MPLA government's enthusiasm for supporting Swapo by showing that Pretoria could strike deep into Angola in retaliation. Apartheid's enemies saw it only as another example of Pretoria's destabilisation, a perception heightened when five months later a similar attack was made on oil storage tanks in Beira harbour in Mozambique.

With the help of its South African support, UNITA now held most of southeastern Angola and was poised to advance further north. The movement made a major advance on the political front as well when its leader, Jonas Savimbi, was invited to Washington in December 1981 and had a meeting with secretary of state Alexander Haig, who offered him financial support.

Pretoria by now seemed more than willing to give up Namibia, whose administration and defence had become a serious drain on South Africa's resources, but not to abandon it to a Swapo government and its Marxist allies. Botha's government aimed to weaken Swapo militarily and politically while strengthening the internal parties, so that independence could be achieved under a government acceptable to Pretoria.

That ambition had been set back, however, when dissension among the internal parties forced Botha to dissolve the National Assembly and put the governance of the territory in the hands of an administrator-general.

There was a breakthrough at talks in New York in July 1982, when agreement was reached on most of the conditions for implementing Resolution 435. But Crocker could get no support for linking the implementation to simultaneous South African and Cuban withdrawals.

Soon afterwards, though, Fidel Castro offered a 'gradual' withdrawal of his men from Angola once the South Africans had quit Namibia. It was not enough to satisfy Pretoria – PW Botha in September firmly made Pretoria's acceptance of 435 conditional on a Cuban withdrawal – but it was a shuffle in what Crocker saw as the right direction. In October the Cubans shuffled a bit further but imposed conditions, one of them being the ending of South African support for UNITA. All the Gordian strings were now being pulled, one way or another, but not enough yet to untie the knot.

CHAPTER 47

THE BUDS OF REFORM

At the time of their greatest triumph, the Afrikaners faced what was possibly their greatest peril. And, as so often in their history, they reacted not in unity but with dissension and division.

Dominant in government, the civil service and the armed forces, they were also an expanding power in commerce and industry. Risen phoenix-like from the ashes of the Boer War and of the double blow of depression and drought in the thirties, they were stronger politically and economically than ever before. Their culture and identity were more clearly defined as well. But at the same time they were beset on two sides: domestically by a black majority demanding what could only end up as black supremacy and perhaps the extinction of Afrikanerdom in any meaningful form; externally by a hostile world bent on their submission to the black demand.

Many Afrikaners, even the authoritarian PW Botha, appreciated that the 'total onslaught' could not in the long run be defeated through head-on confrontation. The assault must be turned through compromise, firstly and obviously in the domestic race policies. Vorster had already begun the process as early as 1977 when he appointed the committee that came up with the idea of separate governments for whites, coloureds and Indians, with the blacks represented through the independent bantustans.

The concept, further refined by a committee headed by 'political scientist' Dennis Worrall, was put to Parliament in 1982. In giving the coloureds and Asians a form of parliamentary representation, the Botha government was evidently hoping to dissuade them from aligning themselves fully with the black majority against the whites. Being fewer than the whites, they could without much risk be brought into the white political fold – but only into its outer circle, with limited influence. And not at all into the social fold; the Group Areas Act would still keep them living and doing business in the separate areas demarcated for them. National Party visionaries presumably looked ahead to a time when the public mood would accept handing some of the white land to the coloureds and Indians to complete the territorial division.*

The proposals were rejected both by apartheid's opponents in the ANC, the PAC

---

*Paradoxically, these efforts to rationalise segregation had already been compromised by military demands. Coloureds and Asians comprised 20 per cent of the SA Navy's personnel by 1979, and black South Africans (as distinct from the Namibians serving in the SWATF) would soon be deployed in Namibia and Angola.

and the outside world, for whom they were inadequate, and by right-wing Afrikaners, to whom Botha's vision of 'healthy power-sharing' was anathema. Dr Andries
Treurnicht, leader of the National Party in the Transvaal, broke away and formed
the Conservative Party in order to oppose the reforms.

This was a damaging blow to patiently constructed Afrikaner unity but not to
Botha's vision of white salvation. Most Afrikaners as well as most English-speakers
approved the proposals in a whites-only referendum in 1983. Not surprisingly, the
coloureds and Asians felt differently, for the new structure ensured that the white
parliament would always be larger than the others and would have the right to
block any further constitutional change it found unacceptable. The proposals were
rejected by most of the coloureds and Asians, and only a small minority of them
participated in the elections for their respective parliaments in 1984.

The ANC and PAC meanwhile continued their political and armed resistance.
Pretoria reacted by intensifying its repression of internal dissent and by retaliation
against the neighbouring states that provided bases or transit routes for the insurgents. In July 1982 a quarter of the Zimbabwe air force's planes were destroyed by
time bombs attached to the aircraft at the Thornhill base near Gweru. A few weeks
later three former Rhodesian soldiers serving with the SADF were killed when intercepted inside Zimbabwe while on a sabotage mission.

In December 1982 SADF commandos attacked 12 houses and flats, believed to
be occupied by ANC insurgents, in Maseru. Some forty people – accounts differ
– were killed, among them ten Basotho, including women and children. The SADF
claimed to have seized guns and explosives and plans for attacks on the Bloemfontein railway station and other targets.

MK scored a notable psychological success in 1982 by exploding a number of
limpet mines at the nuclear power station at Koeberg near Cape Town, causing
damage that delayed the commissioning of the plant – a prestige-winner for the
apartheid government – by 18 months. More attacks were made on police stations, railway and power lines and other non-civilian targets. Police stations became
fenced and fortified, and oil storage depots were ringed by tall, chain-mail fences
as a defence against rockets. All of this added to the rising cost of defending apartheid.

For all Pretoria's talk of 'total onslaught', however, it was a half-war that was being
waged in southern Africa, paradoxical in that South Africa and its neighbours were
trading insurgency and counter-insurgency at the same time as they were trading
in services and commodities, in tourism and labour.

The 'railway diplomacy' with which Pretoria had hoped to use its transport system to win friends in Africa had been undercut by the rise of insurgency from the
neighbouring countries. Against that, Pretoria's support for Renamo's sabotage operations was forcing Zimbabwe and Zambia into ever-greater dependence on the
South African railways and ports for their foreign trade.

Zimbabwe took a more direct role in the conflict by stationing troops in Mozambique to help guard the vital oil pipeline from Beira to Mutare and the railway
from Maputo to Zimbabwe, both of which Renamo had sabotaged.

Estimates of the cost of Pretoria's destabilisation rose with the inclusion of every item its opponents could think of, whether directly attributable or not. Early in 1984 the Maputo government claimed its losses from Pretoria's destabilisation amounted to more than $4-billion US, more than three times Mozambique's foreign debt. It attributed the losses largely to an enforced drop in South African trade through Maputo, to a deliberate squeeze in the recruitment of mineworkers for the South African gold mines, and to the scrapping of the system whereby half of the miners' wages were paid in gold in Maputo. These claims were less questionable than the inclusion in the total of hundreds of millions of dollars in damage to schools, shops, clinics and other infrastructure by a Renamo depicted purely as Pretoria's agent, with no political aims of its own.

In order to foster the myth that its regime was unchallenged politically, Frelimo portrayed Renamo as nothing more than bandits. It is probably truer that unseating Frelimo was always fundamental to Renamo's declared ambitions, vaguely expressed though its political principles always were. It was found convenient in Maputo to overlook the possibility that Renamo's insurgency might never have developed had Frelimo accepted free and fair elections rather than effectively seizing power after the flight of the Portuguese. Renamo remained a viable political party, providing Frelimo's parliamentary opposition, early in the next century, supported mainly in northern Mozambique where its insurgency had been most active.

In the early eighties South African military support was going not only to Renamo and to UNITA in Angola but increasingly also to Super-ZAPU in Zimbabwe, and also to the Lesotho Liberation Army that was seeking to overthrow Leabua Jonathan's government in Maseru. At the same time the SADF's direct strikes at Swapo in Angola continued.

Both the South African and Namibian liberation movements stepped up their own attacks. In February 1983 Swapo's Plan forces made their biggest incursion into Namibia, spearheaded by an elite 'Volcano' unit specially trained in Angola by East German, Russian and Cuban instructors, and northern Namibia experienced some of its bloodiest fighting.

In May the ANC exploded a car bomb outside an office block in downtown Pretoria housing SADF personnel, killing 17 people in the street and wounding 215. Almost all were civilians. The ANC justified it as an attack on a military target, but the government – and perhaps most white South Africans too – saw it as a frightening entry into urban terrorism, despite the ANC's professed policy of not striking at civilians.

Pretoria retaliated with an air raid on a group of buildings near Maputo, and claimed that 42 ANC members and 17 Mozambicans were killed and major ANC insurgency facilities destroyed. Outsiders wondered how such specific casualty figures could have been obtained.

By 1983 the heightened military activity in the sub-continent had inspired serious peace negotiations both on the Mozambican issue and on the Angola-Namibia issues. Negotiations facilitated by the US in Cape Verde and Lusaka had produced agreement on the reciprocal withdrawal of SADF and of MPLA and Cuban troops to create a 297-km buffer zone in southern Angola.

The linkage idea and South Africa's support for UNITA remained stumbling blocks to further negotiation, however, especially as UNITA was making important military advances, giving it control of the southern quarter of Angola and the entire border with Zambia, and the ability to block the Benguela railway.

So great a threat had the movement become that Swapo was now required by the Luanda government to deploy most of its Plan forces against UNITA rather than the prime targets in Namibia.

Alarmed by UNITA's advances, the Kremlin sent shipload after shipload of planes, tanks, missiles and other sophisticated armaments to boost the MPLA's strength.

Pretoria's efforts to form a broad coalition of internal parties to oppose Swapo politically in Namibia led in August 1983 to the formation of a Multi-Party Conference (MPC). The move backfired, however, when the MPC rejected Resolution 435 and demanded a Lancaster House type of constitutional conference. Pretoria stood fast by 435.

South Africa in December 1983 launched what it said was a successful preemptive strike, codenamed Askari, against Plan preparations for a major operation. Deploying more than two thousand mechanised infantry, the SADF was surprised to come up against strong resistance from Cuban troops with the Fapla forces – using battle tanks in an offensive role for the first time against the South Africans.

As the year ended, Pretoria made a surprise offer to pull its troops out of Angola (where they now had a semi-permanent presence) on condition that Swapo was not permitted to exploit the withdrawal. At an American-brokered meeting in Lusaka in February 1984, South Africa and Angola agreed to a simultaneous withdrawal from southern Angola of South African, Swapo and Cuban forces, monitored by a joint commission (the JMC). While the SADF was withdrawing, however, Swapo seized the chance to infiltrate Plan fighters into Namibia, and as a result the reciprocal withdrawal was stalled for the best part of a year while the negotiations sputtered acrimoniously on.

To its other concerns, Pretoria had now added the growth of ANC guerilla training camps in Angola. MK units were required to earn their keep by fighting alongside Fapla troops (though they never played a major role in the hostilities).

Botha's government claimed a signal success against the ANC with the loudly trumpeted signing of the Nkomati Accord with Mozambique in March 1984. The main condition was that Maputo undertook to stop backing the ANC and Pretoria to stop aiding Renamo. With South Africa's help, Frelimo and Renamo made tentative efforts to negotiate a settlement, but these were inconclusive.

Domestic resistance to the apartheid government was meanwhile growing, with work boycotts and continued rioting and school-burning in the townships. Black resistance had become further organised with the formation of the United Democratic Front (UDF) to oppose the three-parliament system.

The relatively favourable reaction to the Nkomati Accord, the domestic reforms and Pretoria's efforts to find a solution in Namibia prompted PW Botha to make a visit to Europe in June 1984 – the first by a South African prime minister since the departure from the Commonwealth. Rather than being welcomed as a reformer and peacemaker, however, he was received coolly almost everywhere and snubbed outright in France.

Still the outcast, apartheid South Africa was left to seek consolation in friendships with other pariahs: the dictators of Paraguay and Chile. Rather than conferring material benefits, these liaisons emphasised South Africa's isolation in the world.

★ ★ ★ ★

In November 1984 three black Americans of some prominence gained entry to the South African embassy in Washington on the pretext of a meeting with the ambassador, Brand Fourie. Once in his office, they announced their intention to stage a 'sit-in' against apartheid.

The invaders – Randall Robinson of an organisation called TransAfrica, Dr Mary Berry of the US Civil Rights Commission, and Walter Fauntroy, the District of Columbia representative in Congress – were inviting charges of trespass and of flouting the law prohibiting political demonstrations at a foreign embassy. Their sit-in was brief, however; once the TV cameras were in place they happily submitted to the police handcuffs, knowing that the publicity would further their cause and/or personal ambitions.

Arrest was one thing; prosecution, however, was another – a can of worms the District of Columbia authorities declined to open. After a night in the police cells the sitters-in were quietly released.

Once it became clear that nobody was going to be prosecuted for demonstrating outside the embassy, getting arrested there became fashionable in certain circles, a valuable credential for both political respectability and social prestige. There was a daily parade of volunteers to be handcuffed – hopefully on television – before being taken off in the paddy wagon to be discreetly shooed away at the police station. In the first four months more than two thousand people of many walks of life, from senators to janitors, Republicans as well as Democrats, were 'arrested' at the embassy gates.

It was a charade, empty in a legal sense but politically bountiful. For many of the volunteers it was just a frolic in political correctness, but for political opportunists like Robinson and Fauntroy it was a windfall to be harvested to the full. For serious opponents of apartheid, it was an honourable mission. Skeptics at first said it wouldn't last a month but it went on for a year.

The Washington demonstrations exemplified an almost explosive expansion of the South African issue in the United States in the early eighties. At a time when Vietnam was fading in memory and there were few other issues to seize public attention, the struggle against white supremacy in South Africa stood out invitingly to American politicians and cause-seekers. It was an empty bandwagon waiting to be boarded – by Democrats looking for material to counter Reagan's landslide re-election in November 1984, by black Americans searching for fresh inspiration for their fight against racial discrimination in their own country, and by college students emerging cause-hungry from a long post-Vietnam hibernation.

The cause had been discovered by a few students as early as the seventies, when they had begun a campaign for their universities to withdraw their investments from companies with South African subsidiaries. Promoted also by church and human rights activists, the disinvestment campaign had by 1984 spread into bigger fields, with city and state governments selling their stocks in companies with South African connections. By the end of 1985 pension and other investments totalling some $4,5-billion had been withdrawn from such companies.[1] Growing parallel with these actions was a well-organised and widely supported campaign to force disinvestment through resolutions put up by stockholders at companies' annual general meetings.

South Africa was now the target of perhaps the most intensive international campaign of political and economic attrition ever directed at a single state.

Concerted actions by Third World and Warsaw Pact countries, largely supported by First World governments, had driven South Africa out of almost every political and sporting body in the world and out of most non-governmental organisations. The only support of any consequence that Pretoria could claim was among conservatives in the US, Britain and Germany, and that was largely for reasons of self-interest.

Gone were the heady times when foreign capital had poured into South Africa to enjoy the benefits of abundant minerals and cheap labour, specifically, returns three times more than the average in the developed countries. Those returns had been reduced by economic decline and political uncertainty caused by internal and external resistance to white supremacy. The gold price had dropped to R300 by June 1982, and the state current account had plunged sharply into deficit.

Past prosperity had been built on a colonial-style economy dependent on cheap and compliant labour. But now the cost of that labour was rising, accelerated when economic pressures forced the government to open trade unionism to blacks in 1979. Also rising was the cost of the efforts to keep the black labour compliant to the dictates of white government and commerce. State revenues were increasingly being diverted to security institutions – military, police, prisons and intelligence. By 1985 the defence budget alone had risen to R4 274-million, representing a hundred-fold increase over 25 years. An increasing proportion of these costs was having to be met by the taxpayers – white wage-earners as well as corporations. The squeeze between taxes and foreign disinvestment pressures was making South Africa less attractive to investors, and foreign capital was flowing out.*

All of this meant that the cost of implementing apartheid was beginning to exceed its economic benefits. The cheap labour element of apartheid was diminishing, leaving as chief rationale only the element of ethnic separation.

While South Africa was still being protected by British and American vetoes from UN economic sanctions, the disinvestment campaigns in the US and Europe

*Security demands had risen to a point where manpower needs could no longer be met from the white male population alone. Efforts to recruit women had had little success, and the government had turned increasingly to black volunteers for the armed forces. By 1985, blacks and coloureds comprised nearly a third of the army's strength.

were indirectly exerting strong pressure on Pretoria to speed up reform. A telling blow came when Citibank, one of America's biggest, began to phase out loans to South Africa after New York City had ceased depositing its funds in any bank lending to the apartheid state.

A hardening of attitudes in Congress was reflected in a letter 35 conservative members sent to Ambassador Fourie declaring they would no longer oppose sanctions. Reagan heeded the signals. While still opposing sanctions and disinvestment, he called for the ending of forced removals and of detention without trial, and for dialogue between whites and blacks.

The European Community demanded an immediate end to the emergency and the freeing of detainees. EC members recalled their ambassadors for consultations – in diplomatic practice a signal of strong disapproval and/or warning.

Sentiment in the United States against apartheid reached a level that persuaded Republican members of Congress in 1985 to support a Democrat-sponsored Anti-Apartheid Act barring new investment in South Africa, loans and computer sales to the government, and the importing of Krugerrands. When the Republican-dominated Senate endorsed a compromise version postponing the investment ban for a year, Reagan, realising a veto might be overridden, implemented the compromise measures in an executive order.

Anti-apartheid feelings were being inflamed in the US and elsewhere by frequent television images of the riots and demonstrations that had become endemic in South Africa, prompting Pretoria in December 1985 to ban TV coverage of disturbances.

In 1986 Democrats, again supported by Republicans, introduced in Congress the Comprehensive Anti-Apartheid Act (CAAA), a stronger measure than Reagan's compromise executive order of the previous year. This time Reagan vetoed the measure, but Congress overrode his veto and passed the act into law. It banned imports of South African coal, iron, steel, textiles, agricultural products, uranium and armaments, revoked South African Airways' landing rights, and prohibited oil exports to and new investments in South Africa.

Passage of the CAAA climaxed the sanctions campaign in the US. Thereafter, Congressional support for tougher measures waned. By that time, both the Pretoria government and the ANC were moving towards negotiation, but so covertly and tentatively that few were aware of it.

Like it not, government was being forced to react to the evidence of apartheid's decline: the failure of the bantustan and influx control systems, the breaching of the job reservation and trade union barriers, the recruitment of blacks into the armed forces.

★ ★ ★ ★

Alongside its temporal failure, apartheid was increasingly being questioned on moral grounds by some of its own adherents, notably in the Dutch Reformed churches where for centuries white segregation and supremacy had found clerical approval,

391

even supposed divine purpose. The opposition of the other churches to white supremacy had been a given since the days of Van der Kemp and Philip. But it had
seldom since then been militant. More recently the Anglican monk, Father Trevor
Huddlestone, had become a thorn in the flesh of the government, and indeed of his
own church, which he accused of sleeping through apartheid, 'though it occasionally talks in its sleep'.

After Sharpeville, the volatile Anglican archbishop in South Africa, Joost de
Blank, had threatened to pull his church out of the World Council of Churches if
the council didn't expel the DRC. He succeeded only in embarrassing his church.
Six months after Sharpeville, the eight South African member churches of the
WCC attended a conference in the Johannesburg suburb of Cottesloe. The DRC
delegation supported the conference's final declaration opposing the exclusion of
any Christian from any church on the grounds of race, and criticising the migrant
labour system, job reservation and exploitation of blacks.

A furious Verwoerd lambasted the DRC delegates, who were repudiated in a decision of the DRC to withdraw from the WCC. But doubt had been seeded in the
body of the church that had become known as 'the National Party at prayer'. Not
that the DRC endorsed racial injustices, rather it condemned them, but it saw no
injustice in the principle of separate development, for which it perceived scriptural
justification.

In 1968 the South African Council of Churches (SACC) published a 'Message to
the People of South Africa', a criticism of racial separation which the government
saw as so threatening that Prime Minister Vorster warned the council of reprisals
if it persisted in doing 'the kind of thing here in South Africa that Martin Luther
King did in America'.[2]

The Presbyterian Church in 1981 gave its blessing to mixed-race marriages in
defiance of the law forbidding them. Two years after the World Alliance of Reformed Churches had declared apartheid a heresy in 1983, a gathering of theologians and church leaders issued the Kairos Document branding the apartheid
government an enemy of God's people.

Revision was under way even in the inner temple of apartheid, the DRC. In
1984 the church's Western Synod abandoned scriptural justification for apartheid
and advised the DRC flock to 'confess their participation in apartheid with humility and sorrow'.

Whether the churches were carrying their white congregations along with them
is arguable; it certainly was not indicated by the ever-larger vote for the apartheid
government in the white general elections. That vote, however, came essentially
from fear. The whites could not easily seek security in morality rather than power,
not until the fear was ameliorated at least by hope.

Temporal salvation must come before spiritual salvation.

CHAPTER 48

ONE MAN'S RUBICON

What is known as classic apartheid had been practised as state policy for nearly forty years before its adherents began seriously to question its viability. And then it was more on grounds of practicality than of morality.

Either way, it involved a revision of notions of white supremacy that had gone largely unchallenged for some three centuries. For most of this time, the concept of racial supremacy had been treated by its supporters partly as convenience, partly as gospel.

But as apartheid became more vigorously opposed domestically and internationally, its convenience became less tenable and its morality more open to question. And then even its practitioners began to question it on both counts and to consider radical changes of direction.

Within both the apartheid government and the ANC, the realisation was growing that neither of them could achieve their objectives through violence. The government was too strong to be overthrown militarily, and black resistance was too widespread, determined and diffuse to be stamped out by force.

Once the re-thinking began, its momentum increased exponentially, progressing to reform that became revolution. Nelson Mandela's release from prison came little more than five years after apartheid's ideologues in academia had quietly raised the idea of negotiation and it had tentatively been accepted by the watchdogs of white supremacy, the Broederbonders and the National Intelligence Service. Within another five years the whites had voluntarily handed political power to the blacks.

Throughout their history, the Afrikaners have shown themselves to be essentially pragmatists and survivors. For most of them, Masada was never an option. They would rather seek the most practical way to come to terms with the demand for majority rule, to do a deal with the ancient bogie of black power.

The first tentative moves were being made by 1984. By then the UDF had been formed to oppose the tricameral parliamentary system, and the black campaign to make parts of South Africa ungovernable was under way – and seriously worrying the government and its security forces. NIS officials began to sound out the idea of talks with Mandela. Other government officials had secret and informal meetings with ANC or UDF representatives in South Africa.[1]

Sensing these subterranean shifts in Afrikanerdom, the ANC's exiled leadership invited two prominent academics, Prof. Willie Esterhuyse and Prof. Sampie Terreblanche, to Lusaka for talks. Botha, however, thought this was going too far and too fast, and blocked the trip. He came up with his own idea: an offer to free Mandela if he rejected violence. Mandela predictably refused the bribe. While he and some in the exiled leadership favoured negotiation, they were not prepared to abandon armed struggle. Rather, it would be used as a means to bring about a political solution within the ambit of the ANC's long-held policy of non-racial democracy.

At a major conference at Kabwe in Zambia in June 1985 the ANC decided to raise the pressure against white hegemony by departing from its policy of avoiding civilian targets. The ANC armed wing, MK, was authorised to attack civilian targets such as prominent government supporters, state witnesses in political trials, and farmers cooperating with the police and army in counter-insurgency operations.

The decision flouted the ANC's acceptance of the Geneva Convention protocol binding it to avoid attacking civilian targets, although this might have been excused by the ANC leadership on the grounds that Pretoria for its part had consistently treated captured insurgents not as prisoners of war but as common criminals, liable to execution.

Since it was difficult precisely to define individual targets of the kind envisaged at Kabwe, the decision effectively gave MK cadres licence to make the choice on the ground. Unable to take on the much stronger security forces, MK resorted largely to the indirect weapons: bombs and, to a lesser extent, land mines. Since both target randomly, numbers of civilians, blacks as well as whites, were killed indiscriminately.

The Kabwe decision was a difficult one for the ANC leadership to take after the years of mainly scrupulous avoidance of civilian targets despite growing state violence. However, apartheid's gauleiters were considered to have taken advantage of ANC pacifism with ever more ruthless measures to crush opposition. Furthermore, it was considered that the whites supporting the government in denying basic rights to blacks should experience something of the suffering that in the process was being inflicted on the blacks. Only then might white public opinion find reason and need to demand that the oppression be ended. White privilege, it was reckoned, would not be relinquished unless it became too painful to retain.

Historians will in time no doubt measure the Kabwe decision against the extent of black suffering and of black frustration after generations of moderation and spurned overtures. But also against white fears, based largely on the belief that, for all the talk of non-racial democracy, the only alternative to white supremacy was black supremacy, which seemed to offer no guarantee of democracy or of respect for white interests. True, the Freedom Charter had offered non-racial democracy, but no special protection for whites. Neither had the Lusaka Manifesto specified how this protection might be provided.

It is debatable whether whites were made more amenable to negotiation by the attacks that followed Kabwe, such as the land mine explosion near Ellisras in the northern Transvaal that killed two whites in January 1986, or the bomb blast in a mall at Amanzimtoti in Natal – said to have been in retaliation for the South African raid on Maseru in October 1985 – that sent shards of glass scything among shoppers.

In May 1986 a bomb explosion at the Benmore shopping centre in Johannesburg caused heavy damage but no casualties. Three civilians were killed and 69 injured by a car bomb exploded outside Magoo's Bar in Durban in June. Two weeks later 20 civilians were injured in a limpet mine explosion in a restaurant at a Holiday Inn in Johannesburg. There was another land mine explosion in October in the Eastern Transvaal in which four soldiers were injured. Six months later four persons were killed in a land mine blast in the northern Transvaal.

Because of the sensitivities on both sides, the first moves towards negotiation were made with the knowledge neither of the white public in South Africa nor of the ANC membership at large. The early exchanges were inspired by the mutual recognition at leadership level that the racial problem in South Africa could be resolved neither by classic apartheid nor by insurgent resistance. But they were made in secret for fear, on both sides, that negotiation would not be well received amid the prevailing black anger and white fear.

White fears had indirectly been heightened by the intolerance and violence among rival black groups, especially the use of the 'necklace', the method of kangaroo court execution in which the victim was burned alive by having a petrol-filled tyre placed round his neck and set alight. Bishop Tutu and others condemned the practice but, to their eternal shame, some ANC leaders defended it as a justifiable punishment for 'collaborators'. In doing so they descended to the moral depths inhabited by apartheid's torturers and assassins.

At the Kabwe conference, the ANC balanced its escalation of violence with an acceptance of the need to win whites to the ANC's way of thinking by persuasion rather than coercion. This seeming contradiction reflected a growing view among moderates that the ANC's aim of a non-racial society might better be achieved by convincing the whites and their government that they could abandon apartheid without sacrificing their security and their culture. The ANC was, in Patti Waldmeir's words, 'torn between those … who were intent on striking fear into white hearts and those … who preferred to charm the whites all the way to defeat'. The conference, she said, 'followed a confusing path between the two positions. While calling for the extension of violence to white areas, it also hinted at an apparently contradictory strategy of engagement.'[2]

The seeds of negotiation were being sown on both sides of the racial divide. Among the whites, it was not only Afrikaners who were coming to favour dialogue. The English-speakers, having been displaced from political influence, expressed their views mainly through the parliamentary opposition and big business. In the corporate world there was growing concern at the economic damage being done by apartheid and the campaigns against it.

Feelers were put out, and in September 1985 a group of South African businessmen led by Gavin Relly of the Anglo-American Corporation met the ANC president, Oliver Tambo, and other exiled ANC officials in Zambia. The meeting was a revealing manifestation of the change in commercial thinking. The old dependence on cheap black labour had been abandoned, or at least modified, in the face of the changes in international moral codes and economic realities. Not the least of these was the growing bargaining power of the blacks as the unworkable apartheid system began to collapse under its own weight, resulting in the legalisation of black trade unions and the breaching of job reservation. There were simply too few whites to provide the economy's motive skills, and once these were opened to blacks apartheid became impossible to sustain.

Those in PW Botha's corner held a narrower view, however. Negotiations were not to be about surrendering power to the blacks but about persuading them to accept segregated societies. And the ANC must not be allowed to enter any negotiations from a position of strength. Both the domestic crackdown on the ANC and the strikes at its foreign bases and backers were therefore intensified.

Botha's reaction to the escalation of domestic violence was ambivalent. While offering further cautious reforms he declared a state of emergency in July 1985 in the parts most severely affected. Thousands of people were detained without trial under tough new legislation.

Nonetheless, Pretoria's seeming acceptance of reform, hesitant though it was, encouraged strong expectations, both at home and abroad, of further concessions. It was widely anticipated that Botha would announce major reforms at a provincial congress of the National Party in Durban in August 1985.

Heavy hints dropped in Western capitals by foreign minister Pik Botha fanned the expectations there. So great was the interest that the president's speech in Durban was televised live on major networks in America, Britain and Germany. Never before had a South African leader been given so huge an international audience. The world waited to see Botha cross his Rubicon and take his country into a bright new future.

★ ★ ★ ★

To an expectant country and an eager world, it seemed that PW Botha either did not see a Rubicon at Durban or he quailed at its edge. His address to the National Party congress was dismissed as containing neither significant announcement nor statesmanlike exposition; only a finger-wagging repetition of hackneyed party themes and a declaration that reform would not be hastened to satisfy external opinion, that the whites would not be led into 'abdication and suicide'.

Political analysts opined that Botha pulled back at the last moment because conservatives in his party had become alarmed at the pace and scale of his reforms. Yet buried in his speech were reformist overtures that were actually far-reaching in the context of the time, departures from apartheid policy that would have seemed radical, even heretical, to earlier purists like Malan and Verwoerd.

He declared his government's willingness to 'share its power of decision-making with other communities' and at the same time hinted at permanent residence and political rights for blacks living in the white areas. He also held out the prospect of 'one citizenship and a universal franchise' in a united South Africa.

His successor, FW de Klerk, later wrote that Botha had in effect 'announced that the government had decided to abandon the policy of grand apartheid that had been so meticulously designed by Hendrik Verwoerd 25 years earlier.'[3]

For a world primed for explicit sensationalism it was all too veiled, however, and it reacted with disappointment and condemnation. At a time when the UDF was striving to make his country ungovernable, when the ANC was notching up its violence, when the world was baying at his borders, the world may have been expecting too much from a man who characteristically reacted obstinately to coercion. But the world was concerned not with personalities but with principles.

Two weeks before the Durban conference, the American bank, Chase Manhattan, had decided to blacklist the South African private sector. When other major international banks followed suit, refusing to roll over maturing short-term loans to the private sector, loans representing nearly two-thirds of South Africa's foreign debt, the value of the rand plummeted. The Johannesburg Stock Exchange closed for three days. Pretoria imposed a four-month moratorium on repayments of foreign debt while it tried to reschedule the debt. Faced with the alternative of default, the banks agreed to an extension of the loans for a year and a partial repayment of principal.

Chase Manhattan later asserted that the decision was made purely on financial, not political, grounds, but the effects were the same anyway. Pretoria was now forced to accept that political intransigence at home could be maintained only at the expense of international financial security.

The disappointment at Botha's Durban speech seemed justified when his offer to share decision-making with blacks appeared to be nothing more than coopting them to his advisory President's Council. If Botha and his cabinet thought that was enough for the time being, the rest of the world thought otherwise. The pressures mounted.

While Reagan was imposing his own strictures on South Africa to avoid having his presidential veto overturned, in Europe the EC countries banned oil and arms exports, curtailed sporting and cultural exchanges, and withdrew their military attaches.

When the Commonwealth leaders met at Nassau in October 1985, strong efforts were made to have full sanctions applied against South Africa. The drive was posited largely on the assertion that black South Africans were willing to suffer the consequences in the interests of ridding themselves of the harsher affliction of apartheid. Though possibly valid, the thesis was unprovable since there was no good way of measuring black opinion, and few blacks were in a position to gauge the likely effects of sanctions. In any event, the proposal was stubbornly blocked by Margaret Thatcher, mindful of Britain's substantial trade with and investment in South Africa.

Instead, a seven-member Eminent Persons Group (EPG) was charged with encouraging internal dialogue in South Africa with the aim of bringing about 'a nonracial and representative government'.

The EPG's formation was founded on the assumption that it was possible to form and maintain a government fairly representative of all race groups, and that a democratically elected government would necessarily be non-racial and remain democratic. It was a bold assumption, given South Africa's history and demograph-ics, and black Africa's recent history, but there was, of course, no realistic alternative at the time.

The EPG was co-chaired by Australian premier Malcolm Fraser and Olusegun Abasanjo, the former head of one of Nigeria's several coup-installed military gov-ernments. Evidently no-one in the Commonwealth saw any irony in the entrusting of the mission to the head of a white settler nation that had systematically oppressed, attenuated, degraded and sidelined its indigenous population, and the former leader of a state that had been roiled by bloody ethnic conflict since its founding, a state in which democracy and racial and religious tolerance had rarely prevailed.

Privately, Botha admitted to the EPG that his government was 'reconciled to the eventual disappearance of white domination' provided the rights of minorities were protected.[4] It was an admission he did not yet dare make publicly, however, for fear of his right wing. He did terminate the pass laws, though, and promised to repeal the influx control legislation. These were concessions of enormous significance in the South African political context, but in the context of the world's demands they were relatively small steps.

The EPG seemed close to arranging formal negotiations between the govern-ment and the ANC when SADF forces on 18 May 1986 simultaneously attacked what were said to be ANC houses in Gaborone, Harare and Lusaka. The govern-ments in all three capitals denied that the houses were ANC premises, and the raids were widely seen as an attempt to torpedo the EPG exercise now that it appeared to be making rather more progress than Pretoria's right wing had expected.

Despite the outrage at the raids, the EPG team went ahead with talks with the government's constitutional committee. These foundered, however, on the govern-ment's insistence that the ANC renounce violence, as distinct from only suspend-ing it, before any negotiations could be opened. In apparent exasperation, the EPG came out in favour of economic sanctions.

The government was nonetheless shuffling closer to negotiation with the ANC, but furtively for fear of arousing the right wing. In November 1985 Justice minister Kobie Coetzee secretly visited Mandela in the hospital in Cape Town where he was being treated after becoming ill on Robben Island. Shortly thereafter, Mandela was moved to the mainland, to Pollsmoor prison near Cape Town.

A few months later Coetzee, responding to an initiative from Mandela, began bringing him secretly to his own home for informal talks. Before the year ended the minister was having the world's most famous prisoner driven around Cape Town on secret sightseeing outings. The motive presumably was to soften him up for more serious negotiating. But Mandela, having early in his political career staked out his position on non-racial democracy, had less compulsion to make concessions than the practitioners of apartheid.

Among the latter – the more moderate ones, at least – revisionism was becoming the order of the day. Both the Broederbond and the Dutch Reformed Church were cautiously moving away from apartheid, tiptoeing off the safe paths of practice and dogma into the dangerous darkness where the old bogie, majority rule, lurked.

ANC moderates for their part were looking ever more seriously at persuasion rather than confrontation, to removing the fears of the whites and giving them reasons other than duress to abandon apartheid.

It was in this spirit that a meeting took place in New York in June 1986 between the Broederbond's chairman, Pieter de Lange, and exiled ANC representatives led by Thabo Mbeki, who was later to become the second president of a democratic South Africa. The election of the relatively liberal De Lange in 1983 to head the most vital organ of Afrikanerdom reflected the new thinking within the white tribe.

De Lange had soon felt he had enough support to suggest government policy revisions along the lines of scrapping statutory discrimination and bringing blacks into the political process. He and like-thinkers were realising that the whites' aspirations could not be attained and preserved by military means. Some kind of political deal had to be struck with the black majority.

Though unseen by an outside world howling blindly for the crushing of white supremacy, these stirrings were perceived by ANC leaders now revising their own thinking. It was becoming clear to them that the violent overthrow of white domination would be a long and costly process. Negotiation seemed a more realistic way of achieving democracy. Hence the Mbeki-De Lange meeting.

As a breaking of the apartheid ice the meeting was hugely significant. A negotiated solution was still a long way off, however.

Botha was able to persuade his party in August 1986 to offer blacks living outside the 'independent homelands' their own parliament, but again it was a concession falling far short of black expectations.

Though he had not fully crossed his Rubicon at Durban, Botha had in effect already put one foot on the far side with his limited reforms. Now he stood painfully stretched across the fateful divide between the old order and a new one, between the failed past and a promising future.

Thus extended, he found himself simultaneously seeking compromise and acting tough.

★ ★ ★ ★

In the military-minded political establishment set up by PW Botha in Pretoria, military reactions to perceived threats were more than ever before favoured over political ones. Even in foreign affairs, the views of the generals in the SADF often carried more weight than those of the diplomats, especially in the case of Angola, Mozambique and Zimbabwe.

Both Maputo and Harare denied facilitating ANC insurgency, but this was either disbelieved or their political support for the ANC's cause and for anti-apartheid campaigns in the UN and elsewhere evidently was enough reason for Pretoria's hawks to continue destabilising their countries and promoting dissidence there.

Since South Africa recognised and had formal relations with both governments, Pretoria's intervention on behalf of the dissidents was perforce covert, in intention if not always in effect.

In the case of Mozambique the policy was peculiarly dichotomous. On the one hand, Pretoria's diplomats promoted closer relations, even to the extent of financing major improvements to Maputo port, and facilitating negotiations for a cease-fire and political settlement with Renamo. On the other hand, Pretoria's security establishment continued secretly to supply Renamo in breach of the Nkomati Accord, evidently flying in to bush air strips or air-dropping food, medicines, radios and AK47s captured in Angola.

With the help of this covert assistance, Renamo was able to gain control of much of northern Mozambique. The rebels' persistent sabotage resulted in some two thousand Zimbabwean troops being deployed to guard the road, rail and oil pipeline from Beira to Mutare.

Maputo's accusations of continued South African support for Renamo were routinely denied in Pretoria – until the rebels' headquarters in the Gorongosa district were overrun by government forces in August 1985. Documents captured there provided a cornucopia of evidence of continued SADF secret dealings with Renamo. Though mostly circumstantial, the evidence was strong enough to convince most analysts that at least some elements of the SADF were determined to continue aiding Renamo regardless of any political concerns.

The Botha government's efforts to destabilise the uncooperative neighbours saw the diplomats of the Department of Foreign Affairs being elbowed by the security establishment on a number of fronts besides Mozambique. Botswana, Lesotho and Swaziland all came under strong pressure from Pretoria to sign 'non-aggression' pacts in order to block ANC insurgency from or through their territories. Only Swaziland buckled and signed – but secretly. Agents of the South African security forces thereafter entered Swaziland virtually at will to kill or abduct suspected ANC operatives, and there was hardly a murmur of protest from a Swazi government that viewed discretion as the better part of valour in its dealings with its domineering neighbour.

Meanwhile, the pressure was maintained on Botswana and Lesotho. In a deliberately spectacular raid evidently intended to cow both the Botswana government and the highly active South African exile community there, SADF commandos loudly attacked ten houses and an office building in different parts of Gaborone one night in June 1985.

Defence Headquarters said afterwards the houses had been occupied by 'key' ANC elements. Strangely, no attempt was made to abduct any of them for questioning, which surely would have been more useful than killing them. Instead, the commandos blasted some of the houses with bombs, shot people asleep in their beds, and machine-gunned wardrobes in which others might be hiding. The Botswana government said that of the 12 persons killed in the raid, only five had ANC connections and were minor figures at best.

When Prime Minister Leabua Jonathan of Lesotho proved reluctant to sign a non-aggression pact or to expel the ANC cadres sheltering in his country, the Lesotho Liberation Army (LLA) set up by his political opponents was invited to conduct insurgency from safe houses in South Africa. Water supplies, oil tanks and other infrastructure were sabotaged, either by South African commandos or by the LLA with South African help. Six South Africans exiles were among nine people killed in a commando raid on suspected ANC houses in Maseru in December 1985.

The next month Pretoria tightened the screws by imposing a 'go-slow' inspection of food, fuel and other goods entering Lesotho. By intensifying public dissatisfaction with Jonathan, this virtual border blockade precipitated a coup which put Lesotho under the rule of a military council. The military government largely closed down ANC operations from Lesotho.

Border blockades of varying severity were imposed against Zimbabwe and Zambia in order to dissuade them from aiding the ANC, though never firmly enough to cause serious economic damage, just enough to emphasise that what Pretoria had done to Ian Smith it could also do to Mugabe and Kaunda – and more.

That Pretoria was prepared to go beyond border blockades became evident when early in 1987 South African commandos raided alleged ANC houses in Livingstone on the Zambian side of the Victoria Falls, 650 kilometres' crow-flight from the nearest point in South Africa. Four occupants of the houses were killed.

The accusations of South African dirty tricks became exceptionally vociferous when in October 1986 President Samora Machel of Mozambique was killed when the Russian aircraft returning him from a visit to Zambia crashed just inside the South African border on its approach to Maputo. A commission of inquiry appointed by the South African government but including seemingly independent British and American authorities blamed the crash on pilot error, but its finding was widely disbelieved among apartheid's opponents. Allegations that the plane had been lured off course by a false beacon placed by Pretoria's agents persisted. No good reason has been advanced, however, as to why Pretoria would have wanted to kill Machel. To the contrary, the South African government averred that its relations with Machel and his government had reached their highest level and seemed likely to get better still.

If the beacon theory is true it would tend to support other indications that the dirty tricks departments of Botha's government were assuming Frankensteinian characteristics, operating at times beyond the ken or control of their masters, obsessively pursuing their distorted vision of duty or their addictive cruelty or whatever else it was that led them to their bizarre excesses. After the fall of apartheid the cover was lifted somewhat off these activities, giving glimpses into a horrific state underworld, but nothing came out to confirm the phony beacon theory.

Among apartheid's more ardent enemies, including some in the outside world, the Machel murder hypothesis was accepted without question, received gratefully, even if sadly, as new ammunition for the cause. In these circles, it seems that apartheid was not only an obnoxious policy to be abolished but also a useful demon, performing a function antithetical to that of an icon, an object not of constant reverence but of perpetual execration, a target against which vicariously to vent resentment of other iniquities less assailable than apartheid, or even a vessel for the transference of other guilts, such as continued racism in America and Europe.

CHAPTER 49

PEACE AND WAR

Glasnost and *perestroika* it might be in Moscow as Mikhail Gorbachev pulled the plug on the old Soviet order, but the consequences of his moves were still unclear in Russia in 1985, and even less clear abroad. Least of all were they discernible in a southern African sub-continent still heaving with ideological conflict, in much of which Moscow had a hand, directly or indirectly. Especially was this the case with the warring in Angola and Namibia.

Even in 1986, Soviet arms supplies continued to pour into Angola. Regardless of *perestroika* – or perhaps because of it – Moscow's military commanders remained obsessed with victory in Angola, and perhaps in the associated insurgency in Namibia as well.

Though Pretoria was no longer fighting to retain occupation of Namibia, it was still intent on keeping Swapo and its communist allies from taking power. Swapo, however, was reluctant to compromise, partly because it suspected Pretoria of seeking to retain control of Namibia through a stooge government. Besides, Sam Nujoma evidently wanted to ensure that Swapo would hold absolute power when South Africa left.

It was this tangle of fear, suspicion and ambition that Chester Crocker was trying to unravel. He was not always helped by the European powers' rejection of the linkage concept, or by the dissension over the Angola-Namibia issue among the Washington politicos, Republicans included.

Crocker's patient negotiations had been set back by the collapse of the Lusaka Accord of 1984. Under this agreement, South Africa had promised to withdraw its troops from their deepest penetration into Angola, and the MPLA had undertaken to stop Swapo from advancing Plan combatants into the area thus vacated. South Africa, however, had pulled out of the exercise, claiming the MPLA had failed to keep its side of the bargain.

Pretoria had meanwhile extended its efforts to create a Swapo-proof political structure within Namibia by installing a 'government of national unity' in Windhoek, which then appointed a council to write a new constitution.

As Gorbachev began his reforms in Moscow, the warfare in Angola entered its most explosive stage, a showdown that would test some of the most sophisticated armaments in the primal African bush and push both the Cuban and South African armed forces close to their limits. In July 1985 the Luanda government began

402

the biggest offensive yet launched against UNITA, led by Soviet and Cuban officers and backed by late-model Russian aircraft, tanks and artillery. By September the offensive had rolled UNITA's defences back close to Mavinga, the gateway to Jamba, which UNITA called its capital.

In its heyday, Jamba could fairly have been described as the world's most important collection of grass huts. These few hundred rudimentary buildings scattered through the dry bush of south-eastern Angola were significant beyond their insubstantial structure – and not only to UNITA. Without Jamba and without its leader, Jonas Savimbi, UNITA would have been hard put to keep challenging the MPLA and its red-flagged backers. Jamba gave the movement a base, a headquarters, a capital, a focal point of identity, a home for its political soul. It represented UNITA's ability to survive and therefore to be considered worth continued external support.

If Jamba had fallen to the MPLA, UNITA might have set up another base somewhere else in the bush, but the loss would have been crippling, perhaps mortal, to UNITA's viability. This was why the MPLA offensives were aimed at Jamba – and why the South Africans felt compelled to intervene in strength to prevent it from being overrun. Once Pretoria had become committed to backing UNITA, the defence of Jamba became imperative. The result was an improbable yet effective alliance between a white supremacist state and an organisation professing to embrace 'negritude' as fundamental policy.

Pretoria feared that if Mavinga fell Luanda's planes would be able to use the airstrip there to strike at Jamba, only 270 km to the south. And Swapo's infiltration front would be greatly extended eastward, from Ovamboland to the Caprivi. Remembering Savannah, the SADF was reluctant to commit troops to support UNITA in Angola, but the threat posed by the Fapla advance could not be ignored. As the Fapla offensive approached Mavinga, the SADF was ordered by Pretoria to intervene, and sent in aircraft and artillery. Heavy South African air and artillery bombardments, together with the approach of the rainy season, decided the Luanda forces to withdraw. But the deployment of the SADF gunners in defence of Mavinga was now the thin end of a South African wedge that was rapidly to widen.

A thin American wedge had also been covertly inserted in the form of shoulder-fired Stinger ground-to-air missiles secretly supplied to UNITA by the CIA. The Stingers – and perhaps Tow anti-tank missiles as well – gave UNITA potent defences against the Russian jets and armour but did not negate them. In July 1985 the US Congress, worried by the flood of Soviet weaponry into Angola, had repealed the Clark Amendment, clearing the way for UNITA again to openly receive American armaments. Crocker was opposed to it, fearing it would upset his delicate efforts to balance a South African withdrawal from Namibia with a Cuban evacuation from Angola. He was overruled by the White House, however, and Jonas Savimbi was received like a head of state in Washington in January 1986. Soon UNITA was openly receiving the missiles, shipped through the former Belgian air base at Kamina in Zaire, which the CIA had refurbished.

Potent though they were, the American weapons were small potatoes compared with the T55 tanks, large-calibre multiple rockets, high-level anti-aircraft missiles, MiG jets and helicopter gunships the Soviets were pouring into Fapla's armoury. The Americans never extended their aid beyond the missiles, for sentiment against US intervention in Angola remained strong in Washington and the Reagan administration evidently was reluctant to risk opening to the world the can of worms that was the CIA's covert operations in Angola. It had enough to worry about closer to home with its covert backing of the *contras* in Nicaragua against the Soviet-supported government there. Anyway, as long as the South Africans were willing to commit their own resources to supporting UNITA, and as long as they were doing it with good effect, there was no need for further US intervention. In the end it was indeed the South African armour, artillery and aircraft that saved UNITA and blocked the Cuban and Soviet ambitions in Angola.

The SADF forces, including the infantry, were largely composed of young white South Africans, conscripts taken, in most cases unwillingly, from their jobs and families. Most of them had only a vague idea of why they were serving, but largely accepted the word of their government and military commanders that they were fighting to stave off black and/or communist supremacy.*

Exasperated by the defeat of the 1985 offensive, Moscow sent one of its top generals, Konstantin Shaganovitch, to Angola to take charge of Luanda's forces, supported by 1 000 Russian officers and 2 000 East German intelligence and communication specialists. Shaganovitch ordered another conventional offensive against UNITA, to begin in the second half of 1986.

Pretoria tried to disrupt the build-up for the offensive by sending a seaborne force in June to Namibe harbour, through which some of the Soviet supplies were coming. Fuel storage tanks were blown up, and one Russian freighter was sunk and two others disabled by mines placed by frogmen.

Shaganovitch's offensive, buzzing with tanks and planes, ground to a halt after only two months, his voracious columns starved by the crimping of his supply lines by UNITA and SADF attacks. He pulled back most of his forces to regroup and rearm them from the mass of Soviet weaponry still being shipped and flown into Luanda.

Much of the Soviet weaponry was old stuff Moscow did not greatly value, but the armaments also included late-model aircraft and tanks and sophisticated weaponry, such as radar-guided, high-altitude anti-aircraft missiles new to the battlefield. When some were captured by the South Africans, Western military agencies begged to examine them.

The town of Cuito Cuanavale, with its airfield and road links commanding the approaches to Mavinga and Jamba, had assumed crucial importance as the springboard for offensives against these targets. To counter any such offensive, UNITA infantry made a thrust towards Cuito Cuanavale, supported by South African air raids

*There were black soldiers, though, in Pretoria's infantry: besides the few black South Africans in the special units there were the Angolans in 32 Battalion and the Namibians in the SWATF. In this respect, South Africa, the last colonial power, was imitating its British, French, German and Belgian predecessors in using their colonised subjects to fight for them. The arming of black soldiers to fight alongside whites ones was, however, as revealing a harbinger of apartheid's demise as was the eroding of job reservation in the workplace.

and long-range shelling – a widening of the wedge.

Crocker meanwhile was tirelessly pursuing negotiations but always bumping up against the obsession in Moscow, Havana and Luanda with military victory.

In his next offensive, launched in August 1987, Shaganovitch advanced two forces from Cuito Cuanavale, the main one aiming to cross the Lomba River, beyond which lay Mavinga. Savimbi's troops were hard pressed to stop the main force, prompting Pretoria to intervene with an SADF force of mechanised infantry and artillery under the code name Operation Modular. It was the beginning of the most intensive combat by South African forces since the Second World War.

Two attempts by Shaganovitch's main force to cross the Lomba were turned back by the South Africans and UNITA in heavy fighting. These actions saw South Africa's first use of the G-5 long-range artillery and the ZT3 anti-tank missile developed by Armscor. In another action, the South Africans claimed to have destroyed an entire Fapla brigade that had moved from Cuito Cuanavale along the south bank of the Lomba.

Much of the action along the Lomba was the ground equivalent of an aerial dogfight, but in a forest – tanks smashing down trees; wheeled armoured dodging and circling the tanks, both firing through the trees at close range, sometimes at thirty metres or less. From over the horizon, the G-5s pounded Luanda's forces, their shelling guided by artillery spotters sometimes hidden only a few hundred metres away from the targets.

Having stopped Shaganovitch at the Lomba, SADF strategists decided to hamper a further offensive by pushing him back east of the southward-flowing Cuito River, whose confluence with the Cuanavale River gave the town there its name. For this task, Pretoria decided to send in reinforcements and to back them with its own tanks.

The Fapla retreat from the Lomba enabled the SADF to get its G-5 guns within range of Cuito Cuanavale, and they began to destroy the airfield, forcing the Fapla/Cuban air operations to be moved back to Menongue with a consequent reduction of air time over the battlefield.

At the same time the South African reinforcements for the push against Shaganovitch arrived at the front – more infantry, more multiple rocket launchers and G-5 guns, and the first troop of its self-propelled version, the G-6; also the SADF's battle tank, the Olifant.

The Olifants were blooded in action on 9 November when a brigade-strong SADF/SWATF/UNITA force attacked Fapla forces advancing along the west-flowing Chambinga River, which joins the Cuito River south of Cuito Cuanavale. Again the armour of both sides duelled half-blind, as it were, in thick forest, close combat in which the fastest gun won. The action ended with the Fapla forces retreating towards Cuito Cuanavale.

More Russian weaponry began arriving at the front, including even more modern tanks, the T-62s. But Castro appears now to have revised his view of Cuba's objectives in Angola and of South Africa's determination to defend its own perceived interests. Castro's exasperation with the Russian and MPLA generals had likely increased with each setback. Nowhere in Africa – neither in the Horn, the Congo nor Angola – had his interventions been as productive as he would no doubt have liked. And in Angola it was destined only to get worse as the war increasingly involved the white South Africans, who had the industrial capacity and military skills to fight with great effectiveness, and many of whom saw themselves as a nation fighting for more than ideology – for its very survival.

Castro was furthermore coming under pressure from Gorbachev for a settlement of the conflict, for Moscow, though still pumping weaponry into Angola, was tiring of the costly fruitlessness of it all.[1] And the MPLA was having difficulty keeping up with its payments for Cuba's military assistance. On top of all that, resentment was rising among the Cuban population at the loss of family members in distant Angola.

UNITA meanwhile was taking advantage of Luanda's defeats to resume operations in the centre of the country, and claimed to have more than a third of Angola under its control.

The SADF's effort to drive the enemy back across the Cuito River was launched, with UNITA infantry support, in January 1988. Luanda's forces were pushed back westwards towards Cuito Cuanavale, and dug in at nearby Tumpo. But now it was the South Africans' turn to suffer defeat. Three times in a one-month period SADF/ UNITA forces attacked the Tumpo positions, and each time they were thrown back. The MPLA and Cubans claimed to have inflicted a major defeat on the South Africans in a determined effort by them to capture Cuito Cuanavale. The SADF, however, denied ever intending to take the town, arguing that it would have served no military purpose.

While the South Africans and UNITA succeeded in their primary objective of stopping the Fapla/Cuban advance towards Mavinga, they clearly failed in their subsequent objective of pushing their enemy back across the Cuito River in order to discourage them from any further designs on Mavinga.

All the fighting around Cuito Cuanavale was, however, less decisive than the Lomba River battle, which was the crucial setback to Luanda's ambition to crush UNITA and which may be said to have more materially influenced the events that led to the political settlement under which the South Africans withdrew from Namibia and the Cubans from Angola.

Declaring that its objective of safeguarding Mavinga had been achieved, the SADF began a gradual withdrawal of its forces, which, the SADF claimed, had never much exceeded three thousand troops anywhere in Angola at any time. About fifteen hundred troops are said to have been left east of Cuito Cuanavale to discourage any further Fapla designs on Jamba.

A number of commentators have averred that Castro, seeing no prospect of a military victory except at unacceptable cost, decided in 1988 that it was time for Cuba to get out of Angola. He needed, however, to devise a way to do so without seeming to have been beaten.[2] He is said to have designed a clever, bold but highly risky strategy that if successful would enable him to claim victory over Pretoria and withdraw from Angola with honour. If it failed, the Cubans might either get sucked deeper into the conflict, even into an invasion of Namibia, or find themselves pulling out of Angola without evidence of victory.

Castro may have reckoned that the South Africans were now genuinely ready to quit Namibia in return for a Cuban withdrawal from Angola (and in that he would not have been far wrong). Swapo were virtually certain to win an election in Namibia, fulfilling at least part of the purpose of Cuba's intervention in Angola. The other part, entrenching the MPLA in power in Angola, would probably follow, for UNITA surely could not survive without South African backing.

Castro's strategy appears to have been designed on two levels, one political and the other military. On the political level, he evidently decided to turn Crocker's linkage policy to his own advantage. Havana began making overtures to South African diplomats at the UN for negotiations for a political settlement in Angola, and implicitly accepted that it be linked to a settlement in Namibia. Meanwhile, Castro developed his military stratagem.

While trumpeting the defeat of the SADF attacks at Tumpo as a failure to capture Cuito Cuanavale and a victory for Cuba and its allies, he poured in more Cuban troops. A strong new front was opened close to the border, backed by powerful tank forces with air support from two upgraded airfields, and the whole covered by a radar-and-missile network.

Taken completely by surprise by these moves, the South Africans stationed a battle group on the border opposite the Cuban front and began preparations to call up 140 000 citizen force soldiers in case the Cuban moves presaged an attempt to invade Namibia. As the Cuban and South African armour began heavy fighting, MiG jets made a well-executed attack on the Calueque Dam, destroying earthworks necessary for any evacuation of the South African armour over the dam wall – and incidentally killing 12 SADF soldiers. Castro had executed a psychological and tactical masterstroke, leaving Pretoria facing a possible invasion of Namibia while some of its armour was cut off on the wrong side of the river.

There was no invasion, however. Instead, the Cubans pulled back and so did the South Africans, who by all accounts were only too happy to give Castro an opening for a withdrawal from Angola that would allow them to quit Namibia. With that action, South Africa's war in Angola was effectively over. Castro claimed his victory, and the action switched from the battlefield to the negotiating table, with a meeting in Cairo in June 1988.

Crocker's patient efforts began to pay off when, at a tripartite meeting in New York in July, agreement was reached on a set of basic principles, including most importantly independence for Namibia through free and fair elections and a Cuban troop withdrawal from Angola.

Ahead still lay more than six months of peripatetic and arduous negotiating to work out the details, with the talks shuttling between Cape Verde, Geneva, Brazzaville and New York. The SADF began a phased withdrawal from Angola, sparking fears in African capitals that with the South Africans out of the way Cuba intended to pursue expansionist ambitions beyond Angola and bring the SADF back. Eleven African governments appealed to Luanda to get rid of the Cubans.

407

At the last of five meetings in Brazzaville, agreement was reached on a timetable for a Cuban withdrawal. Finally, at the UN headquarters in New York agreements were signed for the Cuban withdrawal and the implementation of Resolution 435, giving independence to Namibia.

The signing ceremony on 22 December was a UN affair, but presided over not solely by the secretary-general, Javier Perez de Cuellar, but also by the secretary of state, George Shultz, in recognition that the settlement had been fashioned by Americans, even if in the name of the UN.

Crocker got nothing for his efforts but respect, which is probably all he wanted anyway – unless it was acknowledgement by the Western governments that the linkage concept some of them had pooh-poohed had worked in the end. But those who had closely followed his eight years of endeavour might have thought that the Nobel Peace Prize has been awarded for lesser achievements.

The New York accords provided for phased withdrawal of the Cubans from Angola and the SADF from Namibia, monitored by a Joint Commission representing Cuba, Angola and South Africa. A UN monitoring force acronymed Untag would supervise the election by Namibians, on 1 November 1989, of a constitutional assembly. Angola and Cuba undertook to 'use their good offices' to ensure that Swapo's forces stayed north of the 16th parallel.

On that last, shaky premise the whole peace process came close to collapse when Swapo launched what appears to have been a carefully planned attempt to seize power before the election and, like the MPLA's seizure of power in Angola, have it accepted by the OAU – and therefore the UN – as a fait accompli. Before Untag could be fully assembled in Namibia, the first of some two thousand heavily armed members of Swapo's army, Plan, began on 1 April 1989 to enter Namibia from Angola, and fighting erupted over a wide front.

South Africa formally suspended its cooperation in the peace process, demanding that the Security Council compel Swapo to cease the invasion. The fighting continued, however, for four weeks, before Swapo, reacting to strong international pressure (including some from Cuba and the MPLA), brought it to an end.

By military standards, what South Africa called the 'border war' was a low-intensity war fought at relatively low cost. Over the 23 years of the conflict, only 715 security force personnel died on the South African side. There were more deaths among the civilians of Namibia – 1 087 according to official South African figures. Deaths among the Plan and Fapla forces in action against the SADF/SWATF were estimated by Pretoria at something over eleven thousand. Thousands more are thought to have been killed in the fighting in the civil war with UNITA.[3] Cuban losses, never disclosed, are thought to number several thousands.

Military authorities have reckoned that the war did not significantly damage either the South African or the Namibian economies, despite its high cost. The R2-million spent daily by South Africa on the war was a relatively small part of the overall defence budget, and only in one year did it exceed five per cent of the Gross Domestic Product.[4] Running Namibia was more expensive.

For all that, the war had major political effects. It blocked Moscow's intervention in southern Africa long enough for it to be undercut by the decline of the Soviet system. And it pushed South Africa into quitting Namibia, and brought Pretoria closer to negotiating an end to apartheid.

CHAPTER 50

A DESPERATE POWER

The last stronghold of white supremacy in Africa was at its most powerful and yet also at its most vulnerable.

In repulsing the Soviet-backed offensives in Angola, South Africa had confirmed that it was the strongest military power in Africa. That it had achieved this with its own weaponry reflected its economic, technical and industrial strength. Within the country, resistance to white hegemony had largely been suppressed by an extraordinarily ruthless and effective security system.

For all this power, however, the apartheid state was in mortal decline. Its very foundations – job reservation, influx control and most of the other legalistic underpinnings – were crumbling. After 40 years in power, the government had failed utterly in its efforts to solve the racial problem, and it was desperately seeking some other way to preserve a separate white existence. Classic apartheid had been abandoned in almost all its former halls of power – the Broederbond, the church, academia, the press. A growing number of whites within and outside the ruling party were beginning to think the unthinkable – a negotiated settlement with the black majority.

Though their fears of the blacks were greater than ever, the whites were divided on how to deal with the issue. The National Party had won more than 52 per cent of the votes and increased the number of its seats in the 1987 general election, yet faced a growing challenge from the far right – the Conservative Party had won 30 per cent of the vote and replaced the Progressive Federal Party, a comparatively liberal offshoot of Smuts's old United Party, as the official opposition in Parliament.

The 1987 poll appeared to reflect the rise in white fear, as distinct from plain racial antipathy, since 1948. White antipathy to blacks could not be said to have increased much since then – and might even have declined – but white fear of the black majority certainly had risen as blacks had become more assertive and violent in demanding their rights. Taken as a measure of white opposition even to Botha's mild reforms – whether out of fear of their consequences or out of racism – the poll could hardly encourage the government to further concessions.

Organisations even more radical than the Conservative Party had emerged, notably the *Afrikaner-Weerstandsbeweging* (AWB), the militant, Nazi-like organisation whose emblem resembled the swastika and whose members paraded in khaki uniforms and with firearms.

Sensing the drift, Botha in his election campaign had given reform a relatively low priority, behind measures to ease white fears: first, maintaining law and order, and, second, boosting the economy.

The voting appeared to show that the ANC's increased use of violence and the international community's increasing resort to sanctions and boycotts, rather than forcing the whites to reform, were making them more fearful of it, persuading them to tighten rather than open the laager.

While economic sanctions had been offset by some countries – notably Japan and Taiwan – increasing their trade with South Africa, the sanctions overall were harming both current trade and future development. The disinvestment campaigns had resulted in the withdrawal of about half of the American companies operating in South Africa; and those remaining faced the prospect of double taxation under legislation passed by Congress in 1987.

Politically, PW Botha had run into a dead end with his stubborn belief that most blacks would go along with his ideas if they weren't intimidated by black militants (shades of Ian Smith). His idea of negotiation had been to persuade the ANC to stop its 'terrorism' and cooperate in finding a solution preserving segregation. What had not worked in Rhodesia would work in South Africa, it seems, because the whites were more numerous and economically stronger.

If the ANC would not cooperate it would be sidelined by allowing the blacks living in 'white' South Africa to vote for their own parliament, which would be represented with the other race-defined parliaments in a Council of State for decisions on matters of common interest – but with the whites reserving veto powers. In this way, everyone would be given 'democracy' without white interests – neither white privilege nor white cultural survival – being threatened.

The government sought to undermine the ANC's support with a crash programme to build houses and other facilities in the townships and to promote black businesses there. Special constables were quickly trained (and promptly nicknamed *kitskonstabels* – instant constables) to counter the political agitation. These plans failed, however, against the sheer weight of black opposition, especially the ANC's counter-move to make the townships ungovernable, a campaign strongly supported in the townships with boycotts of rent and service payments and of schools, of destruction of government property, and with the killing of those who attempted to cooperate with the authorities. It took a brave man to vote, let alone run for office, when it could mean death at the hands of the 'comrades' – and numbers of such 'traitors' were murdered, often by the dreaded necklace of fire.

An attempt to provide a platform at municipal level for consultation with blacks at a national level foundered on a voter turnout of less than six per cent in municipal elections in October 1988.

Botha's ruthless crackdown on dissidence and the arrest of some twenty thousand people under his 1986 state of emergency had somewhat quietened mass protest in the townships, but they remained essentially ungovernable.

Insurgent bombings increased, killing civilians of all races (49 in 1988). Especially audacious were the bombing of a military depot in Johannesburg in 1987, and a

411

car bomb blast as white crowds were leaving the Ellis Park rugby stadium, in which two whites were killed and many injured. A mineworkers' strike in August 1987, the biggest strike ever in South Africa, had demonstrated the growing strength of the black unions and their inevitable alignment with the struggle against apartheid.

The partial state of emergency that had first been imposed for five months in 1960 and again on a smaller scale for eight months in 1985, was renewed in June 1986 for the full year allowed by the law, and applied to the whole country except the bantustans. Thereafter it became a feature of life in the country for the next four years, being renewed every year until June 1990, when it was extended for five months in Natal only.

A tightening of the emergency regulations in June 1988 sparked foreign indignation that led in the United States to the House of Representatives passing legislation to end economic links with South Africa. The move was not supported in the senate but was a portent of what might come.

From the perspective of the security chiefs, the situation seemed under control. None of the hundreds of attacks carried out by MK had seriously inconvenienced the authorities. Cross-border insurgency was fairly easily contained, and most of the insurgents were quickly killed or captured. All in all, the securocrats could ostensibly claim success for their elaborate new system. Under the umbrella of the State Security Council (SSC), intelligence and security operations were coordinated through a National Joint Management Centre, which in turn received reports and gave instructions to regional Joint Management Committees (JMCs) on which were represented the military, the police and relevant government departments. The JMCs were in turn linked to sub-JMCs and then mini-JMCs embracing municipal authorities. South Africa was closer than it had ever been to being a police state.

The close involvement of the military in government gave rise to the Special Forces, which began as a number of bodies formed from army reconnaissance units (recces) in order to conduct supposedly surgical strikes at insurgents within South Africa and across the border.

From one of these developed an extraordinarily evil body, the Civilian Cooperation Bureau (CCB), a plainclothes organisation that became responsible for many of the worst crimes perpetrated against individuals in apartheid's name. Its title ironically exposed its purpose: to hide the involvement of the military in the assassination of opponents of apartheid.

From its headquarters in an office block in Pretoria, the CCB carried out assassinations by shooting, blowing up or poisoning the victims. Most of these were active opponents of apartheid, but so fearful was the organisation of having its heinous activities exposed that it also murdered CCB operatives suspected of losing their stomach for the work and therefore liable to blow the gaff.

Fear of exposure made the CCB take pains to ensure that the bodies of its victims could not come back to haunt them as evidence in open inquiry. So the corpses were dumped from aircraft far out at sea, or incinerated in bonfires. After one killing, while waiting for their victim's body to be reduced to ashes, the assassins barbecued beef for their supper on a smaller fire beside the bonfire. The odours of roasting from the two fires must for a while have been identical.

The technology of assassination was refined in a Special Forces laboratory-workshop under a programme code-named Project Coast. Technicians devised instruments such as poison-tipped screwdrivers and umbrellas, lethal cans of beer and soft drink, letter bombs, touch-toxins for applying to door handles, deodorants laced with lethal chemicals, letters and cigarettes containing deadly germs, and poisoned T-shirts.

It has been alleged but not confirmed that Project Coast attempted to produce an infertility vaccine that would affect only black people. The evident aim was to curb the black population explosion, which was fast widening the gap between white and black numbers.

By the mid-eighties, the Special Forces squads were operating beyond South Africa's borders as well as within. Often they employed former members of the Rhodesian recce units – who are suspected of involvement in the assassination in Harare in 1981 of Joe Gqabi, the ANC's chief representative there, and in the Inkomo barracks and Thornhill air base operations.

The military's involvement in domestic suppression took an especially ugly turn into the old hostility between the Xhosa and the Zulu, which had become channelled into competition between the Xhosa-dominated ANC and the predominant Zulu organisation, the Inkatha Freedom Party (IFP) led by Mangosuthu Buthelezi.

An ANC member during his university days, Buthelezi in 1970 had accepted appointment as head of the kwaZulu Territorial Authority, an instrument created by Pretoria to bring the Zulu territory into the bantustan system. He was playing a double game, however, aiming to use the bantustan system to preserve Zulu power but at the same time to undermine apartheid from within. He refused Transkei-style independence for kwaZulu until the ANC was unbanned and Mandela released.

The ANC at first tolerated Buthelezi's tactics but broke with him when he refused to endorse its resort to violence. The break led to increasing enmity and violence between Inkatha and the ANC, not only in kwaZulu but also on the Witwatersrand when Zulu migrant workers in the hostels refused to join the 'comrades' in the township revolts.

Contending that the ANC planned to kill him and disrupt his kwaZulu administration, Buthelezi in 1985 asked the government to form a protective unit. From this grew Operation Marion, the creation of a secretive force trained by the SADF in the Caprivi Strip. The force was later blamed for a string of atrocities, of which Buthelezi claimed to have no knowledge.

One of the most horrific was the massacre in KwaMakutha village early in 1987, when the sleeping occupants of a house were sprayed with automatic gunfire in the belief that a suspected MK operative was among them. He happened to be elsewhere that night, but 13 others in the house, mostly children, were killed.

In another bungled operation, a JMC-ordered attack on a house at Trust Feeds near Pietermaritzburg in December 1988, 11 innocent people, among them women and children, were killed. It turned out afterwards that the death squad had hit the wrong house.

From 1984, the government hit squads cut a foul path through South Africa and beyond with mass killings and single assassinations. Among plans to kill a number of the ANC's exiled leadership was a plot in 1986 to assassinate Pallo Jordan and Ronnie Kasrils, then in London, with poison-tipped umbrellas. There was also a CCB plot to assassinate the exiled head of the ANC, Oliver Tambo, during a visit to Harare.

These efforts failed, but there were numbers of successful assassinations, among them the killing of ANC activist Dr Fabian Ribeiro and his wife in Mamelodi township in 1986. Cassius Make of the ANC's National Executive was assassinated in Swaziland in 1988. When Dulcie September, the ANC's representative in Paris, was gunned down at her apartment there in 1988, her murder was commonly attributed to the hit squads. This assumption was questioned in some quarters, however, and remains a subject of controversy. Dr David Webster, a Witwatersrand University social anthropologist, was shot dead outside his home in Johannesburg in 1989, apparently in retaliation for his campaigning against military conscription and detention without trial.

Such killings made headlines but there were many that did not. Because of the secrecy with which the hit squads operated, no accurate count appears to exist of the number of their victims, but the evidence suggests a total of several hundreds.*

The special tragedy of the hit squad murders was that they probably did not and could not have changed anything, neither the resistance to white domination nor the waning of apartheid nor the move towards a negotiated political solution. With the world behind it, the ANC was not going to make radical concessions, certainly not the kind of segregated solution sought by the National Party. As was to be shown when the negotiations came to the critical issue of the exercise of power, and in the governance that followed the final agreement, the ANC had no intention of compromising its own ambition of effective power for the black majority.

The hit squads operated in Namibia in the run-up to the independence election, and conducted an especially pointless rifle and grenade attack on a UN election monitoring office in Outjo, which predictably had not the slightest effect on Swapo's march to power. Neither did the murder of Anton Lubowski, a white lawyer and Swapo member, although doubts were expressed that his killing was the work of the hit squads.

* * * *

The government, keeping a cautious ear on the rumbles on the right, was concerned to keep the moves towards negotiation secret in its own camp. It expressed public disapproval when a large group of dissident Afrikaners went to Dakar in

---

*"A Crime Against Humanity", published by the Human Rights Committee of South Africa in 1998 and edited by Max Coleman, identifies 370 victims of political assassination between 1974 and 1994. This figure does not include the book's list of 38 deaths in police custody between 1984 and 1989, or the 68 known or suspected abductions and disappearances up to 1991. Neither does it include the turned Swapo members dumped from aircraft into the Atlantic after becoming 'redundant', or the suspected Swapo supporters believed to have been summarily executed by the police unit, Koevoet, in Ovamboland.

Senegal in August 1987 to meet with ANC representatives, but did not try to stop them from going. In both its symbolism and its wider effects, that meeting was more telling than the business group's meeting with the ANC in Lusaka in 1985 or another meeting in Lusaka the same year with a delegation from the Progressive Federal Party.

Though still pursuing armed struggle, the ANC had toned it down since Soviet support for it had waned with Gorbachev's decision in 1986 to discourage regional conflicts. Bowing to the international preference for negotiation, the ANC, in a statement issued in October 1987, had mooted talking as an alternative – really as a parallel – to violence.[1] By this time Oliver Tambo and Thabo Mbeki were working on a new strategy: encouraging an anti-apartheid alliance between white businessmen, Afrikaner intellectuals and black homeland leaders.[2]

In 1988 the ANC modified its political stance – again in recognition of Gorbachev's reverse revolution – to the extent of abandoning the idea of state control of the economy and accepting the concepts of multi-party democracy and a mixed economy. These were truly metamorphic changes; without them there could never have been any accommodation between black and white in South Africa.

Mbeki had come to appreciate that the whites were unlikely to change their resistance to democracy unless their fears of it were removed. To the whites, however, his concept of democracy, the universal one, was synonymous with majority rule, in which many whites saw the demise not only of their privilege but also of their culture and identity. Most of them probably still believed the only kind of democracy workable in South Africa was apartheid's vertical version of separate democracies for separate races.

It seemed to these people that between the two alternatives there could be only one viable compromise: a federal system providing for largely self-governing provinces, some of which might be dominated by whites. This ideal was pursued by some whites when it came to negotiating a new dispensation with the ANC despite it being patently unrealistic, given the general economic dependence on black labour and the fact that nowhere did whites outnumber blacks – not even any longer in the cities.

Mbeki had no intention of shattering the illusion, however, and the ANC did not do so until the negotiations had reached a point where a federal system protecting whites had been revealed as impossible except in minor ways.

Meanwhile, the ANC could not overtly abandon armed struggle without upsetting both its own militants in exile and its oppressed members in South Africa. There was in fact a split of sorts between militants such as Mac Maharaj and Ronnie Kasrils, and pragmatists such as Mbeki, who felt it wiser not to keep the militants fully informed of the overtures for negotiation. Thus while Mbeki at the end of 1987 began a long series of secret talks with Professor Willie Esterhuyse in England, Maharaj was launching Operation Vula, in which top ANC members were to be infiltrated into South Africa with the intention of setting up an underground structure in preparation for a popular uprising should negotiation fail.

Esterhuyse's talks were at one point sponsored by the National Intelligence Service (NIS), which Mbeki accepted in the belief that he could use the link with Pretoria to help ease white fears.[3] Later other influential Afrikaners and ANC leaders joined the talks, most of which were held at Mells Parks House, a stately home near Bath that had been made available through the good offices of the British government – and the purse of the British mining house, Consolidated Goldfields. The talks there continued – kept a close secret by both sides – until Mandela's release from prison in February 1990.

Meanwhile, the NIS's head, Dr Niel Barnard, had begun his own secret talks with Mandela at Pollsmoor prison, with the knowledge only of President Botha.

At this stage neither the government nor the ANC was thinking of compromising its ideals. Botha was looking for a way to get Mandela out of jail before he died there and became a martyr, and Barnard wanted understanding of the ANC in order better to combat it. The ANC essentially wanted to persuade Pretoria to hand over power without further damage to the society and infrastructure. But in the process the yeast of compromise was set working.

★ ★ ★ ★

The political fermentation was accelerated after President Botha suffered a stroke in January 1989. It was a cruel thing for him but not necessarily for his country, for Botha, the patriot supreme, had become politically obsolete, an obstacle in the way of the kind of reform that was both necessary and inevitable in South Africa.

By inducing him to step down from the leadership of the National Party, Botha's misfortune opened the way for FW de Klerk to come forward and clear the way for democracy.

Botha's support was in fact already running out within his own party, as was shown by the demands that soon arose for him to resign the presidency as well as the party leadership. Increasingly volatile and irascible, and uncharacteristically uncertain, Botha seemingly had cracked under the strain of trying to adapt the apartheid monolith to the demands of the times, of attempting to make the granite fluid without sacrificing security.

And, in the end, he had to pay the price for having sidelined his own cabinet while empowering the security establishment. That and his abrasive treatment of his ministers and party leaders turned them against him when his stroke made him vulnerable to a palace coup. He rashly exposed himself to the Caesarian knives of his parliamentary caucus when he asked them to appoint a new party leader while he remained executive state president. Unexpectedly, the caucus appointed not one of Botha's choices but FW de Klerk, who believed Botha's leadership style had become a major obstacle to the negotiation that had become imperative. 'He was no longer fit to rule,' in De Klerk's opinion.[4]

Not that De Klerk, who was as conservatively hidebound as Botha, saw himself either as the messiah of democracy or as the heresiarch who would bring down the temple of apartheid. He had no intention of presiding over the surrender of all power to the black majority. He took over the leadership with a commitment to achieve power-sharing with protection of minority rights, which was not much more adventurous, if at all, than Botha's vision of a common citizenship overarching segregated societies.

White right-wingers in time accused De Klerk of indeed having pulled down the temple. All he did, though, was give the final shoves to a tottering structure already undermined by economic and workforce realities, cracked by revisionism, assaulted by angry blacks, and bombarded from without by foreign detractors. Botha, by accepting the concept of sharing power and nationhood with the blacks, had already eroded beyond repair the foundations laid at union in 1910 and then extended by Malan and Verwoerd.

After becoming party leader De Klerk gave a rough verbal sketch of his ideas: '... a totally changed South Africa which would rid itself of the antagonisms of the past and would be free from domination and suppression ... a South Africa in which all reasonable people would unite behind mutually acceptable goals and against radicalism.'

That was broad enough for anyone to read almost anything into it, except continued white supremacy. It was enough to satisfy most of the white electorate in the subsequent general election, though not all – the National Party won again, but with a reduced majority, winning fewer votes than in any election since 1953. Not all the whites were eager to trip into the flowered fields of democracy signposted by the international community.

Much later, after white rule had been ended, De Klerk insisted that his reforms had had a moral as well as a political motive. It is doubtful, however, that moral issues were uppermost in his mind or in the minds of the party caucus when he was chosen above the other party bigwigs who had been tipped for the leadership. He was seen to have the courage to face down the *Groot Krokodil* (Great Crocodile), as PW Botha was often called even by his own supporters, and then to lead the coup, and then hopefully to have the vision and political skill to take the party and the white community out of the dead end into which Botha had seemed to be charging; to devise instead a solution that would satisfy the blacks and the outside world, without jeopardising the whites' culture and (prosperous) way of life.

De Klerk evidently figured that if the whites didn't voluntarily surrender some power while they still had it all, they might end up with none. But in the end that is pretty much what happened – the ANC holds unchallengeable power in government, and the only effective power the whites still have is economic. De Klerk was then accused by some whites of having lost the plot, his own plot, and negotiated away any chance his race had of retaining enough political influence to protect its interests.

When De Klerk took the party leadership he promised a quantum leap, but he was not quite sure where that leap would be going. In his memoirs he speaks of developing a vision of 'a united South Africa where everybody would have equal rights and opportunities and within which our many minorities would not be threatened or suppressed'.[5] He also conceived of a 'universal franchise' but with 'a reasonable distribution of power between the various parties'.

Subsequent events were to prove how fallacious was the idea of sharing power when the ANC's struggle was as much for power as for rights; for the power as a means of securing the rights, perhaps, but essentially for political power. Rights, for instance, had nothing to do with the bloodiest part of the struggle, the contest between the UDF and Inkatha. That was all about power – political power certainly, if not also tribal power.

Botha resigned in August 1989 and De Klerk took over the presidency, only three weeks before the general election of 6 September. De Klerk fought the election on a platform of fundamental reform – ending racial discrimination and negotiating a new constitutional dispensation while maintaining law and order. His party won – yet again with a reduced majority, but enough for a clear mandate for continued reform. With that mandate, he began to dismantle Botha's security system and to restore full political control to the cabinet.

A more immediate test came with a move by church leaders and the UDF to stage a protest march to coincide with the opening of Parliament. Violence was threatened if the march were to be banned. De Klerk took a gamble and allowed the march, and it paid off in the form of a peaceful parade that boosted his reformist bona fides both at home and abroad.

His image was further boosted by his releasing of Walter Sisulu and some of the other Robben Island prisoners in October 1989. Mandela's release became axiomatic, and De Klerk prepared for it with his first meeting with the famous prisoner, demands for whose freedom had long echoed around the world. In December Mandela was smuggled at night from the Paarl prison, where he was now kept in the relative comfort of a warder's cottage, to the presidential office in Tuynhuys. Mandela did not attempt to exert his famous charm on De Klerk, and the two men thereafter never achieved much more than a stiff working relationship. At times it verged on outright hostility, especially on Mandela's part, and eventually collapsed. Not until February 1990, however, did De Klerk announce his historic decision to release Mandela without conditions, to unban the ANC and its associated South African Communist Party as well as the PAC, and to end the state of emergency.

It was breathtaking in its scope; few had expected De Klerk to go so far so soon. But, as he explains in his memoirs, he rejected a step-by-step approach because 'we would have little chance of success in the coming negotiations if we did not grasp the initiative right at the beginning and convince the important players that we were not negotiating under pressure, but from the strength of our convictions'. The step-by-step approach could come later in the actual negotiations.

The acclamation with which the announcement was received around the world became almost euphoric when Mandela walked out of the prison gates nine days later. He did not disappoint a world eager to adore. The vigorous young man who had gone to jail 27 years before came out stooped and grey but exuding dignity and warmth, humility and wisdom, tolerance and strength – a perfect icon.

This was the climax of the struggle that had obsessed the world more than any other since the Second World War, and the excitement of it was carried into the Namibian independence ceremonies seven weeks later. Namibia would soon become just another African country, but for the present it was part of the great story unfolding in the southern sub-continent. Mandela, sprung from prison gloom to celebrity radiance, would be there. Heads of state jetted into Windhoek in numbers far disproportionate to the importance of the state now being born.

They scrambled to find their seats in a chaotic ceremony in a packed stadium on the night of 20 March. De Klerk and Mandela were escorted with difficulty to theirs – and De Klerk got kissed by Yasser Arafat. Chester Crocker, now out of office but invited to the ceremony in recognition of his part in making it all happen, found his seat. But Pik Botha, Namibia's diplomatic warden for 16 onerous years, was gatecrashed out of his, and ended up sitting on the steps.

A sombre De Klerk conducted the formal hand-over to a beaming Sam Nujoma. As the South African flag was ceremoniously lowered for the last time in the country where it had flown supreme for more than seventy years, De Klerk, hand on heart, seemed close to tears. Most of those across from him in the bleachers were closer to jeers.

One by one the flags of white supremacy and colonialism had been lowered across Africa over the past three decades. For the whites born in Africa, the independence ceremonies in Algeria, Kenya and Zimbabwe had traumatically closed their hopes of unending supremacy. Now in Namibia the last of the colonial flags was coming down. All that was left of white supremacy's banners was the one still flying in South Africa; and De Klerk must have known that that one, too, must be hauled down before long. The only uncertainty was the timing and circumstances of its final furling.

Despite some dirty work by the SADF's secret agencies, and despite Pretoria's massive covert funding of the DTA, Swapo had convincingly won the election for a constituent assembly, though not with a majority large enough to dictate the terms of the constitution. Its failure to sweep the board had demonstrated the fallacy and the expediency of the UN's designation of the movement as the only authentic representative of the Namibian people. Namibia ended up with a multi-party constitutional system. Swapo shed the Marxist garments it had expediently donned while getting Soviet support during the Cold War. But Swapo's big majority, sustained in subsequent elections, brought Namibia uncomfortably close, from the whites' perspective, to being a black-ruled one-party state.

A few years previously, such an eventuality would have been anathema to the white minority that had ruled the roost for more than a century, as it had been to the government in Pretoria that had expended white lives and wealth to retain control of the territory. But now the Soviet threat was gone and the ANC's insurgent bases were being removed from Angola in terms of the New York settlement. Pretoria was happy to pull out, and most of the whites were prepared to stay put. Only a few fled to South Africa or Germany. For most of the many whites born in Namibia it was the only home they knew or wanted. They were Africans and content with it, for the present at least.

CHAPTER 51

NO PAIN, NO GAIN

South Africa's transition from apartheid to democracy was a roller-coaster ride that at times stalled in mid-loop and at other stages threatened to fly off the rails.

Before at last reaching multi-racial governance, the country went through black terrorism, white terrorism, coup plots and attempts at rebellion. There was outright mayhem in some black areas. The negotiations were imperilled by breakdowns, walkouts and brinkmanship. FW de Klerk went into his reforms with the ANC refusing to abandon armed struggle – still seeing it as its best weapon – even after the freeing of Mandela and the other jailed leaders. Whites raided an army base and stole weapons, raising again the old spectre of a white rebellion, with elements of the armed forces perhaps joining in.

A major advance was made in May 1990, when ANC and government leaders, meeting at Groote Schuur, Rhodes's old mansion in Cape Town, signed an agreement on the release of political prisoners and the return of exiles. Reform had now achieved an unstoppable momentum; it was now only a matter of deciding its direction – and whose decision that would be.

Before the year was out, the ANC had suspended (but not abandoned) the armed struggle, and De Klerk had ended the state of emergency, granted amnesty to political prisoners, opened his party to all races, and terminated hospital apartheid. That last act didn't mean much to whites who could afford private hospitals, but it was a dismaying prospect to some of those whites with limited means who objected to lying sick alongside a sick black person.

Many whites, however, were ready to accept racial integration, despite their fears and prejudices. Early in 1991 the parent bodies of state-subsidised white schools voted to admit black students whose parents could afford the fees. White privilege was not being abandoned, it was simply being extended to blacks who had some financial means – the vanguard of the black middle class in whom semi-liberal whites saw their salvation.

In this development was visible the pattern the whites hoped to see in the new South Africa – some blacks being lifted to the levels occupied by most whites, rather than all whites being pulled down to the levels occupied by most blacks. It was not something to please adherents of the black consciousness philosophy, but it was a move in a positive direction – classrooms and playgrounds that once were nurseries of racial prejudice were soon becoming the new breeding grounds of racial acceptance.

For a substantial number of President de Klerk's countrymen, however, his steps towards democracy were like the footfalls of doom.

Voting patterns after the National Party's rise to power in 1948 suggest increasing white support thereafter for the party's apartheid policies. At first the party majority could be attributed to gerrymandering, but as white rule came increasingly under attack more white voters, especially English-speaking ones, swung fearfully behind the perceived security of the strong and defiant party of apartheid.

By the nineties, however, whites had been obliged to measure their fears against the cost of sustaining them in the face of the censure of the outside world and of the blacks' fight for their rights. Perhaps only economists within government and in business were fully aware that the country was slowly bleeding to death as foreign investment dried up and capital already within the country was draining out despite the government's efforts to stem the flow. Besides the economic cost, the psychological cost of maintaining apartheid was beginning to tell. And, in the sports-mad white community, nothing hurt more than the sports boycotts.

Perceptions of white guilt grew alongside the discomfort. Though many whites may have resented or misunderstood the black struggle against apartheid, the determination and scale of the protests had brought home to many of them the enormity of apartheid's offences and the extent of black suffering. The 'cheeky kaffir' who had angrily been dismissed by past generations of whites was increasingly being seen as a person with rights, a victim with legitimate grievance; or, by some, at least as a person whose rights could no longer be trampled with impunity.

At the turn of the decade the majority of the whites were ready to see apartheid abandoned as long as it could be done without jeopardising their own rights – and, hopefully, their privileges. How that was to be done was a Chinese puzzle that the politicians must solve – but in a manner acceptable to the white voters. Even in the incongruous South African social pattern that slotted democracy for whites alongside autocracy for blacks, the white politicians were obliged to be as sensitive as those in any other democracy to the concerns of their constituents.

Paramount among these concerns were cultural, economic and physical security. The privileges of the white way of life were of less concern. Most whites in fact had taken them so much for granted, so much as a natural and rightful part of life, that they had seldom been clearly defined by those who enjoyed them. The blacks, though, had made their own definition of these privileges. They saw them as whites possessing most of the land – land seized from the blacks – and as having blacks work for them for low wages; as whites having sole access to mineral wealth, to bank loans, to technology and skills; having the freedom to travel, trade and live anywhere they liked in most of the country; having a superior education; having better medical care; having good pensions; in general, having a better quality of life – better houses, clothes, cars, shops, food, restaurants, hotels – and all seemingly with the profits made from cheap black labour.

It is unlikely that many blacks considered the extent to which the whites' prosperity was due to their own efforts and initiative rather than to black labour; whether, without the black labour, the whites in South Africa would have been any worse off than those in other countries of white settlement – the United States, Canada, Australia and New Zealand – where the settlers had not become reliant on an inexpensive indigenous work force.

Still, going into the nineties, it is probable that a large proportion of the whites in South Africa were prepared to sacrifice those privileges that could be identified for sacrifice in order to gain peace in their own country, international acceptance and a well-ordered democracy. There was a growing – though not general – acceptance that it simply was not possible for the whites to give up political power without giving up privilege as well.

Most whites remained fearful that in a straightforward one-person-one-vote democracy, the disparity in numbers would deny them political influence other than the indirect influence of economic power, and give them no say in the choosing of the government and in its style of governance. Whites would lose the power to control their own lives – like the whites in Kenya, Zimbabwe and Namibia.

So, like those whites, the South African ones sought to devise a system of qualified democracy that would meet the basic criteria of classic democracy but still give them some control over the running of their country and their lives. But, as it had been elsewhere, it was a hopeless ambition, given the ANC's insistence on majority rule and the fact that the outside world didn't much care what happened to the white South Africans once they had crawled out of the malodorous shell of apartheid.

The alternative of armed revolt against De Klerk that was pursued by white right-wing extremists may have been more realistic than attempts at a qualified democracy, but was equally improbable of success. The army's loyalty to De Klerk was uncertain, but probable, for most of the generals had accepted the dismantling of the National Security Management System that had been one of his first acts as president, together with the appointment of a judicial inquiry into the hit squads and the military's secret projects.

Right-wingers involved in the secret projects subversively continued some of their activities, covertly aiding the Inkatha factions fighting ANC supporters in Natal and in Witwatersrand townships. After this had been exposed by the independent press, De Klerk sidelined his two top security ministers, downgrading General Magnus Malan from Defence to Forestry and Adriaan Vlok from Law and Order to Correctional Services. That way he was not seen to be bowing to the ANC's earlier demand that the two be fired. At the same time, though, he was unintentionally facilitating the ANC's objective of weakening the government security forces in case the movement did not achieve its aims through negotiation and it became necessary to implement Operation Vula.

Early in 1991 the De Klerk government accepted Mandela's proposal of negotiations aimed at the appointment of a constitutional committee. But not until December would it be possible for the talking to start.

In the intervening period the death toll in political violence continued to rise, reaching a figure of some five thousand in the previous five years. Accusing the government of fomenting the violence or failing to prevent it, or both, the ANC suspended negotiations and began a campaign of mass action to press Pretoria to stop what it termed Inkatha's aggression.

Within Inkatha, however, there was a belief that the violence was instigated by the ANC in an effort to neutralise the Zulu movement, seeing it not as a partner in the fight against white rule but as an obstacle to Xhosa domination of majority rule.

While blood ran in the townships and in the rural areas of Natal and kwaZulu, reform advanced in white politics. The government repealed two legislative foundation stones of apartheid – the Land Acts of 1913 and 1936, and the Population Registration Act – together with a host of other racial regulations, leaving apartheid teetering only on the old white supremacist constitution.

The violence ostensibly ended with the signing in September of a National Peace Accord, but in fact continued sporadically. The talking began on 20 December 1991, when most of the political parties met at the World Trade Centre at Kempton Park near Johannesburg to launch the Convention for a Democratic South Africa (Codesa). For varying reasons, the IFP, PAC, the Conservative Party and some smaller groups stayed away.

The attendance meant that South Africa's new dispensation was to be negotiated more or less in the middle of the political spectrum – but with the SA Communist Party coming in on the ANC's coattails. The communist presence was anathema to whites steeped in Red Peril notions, but De Klerk had known from the time he unbanned the proscribed parties that he could not except the SACP since some of the senior ANC officials were also SACP members; and excluding the SACP would have left the ANC free to continue insurgency in the SACP's name.

★ ★ ★ ★

FW de Klerk took his people to the edge of white rule and asked them to jump. And they jumped.

In the referendum for whites that he held in March 1992, De Klerk asked for the voters' backing for continued reform through negotiations for a new constitution. The voters, not knowing exactly where he would take them, in effect were being asked to leap from the relative security of white supremacy, from entrenched privilege, from centuries of custom and practice, into a void where the only certainty was a black majority demanding the political dominance inevitable with majority rule.

De Klerk called the referendum when a reaffirmation of his reform mandate was made virtually obligatory by the shock defeat of his party in by-elections in two formerly safe seats. Given the by-election results, he was taking a big risk. He pledged to resign if he failed to get majority support. But in his campaign he made it clear he was seeking reform stopping short of majority rule. His party's slogan was, 'Vote yes if you're afraid of majority rule.'

Despite heavy campaigning by the right wing for a negative vote, De Klerk got an emphatic 'yes' – a majority of two-thirds in a turnout of 86 per cent of the national white electorate. Clearly the by-elections had not reflected the national mood.

The referendum vote again mirrored the division in white society that had been manifested in the 1989 poll. On the one side, a relatively small but increasingly active group of right-wingers passionately opposed to change. On the other side, the great bulk of the whites, gathered under the broad banner of change, most of them fearful, some fatalistic and some optimistic.

These people knew they had to seek security somewhere other than in the white supremacy on which their forefathers had prospered for centuries but which was now crumbling. They had begun to accept that reality when they had accepted Botha's reforms. But those had been defined changes, made unilaterally by a dominant regime. Now they were being asked to follow De Klerk into unknown places, into negotiation with a violent adversary. They put their trust in De Klerk to lead them to safe ground – hopefully somewhere where blacks might gain their rights without threatening those of the whites.

Had the voters known how it would turn out a few years down the line, with the ANC firmly in power and the whites being pushed ever further into the political corners, they might not have given De Klerk his mandate in 1992.

The consequences of a 'no' vote are widely open to conjecture – perhaps at best an effort to find another formula for compromise, at worst a descent into unprecedented violence and economic decline, a pit from which the whites would have been hard put to save anything they valued – the blacks too, for that matter.

The whites voted 'yes' mainly because they knew they had no realistic option, but probably also because most of them had come to reject apartheid for its injustices and its inhumanity – and its impracticability. They wanted to clear their consciences and to throw off the humiliating polecat image in the world. It was a brave and principled vote, all things considered, and a hugely pivotal action. It was overshadowed later by their acceptance of the constitution that brought democracy at last. But without that crucial vote in the 1992 referendum the democracy of 1994 might not have been achieved, certainly not as quickly and, if achieved at all, probably with infinitely more bloodshed and damage.

Having got his mandate, De Klerk was confident he could answer the voters' prayers. He envisaged a constitution providing for a government shaped by the proportion of the overall vote that was won by each party. The cabinet posts would be allocated accordingly, and all cabinet decisions would be by consensus. The presidency would rotate among the leaders of the various parties. Minorities (whites, coloureds and Asians) would get additional protection through having extra seats in an upper house of parliament that would have veto rights over legislation passed by the lower house. Certain legislation (that is, anything potentially harmful to white interests) would require larger majorities for passage than other measures.

De Klerk also wanted a federal-type structure giving the provinces strong powers outside those of the central government, a separation of powers between parliament and the executive, an independent judiciary, and a Bill of Rights protecting property rights among others.

Some of De Klerk's demands had already been conceded by the ANC at Codesa, but not those surrounding the crucial issue of the white veto and power-sharing, to both of which the ANC was adamantly opposed.

De Klerk figured he could get enough voter support among all races – whites, Asians, coloureds and 'moderate' blacks, including those in the bantustans – to have his ideas endorsed by an elected constituent assembly and written into the new constitution. So confident was he that he supported the idea of an interim constitution providing for the election of a constituent assembly and an interim government operating on a power-sharing basis for at least ten years.

What he envisaged, it seems, was ten years of negotiation, of amending, of compromising, allowing the antagonisms and conflicts of centuries to settle into a political dispensation acceptable to all races.

As events were to prove, it was an unrealistic concept, as pie-in-the-sky as had been the Smith government's plans for protecting white interests in Rhodesia. The ANC was simply not prepared to accept what it saw as white veto rights over majority rule – certainly not when there was strong opposition within the ANC and its supporters to the very idea of negotiation with the whites, and, rather, continued support for the violent seizure of power. Mandela had indicated that the ANC was willing to take measures to allay white fears, but he rejected De Klerk's ideas as a 'loser take all' concept.

At the time, though, De Klerk thought his chances were good with the electorate in general. Perceptions and imperatives had changed in recent years. The collapse of the Soviet Union had deprived insurgency of much material and moral support. The unbanning of the ANC, the release of Mandela, and the start of negotiation for a new dispensation had deprived armed struggle of legitimacy and international tolerance. De Klerk himself had become something of a hero in an outside world where formerly his government had been a pariah.

Within weeks of the referendum, the Codesa talks ran into deadlock, unable to find a constitutional compromise between the ANC's desire for total power through one-person-one-vote democracy and the government's demand for longrunning white veto rights to curtail that power.

De Klerk has asserted that the centre of gravity in the ANC-SACP-Cosatu alliance now shifted to the radical elements, bent on toppling the government through the 'Leipzig option', imitating the strikes, civil disobedience and occupation of government buildings that had contributed to the fall of the East German government.[1]

Certainly the search for democracy had by now run into the rising storm of black politics. Despite its 19 participating parties, Codesa was not fully representative. Besides the Afrikaner right wing, the conference was being boycotted by the Inkatha Freedom Party because, while the IFP had been granted representation as a political party, the Zulu monarchy, representing the Zulu nation, had not. Buthelezi's aim throughout the transition to democracy seemingly was to preserve as much power and autonomy as possible for the Zulus, the largest ethnic group. Possibly he suspected a plot to secure Xhosa dominance through the ANC or, like the Afrikaners, he was determined to preserve his peoples' ethnic identity and influence. At one point in the negotiations Inkatha attempted to assert a right to have kwaZulu secede as an independent kingdom.

The friction between Inkatha and the ANC was covertly fanned by white right-wingers in the security forces, and this activity appears to have been stepped up in response to a decision by the ANC to conduct a campaign of 'rolling mass action' to force immediate acceptance of an interim government and elections for a constituent assembly dominated by blacks.

When Zulu migrant workers massacred more than forty supposed ANC supporters at the Boipatong squatter camp near Johannesburg in June 1992, the ANC accused the police of aiding or at least not intervening in the four-hour slaughter, and walked out of Codesa in protest. The subsequent mass action campaign culminated in a two-day general strike and a march on the Union Buildings by 60 000 people in August.

The campaign was then turned to the 'independent homelands', which in their present form gave the Pretoria government a chance of garnering black votes in an election for a constituent assembly. First targeted was the Ciskei where the ANC had been blocked from political activity by the military junta headed by Brigadier Oupa Gqozo. In September, leaders of the ANC and its partners took some seventy thousand followers on a march on the Ciskei capital, Bisho, evidently with the intention of exercising a 'Leipzig option'. Defying a magisterial order not to go further than the stadium on the outskirts, and ignoring the Ciskei soldiers barring the way, a group tried to run through the stadium to reach the town. The troops opened fire, killing 28 and wounding some two hundred of the marchers.

The Bisho shooting evidently cooled political tempers and persuaded the ANC extremists to call off a planned march on the kwaZulu capital of Ulundi, which would probably have led to a much bloodier clash.

After Bisho the emphasis in the negotiations shifted from Codesa's multi-lateral style to direct exchanges between the government and the ANC as the main players. Behind the parties' hostile public posturing, talks were continued covertly between the two men who would play the leading roles in the shaping of the final settlement: Cyril Ramaphosa, the lawyer-trade unionist who had become the secretary-general of the ANC, and Roelf Meyer, also a lawyer, a minister in De Klerk's cabinet and a formerly conservative Afrikaner who was beginning to feel there might be no way round majority rule.

The informal Ramaphosa-Meyer exchanges were known as 'the back channel', and indeed they did channel the negotiations into a settlement, but it was not the settlement most whites had envisaged when they gave De Klerk his mandate in the referendum.

CHAPTER 52

SUNSET ON SUPREMACY

South Africa's last steps to democratic glory were not so much a proud march as a perilous, agonised, bloodied stagger – for blacks as well as whites. But while the blacks could look ahead to the virtual certainty of majority rule, the whites could only cling to tremulous hope. Or, as a few did, resort vainly to pointless violence.

The violence by whites may in part have been in reaction to the cries of hatred and vengeance that rang out from the ranks of black militancy, chants of 'One settler, one bullet!' and 'Kill the farmer, kill the Boer!' at black gatherings – and which were replayed through the news media.

For all the guilt they might be feeling about their past treatment of the black people, whites in general most likely resented such threats and demonstrations of animosity just when they figured they were trying to put things right. Whether the chants deterred them from risking their future in the peace process, or whether they had the opposite effect of scaring them into seeking security in a negotiated solution, is impossible to know.

It was clear that the slogans did not represent black views in general. But what perhaps made them more alarming was that they were widely shouted at a time of the worst violence the whites had experienced since the Frontier Wars of the previous century. More whites were killed and wounded in political attacks in the last 16 months of the peace process than in any other period in the experience of those then living. The numbers – some fifteen killed and more than ninety wounded – were tiny compared with the thousands of blacks killed by apartheid's security forces and in political violence between blacks. But the psychological impact on the white population was severe. Against such a demonstration of racial hostility the whites had to hold fast to their courage as their leaders negotiated a new dispensation bereft of the security that had been provided by dominance.

Almost all the attacks were carried out by members of the PAC's armed wing, the Azanian People's Liberation Army (Apla). It is arguable whether this naked terrorism had any more rational purpose than the random attacks made by white rightwingers on black people in the run-up to democracy and in its aftermath. The purpose of the Apla killers was never defined, other than vague notions of frightening whites into vacating all the land taken from the blacks. The white extremists who randomly shot blacks in the streets had an even less specific purpose, unless it was to induce blacks to abandon their demands for black power. In neither case, of course, did these actions help to make for a better future for the country.

Taking advantage of its unbanning, the PAC had laid plans for what it grandiosely called Operation Great Storm, an anti-white campaign directed primarily but not solely against farmers The slaughter began in 1992 with a hit on a Christmas party for elderly people at the King William's Town golf club, in which four were killed and 17 wounded. As in the subsequent attacks, the weapons used were AK47s and hand grenades, evidently supplied by the Transkei defence force. A number of white farms in the Eastern Cape were attacked, as well as a restaurant in Queenstown.

In March the next year Apla attacked the Yellowwoods Hotel near Fort Beaufort, killing a white student and wounding others. In April two German tourists were ambushed near Mount Ayliff and wounded. In May five whites were killed and seven wounded in an attack on the Highgate Hotel in East London. In July the AKs and grenades were turned on worshippers at a service in St James' Church in Kenilworth, Cape Town, where 11 were killed and 56 wounded.

Attacks on whites travelling through the Transkei reached a level that prompted the government to set up roadblocks on the border and warn whites against driving through the territory.

In August members of the PAC-aligned Pan Africanist Students Organisation (Paso) clubbed to death an American exchange student, Amy Biehl, in Guguletu township near Cape Town after she had driven black friends to their homes there. At Beaufort West, eight passengers on a long-distance bus were wounded when Apla members fired on it.

In September, Apla cadres raided the Riverside Lodge hotel at Ladybrand in the Free State, told black staff they were looking for whites and, finding none, shot up and petrol-bombed the buildings.

In December, the Apla terrorists hit the Heidelberg Tavern in the Cape Town suburb of Observatory, machine-gunning the patrons in a bar, not all of whom were white. Four were killed and four wounded.

The Apla attacks sparked a retaliatory raid by the SADF on a house in Umtata suspected to be a base for some of the attacks. However, the sleeping forms the attackers riddled with bullets turned out to be those of five young students aged between twelve and seventeen. The SADF made a clumsy but subsequently discredited attempt to pretend that the students had reached for weapons.

Repeated allegations that elements in the security forces were still involved in dirty tricks had proved difficult to substantiate. Then in November 1992, Judge Richard Goldstone, who had been assigned by De Klerk to investigate allegations of covert political violence by security force elements, discovered that a secret branch of military intelligence, the Directorate of Covert Collection, had been living up to its name by engaging in covert activities against the ANC. Goldstone's find supported allegations that a mysterious 'third force' had been secretly fomenting violence.

De Klerk reacted by appointing Lieutenant-General Pierre Steyn, the SADF chief of staff, to investigate the military's intelligence-gathering activities. Steyn came up with circumstantial evidence that SADF units had indeed been involved in arming elements within Inkatha, fomenting violence and discrediting the ANC.

He produced a list of suspect personnel, including senior officers.

De Klerk was caught between the need to root out 'third force' activities and the need to maintain the morale and effectiveness of the SADF, which he saw as both the government's 'ultimate power base and the ultimate guarantor of the constitutional process'. In what has been described as 'the night of the generals', he sacked 23 senior officers, among them two generals and four brigadiers. Some of those dismissed later successfully sued the government in court.

After the collapse of Codesa, De Klerk had set about getting the ANC back into substantive negotiations. These led to the signing in September 1992 of a Record of Understanding in which the government agreed to three ANC demands: the release of political prisoners (including some serving time for terrorist killings), the fencing of the Witwatersrand hostels occupied by Zulu migrant workers, and a ban on Inkatha members carrying traditional weapons in public.*

De Klerk saw the agreement as a climb-down by the ANC from its original 14 demands. Outside observers saw it as a climb-down by De Klerk. Even he recognised that the last two demands were aimed at driving a wedge between himself and Inkatha. Granting the last two demands would inevitably antagonise Inkatha, even though the last one was unenforceable.

Buthelezi was indeed angered. He pulled out of the negotiations and led several thousand Zulus on a protest march through downtown Johannesburg – all defiantly brandishing traditional weapons. Buthelezi went on to join Inkatha with right-wing Afrikaner groups – the Conservative Party, the Afrikaner Freedom Foundation and the Afrikaner Volksunie – in a new Concerned South Africans Group (Cosag).

The Record of Understanding had manifested the ANC's growing strength in the negotiations, but had not materially advanced them. The key to unlocking the impasse came through the unlikely agency of Joe Slovo, secretary-general of the SACP and commander of MK. Slovo's impeccable 'struggle' and ideological credentials enabled him to float the idea of inserting in the negotiated package 'sunset clauses' providing for job and pension guarantees for white civil servants and security force members, amnesty for apartheid crimes, and a transitional government of national unity. In subsequent negotiations the transitional government's term was fixed at five years – only half of the term De Klerk had envisaged for transition to majority rule.

The sunset clauses probably fell short of the expectations of the whites who had supported De Klerk in the referendum and the elections. In accepting them, De Klerk had accepted majority rule thereafter. All that was left to negotiate were the safeguards for the whites, and in that the whites were now dealing from a weaker position than ever.

Acceptance of majority rule was, however, an idea that had been growing on the government side for some time, most importantly in the mind of Roelf Meyer,

---

*The freeing of political prisoners could not be confined to blacks, and among the whites freed was a notorious murderer, Barend Strydom, who had shot to death a number of black people in a public square in Pretoria for no reason other than to protest against the undermining of racial segregation. Evidently recognising no guilt in his act, this twisted and callous killer went on to become a leading right-wing activist through an organisation called the Wit Wolwe (White Wolves).

cunningly fertilised by Ramaphosa. De Klerk, clothed in the new respectability bestowed by Mandela's release, had been welcomed in European capitals, but it had
been impressed on him that his idea of a white veto over black power was not acceptable there. The Europeans would not go beyond protection of minorities under
majority rule, though the protective measures were never spelled out – if they had
even been defined in European minds.

After Codesa's collapse the negotiations became known formally as the Multi-
party Negotiating Forum, more commonly referred to simply as the World Trade
Centre talks. But now they were approaching final agreement – a conclusion that
was almost wrecked by yet another act of extremist idiocy.

★ ★ ★ ★

The news that Chris Hani had been assassinated by a white man swept like fire
through the townships. Suddenly, South Africa was on the edge of unprecedented
violence, perhaps even a race war.

Hani was more than just a hero of the liberation struggle, he was a man for the
future. He was a populist, but a principled one and widely admired. Young, handsome, engaging, charismatic, tough and bright, Hani was clearly destined for leadership at a high level come democracy. Some saw him in time succeeding Mandela
as president.

More important immediately to the politicians on both sides was that, despite
having been MK chief of staff, he had become a voice of moderation with a special
appeal to the young. He had been seen as the man who better than any other could
restrain youths impatient with negotiation and itching for the violent overthrow of
white rule now that it had lowered its guard. He had recently been urging the PAC
to halt its attacks on whites.

Perhaps it was his very popularity as well as his background in MK and the Communist Party (of which he was general secretary) that made him a target of the
white right. The motive for the murder was never explained, but among the conjecture was the suggestion that it was intended to provoke a black uprising that would
compel the government to use the military to quell it and, hopefully, in the process
crush the ANC and put white right-wingers in command of government.

It was indeed a white right-winger, a Polish immigrant named Janusz Walus, who
on 10 April 1993 shot Hani in the head outside his home in Johannesburg and sent
shock through the entire country. Few could have been oblivious to the implications. For the peace process to survive, it was imperative that a strong leader try to
calm black anger. De Klerk was head of state but he was hardly the one to do what
was now necessary. He wisely stood back and asked Mandela to go on television.

In one of his more memorable speeches, Mandela appealed to blacks and whites
to stand together in the cause of their common freedom.

The ANC could not leave it at that, of course – it had an angry constituency
to answer to – but it went rather further than the government liked. Ignoring the
probability that the assassination was the work of a few extremists rather than agen-

cies of the government, the ANC exploited Hani's death to increase pressure on the government to make concessions in the negotiations. The ANC pulled out of the talks and declared a six-week campaign of mass action. There was a highly emotional funeral and some demonstrations and rioting. But in the end reason prevailed over emotion and expediency, for most blacks no doubt perceived that they might be about to win through negotiation what they had failed to win through armed struggle, and there was no profit in a return to violence.

Walus and his co-conspirator, Clive Derby-Lewis, an English-speaking member of the Conservative Party, were in time convicted of Hani's murder and sentenced to death, but saved by the ANC's abolition of the death penalty when it took over governance.

Meanwhile, Hani's death seemed to galvanise the negotiations at Kempton Park. What was perhaps the crucial concession came with agreement on the date of the first democratic election. In July (when De Klerk and Mandela were in the United States separately meeting President Clinton and jointly receiving the Philadelphia Peace Medal) the election date was fixed at 27 April 1994.

That left less than a year in which to finalise the new constitution and prepare for the election. The election could not now be postponed without risking violent black protest, which the ANC was willing and able to arouse if need be. The government negotiators were aware also that a postponement might invalidate Slovo's sunset clauses.

In agreeing to an election date without first getting final agreement on what it considered the crucial elements of the constitution – those protecting white interests – the government had painted itself into a corner. Agreement had not been reached on language and property rights and, most important, on whether and to what extent the country would have the federal system that the NP and the right-wing parties considered essential for protecting white interests against a central government that almost certainly would be dominated by the ANC.

Five of the parties to the negotiations – the IFP, the Conservative Party and the governments of kwaZulu, Ciskei and Bophuthatswana – were not prepared to share the government's corner, and walked out of the talks.

The AWB had already shown its displeasure with the negotiations by crashing an armoured vehicle through the plate-glass doors of the World Trade Centre in June and assaulting black delegates within. The attack achieved nothing other than to demonstrate the AWB's inability to conceive of anything but witless violence as a means of solving racial problems.

Afrikanerdom was now more widely split than ever before. The AWB was the lunatic fringe. Outside of the National Party, most Afrikaners were represented by the Conservative Party. General Constand Viljoen, the former chief of the SADF, and other retired generals had in May brought some twenty conservative Afrikaner organisations into a new alliance, the Afrikaner Volksfront (Afrikaner People's Front), which sought to establish an Afrikaner homeland, a *volkstaat,* within South Africa. To this end it opposed the dissolution of the bantustans, seeing them as black precedents for what the AV wanted for the whites.

431

All the other parties opposed to the incorporation of the bantustans into South Africa – Inkatha, the Conservative Party and the governments of kwaZulu, Bophuthatswana and Ciskei – joined Viljoen's Afrikaner Volksfront in October to form a Freedom Alliance seeking the right to self-determination for the various ethnic groups.

By September the negotiators had agreed on the formation of a Transitional Executive Council (TEC), in effect a multi-party interim government, but with limited powers, which would help run the country in the run-up to the April 1994 election. It would also be responsible for creating a level playing field for the election.

Formation of the TEC was opposed altogether by the Conservative Party, Bophuthatswana, the Ciskei and Inkatha. It was carried, however, on the principle of 'sufficient consensus', a bulldozing mechanism contrived by the ANC and NP to avoid the negotiations being hung up by objections from the minor parties. The TEC was formally authorised by Parliament on 23 September.

It was agreed that the April poll would elect a Government of National Unity (GNU), which would hold office for five years, reaching parliamentary decisions on a basis of consensus. The GNU would be bound by an interim constitution, which would hold effect until a new one was written by the parliament elected in April.

The interim constitution was duly completed by the negotiators by the middle of November and enacted by Parliament in December. De Klerk believed the all-important federal issue had been fixed at a point giving the provinces powers and autonomy more consistent with a federal system than a unitary one. 'We would have liked,' he says in his memoirs, 'to have seen something closer to the power-sharing in the Swiss and Belgian models; we would have liked more clearly defined rights for the regions and minorities.' But the interim constitution offered 'a reasonable assurance of continuing security' for the whites.[1]

While some whites felt betrayed by De Klerk and his team, the outside world welcomed the settlement. It hailed the reforming of the apartheid sinner, and gave absolution for the sinner's confession of wrongdoing – though no apology had yet been forthcoming. Only much later would individuals in the apartheid government say they were sorry for it. But apology was something that was wanted only by the victims of apartheid, not in the wider world. There, the polecat was deemed de-odorised and was restored to respectability. The UN lifted all sanctions except the oil and arms embargoes. De Klerk was awarded the Nobel Peace Prize jointly with Mandela, and on the way to Oslo for the ceremony stopped in London for meetings with Queen Elizabeth and Prime Minister John Major.

CHAPTER 53

SEARCHING FOR THE PHANTOM STATE

The ancient fear strongly threaded through the Afrikaners' history and culture, the fear of being overrun by the black masses, had suddenly became immediate and menacing as the 20th century drew to its close.

The *verligtes* had followed De Klerk's dim light into the uncertain gloom of negotiation. The more moderate of the right-wingers had joined Constand Viljoen in the search for the ultimate laager, a white homeland. A few extremists did as their ancestors had done when faced with an imminent black threat: they reached for their guns – and, more often now, for the bomb, the ultimate weapon of the terrorist.

Not that the white extremists necessarily saw themselves as terrorists any more than did the MK and Apla cadres. Perhaps they, too, saw themselves as freedom fighters, fighting for a just cause. All Afrikaners, especially the conservatives and particularly those on the far right, had been incensed by the killing of whites. When on top of that a government of their own kind was perceived to be bowing to black militancy and international pressure and shamefully bargaining away the white heritage and white security, jeopardising the *volkstaat* ambition, it was too much for some Afrikaners.

The bombings began as early as 1991, when right-wingers blew up the Hillview High School in Pretoria (because they had heard it was going to admit blacks), Cosatu's Pretoria office (targeted for its perceived communistic affiliation), and the post offices at Verwoerdburg and Krugersdorp (state premises selected in order to convey to the government the right-wingers' displeasure at its doing deals with the ANC).

The Freedom Alliance's efforts to have the bantustans retained as precedents for a *volkstaat* suffered a serious blow when the Kempton Park negotiators in December 1993 approved the draft bill for reabsorbing the homelands into South Africa. The bantustans were being destroyed as expediently as they had been created. But the setback to the *volkstaat* ambition spurred a new spate of bombings, ten of them severing railway lines and disrupting normal traffic.

In a less valorous deed, a group of AWB members in 1993 ambushed a car near Randfontein and shot the black occupants, killing four and leaving three for dead.

The AWB found its own blood being shed for the first time in a debacle at Mmabatho, capital of Bophuthatswana, in March 1994. President Lucas Mangope's refus-

433

al to have his bantustan reincorporated in South Africa, and to let his people vote in the election there, had caused his state to begin falling apart. Civil servants went on strike, and when disaffected policemen mutinied, looting began. General Viljoen, Mangope's partner in the Freedom Alliance, offered the services of the Afrikaner Volksfront's armed wing to help maintain order. The AWB was specifically ordered to stay out of the affair; Viljoen and Mangope did not want their plans disrupted by those murderous clowns.

Eugene Terr'Blanche, the buffoonish leader of the AWB, promised to obey the instruction, then promptly disobeyed it, sending some one thousand armed members to Mmabatho, riding in a motley array of civilian vehicles and armed with hunting rifles, shotguns and pistols. Their ostensible purpose was to join Viljoen's force and help save the homeland. For some it evidently was simply an opportunity to vent their basic animosity towards black people by shooting at the first ones they came across. After two local women had been shot dead, the AWB force was ordered out of the territory by the (white) commander of the Bophuthatswana Defence Force (BDF).

They truculently did so, but as they drove out in convoy they fired indiscriminately at black people in the streets, including women and children, and exchanged fire with BDF soldiers. At least eleven black civilians were killed by the AWB, and some two hundred wounded.

One car dropped out of the departing AWB convoy, its driver wounded by BDF fire, and its three occupants ended up grovelling before BDF soldiers and South African journalists. Then a Bophuthatswanan policeman, infuriated by the AWB's wanton killing of his civilian compatriots, ran up and shot all three of the AWB members dead as they lay in the dust. That little tableau, watched by South Africans on television, typified the extreme white right's stand against black rule – confused, violent, often cowardly and, in the end, pathetic.

At the request of the BDF commander, the SADF deployed troops to restore order and escort Viljoen's force of about three hundred and fifty – which had remained disciplined and passive – out of the town. The next day the South African foreign minister, Pik Botha, two members of the Transitional Executive Council and a contingent of SADF troops flew in helicopters to Mangope's country retreat and informed the tearful president that he was being deposed.

The bellicose AWB intrusion into the affair might have been a blessing in disguise for the Pretoria government, for without it Viljoen's forces might well have helped re-establish order in Bophuthatswana and kept Mangope in power. Pretoria would then have had to decide whether the peace process could continue without Bophuthatswana or whether it should send in troops to depose Mangope by force – troops that might have refused to fire on Viljoen's men, their former comrades-in-arms.

Soon after Mangope's collapse, the Transkei and Ciskei meekly followed Bophuthatswana into political liquidation, leaving Venda so exposed it followed suit. The black models for a white *volkstaat* had ceased to exist.

The loss of its bantustan members was a setback for the Freedom Alliance, and made it vulnerable to efforts by De Klerk to woo it back into the Kempton Park negotiations and the April election. He and Mandela knew that an election without the remaining Freedom Alliance parties would be compromised. De Klerk had accordingly persuaded Mandela to agree to amendments to the interim constitution, recognising the principle of self-determination (which some might see as opening the way for negotiations on the establishment of a *volkstaat*). The provinces would get greater powers more in line with a federal system, including the right to frame their own constitutions.

The bait was enough to hook Constand Viljoen and get him back to Kempton Park. He broke with the Alliance and the Afrikaanse Volksfront and formed a new party, the Freedom Front, with which to contest the election, thereby perhaps helping to avert a civil war in South Africa.

In the run-up to the election, AWB members set off three powerful car bombs. The first, detonated outside a hotel in Bree Street in downtown Johannesburg, killed nine people, injured more than ninety and caused severe damage. The next day a bomb outside a supermarket in Germiston killed ten people, injured others and wrecked the building. During the election, the entrance to the international departures section of Johannesburg's main airport was wrecked and 21 people injured by a third bomb.

All three bombs had been made at a farm near Ventersdorp in the Western Transvaal, which province the AWB had decided to make a *volkstaat*.[1] AWB members had been summoned from across the country to come and help create and defend the Afrikaner homeland, bringing their families and abandoning their jobs and their homes on the assurance they would find new ones in the new state. The expectation was that once the *volkstaat* was declared, a large proportion of the SADF would come over in support, providing the armour and heavy weapons necessary to defend it.

Hundreds of AWB members did come, some from as far as Natal and the Free State, but mostly from the Transvaal. The families spread themselves in camp sites over a number of farms while the menfolk prepared for war – with their pistols and sporting guns and their pickup trucks. One estimate was that there were as many as four hundred families. Many AWB members, recognising the foolhardiness of the venture, refused the summons.

It was indeed a silly and pathetic exercise. After the bombings, police raided the main assembly point, made numbers of arrests, and seized firearms and ammunition. There was no resistance. The rebellion was over before it had really begun. The families folded their tents and went home – those that still had homes, that is. Some of those who had sold their houses and given up their jobs ended up destitute.

★ ★ ★ ★

Though the AWB's *volkstaat* ambitions had collapsed in the shambles at Ventersdorp, Viljoen and others still earnestly pursued the impossible dream.

It had seldom been a viable ambition throughout the centuries of Afrikanerdom's creation. It would have been realised had the British not occupied the Cape and become the monkey on the back of the dream, clinging perniciously wherever the Afrikaners went. Even then it might have become viable had the Afrikaners appreciated the importance for themselves of distinguishing between white separateness and white supremacy.

But far back in the past the dream and its followers had become so enmeshed in the existence and the rights of the black majority – in the similar black dream – that the two had become almost inseparable. When white supremacy became unsustainable, so too did white separateness, for the one had never been distinguished from the other.

With De Klerk maintaining his party's rejection of the *volkstaat* notion, Viljoen tried to enlist the support of the other major broker, Nelson Mandela. The irony was enormous – here were conservative Afrikaners, the former standard-bearers of apartheid, supplicating its former victims for a small place in the sun.

ANC leaders politely discussed the *volkstaat* idea with Viljoen, and early in 1994 agreed to form a Volkstaat Council to keep the matter open. But it is doubtful that they ever seriously contemplated agreeing to a *volkstaat*, for, while they professed sympathy for the Afrikaners' situation and ambitions, they probably could not see how a viable white homeland could be fitted into a greater South Africa, neither politically, demographically nor geographically.

In any case, the ANC could not give the *volkstaat* concept any political credibility without lending a similar credibility to Buthelezi's ambition for a federal system giving kwaZulu a large degree of autonomy – and perhaps even allowing for secession as an independent state. (An explicit request for independence was in fact made to De Klerk early in 1994 by King Goodwill Zwelithini and Buthelezi – and was refused.)[2]

Any substantial devolution of power through a federal system, especially devolution of power to kwaZulu, would have impaired the ANC's ideal of a unitary state in which it would have power unchallengeable by the provinces except on minor issues. Some in Inkatha evidently believed that a Xhosa-dominated ANC secretly aimed to extend Xhosa influence across the whole country, and few Zulus were prepared to submit meekly to Xhosa domination. The ANC appeared to believe, however, that only a strong central government could maintain a viable state and preserve democracy in the ethnic jumble that was South Africa.

The federal concept had more relevance for Inkatha than for the whites, for only in kwaZulu did the demographics offer any chance of ethno-territorial independence – though even the Zulus were divided on the issue, as was shown by the bloody clashes between Zulus supporting Inkatha and Zulus supporting the ANC.

Only in the Western Province, the only province where blacks were not in the majority, could the racial proportions have offered the whites any hope of self-rule, and then only in partnership with the coloureds. It was too late for that in the nineties, however, despite the white Afrikaner's belated recognition of the coloureds as *bruin Afrikaners*.

The National Party had evidently figured by 1993 that the demographics ruled out any possibility of the whites gaining a measure of self-determination through a confederation. The party looked instead to an acceptable devolution of power through constitutional devices, especially a devolution of power to provinces that would give whites a better chance of protecting their interests than they would have with the ANC exercising all powers in a unitary state. The terms of that devolution, however, were so vaguely defined at Kempton Park that the National Party negotiators left themselves open to accusations by fellow Afrikaners of having been outwitted by the ANC.

Some whites evidently felt in the end that De Klerk's team had failed to exploit a potentially strong alliance with Inkatha against the wily and hard-nosed ANC negotiators. After all, both the IFP and the government favoured devolution of power.

It was also felt that De Klerk failed to make full use of the power of the military as a bargaining chip. Certainly the ANC was very much aware of the SADF's strength, and was seriously worried that it might stage a coup in collaboration with right-wing civilians, especially those in the commandos – trained reservists who kept their army rifles at home and could be called up at short notice.

Theoretically, coup leaders might have drawn on a large pool of trained white soldiers under arms, considerably more than the few thousand MK cadres in the country. And they would have had at their disposal Africa's most powerful armaments. But a white coup would have angered most blacks and very likely have aroused black resistance on an unprecedented scale, mass insurgency beyond the power of tanks and planes to put down. The country would have been thrown into civil and economic chaos. The international community would have reacted with outrage and sanctions, if not even with military intervention.

There was a suggestion, never substantiated, that the United States had forces secretly standing by in Botswana ready to intervene in the event of a coup attempt. The notion may have been linked to reports that the US had helped Botswana secretly build a large military base and airfield, bigger than anything required by the Botswana forces, in an isolated part of that country. The US has denied placing intervention forces in Botswana, however.

There were indeed tentative efforts to instigate a military coup in South Africa but they never came close to getting off the ground. General Malan, the former defence minister, is reported to have said that a number of people asked him to promote a coup and offered to finance it, but he advised them to use the ballot box instead.[3] It seems clear that the great majority of the whites were opposed to any coup. They had lost faith in white domination, and preferred to put their faith in the negotiators fashioning a system that would give them protection without any more guilt and condemnation.

It appears that any coup attempt would in any case have been put down by the SADF. Lieutenant-General George Meiring, the chief of the SADF at the time, says he took the attitude that he served the government of the day and made it known that he would use his forces to put down any attempt at white insurrection. He specifically informed all those likely to have coup ideas, including Viljoen, that he would stop any such attempt.

Viljoen has admitted to having ordered his followers to commit a few acts of sabotage, such as blowing up powerline pylons, and to having felt that these acts helped persuade the ANC to make concessions at Kempton Park. But he said the Afrikaner Volksfront never seriously considered a coup because there would not have been sufficient support for it either in the SADF or among the white public.

There were, however, widespread fears among whites of some kind of upheaval at election time. Many began hoarding canned food, candles and other commodities likely to become scarce in a breakdown of civil order. After the election they were left wondering what to do with their piles of long-lasting comestibles.

Besides the AWB's nefarious activities, the election campaign was conducted against a background of continued ANC-Inkatha violence. The fighting in Natal prompted De Klerk to declare a state of emergency there on 31 March. On the Witwatersrand clashes continued between Zulu hostel dwellers and 'self-defence units' formed by township residents. On the commuter trains serving the townships, passengers were stabbed, shot and thrown from moving carriages. Other people were shot from moving cars as they walked in the streets. Goldstone's inquiries found that much of this violence was deliberately instigated by the police dirty tricks body known as the Vlakplaas Unit. De Klerk suspended three police generals implicated by Goldstone while the judge continued his probe.

The Inkatha-ANC violence burst spectacularly into downtown Johannesburg a few weeks before the election, when several thousand Zulus, again armed with traditional weapons, marched through the streets in a demonstration of ethnic assertion. When they made an extraordinarily provocative approach to the ANC headquarters in Shell House, guards within the building opened fire, killing a number of Zulus. More were killed later when the marchers massed in the city's central square, the Library Gardens, and came under fire from unknown snipers in office blocks overlooking the square.

Faced with the reality that the election could not be held in kwaZulu, De Klerk called a meeting with Inkatha and the ANC at which it was agreed that Inkatha's demands for recognition of the Zulu kingdom would be submitted to international arbitration. The two arbiters selected – those two 'old Africa hands' Henry Kissinger and Lord Carrington – duly arrived in South Africa but were never given anything to arbitrate. Inkatha, which wanted the final constitution agreed before the election, insisted that the poll be postponed pending the outcome of the arbitration. Both Mandela and De Klerk refused, however, and the arbitrators departed.

With only a week to go to polling, Inkatha suddenly agreed to participate in the election provided the Zulu monarchy was recognised in the interim constitution and in the future constitution of kwaZulu and Natal. De Klerk and Mandela agreed. Any unsettled aspects of the issue would be referred to international arbitration after the election.

The constitutional changes made necessary by this development were approved by Parliament only two days before the election. Meanwhile, the Independent Electoral Commission had heroically managed to put stickers on millions of ballot papers to incorporate Inkatha's candidacy.

A few weeks previously, Constand Viljoen had also had a change of heart. Evidently on the basis of Mandela's assurances that the Afrikaners' interests would be catered for, Viljoen pulled out of the Afrikaanse Volksfront and the Freedom Alliance and entered the election with a new party, the Freedom Front.

Only the Conservative Party and the far-right groups were standing out in the cold as South Africa's blacks and whites entered their first election together.

CHAPTER 54

DEATH OF THE DINOSAUR

Cross by cross, in polling stations around South Africa, black voters marked out the graveyard of minority rule. In two days of voting, they cancelled out nearly three hundred and fifty years of white supremacy.

It was the day of the great levelling, a day when the former oppressors and oppressed lined up together for democracy. Blacks queued to vote for the first time in a general election, and for the first time whites waited with them and behind them in the line.

Whites had queued behind blacks in post offices and banks after petty apartheid had been abandoned, but this was different. Now it was grand apartheid that was being despatched to history and so it was an extraordinary queuing, never to be repeated with the same splendid significance.

In the happy catharsis of the voting lines, the AWB bombings, for all their damage, were but distant groans, the death rattle, so to speak, of white hegemony.

Besides their basic electoral purpose, the queues took on functions not normally associated with polling; they became both bridge and meeting place. Whites who had not before spoken much to blacks, not even their black employees, now had long conversations with black strangers in the slow shuffle to the polling stations. In most cases it was not a permanent transformation, and the old ways were largely resumed on the other side of the polling booth. But it was a breakthrough, a precedent for wider intercourse and acceptance in the future.

The two days of voting, 27 and 28 April 1994, were cathartic in different ways for the different races. For the blacks, the crosses on the two ballot papers – one for the national parliament, and one for the particular provincial legislature – manifested their release from subjugation. Each cross was placed, perhaps hesitantly for the first time, but certainly with both relish and reverence and a sense of triumph. The whites affixed their crosses confidently enough, having voted before, but with trepidation rather than triumph. But for them, too, the poll had special significance: it promised the absolution of their sins and confirmed their release from guilt, censure, boycott and sanction, and their acceptance back into world society.

Neither logistically nor democratically was it a perfect election. In many areas it was shambolic. In the campaigning, there was obstruction and intimidation. Candidates and canvassers were prevented by opposition militants from entering some areas. In the polling, there was at some stations a shortage of ballot papers, ballot boxes and officials. There was stuffing of ballot boxes on a relatively large scale. Adults who had no identity documents were issued with special voting cards, and many obtained and used more than one. Ineligible juveniles cast ballots. De Klerk later asserted that as many as one million of the 19,5-million votes cast were illegal.

Some National Party officers wanted to challenge the results in the courts, but it was decided that this would not be in the interests of the country. They accepted that, for all its faults, the outcome was pretty much what it would have been in a well-ordered election. More importantly, the ANC had not won the two-thirds majority needed to prescribe the terms of the final constitution.

The ANC won 62,6 per cent of the votes, enough to govern but not to dictate. The National Party, which had never expected to win the election but had hoped to get a third of the votes, ended up with 20,6 per cent. The big Zulu vote, probably with some white support, gave the IFP 10,5 per cent, and enough provincial votes to gain control of kwaZulu-Natal. Viljoen's Freedom Front, winning the votes of those conservative Afrikaners who cast ballots, got only 2,2 per cent. But that was still more than the 1,7 per cent of the Democratic Party, the party of the English-speakers. Many of these, it seems, had voted for the NP in an effort to provide at least one strong party to temper ANC power. The PAC came in with 1,2 per cent. The African Christian Democratic Party, the only one of the fringe parties to get into parliament, scraped together 0,5 per cent.

The result more or less reflected the ethnic breakdown of the voting, with the ANC getting the great majority of the 14-million black votes and a large proportion of the 2-million coloured and 500 000 Asian votes. The National Party got most of the 3-million white votes, a substantial part of the coloured vote, a fairly large slice of the Asian votes, and a not-insignificant number of black votes. The party estimated that it had won as many as six hundred thousand black votes, and figured it would have got more had there been less intimidation of its candidates and a more efficient functioning of the electoral system.

De Klerk claimed that the National Party emerged as the most multi-racial party, having got more than half its votes from 'people of colour' (he, too, was using the new term for people his party had once called non-whites). He also presented the National Party as the third-largest black party after the ANC and IFP, having won nearly three times as many black votes as the PAC.[1] (What, one wonders, would Hendrik Verwoerd have thought of *that*?) The ANC, of course, professed not to be a black party, but De Klerk evidently could not accept that.

The ANC had won control of every province except kwaZulu-Natal, which had gone to the IFP, and the Western Cape, won by the NP.

For conservative Afrikaners, the whole negotiating process and election had been a series of disasters. Constand Viljoen had obtained from the ANC an agreement to keep the *volkstaat* idea on the table, but the contract had virtually no practical meaning. Wherever situated and however constituted, the *volkstaat* could never be more than a cultural theme park. The interim constitution gave some protection to the Afrikaans language, but in the new South Africa it was clearly going to be at best secondary to English in official use.

One of the bitterest of the pills the right-wingers were having to swallow was the carving up of the Transvaal, the old Boer republic that had subsequently existed for 84 years as a province of the Union. Now it was being split into three of South Africa's nine new provinces and part of a fourth, all controlled by the ANC under black prime ministers. The Orange Free State was left intact within its old republican and provincial boundaries, but it, too, was now under ANC control.

For those on the extreme right, the nightmare had become reality. Black domination, the ancient phobia that had haunted whites since Van Riebeeck stepped ashore, had at last overwhelmed the Afrikaners. All that was left of what they had for centuries cherished was now in their churches, their museums, their backyards and their memories. They could not trek again to find escape for there was no place to go any more in Africa – except into the non-racism offered by the ANC. The last Great Trek could only be a metaphysical one into that part of Africa the Afrikaners had never willingly entered: brotherhood with the blacks – economic certainly, political probably, cultural increasingly, genetic perhaps. But it would not be a journey undertaken soon, certainly not the last part.

Most Afrikaners, however, entered the new dispensation with their customary pragmatism. The flaws in the Kempton Park agreement and in the interim constitution would not become materially discomfiting – if at all – until the new order settled and jelled. Meanwhile, it was a matter of making the best of whatever faced them – and that was largely true of the English-speakers as well.

It perhaps came easily in the euphoria of the moment, especially in the exhilaration of Mandela's inauguration in auspicious sunshine, when the massed choirs sang in full African glory, when the foreign delegates came in bright panoply to confer the world's blessing on the new order, when the planes trailed the new flag colours above the Union Buildings, and the bemedalled brass of the white military establishment saluted their new chief.

The generals' pledge of fealty was backed by armed jet fighters patrolling the sky above Pretoria throughout the ceremony, with orders to shoot down any unauthorised aircraft, and by some nine thousand troops policing a wide radius on the ground. The white military establishment was holding true to its new allegiance.

Had the ANC negotiators known that they could count on the loyalty of the SADF they might not have made the concessions they did at Kempton Park. According to Patti Waldmeir, the American journalist who chronicled South Africa's transition to democracy, the ANC agreed to guarantee the jobs and pensions of white civil servants, including the security forces, and to include De Klerk in government as a deputy president, because it believed it could not rule without the National Party to guarantee the cooperation of the security forces and the civil service.[2] Shortly after the election, however, senior ANC members began questioning whether these concessions had been necessary as Afrikaners pragmatically accepted the new reality.

De Klerk for his part is reported to have questioned whether his side should have conceded so readily to the ANC's demands. According to one account, De Klerk remarked in an aside to General Meiring at the inauguration ceremony: 'We really needn't have given in so easily.' And Meiring in response pointed out that De Klerk had neglected to use the military as a strong base for negotiation.[3] Assuming the accuracy of this account, De Klerk's casual observation was an astonishing revelation, an astounding epitaph to white supremacy. Perhaps its explanation is to be found in suggestions that De Klerk's judgment had been clouded by vanity while he, the former pariah, toured the Western world to collect applause to add to his Nobel laureation; or the assertions that Roelf Meyer had simply been too naive to withstand the cunning ANC negotiators.

By May 1994 it was too late, of course, for anything but the 'what if' game. White political power was gone forever. The last keep of the white fortress in Africa had surrendered.

★ ★ ★ ★

White rule in Africa formally ended with Mandela's inauguration, but procedurally it had concluded six days earlier with the last meeting of De Klerk's cabinet, the last of the continent's white cabinets. Perhaps for the first time in their country's history, ministers shed tears at the cabinet table.

They were weeping not so much for the end of some three and a half centuries of white rule in South Africa as for the end of nearly fifty years of Afrikaner supremacy and, perhaps even more, for the final defeat of the long struggle for Afrikaner nationhood.

Afterwards, De Klerk moved from the presidential suite in the west wing of the Union Buildings to a less prestigious suite in the east wing. Those offices had been allocated to him as the junior of Mandela's two vice-presidents, a position dictated by his party having won the second-largest vote in the election. Mandela and Thabo Mbeki, the senior vice-president, took over the west wing.

This was how it was going to be for the whites from now on – junior partners in everything except commerce and industry.

It was a humiliating demotion for De Klerk, but entirely in accord with the settlement reached at Kempton Park. So, too, was his downgraded seat at the cabinet table over which he had once presided. He evidently accepted it all in the belief that it offered the best hope of looking after the interests of the whites in the new dispensation. His acceptance, and the good grace with which it was done, were in keeping with the courage with which he had gone about the assignment that fate had handed him: the job of terminating white supremacy – the most consequential and agonising task ever demanded of a white politician in South Africa.

There was more than demotion for De Klerk to endure. He went into the five-year interim government of national unity convinced it was a form of power-sharing, but in fact it wasn't. He had given way to majority rule in the belief that he had been able to protect white interests by persuading the ANC to share power to a degree. The ANC, acknowledging its inexperience in government, did indeed accept that white civil servants must continue to manage affairs for the time being – though under black heads of department. And it put the vital finance ministry in

443

the hands of an apolitical white businessman. But the ANC took for itself the primary levers of power, the security ministries, and gave the NP the departments on the fringes of power, such as energy and agriculture.

What De Klerk perhaps failed fully to appreciate was that the Kempton Park negotiations were about surrendering power, not about sharing it. At Kempton Park the NP had attempted to retain some power for the whites in the only way left – parliamentary vetoes defined specifically in the constitution. The ANC, however, had rejected this as a form of racism. It would not have helped for the NP to argue that majority rule was equally racist in that it gave the blacks power over the whites as much as apartheid had given the whites power over the blacks. To that the ANC might have responded that numbers were of no consequence in a party or a society in which race was unimportant. The ANC, after all, not only espoused multi-racialism but had whites among its members and in its leadership.

Some whites reckoned that the ANC's equating of majority rule with democracy was a facile exploitation of the racial imbalance in order to gain race-based political power – a distortion of the very meaning of democracy. The ANC might have replied that it was the whites who were flouting the spirit of democracy by demanding special treatment for themselves when democracy was essentially about equal treatment for all. It was open to opinion whether the whites were holding themselves more equal, in the Orwellian sense, than the others in that they demanded special protection, or whether the blacks were doing so in that they had power over the whites.

The ANC did accept a measure of special protection for the whites in the constitution, but only in matters such as language rights that were peripheral to the exercise of power. That prerogative remained firmly in the hands of the elected government, which was always going to be dominated by blacks.

There will always be questions attached to the race issue that cannot be answered except as expressions of opinion. For instance, had the whites generations ago made power more a matter of policy than of race, would they have ended up less fearful about their future than they were in May 1994? Or would the black majority simply have taken over the power, once given the chance to do so, and used it primarily for their own advantage, as the whites did? To what extent would the blacks have respected the customs and interests that make up white culture?

Perhaps the closest these questions will come to being answered, and then only indirectly, will be in the manner in which the blacks, now that they have the power, exercise it in respect of the whites. In the first decade of black rule the whites had not much to complain about as far as the preservation of their rights and way of life was concerned. During the struggle to overthrow apartheid, its opponents often quoted the passage from Alan Paton's *Cry, the Beloved Country* in which Reverend Khumalo expresses the fear that by the time the whites stop hating and turn to loving, the blacks will have turned to hating.

It did not turn out that way in the sense of hating. The blacks did not take hatred into their new freedom. Despite all the suffering and indignity inflicted on their people by apartheid and the systems that preceded it, the blacks in the main wiped the slate clean in April 1994. There was residual hatred of systems and events of the past, but not of whites in general, not of the whites of May 1994. There was resentment of residual inequity and envy of unequal wealth, but very little animosity of race, not at first, at any rate.

Notable exceptions would be verbal attacks on whites by black politicians and the large number of white farmers murdered over the next few years in what some saw as a campaign, presumably by PAC extremists, to drive them off the land. One thing the whites didn't have to worry about in the new democracy was that old menace, the SA Communist Party. The collapse of the party's ideological mainstay in Russia had drawn the few teeth the SACP could ever claim. The NP, which only a few years previously had had Reds-under-the-bed nightmares, now had no serious qualms about having Reds *in* the bed – the NP's ministers were sitting at the cabinet table with senior members of the SACP. As a partner of the ANC, the SACP, which could not have won a single seat on its own, ended up being able to claim 12,5 per cent of the parliamentary seats. On the other hand, numbers of ANC stalwarts who had formerly genuflected to the hammer and sickle now embraced social democracy, the philosophy to which the ANC as a whole was now turning.

It was anything but smooth sailing in the interim government, however. Suspicions and resentments from the old order were carried into the new. The prickly relationship between De Klerk and Mandela verged on the hostile, and they often fought in the cabinet room. Though it was De Klerk who had freed him and ended apartheid, Mandela evidently was never able to get over his dislike of the man, or never came to understand him. On a number of occasions he attempted to bully De Klerk in public, both in South Africa and overseas.

The ANC and the NP appear to have had differing concepts of a government of national unity, and especially of the working of consensus. According to De Klerk, the ANC used the majority bestowed by the election result to get its way whenever it chose to do so on any particular issue, ignoring the provision in the interim constitution that cabinet decisions should be by consensus. The NP therefore felt it had a right publicly to criticise decisions that the ANC majority had steamrollered through the cabinet over the NP's objections. The ANC seems not to have recognised any such right. On a general basis, Mandela appears to have been unable to reconcile De Klerk's defence of white interests with his own espousal of non-racism.

These differences led to the NP at least twice contemplating withdrawing from the interim government. It came close when, at a cabinet meeting, Mandela furiously accused De Klerk of undermining government policy in several respects. De Klerk, insisting that all the accusations were spurious, angrily walked out of the meeting. Only peacemaking overtures from senior ANC members prevented the NP from walking out of the government itself.

But a breaking point was eventually reached when the interim government came to vote in May 1996 on acceptance of the new constitution that it had drawn up in its capacity as a constitutional assembly. The NP considered casting a negative vote because of the ANC's continued refusal to accept power-sharing at executive level and government decisions by consensus. It was the old power-sharing issue that the NP had fudged at Kempton Park in the hope that it could be resolved in the interim government. Now, two years later, it had come back to haunt the party, for the ANC had not budged on the issue during the framing of the final constitution, and the NP had been unable to get enough support from the other parties to outvote the ANC in the interim government.

If the NP rejected the new constitution it would have to be submitted to a national referendum, where its objections would obviously be overruled by the black majority. So the party voted for adoption of the constitution and then withdrew from the government. The NP was actually divided on the question of withdrawal, but De Klerk in effect forced the issue by announcing his decision to resign as deputy vice-president in order to become leader of the opposition – a role he had largely been playing anyway in the cabinet, to Mandela's annoyance.

★ ★ ★ ★

When white domination in South Africa ended, the credit for the achievement was justifiably given largely to the black people who had been its victims and principle opponents, and to the external forces that had helped them in their struggle. A not inconsiderable part was played, however, by whites themselves – not by the great body of the whites, who either actively or passively supported apartheid, but by a relatively small number of activists, some of whom risked liberty and life to fight apartheid.

Opposition to white hegemony was always rare among whites. It was rare indeed at the time when Dr John Philip, the missionary, riled the white frontiersmen with his campaigns against their injustices, still singular when Bishop Colenso split the Anglican church in the 1860s with his support for the customs of the Zulu and their resistance to white hegemony. It was barely tolerated in the age of moral ambivalence during which Olive Schreiner the writer expressed her criticisms. White supremacy was barely challenged until after the Second World War. When the Torch Commando then made its flame-lit marches against Dr Malan's fast-unfolding policies, its members were demanding not democracy for all but only a less precipitate and absolute approach to white supremacy and more time to find some sort of compromise – more or less the same stance as that of Smuts's United Party. Alan Paton's Liberal Party took a more principled position at its founding in 1953 but held back from advocating democracy, proposing instead a qualified franchise. Only in 1960 did it embrace universal suffrage, but that got even less support from whites and the party disbanded when the government banned mixed-race political parties.

Paton was representative of a relatively large proportion of whites who were opposed to apartheid but equally opposed to the use of violence to overthrow it. For this they became, as Helen Suzman put it, 'very unpopular both with liberation struggle people inside the country and with many of our friends outside South Africa'.[4]

The restrictions on free politicking left white opponents of apartheid with no alternatives but to conform or go underground, which some did, forming the African Resistance Movement (ARM) and turning to sabotage even before the ANC's MK resorted to violence. John Harris, the only white person executed for sabotage, was an ARM member when he placed his bomb on a passenger train platform at Johannesburg's Park Station in 1964, killing an elderly woman and maiming her young granddaughter as they waited for a train. Other members of the organisation were sentenced to prison terms of up to 15 years. The ARM's membership consisted substantially of university students espousing far-left ideology, but more of the white students preferred to oppose apartheid non-violently through the National Union of South African Students (Nusas), which specifically condemned acts of sabotage. Its leaders were nonetheless banned and otherwise harassed by the government, and the ranks infiltrated by police spies.

Some white faculty members at the universities actively opposed apartheid on their own, and at least two, Rick Turner and David Webster, paid for it with their lives when they were shot at their homes by government assassins.

It took considerable courage for whites to work actively against apartheid, for they stood out in a white society largely supporting or passively condoning the policy and in which they were vulnerable to official spying.

Numbers of whites were imprisoned under the detention-without-trial regulations that were one of the most effective instruments devised by the apartheid government to counter dissent. It gave the authorities the right to hold suspects without the publicity of a trial or even confirmation of arrest, and to subject them to tortures that in some cases killed them or caused them to commit suicide. In one of the most notorious cases, Dr Neil Aggett, a prominent trade unionist, died after being detained under the government's crack-down on strike activity.

A few courageous white people sheltered and otherwise aided black ANC activists on the run from the police. Others were obliged to go on the run themselves, fleeing into neighbouring territories to continue resistance from there or further afield in Britain or Europe. Even there they were not necessarily safe from apartheid's murder machinery, as Joe Slovo learned when his wife Ruth First was killed by a parcel bomb in Maputo in 1982; as Marius Schoon learned in 1984 when his wife and infant daughter were killed by a similar bomb sent to him in Lubango, Angola; as Albie Sachs learned when he lost an arm to a car bomb in Maputo in 1988.

Among the whites who became involved in the armed struggle against apartheid, Hein Grosskopf was no doubt regarded by most of his white countrymen as one of the most notorious. Having fled the country to join the ANC, he was sent back to explode a car bomb outside an army base in Johannesburg in 1987, injuring 26 people, mostly civilians. Then he escaped by way of Botswana to another 13 years in exile in the United Kingdom.

Perhaps the most widely known white political prisoner was Bram Fischer, an Oxford-educated advocate descended from prominent Afrikaners of the Orange Free State but whose social convictions led him to become a leader of the Communist Party. After defending the accused in the Treason Trial and the Rivonia Trial he was arrested for his own political activities, but jumped bail and continued working underground against apartheid. Caught again, he was sentenced to life imprisonment and released only after becoming terminally ill. He has been celebrated as a staunch opponent of white supremacy, but some believe him to have been motivated primarily by his dedication to communism.

White women were active in the struggle against apartheid, but again in small numbers, both in exile and in the domestic underground. Some ended up in jail. Jean Middleton, who was sentenced in the same group as Bram Fischer, spent four years awaiting trial and serving her sentence. She recalled how she and five other white women jailed for their Communist Party affiliation were sent to the Barberton prison, where they were made to spend their time washing the canvas prison clothes of male prisoners, which often were streaked with blood from their beatings.[5]

No white opponent of apartheid was more greatly honoured than Reverend Beyers Naude, also an Afrikaner of impeccable family connections, and who became a living symbol of non-racism. Like his father, he was both a minister in the Dutch Reformed Church and a member of the Broederbond. The crucial turning point in his life came when Prime Minister Verwoerd ordered the DRC delegates to the Cottesloe Conference of 1960 to recant the conference's rejection of the theological justification of apartheid. Alone among them, Beyers Naude refused to recant, and was hounded from his congregation and church. The Christian Institute, which he founded as a theological vehicle for racial reconciliation, was banned, along with Naude himself. He worked underground to support ANC activists, and joined the DRC's black sister church. When the negotiating with the government began he was asked by the ANC to become a member of its team. On his death in 2004 he was given a state funeral by the ANC government, among whose members he was known affectionately and respectfully as Oom Bey. At his request his ashes were scattered in Alexandra township.

Naude was one of the few heroes the blacks could find among their white countrymen at the end of the struggle for democracy, and they embraced him as one of their own. The same embrace could not be extended to all the whites who had sacrificed their supremacy, if not immediately their privileges, since no-one could be certain which of them had done it resentfully and which willingly.

CHAPTER 55

CHIMURENGA

Whites in South Africa who were uneasy about their situation under black rule could consider themselves more fortunate than those in Zimbabwe. Under the autocratic governance of Robert Mugabe and his oligarchic Zanu(PF) party, the fortunes of many of the Zimbabwean whites had nose-dived.

The reconciliation offered to the whites by Mugabe when he took power in 1980 was short-lived. Within a year he was castigating the whites, seemingly irritated by their failure to share his social and political views – and possibly by the insurgency fomented by Pretoria in the first few years of Zimbabwe's independence. A white parliamentarian suspected of plotting against Mugabe was jailed and tortured. So were the white commanders of the air force after being blamed for the aircraft sabotage at Thornhill that had actually been carried out by Pretoria's agents.

Intolerant of any political competition, Mugabe especially resented the opposition of Ian Smith and his white right-wingers of the old Rhodesian Front. He was incensed when in their new guise, the Conservative Alliance, they won 15 of the 20 white seats in 1985 in the first parliamentary election after independence. Those whites who were unwilling to accept African governance should leave the country, he said. When Smith criticised Mugabe's government while on an overseas trip, his passport was withdrawn.

Besides his racism, Mugabe was an incompetent ruler, and the whites became the scapegoats for his follies. The condemnation of their supposed offences became a cover for his mistakes and his misdeeds against his own black people.

Backed by a coterie of sycophants and venal opportunists, his fixations caused thousands of deaths, wrecked the economy, jeopardised the wellbeing of the whole sub-continent, and brought the scorn and censure of much of the non-African world down on his government. And the whites, who, for all their faults, had the means to help keep the country prosperous, were reduced to flight from it or to fearful obscurity within it. What had been the second-largest white population in Africa, numbering close to three hundred thousand at its height, was reduced to about seventy thousand after 20 years of Mugabe's mad rule.

It seems that Mugabe and his cohorts eventually found themselves caught in a tunnel of oppression and corruption they could not back out of without exposing themselves to punishment for their crimes. They could only go forward into further misdemeanour and destruction, led by a man whose own psyche appeared to be going ever deeper into paranoia.

Mugabe's intolerance – or fear – of opposition was initially turned against his main rival, Joshua Nkomo's ZAPU party and its armed wing, Zipra. His chosen instrument was the 5th Brigade, an all-Shona, Korean-trained force he created for the purpose. In a campaign of utmost horror and brutality, the 5th Brigade swept through Matabeleland in 1983 and 1984, killing, torturing, raping and harassing the Ndebele. At least four thousand people were murdered. Truckloads of bodies were dumped down mine shafts. Food supplies were withheld in order to cause famine. ZAPU was harassed into political impotence, then swallowed by Zanu(PF) and Nkomo sent into obscure retirement.

Mugabe spent huge sums on education and health care, then found his treasury did not have much left for other governance. Foreign earnings declined with falling prices of the principal exports and with competition from South African products. Only a trickle of foreign investment came in.

Until he could steer the blacks out of the backwaters into which they had been trapped by white exploitation and their own technical backwardness, Mugabe needed the resources of the whites to keep Zimbabwe in or near the world's economic mainstream. But as economic and political problems grew he turned increasingly to anti-white racism and to the suppression of the independent news media. Opposition and criticism were harshly discouraged, though not entirely prohibited.

With near-absolute power came corruption to match, with Zanu(PF)'s elite bending and ignoring law and sound practice in order to enrich themselves.

Land redistribution, which Mugabe had held up during the freedom struggle as one of its main causes, became an instrument of patronage for protecting his power. Through the first ten years of his rule, he gave little attention to the land issue. Some fifty-two thousand black families were indeed settled on some of the 6,5-million acres bought from white farmers, but this was little more than the population increase in the tribal reserves in a single year.[1]

Under the Lancaster House settlement, Mugabe had reluctantly agreed to pay, at market prices, for land expropriated from consenting white farmers, but on the understanding that Britain would provide the funds. No amounts were ever specified. From 1980 any commercial farm coming on the market had to be offered first to the government. More than 80 per cent of the white-owned farms are said to have changed hands between 1980 and the time the land issue became a crisis in the second decade of Zanu(PF)'s rule.[2] Thus the government could have acquired any of these farms from willing sellers, but in most cases neglected to do so.

Only when he saw political advantage in it in the late nineties did Mugabe inflame the land issue. At the time, the government possessed 70 farms bought from whites, totalling about three hundred thousand hectares, which it had not got around to allocating to black farmers. The British government by 1995 had paid out 47-million pounds for land purchases, of which the Zanu(PF) government spent 44-million pounds and returned the unspent 3-million pounds.[3]

When the ten-year protective clauses of the Lancaster House agreement lapsed in 1990, Mugabe passed legislation to allow the expropriation of land at a price decided by the government, with no appeal to the courts permitted. Concern began to stir in the hitherto complacent ranks of the Commercial Farmers' Union, representing more than four thousand white farmers and several hundred black commercial farmers. Until this time the CFU had been content to accept the outrageously disproportionate division of land in Zimbabwe. Many of its members owned vast acreages, not all used, and some individuals held a number of large farms. The CFU now made tentative proposals for a rational programme of land redistribution, but neither the CFU nor Zanu(PF) was much concerned about the issue and took it no further.

The land issue became prominent, however, when independent newspapers in 1995 exposed the distribution of choice land expropriated from whites to members of the Zanu(PF) 'waBenzi', most of whom had neither the time, inclination nor skills to till the soil, and simply left it fallow. An appalled British government refused to provide any more funds unless expropriated farms were allocated only to needy blacks.

★ ★ ★ ★

Mugabe's most serious challenge came not from the whites but from his own side, the war veterans, the former guerillas who had fought for him in the bush war and then been left to unemployment and hunger. Their resentment turned to anger and street protests in 1997 when the fund established to compensate victims of the war was forced to suspend payments because it had been looted by cabinet ministers and other Zanu(PF) bigwigs.

The veterans demanded not only the resumption of the compensation payments but in addition large gratuities, monthly pensions and land, otherwise they would invade white-owned farms.

The cost of meeting the veterans' demands, a staggering Z$4-billion, was beyond the government's means. But without the veterans on his side, Mugabe would be politically emasculated. He gave in to their demands and imposed a special tax to meet the cost – and which immediately brought protests from the trade unions. To obtain land for the veterans he designated 1 500 white farms for expropriation without compensation. Totalling some twelve million acres, the farms comprised more than a third of the land owned by the 4 500 white farmers remaining in the country.[4] Mugabe declared that farmers whose land was seized should seek compensation from Britain.*

Amid growing international concern over his land policies, representatives of the United Nations and other agencies, and of 23 foreign governments, met in Harare with Zanu(PF) officials to try to work out a rational land reform plan. Agreement was reached on a two-year programme, financed by foreign donors, to buy 700 000 acres from white farmers who had already signalled a willingness to sell. Before the scheme could get off the ground, however, the government announced the seizure

---

*Throughout the ensuing land crisis, Mugabe persistently depicted the white commercial farmers as British citizens, though most were born Zimbabweans – some had a claim on British citizenship through parentage.

without compensation of a further 841 white farms. Mugabe, it seemed, was not interested in orderly land reform but only in using land seizure as a political tool in his efforts to stay in power.

He had in the mean time found a new way to make money – not for his exchequer, but for himself and his political cronies. In return for access to the mineral and timber riches of the Democratic Republic of the Congo (formerly Zaire), Mugabe sent Zimbabwean troops to support President Laurent Kabila's ailing regime in its fight against rebels. The presidents of Namibia and Angola were persuaded to join the venture. The high cost of this enterprise to Zimbabwe's financially strapped government so alarmed the International Monetary Fund that it refused to make any more loans to Harare.

Domestic opposition to Mugabe's policies was meanwhile growing. In 1999 the trade unions joined civic bodies in forming a National Constitutional Assembly to campaign for a constitution protecting democracy. As a counter, Mugabe established his own commission, dominated by party hacks, to revise the constitution. The party majority forced through a new draft retaining the president's wide powers and enabling him to seek re-election for two more five-year terms. The government was absolved of any obligation to compensate white farmers for seized land, and the obligation was specifically placed at London's door.

The farmers, seeing this move as a negation of their Zimbabwean citizenship, emphatically rejected it.[5] In any case, the Labour government in Britain had already disclaimed any inherited obligation from Rhodes's time to pay for land redistribution in Zimbabwe. The secretary for international development, Clare Short, had explained in 1997 that 'we do not accept that Britain has a special responsibility to meet the cost of land purchases in Zimbabwe. We are a new government from diverse backgrounds without links to former colonial interests.'[6*]

The draft new constitution was put to the electorate in a referendum in February 2000, with the aim of paving the way for Zanu(PF) to win the parliamentary election due in four months' time. In its campaign the party sought to put the blame for the country's economic woes on Britain, the IMF and the World Bank, but primarily on Zimbabwe's whites – businessmen and industrialists as well as farmers. The voters, however, seized the chance to express their opinion of Zanu(PF)'s governance. Only a quarter of the electorate voted, but 55 per cent of the votes went against the government. Not only were the constitutional proposals rejected by urban blacks but there was a heavy negative vote in rural constituencies thought to be Zanu(PF) strongholds.

Zanu(PF) leaders were left in a state of shock. Facing the possibility of their profits and privileges being swept away in the coming election, they targeted those consid-

---

*In February 2002 Baroness Amos, the under-secretary of state, reaffirmed the British government's willingness to help finance land reform, besides the 500-million pounds it had given in unrelated aid since Lancaster House. In a radio interview during a visit to South Africa, Amos said Britain had tried for many years to support land reform but the Zimbabwean government had not cooperated. She said agreement appeared to have been reached in the inter-government conference in 1985 and again in the discussions in Nigeria in 2001, when the Zimbabwe government gave undertakings which had since been broken. Amos described Mugabe's attitude as 'illogical and difficult to understand'.

ered responsible for the 'no' vote: the white farmers and industrialists and their black workers, as well as educated blacks such as teachers and nurses. These groups, however, now had a champion: the Movement for Democratic Change (MDC) formed recently as a political party under the leadership of trade unionist Morgan Tsvangirai.

Within weeks of the referendum, Zanu(PF) gangs began to invade white farms across the country, seizing land and harassing the farmers. Many of the farms invaded had not been officially listed for expropriation. The CFU got a high court ruling that the invasions were illegal, but the government simply ignored it. By the end of March 2000 there were an estimated eight thousand 'war veterans' squatting on white farms.

Many of the squatters were obviously not war veterans, being too young to have fought in the war. They were the first of an army of thugs hired by Zanu(PF) to harass white farmers, to evict many from their farms, and loot and burn their homes and farm buildings, to steal their cattle and vehicles and to attack their workers. Numbers of the workers were murdered, and tens of thousands were driven from their homes and left jobless. Throughout the rampage the police, acting on instructions from the government, refused to intervene. The government ignored more high court rulings that the land invasions were illegal.

At a party rally at Bindura in April, Mugabe accused the whites of spurning the hand of reconciliation he had offered in 1980, of engineering his defeat in the referendum, and of financing the MDC. He termed the whites 'the monster behind' the MDC, and promised a relentless struggle to seize their land and crush the party.

The Bindura speech triggered a month of terror for the white farmers. Invading gangs began assaulting farmers and looting and wrecking their farms. White farm families in the Mrewa district began to flee to the relative safety of the towns. Three white farmers were murdered by the gangs. Whites with a claim to British citizenship began queuing at the British High Commission in Harare in an effort to escape what seemed to be a government-orchestrated pogrom. At the celebration of the 20th anniversary of independence on 18 April, Mugabe advised the white farmers: 'You are now our enemies.'

In the campaign for the parliamentary election of June 2000, Zanu(PF) thugs were blatant in their intimidation of MDC supporters. This time, however, it was ineffective. The party won only 48 per cent of the vote, just one percentage point more than the MDC. But with its 30 gift seats, Zanu(PF) entered the new parliament with 92 of the 150 seats. The MDC immediately began legal proceedings to challenge the results in about a third of the constituencies on the grounds of intimidation and procedural irregularities.

Foreign observers, including teams from the European Union and the Commonwealth, found that the poll was neither free nor fair. In the chorus of condemnation one discordant note rang out: the observers sent by South Africa's ANC government declared the election had been held in 'absolute peace' and broadly reflected the will of the Zimbabwean people. The observers seemingly were reflecting the ANC's determination to neither see, hear nor speak of the manifest evil in the Zimbabwean dictatorship.

★ ★ ★ ★

Twenty years after colonial Rhodesia became independent Zimbabwe, two decades after political power had passed from the whites to the blacks, Mugabe launched what he called the Third *Chimurenga*, the third war of liberation.

Like the two previous *chimurengas*, this one was a war against the whites, but this time against white economic rather than political domination. It was waged not with spears like the first *chimurenga*, the uprising of 1896 against Rhodes's conquest, not with AK47s like the second, the guerilla war against Ian Smith's regime. This time it was waged with the political power won in the second *chimurenga*.

The third one had effectively begun with the farm invasions orchestrated by Zanu(PF), but Mugabe did not formally declare it as a *chimurenga* until after his party's near-defeat in the parliamentary election of 2000. Then the Third *Chimurenga* emerged as a tactic to counter the alarming trend manifested in the election.

The first aim of the new war was to ensure that Mugabe's personal power would not be terminated in the presidential election of 2002, an ambition shared by the clique of party bosses who ran the government and were as much addicted to power and its material benefits as Mugabe was. The opening offensive took the form of a programme to fast-track the acquisition of white farms and accelerate the squatter invasion of farms not formally designated for expropriation. The number of commercial farms to be expropriated was increased to 3 000 – about two-thirds of the white farms.

To the harassment of the white farmers was added humiliation; farmers who had not been chased off their farms were forced to attend 're-education centres' at seized farms and, sometimes together with their wives and children, made to dance and sing Zanu(PF) songs.

Mugabe's rule was further challenged by food riots in Harare, a general strike called by the trade unions, and an impeachment motion introduced in parliament by the MDC.

His anger was turned to the judiciary when the courts rejected a government attempt to block the MDC's challenges of the parliamentary election results and upheld the findings of illegality against the land invasions. A campaign of vilification was unleashed against the white judges, forcing two to quit the bench, which was then packed with party stalwarts who began to reverse the earlier court rulings against the land invasions.

The government next moved to prevent the public from receiving information through means other than the state-controlled news media. Editors and reporters of the independent newspapers were arrested, the presses of the *Daily News* were blown up, and some foreign correspondents were expelled.

Mugabe meanwhile turned up the heat on the whites, denouncing the commercial farmers as 'white devils' and urging his party to 'strike fear in the hearts of the white man, our enemy'. Some twenty white farmers of the Chinhoyi district were jailed on spurious charges in March 2001 and later shuffled into court barefooted, shaven-headed, handcuffed and manacled as TV cameras recorded the scene for the evening news.

Their arrests were the signal for mobs to rampage though the town of Chinhoyi, assaulting all whites encountered. The entire white population of about a hundred and fifty fled the town. About fifty white farms in the district were invaded, looted and wrecked. The white families fled in small convoys as pillars of smoke rose all around from their burning farms. When the refugees found themselves unable to get through Zanu(PF) gangs on the roads, three small aircraft were chartered to fly the families out to safety.

White farmers in general were now being forced to realise that they were partly to blame for their predicament. When Mugabe had initially adopted a laissez faire attitude to land reform as he rolled in the clover of power, the white farmers had gone along with him, ignoring the ticking time bomb that was the black peasantry's desperate need for land. Through their failure to take a proactive stance on land reform they had made themselves vulnerable to Zanu(PF)'s attacks when it became politically expedient for Mugabe to launch them.

The folly of the farmers' attitude was plain even to Maria Stevens, the wife of the first white farmer to be murdered in the land invasions. Three months after the death of her husband, David, she told a journalist that 'the farmers, living in their big houses and driving their flashy cars, should have realised they would eventually be targeted and done something to distribute some of their land and wealth.'[7]

Mrs Stevens was one of a number of white refugees from the farms who were attending 'stress seminars' being held by a psychologist, David Harrison, at the CFU's headquarters in Harare. Harrison said one of the stress reactions of his patients was a feeling of guilt about owning the best of the country's farmland.

By June 2001 the farms of about ninety-five per cent of the CFU's members had been placed under expropriation orders.

The harassment of whites went from barbarity to lunacy when Mugabe turned his malevolence on the urban whites. Zanu(PF) thugs invaded business premises and foreign aid agencies in Harare and other towns. Factories, offices, shops, restaurants, hotels, department stores, a private hospital, a dental surgery, a children's home and a health club were among the premises invaded on the pretext of righting employees' grievances. Offices and factories were looted, and millions of Zimbabwean dollars were extorted under threat of violence. Some businessmen closed their firms, leaving their staff jobless, and some fled the country.

A European Union delegation that went to the foreign ministry to protest against the government's looting of EU food aid was told that NGOs sympathetic to opposition parties could expect no protection. The Canadian director of the Care International agency was abducted to a Zanu(PF) office, and when the Canadian high commissioner intervened he was assaulted.

Zimbabwe was now experiencing the unique phenomenon of mob rule orchestrated by government, a paradoxical situation of official anarchy, of lawlessness by the makers and custodians of the law, of banditry by the state.

In the early years of his regime, Ian Smith had refused to deal with Mugabe and his party on the grounds that they were nothing but opportunistic thugs pretending to be liberators. Mugabe seemed now to be proving him right.

The Zanu(PF) boss appeared to be unmoved by 'smart' sanctions that had already been imposed individually on him and his cohorts by some Western states.

While resentfully tolerating the newly strong opposition in parliament, the ruling party used totalitarian-style measures outside it in an effort to hamstring opposition. Notable among these was the formation of a youth movement, informally known as the Green Bombers from the colour of their uniforms. Trained and indoctrinated at special centres, the Green Bombers were deployed to intimidate and assault MDC supporters and to herd people into 're-education' centres for *their* brainwashing – a tactic of exponential indoctrination.

An intriguing aspect of Mugabe's attitude is that while decrying the white conquest and land-grabbing in Rhodesia he never similarly denounced the Ndebele conquest and land-grabbing, which occurred a mere 50 years before the whites arrived and also resulted in the subjugation of the Shonas.

Fewer than a third of the white farms were still being operated by their owners by mid-2004. Once a vibrant exporter of food and other agricultural products such as tobacco and flowers, Zimbabwe had become a famine-ridden beggar, with some rural people reduced to eating insects and grass. In this situation, the government turned food into a political weapon, hijacking international aid shipments and distributing the food only to those with Zanu(PF) membership cards.

Many of the seized farms had been abandoned to the weeds, for most of the invaders had neither the inclination, experience nor wherewithal for farming. Those peasants who had been allocated plots had no tools, seeds or fertiliser to cultivate them. Little of these was provided by the bankrupt government. Tens of thousands of workers once employed on the farms had, with their families, been made destitute.

The attacks on the white farms and businesses had destroyed much of Zimbabwe's productive capacity and much of the population's earning capacity, leaving more than seventy per cent of the working population unemployed. There had been a flight of capital and skills. Tourism, which had the capacity to be one of Zimbabwe's main industries and foreign currency earners, had shrunk drastically. The foreign investment vital for economic viability had dried up. Zimbabwe was faced with having to import much of the grains, beef and other foods it had once exported, but had insufficient foreign exchange for this purpose or for buying petrol and electricity. Hospitals were desperately short of drugs and equipment – and of doctors and nurses, many of whom had fled the country.

By mid-2003, inflation had soared well beyond two hundred per cent. The Zimbabwean dollar, at par with the British pound in 1980, had sunk to a black market value of well over two thousand to the pound.

In an act of supreme insanity, the government had in 2002 ordered all farmers whose lands had been listed for expropriation to cease production and quit their farms within a month. Hundreds refused to abandon their livestock and standing crops, and large numbers of them were arrested.

★ ★ ★ ★

The best place to ambush your enemy is, of course, where he least expects it. And Robert Mugabe knew that British premier Tony Blair would not expect to be bushwhacked at the World Summit on Sustainable Development – the Earth Summit of September 2002.

So it was there that Mugabe sprang his ambuscade, before the presidents and prime ministers assembled at Sandton near Johannesburg to discuss what some delegates saw as nothing less than the future of the human race. His cohort in the Congo venture, President Sam Nujoma of Namibia, fired the first shots for Mugabe.

'Here in southern Africa,' Nujoma said, 'we have one problem … Blair is here … the man who went out to campaign for sanctions against Zimbabwe while the British owned 80 per cent of Zimbabwe's land.'

Nujoma, suitably briefed, was perpetuating Mugabe's fictional assertion of British ownership, which ignored the fact that most of the white farmers were Zimbabweans, not Britons, and owned only 39 per cent of the land at independence and even less at the start of the land crisis. The figure has later been put as low as 21 per cent,[8] but by 2002 'ownership' had become an uncertain term in respect to land in Zimbabwe. Nujoma's attack was warmly applauded by African delegates nonetheless.

Mugabe then came in with an even ruder blast revolving around his oft-repeated accusation that Blair was seeking to restore something of Britain's colonial influence in Zimbabwe. 'So, Blair, keep your England and let me keep my Zimbabwe,' he cried, and sat down to enthusiastic applause by African and other Third World delegates, who then pressed round to shake his hand.

The fervency of Mugabe's acclamation by his fellow Africans surprised and puzzled some delegates and observers. They could hardly have been hailing Mugabe as a great leader or statesman, not as any kind of saviour or savant, for he was none of these. Were they applauding him only for publicly tweaking the nose of the British lion, thin-maned and blunt-toothed though it might now be? Were he and Nujoma seen to be giving the finger not only to Britain but to all of the First World, to the developed countries they believed had grown rich on colonial exploitation and now kept the Third World down through debt manipulation, closed markets, export subsidies and other economic trickery?

If they were lauding him simply as the black leader who kicked white butt in Africa that would be understandable, given the history of white oppression of blacks across the continent. But in cheering Mugabe they were ostensibly excusing all his crimes – the Matabeleland holocaust; the suppression of opposition through murder, torture and intimidation; the sacrifice of property rights for political gain; the creation of famine and its use as a political tool; the wilful destruction of his country's economy, the suppression of freedom of expression, the top-level corruption, the thousands of deaths at his door.

Did the Africans really condone Mugabe's atrocities? Or did they believe his spin, despite the plain evidence that he had concocted the land crisis for political purposes after not bothering much about land reform for 20 years? That no specific figure was agreed on at Lancaster House for British compensation for land reform? That Britain, after paying out more than forty million pounds, had refused to give more unless white farms were no longer seized illegally in defiance of the courts, and no longer distributed among Mugabe's family and party elite? That Britain had set aside another 36-million pounds for land reform conducted properly and legally, and might still be willing to pay it?

The clapping and handshakes at Sandton were not the only manifestation of Mugabe's continued support among Africa's politicians. It was again shown, for instance, a full two years later at the Southern African Development Community (SADC) summit in Mauritius in August 2004, when delegates again backed his 'land reform' programme.[9] Support for his policies has also come at other times from individual African leaders.

Mugabe's African backing is of special interest to the white Africans, for whom it must represent an important element of the milieu in which they seek acceptance, a significant indicator in their search for their place in the continent of their birth, identity and destiny. Their ancestral roots in Europe severed or withered, these whites are now locked into Africa, into its cultures, its politics and its moral stances, into its rights and wrongs, its weaknesses and strengths. When the African Union adopts positions, continentally and in the wider world, it does so for all the Africans, white as well as black. Where Africa goes, its whites go too. But they remain uncertain whether they go as compatriots or as unwelcome passengers, whether they are seen to have an equal birthright in Africa.

Some Westerners, like many white South Africans, were especially puzzled and disappointed by the official attitude of South Africa, the state most affected by Mugabe's excesses and the one best placed to moderate them. Comments in the public arena in South Africa suggested that the Mbeki government's attitude to Mugabe was seen by many whites as a kind of weathercock of its policies insofar as these might affect them, or at least of its respect for democracy. Before Zimbabwe's prosperity had been ruined by Mugabe, his country had been South Africa's chief trading partner in Africa. President Thabo Mbeki held much the same power of disruption over landlocked Zimbabwe's economy that Vorster had held – and effectively exercised – over Rhodesia's. There were, of course, political and economic reasons for Mbeki to refuse to use those powers. But many of his white countrymen appeared to consider it less understandable that he should refuse even to condemn Mugabe's actions, if not on moral grounds then because of the danger that economic collapse in Zimbabwe would harm South Africa's own economy and perhaps flood it with refugees.

Mbeki's stance was presumably not based on the sentiments attributed to his foreign minister, Nkosazana Dlamini-Zuma, who was quoted in a radio report as saying in October 2002 that it would be 'unrevolutionary' to criticise Mugabe's land reform programme. It seems more likely that Mbeki was influenced by his strong belief in pan-Africanism, in African solidarity and in cooperative approaches to the solution of Africa's problems. It was perhaps based also on his reluctance to be seen elsewhere in Africa – and, indeed, by powerful elements within his own party – as a tool of white racism and European neo-colonial ambitions.

Mbeki preferred to pursue 'quiet diplomacy' – which Mugabe did not hesitate to exploit to his own advantage, breaking a number of promises to mend his ways, and seeming to critics in the South African news media to be outsmarting Mbeki at almost every turn. When challenged on this, Mbeki insisted South Africa had no right to intervene in Zimbabwe's internal affairs or dictate policy to Harare. That, however, was not necessarily what his critics wanted. They expected him at least to condemn Mugabe's misgovernance, corruption, human rights violations and atrocities. Some whites recalled that Mbeki had never objected to outside intervention in South Africa when apartheid was the target. Were Mugabe's crimes less heinous, they asked, than those of apartheid? Or did Africans have different standards of morality for whites and blacks?

Mbeki might have reversed the latter question. For instance, he suggested to one interviewer that the murder of 12 white farmers in Zimbabwe had been condemned largely because they were white. If 12 black farmers had been killed, he said, there would have been no outcry. While that is certainly true, it cannot be true of the thousands of black Zimbabweans killed at Mugabe's behest, or the hardships and cruelties he inflicted on many more of them, and of his ravaging of the country's economy.

Mbeki's stance on the Zimbabwe issue was especially puzzling in that it was undermining one of his prime projects: the New Partnership for Africa's Development (Nepad), the plan for donor-assisted rejuvenation in the continent that he was promoting together with the presidents of Nigeria, Senegal and Algeria, and which depended on the support of the developed countries for its success.

Whatever uncertainty or obfuscation there might be in respect of Britain's Lancaster House obligations, the facts of the crimes of Mugabe and his Zanu(PF) cohorts were beyond dispute. They were recognised and condemned in much of the world outside Africa. The UN, for instance, stopped development funding in Zimbabwe until the rule of law was restored there. Zimbabwe's membership of the Commonwealth was suspended and efforts made to have it terminated. The European Union halted aid and sponsored a condemnatory resolution in the UN Human Rights Commission (a resolution blocked by South Africa and the other African members).

The United States expressed disapproval of Mbeki's quiet diplomacy and urged him to take a firmer stand. It had threatened 'intrusive, interventionist measures' to deliver food in Zimbabwe if Mugabe continued to starve his political opponents. Washington also promised generous aid if Zanu(PF) cooperated with the MDC to set up a transitional government to rule pending new elections. EU members and other Western nations imposed 'smart' sanctions such as travel and banking bans on Mugabe and other Zanu(PF) leaders.

What was clearly disturbing to Mugabe's critics was the evident inability, or unwillingness, of black politicians to distinguish between, on the one hand, the need for genuine land reform in the case of land seized by white settlers and, on the other hand, Mugabe's crimes, which had little to do with land reform and everything to do with human rights violations. Supported by some of his fellow African leaders, Mugabe had oppressed most of his own people. It would make no sense if they were motivated by lingering resentment of the white supremacy of the past, for that had nothing to do with what Mugabe and Zanu(PF) were doing to Zimbabwe. In this, the whites were among the victims, not the perpetrators.

CHAPTER 56

AS JUNIOR PARTNERS

A decade after white supremacy ended in Africa, the remaining whites had largely come to terms with black rule. And black rule had so far treated them rather well – with the horrendous exception of Zimbabwe.

There the whites' numbers – close on three hundred thousand when the country came under black rule in 1980 – and their economic leverage should by normal reasoning have given them a measure of political influence and social respectability. These factors, however, became a disadvantage rather than an advantage for the whites as Zanu(PF)'s leaders came to see them as a threat to their autocratic ambitions. The whites came to be viewed as enemies rather than assets.

Most of those whites unwilling to live under black rule had left the country soon after 1980. But then Zanu(PF) turned its animosity even to the whites who accepted black rule. By mid-2003, about three-quarters of the whites had fled to less hostile places. Estimates of the number remaining varied between one hundred thousand and thirty thousand, with the most common estimate somewhere around seventy thousand.

It was widely believed that Mugabe and his cohorts had set out to drive the whites from the country. In this view, the ruling party was unconcerned about the consequent stoppage of funds from the Western donor agencies, reckoning that the aid would be resumed once all the whites were gone and Zimbabwe had become just another black country with desperate need.

According to the chief executive officer of the Commercial Farmers' Union, Gerry Davidson, the policy of driving out the whites was explicitly stated to a CFU official by the minister of local government, Ignatius Chombo, in 1998.

The minister of information, Jonathan Moyo, appeared to have been referring to such a policy when in July 2003 he told a party meeting at Bikita West: 'We like democracy but we hate the MDC because they are working with the white man, who is powerful and whom we are sending away from our land.'[1]

Whatever the government's aim, it had wreaked devastation among many of the country's whites (and even more severely, of course, among the blacks). Hundreds of the white farmers driven off their land were left with no other source of income, unable even to sell their tractors and machinery in a market glutted with such equipment but bereft of buyers. Living in rented accommodation in the towns, some survived on their dwindling capital, others on the charity of relatives. Some had buried generations of ancestors in the country but now would leave it if they could.

Equally desperate were the elderly whites whose pensions had been ravaged by runaway inflation that exceeded 230 per cent in 2003. Too poor to leave, and often with nowhere to go anyway, they existed on less than they once had fed their black servants. Like the dispossessed farmers, they were pitiable relics of 'the Rhodesian way of life'.

Not all the whites in Zimbabwe were in dire straits. Some had grown rich under Mugabe's rule, together with a black elite. Their wealth, however, had not always come from productive enterprise, for normal commercial and industrial activity had been crippled by Zanu(PF)'s actions. Some of the white *waBenzi* had profited from their ability to generate foreign exchange in a situation where, as one observer put it, 'the only stability lies in access to US dollars' – the US currency being officially valued in August 2003 at Z\$800 but fetching Z\$2 500 on the black market. The scarcity of domestic cash made it possible to make money in the lively black market that existed even in that sector. And gains could be made from another febrile phenomenon of Zanu(PF)'s rule: a volatile stock market attracting sometimes desperate players who saw no other way of making money.

The few whites with money still lived the good life, with swimming pools, servants, and holidays abroad. But it seemed there were now more rich blacks than rich whites. White privilege, if not quite dead, was dying, eroded by political events and the emergence of a black middle and business class. Privilege now existed more in wealth than in skin colour.

Few white doctors, lawyers and other professionals remained in the country. Only a handful of white academics were left at the University of Zimbabwe. Most of the white teachers in the private schools were said to have emigrated. Only four or five whites remained in the civil service, tied desperately and despairingly to their pensions.

The children of whites too poor to emigrate or to afford private schools were learning new facts of life in the black-dominated government schools. The Europe of their ancestors was becoming ever more distant to them, and Africa ever more preponderant. Increasingly, however, young whites were leaving and the white population was becoming older. The old-age homes, though struggling financially, were said to be filled with elderly whites, often left behind by fleeing families because they could not face the trauma of starting anew overseas.

Some hundred and sixty young white farmers, unwilling to leave the continent of their birth, had emigrated to Zambia or Mozambique, where their agricultural skills had been welcomed, and were reported to be making a go of it in a hard but free life.

Much of the 11-million hectares seized by Zanu(PF) from white farmers – 90 per cent of the total area they once farmed – was largely desolate. Very few of the many country clubs that once were the hub of white, rural social life were still functioning. Some of the others had been turned into beer halls, some abandoned to dilapidation. Most of the few whites left on the land continued to be subjected to harassment and the threat of eviction. By August 2003 only about two per cent of the white-owned agricultural land had not been listed for expropriation – only because the deeds office had lost their title deeds, according to Davidson. Even large estates run by big corporations – sugar and timber plantations and cattle ranches – had been listed. Urban business and industrial concerns were left wondering whether they would be next. Many of the small family businesses had already closed.

The sports once enjoyed by whites were mostly moribund, only cricket being able to field a team in international competition – and even that disrupted by racial dispute.

'There is no laughter here, no fun and few jokes,' said one white resident of Harare. 'In a situation where their children have no future here, most whites who are left are deeply depressed and long to go.' Another took a different view, however, saying that many of those whites remaining were cautiously optimistic. 'One often hears people say they've been through this much, they might as well see it through to the end. And roots go surprisingly deep. People are reluctant to leave, hoping against hope that "It'll come right".'

For all their racist sins, the whites had been a virile, productive and constructive part of Rhodesian and then Zimbabwean society, helping to make the country one of the most prosperous in Africa. They had the capacity and the willingness to continue that role after 1980, having begun a cathartic adjustment to black rule. White racism did not, of course, suddenly die with Mugabe's victory. It remained as an ugly thread in the social fabric. Even in the benign early days of majority rule there was no move among the whites to apologise for the past misdeeds of their kind, no talk of reparation, no urgent move to rectify the imbalance of land ownership.

Most of the whites who stayed on in Zimbabwe after Mugabe's victory probably retained the primal white fear of black domination but evidently had been prepared to take a chance on it not turning out as badly as they had always feared. They could not but recognise the grievances blacks had from white rule, but they were willing to trust their fate to black forgiveness and tolerance. Their acceptance of black supremacy had been an essential first step towards a society in which race would be an incidental rather than a cardinal factor. Zimbabwe had been pointed in the direction of a racism-free society, and it had seemed an attainable goal. The Zanu(PF) government had the option of forgiving the past, even if not forgetting it, and of making the most of what the whites, now reforming and politically innocuous, could offer to the country. But that was not a concern at Zanu(PF)'s ostentatious, skyscraper headquarters in Harare once the whites came to be seen as obstacles to the ruling clique's ambitions.

If things had gone badly for the whites in Zimbabwe, however, they had gone rather better for those in the other main areas of white population, in Kenya, Namibia and South Africa.

★ ★ ★ ★

Compared with those to the south, Kenya's whites were old hands at living with black rule. When the whites in South Africa began adjusting to majority governance in 1994, those in Kenya had already had some thirty years of it. They had 17 years more than the whites in Zimbabwe, 27 years more than those in Namibia.

The Kenyan whites had had plenty of time to come to terms with the realities of their situation since the rug of privilege had been pulled from under them by Britain's granting of independence to the colony in 1963. The principal reality, of course, was being hugely outnumbered by the blacks – about three hundred to one – more so than were the whites in the other countries of settlement.

At independence in 1963 the Kenyan whites therefore had even less political influence, as measured by proportional vote, than those in the other countries. In the beginning, even before Jomo Kenyatta's KANU government began to edge towards effective one-party rule, the whites had only their economic strength for political leverage. Even that leverage diminished as the blacks, freed from the constraints of white domination, began to acquire some economic muscle of their own.

Besides being outnumbered by the blacks, the Kenyan whites, unlike those in the other three countries, were outnumbered nearly two-to-one by the Asians and Arabs, who had always had considerable economic strength of their own. After independence the whites had to compete politically and economically on more or less equal terms with these groups, whose influence they had previously managed to restrict through the power vicariously bestowed on the whites by colonialism. Both whites and Asians had to seek their future within the constraints of black politics. Some figured they had to choose between sinking or swimming in the flood of official corruption that rose after Kenyatta took office, and ran even stronger after he died in 1978 and was succeeded by Daniel arap Moi. Many chose to swim. For these, prosperity depended on the closeness of their ties with those in power, and that association often involved collaboration in the official venality that became endemic after independence.

Many of the successful Kenyan whites have had highly questionable links with arap Moi's family, and closely supported him despite the corruption and brutal repression of his regime. Knowledgeable analysts reckon that most of the whites voted for Moi in all his elections and again voted (unsuccessfully this time) for his chosen successor, Jomo Kenyatta's son, Uhuru, in the election after Moi's retirement in 2002. Whites who openly criticised Moi's wrongdoings ran the risk of being ostracised in certain white circles.

Almost without exception throughout Africa, independence from colonial domination, from imposed European moral codes, was followed by governmental corruption, top-down turpitude that permeated the social structure. The former colonial masters saw this as intrinsic to 'the African nature' but it might in fact have had more to do with the destructive effect of colonialism on ancient African social structures. Whatever the causes, it became the African way and Kenya followed it. Those with moral objections – dissenting blacks as well as whites and Asians – lacked the political power to oppose it.

Amid the corruption in Kenya swirled black political and tribal rivalries. The whites watched from the sidelines as these disturbed the country almost without pause after independence. The democracy purportedly installed by the departing colonial power came under increasingly autocratic influences as KANU (again following another post-colonial pattern in Africa) sought to retain power against dissenting challengers. Moi's dictatorial style of government was confronted by an attempted military coup in 1982, by intermittent riots by university students over the years, and by a number of incipient uprisings, all quashed.

To some extent the decline into corruption and autocracy was discouraged by Kenya's dependence on foreign aid and investment. Eschewing the Cold War alliances with the Soviet Bloc favoured by many other African countries, the Nairobi government fostered relations with Britain and more especially with the United States. These moves helped ease the minds of the whites who had elected to remain in Kenya under black rule. But eventually corruption and the suppression of dissent led first to protests by international human rights groups, and then to the withdrawal of funds by Western donors.

White confidence was nevertheless bolstered, in a somewhat ironic way, by the fact that with KANU's autocracy came a firmness of governance that helped to instil confidence in the continued stability of the country. That and the traditional attractions of life in Kenya helped slow the exodus of whites that had begun immediately after independence. From the high point of around eighty thousand, the white population was down to fifty thousand by 1979, according to the census of that year. By 1997 it was put at some thirty-five thousand.

Today, in the absence of a specific census count, estimates must suffice. Estimates of the number of whites having Kenyan citizenship vary between six thousand and eighteen thousand. There are several thousand more residents with British passports. Some twenty thousand Britons are registered with the British high commission but it is thought there could be another twenty thousand or so not on the commission's books. Many of these, however, are Asians holding British citizenship.

By any estimate, there are fewer whites with Kenyan citizenship than whites who are not citizens – that is, long-term residents and short-term expatriates (called 'two-year wonders' by those locally born or long resident).

In Kenya itself there is uncertainty about the definition of a white Kenyan. It obviously applies to those with Kenyan citizenship, whether they have several generations behind them or, like some, have been in the country for only ten years. But those who reside without citizenship, such as the many who came as expatriates and stayed on to work in business, would not necessarily be regarded as Kenyans by the old-established 'up-country' families, so called because their forebears were among the pioneers who settled in the White Highlands.

White settlers in Kenya were mostly from the upper and upper-middle classes of British society, partly because they needed a fairly large income to cover the cost of settlement in virgin territory. They came mostly to open up plantations or ranches, a few as traders – all occupations requiring rather more capital than most small farmers, shopkeepers or artisans in Britain could raise. The subsequent development provided few opportunities for British artisans, the Asian *fundis* having cornered the market in most of the manual trades.

Once the basis had been established, it became a pattern. There is a jocular but not entirely inaccurate saying that when British ex-servicemen were settled in Africa after the Second World War, privates and n.c.o.'s were given land in Rhodesia, officers were given land in Kenya.

White society in Kenya is still presided over by those with a claim to aristocratic or 'up-country' lineage. Those who can claim to be 'up-country' form a special group in which status might be enhanced by noble lineage but is not dependent on it. As in all places of European colonial settlement, from Sydney to Boston, the descendents of the first settlers claim a special cachet, not necessarily one of elitism, for money can buy that, but rather of precedence and rarity. It is not necessarily a matter of snobbery, for it could be said to go beyond that, but the two often coincide.

The snobbishness that is discreetly prevalent in the white 'establishment' is largely a hangover from the era when Kenya Colony was considered a playground of the British aristocracy. The collective self-esteem inherent from that era has been reinforced by the British royal family's love of Kenya, manifested in a number of visits beginning with the Prince of Wales's two hunting safaris in the thirties. In a sense, the second Elizabethan reign began in Kenya, for the princess who became queen was in Kenya, in the Tree-Tops Hotel near Nyeri, when she learned of the death of her father and of her accession to the throne. Queen Elizabeth came again to Kenya, as did the Queen Mother, and Prince Michael of Kent, Prince Charles and Prince William, the royal fondness extending from colonialism into independence. It might truly be said that no part of the former British Empire has been more visited by British royalty – out of desire rather than obligation – than Kenya.

Kenya's social upper crust was never easily penetrated by those who were not white. But it is snobbery, rather than racism, that now decides acceptance in a Kenya ruled by blacks. Racism does exist, of course, and among blacks as well as whites, but in what one white Kenyan has described as 'patrimonial/patrician terms rather than the loutish manifestations you would see in the United Kingdom'. It is almost unheard of for a multi-generation white Kenyan to marry a person of colour, but somewhat more common for expatriates to do so. A substantial number of expatriates gained Kenyan citizenship by marrying outside their race. They tend not to be accepted socially, however, by the white 'establishment'.

Before independence, the social exercises of the whites were, of course, a matter of indifference to the indigenous Kenyans in their resentment of European hegemony, not least to those Kikuyus who launched the Mau Mau rebellion. Besides political power, the return of the land taken by the whites was a main objective of the struggle against colonial and white domination. Since the whites at the time of independence were heavily engaged in agriculture, the Kenyans, even more than the whites in Rhodesia or South Africa, were severely affected by the post-independence redistribution of land. And the prime land, certainly in Kikuyu eyes, was in the White Highlands.

Today the White Highlands are a memory, in terms of both race and nomenclature. Not for a long time has anyone applied the term to the region. It was never a term much accepted by the black people who lived in and around the region. It was more an appellation applied by the whites to what they regarded as a preserve for their kind, a region where blacks would work on but never own the land. It was always spelled with capitals, affirming the ownership as well as the altitude.

The term became inappropriate for obvious reasons at independence, and it became increasingly inaccurate as blacks began to take over the white farms. It was then that Kenyans began to use the term 'up-country'.

Most of the White Highlands estates bought out by the KANU government with the funds provided by the British government were distributed among the Kikuyu to be farmed as subsistence *shambas*. Some came to be operated on a commercial basis by wealthy black owners. A number of farms remained in white hands, some still held by descendents of the settlers. Most of the whites, however, ended up in ranching and sisal-growing in the lower country, rather than in the coffee and pyrethrum production predominant in the highlands.

Around the turn of the century, some twenty vast cattle ranches in the Laikipia area, about 250 km north of Nairobi, were owned by whites (though they are said to have been forced to give shares to Moi). There were still numbers of white farmers in Timau, around the Mara, south of Lake Kajiado, in Naivasha, Nakuru, Njoro and Limuru, but they tend to keep a low profile.

Most of the Afrikaners whose forebears came up from South Africa to settle around Eldoret found the prospect of black rule intolerable. They sold up and trekked south, abandoning the graves of their fathers, going back to the land where earlier forefathers were buried. Only one remains – and continues to farm profitably and peacefully.

White land tenure throughout Kenya remained uncertain, however, in the face of mounting challenges by blacks, and attempts by minor politicians to incite Zimbabwe-style invasions of white farms. The government continued to back the remaining 999-year leases and insisted that private property ownership would be protected. Some sixty squatters who invaded a white-owned farm in 2002 were each sent to jail for a month. Demands by blacks for land held by whites have continued, however. By 2004 police were being called out regularly to chase off Masai cutting fences and driving their cattle onto white-owned ranches west of Mount Kenya, claiming the land belonged by ancient right to their people. Scores of Masai were arrested during a number of violent protests, but the invasions continued, making the ranches largely unworkable.

Aside from the land problems, whites generally continued to prosper in Kenya. While lifestyles were no longer as flamboyant and luxurious as some once were, there was wealth among the whites, even if sometimes tainted. A number of whites maintained exclusive retreats on the coast and in the game parks. Something of the Happy Valley ethos persisted, though no longer in that area and not with the same dedication.

Everywhere they had settled in Africa, whites feared black rule for both political and social reasons, and prime among the latter were the questions of education for their children and health care for their families. To some extent their fears of a degradation of amenities were realised in both areas, and those who could afford it often made use of better schools and hospitals in other countries. Some of the wealthier Kenyans sent their children to boarding schools in Britain or South Africa, but others made use of excellent private 'prep' schools, notably the Banda, and others again sent their children to the state schools. For tertiary education, however, universities in Britain, South Africa and even Australia were often preferred to the one in Nairobi. Some whites favoured South African or British hospitals for treatment of more serious ailments, although private clinics of a good standard were available for those who could afford them.

Sport, once the preserve of the whites, had been entered by blacks in most fields except rugby and tennis. Cricket prospers sufficiently for Kenya to have been accepted at international level, playing in the one-day matches of the ICC World Cup competition, though not initially in full-scale Test matches.

European culture was largely thrown back on itself in black-dominated Kenya, dependent for stimulation at long range from Britain and on transient infusions from tourism. The decline in white numbers meant a concomitant decline in cultural structures.

Still, aside from the simmering tribal rivalries, racial tolerance had by and large become the norm in Kenya. Given stable and honest government – and past experience everywhere in Africa seemed to militate against it rather than encourage hope for it – the whites in Kenya might feel, going into the 21st century, that they had a place in the sun not only for themselves but for their children as well, a good place for white Africans.

★ ★ ★ ★

Namibia slipped quite easily from war to peace, from freedom struggle to independence, despite the struggle having lasted 23 years. And the country's whites on the whole slipped as easily into the new dispensation.

One reason for the smooth transition was that the war had always been more an external than an internal matter. It was South Africa's war more than Namibia's. Once the South Africans had gone away, the Namibians were free to forge their own destiny. Another reason was that the 'border' war had never spread deeply into Namibia. The insurgency had been sporadic and not greatly disruptive of anything except political concerns – and Ovambo lives and families. The greatest economic damage, ironically, was caused at the end of the war by the departure of the SADF and its big-spending commissariats and troopies.

At independence in 1990, some whites, seeing Swapo as an anti-white, communist organisation, sold up and fled, mostly to South Africa and Germany. Most of the whites, however, remained, held by ties of birth, family, business interests, jobs, or simply the fascination that Namibia exercises over those who have known the country.

Many of the emigrants soon came back, for Swapo at first seemed not quite the ogre expected. The Marxist sympathies once professed among its leadership waned once the movement found itself switching from insurgency to governance. Free enterprise became acceptable, as did the enticement of capitalist investment from abroad. There was nothing in Namibia like the official black racism that became rampant in Zimbabwe. Not that race relations were smooth and untroubled – given Namibia's history, it would have been surprising if they were.

Whites' unease was centred largely on their first president, Sam Nujoma. While ostensibly advocating a 'forgive and forget' policy by both sides, Nujoma was not above attacking whites for being 'arrogant' and 'imperialist'. His party antagonised many Afrikaners, brown and white, by making English the sole official language despite Afrikaans being the universal medium of communication.

Only a year after independence, a human rights group staged a march in Windhoek to protest against what it said was Swapo's disregard of human rights. It accused the government of turning from reconciliation to confrontation, of labelling white Namibians as racists and colonialists, of advocating an end to teaching in Afrikaans, of attacking foreigners and homosexuals, and of undermining the judiciary and freedom of expression. In all of this there were echoes of Zimbabwe.

Most worrisome, in the view of some whites, were the similarities between the land issues in Namibia and Zimbabwe, for in southern Africa white ownership of the best land is an elemental factor in politics. As in Zimbabwe, the Namibian independence agreement had left most of the countryside divided between private farms, held mainly by whites, and communal lands occupied by blacks (60 per cent of the population) on a tribal basis. As in the case of other African governments, it suited Swapo at first to maintain the communal system for it gave the party greater influence over the rural votes in that it controlled the chiefs who in turn controlled the allocation of the communal lands. Not all rural residents supported this system, however. In 1999 about a thousand of them marched in Windhoek to protest against a bill they reckoned was designed to strengthen the position of the chiefs.

In Namibia, as in Zimbabwe, land reform was not at first pushed with urgency, despite most of the best farmland being held by whites after in most cases having been taken from the original indigenous owners by force or fraud. By 2002 the government had settled only 30 000 blacks on purchased land, while some two hundred thousand applicants were still waiting for an allocation. By 2004 the waiting list was said to have grown to two hundred and forty thousand.

Land reform was inhibited to some extent by the constitutional requirement that land be acquired from willing sellers rather than through expropriation. Namibia in any case consists largely of semi-desert and low-rainfall grassland, and little of it is suitable for intensive farming or extensive crop-growing. Most of it is good only for cattle or game farming or wild-life tourism, all requiring big acreages and big capital. Relatively few disadvantaged blacks could be put into this kind of farming, and therefore Swapo could expect relatively few votes from land reform. Job creation through the promotion of urban commerce and industry offered greater political rewards. Furthermore, most of Swapo's support was among the majority Ovambos, none of whose land in Namibia (as distinct from Angola) had been taken by white settlers.

Land reform efforts were complicated by the fact that much of the white-owned land was held by German citizens. An agreement with Bonn required the Windhoek government to acquire any such land by purchase at market value in hard currency payable in Germany, and such deals were made unattractive by the unfavourable exchange rate. Besides, much of the German-owned land was used for wild-life tourism and hunting, which brought in valuable foreign currency, and few black Namibians had the means or expertise to take them over.

The unequal ownership of land was nonetheless a political issue that Swapo could not ignore, and Nujoma found it politic occasionally to attack white farmers for not cooperating with land reform and for pricing their land too high. Only a year after independence, he challenged the whites' right to own land, saying they had not brought any farms, 'any sand in their bags', when they came to Namibia as foreign settlers.

Each attack sent tremors of concern among the 4 000 white farmers, but not strongly – until his dramatic backing for Mugabe at the Earth Summit in Sandton. The reaction to his outburst there was made stronger than it might otherwise have been by the fact that at a party congress a week earlier he had supported Mugabe's land-grabbing, and had made what news reports described as a vitriolic attack on 'arrogant white farmers' in Namibia. He announced an intention to seize 192 farms from absentee landlords. That was different from Mugabe's invasion of occupied and productive farms. Still, the similarity between Nujoma's and Mugabe's attitude to white land ownership was unmistakeable.

Unease grew among whites when in March 2004 the government announced plans for the compulsory expropriation of white farms, pointing out that 80 per cent of the arable land was still in white hands. The Institute for Public Policy Research in Windhoek had estimated in 2002 that at the current rate of land reform (only 7,4 per cent of the commercial farmlands allocated to blacks since independence in 1990) it would take 60 years before blacks owned even half of the commercial farms in Namibia.[2] The institute said then that despite legislation requiring prospective sellers to offer their land to the government first, the government had taken up little of the farmland on offer. Only a third of the funds budgeted for land acquisition had been spent.

Cabinet ministers, however, were quick to buy farms with the low-interest loans available under the land reform programme. Nujoma owned several himself.

According to the opposition Congress of Democracy party, Swapo was using the white farmers as 'scapegoats to divert attention from the real issues of poverty and unemployment, as Zanu(PF) did in Zimbabwe'.[3] The farmers themselves were never sure how much of Nujoma's anti-white utterances were just political grandstanding. He told one interviewer, for example, that all Namibians, irrespective of colour or race, were entitled to the land. Only foreigners, he said, would be barred from owning land.[4]

Nujoma retired in 2004 and was succeeded as president by Hifikepunye Pohamba, but his policies were expected to continue unchanged, for Pohamba was widely regarded as his stooge.

For all their fears, whites found that their lifestyles remained largely unchanged in the first decade of independence, largely because of their dominance in the economy and because of Swapo's generally sound governance.

Whites worried about government corruption and the decline in public services and amenities. Some whites who could afford it sent their children to private boarding schools in South Africa, and made use of the private hospitals there. In Namibia itself there were private hospitals of a high standard – and high prices – served by visiting specialists from South Africa. Those with limited means made do with the public facilities – and privately complained about them.

Few whites evidently were discontented enough or fearful enough to emigrate. The white population stayed fairly constant at some eighty thousand in a total population of just under two million scattered over a country bigger than France. Even at only about six per cent of the population, their numbers – and therefore their influence – were proportionately greater than the fewer than one per cent left in Zimbabwe at the turn of the century, and the even smaller proportion in Kenya.

In a society where half the population lived below the poverty line and the unemployment rate hovered close to forty per cent, the whites' virtually exclusive possession of skills and capital made it relatively easy for them to retain their privileges. But privilege, of course, never rests easy where the haves are grossly outnumbered by the have-nots, and when the disparity between them is huge. Like their counterparts in South Africa, white Namibians could find their greatest security in devising ways to improve the lot of the have-nots rather than simply welcoming the black haves into the ranks of the elite. But in any such endeavour they were hamstrung without political power. That was their dilemma.

CHAPTER 57

A GAP UNBRIDGED

The white South Africans abandoned apartheid because they came to recognise both its wickedness and its impracticability. In the latter respect it was perhaps something like a man giving up rape because he had become diserectile. There was nevertheless a strong moral element in the whites' acceptance of reform. And in this there was necessarily some acknowledgement of guilt.

The whites had become accustomed to guilt, or at least to accusations of it. They had lived in its shadow through 40 years of worldwide castigation, through sanctions and isolation. The older ones had experienced it for most of their lives, the younger ones had known nothing else.

Probably very few of those whites who admitted some guilt for apartheid would acknowledge having acquired it by commission, by direct involvement in one of its heinous applications, such as security police torture or mass removals. Many more might accept the guilt of having voted the National Party back into power in election after election despite the enforcement of apartheid becoming more atrocious in direct proportion to the resistance to it. Some might acknowledge a measure of guilt through thoughtless indifference to the iniquities of the policy. Most would no doubt plead ignorance of the worst aspects of apartheid, perhaps offering as excuse the strict secrecy and censorship laws. But of course it wasn't only the atrocities that the world condemned but also the fundamental immorality of the policy. And by the time democracy came, no living white South Africans could claim ignorance at least of the manifest injustice and cruelty that had surrounded them and permeated their lives since birth. Nothing, and least of all any belief that black people were inferior, could be used as justification for the discrimination, deprivation and exploitation that were visible to every white person.

Most whites, if they gave sufficient thought to the matter, would accept that they benefited from the official exploitation of blacks, no matter how indirectly or even innocently. They were not in agreement, however, over the related issues of reparation, restitution and reconciliation.

Miraculous though it was, the political settlement was never going to be enough in itself. There had to be a moral equivalent as well. The surrender of power to the blacks could not be the end of it. There had been too much hatred, strife, killing, damage and hurt for the blacks and whites to simply close the past and try to get on with each other in the new democratic dispensation.

If the new order was to have a good chance of success, the guilt would have to be confessed, apologies made, and the victims reconciled with the perpetrators. Reparation would have to be made for the deaths, suffering and humiliation inflicted on the blacks, and for the opportunities denied them. There would have to be at least some restitution of the land and labour taken without adequate recompense.

That was the Ideal. But idealism is usually more abstract than concrete, and perhaps more so when racial differences are involved. After a decade of democracy no-one could fairly claim that reparation, restitution and reconciliation had been accomplished.

The moral settlement was attempted informally – and perhaps most successfully – in innumerable private and commercial contacts across a colour line that was not supposed to exist any more but of course still did in many ways. Formally the attempt was made through the Truth and Reconciliation Commission appointed by the transitional government in 1995.

In the TRC's hearings, the evils of apartheid became live theatre, fetched out from the dreadful past for recollection, sometimes re-enactment, in the spotlights of democracy. Victims of official torture relived their agonies in vivid description. Relatives of those murdered by the apartheid state wept again as they recounted their loss. Covers were lifted from the activities of the official hit squads and the sinister laboratories and workshops where the technology of assassination had been refined. A few of the perpetrators confessed their guilt, even demonstrated their techniques of torture, offered apology and sought amnesty.

Feelings overflowed often, and at times the hearings came close to becoming emotional circus.

The South African truth commission went further than the similar exercises conducted in the former Latin American dictatorships in that it could examine the misdeeds not only of apartheid's perpetrators but also of its opponents. It could give amnesty not only for the killing of white civilians by the liberation movements – some liberation movement cadres did indeed seek amnesty for their killing of whites through acts of terrorism – but also for the crimes the movements committed against their own members, such as the torture and arbitrary execution by the ANC of suspected spies within its ranks.

Such evidence of even-handedness in the TRC's brief did not entirely satisfy the old guard of the NP, which believed that in its composition and attitude the commission was biased against the former government and unwilling to give any consideration to the ethos and motives behind apartheid. These objections substantially reduced the TRC's chances of success, since they depended largely on apartheid's perpetrators being encouraged to acknowledge and repent their sins.

The chosen path – reconciliation through admission of guilt and expression of remorse – meant that the exercise had to be conducted as both inquisition and confessional, as both a punitive and a curative undertaking. There evidently were differences of opinion, however, over whether the prime concern was to put apartheid posthumously on trial, or whether it was to repair the damage it had left among the living.

Ideally, the TRC would have surveyed and pronounced upon white supremacy in general. But to clean the slate of all the white misdeeds, it would have had to go back to the first European settlements of the 17th century. Reconciliation being a matter for the present and future, the commission necessarily dealt with the post-1948 apartheid, and then only with the especially violent events of the previous decade. It sought particularly to identify those behind the abduction, torture and killing by the security forces at the climax of the freedom struggle, for it was there that the pain was still sharpest and the need for closure greatest.

While some lesser security force members confessed their part in apartheid's crimes, those who were thought by the TRC's investigators to bear the main culpability, the senior generals and the NP cabinet ministers, denied even knowing of them. The chain of responsibility seemed to disappear in the murk of apartheid's last desperate years under PW Botha, when official torture and murder evidently had become a matter of free enterprise, and culpability was blurred in the security system's obsession with concealing its criminality.

Botha, commonly regarded as the arch villain, refused to testify, and privately denied guilt for apartheid or anything else. De Klerk in his testimony condemned the atrocities and apologised broadly for the hurt and harm caused by apartheid. But he refused to say the policy was wrong, arguing that apartheid and the whole matter of reconciliation should be seen in the light of the Afrikaners' historical search for security of identity and culture. That got short shrift from a commission more concerned with culpability than with rationales.

The former foreign minister, Pik Botha, was more forthcoming than his former cabinet colleagues who took the stand. He admitted that the policy of the government – in which he had been the longest-serving foreign minister but also a moderate within the party – 'had no moral basis' and declared that no-one in the cabinet could not have had suspicions of the security force atrocities, and should have done more to prevent them. As for himself, he said: 'I deeply regret this omission. May God forgive me.'

The security force atrocities aside, there evidently was a hope among the TRC commissioners that numbers of whites outside the security forces and government would contribute to the reconciliation process by coming forward to confess guilt and seek absolution for profiting from apartheid or passively accepting it. Few did, probably because most whites hadn't been directly involved in the enforcement of apartheid and many of them didn't think there was much wrong with it anyway. It was only politicians and former security force members who came before the TRC, and it could hardly have been otherwise; the proverbial man-in-the-street could hardly have been expected to testify.

Midway through the three years of hearings, the chairperson, Archbishop Desmond Tutu, implored the whites not to take for granted the 'amazing phenomenon' of the blacks' readiness to forgive. He urged the whites to grab this 'last but most generous offer of dealing with the past', adding: 'Your survival depends on it.' [1]

The archbishop did not spell out precisely what he expected in this regard. He obviously did not envisage white housewives coming in numbers to confess to having humiliated and exploited their domestic servants (though most of them did). Or corporate executives to confess to similar treatment of their black employees (though many of them justifiably could). Or the whites who had been given a better life by cheap black labour (as they all had) to come and express their regrets, one by one.

Most whites were probably content to leave it to the government to devise measures to overcome the hardships still endured by the majority of the black people and to effect restitution. They might well have accepted any reasonable measures, perhaps even onerous ones, after the horrors of apartheid had been dramatised through the TRC.

In its seven-volume report the TRC duly declared the apartheid state to be the prime perpetrator of gross violations of human rights, and specifically fingered a number of its politicians and military and police officers. It recommended certain criminal prosecutions. The commission also found the ANC and PAC guilty of human rights violations during the freedom struggle.

The TRC, concerned as it was with reparations rather than restitution, recommended government payments to identified victims of human rights abuses. It made the broader point that reconciliation and peace would not be achieved until the gap between rich and poor was bridged and restitution made.

Some who had suffered from apartheid would perhaps have preferred Nuremberg-type trials, but the inadequacy of this approach was shown in unsuccessful efforts to convict the generals in court cases conducted outside the ambit of the TRC. The United Nations' declaration of apartheid to be a crime against humanity was of no practical use in prosecuting its perpetrators.

There was disappointment at the absence of an unequivocal admission of the criminality of apartheid by its chief practitioners, especially by De Klerk, the man who had had the good sense and courage to terminate it.

The Afrikaners' principal church, the Nederduits Gereformeerde Kerk in the Dutch Reformed group, had in October 1998 declared apartheid to have been 'wrong and sinful, not simply in its effects and operations, but in its fundamental nature'. A resolution adopted by the church's general synod had branded the theological justification of apartheid as a travesty of the Gospel and a theological heresy.

If apartheid could now be considered sinful and heretical by the church that formerly had provided that theological justification, why could the party of apartheid not do so too? Was it because Afrikaner nationalism was bound up only partly in religion and more importantly in identity and cultural survival, and Afrikaner nationalist politicians like De Klerk could see no evil in efforts to survive? Perhaps this was why De Klerk could apologise for the harm done through these efforts but not for their end purpose. But this surely would be to ignore the exploitation that had run parallel with survival.

★ ★ ★ ★

The division among the whites was highlighted when at the end of 2000 a group of them proposed that all the whites sign a declaration accepting responsibility for the wrongs of apartheid, acknowledging that they benefited unjustly from it and pledging to help repair its damage. They proposed to set up a fund to which whites might contribute individually and from which blacks still suffering the effects of apartheid might be helped.

Numbers of prominent whites signed the declaration. Others, equally prominent, publicly refused. The signatories included judges of the Constitutional Court, academics, business leaders, publishers, educationists, journalists, human rights activists and former politicians. Among those who refused was former president De Klerk, who thought the declaration 'failed to capture the full complexity' of the whites' situation.[2] He thought it would assign collective guilt to the whites and thereby label them as morally inferior. De Klerk said many whites were not contributing to reconciliation because of a growing sense of alienation based on the feeling that they were not entirely welcome in the new South Africa. They were demotivated, he said, by 'being kept in the dock'.

The alienation chord was struck also by another who withheld his signature: Marthinus van Schalkwyk, De Klerk's successor as leader of the New National Party, at the time linked with the former Democratic Party in a new Democratic Alliance.* Van Schalkwyk said the declaration would deepen divisions between whites and blacks and strengthen the 'two nations' concept enunciated by President Thabo Mbeki (who in 1998 had said South Africans appeared to be divided between a white and rich nation and a black and poor one). Van Schalkwyk said the whites must not be reduced to 'hand-wringing apologists'. He saw the declaration as a basis for establishing collective guilt for the whites, and extending it to young South Africans who were not to blame for apartheid.[3]

The leader of the Democratic Alliance, Tony Leon, also refused to sign, saying: 'I have serious doubts about the politics of apology. Where is it going to end?'

The controversy reflected not only the differences among the whites but also the failure of ambitions to reconcile them fully with the blacks. In the reasons given for not signing the declaration may perhaps be found some of the reasons for the failure of the Truth and Reconciliation Commission to realise all the expectations of its creators.

It may be that the TRC failed to achieve measurable reconciliation between the races firstly because its composition was seen as antagonistic by those with whom reconciliation was primarily supposed to be effected: not so much the general white public as the executives and supporters of apartheid. A second reason may have been that no attempt was made to reconcile the different concepts of white guilt: the view of guilt-without-good-reason held by apartheid's victims and prosecutors, and the view of guilt-with-understandable-reason held by its executives.

---

*Van Schalkwyk would later break away from the DA to effect another and even more eccentric alliance with the ANC when that seemed the only way to avoid the demise of the former party of apartheid. And even that move would fail, as had the device of attempting to reinvent the party as the New National Party after 1994; in one of the most ironical of political events, the party was swallowed by the ANC in 2004 and effectively ceased to exist, though Van Schalkwyk remained politically alive, at least for a while, under the ANC's wing.

Full reconciliation between South Africa's blacks and whites was, of course, an impossible dream in the short term. Even in the long term it could not be achieved without a good measure of reparation and restitution. The partial reconciliation achieved through the TRC could be neither effective nor lasting without adequate compensation for the harm done by apartheid and restitution for what was wrongly taken.

There were precedents aplenty for reparations payments, most famously the billions paid by the German government to the survivors of the Holocaust and, with German industry, to survivors of the Nazi slave labour system. In America, the government had compensated its own Japanese citizens for interning them during the Second World War.

South Africa was different, of course. The felonies of white supremacy were older and more complex than the relatively short-lived iniquities of the German Nazis, and in any case were dissimilar. The dispossession and exploitation in South Africa were too deeply ingrained in the social structure, and reached too far back in history, to be extracted and measured for compensation. It was not possible precisely to quantify and evaluate more than three centuries of expropriation of land and labour and abuse of rights. That was a tangle beyond full unravelling.

Reparations could be awarded only to the living and to the estates of the recently dead. But the living in many cases were suffering by inheritance, by extension, from the expropriations and exploitation inflicted upon their distant ancestors, which had left later generations bereft of opportunities and possessions. To quantify that would be impossible.

The attempt had to be made, of course, but how far back should it reach? The TRC's own mandate was taken back no more than thirty years, not even back to the formulation of modern apartheid in 1948, not even one lifetime.

The TRC suggested a number of forms of reparation, including cash payments to identified victims of apartheid excesses by government, and payments by business and white individuals. Some payments were made by the government, but it was accused by human rights groups of being laggardly and stingy in implementing the TRC's recommendations. Government's attitude came across as an unwillingness to divert reparations payments from an exchequer that was hard pressed to finance essential reconstruction and development in the democratic society.

There was a widespread view in the ruling triumvirate that a special responsibility for reparations lay on big business as the main economic beneficiary of apartheid. A strong case could indeed be made out that big business, mining in particular, had not only benefited from apartheid but had actively promoted it and devised some of its mechanisms.

Business did, of course, play a role in bringing democracy to South Africa by initiating dialogue with the ANC while the latter was still fighting apartheid from exile. By that time, however, apartheid had become a handicap as the domestic and international opposition to it had begun to harm trade and industry. The corporate sector now stood to benefit more from democracy than from apartheid, especially if it could persuade the ANC to abandon what was left of its socialist ideals and instead embrace neo-liberalistic capitalism as the best way to bring employment and prosperity to the masses who were the ANC's main constituency.

There is some evidence that the ANC may have been influenced, not only while in exile but after it came to power, by assurances by big business that it would reciprocate the ANC's policy changes with active steps to repair white supremacy's damages to black society. It has since been alleged that big business, having seen apartheid abolished and capitalism entrenched in South Africa, has not shown as much enthusiasm and enterprise in helping to repair the damage and uplift the victims as it showed in achieving its own aims. In terms of unemployment and poverty, the victims are worse off than before, unemployment (most of it among blacks) having increased from 30 per cent in 1994 to 42 per cent in 2004. Nearly half of the black families were reckoned to live close to or within the official definition of poverty. To what extent big business might be blamed for this state of affairs was impossible to measure, however.

The corporate sector did indeed collectively establish a reparations fund, the Business Trust, but by late 2004 it had paid out or done nothing of significance. The TRC suggested a number of ways of exacting reparations from the corporate sector – a wealth tax, a once-only levy or a surcharge on profits. President Mbeki, however, rejected the notion of any of apartheid's beneficiaries being required to contribute to a reparations fund, and said such contributions should be made voluntarily by all South Africans.

In the absence of a formal channel for the payment of individual reparations by whites, either by compulsory levy or voluntary contribution, no assessment could be made of the willingness of individual whites to pay reparations. It seems likely that an appropriate survey would find that most whites were willing to pay some form of reparation if provided with a suitable channel.

An important element of the TRC process was the provision for individual amnesty for crimes committed both in furthering apartheid and in opposing it. Here, too, the issue still festered. Amnesty had been granted to some, but, despite Mbeki's decision in 2003 to close the matter, it refused to stay closed. Demands for amnesty or presidential pardon were still being pressed a year later by persons serving jail terms or still fearing prosecution.

After ten years of democracy, much of the bitterness and resentment created by apartheid remained unappeased. The desire for reconciliation still ran strong among both whites and blacks, however. It was effected with significant success on an individual level, but the mechanisms for promoting it on a national scale had not been created and so the gulf remained formally unbridged, crossed only by the flimsiest of official formations. Time might eventually close the gap if the issue was not disrupted by political protest; but the longer reconciliation remained unrealised, the uglier would be the scars left on the society.

★ ★ ★ ★

With the coming of democracy in South Africa the whites found the old issue of land ownership heaving up from the past like a monster resurrected from a forgotten dormancy, breathing menace at their entitlement.

In the early days of their settlement the whites' affairs were dictated essentially by their need for land and labour. Later, when they had acquired as much of the land as they dared without jeopardising their black labour supply, it became more a matter of labour than of land. The ownership of the land was fixed, but labour supplies remained uncertain, fluctuating with economic and political influences.

For the blacks, however, land ownership had always been a major and unresolved grievance about which they could do little other than to wait for the inevitable end of white domination. When that came, however, they found that the issue was anything but simple to resolve.

The division of the land, made through generations of bloodshed and war, was formalised in modern times by the Natives Land Act of 1913, which pegged most of the country for the whites. Later came the extension of the black homelands in order to further protect the labour supply, and finally there was the redrawing of the homelands in the abortive effort to make them independent bantustans and give the whites undisturbed possession of the rest of the country.

When democracy came to be negotiated in the nineties, the redivision of the land was found to be far more complex than the redivision of political power. The bantustans posed no great problem; after the more intractable leaders had been sidelined, the territories were simply absorbed into the new provinces. But the ownership of the land, all the land in the whole country, could not so easily be resolved, for it was wrapped up in two disparate and intractable systems.

One of them kept the former homelands locked in communal tribal ownership. While this had the advantage of providing a social safety net, it had the disadvantage of keeping those who farmed the land in a medieval dead-end of subsistence agriculture, unable to put up the land as collateral for loans for expansion or improvement. The ANC government could not easily bring the tribal land into the capitalist system prevailing in the national economy without antagonising the traditional leaders, the chiefs and headmen, whose power was derived primarily from their ability to allocate land use.

The other system, the one prevailing in most of the country, put the land in private ownership, almost all white. Land title was inextricably bound up with the respect for property that was intrinsic to Western democracy. Title of most of the white-owned land ran too far back into history, and had run through too many hands, to be successfully challenged except, perhaps, on a communal basis, and even then not always with certainty. It had besides become embedded in the national economy.

This applied even to land seized relatively recently, such as the large expanses of Zulu territory expropriated by the British colonial authorities after the final defeat of Zulu military power at the end of the 19th century, and converted into lush sugar farms by the new white owners and their descendants.

It was the same, though to a lesser extent, even with the land seized from blacks and given to whites by the apartheid government after 1948 under its efforts to remove 'black spots' from what had been declared white areas. De Klerk's National Party government had, however, made a start with land reform by introducing legislation providing for the return of such land to its previous owners by state purchase.

Land reform was nevertheless going to be a can of worms for the first democratic government. Original ownership of the land was in many cases so open to dispute as to be beyond any clinical restitution. Reckless restitution might endanger the economy and the wellbeing of the state. Still, the can had to be opened.

The impracticability of subjecting the modern economy to ancient land ownership claims was recognised by the government of national unity. It was decided to meet legitimate black demands by purchasing land with state funds from willing sellers at market prices. A commission was set up to hear land claims, and a special court to decide claims the commission was unable to resolve. No claim would be considered that went back beyond 1913, the year of the infamous Land Act.

Some activists felt this pegging meant that the fundamental issue of land reform would remain unresolved, for most of the land taken by whites from blacks had been acquired before 1913. Any other way, however, would have entailed a tortuous backtracking into ancient tribal claims whose basis or boundaries would in some cases be tenuous. Almost all land in South Africa had been taken by conquest at one time or another. The whites' conquest was the most recent; was it too recent to be considered the same as the others? There was the further point that arbitrary awards on a tribal basis would strengthen the chief-dominated communal system, from which the government evidently sought to move away.

White farmers' organisations recognised the need for land reform and supported the government's programme, backed by the farmers' main church, the DRC. According to the farmers' bodies, land reform was hampered not by a lack of willing sellers but by the government's failure to allocate enough funds to pay market prices for all the land on offer.

Increasingly the land issue became shadowed by Mugabe's seizure of white farms in Zimbabwe. As the PAC and the radical Azanian People's Organisation (AZAPO) moved towards demanding something similar in South Africa, the ANC repeated assurances that land seizures would not be tolerated. A Landless People's Movement was formed, however, and began to press for faster land reform.

Though rural land invasions were not widespread, they remained a serious worry for the white farming community. They were besides an incipient cause of concern for a government caught between, on the one hand, the need to protect civil order and the economy, and, on the other, the fear of antagonising black constituents by frustrating the black demand for land.

Blacks demanded land either for housing, in most cases in or near the urban areas where they worked, or for farming. Meeting the need for farmland, however, was complicated by the fact that much of the country was agriculturally unsuitable for large-scale settlement. Outside the relatively small high-rainfall areas, most land was suitable only for ranching or game farming requiring large acreages. To settle large numbers of people on such land would be to condemn them to unending poverty.

Even in the wetter regions, blacks given land under the reform programme, but not given start-up capital for livestock, implements, seeds, fertiliser and training, would not be able to farm it beyond a basic subsistence level at best. To thus turn productive commercial farmland into subsistence farmland would put a further dent in the economy. (The government had in fact been criticised by the white farming bodies for failing to provide this assistance when it redistributed land.)

Through the land reform issue ran a seemingly sinister but elusive thread: the murder in recent years of hundreds of white farmers. Since 1997, more than a thousand whites had by mid-2003 been murdered on their farms – an astonishingly high toll, exceeding even the number of whites (troops and civilians together) who were killed during the wars against white domination in either South Africa, Rhodesia or Namibia. At between ten and twelve a month, the murder rate made white farmers in South Africa the most endangered community in the world outside a war zone. It far exceeded that of whites killed in urban areas. At 313 per 100 000, it exceeded the national murder rate of 58 per 100 000.

White farming bodies believed the killings were orchestrated and aimed at driving the whites off the land to make way for blacks. A contrary finding was made, however, by two government-appointed commissions of inquiry. Both commissions reported in 2003 that the murders appeared to have criminal and not political motives. The police service, too, attributed most of the attacks to robbery. The Human Rights Commission in its report nevertheless linked the killings with land reform, urging the government to take measures to stop land invasions and speed up land reform. The white farming community for its part remained largely unconvinced that the murders were not political, pointing out that in several of the attacks nothing had been stolen, while some of the killings had been done with deliberate cruelty.

All things considered, it seemed that the ancient contest for the land was set to continue even into the democratic era.

CHAPTER 58

FREEDOM'S FRUITS

Miracles must by definition be temporary; a sustained miracle becomes the normal. Ten years after the event, South Africa's peaceful transition from white supremacy to democracy, widely hailed as a miracle in 1994, had largely held good.

For that, for their miraculous norm, all South Africans, but the white ones especially, had reason to be thankful. It could have gone the other way. It might still go wrong, but that seemed less likely than it had in 1994. What was created then had been fairly solidly reinforced by subsequent events.

The marvel of 1994 was sustained primarily because it was essentially a grass-roots thing, an upwelling of broad reformist sentiment across the colour line and across the classes, a demand which the politicians had merely to give political shape. This common sense of destiny and purpose persisted after 1994, even a decade afterwards. It might yet be overtaken by rising black resentment if the ANC government is unable significantly to close the gap between white affluence and black poverty. Nonetheless, a decade of majority rule had left the country in much better shape than many whites had expected in 1994.

While there had been serious mismanagement and corruption in government, there had been no critical failure of governance and public order, no coup, no civil war, no economic crash, none of the breakdowns that had been common among other African countries after being freed from white supremacy.

To a large extent this was attributable to the fact that, despite all the handicaps left by apartheid, the ANC was able to draw on a high level of qualification and capability among its members. Furthermore, it had inherited a vastly more developed and prosperous infrastructure than had existed anywhere else on the continent. The fact that these assets had been created partly through exploiting the blacks made them no less valuable to the new rulers. With that infrastructure came a large white population which was generally anxious for the new democracy to succeed – for they had the most to lose if it failed – and ready to commit their skills, energies and resources to that end. No other African country emerging from European domination had enjoyed these advantages, not even Zimbabwe to the same extent.

Whereas in most of Africa the blacks at independence acquired both political and economic control, in South Africa they got only some of each. Rather than being handed everything on a plate by a decamping colonial power, they had to negotiate a transfer of power with a strong and resident white hegemony anxious to retain as much influence as possible. The blacks' political power was therefore to some extent constrained by a negotiated constitution they had no good reason to override.

Compared with the misgovernance in newly-independent Africa, the ANC's rule had been remarkably proficient considering that it came into power as a novice at the game – enabling the whites to feel relatively comfortable even in their political nakedness. There had been a decline in the quality of some state services and amenities, but most whites were inconvenienced by this only when it involved services they could not acquire privately, such as the issuing of passports. Whites were more worried about what they saw as an almost explosive increase in violent crime and by the corruption at all levels of government, even in the cabinet. The government had cracked down on the corruption with some earnestness, however, and it had not been allowed to become as habitual and widespread as in other parts of Africa.

Though most whites probably failed to appreciate it, the ANC government had done much to ensure their security by improving the lot of the black poor by providing housing, clean water and electricity, measures that may have helped take the edge off the anger of blacks still seriously deprived and disadvantaged – for a while, at any rate.

A greatly under-appreciated achievement – a lesser miracle within the major one – had been the reasonably successful merging of the armed forces that had been at each others' throats for nearly three decades – the SADF, and MK and Apla.

White lifestyles had not been much changed by the advent of democracy. The privileges had largely been maintained. They had not, however, been guaranteed; now they were held not with complacency but with apprehension. Economically, the whites remained advantaged and the blacks in general disadvantaged. Politically, however, the balance had been reversed: in that sense the whites were now the disadvantaged ones. The degree of disadvantage depended, of course, on the extent to which the black majority eschewed anti-white racism. And that in turn was difficult to gauge in a situation where affirmative action and other reformative policies had to be implemented to eliminate white supremacy's inequities.

By giving equal protection to all, and not to specific groups, the new constitution effectively enshrined black power over whites by the fact of black numerical superiority. In that mathematical verity had always lain the basis of the whites' fear of the blacks. Now it had come to pass, and all that remained was to find out whether the ancient fear would be realised or fade away. With the white birth rate declining and the black one increasing (assuming the eventual waning of the HIV/Aids pandemic) the disparity in numbers could only widen. But that would not matter much if it was matched by an increasing commonality of interests, a commonality reflected in joint political ambitions.

That ideal had not been reached in the first decade of democracy, however. The white membership of the ANC was still miniscule. For all its professions of non-racialism, the ANC remained essentially the party of those who weren't white. It was the party not only of the 'historically disadvantaged', the victims of white supremacy, but also of the black new rich. Little need evidently was seen to recruit or even reach out to the whites, who mostly still sought their protection in the old white parties, the Democratic Party (later Democratic Front and then Democratic Alliance) and the Freedom Front.

The new constitution had failed to create not only the *volkstaat* sought by some Afrikaners but also the federal system that other whites had wanted as a means of limiting black power. While it gave the provinces more powers than they had held under the previous system, the ANC's voting majority meant these powers were exercised largely at its behest, and consolidated to its advantage in the National Council of Provinces.

Democracy had brought other disadvantages to the whites beside political emasculation. Affirmative action severely limited whites' career prospects in the private sector if they lacked a high level of specialist skill. Whites with little education and no skills became largely unemployable. Whites became ever rarer in the civil service, once the chief employment shelter for whites and the salvation of many – Afrikaners in particular – from poor white status. By 2003 the proportion of whites in the civil service had dropped to 20 per cent from 44 per cent in 1994.[1] Even before democracy, unemployment among whites had increased as blacks moved into an economy fast opening to them. White unemployment rose from one per cent in 1990 to ten per cent in 2004.[2]

The 'poor white' syndrome returned, though less widespread than before. For the first time since the Great Depression of the thirties, whites were seen begging in the streets. An extensive survey conducted in 2003 showed that more than a half million whites – about 10 per cent of the total white population – were living on incomes of less than R3 000 a month. Of these, more than a hundred and twenty thousand, or close to three per cent, were living on less than R1 000 a month – below the official poverty line.[3]

The proportion of destitution was still not as great as in the Great Depression, when a survey carried out in 1932 by the Carnegie Institute for the Dutch Reformed Church found that 22 per cent of the whites might be classed as poor white, and another 32 per cent as economically below normal, that is, unable to provide the basic needs of their families without government help.[4]

Unlike the thirties, when government set up work schemes for poor white victims of the depression, the poor whites of the new era were on their own. Otherwise, they must join the queues of poor blacks to get official relief. Some, too proud or too racist for that, sank deeper into poverty and despair, or sought the soup kitchens of the churches serving mainly whites. Some retreated at first into white slums and then into embryonic white squatter camps.

Faced with the barriers of affirmative action and black economic empowerment, young whites began increasingly to see their future either in a high level of skills or in self-employment – or in some other country where a white skin was not seen as a disadvantage in the job market.

Though white emigration had not reached the level of an exodus, it had contributed substantially to a decline in the white population. Since many of the emigrants were skilled, their loss represented a serious brain-drain, one not being balanced by the small skills influx. While the outflow increased after 1994, there had been a substantial haemorrhage even before then as whites grew more pessimistic about their future in the land of their birth. The outflow could have resulted in about five hundred and eighty thousand white South Africans living abroad as emigrants in 1999, according to a survey published in 2000 by Johan van Rooyen, the most extensive review yet made of white emigration.[5] Three hundred thousand were estimated to be living in the United Kingdom, 125 000 in the United States, 100 000 in Australia, 40 000 in Canada and 20 000 in New Zealand.[6]

Though Van Rooyen does not himself make the point, it is possible to calculate that these people would make up a white diaspora equivalent to more than ten per cent of South Africa's white population. A proportionate extraction from the population of the United States would have some thirty million Americans emigrating; and, in the case of the United Kingdom, about seven million.

Emigration from South Africa after the ANC came to power was at a rate of about nine thousand a year, mostly white, according to official statistics. These show an outflow of about fifty-five thousand between 1994 and 1999. However, Van Rooyen disputes the accuracy of the official statistics, which do not jibe with immigration figures issued by countries where the emigrants settled (often after not disclosing their intentions on leaving South Africa). He says the number of departures in this period might be double the official count, and could be as high as a hundred and sixty-five thousand.

The inflow of white immigrants was, of course, insignificant by comparison.

White South Africans fled their homeland for a number of reasons. These, according to Van Rooyen, included uncertainty about the future, falling standards, concerns about their children's education, the state of the economy, affirmative action and bleak job prospects, and loss of faith in the ANC-led government. But the chief reason was the perception of a threat from violent crime – a factor cited by 60 per cent of emigrants as their reason for leaving.

Many, if not most, of the emigrants were people whose skills opened foreign doors for them, hence the brain drain aspect of the ouflow. Rather than the government attempting to stem the skills haemorrhage by more openly addressing its causes, some of government's senior representatives at first dismissed the departures as 'good riddance' of unpatriotic people. As its damaging consequences became more apparent, however, they tended to mute their criticism.

Beside actual emigration ran the parallel phenomena of pseudo-emigration and psychological emigration, which were slightly different but intertwined. Both forms existed among whites who, unable or unwilling to leave the country, tried to withdraw from or shut out the influences that made others seek new homes abroad. Pseudo-emigrants, fleeing from the physical threat of crime, retreated into tighter security – the fenced and boom-guarded suburbs, higher perimeter walls, more razor and electric wires and dogs, costlier armed response services and so on. Psychological emigrants withdrew on a more abstract level, retreating in their minds as far as possible from the broader society in which they perceived the threats of black domination or even racism, of rejection by the new social mainstream and of cultural deterioration. By not participating in political or other forms of social interaction, by seceding from the wider community, they in fact lessened their opportunities to defend or promote their own interests.

For one reason or another, however, by the turn of the millennium most whites seemed determined to stay and take their chances as Africans of a different colour. For not only had white living standards not been degraded, but for the wealthier ones they had improved. By some measures, there was greater wealth at the top of the social pile than at any other time in South Africa's history. And the fact that the top of the pile was no longer all white gave a sense of security to almost everyone, even of faint hope to some at least of the blacks at the bottom. However, the glaring difference between the sometimes obscene wealth at the top and the excruciating poverty at the bottom did not bode well for social tranquillity in the future.

★ ★ ★ ★

While democracy gave the whites release from guilt and readmission to international respectability, it did not give them much of the accountable government that is supposed to be intrinsic to democracy. If accountability is measured by the ability of the voters to influence or replace their rulers, then the whites had very little of it at either local, provincial or parliamentary level, for by 2004 the ANC held power at all three levels throughout the country, and did not look like losing any of it for a long time. In effect, the whites had democracy only at the pleasure of the blacks, and this would remain the case until the racial differences were no longer material, which would not come about soon.

After a decade of democracy, the South Africans were finding that its political aspects were easier to install than the social ones. If under apartheid the blacks had felt alienated in their own country, many whites evidently felt much the same under democracy. It could not be said with certainty that most whites felt accepted by blacks rather than just tolerated by them. Blacks could perhaps make the same claim in reverse. It seemed that in general blacks were not reaching out to whites any more than whites were reaching out to blacks.

There were significant exceptions, of course, such as that reflected in the letter sent to President Mbeki in May 2004 by 110 prominent Afrikaans-speaking South Africans.[7] Expressing their appreciation for Mbeki's leadership, the group said he had 'enabled all South Africans, including us Afrikaans-speakers, to feel at home in our country and welcome in Africa and the world'. Assuring him of their support in making South Africa a success, the group said he could depend on 'our participation and critical interaction' in this regard. Members of the group are said to have had regular meetings with Mbeki.

At a lower level, however, and especially at the private social level, close interaction between whites and blacks remained exceptional rather than common. Ten years was perhaps too short a time for black bitterness and white prejudice to be wiped away. There was no good reason, however, for anyone to believe that it would not come about in time.

For the present, the whites faced an elemental difficulty in overlaying an African identity on their European cultural inheritance. They were Africans and yet they were not Africans. They were Africans by reason of their birth, and in many cases long ancestry, in Africa. But they were Europeans not only in physical appearance but also in language, habits, traditions, literature, music, dance and other culture. A common national identity based on shared history and interests could indeed be contrived with the blacks in South Africa because of the relatively long and large white presence there. But this was less easily extended to the continental identity – and, beyond that, the diasporan one fostered by the ANC government.

Integration was taking place at various social levels – school, workplace, sport – but it was a slow process that would need at least a full generation to produce clearly visible results. For the present, the whites had no option but to accept affirmative action in all fields and activities as a necessary function of reconciliation and equalising. It was at its very least a form of recompense for the damage the whites inflicted on black social structures through the migrant labour and bantustan systems and the land seizures. Somewhere along the line a price must be paid for the cheap labour and the other advantages of apartheid. Part of the price had already been paid indirectly in the form of a high crime rate that was in part a direct consequence of the ravaging of the black social structures by apartheid and its colonial antecedents.

Affirmative action was borrowed in name and policy from the Americans, but it had different significance in South Africa. For the Americans, it meant giving the black minority a chance to rise out of the disadvantages imposed on them by the dominant white majority, and who would remain the dominant majority. For the white minority in South Africa, however, it meant compensating for the disadvantages they had imposed on the majority – and hoping now for the best under that majority's domination.

It was easier, however, to impose affirmative action in the marketplace than in culture – in sport and the arts. In sport, the opium of the white public, it had to be imposed in the face of resistance to integration on the part of many white administrators and clubs, who feared it would drag their sports down from the international status they had enjoyed for generations. Imposing racial quotas for sporting teams was in turn a more straightforward matter than democratising the arts, which carried the danger of politicising them.

The relative smallness of the white population had meant that in the past the classical culture of the whites, the culture brought from Europe, had depended heavily on state subsidisation. Come democracy, however, some of that revenue had to be diverted to the vital business of repairing apartheid's damage to black society – and to promoting the black culture that most whites had tended to view patronisingly if not disparagingly. The ballet, opera, drama and orchestral companies suffered hard times, but mostly survived in abridged form – and with a growing proportion of blacks in the companies, suggesting that the arts of Europe might remain safe in black hands after all.

The Italian novelist Alberto Moravia declared that 'there is no greater suffering for man than to feel his cultural foundations giving way beneath his feet.' He wrote that in 1972 about black Africa, but his words are equally applicable to the white

Africans today. In the 1994 settlement the whites implicitly accepted an obligation to help dismantle apartheid and repair its damage. The ANC for its part implicitly accepted an obligation to respect and protect the identity and interests of the whites – not their privileges and their lifestyles but their culture, inheritance and legitimate aspirations.

Ten years later the identity of the whites still had political connotations, closely allied to the question of affirmative action. A common identity could not easily be defined or accepted while the majority of the population was being treated preferentially in order to compensate for the disadvantages imposed on it by the former minority power. The whites' acceptance as Africans was thus linked to the question of when affirmative action would end. Affirmative action maintained indefinitely as preferential treatment for blacks would mean the gradual disadvantagement of the whites and their eventual subjugation in second-class status – a reversal of the apartheid situation that would be equally heinous.

After surrendering their supremacy in 1994 the whites in South Africa were left in a situation oddly analogous with that of the blacks in the United States. Both were minorities in a society politically dominated by people of a different race, and whose culture they were required to adopt, or adapt to, despite it being dissimilar to that of their own forefathers.

The analogy is made especially singular by the fact that in all other respects the two groups are dissimilar – the black Americans coming from a background of slavery and African culture, white South Africans from one of mastery and European culture; the black Americans being economically disadvantaged, and the white South Africans economically dominant.

Unlike the African Americans, however, the white South Africans have not come under strong pressure to adopt the culture and language of the majority. Instead, the pressure is in reverse, obliging the blacks to adopt major elements of the culture of the whites, whose language and ways are key to the technological and economic levers essential for black advancement. English has become entrenched as the common medium of communication, though with distinctly African overtones.

It is inevitable, however, that the whites who remain in Africa will gradually become ever more Africanised in their speech, their habits, their entire culture. They have already moved significantly away from their European roots in all these aspects. At the same time, the blacks will become ever more Westernised, moving further away from their tribal cultures, as they deal more closely with the shrinking world outside. The Africanisation of the whites will perhaps be the more gradual process. White Africans they may already be, but they are still greatly different from the black Africans in a number of ways.

The whites have no option, however, but to accept that the milieu in which they are seeking acceptance of their African identity places them not in the First World of their forebears but in the Third World of their fellow Africans, not in the developed world of their cultural heritage but in the developing world of their political inheritance. It is on the African continent, with all its perceived disadvantage, that the native whites must find their future. They must now fight Africa's fights, not Europe's or

America's. They must join their fellow Africans, for instance, in their battle against the legacy of debt that Europe has left them and against the exploitation of Africa that is still exacted by the Western nations through unfair trading practices.

★ ★ ★ ★

Democracy inevitably exposed the whites to the envy and resentment felt by blacks as the whites retained their general affluence while the blacks moved only slowly out of their general poverty, a poverty attributed by some of their leaders solely to exploitation of blacks under white supremacy. This situation was obliquely but famously referred to by President Mbeki when in 1998 he suggested that, four years after the advent of democracy, there were still two South African nations, one white and rich and the other black and poor.

That was certainly true. But many whites were perhaps surprised not at the truth of what he said but at the fact that he felt constrained to state it, implying that the whites were at fault for allowing this state of affairs to continue.

It was, of course, an undesirable situation, as is much remaining from the old order, but it could hardly have been corrected overnight after 1994. It was a situation created over more than three centuries, and it may take more than a single generation to rectify it. It could never have been expected that the blacks and whites would instantly become either culturally or economically homogenised by the advent of democracy. But Mbeki was perhaps thinking not about the perpetuation of the inherent differences but about the perpetuation of the state of mind among the whites that arises from those differences, especially about the whites' slowness in helping the blacks to climb out of the pit of deprivation into which they were kept by white supremacy and exploitation.

It was doubtful that the whites, in general, were oblivious of or indifferent to the hardships still suffered by the majority of the blacks through unemployment, hunger and lack of houses and other amenities. No white could drive past an informal settlement without seeing the warning to his continued privilege that each shack signalled. Most whites, however, would probably have had some difficulty in figuring out just what Mbeki expected them to do to rectify the situation. Neither he nor anyone else in government ever spelled it out. Mbeki might have felt that in this the whites were showing the same attitude as they previously had in passively opposing apartheid but doing nothing concrete to combat it. It was, of course, easier for the whites to acknowledge the evil of apartheid and collaborate in its demise than it was for them to sacrifice its benefits. But some of them might have contended that the onus for transformation lay primarily with the government, which was better equipped for the job, and only secondly with organised commerce and industry. And only much further down the line with white individuals.

White South Africans' anxieties about their future were not eased by Mbeki's persistent criticisms of their attitude to 'reformation' and nation-building. His criticisms may have been inspired by his expressed fear that if the gap between the black poor and the white rich was not closed significantly and soon, black resentment could explode dangerously. Still, the whites in general seemed to feel they had done just about all they could to make up for the past by surrendering power, confessing their sins, putting their fate in the hands of those they once dominated and exploited, and co-operating in affirmative action measures and black empowerment. It appeared that not all blacks saw it in such simple terms, however.

Some blacks believed, perhaps as a result of earlier ANC and PAC propaganda, that the whites had not surrendered power voluntarily but only after being vanquished by the liberation movements backed by international pressures. The termination of apartheid was seen not as compromise but as conquest, and therefore the whites had no claim to concessions. This view ignored the fact that, though white supremacy was indeed doomed when the decision was taken to negotiate a settlement, it was not yet dead, and still had plenty of power behind it. MK and Apla played a relatively minor role in ending white supremacy, never testing the power of the government security forces. White supremacy was brought down by economic and political pressures, by the people in the streets and by the whites' own consciences. MK and the ANC's ex-ile wing gave crucial support and direction to those pressures, of course, and certainly hastened white supremacy's end, but were not the only factors in its demise.

Whether the whites now live under majority rule or black supremacy is essential-ly a semantic matter, for the effects are the same either way. White rule in Africa was called white supremacy because blacks were legislatively barred from equality with whites. Blacks now in power can argue that their rule does not amount to black su-premacy because there are no legal obstacles blocking whites from equality. The real-ity, however, is that in every case blacks call the shots politically and whites don't.

The urgency Mbeki saw for faster transformation remains, however. Bound up with that is a palpable need for whites to identify more with their black country-men, and to sympathise more with the majority who remain disadvantaged, whose daily lives have remained unchanged by the miracle of 1994. The Human Sciences Research Council reported in 2004 that 57 per cent of South Africans were living below the poverty line of R1 290 a month for a family of four.[8] Translated demo-graphically, this meant that the majority of the black majority were living in pover-ty. While democracy had brought prosperity to many blacks, it had left many more of them behind, according to the HSRC's figures. The gap between rich and poor had widened among both blacks and whites.

Another survey estimated that between forty per cent and sixty per cent of the urban labour force lived in squatter shacks in informal settlements.[9]

The shadowy threat that has lurked at the back of white consciousness for cen-turies, the fear of a mass black assertion of demand, has not been removed by de-mocracy. If anything, it has been amplified by the new freedom. It will remain as long as a large proportion of the black people live in poverty and see little chance of getting above it.

CHAPTER 59

FOR BETTER OR FOR WORSE?

Africa's liberation at last from white domination has left a past full of uncertainties, of questions unanswered and issues still awaiting a certain place in history.

Among the questions: did the presence of the Europeans do more harm than good; was colonialism more destructive than beneficial? Where might Africa have been today had the Europeans never come as conquerors, had the Africans been left to their own devices? And the question underlying it all: how was it possible for so few Europeans to dominate so many Africans for so long?

Answers to these questions remain matters of conjecture and dispute nearly half a century after the collapse of colonialism, and a decade after the dissolution of the last of white supremacy.[*] For now, the answers tend to depend largely on the background and outlook of whoever is giving them.

Some might hold that the consequences of colonialism should not be judged by the norms of today when their causes were rooted in the norms of a different time. This line of thought might be extended to the thesis that white supremacy, both in its attitudes and in its practice, was inevitable, given the situation prevailing when the whites first settled in Africa. Most whites of the time would almost certainly have taken the view that to treat the blacks as equals would have been irrational since they were seen to be patently inferior in terms of the Europeans' technology and other concepts of civilisation. Furthermore, equality might have been considered unwise, given that the blacks so greatly outnumbered the whites. Who in his right senses, they might have asked, would freely submit to domination by inferiors?

Notions of black inferiority arose soon after the arrival of the Europeans in Africa, based largely on the indigenous peoples' lesser technical sophistication. The first Europeans to arrive did indeed find social sophistication in organised systems of government, and technical sophistication in skilled metal-working and weaving in some parts of Africa. Whatever respect they had for these attributes, however, appears to have been overridden by the ability their better technology gave them to enslave and exploit the blacks. If egalitarianism was a rare concept in Europe, how

---

[*]While there has in recent years been a tendency in some quarters to use the term 'colonialism' as a catchall for all white domination, the practice overlooks the difference between colonialism and white settlement, and the even greater difference between white settlement in the British and other colonies, and the earlier Afrikaner settlement in South Africa, which was colonial only in the minds of politicians and business interests in Europe, and not in the minds of the settlers who from the late 17th century had identified themselves not with Europe but with Africa.

much less acceptable would it have been, for instance, at the Cape, as the settlers competed with the Iron-Age indigenous peoples for land and resources? Though egalitarian views existed among Europeans long before Exeter Hall, they became dominant only after the Second World War. Only then did white supremacy in Africa become seriously and widely criticised by whites elsewhere.

Africans, of course, have seldom thought otherwise. They commonly view European slavery, colonialism and settlement as malignities without which the continent would have been better off. Few, if any, of the modern African societies have attributed any advances they have made to their colonial inheritance. Rather, colonialism and apartheid became dirty words in Africa, afflictions blamed largely for the generally benighted state of the continent as most of the rest of the world became increasingly sophisticated and prosperous.

Colonialism was accused of having left African states ill-equipped for independence when the Europeans decamped. In the worst scenario of blame, the colonialists left their former possessions plundered of resources, the infrastructures rudimentary, the services minimal, and the inhabitants ill-educated and unprepared for self-government. Deliberately kept down and backward for generations, the people had been left socially crippled.

The largest white settlement, the one in South Africa, was accused of having subjugated the richest part of the continent for the benefit of resident and foreign whites, of having driven the indigenous inhabitants off the best lands and herded them into reserves designed as pools of cheap labour, of having denied them proper education and training and kept them politically emasculated and perpetually subservient to white interests.

The opposing view is that, for all its iniquities, the intrusion of the Europeans left Africa better equipped to stand in the modern world than it would otherwise have been; that the Europeans and their settlers created administrative, medicinal, educational and economic infrastructures which the Africans would not have been able to provide on their own. And that, white privilege and racism aside, the white settlers and their descendents have contributed materially to the development of their countries, to the benefit of everyone living there.

There are no doubt both emotional and political reasons for the reluctance of many black people to acknowledge any benefits from white hegemony. Who could easily associate benefit with oppression, exploitation and humiliation? It was certainly politically imprudent to acknowledge any benefit throughout the long struggles against colonialism and apartheid. Afterwards, when the newly independent states began crashing into misgovernance, autocracy and poverty, colonialism was generally seen – or seized on – as an excuse for these failings. It couldn't therefore be given credit for any benefits.

Whether Africa would have been better off had the Europeans never come can only be a matter of conjecture. That conjecture can, however, be directed fairly convincingly at the notion that European colonialism and settlement on balance did Africa more harm than good.

It is true, of course, that as late as the beginning of the Scramble most of the continent from the Sahel to the Limpopo was largely undeveloped. There were few hardened roads, no railways (at a time when there were more than thirty thousand kilometres of railways in Britain, and more than twenty-five thousand in France), few harbours, no electricity, no hospitals, no schools imparting the knowledge of the wider world (except in the Muslim communities of the Sahel and east coast). Most of these amenities were provided by the colonialists and settlers. They opened markets and created industries. African living standards and life spans were improved by the medical science, new foods and agricultural techniques and economic development brought by the Europeans.

They did all this, of course, mostly for their own ends, certainly in the beginning and only later with some sense of moral obligation. Either way, many Africans believe, it was inadequate because it was essentially exploitive. Whatever benefits the Africans derived tended to be incidental; seldom if ever did the colonialists put the interests of the colonised above their own. Whether the native peoples would have had more of these benefits without colonialism is difficult to determine, since most of the pre-colonial nations and social systems were debased or destroyed by the Europeans.

What can be determined, however, is that when the Europeans began to encroach into the interior, much of Africa had settled into a number of fairly well-defined nation states distinguishable by ethnicity, language and custom. True, borders were in some cases not clearly defined, and conflict between the states at times altered the boundaries and even the dominant race – as has happened in Europe even in modern times. But there was sufficient permanence of habitation, identity and boundaries for there to be a large degree of demographic permanence, though still vulnerable to the vagaries of ethnic competition.

This dispensation would probably have become more or less fixed had the colonial powers not divided the continent into artificial states according to where they bumped noses in their scramble for possession. Boundaries would have tended to follow the natural features that in many instances divided the different ethnic groups. Nations would have tended to be mono-ethnic rather than the artificial and sometimes monstrous aggregates of tribes with differing languages and cultures that the colonialists created by force, and whose development after independence was hampered by the consequent tribal friction. Each nation would have been regulated by the often-elaborate social structures and customs it had evolved over generations – and in this context it is important to note that even if not technologically advanced, many African nations were highly developed in other respects. Almost all had mature and complex languages, effective social and political systems, and strong moral codes.

The pre-colonial societies might not, of course, have constituted ideal states, any more than there has ever been an ideal state in Europe or elsewhere. Some might have continued to fight each other. They might have fallen under dictators and fought civil wars and become as corrupt and bankrupt as did some of the synthetic nations created by the colonialists. There is no good reason to doubt, however, that had the Africans been left to their own devices, but in contact with the wider world, they would have advanced more rapidly than they did under the constraints that colonialism and white hegemony imposed in order to further their own interests above those of the colonised.

The Africans might not, of course, have been able as quickly to provide the development and infrastructure that the colonial powers installed. Ill-equipped with the skills and capital necessary to exploit their own resources and build their own infrastructures, they might indeed have turned to European developers and financiers – and perhaps ended up subject to economic colonialism, something similar to that left by the departing territorial colonialists in the form of today's debt-traps and unfair trade.

Nonetheless, had the European contacts been confined to trade and cultural exchanges and not extended through conquest to artificial subdivision and agglomeration, to subjugation and exploitation, the Africans would presumably have been able to adopt Western technology and synthesise it with their own cultures. Within their natural ethnic, cultural and territorial boundaries, unhampered by colonial constraint and exploitation, they would perhaps have made faster progress in catching up with the Europeans. This generalisation cannot, of course, be extended across the continent, given the wide disparity of African cultures, but it surely would apply to a number of black nations.

For the time it took them to catch up, however, they would have been at a disadvantage against foreign competition both in Africa and abroad. And how long it would have taken them to catch up is again a matter of conjecture, but it could not have been less than a couple of generations.

Basil Davidson, one of the most eminent of the Africanists, has pointed out that Iron-Age Africa faced a developmental crisis even before the Europeans arrived. Thereafter the Europeans destroyed not only the weaknesses of the old African systems but also the strengths. When they withdrew 'everything of basic social meaning remained to be renewed or built afresh'. In this situation, says Davidson, it was inevitable that the Africans would tend to lay all their troubles at the feet of colonialism, 'whereas, in truth, these troubles were inherent in the need to undertake and carry through the far-reaching reconstruction of Iron-Age society which colonialism had provoked but never realized'.[1]

★ ★ ★ ★

The question of why comparatively few whites were able to dominate much larger numbers of blacks for so long – for more than three centuries in one place or another – is one whose answer can essentially be found in the Africans' comparative backwardness in technology. More complex is the matter of why they were backward in this respect – why many sub-Saharan communities had no wheel, no writing, no mathematics, no machinery, no gunpowder, no maritime expertise, no horses, no fine cloths, no stone-masonry or carpentry, no coinage, clocks or other appurtenances of sophistication when the Europeans arrived.

It suited exploitive Europeans to attribute African backwardness to intellectual

494

inferiority, but that attribution has never had any validity. The Africans were technologically backward not because of any intellectual shortcomings but because of environmental and other factors having nothing to do with intelligence. It had more to do with the fact that when the Europeans arrived, most of sub-Saharan Africa was caught in a backwater of time, untouched by the social currents, the exchanges of trade and ideas, that had long been swirling between the Mediterranean and the Far East, and northwards into Europe.

African societies at that time were in different stages of development, ranging from the relative sophistication of those in the north and east who had some form of contact with the wellsprings of technology outside Africa, to those to the centre, the west and the south who were still working their way out of the Iron Age. The isolation of most of these peoples from more advanced societies and ideas was enforced in part by the desert barrier of the Sahara, and by the tsetse fly belt stretching from the Atlantic eastward across the centre of the continent. The trypanosomiasis disease (nagana) carried by the fly being fatal to domestic animals, sustained animal transport across the tsetse belt was impracticable. Human activity in the belt was inhibited by the sleeping sickness transmitted by the fly.

The tsetse-free highlands and coastal belt of the Horn and East Africa no doubt provided a narrow passage for people and their livestock, but once the great Bantu migration had passed through, it presumably became blocked to further passage by powerful communities now settled and hostile to intruders. Thereafter there was probably little or no traffic either way through the highland/coastal passage. The east coastal communities did indeed have regular communication by way of trade across the Indian Ocean with Arab and Indian societies, but their influence did not extend deep into their own hinterland.

★ ★ ★ ★

Human development has depended hugely on the communication of knowledge and ideas, whose advancement in turn required a firm base in food production. A lifestyle based on foods that were neither plentiful nor diverse was not conducive to social development. Geographic factors made this adversity more pronounced in Africa than in Eurasia. The latter landmass has been described as having an east–west axis providing a commonality of latitude and climatic cycles that facilitated food production and the spreading of agricultural expertise and the other expertise that grows from it. Africa, on the other hand, has a north–south axis that is latitudinally cut by climatic and seasonal differences that initially inhibited the spread of agricultural expertise and other knowledge and ideas.[2]

Technological development among African nations was hampered by various other natural handicaps – climates both enervating and subject to extremes of drought and flood, debilitating diseases, and perhaps the communal and conformist social styles enforced by a dangerous environment. In much of sub-Saharan Africa, people moved either on foot or by canoe, but the few rivers were not conducive to north–south exchanges since most ran latitudinally. Efforts to sail by sea around the land barriers would have been hampered by a straight and dangerous coastline that challenges even modern motorised vessels, and by generally unfavourable winds and currents. Maritime ventures were in any case made unimperative by a relative abundance of game, pasture and cropland in the moister regions where most of the people in the central and southern continent lived. The main pressure for onward movement came from population increase, and there was always new land to move into – until the Europeans came up from the south.

In this situation, the arrival by sea of the Europeans and their advanced technology had a time-machine impact on the indigenous peoples. Suddenly the future rushed back to meet them – but they weren't yet ready for it. They were several centuries behind in time; some were where the Britons had been some two thousand years previously, and the peoples of the Mediterranean and Middle East even earlier.

White supremacy in Africa had different levels, ranging from the near-absolute form in apartheid South Africa to the paternalistic semi-citizenship of the French. But in all its forms it was universal and invincible, putting almost all of Africa under the domination of the Europeans and their settlers for nearly a century. It was a domination made extraordinary by the huge disparity in numbers. Other than in South Africa, where the whites at one stage were outnumbered by no more than five to one, the Europeans were always hugely outnumbered, often by thousands to one.

They were nevertheless able to dominate the natives through the superior technology they brought with them, backed by strong economic and political systems. Maritime technology had enabled them in the first place to cross the oceans to conquer foreign peoples and to resupply their outposts there. Superior weaponry and mobility – the gun and the horse and later the steam and internal combustion engine – made possible both the conquest and its perpetuation.

It was essentially from the time warp phenomenon and its coincidence with physical difference that racism was born. The difference, of course, has nothing to do with intellectual capacity, which in turn is not the sole creator of technology, environmental factors also having an influence. And Africans are, of course, no less intelligent than Europeans and can easily adopt technology provided all other factors are equal – which they still are not, not even in America after generations of supposed coexistence between blacks and whites numbering many millions in each case.

Social development tends to be exponential – the more a society knows the faster it increases its knowledge. Most African societies were still in an early stage of this process, compared with the Europeans, when the latter arrived. Tomorrow had come too soon for the Africans, and their struggle to adjust was hampered by the very Europeans who had catapulted them into the future – hampered by white prejudice and the exploitation and social destruction wrought by slavery, colonialism and settler ambitions.

Both whites and blacks have today to cope with inherited burdens: the whites with the guilt of their past supremacy and exploitation, the blacks with the disadvantages remaining from the relative backwardness of their forefathers. It is far easier for the whites to throw off the guilt of the past misdeeds than it is for the blacks to overcome the effects of those misdeeds while at the same time trying to complete the leap in time that was forced by the arrival of the Europeans.

The effects of the colonial conquest in sub-Saharan Africa may to a degree have been shaped by its very lateness, coming as it did, for instance, long after the European intrusion into Latin America (except, of course, for the Cape and the Portuguese footholds in Angola and Mozambique). Argentina and Brazil had been settled by Europeans for some two centuries before they became independent of Spain and Portugal in 1816 and 1822 respectively. Almost all the Latin American states were independent republics by 1844, whereas most of the present African states were not created in their modern form until some four decades later, in the Scramble, and did not gain independence until the 1960s, more than a century after those in South America. This meant that the influence – for better or worse – of European interests, technology and settlement came later to Africa and was of shorter duration. European dominance of the indigenous peoples was, of course, more complete in Latin America than in Africa, but then so was the absorption of the natives into the subsequent societies.

The eventual departure of the colonial powers ostensibly gave the Africans an opportunity to remake the continent in a more rational form than that imposed by the Europeans, closer to what it might have been had the Europeans not arrived. This would have meant dismantling numbers of states and creating new ones more closely following the pre-colonial ethnic and geographical divisions. Whether it was feasible is uncertain, however. Most Africans evidently thought it wasn't, for one of the first decisions taken by the Organisation of African Unity when it was formed in 1963 was to leave the colonial boundaries unchanged. To do otherwise, it was reckoned, would be to attempt to unmake the omelette. It was not only a matter of ethnic differences, but also of economic and infrastructural questions – who would get the mineral wealth and who wouldn't, who would run the trans-border railways, who might be cut off from the sea, who would have to build new capitals, new parliaments and airports, and so on.

There were heavy prices to pay for the OAU's decision. For instance, bloody and damaging civil wars between different ethnic groups forced together by false colonial boundaries, such as the Biafran secessionist attempt in Nigeria and the conflict between the Sudan's Muslim north and Christian / animist south. The most telling case in point is that of the former Belgian Congo. So huge, so rich in resources, so diverse in its tribes and its neighbours is this so-called democratic republic that its inhabitants, together with some of the neighbours and rapacious interests even further away, have been engaged in warfare within the country ever since it obtained ostensible independence in 1960.

A good practical case might have been made for breaking the Belgian Congo into smaller and more natural states in 1960. Politically, however, it might have been considerably more difficult – though perhaps easier than present generations are finding the task of resolving the mess that now exists there. However, the Belgians, even more than the other colonial powers, were more concerned with getting out than with what they left behind.

All the colonial powers, except to some extent the French, left little of their own professed democracy behind when they decamped. They could hardly have done otherwise, colonialism being itself undemocratic, its purposes subjugation and exploitation. The departing British made perfunctory efforts to throw some democratic fabric on their colonial structures, but this hardly sufficed to install the democracy the Europeans themselves had learned through trial and error over centuries. Having destroyed the indigenous social systems, the Europeans left in their place only alien and unworkable semi-systems. Small wonder that democracy didn't at first work in independent Africa, that colonialism was in many cases replaced by autocratic and corrupt systems that were even more immoral than colonialism had been.

The policy professed by the British of helping the Africans to reach their own level of 'civilisation' was in some measure fraudulent in that no strong effort was made to educate and train them until shortly before the Second World War, when colonialism was already doomed and the natives were beginning to demand the freedom to run their own lives. British expenditure on colonial infrastructure was directed mainly at promoting the interests of the British – trade, labour, taxation and law enforcement – rather than those of the colonised peoples. Education was for long left mostly to the missionaries.

If the future rushed up too quickly for the Iron-Age Africans, it came up too quickly for the colonial powers too. Until the Second World War spun the clock forward, they had figured they had plenty of time to achieve whatever objectives they perceived in their colonies. Suddenly the major objective became evacuation as different political, economic and moral imperatives arose in the wake of the war. The European powers almost in bewilderment found themselves abandoning colonial ambitions and concepts and scuttling home.

Colonialism has gone now, as has the Cold War that rushed in to fill the vacuum left by its departure. Apartheid is now history. The Africans are at last being left to their own devices – apart from the handicaps of unfair trade practices and debts still imposed at long range by Europe and the United States. The white Africans who remain are no longer symptomatic of the impact of the time warp. No longer are they part of the problem; they are part of the solution. The question now is whether, or to what extent, this reality will be accepted by the blacks who find themselves in power without having fully overcome the double disadvantage of the time warp and of past white domination.

CHAPTER 60

MOTHER AFRICA

Four centuries after the Europeans arrived in sub-Saharan Africa, four decades after they began withdrawing from their colonies, their genetic sediment survives across the continent, mostly now to its benefit.

The native whites are scattered over the mainland and the offshore island states in pools ranging in size from the millions in South Africa* to the thousands in Kenya, Zimbabwe and Namibia, and the hundreds in Mauritius, Seychelles, Madagascar and mainland states such as Gabon.

All told they probably number around five million, somewhat less than in the heyday of white supremacy. Their numbers are unlikely to increase, more likely to decline. There will be no more white settlers, not in significant numbers. The white settler has been consigned to history.

The settlers now are going the other way – both whites and blacks seeking a new life outside Africa. Thousands of black Africans slip illegally into Europe, many risking their lives in leaky boats on the Mediterranean. In many cases, those blacks with qualifications emigrate legally, to America as well as to Europe, in a brain drain the continent cannot afford. After forty years or so of independence, many of the black Africans, it seems, want to escape from Africa, to the lands where the whites still rule and life is better. If they see irony in this it probably doesn't bother them – they are more concerned with improving their lives, or even with mere survival.

There are mini-migrations within Africa too, notably a steady stream of thousands of Africans into South Africa from as far away as Nigeria and Senegal, looking for opportunity in the richest country on the continent. Their influx is resented by many whites, not only from the basic xenophobia shared with many black South Africans but also because it swells the proportion of the whites' numerical minority, or at least emphasises it.

For all their centuries of settlement in Africa, the native whites are at present more insecure and vulnerable than ever before. Stripped of the power that once enabled their kind to rule all Africa, they live in a state of anxiety about the present and of uncertainty about the future. These fears persist despite their having experienced long periods of black rule – more than forty years in Kenya, 24 in Zimbabwe, 14 in Namibia, and 10 in South Africa. In none of these countries is the whites' Africanness unequivocally accepted, despite their long presence. Some of those in

*About 4 400 000 in the 2003 census, which some academics believe under-counted the whites.

South Africa have an ancestry there stretching back ten generations or more. The forebears of some were born at the Cape when Louis XIV ruled in France and Oliver Cromwell in England. Yet many blacks, while not necessarily seeing the native whites as aliens, still have difficulty accepting them as fellow Africans.

The people of negroid origin who form the great majority in Africa are happy to recognise African fellowship with peoples of a lighter complexion or otherwise different physiognomy, such as the Arabs of the Mediterranean littoral, the Berbers of the Sahel, and the Hamites of the Horn, and they presumably will come to accept also the Caucasians of the south when the stigma of white supremacy has faded enough.

Black reluctance to accept the whites seemingly has less to do with ethnicity than with history, more to do with resentment than with race. Though the blacks of South Africa did not take hatred with them into the new democratic dispensation, they did bring understandable resentment of what white supremacy had done to their kind. The resentments of the past persist long after their causes – though not the effects – have disappeared. While black Africans in general increasingly recognise that colonialism is becoming outworn as a catchall excuse for all their misfortunes and failings, they see good reason to believe that its deleterious effects persist. Certainly the humiliation and exploitation of colonialism and apartheid are woven forever as a bitter thread in the black cultural fabric.

The resentment of white supremacy may not dim until those who experienced it at first hand have all died, perhaps not until their descendants can no longer claim with justification that they are still suffering from its deprivations and exploitation. And that may take more than a generation or two, perhaps not until the whites are no longer perceived to be a minority still unfairly privileged.

★ ★ ★ ★

More than those elsewhere in Africa, the whites in South Africa are an ethnological curiosity, unusual in a number of ways. They had been singular in their minority power and their reprehensible efforts to maintain it, then in their brave surrender of it, and now are notable for their capacity to benefit their continent.

The native whites now live – not always uncomfortably, it must be said – among the debris of their power, their polities displaced, their administrations disbanded, their cultures endangered, their privileges waning, their histories revised and their heroes sometimes reviled, their cities and streets in some cases renamed. Most of this they must accept as part of the process of indigenisation that is essential for them to have a viable future in Africa.

Looking back, they must realise that it probably could not have gone any other way, for European settlement around the world was a numbers game, and in Africa the numbers were against the settlers. Everywhere in the world, the outcome of European settlement has been dictated by the ratio of settlers to indigenous people: the more lightly weighted the ratio against the settlers, the more likely they were to maintain supremacy. Those whose European forebears settled in the Americas and

Australasia multiply and flourish in a mastery so complete that the descendents of the indigenous peoples have in most cases become not much more than incidental nuisances, occasionally tweaking consciences and making hopeless demands for restitution but otherwise ignored. In contrast, Africa, vast and more populous and in some ways more perilous to Europeans, was never fully conquered or settled. As in Asia, the native peoples, only partly and relatively briefly subjugated, again reign unchallenged in the lands of their ancestors, vulnerable only to their own mistakes and to Western economic pressures.

The descendants of the white settlers in Africa, unable to overcome a heavily adverse ratio, face a future not of expanding European culture and identity like the whites in the Americas and Australasia but one of cultural subordination and assimilation. Those for whom emigration is not an option are being absorbed by Africa.

For the relatively large white community in South Africa, an existence separate from the blacks might have been feasible had it been entrenched early on, and had it avoided excessive reliance on black labour and eschewed exploitation of the blacks. When this was finally attempted it was too little and too late, played out pathetically in the pretend-enclave of Orania.

The full Africanisation of the whites will take place slowly, extending over generations. And it will not be a one-way process, not in South Africa, at least. There, the relatively large white population and entrenched European culture have already had a radical influence on indigenous culture and ways of life, and this effect must continue. As the French, Portuguese and British left their languages as the lingua franca in their respective former colonies, so English and Afrikaans have become the general media of communication in South Africa, though with Afrikaans suffering from its tag as the language of apartheid.

The European inheritance in South Africa will continue quite profoundly to influence habits and speech among the black majority. The very verisimilitude of indigenous nations and languages must favour the culture of the whites as a catalyst for the unity that the once-warring indigenous communities must seek if they are to prosper in peace. But the catalyst itself will inevitably undergo change – has already begun to change in the shaping of white accents and attitudes.

The most severe cultural casualties of majority rule were the Afrikaners. For these people, who were a nation by any definition other than that of unchallenged territorial sovereignty, the fate of the numbers has been especially cruel. It has negated their centuries-old search for a place of their own in which to foster their identity and culture. The creation of their nation and language was an extraordinary social achievement, and deserved a better fate – which they might have had even as late as the Second World War had their leaders and their church chosen a less selfish path.

The Afrikaners' search for own land and identity was essentially no different from that of many other ethnic groups in Africa who had done the same. The main differences were that they were white and that they made their effort relatively recently, which meant it was overtaken by events before it could be entrenched in territorial sovereignty.

The Afrikaners are now territorially and politically bereft. The former republics for which their forebears fought and died are ruled by blacks, the Transvaal not even in its old form but carved up four-fold in the remaking of the provinces, even its name scrapped. The Voortrekker Monument has lost some of its sacred character and become a relic of a closed past rather than a beacon to a desired future.

The Afrikaners' language, though still one of the official languages, has had to take a back seat to English, which the ANC government has made the effective lingua franca even though more people speak Afrikaans. The Afrikaners' universities, once citadels of their language and culture, have been homogenised by the government in a uniform tertiary structure in which Afrikaans is no longer an exclusive medium of instruction.

None of these developments will necessarily be fatal to the Afrikaners' culture. They will, however, have radically to revise their concept of the milieu in which it will be practised and preserved. Right up to 1994, and in some cases even afterwards, some Afrikaners had still held faithfully to the old ambition of ethnic and territorial sovereignty. But now they will have to reshape their vision to a purely cultural entity within the wider nation. There is no other option. The old dream is dead, consigned to museums and monuments and, among some of the living, to smouldering but useless resentment. The Afrikaner must surely now seek his cultural salvation outside his skin colour – even if for many that would be the ultimate irony – among the black and coloured people among whom Afrikaans is already widely spoken.

If the present is bitter, the future will be more so for those Afrikaners still stumbling hopelessly through the ancestral delusion of a divinely ordained white separateness. Both their plight and their delusion were pathetically dramatised in the trial in 2003 of a group of right-wingers accused of plotting to overthrow the government. The prosecution charged that they had planned to drive the blacks out of the country, some into Zimbabwe and others out to sea! In one sense this ludicrous escapade might be seen as white supremacy's last dying twitch, a cry of agony, or perhaps a last bellow of defiance and despair, by those white Africans who valued their whiteness above their Africanness and could not bear to see the precedence reversed. The great majority of the Afrikaners for their part are now dedicated pragmatically to making the best of their new situation, to revising their concept of their Africanism and adapting it to the prevailing realities.

The definition of a white African, however, remains pretty much a matter of opinion – though, for that matter, the same is true of the definition of an African. Some see the latter as anyone who identifies with Africa, others require at least birth in Africa. Some extend it to black people in the diaspora who have never been to Africa but with whom many resident Africans evidently feel a stronger brotherly bond than they do with the native whites. The question arises: does a white person of five generations of ancestry in South Africa have a stronger or lesser claim to be called African than a black person of seven generations in the United States or Haiti? The issue may of course be of less importance to black Africans secure in their identity than to white ones still establishing theirs.

The whites' African identity is a matter of circumstance as well as of choice. Most whites with more than two generations of ancestry on the continent find, if they seek to live in Europe – or anywhere else in the white world – that they can do so only as aliens, as immigrants. Even someone with British ancestry going back unbroken to the time of William the Conqueror would be barred by immigration restrictions from open entry to Britain. These bureaucratic barriers were erected after colonialism was dismantled, their purpose largely being to stem a post-colonial flood of dark-skinned former subjects seeking to enjoy some of the British prosperity that their subjugation had helped create. In order to seem not to be practising racial discrimination, the British drew the immigration barriers across their own genetic trail. Thus persons born of more than two generations of whites in Kenya, Zimbabwe or South Africa and who sought to live in the Britain of their ancestors were obliged to join the queue of West Indians, Pakistanis and other former colonial subjects seeking permission to live or work in post-imperial Britain.

This slamming of the ancestral door left many of the Africa-born whites with no choice but to accept their Africanness. However, many, if not most, probably have no desire to live in Britain or anywhere else but the country of their birth – provided, of course, that life in Africa does not become unpleasant for them through economic or governmental degradation or black racism.

For the many who remain, the defining of their African identity is less important immediately than getting on with their lives. They cannot but be aware, however, that their future is shadowed by agonising questions. They now occupy a half-world of their own, held in a state of transition, of suspended identity, neither accepted any longer in the lands of their forebears nor fully accepted by their black fellows.

For some time to come, the white Africans must remain as socially separate and identifiable in Africa as the black Americans are in the United States. They are unlikely soon to become as similar to their black compatriots in accent and habits as London's black Cockneys are to *their* white countrymen. Still, it is only in full acceptance of their Africanness that the whites can find self-realisation and security.

Africa's anthropological history, like that of Europe, has been one of great movements, migrations and conquests that transferred genes and blended races. The genes of Europe are only the latest to be put into the mix. Not yet much mixed, they mostly float on the surface, so to speak, but inevitably they will sink ever deeper. It may take many generations, centuries even, but inexorably the descendants of the white settlers will become ever less European and ever more African as their ancestral links erode and timeless Africa draws them into her great being. It will be a long time, though, before there are no more white Africans.

NOTES

CHAPTER 1

1 Davidson, Basil *Africa in History* (Phoenix Press, 2001) p 145.

CHAPTER 3

1 Shell, Robert C-H *Children of Bondage; a Social History of the Slave Societies at the Cape of Good Hope, 1652-1838* (Witwatersrand University Press; University Press of England) p 324.

2 Ibid p 47.

3 Keegan, Timothy *Colonial South Africa and the Origins of the Racial Order* (David Philip, 1996) p 20.

4 Milton, Giles *White Gold – The Extraordinary Story of Thomas Pellow and North Africa's One Million European Slaves* (Hodder and Stoughton, 2004) p 272.

5 Ibid pp 271-277.

CHAPTER 5

1 Report of the London Missionary Society for 1899, pp 495-6.

2 Keegan p 243.

CHAPTER 6

1 Edgerton, Robert B *The Fall of the Asante Empire* (The Free Press / Simon and Schuster, 1995) p 79.

2 Ibid p 26.

CHAPTER 7

1 Watt, Elizabeth Paris *Febana, The True Story of Francis George Farewell, Pioneer and Founder of Natal* (Peter Davies, London, 1962) p 16.

2 Ibid p 37.

3 Ritter, EA *Shaka Zulu* (Longmans, 1955; Penguin, 1978, 1986) p 369.

4 De Gruchy, John W *The Church Struggle in South Africa* (Wm B Eerdmans Publishing Co. and David Philip, 1986) p 20.

CHAPTER 8

1 Chamberlain, ME *The Scramble for Africa* (Seminar Studies in History, Longman, 1974, 1995) p 25.

2 Livingstone, David and Charles *Narrative of an Expedition to the Zambezi, 1858-64* (John Murray, 1865).

3 Chamberlain p 23.

4 Healey, Edna *Wives of Fame* (Hodder and Stoughton New English Library, 1988) p 50.

5 Cairns, HAC *Prelude to Imperialism: British Reactions to Central African Society, 1849-90* (Routledge, 1965).

6 James p 186.

CHAPTER 9

1 Moorehead, Alan *The Blue Nile* (Hamish Hamilton, 1962) p 235.

2 Edgerton p 110.

CHAPTER 10

1 Edgerton p 144.

2 Chamberlain pp 37-38.

CHAPTER 11

1 Rosenthal, Eric *River of Diamonds* (Howard Timmins) pp 10-12.

2 Thomas, Anthony *Rhodes* (Jonathan Ball, Johannesburg, 1996) p 83.

3 Roberts, Brian *The Diamond Magnates* (Hamish Hamilton, 1972) p 44.

4 Thompson, Francis *Matabele Thompson, His Biography and Story of Rhodesia* edited by Nancy Rouillard (first published by

Faber and Faber, London, 1936; reprinted by Dassie Books / Central News Agency, South Africa, 1957) p 46.

CHAPTER 12
1 Pakenham, Thomas *The Scramble for Africa* (Jonathan Ball, Johannesburg, 1992) p 22.
2 Edgerton p 228.

CHAPTER 13
1 James p 269.

CHAPTER 14
1 Drechsler, Horst *Let Us Die Fighting; The Struggle of the Herero and Nama against German Imperialism* (Zed Press, London, 1980) p 26.

CHAPTER 15
1 Drechsler pp 31–32.
2 Nathan, Manfred *Paul Kruger, His Life and Times* (The Knox Publishing Company, Durban, 1941) p 224.
3 Thomas, Antony *Rhodes – the Race for Africa* (Jonathan Ball, 1996) p 114.
4 Thompson p 104.
5 Drechsler p 97.

CHAPTER 17
1 Judd, Dennis *Empire – the British Imperial experience from 1765 to the Present* (Fontana, 1997) p 158.
2 Nathan p 333.
3 Churchill, Winston S *My Early Life* (Fontana, 1974) pp 190–191.

CHAPTER 18
1 Welsh, Frank *A History of South Africa* (Harper Collins, 1998) p 340.

CHAPTER 19
1 Drechsler p 135.
2 Ibid p 148.
3 Pakenham p 615.

CHAPTER 21
1 *Atlas of World History* (Philip's, London, 1992) p 110.
2 McEvedy, Colin *The Penguin Atlas of African History* (Penguin Reference Books, 1995) p 116.

3 Oliver, Roland *The African Experience* (Weidenfeld and Nicholson, 1991) p 184.

CHAPTER 22
1 Allen, Charles with Helen Fry *Tales From the Dark Continent* (Andre Deutsch / BBC, London, 1979).

CHAPTER 24
1 Huxley, Elspeth *The Flame Trees of Thika* (Penguin Books, 1981) p 8.
2 James p 296.
3 Smith, Ian *The Great Betrayal* (Blake Publishing, London, 1997) pp 4–5.
4 Young, Kenneth *Rhodesia and Independence* (Dent, London, 1969) p 13.

CHAPTER 25
1 Bull, Bartle *Safari* (Penguin, 1992) p 95.
2 Oliver, Roland and JD Fage *A Short History of Africa* (Penguin African Library) p 219.

CHAPTER 26
1 Welsh, p 246.
2 Callinicos, Luli *Gold and Workers* (Ravan Press, 1998) p 49.

CHAPTER 27
1 Hibbert, Christopher *Benito Mussolini* (The Reprint Society / Longmans Green, 1963) p 16.
2 Oliver, Roland *The African Experience* (Weidenfeld and Nicholson, 1991) p 215.

CHAPTER 28
1 Hartshorn, EP *Avenge Tobruk* (Purnell and Sons, 1969) pp 8–18.
2 Gleeson, Ian *The Unknown Force* (Ashanti, 1994) p 153.
3 Klein, Harry *Springbok Record* (South African Legion of the British Empire Service League, 1946) p 89.
4 Macdonald, JF *War History of Southern Rhodesia, 1939-1945* published by the Southern Rhodesian government, 1947.

CHAPTER 31
1 Judd p 332.
2 Wilson, HS *African Decolonisation* (Edward Arnold / Hodder Headline, 1994) p 145.

CHAPTER 32
1 Iliffe, John *Africa – The History of a Continent* (Cambridge University Press 1997) p 236.

CHAPTER 34
1 Wilson p 150.

CHAPTER 35
1 Duffy, James *Penguin African Handbook* (1969) p 421.
2 Chaon, Anne, article in *Le Monde Diplomatique*, republished in *Mail&Guardian*, 21 July 2000.

CHAPTER 36
1 Godwin, Peter and Hancock, Ian *'Rhodesians Never Die'* (Baobab Books, Harare, 1997; first publication Oxford University Press, 1993) p 16.
2 Godwin and Hancock p 46.
3 Smith, Ian *The Great Betrayal* (Blake Publishing, London, 1997) p 55.
4 Flower, Ken *Serving Secretly* (Galago Publishing, 1987) p 51.
5 Ibid p 32.

CHAPTER 37
1 Gavshon, Arthur *Crisis in Africa; Battleground of East and West* (Pelican Books, 1981) p 19.

CHAPTER 38
1 Wilson p 182.
2 Barber, James and Barratt, John *South Africa's Foreign Policy – The Search for Status and Security 1945-1988* (SA Institute of International Affairs / Southern Book Publishers, 1990) p 142.
3 Smith p 160.
4 Steenkamp, Willem *South Africa's Border War 1966-1989* (Ashanti, 1989) p 36.

CHAPTER 39
1 Flower p 159.
2 Smith p 171.
3 Legum, Colin *After Angola – War Over Southern Africa* (Africana Publishing Co., New York, 1978) p 15.
4 Heitman, Helmoed-Romer *South African Armed Forces* (Buffalo Publications, 1990) p 204.

5 Flower p 162.

CHAPTER 40
1 Steenkamp p 46.

CHAPTER 41
1 Johnson, RW *How Long Will South Africa Survive?* (Macmillan South Africa, 1997) p 276.
2 Ibid pp 240-241.
3 Flower p 164.
4 Legum p 50.

CHAPTER 43
1 Moorcraft p 140.
2 Renwick, Robin *Unconventional Diplomacy in Southern Africa* (Macmillan, 1997) p 20.
3 Flower p 219.
4 Cole, Barbara *The Elite – Rhodesian Special Air Service – Pictorial* (Three Knights Publishing, 1986) pp 130-132.
5 Renwick pp 11, 12.
6 Ibid p 31.
7 Flower pp 238, 239.
8 Renwick p 60; Flower p 247.

CHAPTER 44
1 Flower p 258.
2 Ibid p 264.
3 Godwin and Hancock p 271.
4 Ibid p 270.
5 Smith p 335.
6 Cole pp 153-156.
7 Reid-Daly, Ron 'War in Rhodesia', chapter in *Challenge* (Ashanti, 1989) p 176.
8 Smith p 350.
9 Carrington, Peter *Reflect on Things Past; the Memoirs of Lord Carrington* (Collins, 1988).
10 Thatcher, Margaret *The Downing Street Years* (Harper Collins, 1993).

CHAPTER 45
1 Johnson, Phyllis and Martin, David eds *Destructive Engagement* (Zimbabwe Publishing House for Southern African Research and Documentation Centre, 1986) p 44.

CHAPTER 46

1 Crocker, Chester *High Noon in Southern Africa* (WW Norton, 1992) p 36.

2 Ibid p 40.

CHAPTER 47

1 Minter, William 'US/SA in the Reagan Era', chapter in *Destructive Engagement* p 312.

2 De Gruchy p 118.

CHAPTER 48

1 Waldmeir, Patti *Anatomy of a Miracle* (first published 1997 by Norton in USA and Viking in UK) (Penguin Books) pp 51, 71-72.

2 Ibid pp 65 and 66.

3 De Klerk, FW *The Last Trek – A New Beginning* (Pan Books, 2000) p 104.

4 Barber and Barratt p 329.

CHAPTER 49

1 Bridgland, Fred *The War for Africa* (Ashanti, 1990) p 228.

2 Heitman, Helmoed-Romer *War in Angola. The Final South African Phase* (Ashanti, 1990) p 338; Bridgland p 341; Barber, Simon *Cape Times*, 27 July 1989.

3 Steenkamp p 185.

4 Ibid p 185.

CHAPTER 50

1 Davenport, TRH *The Transfer of Power in South Africa* (David Philip, 1998) p 5.

2 Waldmeir p 66.

3 Ibid p 77.

4 De Klerk p 146.

5 Ibid p 161.

CHAPTER 51

1 De Klerk pp 239, 247.

CHAPTER 52

1 De Klerk p 291.

CHAPTER 53

1 Stiff, Peter *Warfare by Other Means* (Galago Publishing, 2001) pp 572-584.

2 De Klerk p 307.

3 Hamman pp 209-213.

CHAPTER 54

1 De Klerk p 336.

2 Waldmeir p 271.

3 Hamman p 227.

4 Speech in Pietermaritzburg commemorating tenth anniversary of Paton's death (extract published in *The Sunday Independent*, 6 September 1998).

5 Middleton, Jean *Convictions: A Woman Political Prisoner Remembers* (Ravan Press, 1998).

CHAPTER 55

1 Meredith, Martin *Robert Mugabe – Power, Plunder and Tyranny in Zimbabwe* (Jonathan Ball, 2002) p 121.

2 Blair, David *Degrees in Violence. Robert Mugabe and the Struggle for Power in Zimbabwe* (Continuum, London and New York, 2002) p 177.

3 Ibid.

4 Meredith p 139.

5 Blair p 53.

6 Ibid p 133.

7 *The Star*, Johannesburg, 26 July 2000.

8 Blair p 174.

9 Reuters report in *Cape Times*, 17 August 2004.

CHAPTER 56

1 Report in *The Herald*.

2 Article by John Grobler in *Mail&Guardian*, September 2002.

3 Article by Jane Flanagan in *Mail&Guardian*, 23 September 2002.

4 Interview with Thomas Knemeyer of *Die Welt*, reprinted in *Mail&Guardian*, 26 December 2002.

CHAPTER 57

1 Speech to the Cape Press Club on 21 October 1997.

2 Letter to *The Star*, 13 December 2000.

3 Article in *The Star*, 22 December 2000.

CHAPTER 58

1 *Mail&Guardian*, 9 July 2004.

2 University of SA Bureau for Market Research, quoted by Sapa in *Cape Times*, 27 July 2004.

3 SA Advertising Research Foundation

All-Media Products Survey.

4 Millin, Sarah Gertrude *The People of South Africa* (Constable, 1951) p 193.

5 Van Rooyen, Johan *The New Great Trek – The Story of South Africa's White Exodus* (University of South Africa, 2000).

6 Ibid pp 137–166.

7 *Sunday Independent*, 30 May 2004.

8 *Mail&Guardian*, 16 July 2004.

9 Ibid.

CHAPTER 59

1 Davidson pp 307–323.

2 Diamond, Jared *Guns, Germs and Steel* (Vintage, 1998) pp 176–191.

SELECT BIBLIOGRAPHY

Africa South of the Sahara – 1992 and 1993 yearbooks (Europa Publications Ltd, London).

Allen, Charles with Helen Fry *Tales from the Dark Continent* (Andre Deutsch / BBC, London, 1979).

Axelson, Paul *Vasco da Gama – The Diary of His Travels Through African Waters, 1497-1499* (Stephen Phillips (Pty) Ltd, Somerset West, 1998).

Barber, James and Barratt John *South Africa's Foreign Policy – The Search for Status and Security* (SA Institute of International Affairs / Southern Book Publishers, Johannesburg, 1990).

Blair, David *Degrees in Violence; Robert Mugabe and the Struggle for Power in Zimbabwe* (Continuum, London and New York, 2002).

Bridgland, Fred *The War for Africa – Twelve Months That Transformed a Continent* (Ashanti, Gibraltar, 1990).

Briggs, Asa *A Social History of England* (The Viking Press, New York, 1983).

Brown, James Ambrose *The War of a Hundred Days; Springboks in Somalia and Abyssinia 1940-41* (Ashanti, Rivonia, 1990).

Brown, James Ambrose *They Fought for King and Kaiser; South Africans in German East Africa, 1916* (Ashanti, Rivonia, 1991).

Buckle, Catherine *African Tears – The Zimbabwe Land Invasions* (Jonathan Ball, Johannesburg and Cape Town, 2001).

Buckle, Catherine *Beyond Tears – Zimbabwe's Tragedy* (Jonathan Ball, Johannesburg and Cape Town, 2002).

Bull, Bartle *Safari* (Penguin Books, London, 1992).

Burger, John *The Black Man's Burden* (Victor Gollancz, London, 1943).

Cairns, HAC *Prelude to Imperialism; British Reactions to Central African Society 1849-90* (Routledge, London, 1965).

Callinicos, Luli *Gold and Workers* (Ravan Press, Johannesburg, 1998).

Cameron, Trewhella general ed *A New Illustrated History of South Africa* (Southern Book Publishers, Johannesburg / Human and Rousseau, Cape Town and Johannesburg, 1991).

Cary, Robert *Charter Royal* (Howard Timmins, Cape Town, 1970).

Caute, David *Under the Skin – The Death of White Rhodesia* (Penguin Books, London, 1983).

Chamberlain, ME *The Scramble for Africa* (Longman's Seminar Studies in History, Longman Group, Harlow, Essex, 1995).

Cole, Barbara *The Elite – Rhodesian Special Air Service – Pictorial* (Three Knights Publishing, Amanzimtoti, 1986).

Crocker, Chester *High Noon in Southern Africa – Making Peace in a Rough Neighbourhood* (WW Norton, New York, 1992).

Davenport, TRH *South Africa – A Modern History* (Macmillan South Africa, Johannesburg, 1987).

Davenport, TRH *The Transfer of Power in South Africa* (David Philip, Cape Town, 1998).

Davidson, Basil *Africa in History* (Phoenix Press, London, 2001).

De Gruchy, John W *The Church Struggle in South Africa* (Wm B Eerdmans Publishing Co., Grand Rapids, Michigan / Wm Collins Sons and Co., London / David Philip, Cape Town, 1986).

De Klerk, FW *The Last Trek – A New Beginning* (Pan Books, London, 2000).

De Villiers, Marq *White Tribe Dreaming – Apartheid's Bitter Roots as Witnessed by Eight

Generations of an Afrikaner Family (Penguin Books, London, 1990).

Diamond, Jared *Guns, Germs and Steel – A Short History of Everybody for the Last 13 000 Years* (Vintage / Random House, London, 1997).

Digby, Peter KA *Pyramids and Poppies; The 1st SA Infantry Brigade in Libya, France and Flanders, 1915-1919* (Ashanti, Rivonia, 1993).

Divine, David *Six Great Explorers* (Hamish Hamilton, New York and London, 1954).

Edgerton, Robert B *The Fall of the Asante Empire – The Hundred-Year War for Africa's Gold Coast* (The Free Press / Simon and Schuster, New York, 1995).

Flower, Ken *Serving Secretly – Rhodesia's CIO Chief on Record* (Galago, Alberton, 1986).

Fox, James *White Mischief* (Penguin, London, 1988).

Garraty, John A and Gay, Peter eds *The Columbia History of the World* (Harper and Row, New York, 1972).

Gavshon, Arthur *Crisis in Africa: Battleground of East and West* (Pelican Books, London, 1981).

Giles, Milton *White Gold, The Extraordinary Story of Thomas Pellow and North Africa's One Million European Slaves* (Hodder and Stoughton, London, 2004).

Godwin, Peter and Hancock, Ian *Rhodesians Never Die – the Impact of War and Political Change on White Rhodesia, 1970-1980* (Baobab Books / Academic Books Pvt Ltd, Harare, 1997).

Grace, John and Laffin, John *Fontana Dictionary of Africa Since 1960* (Fontana Press / Harper Collins, London, 1991).

Greater South Africa; Plans for a Better World – The Speeches of General J.C. Smuts (The Truth Legion, Johannesburg, 1940).

Grun, Bernard *The Timetables of History* (Touchstone / Simon and Schuster, New York, 1982).

Hamman, Hilton *Days of the Generals – The Untold Story of South Africa's Apartheid-era Military Generals* (Zebra Press, Cape Town, 2001).

Hartshorn, EP *Avenge Tobruk* (Purnell and Sons, Cape Town and Johannesburg, 1969).

Healey, Edna *Wives of Fame* (Hodder and Stoughton New English Library, London, 1988).

Heitman, Helmoed-Romer *War in Angola*

– *The Final South African Phase* (Ashanti, Gibralter, 1990).

Hibbert, Christopher *Benito Mussolini* (The Reprint Society / Longmans Green, London, 1963).

Hobsbawm, Eric *The Age of Extremism, 1914-1991* (Vintage Books / Random House, London, 1996).

Hochschild, Adam *King Leopold's Ghost* (Macmillan, London, 1999).

Hockly, Harold Edward, *The Story of the British Settlers of 1820 in South Africa* (Juta, Cape Town and Johannesburg, 1966).

Horne, Alistair *A Savage War of Peace – Algeria 1954-1962* (Pan Books, London, 2002).

Horrell, Muriel *Action, Reaction and Counter-Action – A Brief Review of Non-white Political Movements in South Africa* (SA Institute of Race Relations, Johannesburg, 1971).

Iliffe, John *Africans – The History of a Continent* (Cambridge University Press, Cambridge, New York and Melbourne, 1995).

James, Lawrence *The Rise and Fall of the British Empire* (Abacus / Little, Brown, London, 1995).

Johnson, Phyllis and Martin, David eds *Destructive Engagement – Southern Africa at War* (Zimbabwe Publishing House for Southern African Research and Documentation Centre, Harare, 1986).

Johnson, RW *How Long Will South Africa Survive?* (Macmillan South Africa, Johannesburg, 1977).

Judd, Denis *Empire – The British Imperial Experience, from 1765 to the Present* (Fontana / Harper Collins, London, 1997).

Keegan, Timothy *Colonial South Africa and the Origins of the Racial Order* (David Philip, Cape Town and Johannesburg, 1996).

Klein, Harry *Springbok Record* (SA Legion of the British Empire Service League, Johannesburg, 1946).

Kros, Jack *War in Italy – With the South Africans from Taranto to the Alps* (Ashanti, Rivonia, 1992).

Kruger, Rayne *Good-bye Dolly Gray – The Story of the Boer War* (Cassell, London, 1961).

L'Ange, Gerald *Urgent Imperial Service; South African Forces in German South West Africa, 1914-1915* (Ashanti Publishing, Rivonia, 1991).

Lamb, David *The Africans* (Vintage Books / Random House, New York, 1987).

Legum, Colin and Hodges, Tony *After Angola – The War Over Southern Africa* (Africana Publishing Company / Holmes and Meier, New York, 1978).

Legum, Colin ed *Africa Handbook* (Penguin Reference Books, Harmondsworth, Middlesex, 1969).

Legum, Colin *The Battlefronts of Southern Africa* (Africana Publishing Company / Holmes and Meier, New York, 1988).

Livingstone, David and Charles *Narrative of an Expedition to the Zambezi, 1858-1864* (John Murray, London, 1865).

Lovett, Richard *The History of the London Missionary Society, 1795-1895* (Henry Frowde, Oxford, 1899).

Mandela, Nelson *Long Walk to Freedom* (Abacus, London, 1995).

McEvedy, Colin *The Penguin Atlas of African History* (Penguin Books, London, 1995).

Meredith, Martin *Robert Mugabe – Power, Plunder and Tyranny in Zimbabwe* (Jonathan Ball, Johannesburg and Cape Town, 2002).

Mervis, Joel *South Africa in World War II* (The Executive / Times Media Ltd, Johannesburg, 1989).

Moorcroft, Paul L *African Nemesis – War and Revolution in Southern Africa, 1945-2010* (Brasseys (UK) Ltd, London and Washington, 1994).

Moore, Dermot and Bagshawe, Peter *South Africa's Flying Cheetahs in Korea* (Ashanti, Rivonia, 1991).

Moore, RI ed *Atlas of World History* (Philip's / Octopus Illustrated Publishing, London, 1992).

Moorehead, Alan *The White Nile* (Hamish Hamilton, London, 1960).

Moorehead, Alan *The Blue Nile* (Hamish Hamilton, London, 1962).

Morris, Donald R *The Washing of the Spears* (Jonathan Cape, London, 1966).

Narrative of Discovery and Adventure in Africa (Thomas Nelson, London, 1840).

Norwich, Oscar I *Maps of Southern Africa* (Ad Donker and Jonathan Ball Publishers, Johannesburg and Cape Town, 1993).

Okoth, Assa *A History of Africa* (Heinemann Kenya, Nairobi, 1979).

Oliver, Roland *The African Experience* (Weidenfeld and Nicholson, London, 1991).

Oliver, Roland, and Fage, JD *A Short History of Africa* (Penguin Books, Harmondsworth, 1962).

Pakenham, Thomas *The Boer War* (Jonathan Ball, Johannesburg and Cape Town, 1993).

Pakenham, Thomas *The Scramble for Africa* (Jonathan Ball, Johannesburg and Cape Town, 1992).

Perham, M and Simmons J *African Discovery* (Penguin, Harmondsworth, 1942).

Renwick, Robin *Unconventional Diplomacy in Southern Africa* (Macmillan, Basingstoke and London, 1997).

Ritter, EA *Shaka Zulu* (Penguin Books, Harmondsworth, 1978).

Rivett-Carnac, Dorothy E *Thus Came the English in 1820* (Howard Timmins, Cape Town, 1963).

Roberts, Brian *The Diamond Magnates* (Hamish Hamilton, London and New York, 1972).

Rosenthal, Eric *River of Diamonds* (Howard Timmins, Cape Town, undated).

Royle, Trevor *Winds of Change – The End of Empire in Africa* (John Murray, London, 1996).

Ruark, Robert C *Horn of the Hunter* (Arrow Books / Hutchinson, London, 1963).

Shell, Robert C-H *Children of Bondage – A Social History of the Slave Society at the Cape of Good Hope, 1652-1838* (Witwatersrand University Press, Johannesburg, 1994).

Simons, Jack and Ray *Class and Colour in South Africa 1850-1950* (International Defence and Aid Fund for Southern Africa, 1983).

Smith, Ian *The Great Betrayal* (Blake Publishing, London, 1997).

Sparks, Allister *Beyond the Miracle – Inside the New South Africa* (Jonathan Ball, Johannesburg and Cape Town, 2003).

Steenkamp, Willem *South Africa's Border War* (Ashanti, Rivonia, 1989).

Stiff, Peter *Warfare by Other Means – South Africa in the 1980s and 1990s* (Galago, Alberton, 2001).

Stockwell, John *In Search of Enemies – A CIA Story* (WW Norton, New York, 1978).

Symons, Julian *England's Pride – The Story of the Gordon Relief Expedition* (Hamish Hamilton, London, 1965).

Tabor, George *The Cape to Cairo Railway and River Routes* (Genta Publications, 2003).

Taylor, Don *The British in Africa* (Robert Hale Ltd, London, 1962.)

The Horizon History of Africa (American Heritage Publishing Co. Inc., New York).

Thomas, Antony *Rhodes – The Race for Africa* (Jonathan Ball, Johannesburg and Cape Town, 1996).

Thompson, Francis *Matabele Thompson, His Biography and Story of Rhodesia* (Dassie Books / Central News Agency, Johannesburg, 1957; first publication Faber and Faber, London).

Turner, John W *Continent Ablaze – The Insurgency Wars in Africa 1960 to the Present* (Jonathan Ball, Johannesburg and Cape Town, 1998).

Van Rooyen, Johan *The New Great Trek – The Story of South Africa's White Exodus* (University of South Africa, Pretoria, 2000).

Waldmeir, Patti *Anatomy of a Miracle* (Penguin Books, London, 1998).

Walker, Eric A *A History of Southern Africa* (Longmans Green and Co. Ltd, London, revised issue, 1962).

Watkins, Ronald *Unknown Seas – How Vasco da Gama Opened the East* (John Murray / Hodder Headline, London, 2004).

Watt, Elizabeth Paris *Febana – The True Story of Francis George Farewell: Explorer, Pioneer and Founder of Natal* (Peter Davies, London, 1962).

Welsh, Frank *A History of South Africa* (Harper Collins, London, 1998).

Woodham-Smith, Cecil *Queen Victoria, From her Birth to the Death of the Prince Consort* (Alfred A Knopf, New York, 1972).

Young, Kenneth *Rhodesia and Independence* (Dent, London, 1969).

INDEX